MW00388822

The Center for Creative Leadership
Handbook of Coaching in Organizations

The Center for Creative Leadership Handbook of Coaching in Organizations

Douglas D. Riddle
Emily R. Hoole
Elizabeth C. D. Gullette
Editors

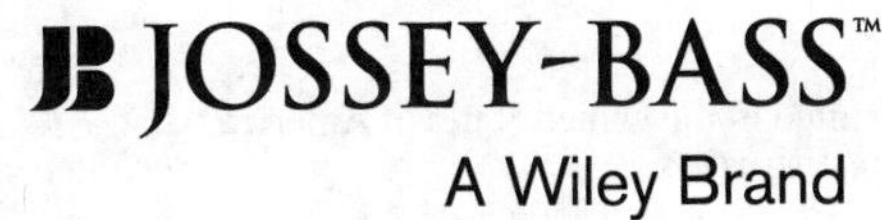

Cover Design: Wiley
Cover image: © iStock.com/Orla

Published by Jossey-Bass
A Wiley Brand
One Montgomery Street, Suite 1200, San Francisco, CA 94104-4594-www.josseybass.com

Library of Congress Cataloging-in-Publication Data

The CCL handbook of coaching in organizations / by Douglas D. Riddle, Emily R. Hoole, and Elizabeth C.D. Gullette, editors.
1 online resource.
Includes bibliographical references and index.
Description based on print version record and CIP data provided by publisher; resource not viewed.
ISBN 978-1-118-84148-8 (cloth)—ISBN 978-1-118-84163-1 (pdf)—ISBN 978-1-118-84149-5 (epub)
1. Executive coaching. 2. Leadership. 3. Mentoring in business. 4. Employees—Coaching of.
I. Riddle, Douglas Duane Jacobs, 1949- II. Hoole, Emily R., 1968- III. Gullette, Elizabeth C. D., 1969-
HD30.4
658.3′124—dc23

2014042973

Printed in the United States of America
FIRST EDITION
HB Printing 10 9 8 7 6 5 4 3 2 1

CONTENTS

Dedicated to the human resource professionals who invest their hearts, minds, and hands for the betterment of their workplaces

FOREWORD

Few other elements of corporate preparation for global leaders have more impact than coaching. And few organizations have had more impact in shaping the thinking about the development of leaders within the coaching context than the Center for Creative Leadership.

Research tells us that coaching, when done well for the right reasons by talented coaches with clear goals and within strong ethical guidelines, works. Leaders tell us that one of the ways to develop what they find most effective is through coaching. Organizations can point to the positive effects of coaching for not only the leaders being coached but also their teams and the fabric of their very culture.

Recently I had the great privilege of researching what great companies know about consistently developing effective leaders who are different from the rest. The report, *DNA of Leaders: Leadership Development Secrets,* profiled the leadership development programs and philosophies at Accenture, L'Oreal, Shell, Siemens, American Express, the Coca-Cola Company, Wipro, Unilever, Intel, IBM, McDonald's, Proctor & Gamble, Hewlett Packard, General Mills, Caterpillar, Cardinal Health, and BASF. They had much in common: a clear understanding of what leaders need to be and do at their organization; linkage to the organization's values; active involvement and support from senior leaders; and the strong use of analytics and the continual assessment not only of development programs' effectiveness but also the impact on business results. What they also had in common was a commitment to supporting leaders on a personal basis through structured coaching programs, a key element of their overall structure. As part of that same study, we asked business leaders what leadership development experiences they believed had the greatest impact. Their top six choices were mentoring, action learning, rotational programs, international assignments, executive coaching, and informal feedback. Clearly coaching is top of mind; action learning, rotational programs, and international assignments all require an element of coaching and feedback to be truly successful.

Practitioners will find in this book the distilled wisdom that comes only from having built or witnessed hundreds of successful coaching programs and thousands of individuals who have been transformed by them. This highly accessible and comprehensive handbook is logically framed around three core elements: the human resource leader as a coach, building a coaching culture, and specific coaching applications. More than a blueprint to simply replicate a model, it is a launching pad for what could be.

The CCL Handbook of Coaching in Organizations has much to offer human capital executives charged with creating the environment in which leaders are successfully forged in a crucible of development and then sent forth into the complex, ever changing, unpredictable world that awaits them. There is probably no more critical task than to build the leaders every organization needs to drive its success; coaching is a powerful tool to accomplish that task. I know that you will find this new work to be of great value.

Rebecca L. Ray
Executive Vice President, The Conference Board

THE AUTHORS

Amy Lui Abel is managing director of human capital at The Conference Board. She leads research efforts focusing on human capital analytics, leadership development, labor markets, strategic workforce planning, talent management, diversity and inclusion, human resources, and employee engagement. She has taught at New York University Stern School of Business and served on the board of directors for the Association for Talent Development New York Chapter. Amy has published widely and holds several degrees, including a doctorate from New York University.

J. Ross Blankenship is a principal at Bespoke Partners, a retained executive search firm, where he leads the assessment and development practice. He also works as an executive coach with the Organizational Consulting Center and is completing a practicum on coaching and research at the Center for Creative Leadership. Ross has an MS in consulting psychology and is pursuing his PhD from the California School of Professional Psychology. He is a member of the Society of Consulting Psychology and the Society for Industrial and Organizational Psychology.

Lize A. E. Booysen is professor of leadership and organizational behavior at Antioch University, teaching in the PhD in leadership and change program. She is an internationally recognized scholar in the field of diversity, race, gender, leadership development, and coaching. Lize holds a doctorate in business leadership from the University of South Africa, as well as master's degrees in clinical psychology, research psychology, and criminology (University of Pretoria). She is also a visiting professor, Faculty of Management, at the University of Johannesburg, and executive coach at the Center for Creative Leadership.

Monica Bortoluzzi is a design faculty and leadership coach in the Center for Creative Leadership's EMEA office. She designs customized leadership solutions and interventions for clients and bring these designs to fruition. Since joining the center, she has helped more than thirty organizations expand their leadership capabilities and align their values, objectives, and human potential. Monica holds a master's degree in human resources management and organization from ESIC (Business & Marketing School, Madrid) and an MSc in philosophy from the University of Venice.

Erica Desrosiers is senior director of global talent management at Walmart, where she is responsible for the global talent review and succession process, performance management, selection, executive coaching, 360-degree feedback, and other developmental assessments. She earned her master's and PhD in industrial organizational psychology from Purdue University. She is a member of the Society for Industrial and Organizational Psychology and has published and presented in the areas of leadership development, performance management, 360-degree feedback, and executive coaching.

Robert Elsey is a director at AlixPartners and former senior faculty at the Center for Creative Leadership. He consults and partners with Fortune 500 companies to diagnose, design, implement, and evaluate talent-focused initiatives across all organizational levels. A psychologist and board-certified executive coach, Rob is a member of the American Psychological Association and Society of Consulting Psychology, and holds a PhD in clinical, educational, and school psychology from the University of Northern Colorado. He is a coauthor of the book *Change Now! Five Steps to Better Leadership*.

Barbara Fly-Dierks is senior faculty and coaching talent manager for the Center for Creative Leadership's Central North American Region. She is responsible for the recruitment and selection of adjunct coaches and the training, qualification, and continuing quality of internal and adjunct coaches. In addition, she serves on key global account teams to ensure continuity, brand fidelity, and quality of coaching across regions. Barbara is a licensed psychologist, with a bachelor's degree in psychology from the University of Colorado, Colorado Springs, and an MA and PhD in counseling psychology from the University of Denver.

Candice C. Frankovelgia is a coaching portfolio manager and senior faculty member with the Center for Creative Leadership. She is a leadership development and coaching skills trainer, executive coach, and designer of custom team and individual coaching engagements. Candice holds a doctoral degree in clinical psychology from the Illinois School of Professional Psychology. Previous publications include contributions to the *Harvard Business Review Guide to Coaching Your Employees* (2013), *The Center for Creative Leadership Handbook of Leadership Development* (2010), and *The Center for Creative Leadership Handbook of Coaching* (2006).

William A. Gentry is a senior research scientist at the Center for Creative Leadership and the coordinator of internships and postdocs there. He is also an adjunct assistant professor in the Psychology Department at Guilford College and an associate member of the graduate faculty in the organizational sciences doctoral program at the University of North Carolina, Charlotte. Bill holds a doctorate in industrial-organizational psychology from the University of Georgia.

Elizabeth C. D. Gullette is vice president in leadership and organizational effectiveness at AlixPartners and previously served as senior faculty and coaching practice leader at the Center for Creative Leadership. Beth holds PhD and MA degrees in clinical psychology from Duke University. She is a licensed psychologist and member of the American Psychological Association, Society of Consulting Psychology, International Society for Coaching Psychology, and Triangle Organization Development Network in North Carolina, where she served several years on the board.

Jennifer Habig is a design and delivery manager for the Center for Creative Leadership and oversees quality for all leadership solutions in western North America and South America. Previous to this role, Jennifer coached individuals and leadership teams; delivered large-scale, global executive coaching programs; and helped create new products for the coaching portfolio, including the Coaching Evaluation Assessment, which measures the impact of executive coaching engagements. Jennifer holds an MS in industrial/organizational psychology and is a Board Certified Coach through the Center for Credentialing and Education and a member of the American Psychological Association.

Emily Hoole is group director of global research and evaluation at the Center for Creative Leadership. She leads the center in setting the strategy for global research and evaluation to both align with and anticipate clients' needs regarding leadership and leadership development to address critical challenges and issues. Emily holds a BS in political science, an MPA, and a PhD in assessment and measurement from James Madison University. She is a member of the American Educational Research Association, American Evaluation Association, and Academy of Management.

John B. McGuire is a Center for Creative Leadership senior fellow and a researcher, practitioner, and speaker specializing in organizational leadership. His use of applied research has advanced feasible organizational change, increasing the probability of success through advancing interdependent, collaborative capability. John is coauthor of *Transforming Your Leadership Culture*, chapters in such books as Harvard Business School's *The Handbook for Teaching Leadership*, and articles in the *Harvard Business Review*, *CEO Magazine*, Forbes.com, the *Washington Post*, and *Leadership Quarterly*. John holds master's degrees from Harvard and Brandeis universities.

Sherlin V. Nair is a research consultant with The Conference Board and supports projects in human capital, talent management, and leadership development. She has coauthored research reports and articles and has several years of work experience in business operations and training with global organizations like GE Capital, Dell International Services, and Dale Carnegie Training India. She holds a postmaster's degree from New York University in workplace learning.

Johan Naudé is a coaching talent manager at the Center for Creative Leadership and a consulting and coaching psychologist with twenty years of experience working with organizations in the private and public sectors. He has trained coaches in the Americas, Europe, Asia, and Africa and supervises a dispersed network of professional coaches. He has worked with organizations to design and deliver coach training for HR, leaders, and managers. Johan also consults to organizations seeking to build internal coaching capability and capacity, including the systems required to manage internal and external coaching pools.

Kevin O'Gorman is a senior faculty member and organizational leadership portfolio manager at the Center for Creative Leadership. His interests and expertise include leading interconnected, global social systems, organizational performance, executive leadership, strategy, mergers and acquisitions, transformation, agency, and culture across industries. Kevin spent twenty years as managing director of Ideation, a San Francisco–based global consulting, coaching, and training firm. He conducted doctoral work at the Business School at Trinity College in Dublin, Ireland, and holds an MA in counseling psychology from Antioch, New England.

Florence Plessier is a coaching practice leader and leads the development of the coaching portfolio of the Center for Creative Leadership's EMEA office. She has worked as an executive coach over the past ten years and has held HR business partners and/or internal coach positions in corporations such as

StorageTek, Motorola, and STMicroelectonics. Florence holds an MBA from Toulouse Business School and graduated from Corporate Coaching University. She contributed to *The Discipline of Teams* and *Organisation and Management* and coauthored *Becoming a Leader-Coach*. Florence is a member of the International Coach Federation as a Personal Certified Coach.

TZiPi Radonsky is a rabbi leadership coach at Watering the Tree Outside the Fence. Her primary focus is building partnerships through deep listening, setting boundaries, being curious, and the use of positive and improvisational thinking. She published *And: Building a World of Connection through Jewish Mystical Wisdom* and *Spiritual Pilgrim Discovers Home*. She holds a doctorate in counselor education from the University of North Carolina at Greensboro and is adjunct faculty at the Center for Creative Leadership as a coach and trainer.

Lyndon Rego is the global director for the Center for Creative Leadership's Leadership Beyond Boundaries initiative, an effort to democratize leadership development that spans twenty countries and interacts with youth, grassroots populations, government, entrepreneurs, and social change makers. Lyndon has an MBA from the University of North Carolina at Chapel Hill and an MA in communication from the University of North Dakota. He received the 2013 OD Network award for Outstanding Achievement in Global Work. He writes and speaks on issues at the intersection of social innovation, complexity, and leadership.

Philomena Rego is a leadership facilitator and coach who has worked in the United States, Asia, the Caribbean, Africa, and South America. These efforts include programs for nonprofit and government leaders, leadership trainers and coaches, and teachers and students. For more than a decade, she has worked to advance the rights of and empower women and marginalized people in the United States and India. Philomena is certified by the International Coach Federation and the Coaches Training Institute. She has a master's in social work and in sociology.

Douglas D. Riddle is the global director of coaching services at the Center for Creative Leadership. He has directed the expansion of coaching services to include coach training, team coaching, executive leadership coaching, executive integration, and coach assessment. Doug serves as senior advisor to the Harvard Institute of Coaching, senior advisor for Project Rising Sun, and is the moderator of the Leadership Coaching LinkedIn group. He is a member of the Society for Consulting Psychology and the International Society for Coaching Psychology and is licensed as a psychologist in California.

Maggie Sass is a faculty member and part of the coaching portfolio group with the Center for Creative Leadership. In this role, she specializes in programs that train leaders how to achieve lasting results through others and teach coaching skills to managers. Her research focus, including her doctoral work, is on coaching ethics in executive coaching and internal coaching programs. Maggie is completing her PhD in consulting psychology at the California School of Professional Psychology.

Patrick Stichelmans is coaching talent director EMEA at the Center for Creative Leadership in Brussels, Belgium. In this role, he manages the coach community in Europe, the Middle East, and Africa, including recruitment, training, and the quality of work of around 150 internal and associate coaches. He also coaches regularly in leadership programs targeted at senior leaders. Patrick earned a master's degree in clinical psychology from the Free University of Brussels.

Patrick Williams is the founder of the Institute for Life Coach Training, which specializes in training psychotherapists, psychologists, counselors, and other helping professionals in building a successful coaching practice. A licensed psychologist, he began executive coaching in 1990 with Hewlett Packard, IBM, and Kodak. He coauthored *Therapist as Coach: Transforming Your Practice* and *Total Life Coaching: 50+ Life Lessons, Skills, and Techniques to Enhance Your Practice and Your Life*. His newest book, with Diane Menendez, is *Becoming a Professional Life Coach: Lessons from the Institute for Life Coach Training.*

Joel F. Wright is early leadership development director at the Center for Creative Leadership. He and the early leadership team work with youth-serving organizations, schools, colleges, communities, and foundations to create leadership and coaching curriculum and train-the-trainers programs and to engage in research and innovation partnerships. He writes, presents, facilitates, designs, and delivers on youth leadership development. Joel graduated from Wittenberg University with a bachelor's degree in history.

INTRODUCTION

When people think about coaching in leadership, they often assume the reference is to executive coaching: one professional coach working with one leader. This may be a consequence of the fact that the profession of coaching has driven the growth of the field. We believe it is valuable to think more broadly about coaching and recognize that the applications of this kind of interaction should not be limited to executive coaching. At the Center for Creative Leadership, we look at coaching as a certain kind of relationship, worked out in certain kinds of conversations, that has value far beyond what takes place between professional coach and the person being coached. In fact, the most powerful coaching conversations with the greatest impact on leadership challenges are often the ones that take place in the hallways, cafeterias, offices, and other organizational workspaces. These conversations are conducted by thoughtful leaders and managers who recognize the importance of coaching relationships for the advancement of leadership capability at all levels in the course of the organization's everyday work.

For our purposes, coaching is a helping relationship with a developmental focus played out in conversations that stimulate the person or group being coached to greater awareness, deeper and broader thought, and wiser decisions and actions. The conversations are developmental because they always have in mind the improvement of the person's perceiving, thinking, and reflecting, as well as the solution to the concern at hand. It is a helping relationship because the benefit is clearly focused on the value to the person being coached and her leadership responsibilities. Coaching conversations are an important means by which experiences are turned into learning, and nearly anyone can conduct them. Friends, mentors, coaches, teachers, and leaders of every stripe have greater impact on the thinking, feeling, and behavior of others when they listen carefully, respond thoughtfully, and are careful to resist imposing their own solutions. We can all coach. We can all create openness to new thinking and action.

At the core of this book is an idea: human resource leaders can create the conditions that permit the growth of a developmental culture and of climates that encourage individual and organizational learning. They can do this through implementing coaching systems based on lessons derived from organizations all over the world, in many sectors and industries, of all sizes. Coaching, mentoring, and other developmental activities are only part of the total work of human resource professionals; they are important to the health of the organization and the growth of those being coaching, and they are an essential element of organizational change. Furthermore, we believe that human resource professionals are ideally located within the organization to activate a variety of resources leading to leadership growth.

CCL research has consistently shown the consequences of trying to execute brilliant business strategies without the benefit of adequate leadership. The realization that implementation of business strategy requires a corresponding leadership strategy has shaped CCL's research and portfolio for over a decade. However, this book recognizes that it is nearly impossible for any internal HR professional to know all that is necessary to implement practical and effective coaching systems. We have gathered in this book experience and research from all over the globe in one place for busy HR and organizational development leaders who recognize the need for coaching as one piece of a comprehensive orientation toward development.

This book focuses on the opportunities and challenges of the professionals working within an organization responsible for doing coaching or implementing coaching systems. The key word is *system*, because we have come to appreciate an ecological perspective, which always seeks to broaden the attention beyond the current definition of a given situation. For instance, an HR leader may be called on to coach an executive who is in danger of derailing. In years past, the leader might have been content to counsel the individual, warn him of his potential fate, and consult with him until he either changes or flames out. An ecological perspective changes that approach and helps HR leaders recognize that they sit at the crossroads of a rich set of resources and are likely to be much more effective by activating the help of others, all for the benefit of the executive and the organization. HR leaders who think in terms of the system will help derailing executives enlist the involvement and support of many others.

Although it has become popular to seek alternative terms to describe the HR function within organizations (Google's People Operations, for instance), we consistently refer in this book to the functional group as human resources. Because of the variety of foci within HR departments or groups who are responsible for organizational development, learning and development, training and development, and the like, we have not imposed any particular constraints on the chapter authors, who come from a broad range of organizations and research and practice settings. You may see terms such as *human resource business partner*, *human resource coach*, or, as in the case of this Introduction, *human resource leader*. The common element in all of these labels is that they signify people in HR roles who are responsible for developing their organization's leaders.

This book originated in the persistent cries for help of clients and colleagues all over the world who have faced the challenges of implementing coaching systems or doing coaching. Human resource professionals have unique multiple roles in that they are often expected to coach and simultaneously create and manage systems of coaching. As we reviewed the literature on coaching and its applications within organizational life, the need for guidance based on CCL's global experience with organizations of every kind became clear. In particular, the multiple, competing roles of human resource leaders demonstrated the need for a book that addressed the requirement to be both a coach and manager of coaches and coaching.

This book has three parts.

Part 1 focuses on the creation and management of coaching programs. Most organizations have come to realize that coaching activities have to include mentoring and peer coaching as well as developing the coaching competence of managers. The HR professionals responsible for advising senior leadership on development strategies and responsive talent management to achieve business results have told us they need resources to educate others on the conditions and activities important for successful initiatives. What are the best ways to begin or expand programs that can equip leaders for meeting rapidly changing market conditions? How can coaching address dynamic cultural changes that accompany new generations or the internationalization of the workforce? We share the lessons of our experiences with organizations in over 130 countries and with over thirty thousand leaders a year to put at your disposal in chapters 1 to 5 the best practices for creating and managing comprehensive leadership development solutions that incorporate coaching and describe the most critical pitfalls.

Part 2 addresses the need for all human resource leaders (or, as we refer to them, human resource business partners) to coach others. Human resource business partners (HRBP) are responsible for advising and helping other leaders throughout their organizations on the most delicate and sensitive issues, while simultaneously guiding processes of talent management and selection. In one afternoon, an HRBP leader may preside over a talent review of middle managers and coach a senior vice president on conflict between her direct reports. The next morning may require that same HRBP to lead a team in assessing its decision processes and finding solutions for its reputation as a bottleneck hindering the organization's agility. These multiple roles and competing challenges with political, ethical, legal, and interpersonal factors are unique to human resource departments. Coach training that doesn't address the conflicts and the complexity of that office will not properly equip HRBPs with what is necessary to do the job.

Part 3 tackles some specific applications of coaching that have grown more important in recent years and addresses them from the viewpoint of the internal professional. Team interventions, including action learning and senior team coaching, are examined here, as are special populations, such as senior executives.

We hope that you will find this handbook to be comprehensive enough that you will rely on it for developing appropriate coaching strategies that will contribute to your success in your organizations. But we also hope it is practical and sufficiently detailed that you will find specific, immediately useful guidance for the special challenges you face every day. Finally, because human resource experts are often the champion for smart leadership and advisors to managers and senior leaders and everyone else who needs to lead, we intend for this book to be broadly shared.

The Center for Creative Leadership Handbook of Coaching in Organizations

PART ONE

Toward a Coaching Culture

Creating and Managing Coaching Programs

The challenge of promoting the necessary culture, talent, and leadership to support business strategies in today's complex organizational environments makes one-off and ad hoc coaching activities inefficient and ineffective. This is particularly true when it comes to coaching, because coaching is often delivered one-on-one or to only a few people in an organization, and it can easily remain hidden and disconnected from broader organizational goals and initiatives. A strategic, systemic approach to coaching, by contrast, is more likely to lead to sustainable results in terms of outcomes and the organizational impact that it is hoped will follow. Indeed, an ultimate goal for many organizations is to extend the benefits of coaching throughout its culture—to create a coaching culture—such that developmental conversations, reflection, and multilevel learning become embedded in the everyday behavior and attitudes of organizational leaders at all levels. Potential benefits of such a culture go beyond individual performance and development to team and organizational performance, as well as to employee retention and engagement. Moreover, a coordinated, systemic approach to coaching allows for visibility, management, and evaluation, the better to ensure an appropriate use of resources and a return on the investment of those resources.

So how do you, as an HR leader, plan and drive the development of a coaching culture within your organization? What are other companies doing that you could learn from? What range of coaching-related activities could contribute to an integrated approach to embedding coaching and learning into the culture of your organization? How do you decide what your organization needs and what it is ready for? How do you leverage outside resources as part of the equation, and how do you manage internal resources that are part of developmental activities? And, finally, how do you evaluate the effectiveness of any of these coaching-related initiatives in your organization to ensure that they are delivering the return intended?

Part 1 serves as a resource for you, the HR leader, as you consider these questions in the context of your organization. It can also be a resource to you as you consult with and educate the senior leadership of your organization as you work to incorporate coaching into its talent and leadership strategy. Chapter 1 lays the foundation for thinking through the nuts and bolts of developing and managing coaching programs by providing some benchmark data from the most recent Conference Board survey on the internal use of coaching in organizations, including recent trends and thoughts on future directions. Chapter 2 dives into the needs and readiness assessment processes, prompting you to ask the questions necessary to clarify the unique demands of your specific context and the indicators of readiness or challenge that should be taken into account in developing next step plans for your organization. Chapter 3 serves as a "thought partner," with which you can interact to consider the variety of activities or components that might contribute to a coaching culture and which ones and which combinations make the most sense for your organization given its strategic goals.

Having comparative data on other organizations' coaching activities and assessing the needs and readiness of your own organization are important elements to ensuring that quality in your development efforts is only half of the coaching culture equation. Understanding the value and impact of coaching initiatives at the individual, team, and organizational levels is the other half. The topic of evaluation is covered in chapter 4, including models for the evaluation of coaching, best practices, and a new instrument recently developed at CCL, the Coaching Evaluation Assessment (CEA), for understanding coaching impact and the quality of coaching. This part ends with chapter 5, which covers the complicated topic of managing pools of coaches, from recruitment and selection to supervision and accreditation. Drawing on years of CCL's own experience and that of HR leaders within its client organizations across the globe, part 1 offers proven cutting-edge advice to you as you design your own approach to a coaching culture.

All of the authors who contributed chapters to this part provide well-grounded resources, drawn from research and experience, trial and error, successes and failures, and their work will give you a head start in the do-it-yourself process of creating a coaching culture that fits with your organization's values and goals.

chapter
ONE

The Rise of Coaching in Organizations

Amy Lui Abel and Sherlin V. Nair

Workplace dynamics have dramatically changed over the past two decades. Globalization, increased competition and regulations, emerging technologies in the cloud, global connectivity and social media, evolving workforce demographics, and a shorter shelf life of knowledge have not only shrunk world borders but have also all converged to make the workplace more fluid, complex, and ambiguous (Meister & Willyerd, 2010). These sweeping changes may have unleashed the need for a new breed of leaders with new skills and competencies. Gone are the days of superhero CEOs who swooped down to rescue organizations (Senge, 2000). Globalization and inter- and intraconnectedness have destroyed the cult of the hero-leader and made it mandatory for organizations to develop leadership capabilities throughout the organization.

Businesses today operate in an environment where the pace of work will continue to accelerate, talent will be the single most important factor in driving competitive advantage, and the skills and capabilities needed tomorrow may not exist today (Elliott, 2010). This focus on talent and human capital in an evolving business environment has also been the primary and most critical challenge that CEOs globally have identified (Mitchell, Ray, & van Ark, 2013). This was the most important insight to emerge from the responses of 729 CEOs and presidents from across the globe to the 2013 edition of The Conference Board CEO Challenge survey.

We thank Jordan Stabley, research assistant, The Conference Board, for his timely help and support on this project.

Building internal strength and creating value requires an unflinching focus on people, as well as an enterprise-wide dedication to excellence, regardless of the task or the external landscape. For leaders to focus on the human side of business and manage in a highly future-oriented business environment requires them to have new competencies: the ability to lead change, possession of a global thinking and mind-set, the ability to retain and develop talent, and collaboration with others (see exhibit 1.1).

Despite the critical need for leaders to demonstrate these competencies today and be prepared for the future, a recent study conducted by The Conference Board (Abel, Ray, & Roi, 2013) to examine strategic leadership practices found that 40 percent of leaders were not prepared at all or only marginally prepared to meet the business challenges of the next twelve to twenty-four months (see figure 1.1). For any one organization, this could mean that a large number of the leaders do not have the required competencies to meet strategic business goals and objectives. In addition, this lack of preparation of leaders may have further impacts on organizations, especially in the United States and Europe, that will soon have to also face the inevitable vacuum in the senior leadership pool created as the baby boomers begin to retire. With only 9 percent of leaders identified as very prepared to address current and future dilemmas, the study exposes gaps in leadership developmental efforts and a need for organizations to develop their new and existing leaders in order to promote continuity and seamless business growth (see exhibit 1.1).

Figure 1.1
Preparedness of Business Leaders to Meet Upcoming Challenges

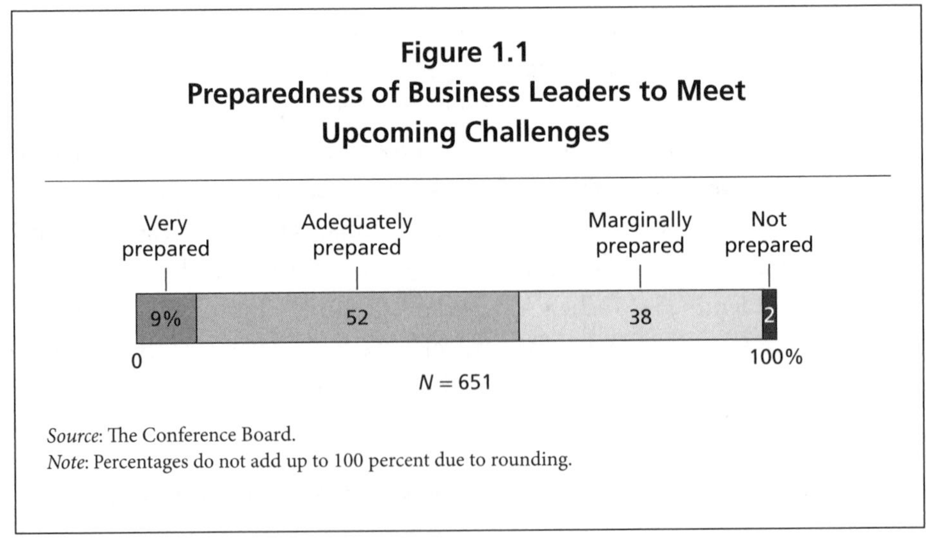

Source: The Conference Board.
Note: Percentages do not add up to 100 percent due to rounding.

Exhibit 1.1
Research Insights: Impact of Leadership Development

Leadership development programs have become laboratories of change. Leaders going through executive developmental programs are introduced to skills and competencies that will help them empower and engage their workforce. Leaders may be born, but there's a growing school of thought that because most aspects of leadership are behavioral, leaders can be developed through a well-crafted leadership development program (Watkins, 2012).

Several studies show the benefits of a successfully implemented leadership development program to improve business outcomes (Coffman, 2000), including these:

- Retention
- Productivity
- Profitability
- Customer loyalty
- Safety

Additional impacts include (Lamoureux, 2007):

- Driving organization and bench strength
- Improving the efficiency and effectiveness of leaders
- Increasing the successful execution of business strategies
- Improving management communication and alignment

Studies by the CCL highlight four benefits of investing in leadership development programs (Center for Creative Leadership, 2008):

1. Improved bottom-line financial performance
2. The ability to attract and retain talent
3. A performance culture
4. Increased organizational agility

With numerous studies drawing a direct linkage from leadership, to profitability, to financial success, few would argue against the need for an explosion and proliferation of new leadership development methods.

INTERNAL COACHING FOR ACCELERATED LEADERSHIP DEVELOPMENT

Based on context and need, leadership development approaches have changed over time. While classroom-based programs and seminars on functional knowledge may have worked in the past, fierce global competition and transitions require organizations to depart from one-size-fits-all solutions toward personalized and customized approaches that target leadership and organizational changes (Byrne & Rees, 2006). Holistic development (Michaelson & Anderson, 2008) has replaced professional growth, which means that personal mastery and work/life integration are considered as important as leading high-performance teams and creating the best places to work. Holistic behaviors and competencies enhanced through targeted approaches can help leaders balance corporate and individual goals, thereby gaining a competitive advantage in the workplace.

The CEO Challenge report highlights the top three human capital strategies to address talent needs: grow talent internally, provide employee training and development, and raise employee engagement (Mitchell et al., 2013). These strategies can be implemented using approaches that have been found to have the most impact for developing leaders: executive coaching or mentoring, action learning initiatives, and focused skill development (Abel et al., 2013). An analysis of these approaches shows that experience-based learning has greater impact than all other types of learning, a finding also explored and supported in depth in CCL's recent book, *Experience-Driven Leader Development: Models, Tools, Best Practices, and Advice for On-the-Job Development* (McCauley, DeRue, Yost, & Taylor, 2013). Experiential learning is learning through action, through experience, and by doing. Unlike traditional classroom situations where instruction is highly structured, instruction in experienced-based learning is designed to engage leaders in direct experiences tied to real-world problems and situations. In this approach, leaders are evaluated on how well they function individually and collectively and in their ability to translate challenges into decisive actions and goals.

Executive coaching is an experiential and individualized leader development approach that is used to build a leader's capability to achieve short- and long-term organization goals. It is conducted through one-on-one and group interactions, driven by data from multiple perspectives, and is based on mutual trust and respect. The organization, the executive, and the executive coach work together in partnership to achieve individual and organizational goals (Executive Coaching Forum, 2008). While coaching is a way for leaders to continue to develop and become more effective, it may no longer be considered a remedial tool to help failing executives solve serious behavioral and technical problems. It is most useful for succession grooming, performance coaching, interpersonal skills development, business etiquette grooming, promotion support, transition management, and conflict resolution. Executive coaching, integrated with a holistic menu of leadership assessment and development tools, may help release many leaders' potential and build an environment that understands, values, and engages leadership capabilities at every level of the organization (Foster, 2014).

Trends show that there may be growth in organizational investments for executive coaching in the future (see table 1.1). According to The Conference Board report on executive coaching, the organizational focus on coaching will continue to grow in the next five years (Abel & Nair, 2012).

INTERNAL COACHING

Internal coaching is a one-on-one developmental intervention supported by the organization and provided by a colleague within the organization who is trusted to shape and deliver a program yielding individual professional growth (Frisch, 2001). Coaches are engaged by organizations to help leaders align personal

Table 1.1
Future Investments in Development Approaches

Developmental Approach	
Executive coaching or mentoring	48%
Action learning initiatives (business challenges, simulation)	41%
Focused skill development	33%
Executive assessments	31%
Executive education/academic university programs	28%
International assignments	28%
Rotational programs	22%
Social learning	5%

Source: The Conference Board.

Note: The question asked was, "Where is your organization allocating greater resources in the next twelve months?" $N = 654$. Multiple selections allowed.

development with business strategy. Until recently, executive coaches were almost always external to the organization. However, recent trends and research suggest that coaches are being developed internally to create greater capacity for the ever-growing demand for ready leaders. In a survey conducted in 2010, 61 percent of companies said that they expected to rely more on internal coaches in the next few years. This reliance on internal coaching increased to 72 percent when companies were asked again in 2012 (see figure 1.2).

The reasons driving increased reliance on internal coaching may include the following factors:

1. A need to develop more leaders lower in the organizational hierarchy
2. An increased demand for coaching
3. Internal coaches better understand the business and culture
4. A need to reduce external spending

While costs and external spending may have been assumed to be prime reasons for choosing internal coaches in this slowly recovering economy, these findings clearly indicate that the need to cut costs is not as much a consideration for organizations as the growing need to develop leadership capabilities across all organizational levels and functions.

Figure 1.2
Percentage of Companies' Expected Use of Internal Coaching

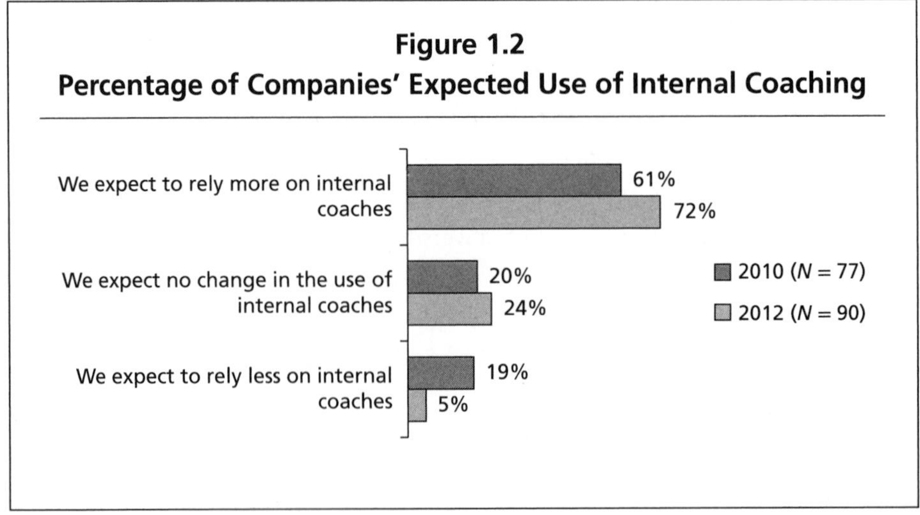

INTERNAL COACHING VERSUS EXTERNAL COACHING

The Conference Board 2012 Executive Coaching Survey revealed that organizations consider the interplay of a number of factors when choosing between using an internal coach and hiring an external coach (see figure 1.3). The top two issues related to this decision deal with the type of development need and the level of coachee. The other determinants are costs, availability of a coach, and coachee preference.

Based on an analysis of the factors leading to increased use of internal coaching and the determinants that help organizations choose between internal and external coaches, it would appear that organizations may use internal coaching more frequently to develop emerging leaders and potential leaders identified earlier in their careers and groomed to assume diversified leadership roles in the future. External coaches may still be used extensively to coach the executive and C-suite levels of an organization.

While organizations in the past may have hired external coaches to "fix" a high-performing leader with a serious issue, both internal and external coaching also encompass assignments focused on transforming a leader with good performance into a high-performing leader (Abel, 2011). Based on an analysis of the advantages and limitations of both internal and external coaches shown in table 1.2, it is important for organizations to remember that it is not so much a question of which type of coaching is better and that the two types of coaching

Figure 1.3
Primary Determinants When Choosing between Internal and External Coaches

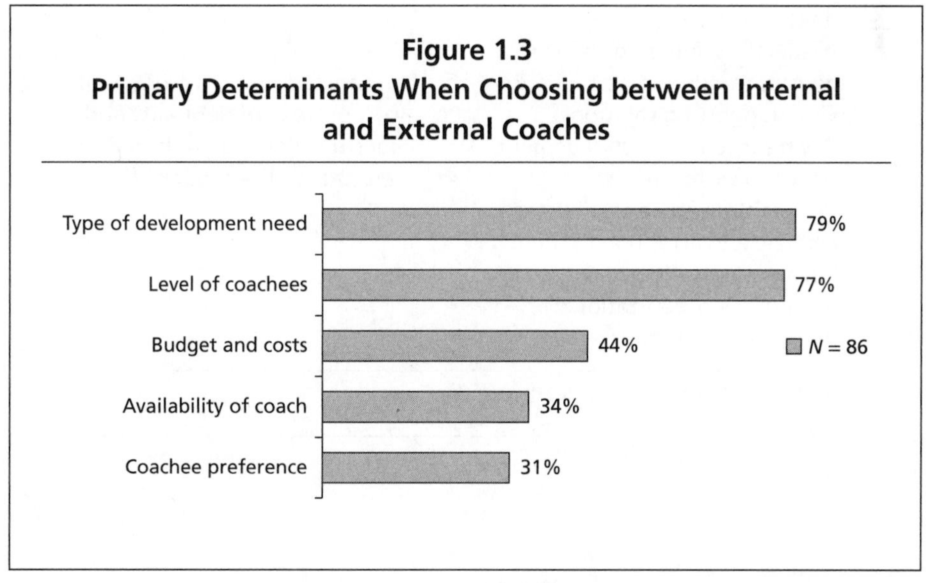

Table 1.2
Comparing External and Internal Coaches

Internal Coaches	External Coaches
• Have an insider view of the company's culture, processes, goals, and important stakeholders • Have a keener sense and awareness of the executive's developmental need based on internal performance data • Help save cost since coaching becomes part of their job description, with no extra expense for the business • Are easily accessible and flexible • Can see leaders in action and be able to provide just-in-time responses • May have varying levels of formal training and experiences and may have less credibility • Can have a difficult time earning a coachee's trust and confidence for fear of information leakage within the organization • May lack cross-organizational perspectives and insights into industry trends and best practices when suggesting solutions • May treat coaching engagements as secondary to their other deliverables and hence allocate less time and attention to them • Can have less influence if they are lower in the organizational hierarchy than their coachees	• Can bring an outsider's perspective to issues and are better able to be objective and neutral • Are not bound by internal constraints or "political agendas" • Can be very expensive • May be less available for quick and easy access • Are more likely to be professionally trained and certified as a coach • May instill greater faith in confidentiality, increasing their credibility and trust with coachees • Can provide external benchmarking criteria and insights into industry trends • May suggest external networks, associations, and resources relevant for coachee development • Operate only for a finite period of time • May be subject to the organization's concerns about corporate confidentiality and sensitive data being shared external to the organization

Sources: Abel (2011); Abel and Nair (2012).

need not be viewed as competing with each other. Both types of coaching can be included within the broader leadership development strategy.

INTERNAL COACHING PRACTICES

The demand for flexible but targeted leadership development options and the widespread acceptance of coaching in organizations have paved the way for the growth of internal coaches who, as either a formal or informal part of their job, develop leaders within their own organization. While no definitive guidelines exist for the design, development, and implementation of internal coaching programs, The Conference Board 2012 Executive Coaching Survey results provided insight into the emerging role of internal coaches and their current coaching practices.

Profile of Internal Coaches

The survey revealed that internal coaches were mostly HR professionals who coached on a part-time or full-time basis. Managers and coaches from the business units were also found to coach as part of their job responsibilities, but their numbers were significantly lower than coaches from the HR functions (see figure 1.4). HR partners have historically been doing some form of coaching already. But now, with increased focus on using internal coaching as an effective

Figure 1.4
Profile of Internal Coaches

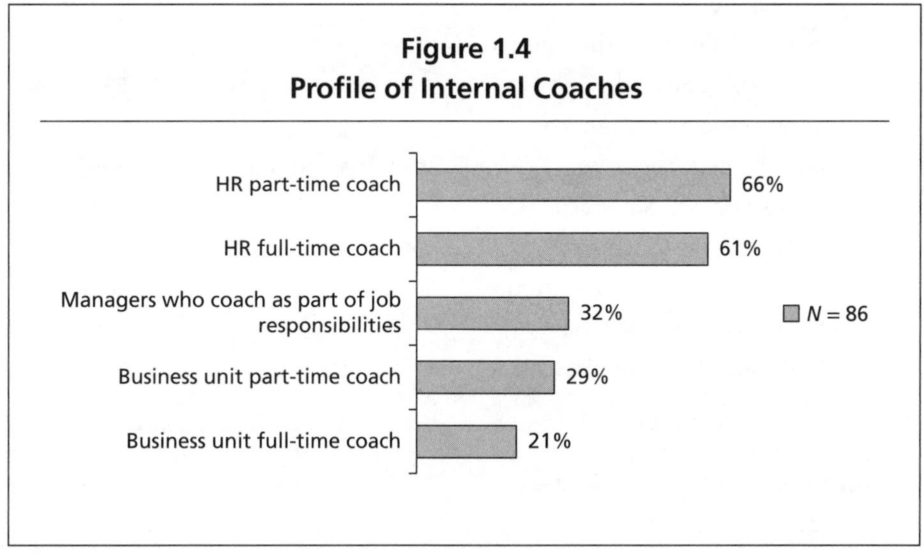

tool for leadership development, the process is becoming more formal and coaches are offered training and support when needed.

Selection of Internal Coaches

Organizations select internal coaches based on a variety of factors, such as credibility as a coach (84 percent), prior training and experience in coaching (70 percent), and strong people skills (70 percent). Business acumen and strong executive presence are also important, emphasizing the need for internal coaches to build on their business knowledge in order to earn the trust and respect of businesses and leaders whom they support (see table 1.3). Prior training and experience with assessment tools, formal coaching certifications, and academic degrees ranked lower on the selection criteria scale in our survey, which may not necessarily suggest a disregard for formal certification programs and education but relatively less emphasis in comparison to the other factors. Membership in coaching and related

Table 1.3
Criteria for Selecting Internal Coaches

Criterion	
Credibility as a coach	84%
Reputation for being a strong people manager or feedback provider	70%
Prior training and experience in coaching	70%
Business acumen	59%
Strong executive presence	58%
Prior training and experience with assessment tools	49%
Interest of internal coach	46%
Formal coaching certifications, academic degrees	36%
Minimum performance criteria	28%
Minimum tenure criteria	17%
Professional coaching association memberships	12%
Other	2%

Source: The Conference Board.

Note: $N = 86$. Multiple answers were allowed.

professional organizations was ranked the least significant criterion considered when selecting internal coaches.

Organizations have found that many individuals are already coaching informally or have demonstrated passion for coaching and have developed a reputation for being strong people developers. Though they would appear to be natural recruits, their eventual selection as internal coaches is determined by their credibility as a coach.

Preparation of Internal Coaches

Although formal certification was not a crucial selection criterion in figure 1.5, it has been found that many internal coaches come with an academic degree in organizational psychology, HR, or adult learning, as well as experience with organizational development and consulting efforts. From an organizational perspective, since internal coaching is a relatively new field of leadership development, there is an apparent lack of consistency in the preparation of internal coaches (see figure 1.5). The most common types of preparation for internal coaches that companies reported in the survey are informal briefing by stakeholders (26 percent), an internal certification program (24 percent), and a formal orientation program (20 percent). Lack of any form of institutionalized standards or processes in 19 percent of companies raises serious concerns about the quality, credibility, and selection of coaches. However, trends show that the

Figure 1.5
Preparation of Internal Coaches

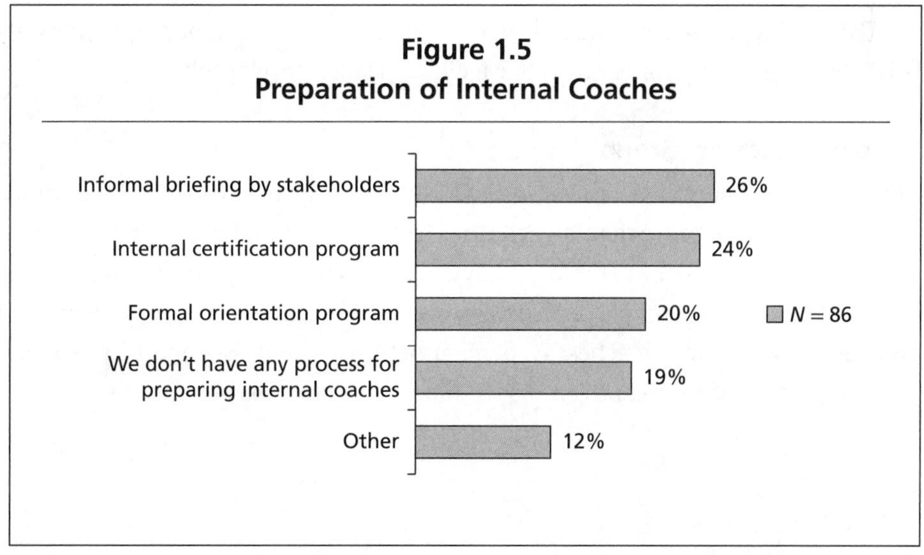

professionalism and credibility of the practice of coaching are slowly increasing as organizations develop standard criteria for internal and external certification processes, articulate competencies, and create foundational training curricula for coaches.

Types of Internal Coaching

Leaders have varying types of developmental needs. To address these diverse needs, internal coaches engage in different types of coaching. The study identified these most commonly used types of coaching:

- 360-degree debriefing and other assessment tools (e.g., DiSC, Myers-Briggs Type Indicator, Hogan)
- Career coaching (e.g., providing future direction, addressing job-fit issues)
- Development-focused coaching (e.g., building on strengths, preparing for new experiences)
- Performance-focused coaching (e.g., changing behaviors or building new skills to improve performance)
- Onboarding coaching (e.g., helping new leaders align to the organizational structure and vision)
- Transition coaching (e.g., new internal job, business function, or geography)
- Team coaching (e.g., enhancing effectiveness of intact teams)

Exhibit 1.2 provides an example of how one company developed and refined its own 360-degree assessment to better facilitate leader development.

Size of Coaching Group

The number of internal coaches selected to support organizational needs can range from one coach to more than fifty coaches (see figure 1.6). The study revealed that 37 percent of companies employed anywhere between one and five coaches per year; 24 percent of companies between six and fifteen coaches; 7 percent used sixteen to twenty-five coaches; 12 percent between twenty-six and fifty coaches; and 16 percent of companies employed more than fifty coaches per year.

Exhibit 1.2
Fidelity Investments: 360 Degrees of Coaching

In 2011, Fidelity Investments implemented a newly revised leadership development competency model and an enhanced, customized 360-degree tool for leaders. Because the company was committed to providing all leaders taking the assessment with an in-depth debriefing of the results, Fidelity established a process to train and certify internal debriefing facilitators and coaches.

Previously all leaders who took an older 360-degree tool received a debriefing with someone from HR to discuss the results and implications. That HR professional would also coach the leader in developing an action plan. However, there was significant variance in the quality of debriefings and coaching provided, in part because any HR professional who completed a one-day certification workshop was allowed to conduct this debriefing and coaching session. In an effort to raise the quality of the debriefing coaching sessions for Fidelity's new leadership competency 360-degree tool, the organization redesigned the qualification and certification processes for their internal debriefing of facilitators and coaches.

A separate competency model was developed for the practice of debriefing facilitation and coaching. Heads of HR across business divisions were asked to nominate HR generalists who demonstrated "natural coaching abilities" and a mind-set to be a coach. Approximately 10 percent of the eligible HR generalist population was nominated. These few nominated individuals had to complete a newly designed certification program prior to starting a coaching assignment.

The certification process had two components. The first provided participants with details about the design and approach of the 360-degree tool, content about coaching skills, and the opportunity to practice these skills while receiving feedback in small group exercises. The second component involved pairing up participants to go through the entire process and then discuss the 360-degree tool and its results. This real-life "simulation" provided participants with the experience of what a leader would go through, an increased understanding of the 360-degree tool itself, and a framework that encouraged them to be more empathetic as they delivered potentially

(*continued*)

Exhibit 1.2 (*Continued*)

difficult feedback to individuals. "The internal coach needs to model development, openness to growth, and continuous learning for themselves and those they work with," explains William H. Hodgetts, vice president of enterprise coaching and assessment at Fidelity Investments.

During the simulation exercise, a master coach assessor observed and evaluated the participant's coaching approach. Nominated individuals who attended this program were not automatically certified simply because they completed the course. While a majority of nominated HR professionals did become certified, it was the master coach assessor who made the final determination of whether a participant was ready for certification. A master coach assessor is another level of internal certification offered within the organization.

Evaluation of coaching sessions from individuals shows consistently higher satisfaction levels and much less variance in ratings of coach performance since the launch of the new certification process. Internal coaches have also provided anecdotal feedback on their own increased effectiveness in coaching discussions and their desires to continue their development as a coach by pursuing additional external training programs.

Fidelity recently certified sixty additional debriefing facilitator coaches as the demand for internal coaching support continues to increase. In the four years since its inception and launch, Fidelity's Leadership Success Profile 360 tool has gained widespread use throughout the organization, both as an assessment used with individual leaders and as part of the organization's high-potential leadership development programs. Internal coaches continue to support the debriefing and action planning activities around the 360-degree results. In the high-potential leadership program, internal coaches are also enhancing their roles beyond the debriefing by assisting in action plan development, ensuring alignment between the action plan and the direct manager's goals, and working with high-potential leaders throughout the year to implement and evaluate results of the action plans. What began as a limited internal coaching role for debriefing facilitation is gradually expanding to encompass additional coaching activities.

Source: Abel (2011).

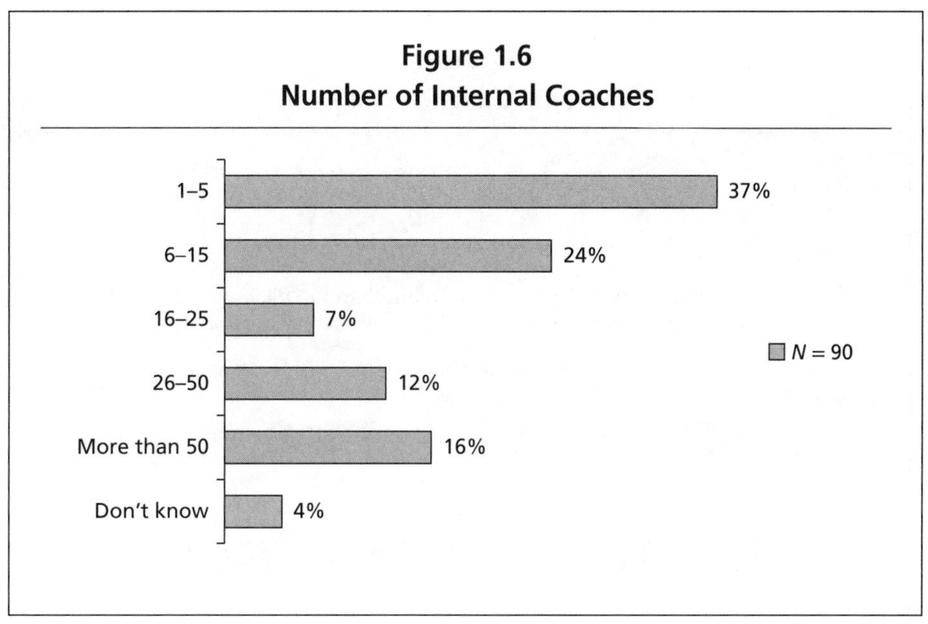

The number of coaches employed by an organization is also related to the company's revenue. An analysis of the number of full-time and part-time coaches by company revenue reveals that the smaller the company, the lower the number of coaches employed per year, which is not surprising (see figure 1.7). Most companies with revenues under $5 billion engaged one to fifteen coaches per year. Companies with revenues between $5 billion and $10 billion were found to hire more than fifty coaches per year. There was a greater range in companies with revenues of more than $10 billion, which were found to hire anywhere from one to more than fifty per year. Larger companies with more employees were expected to have more internal coaches to cover larger populations of leaders and their teams.

Average Length of Time per Month Spent Coaching

In 41 percent of companies (see figure 1.8), internal coaches spend one to two hours coaching per month while 20 percent of coaches spend three to four hours in coaching. This is interesting, especially in comparison to The Conference Board 2010 Executive Coaching report (Pomerleau, Silvert, WanVeer, Desrosiers, & Henderson, 2011), which found that most coaches were spending three to four hours per month coaching their coachees. At the lower and higher extremes, coaches were found to be active for less than one hour per month in 3 percent of companies,

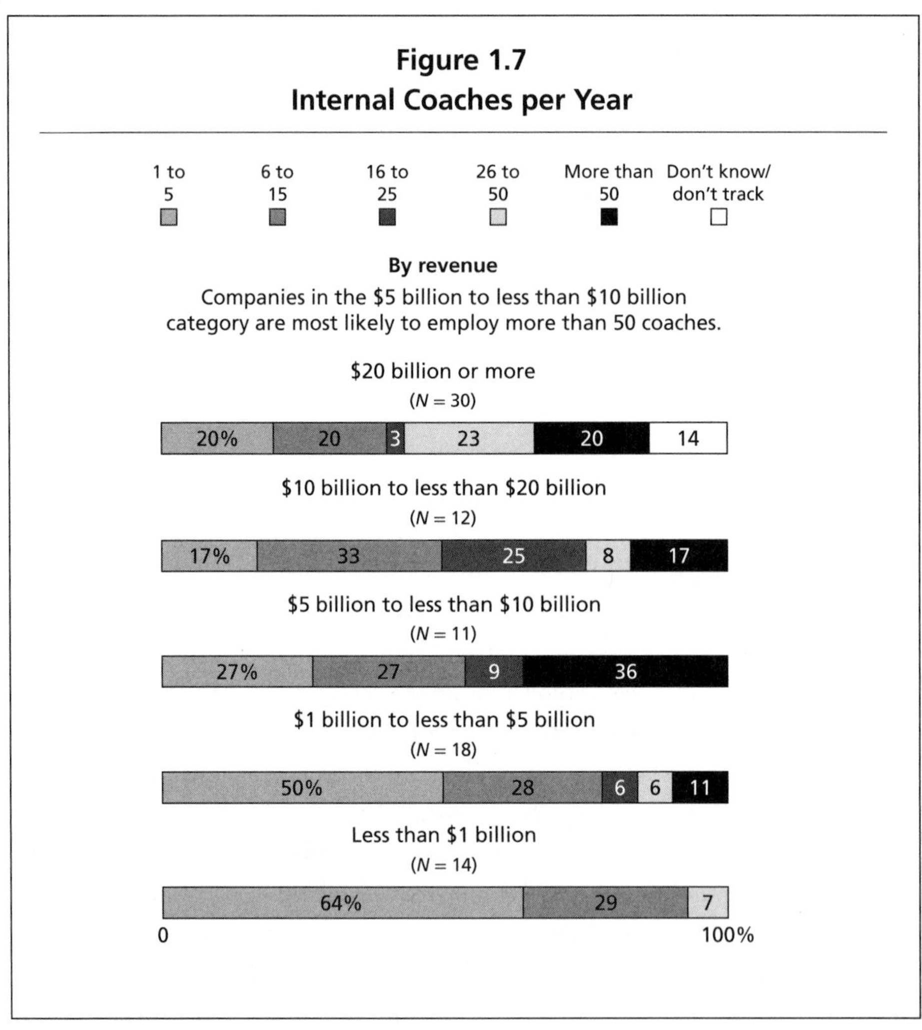

whereas in 9 percent of companies, coaches spent at least eight hours a month actively coaching.

Ongoing Development Opportunities

An internal coaching program can be a cost-effective tool for developing talent. If structured properly, it can be an effective method for developing leaders. The effectiveness of internal coaches can be increased by providing them with ongoing developmental opportunities (see table 1.4), such as sharing new coaching tools and practices, peer support groups and mentoring programs, and sharing themes

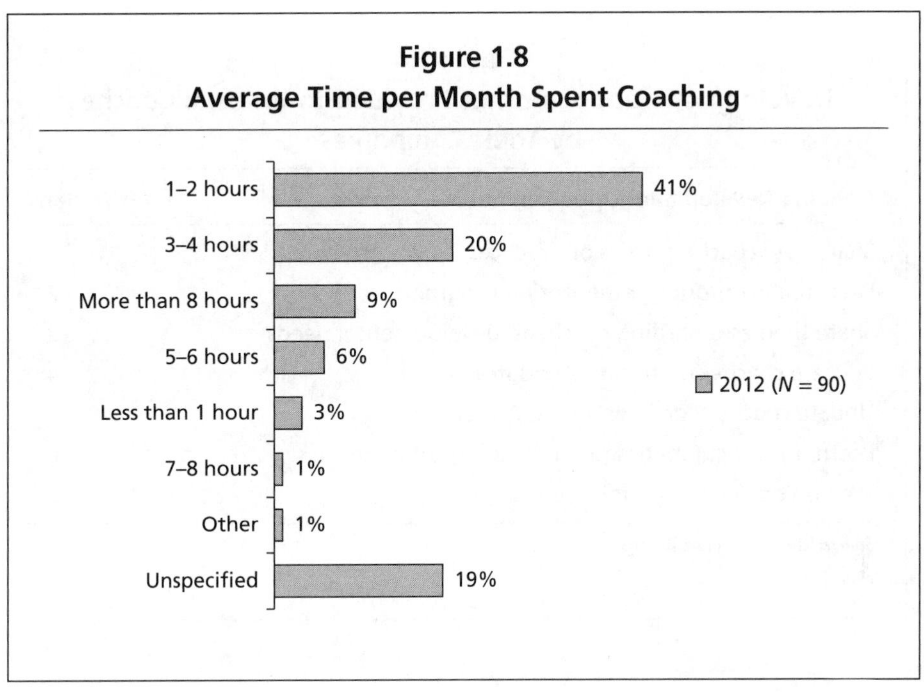

regarding their coachees' developmental needs. The other ongoing opportunities for organizations to enhance the quality of their internal coaching include educating coaches on business updates, providing regular and ongoing updates on coaching policies and procedures, and creating learning curricula based on coaching competencies. Learning from others, especially other coaching experts, is helpful for refining skills and working through issues that arise during coaching engagements. Being ill informed about industry trends and practices may not only affect a coach's ability to do his job well, but may also affect the coachees who rely on the coaches to guide them through complex developmental challenges and provide them with candid directions and best practices for future.

Charge for Use of Internal Coaches

While the developmental need and level of coachee have already been identified as key factors contributing to the rise of internal coaching, another factor may be that only 10 percent of companies "charge back" to the coachee's line of business for the services provided by the internal coaches (see figure 1.9). In 74 percent of companies, no line item engagement charges are incurred for the use of internal coaching, while in 11 percent of companies, even if the coach's time is paid for, it is

Table 1.4
Development Opportunities Provided to Internal Coaches by Their Companies

Ongoing Development Opportunities	Rank
Share new coaching tools or practices	1
Peer support groups or mentoring programs	2
Share themes regarding coachees' developmental needs	3
Educate coaches on business updates	4
Update coaching policies and procedures	5
Learning curriculum based on coaching competencies	6
We don't offer any ongoing development	7

Source: The Conference Board.

Note: $N = 86$.

charged through the wider central corporate budget with minimal impact on the direct business unit. This can be a contributing factor for the continued reliance on and growth of internal coaching. However, as internal coaching takes center stage and becomes part of the organizational norm for development, it will be interesting to see if costs emerge as an important part of the business conversation and if internal charges will be handled differently in the future. Exhibit 1.3 offers an example of how one organization has used internal and external coaches to gain momentum and achieve success.

Evaluation of Internal Coaching

Evaluation, a critical part of the executive coaching process, is necessary for the establishment of accountability, the determination of returns on investment, the linking of behaviors to performance goals, and fine-tuning the coaching process, as discussed in detail in chapter 4 of this book. According to David B. Peterson (2009), director of executive coaching and leadership at Google, "Coaching is a time-intensive and expensive engagement, and organizations should insist on getting regular and formal progress reviews, even if they are only qualitative" (p. 95).

Figure 1.9
Charge Back for the Use of Internal Coaching

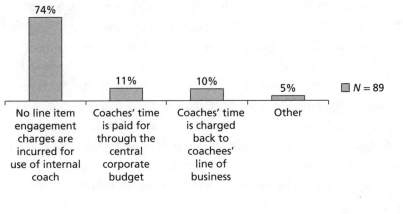

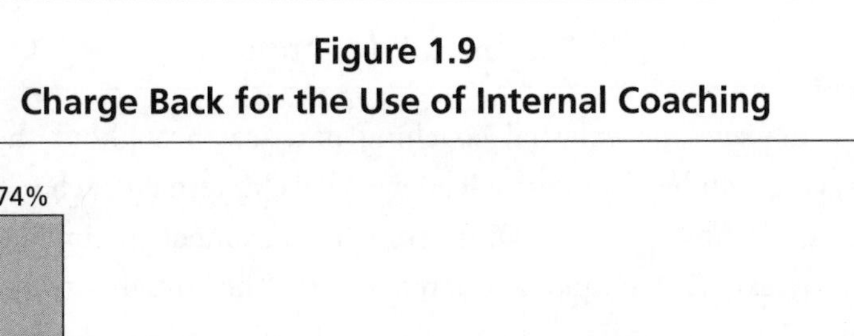

Exhibit 1.3
Gaining Momentum: Executive Coaching Practices at Ernst & Young

Ernst & Young (EY), one of the Big Four accounting firms with assurance, tax, transaction, and advisory services, is one of the largest professional service firms in the world, employing 152,000 people worldwide.

EY recognizes coaching as a core component of how it develops its people. The organization is gaining momentum with targeted use of external coaches and the growing use of internal coaches. Executive coaching is "seen as a desired benefit for high-performers and a valuable asset to the firm," noted Jackie Bayer, former director of the Americas' Executive Coaching Team. Coaching also serves as a means of support for new partners, newly titled partners taking on the firm's leadership positions, and partners on overseas assignments, as well as legacy partners who are nearing retirement. Focused coaching is used to help leaders transition to new roles and overcome barriers to accelerated performance and growth.

(continued)

Exhibit 1.3 (*Continued*)

EY manages its external coaching practice throughout the coaching engagement to best support a leader's needs. External coaches are selected based on their experience with senior management in similar industries, business experience, and good references. The initial screening process includes a standardized interview protocol that is conducted at the enterprise level, and selected coaches are added to the firm's directory. Contracting and monitoring of engagements are handled locally. Although there is an existing companywide onboarding orientation process for external coaches, most onboarding occurs informally by stakeholders since new coaches are brought in at the local office level. Fees for external coaches are set at the enterprise level with global differences. While travel expenses are compensated for, travel time is not, and assessment fees are paid on approval. Currently evaluation of coaches is conducted informally at local offices, with progress monitored and results evaluated. Over the past five years, dependence on external coaches has diminished, with such coaches being brought in for special development needs or when an internal coach is unavailable.

In a shift of coaching practices, EY has developed a robust internal coaching team made up of full-time professional coaches. Internal coaches coach the senior-level partners in leadership transition and oversee the selection, training, and development of new part-time internal coaches who support lower levels of executives to reach deeper in the organization. While internal coaches are chosen from the senior ranks of the HR organization, their eventual selection is based on tenure with the firm, an understanding of the firm's business and culture, high performance in past roles, and a reputation for strong people and coaching skills.

Once they are selected, internal coaches undergo a forty-hour rigorous training program spread out over six months. The program includes classroom training of coaching skills, telecourses, action learning groups, one-on-one mentoring sessions, and written and oral exams. For continued development of internal coaches, the firm conducts education conferences

Exhibit 1.3 (*Continued*)

periodically, provides financial support for external learning, and maintains a virtual community of practice for anyone involved in or interested in coaching within the firm. The evaluation process for internal coaches is well developed and involves formal evaluations by survey and interviews at the midpoint and end of an engagement.

Source: Abel and Nair (2012).

In The Conference Board 2012 Executive Coaching Survey, the fact that 28 percent of companies said they had no evaluation process in place to measure the coaching effectiveness of the internal coaches may well be a reflection of an internal coaching process still in its nascent stages of development (see figure 1.10). However, in 69 percent of companies, internal coaches are given evaluations formally (31 percent) or informally (38 percent). Informal evaluation usually involves conversations with critical stakeholders, while formal evaluations measure the effectiveness of coaching deliverables agreed on before the start of the coaching

Figure 1.10
Evaluation of Internal Coaches

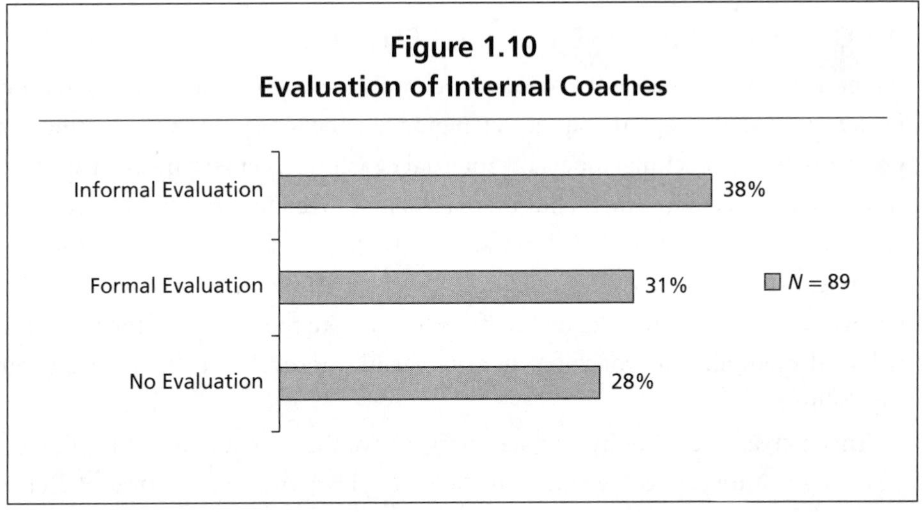

engagement. Organizations keen on developing a robust coaching practice may also consider the following evaluation methods:

- Assessments or surveys of coachee satisfaction
- Assessments or surveys of behavioral change by managers of coachees
- Turnover rates and retention rates for coachees
- Promotion rates of coachees after coaching
- Business performance (revenue or operational metrics) of coachees
- Employee engagement scores of teams or divisions of coachees

Formal Recognition for Efforts

Internal coaches were recognized in different ways by companies in The Conference Board survey. Common practices include recognizing internal coaches by including their coaching responsibilities in their individual performance goals or giving them credit during annual events or performance reviews. A small number of companies also offer bonuses and other monetary benefits. While it could be seen that many companies have some form of a recognition program in place, an equal number do not. Coaching efforts that are unaccompanied by any kind of formal recognition programs for sustained periods of time may result in a motivational freeze, thereby affecting the quality of the coaching partnerships over time.

A COACHING CULTURE FOR THE FUTURE

As markets and businesses become more complex and global, the need to develop leaders who can adapt to rapidly changing business realities will continue to grow. Executive coaching, especially internal coaching, is emerging as an effective response to this environment, but there remains a need to formalize its processes and structures. Creating benchmarks and standards for the certification and training of internal coaches, measures to chart the effectiveness of coaching engagements, and clearly defined metrics to evaluate the impact of the programs will add credibility to coaching as a powerful approach for enhancing talent capabilities.

This increased credibility and acceptance have the potential to contribute to a coaching culture across the enterprise, allowing leaders and executives at all levels to reap its benefits for greater organizational impact and individual success. A coaching culture can promote dialogue and feedback between leaders and teams at all levels of the organization, not just for the few. Forward-looking organizations are already seeking insights and approaches related to successfully supporting and encouraging a culture of coaching to prepare their employees for the challenges of the future.

SUMMARY OF KEY FINDINGS

- Human capital is the main challenge identified by CEOs across the globe. The top three strategies identified to address these talent challenges are develop talent internally, provide employee training and development, and raise employee engagement.
- Top competencies for leaders to adapt to current and future business demands are leading change, retaining and developing top talent, and a global mind-set. These competencies are in direct response to emerging trends like globalization, changing demographics, and technological advancements.
- Companies are investing in leadership development approaches that show maximum impact: executive coaching, action learning programs, and focused skill development.
- Organizations can create and deliver solutions that are personal, customized to address distinct regional and global needs (as one size does not fit all), and multifaceted in nature. Executive coaching can be used as an effective tool for preparing leaders who are unprepared or only marginally prepared to meet the business challenges ahead. Future challenges also include creating a successful pipeline of competent leaders.
- Of those using internal coaches, almost three-quarters expect to increase their use over the next few years.
- When senior leaders are choosing between internal and external coaching, the type of developmental need and the level of the coachee are important factors for them to consider in decision making.
- According to survey participants, the most common types of internal coaching are 360-degree debriefing, development-focused coaching, and other assessment tool debriefings.
- In terms of efforts to support their internal coaches, respondents ranked sharing new coaching tools and practices, peer support groups or mentoring

programs, and sharing themes regarding coachees' developmental needs as their most important development opportunities.

- There is further need to structure and formalize internal coaching programs, especially in relation to selecting and preparing internal coaches, the average length of the program, the evaluation process, and the formal recognition of internal coaches for successful implementation of coaching engagements.
- There is typically no charge-back to the business unit for the use of internal coaches currently; this practice may evolve as internal coaching becomes more common within organizations.
- Creating a coaching culture requires a multifaceted strategy of training and supporting managers to adopt a coaching style, investing in developing coaching capability in senior leaders and HR professionals, and preparing internal coaches for maximum impact.
- While best practices are helpful, it is important to remember that coaching is less about transactional and technical perfections and more about who is engaged in coaching and about the quality of partnerships created between the coach and the coachee.

Our hope is that organizations use these studies not only to benchmark against their own practices but also to create engagements that have results to support an individual's development and the organization's bottom line.

chapter
TWO

Assessing Your Organization's Need for Coaching

Emily Hoole

A basic assessment regarding the need for coaching in an organization begins with the business strategy and the clarification of a leadership strategy to support the business strategy. CCL's work with clients starts with an understanding of key business drivers and the implications for leadership and leadership development. Understanding the leadership needs of the organization, including the quantity and quality of leaders, skills and behaviors necessary, and collective leadership capabilities and leadership culture necessary for success, may uncover opportunities for coaching as a possible solution in meeting certain goals.

These coaching solutions may address leadership strategy goals at multiple levels. In a high-growth market where the number of leaders needs to increase 10 percent each year, coaching can be used to accelerate and support leaders moving up quickly. Organizations working to turn an organizational capability, such as innovation or execution, into a competitive advantage may leverage internal coaches, team leaders as coaches, or managers coaching employees at all levels. When coaching is identified as a possible solution linked to leadership and business strategy, the organization's readiness and capacity to support the coaching approach are necessary to ensure the most appropriate fit, build support, and increase readiness in a way most likely to support success.

This chapter is organized as a series of steps to assess the fit of coaching in the organization and the organizational readiness and capabilities necessary for success:

Step 1: Assess your current organizational stage of coaching.

Step 2: Determine if coaching is the right solution.

Step 3: Assess and build your organizational readiness.

Step 4: Review your internal capacity.

Step 5: Build the case for coaching.

Engaging in all of these steps will ensure that you have taken the relevant elements into account when moving forward with any type of coaching effort within your organization. Success starts with understanding where the organization is; building readiness and capacity; aligning stakeholders, including the target audience for a coaching intervention; and articulating what results are expected and how these results will be measured. We begin the process by examining the current stage of coaching within your organization.

STEP 1: ASSESS YOUR ORGANIZATIONAL STAGE OF COACHING

Deeply understanding the current state and use of coaching within the organization is necessary for effective planning of the next steps in the coaching journey. We have found five levels of coaching use within organizations (Riddle & Pothier, 2011) depending on the experience and maturity of the HR function (see figure 2.1). These levels also differ based on the leadership culture and perspective of leadership as individual, collective, or systemic. When an organization moves from a view of leadership as individual to a more systemic view of leadership as a collective social process (Drath et al., 2008), this new understanding opens up opportunities to use coaching as an organization-wide capability rather than continuing to view it as an individual intervention from an outside professional.

Organizations at the early stages of coaching use coaching in an ad hoc fashion. As a result, they lack a comprehensive perspective regarding current coaching efforts within the organization that would permit an understanding of the overall value or impact of what is occurring. There is typically a lack of alignment with systems and strategy at this stage, but the positive perceptions regarding the coaching that is occurring provide a springboard to move to the next phase.

Figure 2.1
Organizational Levels of Coaching

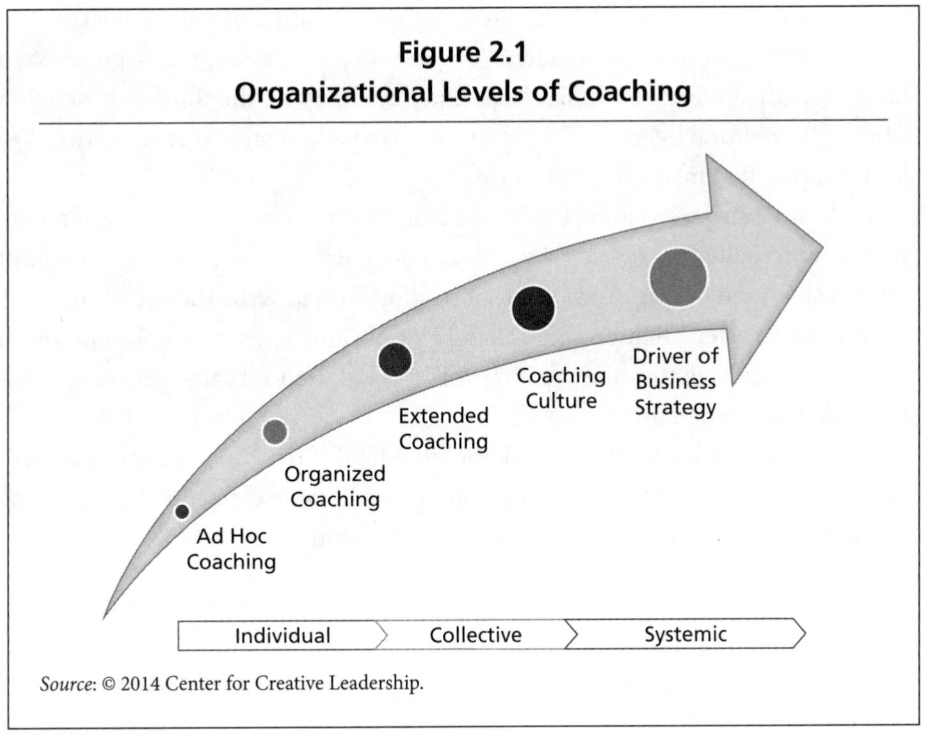

Source: © 2014 Center for Creative Leadership.

After coaching efforts have proliferated within an organization, there is often a movement toward centralization of coaching to better understand the investment and return and to ensure quality and consistency. At this organized coaching stage, organizations typically develop a point of view regarding the use of coaching and a philosophy to guide the work.

When organizations move to the extended coaching stage, coaching skills and behaviors are viewed as a fundamental expectation of leaders, and these expectations are incorporated into performance and reward systems. The perspective regarding coaching shifts from something that is done to leaders to a belief that coaching is something leaders do. More focus is placed on supporting leaders through transitions or challenging assignments in addition to the use of coaching to close competency gaps.

Organizations moving into the coaching culture phase systematically use coaching cascaded throughout the organization to enhance the overall culture and link day-to-day coaching behaviors and skills to business strategy or goals. A long-term commitment to coaching is evident, and senior leaders are seen to embrace and role-model coaching behaviors. Established standards and sophisticated processes are evident. Organizations that reach this point often have a long history of coaching efforts and have invested the time and energy in shifting the cultural beliefs of the organization to get coaching recognized as a key leadership skill to measure and reward.

In the final stage, coaching becomes a true driver of business strategy. It moves from an internally focused activity between people in an organization to a type of relationship used to transform external relationships as well. The use of coaching approaches in sales situations is an example. Coaching approaches become key to inquiry processes within the organization and are used for large-scale organizational development efforts.

Exhibit 2.1 can be used as a quick tool to establish the current stage of organizational coaching use within an organization and point to elements characterizing higher stages of coaching to target as an organization continues to evolve.

Exhibit 2.1
Checklist to Determine Organizational Stage of Coaching

Level 1: Ad Hoc Coaching

- ❑ Various departments and HR groups use external coaching to meet individual leader needs.
- ❑ Coaching with individual leaders focuses on leadership gaps.
- ❑ The organization often initiates coaching with a focus on derailing or failing employees.
- ❑ A key expected outcome is retention of high-potential leaders.

Level 2: Organized Coaching

- ❑ Administration is more centralized, and there is an understanding of the scope and scale and the investment in coaching.
- ❑ Policies and standards for coaches exist and are used to maintain quality.
- ❑ Coaching focuses on accelerating leader development and supporting leaders in new assignments or through challenging assignments.
- ❑ The balance of external to internal coaches is weighted more heavily toward external experts.

Exhibit 2.1 (*Continued*)

Level 3: Extended Coaching

- ❑ Coaching is an expectation of leaders in the organization, and this is recognized in performance and reward systems.
- ❑ Advanced development of internal professionally trained coaches and a strong mix of internal to external coaches are used throughout the organization.
- ❑ Use of coaching is aligned with and supports talent management and leadership development systems.
- ❑ There is a greater use of team coaching for development and change management.

Level 4: Coaching Culture

- ❑ Coaching is seen as a key organizational capability to advance organizational goals such as innovation.
- ❑ Coaching skills and behaviors are an expected part of the day-to-day way people work together.
- ❑ Multiple coaching approaches are used and cascaded throughout the organization.
- ❑ Organization and senior management have a long-term commitment to coaching.

Level 5: Driver of Business Strategy

- ❑ Coaching is a recognized part of critical relationships (such as sales) internally and externally to advance the business strategy.
- ❑ Coaching is used as a key lever in organizational change processes.
- ❑ Full engagement and modeling of coaching by the CEO and top team is visible throughout the organization.
- ❑ Coaching conversations are used throughout the organization to generate creative thinking and new solutions at all levels during the strategy development process.

Beginning with a clear sense of what stage the organization is in is the essential first step, followed by evaluating the potential use of coaching against other possible solutions. Knowing your organizational stage of coaching can point to realistic next steps in determining appropriate coaching solutions to move the organization toward the next higher stage.

STEP 2: DETERMINE IF COACHING IS THE RIGHT SOLUTION

Assuming the organization has a clearly articulated leadership strategy identifying the individual behaviors and collective capabilities necessary to drive business strategy, it must still determine if coaching is the right solution at this time. Often specific types of developmental interventions become preferred methods by senior leaders and human resources because of previous experience, without sufficient attention to matching identified needs and issues with the most appropriate approach. In many cases, coaching may be used as a hammer for every issue that may be seen as a nail. Organizations should explore a full range of alternative developmental interventions to determine the most appropriate approach.

For example, leadership development programs may be a better fit for the organization when common gaps exist within a leadership group, such as at the front line or within middle management, or when there is a clear need to get a level of leadership aligned and working toward the same strategy. A shared leadership development experience can build and reinforce leadership expectations and culture, as well as create essential leadership networks necessary within the organization. In this case, coaching can be used as part of a transformational leadership experience to support the individual needs of leaders as they go through a more standardized leadership development process.

Management training, along with leadership development, may be the correct approach when larger numbers of individuals transition from an individual contributor role to a first-time-manager role. When new operationally focused initiatives are launched, such as Lean or Six Sigma, management training to quickly "skill up" a target group supported by technical coaching for implementation may be called for. Other issues best addressed through management training are areas such as time management, business acumen, strategic planning, supervision, and implementing organization-specific processes around performance and talent management. At times, some of these areas may arise in an individual coaching engagement, but when a broad need exists within an organization, coaching may not be the initial response to select.

In organizations that are struggling with issues of accountability or shifting a culture to a results orientation, performance management may be what is needed. An organization may be implementing a new strategy and needs to create strong alignment or individual, team, and organizational performance, yet its managers throughout the organization lack this capacity. Implementation of a strong performance management process and supporting managers in creating a clear line of sight for employees between day-to-day actions and organizational goals may be the key lever to driving business strategy. Coaching by HR may be needed to support such an effort, so in many cases, coaching may be part of a broader solution. Often HR may consider the use of coaching for an individual leader experiencing performance issues with the belief that executive coaching can "fix" the leader and the issue. We strongly believe external coaching should not be used to shift the responsibility for dealing with performance issues from the organization and the individual's manager to an external party. These issues should be dealt with through the organization's internal performance review process. Table 2.1 provides the pros and cons of different types of organizational interventions.

After multiple options have been explored and the pros and cons of each weighed, a clear understanding should exist regarding the fit of coaching as the solution or as a part of a broader solution to achieve the organization's talent and business strategy prior to moving to a development and implementation phase.

During this needs assessment phase, HR should work on clearly identifying the intended population for a coaching initiative. This population may be based on level, from first-time frontline leaders all the way through senior management, or be based on needs, such as onboarding new leaders, supporting executive integration at senior levels, or cascading cultural change throughout the organization. Other common targets for coaching efforts are those with high potential to accelerate their development and support them through the course of challenging assignments. Coaching can also send them a clear signal regarding their value in the organization and can function as a retention tool as well as a development tool. But an organization must be clear regarding the intended outcomes for its investments in coaching and measure the impact rather than making vague assumptions or just hoping an effort will achieve its intended outcomes. (Effectively tackling the challenge of evaluating coaching interventions is addressed in chapter 4.)

So if frontline leaders are the target population, what is the most appropriate coaching intervention? Will they receive executive coaching, a very costly proposition within most organizations? Or will they be the level targeted for skill-building

Table 2.1
Pros and Cons of Different Types of Interventions

	Coaching	Leadership Development Programs	Management Training	Performance Management
Pros	Individually tailored to meet each leader's development needs. Many coaching options exist based on need and intent. Coaching can be provided by an external professional, internally certified coaches, or managers as coaches. Use at the team level can improve collective functioning and efficiency. Use at the executive team level can support organizational change efforts and overall organizational performance.	Can efficiently reach a target group and introduce or develop participants to a common leadership framework deemed critical in an organization. Can build or reinforce a common leadership culture, including expectations and norms. Builds networks and relationships within the cohort if delivered face-to-face.	Can efficiently skill up participants when a new system or process is introduced. Effective when people move into a management role for the first time to introduce management expectations and internal processes such as talent or performance management. Can build or reinforce a common management culture, including expectations and norms. Builds networks and relationships within the cohort if delivered face-to-face.	Can create internal alignment throughout the organization in day-to-day actions.

Table 2.1 (*Continued*)

	Coaching	Leadership Development Programs	Management Training	Performance Management
Cons	Large-scale executive coaching, either external or internal, can be resource intensive to scale compared to other approaches. Executive coaching does not typically happen in a cohort format, so cross-sharing among leaders to build collective capability does not occur. Requires sustained commitment from the leaders being coached.	Can be a one-size-fits-all approach that does not meet the individual needs of each leader. Interventions typically not long enough or intensive enough to bring about a significant amount of change and growth as desired by the organization.	Can be a one-size-fits-all approach that does not meet the individual needs of each leader. Used alone, management training may not provide all of the relevant development necessary for leaders to be successful. Can cover the "what" but often leaves out the "how" of the work.	Risks emphasizing current performance over needed skills and competencies for the future, leaving development out of the loop. May focus too much on results, not on how the results are achieved, creating or reinforcing a negative culture.

programs so they can begin fostering a stronger developmental coaching culture? Maybe the introduction of a peer coaching process at the frontline level is the best means of achieving the organization's goals. Clarity regarding the target population linked with desired outcomes greatly increases the likelihood of success in launching coaching efforts.

Onboarding or executive integration may be an identified target for coaching. (Chapter 15 focuses on the use of coaching to enhance the onboarding and integration of new leaders into an organization.) If past internal promotions or those hired from the outside have struggled in moving into these roles successfully and turnover is an issue, this approach may provide significant benefits in addressing such costly issues. An executive integration coaching approach may also yield significant benefits in accelerating a new executive to full performance much more quickly compared to a traditional onboarding process.

High-potential leaders are quite commonly identified by HR as the target population for coaching for a variety of reasons. Leadership talent is generally at a premium within organizations, so developing and retaining internal leaders with future capability builds bench strength and organizational agility to move quickly when growth opportunities emerge or an enterprise-wide reorganization occurs. (Chapter 7 focuses on the systemic use of coaching to support high-potential development and overall collective capability. Mentoring, discussed in chapter 14, can also be a fruitful approach for the development of those with high potential.)

One possibility that targets lower levels in the organization but still focuses on future bench strength is to consider the use of coaching for aspiring leaders. A variety of options for this audience may exist, from mentoring or peer coaching programs to targeted coaching by their managers or internal coaches. Coaching could play a role in identifying high-potential individuals within this audience or preparing this target group for future development efforts. (Chapter 19 offers an interesting look at some creative, nontraditional approaches to developing leadership capability in young people.)

In alignment with organizational goals, specific populations of individuals, as opposed to specific levels, may be a key target. This can include women if an organizational imperative is to increase the number of senior women leaders or to create a more robust and diverse leadership pipeline. Globally, legislative approaches to gender equity are on the rise, while in certain regions, rapid economic growth is driving the need to develop and retain all available talent. Rapid regional growth creates challenges for global organizations to develop the sufficient number and quantity of leaders needed. Coaching, in alignment with a leadership strategy that has identified the pipeline needed within certain regions, countries, and levels, can support the organization's strategic growth drivers.

Team coaching can be indicated if critical standing or ad hoc teams need support to operate most efficiently and effectively or to develop collective capabilities to achieve group goals. Building collective capability within teams may be a goal of an organization-wide change effort through teams working directly with a coach or building the capability of the team leader to coach the team toward a new level of performance. (Chapter 16 covers team coaching and the process and outcomes of teams which could be the focus for the work. Chapter 18 discusses even broader efforts to develop collective leadership capability as part of the organizational transformation work that begins with executive teams and cascades down.)

If, after close examination of all options, coaching is decided on as the most appropriate approach with a clear target audience and agreed-on goals, the next step is to assess and build the organization's readiness to successfully implement a coaching effort.

STEP 3: ASSESS AND BUILD YOUR ORGANIZATIONAL READINESS

A variety of readiness indicators exist related to the current organizational context that are relevant in assessing whether now is the right time to implement coaching in an organization. Previous positive experience with coaching and other types of developmental interventions can provide a more fertile context to seed coaching efforts. If leadership or management development is common at the enterprise, division, or functional level, coaching can be seen as the next iteration of the development process within HR or the training and development function.

Before considering a coaching intervention, determine the number and intensity of current change efforts occurring within the organization. A year-long implementation of a new enterprise resource planning system or a significant rebranding effort may suggest that coaching may not receive the focus and support required for success unless it is directly aligned with such efforts. This may also be the case if another major development initiative rollout is planned or under way. When overall efforts are not aligned, managers are unsure where to invest their limited time and resources, inadvertently reducing the overall impact of multiple efforts. For example, when a comprehensive talent development architecture is being launched, consider sequential timing in introducing coaching or mentoring, making sure the work is aligned with the talent and performance systems and succession management. Taking this approach advances an organization in its organizational level of coaching to the extended coaching stage or higher.

A common finding when organizations assess their readiness for coaching is the lack of a clear model of leadership expectations or competencies

(Hunt & Weintraub, 2007). This is often a first step an organization must take, especially if recent organizational changes have significantly shifted what leaders must be able to do in order to accomplish a new strategy or direction. Coaching is most effective when leadership expectations and accountabilities are clear. This leads to greater alignment of the coaching and developmental goals with the organization's needs. Another readiness indicator often related to clarity of leadership expectations is previous experience of the organization with 360-degree assessments. When 360-degree assessments and related feedback processes are used within an organization, coaching starts from a familiar place for the individual and the organization. If previous 360-degree interventions were not successful, the causes of failure need to be identified and addressed prior to launching a new effort, since assessment is a critical component of most formal coaching processes. If a bias against 360-degree assessments, even for developmental purposes, is strong within an organization, a different methodology, such as peer coaching or mentoring, may be a better starting point for introducing coaching approaches.

Prior to implementing a coaching approach or intervention, it is worth considering several factors that can contribute to the success of the effort. The first of these is that the intervention has clearly articulated goals with significant buy-in from key stakeholders. This clarity of purpose and stakeholder support builds political support and understanding for the work during implementation and into the sustaining phase. Building and implementing an evaluation plan for the effort is also a critical success factor. Ongoing evaluation will strengthen and improve efforts over time and provide evidence of impact and value when financial times get tough or if coaching is called into question. Finally, identifying possible barriers to the success of coaching at the organizational and individual leader level before implementation ensures a smoother implementation and increases the positive impact of coaching. Some possible barriers can include lack of boss support and engagement in coaching; inadequate funding, especially if departments or business units are expected to pay for the cost of the intervention; the inability of the leader to make time for the coaching process; and low readiness among those selected for coaching. Designing adequate processes, from formally incorporating boss support into the executive coaching process to the appropriate selection of leaders ready to commit the time and effort to get the most out of coaching (whether this is executive coaching, peer coaching, mentoring, or coaching skill building), increases the likelihood of success and builds positive regard for such efforts within the organization.

Developmental Climate

CCL's research and experience working with thousands of organizations for over forty years has taught us, and the organizations we work with, the importance of the developmental climate in the organization for any type of intervention (Berke, Kossler, & Wakefield, 2008). Coaching interventions or programs are no exception. Exhibit 2.2 can be used to conduct a review of the development climate elements we have identified as important to implementing and sustaining coaching efforts, as well as any large-scale development efforts. Few organizations will have all of these elements in place, but the more they do have, the greater the likelihood of success in implementing developmental programs.

Exhibit 2.2
Developmental Climate Checklist

- ❑ A culture of feedback exists, and people give honest feedback to each other in the organization:
  - ❑ Individuals in the organization work together to foster individual and collective learning (Peterson, 2011).
  - ❑ Project debriefings or after-action reviews are used to honestly assess success and identify issues for continuous organizational learning.
  - ❑ The organization has an ongoing feedback process regarding performance and development rather than just once a year during performance review time.
- ❑ The organization provides an environment of challenge:
  - ❑ Stretch assignments and challenges are used for development.
  - ❑ Recognition of coaching (formal or informal) is a key part of ensuring that leaders learn from stretch and developmental assignments.
- ❑ A supportive climate for development exists in the organization:
  - ❑ The importance of developing others is a leadership expectation and is tracked and measured.
  - ❑ Development is included in performance systems and reviews.

(continued)

Exhibit 2.2 (*Continued*)

- ❑ The organization takes a long-term perspective when planning for development—looking five or ten years out, not just tomorrow.
- ❑ The ability to learn, grow, and adapt to new situations is valued among employees.
- ❑ This leads to an environment in which employees act as self-directed learners, taking responsibility for their own learning and development (Peterson, 2011).

❑ Within the organization, people's development is tracked and rewarded:

- ❑ Tools and resources are readily available to employees.
- ❑ Development programs are available.
- ❑ Individuals receive recognition from their manager for development.
- ❑ Managers are formally held accountable for developing others.
- ❑ The organization provides opportunities for people to stretch and develop early in their careers.
- ❑ The organization has identified key transition points for career development.
- ❑ The organization plans development activities for the key points in an employee's career where these activities can have the most impact.

❑ Senior management believes development is important:

- ❑ Senior leaders serve as role models for development.
- ❑ Senior leaders are visible in coaching and mentoring others.
- ❑ Senior leaders actively participate in development programs.
- ❑ Senior leaders conduct talent reviews and are committed to developing internal talent and promotion from within.
- ❑ Senior leaders view development of employees as a key part of overall business strategy.
- ❑ Senior leaders do not let short-term business pressure interfere with development of people.

Peterson (2010) highlights three critical factors in creating a development pipeline that are relevant to assessing coaching readiness in an organization:

1. Do people have insight into what to develop?
2. Do those targeted have the motivation and willingness to invest the time and energy it takes to develop themselves?
3. Do people have the capabilities and skills necessary for success?

HR should spend time ensuring these conditions exist within the target audience. Otherwise, the proposed effort may be at risk, so time should be spent building awareness and motivation prior to beginning coaching.

Research also indicates that having a clear definition of what coaching and mentoring means within the organization is necessary for long-term success. The Human Capital Institute's (2012) study on challenges to the effective use of coaching in organizations found the lack of a clear definition of coaching to be a fundamental challenge. This includes clarifying if the organization will leverage coaching for performance or coaching for development, or both. Coaching in an organization could mean a manager coaching for performance or development, senior executives coaching and mentoring those with high potential, or the use of internal certified coaches or external coaches, or all of these together. Identification of who coaches and for what purposes within an organization helps people understand expectations and uses. As an organization transitions upward in the organizational stage of coaching framework illustrated in figure 2.1, the definition of who is a coach broadens. Assessing where your organization currently is in people's understanding and expectations of coaching allows you to begin the process of shifting perspectives and mind-sets to a higher level of sophistication. When considering global coaching initiatives, identifying differences in perceptions of coaching from a cultural context is necessary. Some cultures have less familiarity with coaching as a performance or development method. Other regions, divisions, and cultures may have experienced coaching only as a method to address individual performance issues. Different perceptions regarding coaching—what coaching is, who provides coaching, and what coaching can achieve—can drastically boost the implementation and success of coaching efforts globally.

Organizational Climate

The overall organizational climate can also have an impact on the success or failure of coaching efforts beyond the developmental climate of an organization.

Key factors related to organizational climate and coaching include openness of communication, trust, engagement and morale, and clarity of the organization's mission and goals. The level of transparency of communications within an organization is related to developmental climate and highly correlated with trust in an organization. Transparent communication from senior leaders ensures employees that there are no hidden agendas that may derail a coaching intervention. Trust is a critical success factor, and sufficient levels must exist within the organization. A low level of organizational trust breeds suspicion of coaching efforts as a management ploy and can lead to lack of engagement in the process (Hunt & Weintraub, 2007; Hanson, 2007). Organizations with a low level of trust may also be experiencing low levels of morale and engagement, and coaching efforts may be viewed with suspicion. In these cases, coach skill-building efforts that focus on managers' coaching and developing their direct reports, and being held accountable to do so, can assist in creating higher levels of engagement if employees view managers as sincere in caring about their performance and development. Linking coaching to business strategy and strategic drivers creates alignment of coaching efforts. If the organization lacks clarity of mission and goals, then the ability to link coaching in whatever form (e.g., executive coaching, managerial coaching, mentoring, peer coaching) to a clear line of sight for employees may be missing. If people are unsure about the direction of the organization, this needs to be clarified prior to a large-scale coaching effort.

If, after careful review of organizational and individual factors, it is clear that sufficient readiness exists in the organization to move forward with implementing a coaching intervention, the internal capacity of the HR department or group tasked with developing, implementing, monitoring, and evaluating coaching efforts should be examined and their capacity developed or enhanced if needed. Coaching interventions often need very different capabilities for implementation compared to traditional training and development activities.

STEP 4: REVIEW YOUR INTERNAL CAPACITY

As important as the organizational characteristics necessary for success are the internal capacity and capabilities of those who will be responsible for implementing the coaching. The group or individual who will be responsible for implementation should have an understanding of coaching systems and process, as well as experience with coaching. These individuals need to be able to explain in detail the coaching process and benefits to leaders who will be coached and to their managers. Internal capability to manage pools of coaches, including the complex process of tracking coaching engagements, whether by external or internal coaches, or the ability to manage an external coaching vendor, is essential. (See Chapter 5 for a detailed discussion of managing coaching talent pools.) We have seen coaching efforts struggle when those tasked with the responsibility don't understand the coaching process and are unable to convey the specifics to those involved or articulate the value to key stakeholders in the organization. While not a requirement, staff with an organizational development or leadership development background or educational qualification can be a bonus. In the absence of previous experience implementing coaching, experience with other types of developmental interventions and implementing and sustaining such efforts can form a basis to build on. Some key personal characteristics can be a strong sense of self-efficacy and the ability to advocate for and represent the work well to key stakeholders. A willingness and ability to influence coworkers and stakeholders can also be critical.

Resource implications are an important aspect to consider when determining readiness and ability to develop and implement coaching. There should be clarity regarding who will be responsible for developing, implementing, and funding coaching programs. Options include funding at the corporate, divisional, or departmental level. Alignment and agreement are essential if the programs are centralized in terms of administration but paid for out of different budgets. In this instance, the value of coaching needs to be clearly evident so leaders will invest their limited time and resources.

Tracking coaching utilization requires sophisticated processes, as well as financial systems able to track coaching expenditures, especially if department charge-backs are involved. There should be sufficient budget available for adequate staffing to administer programs and processes. Coaching programs can be time intensive to implement and monitor. Administrative support, program oversight, management of coaching pools, and overall program management are critical functions to staff for success. Alternatively, adequate staffing to partner with a coaching vendor or provider should be designated if this route is taken. Communications planning and resources should also be taken into account, as well as coordination and integration with talent and performance systems, especially if these reside outside the functional team or area implementing the coaching. The ability to scale or implement coaching as a customized process across multiple geographies, business units, or functions in a standardized and quality manner is a challenge within larger organizations with staffing and staff development implications (Human Capital Institute, 2012). In the end, for coaching to have the desired impact for leaders and organizations, a long-term commitment from a funding and staff perspective should be evident before investing and moving forward.

STEP 5: BUILD THE CASE FOR COACHING

The final stage in building readiness to engage in coaching work in a systematic way is establishing a clear case for coaching within the organization and strong support at the senior levels. Often if senior leaders have personal positive experience with coaching through executive coaching or coaching as part of a transformational leadership development experience, they understand the value and benefit of coaching to individuals and organizations. Another key means of building senior-level support for coaching is a clear understanding by senior management of how coaching can drive organizational goals. If the proposed coaching solution, whether executive coaching for high-potential employees, a mentoring program for emerging leaders, or coaching skill development for managers, is linked closely with business and talent strategy, the effort will more likely be endorsed and supported by leaders at all levels.

Beyond the personal experience of senior leaders, previous use of coaching within the organization can lay either a positive or a negative foundation for future efforts. If coaching has previously been used in the organization only for leaders perceived to be failing or derailing and those efforts are not viewed positively, then a negative perception regarding coaching may exist. Leaders within the organization may not want to engage in coaching if they believe this will be negatively perceived and have an adverse impact on their career. In this case, efforts must be taken to shift that perception. This is where positive experiences of senior management with executive coaching can be powerful if these leaders are willing to publicly share their stories and visibly support coaching as a positive developmental experience for high-performing or high-potential leaders. If previous coaching efforts were developmental in nature and perceived to have had a positive impact, then some groundwork may exist on which to build future coaching efforts.

Identifying and promoting the expected positive benefits of developing a coaching culture, combined with previous positive experiences, can build a compelling case. Leaders responding to CCL's survey (Anderson, Frankovelgia, & Hernez-Broome, 2009) on coaching cultures reported a variety of benefits to creating a coaching culture, including:

- Increased employee engagement
- Increased job satisfaction and morale
- Increased collaboration
- Improved teamwork
- Increased bench strength

Determining what outcomes at the individual, group, and organizational level will be affected through coaching is essential to developing a compelling case. When a clear understanding of the time and financial resources required to implement a coaching solution exists along with agreement that the return is worth the investment, a strong case can be made for coaching in the organization and the next steps toward implementation can begin.

CONCLUSION

Systematically assessing an organization's need and readiness for coaching as a potential driver of the business strategy is a critical pre-condition to implementing a coaching program of any type. When guided by a clear set of steps, as laid out above, that clarify the connection between coaching and business strategy as well as the organization's current state, resources, and capacity, an HR leader is better prepared to fully leverage the potential benefits of coaching for the good of the organization and to sustain these benefits over time.

chapter
THREE

Creating an Integrated Coaching System

Douglas D. Riddle

The value of coaching is amplified significantly when it is expressed in integrated, comprehensive systems. I am referring to leadership development processes that make systematic use of coaching in multiple modalities exercised by different individuals and groups within the organization. Such systems start from the recognition that coaching is a central attitude and mind-set for learning organizations and is fundamental to the development of effective leadership. Coaching works by leveraging relationships and conversations to elicit a variety of mental processes in those who are coached, such as an exploration of alternatives, persistence in problem solving, initiation in solution seeking, and cross-boundary collaboration. These benefits of coaching do not always require a professional executive coach. In fact, they may work better when they are part of the warp and woof of an organization's cultural fabric. Human resource and learning and development professionals are ideally positioned to move coaching beyond its singular association with professional executive coaching and lead its application to a variety of developmental needs.

This chapter is intended to be used as a kind of thought partner as you consider your own organization and the ways you can extend coaching as a professional service and a key element of leadership culture. It is not my intention to prescribe a particular model or system, but rather to stimulate your own discovery and design by sharing CCL's experiences with organizations around the globe that are stepping up to maximize the impact of coaching for developing leaders. I want to arm you with resources that can help you take advantage of your unique situation and the opportunities already at work in it. If I am successful, you may come to see this chapter as a practical and thoughtful source of dialogue. I'll share what my colleagues and I have seen that works in organizations, but advise against your trying to copy these unless your company or organization is the same as the organizations we profile. The objective is to stimulate you to think creatively about your own circumstances.

We have found it extremely valuable as well as cost-effective to have coaching systems with multiple elements, but we have yet to encounter an organization that has made full use of the range of coaching modalities discussed here. As coaching practice expands and our understanding of the underlying dynamics of coaching relationships and coaching conversations grows, we at CCL expect a greater number of organizations will engage in more complete use of the possibilities raised by these approaches, but most of the illustrations that follow show the value of this direction, not its completion.

MAKE SYSTEMS INTEGRATED AND COMPREHENSIVE

Overly simple approaches to coaching tend to focus on the modality that's familiar to a leader in the organization. The popularity of executive coaching has led many organizations to limit their use of coaching to engaging pools of executive coaches or to starting formal mentoring programs. In the least effective applications of coaching, organizations rely solely on the use of external coaches for executives and do not provide other leadership development or learning experiences. That would be acceptable if all the learning that executives need comes as the result of reflection and engagement with another person about circumstances, but coaching is not always the best way to learn. For instance, coaching would not be the preferred method of learning the basics of management or what the best practices in one's industry are. In addition, few executive coaches are as deeply versed in the internal dynamics and the culture of the organization as internal professional staff or potential mentors, so those domains of learning are not adequately addressed in executive coaching by external professionals.

Executive coaching can be a very cost-effective, high-impact solution for some leaders in some situations, but it is a much more expensive or ill-advised approach for many others. Overreliance on this modality excludes many people from this effective approach to leadership development, particularly those for whom the organization may decide that executive coaching is too expensive. The fact that executive coaching is so personalized makes it less valuable when there is a need for uniform leadership development across a large enterprise. Neither is it useful when it has been seen as either a solution for derailment or a perquisite for the highly compensated. No one wants it in the first case and everyone does in the latter. Other problematic approaches include providing a standard executive coaching package to everyone at a certain level in the organization. This sometimes takes place in executive education when every participant is given some fixed number of sessions. Of course, in any given cohort, some people will benefit from many sessions and others will find even one session of no great value. Differences in circumstances, learning style, developmental challenges, and opportunities all can undermine well-intentioned executive coaching programs. While it might make sense to provide coaching for all executives coming into new roles, designing a coaching program with a certain number of sessions may not be wise. Instead, it might be more useful to think about the accomplishment of specific tasks or milestones associated with successful integration (Riddle, 2009). This is why we recommend a comprehensive, well-integrated system of coaching services as the most effective use of coaching for leadership development and change.

VALUE OF MULTIPLE MODALITIES IN A SYSTEMS APPROACH

By seeing that coaching is potentially many things—a professional service, a kind of relationship, a managerial and leadership skill—an organization may create a highly effective system when it takes advantage of these diverse modalities. The interaction among the various modalities allows the greatest impact on creating a learning organization in which learning from experience is maximized for everyone.

Begin by Defining Coaching More Broadly

How does this work? Seeing coaching as a set of skills, competencies, and behaviors as well as a professional service allows your organization to leverage multiple resources as needed. This multidimensionality of coaching lends itself to system effects much greater than the sum of the various parts. For example, the impact of professional interventions can have a short life if the organization's environment is not ready to take advantage of an executive's growth. When the executive's manager has developed coaching skills and the HR business partner of the executive is equipped to provide some kinds of coaching for the executive and her team, the continued interactions within the system amplify the impact. The possibility of a virtuous cycle relies on the interactions of complementary elements. A coaching system intelligently leveraging those complementary elements through explicit reliance on systems thinking is the mechanism for such a virtuous cycle.

Leverage Existing Natural Processes

Consider that the engagement of external professional coaches requires budgeted funding and significant internal resources to manage (or requires hiring a firm that can ensure quality and manage the processes). However, mentoring programs can often build on the casual, informal mentoring relationships already in place in an organization. Rather than significant financial resources, attention to preparing mentors and protégés to make the relationships healthy and useful for both is required. Similarly, peer coaching can be structured with one-to-one relationships or in small cohort groups and may need only some basic training or guidance of the participants to avoid common pitfalls that might give the process a bad reputation. Sometimes it is best to work on improving the naturally occurring developmental relationships rather than creating a new program. Initiatives built on naturally occurring relations are not expensive from the viewpoint of initial funding. So whatever the size of your organization or the kinds of resources or constraints you face, a thoughtful, comprehensive approach can allow you to use what you have in an effective way. The key is in taking advantage of system effects when possible and smart choices about applying the right coaching services to the right opportunities.

Extend the Life of Developmental Efforts

Another advantage of systems of coaching incorporating multiple modalities is that they can have staying power because they build on these naturally occurring processes. They can be self-sustaining. This can be important as we go through business cycles. Companies might abandon leadership development programs because expensive top-down approaches cannot be justified when the business cycle is heading down. Investing resources of time and energy in multiple channels allows those nurtured in the rich soil of volunteerism and within social networks to thrive. They also take development right to the neighborhood where leadership is practiced. Where managers are prepared to be good coaches, their people learn from experience and apply the lessons in the place where they are learned. Most leaders recall lessons they learned from their experiences in the workplace, including challenges, and they especially remember the ones that have had the greatest impact on their leadership (McCauley, 2013).

Reflection

- Do you know what informal mentoring or mutual development activities are already taking place in your organization?
- What developmental initiatives has your organization abandoned in difficult financial times?
- What traditions of leadership development have persisted in spite of market cycles?

COMPREHENSIVE VISION

An important place to start is with a vision of what is to be accomplished through the creation of an integrated system. Behind this view is the assumption that adaptation to an accelerating environment of change requires leadership that is particularly effective at learning on the fly and adapting strategy and tactics to respond to what is learned. No one approach can affect enough leaders throughout an organization. No program can create enough critical mass of leaders equipped to change and respond together across limiting assumptions and boundaries. Neither can any single approach address the wide range of starting places and readiness of leaders who all need to be aligned on thinking and acting.

Search the Gap for a Compelling Vision

In one regional chemical company, the senior leadership team came face-to-face with the consequences of long-term incumbency in their leadership team. The most pressing consequence was the concentration of expertise and experience in a small number of aging leaders and the large gap between their knowledge, relationships, and impact and those of the next cohort. We were enlisted to propose an executive coaching process and provide a pool of leadership coaches who could accelerate the learning of the next cohort. Our discovery process confirmed that the gap was as large as senior leadership thought. As we surfaced the details of the need, we found that a specific problem was lack of adequate knowledge about the industry. However, we also discovered that some in the cohort were in active mentoring relationships and were further advanced than their colleagues. Since executive coaching was unlikely to provide the right forum for increasing knowledge about the industry and there was already some effective use of internal coaching, we proposed a hybrid process. The senior team took the discovery data and recognized they were aiming at a whole new understanding of the nature of leadership in the company. The result was a formulation of this vision: *Every leader a mentor.*

That key shift in perspective arose as the result of a detailed understanding of the problem that had surfaced, but it also required a lens of health—a perspective based on the assumption that even ineffective organizations have some healthy processes in place. Ignorance of the ongoing healthy natural processes and relationships within an organization often leads to the adoption of unsustainable, ineffective, expensive programs. If a profitable enterprise has been around for any significant length of time, it has many good elements that may provide a platform for renewal. Smart analysts and consultants start with an assumption that building on what is already working will always yield better results than simply doing the opposite of what is not working.

Workplace as the Primary Locus for Development

We know that when queried, leaders point overwhelmingly to experiences of challenge in the day-to-day work of managing and key relationships for the source of their leadership lessons (McCauley, DeRue, Yost, & Taylor, 2013). Therefore, a vision for leadership development that makes the workplace the primary classroom and the relationships between leaders the nexus for reflective coaching conversations can open a world of possibility. Although approaching fad status in business a couple years ago, the quest for a "coaching culture" (Knights & Poppleton, 2008) pointed to a growing awareness that leadership development can be an ongoing, fully embedded process for the benefit of company performance. As long as the coaching emphasis is not driven by some trivial idea that a coaching culture is a "nice" culture and those who coach are nicer, the focus on leaders who can draw out the best thinking of others is a useful one. This kind of vision of a culture driving business or mission results is what I mean by a *comprehensive vision.*

Expansive Conversations

A culture incorporating coaching mind-sets and behaviors has a number of benefits for organizations bent on succeeding in a fast, interconnected, and rapidly changing world. A coaching culture is manifest in all the interactions that take place between people in the organization, particularly in conversation. When the people of an organization expect from and offer to each other conversations intended to expand the thinking and doing capacity of each person, we might say that the culture reflects a coaching orientation. Against this, many of us have experienced the irritation associated with a colleague or friend trying to give advice without fully understanding the complexity of our situations or a boss advising some simplistic action to solve a leadership problem.

The irritation or frustration evoked by others telling us what to do when we need to think through alternatives is an indication that coaching conversations are needed. In a coaching conversation, a manager might turn a question back to the questioner because she is confident the questioner will benefit from struggling with the lack of an answer or needs to broaden the range of resources he consults. By asking the questioner what he thinks he should do or what alternatives he has considered, she is expanding his capacity for creatively focused problem solving. She responds to a question with the mildly frustrating use of another question, but her question stimulates his internal mental search and returns the responsibility to him. Furthermore, she is conveying a basic confidence in the intelligence and resourcefulness of that person. In essence, she is communicating the implied message, "I believe you can figure this out yourself. You don't need to be dependent on me."

Responses that presume more autonomous initiative and capability can have a beneficial effect on a colleague's confidence as well. When leaders consistently communicate their expectations that those who work with them can solve their own problems and can find creative solutions to important challenges, the climate of mutual encouragement can unleash substantial group energy. Using coaching approaches to everyday conversations can turn even trivial or mundane exchanges into opportunities for learning and development. An environment reliant on learning at its core encourages people to work together creatively and nurtures innovative solutions to organizational challenges.

Reflection

- How is the expression of your current corporate culture creating upper limits to effectiveness?
- What kind of attitudes, thinking, and behavior would foster greater engagement and creative thinking among your leaders?
- In what ways are your leaders demonstrating a constant attention to developing others?

COMPONENTS OF AN INTEGRATED COACHING SYSTEM

The following elements are those most frequently found in an integrated coaching system:

- *Executive coaching*: One-to-one coaching by a trained external professional
- *Mentoring*: An experienced leader meeting with someone more junior to help him or her benefit from the greater experience
- *Peer coaching*: Meetings of equals to support and challenge each other's growth
- *HR coaching*: The interventions human resource professionals are called on to address individual, interpersonal, and group problems within the organization
- *Manager as coach*: Managers using coaching approaches as an element of their leadership
- *Digital goal tracking and reminder systems*: Digital and Internet reminder services to support goal achievement for individuals
- *Team and group coaching*: Interventions by a professional to improve the functioning of groups

Let's consider each of these components and make note of benefits, limitations, and some lessons we've learned in designing them.

Executive Coaching

Executive coaching has received the most press, perhaps because so many people hold themselves out to be coaches. How will you determine whether a coach is qualified and could meet your needs? Evaluating qualifications and credentials of coaches poses a significant difficulty for consumers because of the multitude of competing credentials. While some groups have been working to establish common standards for training and experience for coaches, many training organizations "certify" coaches without any evidence of effectiveness or reasonable standards of professional practice. Many of these organizations have idiosyncratic approaches to coaching that may be driven solely by the need to differentiate themselves within the marketplace. They create a unique brand of coaching with an unusual language that ignores the accumulating body of research and experience about coaching. Almost none have any evidence of effectiveness, and few have genuine filters to limit unprepared or incompetent coaches.

Executive coaching by well-qualified external or internal professionals provides the highest level of confidentiality necessary for sensitive situations. Because of the expense and the concerns about confidentiality, most coaching of very senior leaders is conducted by external professional coaches. However, increasingly we have many more internal professional coaches working with leaders in companies that have longer experience with coaching. In particular, companies that have invested in ensuring a high level of professional discretion by hiring or educating internal coaches and companies in which senior leaders want to demonstrate their commitment to coaching are more likely to present expanded use of internal coaches.

The attention given to executive coaching by popular and business media has raised another challenge. As with any other powerful intervention, the temptation arises to try to apply executive coaching to any leadership challenge, whether appropriate or not. Inappropriate uses of executive coaching include assigning a coach to "rescue" or restore the effectiveness of an executive on whom the organizational leadership has already given up. More frequently, conflict-averse leaders may send a leader for coaching when they have not tackled the thorny challenges of direct, clear feedback in the face of unacceptable behavior. Coaching should not be used to replace managing simply because a leader doesn't know how to deliver straightforward information to others. In other words, coaching should not be substituted for basic management practices such as setting standards and requiring adequate performance. Repeatedly we have been called on by conflict-avoidant companies to "fix" someone whose manager never held this person accountable for his behavior or results. Worse, unqualified or unethical coaches have been willing to take on such assignments even when they are patently ill considered. Before considering hiring an executive coach, assess whether you are dealing with a coaching problem or a managing problem.

The next challenge with executive coaching relates to how useful and valuable leaders find it. A coach who has had beneficial results with one leader may find it easy to persuade others in the organization that they also need her services. This becomes a problem when coaching services are not well managed and lack a clear strategic intent as part of integrated leadership development. More than one organization has discovered an accumulation of substantial unregulated expenses due to executive coaching. The reason? They never established effective processes to manage coaching availability based on consistent principles in support of the business purpose or organizational mission. I ask my clients to consider questions such as these:

- What is the range of issues and opportunities for which coaching will be offered as a solution?

- Who will be eligible?
- How will decisions about coaching be made to ensure alignment with business and leadership strategy?
- How will results be evaluated and their value determined?
- How will the value be integrated with other processes of leadership development?

These are some of the management questions that should always accompany executive coaching services.

Executive coaching makes unique contributions to leadership development and is particularly powerful in that context. When there are concerns about sensitive political or interpersonal conditions that might affect leadership stability, executive coaching can be an essential response. It offers the most consistent approach for confidentiality and addressing personal behaviors and habits that require persistent effort for modification. More sessions can be added as needed, increasing the flexibility of any intervention. Also, the complex interpersonal dynamics and unusual developmental challenges of some leaders and leadership cultures may require the specialized expertise of a proven executive coach. For instance, when introducing comprehensive leadership development initiatives in organizations without a history of them, the most senior leaders may merit executive coaches if they are to model developmental leadership. Developmental leadership demonstrates concern for the learning and development of others, as well as their current performance. We have also found that the use of external executive coaches for executive integration (or onboarding) can be important because external coaches can push processes that may be challenging for internal staff to manage (Riddle, 2009). They provide a safe conversational environment for dealing with the inevitable challenges associated with stepping into new executive positions and allow the emergence of thoughtful solutions to frustrating discoveries.

At the same time, internal executive coaches can form trusting relationships through more casual interactions in meetings and conferences that may lead to deep and powerful coaching relationships. While the great majority of coaches for senior leaders are external professionals, we have seen top internal coaches become trusted advisors across levels and business units. The ready availability and demonstrated competence in a variety of leadership settings can establish the high credibility of internal coaches. Coaching sessions may not require the formal contracting of an external coach and may proceed as needed without any predetermined plan. When the coach and person being coached are both clear on the nature and limits of confidentiality required by their roles, the familiarity of an internal coach can contribute to a dependable sense of safety and comfort that is hard for any external coach to offer. In addition, the opportunities to run into each other in the workplace might provide a subtle nudge of accountability because of the dynamics developed in a coaching relationship.

While executive coaching should probably never be the sole leadership development avenue available within an organization, it occupies an indispensable place. Whenever very senior leaders experience developmental challenges and the consequences of not addressing them justify the expense, executive coaching should be available. As an HR leader, ensuring that you have internal or external coaches available for such opportunities will save your organization significant money and trouble associated with unrealized talent and with individual leader growth neglected.

Mentoring

Mentoring is taking place right now in many places within your organization, whether you have a formal program for it or not. Mentoring occurs naturally as junior members of your staff seek out the knowledge and wisdom of more senior people. In addition, the urge to share one's experience and the lessons learned is a high source of motivation for older leaders. Great mentoring programs build on a foundation of this naturally occurring practice. Poor mentoring programs overregulate the elements of the mentoring relationship that don't require regulation and underprepare mentors and protégés for the work of mentoring. The responsibility of those who would organize mentoring programs is to create a place where people can meet each other, establish ground rules for setting expectations, and provide regular, easily accessible training for maximizing the mentoring conversations. (See chapter 14.)

Mentoring is a critical element of ensuring that knowledge and experience don't leave the organization as leaders retire or move. Without an emphasis on mentoring, most organizations are losing vast amounts of very expensive experience and industry knowledge. The advantages of giving attention to supporting mentoring are having more people participating (even those who are not naturals at mentoring relationships are given tools enabling them to contribute), and more targeted learning takes place as guidance or structure is provided. We have found the most effective onboarding approaches are executive coaching and mentoring, along with a structured protocol that builds the tools and mind-set that leaders need in new roles.

Affirming and expanding mentoring opportunities is critical for the retention of the dynamic intellectual property of the organization held in the experience and memories of senior leaders. No matter how much effort you have devoted to the creation of knowledge management systems, they can never capture the rich and contradictory wisdom accumulated through experience. It is much less expensive to learn from others' mistakes than to make your own, but mentoring is one of the few ways that the real lessons of experience can be communicated. Key to effectiveness is building mentoring on healthy reciprocal relationships. The quality of caring that often grows in mentoring relationships can unlock stories and lessons that use a senior leader's foibles as well as successes for the benefit of the protégé. While these are often the most powerful and useful lessons, they are the most difficult to surface and the least likely to yield to formal attempts to catalogue them.

In addition, mentoring is one of the only ways that the political dynamics and culture land mines are made visible to junior leaders. Most trouble spots are hidden by a layer of anxious civility or intentional amnesia, so an experienced guide can make all the difference in the safe passage of the leaders who follow. We have evidence that the inability to read the political dangers and realpolitik of an organization is a common source of derailment of leaders (see chapter 6). The special sensitivities of senior leaders are known to only a few, and it is easy to misstep unintentionally yet with serious consequences. My own mentors have been most helpful in steering me away from unnecessarily risky ways of raising questions.

Related to this, mentoring also creates a dialectic between experience and innovation in which more junior leaders can avoid errors of the past and more senior leaders are stretched with new ideas. The dynamic tension generated in mentoring relationships can be valuable because the best forms of innovation attend to both poles. The mentoring relationship also meets the spiritual and emotional needs of mentors and protégés. Mentors are often motivated by the need to leave a legacy. Protégés are often reassured and gain confidence from the longer time perspective of their seniors.

Third-party assignment of mentors is a common approach and can help people who are shy make the connections they need. Assigning mentor-protégé pairs results in a small percentage of outstanding relationships, a few ineffective relationships, and the bulk of the relationships somewhere in between. You can improve the odds by training and supporting mentors and protégés. Because these are human relationships with all the complexity and messiness implied by that, no single model of support or accountability will work for everyone. We have found that providing some simple structure, including a requirement for agreements about the logistics, content, and mutual obligations, can help. In addition, the stalling, or loss of momentum, that may take place when the initial magic or tension is gone can be reduced by requiring growth or learning goals to be agreed on by the parties. Insofar as possible, organizers of mentoring programs can have the best success by creating many opportunities for potential mentors and protégés to get to know each other and define what they seek and what they can contribute.

Educating potential protégés on how to maximize their choice of mentors ought to be part of all leadership development programs. The temptation to get advice and become known to the most powerful and visible leaders can undermine the intent for growth. Issues of emotional fit and appropriate expectations may be much more important than access to the CEO or other senior leaders. In one program, two leaders were able to work with the chief executive. One was delighted and the other deeply disappointed. The difference? The disappointed protégé hoped for a kind of personal transparency and emotional connection that the CEO was unable to provide. The CEO was the consummate political operator and a charismatic figure who was personable and gave the impression of openness only in public settings. In one-on-one encounters, she was guarded and ill at ease, often falling into party-speak or attempts at helpful advice rather than genuine sharing of experiences and lessons. The delighted protégé adjusted his expectations to focus on the realistic contribution that the CEO was able to make to him.

Peer Coaching

Peer coaching is underused in many organizations. Its value lies in the creation of an emotional climate of safety and confidence that is the result of collegiality and shared experiences. Because peers are of necessity in similar situations within their careers or in their time with the organization, they can share lessons, identify with each other's problems, and reduce the sense of isolation that accompanies employment change. When organized thoughtfully, peer coaching can also create cross-functional relationships that can contribute to the agility of the company as it seeks to solve business problems requiring collaborative approaches. Peer coaching across companies where corporate secrets are not at stake can contribute to more flexible and creative thinking. This is sometimes accomplished through leadership development programs provided by professional societies or similar settings in which peers from a region make connections that serve them throughout their careers.

When creating opportunities for peer coaching, recognize the many different ways of structuring the programs depending on the benefits sought. For instance, when a more structured process is needed to ensure consistency in leadership culture and strategic direction, peer coaching might be best organized on the basis of coaching groups. Coaching groups can be composed purely of peers or organized using a trained facilitator, external coach, or well-prepared senior executive. If the targets for advancement relate to encouraging personal investment and individual leader growth, partnering peers in dyads may be preferable.

The point of peer coaching is to leverage collegial relationships for mutual development. Simply by being promoted within the organization, peer coaching can increase the confidence of leaders because it represents a vote of confidence in their shared intelligence and emergent wisdom. This can be particularly important when junior leaders appear reticent to connect with each other out of concern for an overly competitive environment. Some companies still rely on spurring competition between junior staff as a motivational tool, but few sectors or industries provide a context in which such a dog-eat-dog approach can yield the innovation and energy needed to compete effectively. One way to undermine the fearfulness and distrust marking such environments is to form guided and well-supported peer coaching networks. Admittedly, those networks work best when participants can form an early emotional connection with their colleagues through program kickoffs including off-site joint professional growth experiences or strategy development. One result of this approach is that participants acquire an expectation of social interaction around mutual development.

Custom leadership development programs always benefit from the addition of peer coaching networks of one form or another. While valuable from the standpoint of ensuring a higher level of goal achievement and behavior change from participation in the program, they may be more valuable as a bridge to organizational impact. The mutual accountability and opportunities for shared vulnerability afforded by ongoing meetings with peers working together on professional growth can forge loyalties to each other and consequently to the organization. These loyalties are necessary for the trust and open communication collaborative leadership requires. In a major health care center, both the senior leadership and CCL have been pleased to see peers from across the organization continue to meet and work together to solve significant organizational challenges years after the program ended.

Peer coaching seems to benefit from assigned pairings, unlike mentoring programs, where I have found that increasing individual choice can help make them more successful. One reason to assign pairings is that few junior leaders know enough about their peers in other divisions or departments to make interesting choices. Another reason that assigned pairings work well in peer coaching is that such pairings communicate clearly that the partners are obligated to make the peer relationship work. The relationship might require partners to stretch themselves, but that is all part of their growth as leaders. As much as possible, you should pair peers from different parts of the organization but with similar levels of experience and authority. Also, expecting a modest amount of structure including frequency of meetings, the establishment of agreements on how and how much they will share, and the requirement that goals be made, communicated, and tracked seems to be beneficial.

Human Resource Coaching

In effective coaching systems, the human resource professionals (or learning and development or organizational development groups) are seen as the go-to people for coaching. They have established a reputation as thought partners in matters related to leadership and management. Robust human resource coaching requires providing global standard coaching education and skills training to internal human resource professionals who have reasonable emotional intelligence. Organizations that go this route significantly reduce the need for external professional coaches, making much more cost-effective coaching solutions available when indicated, as discussed in detail in chapter 1.

In recent years, concerns about the dual roles of most HR leaders have lessened as professional standards and ethical practices have become more widespread. Most HR leadership coaches now can be clear about the limits of confidentiality, but they also have permission within their organization to observe strong boundaries between what they learn in coaching situations and what they have to do when evaluating leaders. Although some cross-influence is inevitable, internal professional coaches are no less able to clarify what cannot be confidential and thus help those being coached make wise decisions about how to use the coaching conversations. In addition, their ready availability in the workplace means that more in-the-moment coaching conversations, some taking only a few minutes, can contribute to a more thoughtful and effective leadership environment.

Our experience with human resource professionals across the globe and in CCL's Coaching for Human Resource Professionals program suggests some important considerations when it comes to human resource coaching:

- Formal coaching training is essential. The complexity of the dynamics associated with internal coaching requires a firm foundation in coaching skills, ethical thinking, and systems dynamics. It is still unusual to find this content and the practice needed in HR certification programs or academic programs, and natural ability is not enough.
- Collegial supervision is just as important as good training for maintaining one's balance in the face of the competing demands on the internal coach. This can take the form of a professional supervisor or a colleague with similar responsibilities.
- There is a constant need to educate the organization and the "clients" about the coach's role and scope of responsibility because the internal coach is always balancing the sometimes contradictory requirements of the work. How do human resource coaches ensure the minimum intrusion of private information into the talent management responsibilities for which they are obligated? At talent review time, your colleagues and business managers will be looking expectantly for insights you've gained in your privileged position. At the same time, those you've coached will expect you to pretend you know nothing personal about them or advocate on their behalf. It is only as you persistently affirm the boundaries between these roles that others can cooperate and support you in the ethical and practical choices required.
- A key contribution of the HR professional coach is the promotion of direct and clear communications between parties who might otherwise be unable to resolve differences. The HR coach can encourage those who come to her with complaints or problems to take their concerns directly to those involved.

Manager as Coach

In companies with a strong focus on coaching culture, leadership roles include the expectation of mentoring. However, all effective managers know when to use coaching approaches to develop their people. This is also an important part of the culture for agile, innovative organizations: managers know when to direct and when to coach. When managers use coaching skills, they create space for those whom they manage to think more deeply, access a wider range of resources, and work through to more creative solutions to their challenges. While many managers are naturally good at this because they've been coached well, many more are not good at elicitation and have never had adequate training. Because it appears quicker and easier to simply tell people what to do, it is natural to not coach. Until coaching becomes an implicit and explicit expectation for managers in your organization, it will be underused. However, managerial coaching is ultimately the most powerful application of a coaching modality because it pervades the day-to-day functioning of the company. It touches everyone, including your customers and clients.

A specific application of coaching to managerial work is offered by onboarding processes. Coaching can make a large difference in the success of those newly hired or newly promoted leaders. We have often been engaged to provide external professional executive coaches in structured processes of leadership integration. However, a few organizations have developed formal processes in which the manager, an HR professional, and a mentor (or one of these) take a new leader through a systematic learning process to equip her with the tools she will need for early success in her role.

As you are looking to advance the use of coaching skills by managers, you will focus on communicating the benefits to them, their people, and the organization. In our view, coaching skills lay the foundation for positive relationships between leaders and followers (Sahin, 2012). Because coaching approaches to management convey the confidence that managers have in the abilities and attitudes of their people, coaching is an essential skill set for those who care about creating a positive, energized, and innovative workplace. In contexts in which workers are not equipped with the proper training and tools to accomplish their goals, directive guidance by managers may be necessary. However, employees who are reasonably well prepared and understand the objectives and needed outcomes often do better when given the freedom to devise their own solutions to achievement needs.

Coaching approaches, with their emphasis on thoughtful inquiry and encouragement of self-reliance, can create the space that allows managers to focus on their leadership responsibilities and give less energy and time to directing the activities of those who report to them. The possibility of working smarter, and not harder, is realistic only when a manager can step back from highly directive relationships and allow team members to figure things out for themselves. Also, coaching approaches, because they encourage the person being coached to think through the questions to be answered, help those coached to learn the thinking processes of the manager and not just to follow the instructions provided.

Finally, coaching approaches with performance reviews can change the tenor of these interactions (Hart, 2011). A manager who uses coaching regularly is already asking employees what they think should be done and to self-evaluate their actions and outcomes. When this approach is extended to performance reviews, the possibility of uninformed surprise at the evaluation of one's performance is attenuated. Periodic reviews become exercises in mutual discovery, not the fraught delivery of unexpected news of disappointment or potentially empty praise.

It is my experience that the use of coaching throughout an organization seldom exceeds the modeling demonstrated by senior management. In interviews across multiple organizations at all levels and in many industries, I have found that the amount of coaching by managers is predicted by the extent to which their own managers exercise these skills. The level of humble inquiry and smart coaching used by senior executives sets some kind of upper limit to the use of coaching throughout the organization. As a result, we have taken to insisting on building coaching and mentoring expertise and practice into senior team interventions for the greatest impact on organizational culture. While having good coaches in the senior suite is no guarantee the organization will have a culture eliciting the best energy from the rest of the workforce, it does set a higher ceiling for organizational development.

Digital Goal Tracking and Reminder Systems

While many online knowledge management systems are only static repositories of knowledge, more and more of those systems employ query processes that can respond to the immediate needs of the person accessing the system. In addition, more organizations are using online services, including social networks, that could allow more involvement of peers in addressing leadership questions. So far our experience indicates these are being used primarily to locate organizational knowledge or resources hidden by poor indexing or just difficult to find because of the absence of good knowledge management systems. However, once people begin to address leadership and people management questions, they have the potential to create a kind of virtual coaching community.

This is not to minimize the value for some people of online resources (e.g., video, articles) for helping them think through what they need to do. A naive expectation that people will simply and easily apply what they learn from those sources results in few systems that are designed to help the user's thinking and application processes, and we expect more knowledge systems to provide that kind of help. Along these lines are online cueing systems that provide goal reminders that employees set. These reminders are useful when people voluntarily use them, but they can feel like an extra burden when required of everyone, including those who are demotivated by external reminders. When they are included in existing knowledge management or people management systems, the incremental additional cost is minimal and automated systems and online resources should be included in an integrated system of coaching.

Because leadership appears to operate most effectively on the foundation of strong relationships, I think that digital or electronic tools for learning may be best seen as adjunctive to learning experiences built on face-to-face interactions. This may require not teachers or coaches in the room but the guidance of a manager with a coaching mind-set to encourage their use. Online and asynchronous tools have been some of the fastest-growing uses of new technology, driven by the expectation of lower cost for large-scale application. However, we are also seeing more multimodal coaching experiences in which technology may provide reminders that pop up as a result of being preset to trigger interaction with coaches or colleagues remotely. The integration of digital tools in coaching is widespread yet still in its infancy. Generational differences in comfort with online resources still appear to be a factor in uptake as well, though the ubiquity of screen-based tools and the significant improvement of platform-agnostic resources is increasing their use. We encourage the use of digital resources in coaching relationships in several simple ways:

- Setting, recording, and holding oneself accountable for goals is easily accomplished through shared services. Coaches and those they coach can work together on shared documents, and reminders can be scheduled for future dates to ensure that good intentions become accountabilities.
- Books, articles, and video resources can be made regularly available so shared knowledge and experience can be the foundation for deeper thinking and action as a result of coaching. Seeing the interactions targeted in exemplary video presentations can help those being coached to acquire new habits more readily.

- The ability of a person being coached to record (audio or video) her own behavior provides the opportunity for powerful self-observation and the increased impact of feedback from a coach on directly observed behavior. The ready availability of videorecording on phones, tablets, and laptop computers makes this available to everyone everywhere.

Team and Group Coaching

While executive coaching or mentoring is often thought of as a one-to-one kind of interaction, leadership involves groups. This has led to new thinking about mentoring as a social phenomenon and the ideas of community mentoring (Kram & Higgins, 2009). However, coaching has unique value as a process within the groups and teams that power the work of the organization. Coaching can be something that the leader of a team contributes to the team process, something that an HR partner guides within a team, or a separate set of resources and activities used periodically to accelerate team learning. This is typically the purview of organizational development professionals because few other internal HR leaders have the experience or training in group process and team development. This is also an area where we have found that teams and groups are most comfortable calling on external professionals to engage the team in creating the right climate and culture for its success. Team coaching is in high demand in almost all of our client organizations. We suspect it reflects how difficult it can be to think and act collaboratively because our whole landscape has become more diverse. The challenge is not getting different ideas and approaches so much as working together to get alignment with the range of assumptions, experiences, and orientations we represent.

I think it is useful to add team and group coaching when seeding culture changes through an organization (see chapter 18). Beginning with the senior executive team, coaching the whole group can make group awareness possible when normal human dynamics tend to lead to scapegoating or blaming individuals for poor climates and ragged performance. A coach, whether external professional, internal organizational development professional, or member of the group who has sufficient stature to be listened to, draws the attention of the group to the ways they work together (or don't), the ways they approach problems or avoid them, and the level of respect evidenced by receptive attention afforded each other. These dynamics of ongoing group process are extremely difficult to get on the table for deliberate, conscious modification without someone being responsible for taking an observer role in the midst of the process. The reality is that most teams never talk about how they are working together and how they want to function. Seldom do teams address these important aspects of their functioning unless they have broken down or enlisted a professional to challenge them.

This work requires specialized training for professionals from cultures that frame the world in individual terms or as dyadic relationships. Groups are much more complex because social dynamics that affect how we operate in the presence of others and the development of group identity make a large difference in our individual behavior that can only imperfectly be explained through ideas of personality. Issues of power, influence, politics, alliances, and justice are the language of groups, and results are the measure of success. Coaches who are trained in individual models of change may not be equipped to address group, team, and organizational change and may continue to rely on descriptions based on the aggregation of individual data. When we see group change efforts that start with personality assessments (such as the Myers-Briggs Type Indicator), they will only tap into the individual aspects of the groups functioning. Group dynamics are not readily accessible from a personality framework.

Not all teams will benefit from team coaching. Like any other intervention, the starting condition determines the appropriate intervention. In a number of organizations, we've seen senior leaders who were unhappy at having been sold team coaching for relatively effective teams by previous consultants. They were not unhappy at the prospect of improving the performance of their teams, but unhappy that former team "coaches" had shifted the focus of attention within the team from its leadership performance to an exclusive focus on how they got along with each other. While easy, conflict-free relationships may have advantages, such peace is not necessary for effective team functioning. Effective teams have a high commitment to their mission and to working well with each other. Conflict is an inevitable characteristic of dynamic teams and should be managed and or leveraged for better ideas, not avoided.

Team coaching benefits teams when they need to pull together in the same direction and there's a need for great direction, alignment, and commitment. Conflict that leads to ineffective meetings, personal attacks and blaming of others, and excuses rather than mutual determination for solutions are other indicators that team coaching may be a useful initiative. However, team coaching can be most effective simply because a group recognizes that high-performing individuals can amplify their efforts by taking responsibility for the group process.

These are the modalities or applications of coaching we encounter in our leadership work. More are likely to emerge as we find more ways to use coaching, but the key is tailoring the kind and form of coaching to your situation. It is also leveraging the amplification of impact when they are used together.

Reflection

1. What mode of coaching is most used within your organization? Could its effectiveness be leveraged through the addition of another mode?
2. How are different modes of coaching being coordinated or extending each other in your organization?
3. How well are the various coaching services available being communicated?

We've found it helpful to tie the form of coaching to the kind of impact we're seeking as we create designs for comprehensive systems of coaching. Although our conviction is that multiple forms reinforce each other, each also makes a unique contribution to development. As you think about the development of your coaching system, review the benefits listed for each form and use them to shape how you want to sequence expanding their use.

STRATEGIC APPROACH

This section presents a particular approach to the implementation of a more integrated use of coaching within your organization. I am applying the results of experience with many organizations, but I encourage you to take seriously that your organization is unique and deserves a well-thought-out approach addressing the environment in which you operate. This is approached from the assumption that you are an individual leader of human resources or part of a team that believes in the power of creating a learning environment and would like to increase the use of coaching approaches in your organization.

Stepwise Development

In a brief form, here are some steps we've found useful when embarking on a significant expansion of coaching:

1. Develop a compelling vision of the kind of company you need to be. Give thought to how it needs to operate and what kinds of leadership will be needed to fulfill the vision.

2. Assess current gaps and opportunities for advancing leadership development. (Chapter 2 provides detailed guidance on assessing your current situation.) Using CCL's five-stage model, determine where you are now in implementing coaching in a comprehensive, integrated fashion (Riddle & Pothier, 2010).
3. Engage in appreciative inquiry to locate formal and informal current uses of coaching approaches.
4. Create a well-plotted strategy based on the broad vision and the results of assessment.
5. Use disciplined management systems that can ensure ease of use for everyone involved. Devoting adequate administrative and process or project management resources will pay off right away. Neglecting the practical questions of how people find out what and how they can participate will undermine even the most brilliant programs.
6. Start small and develop over time. When you can, choose to elevate attention on current positive activities over starting new programs. Build initial programs on existing platforms.
7. Win supporters first and continuously.
8. Create cross-functional advisory groups for all new initiatives:
   - Use them to generate market data within your organization.
   - Use them to develop rules to ensure application of the right approaches for the desired outcomes.
   - Use them to identify meaningful targets for evaluation of success.
9. Build evaluation into the whole system. (See chapter 4.)
10. When possible, start at the top (you may never exceed the leadership performance of the senior team). If you have access, engage the board (ultimately responsible for the success of the firm).

Eye on Strategic Vision

The need to deliver something has led many human resource professionals to settle for creating a successful course or program of leadership development. While these may themselves be useful, without a strategic vision, they miss the larger value created when more employees are affected and the potential for greater organizational impact. This is particularly true in the case of executive coaching when limited to a few top leaders. This can be a great entry point for a more comprehensive system, but should be selected with care to ensure that however you begin, it can be leveraged for greater impact.

Build as Fast as Your Political Support

Start small and never outstrip your political support. Starting small may mean beginning with nothing more than a discovery shaped by appreciative inquiry (Cooperrider & Srivastva, 1987) to uncover where good things are already at work. It is likely that mentoring is taking place in many corners of the organization. There may be managers who are stimulating their teams through wise questioning and creating space for growth by letting their people solve problems instead of giving them answers. Perhaps leaders are meeting together to discuss their dilemmas and share ideas in meetings that are like peer coaching. Maybe some of your colleagues in human resources or organizational development are doing substantial coaching of leaders. It is always better to acknowledge and build on what is working based on available evidence.

POLITICS IS EVERYTHING

Humans are political animals. We care about the ownership of ideas and influence, we compare ourselves to others, and we operate at all times in a social garden. Learning political savvy means learning to care about how choices we make as an organization or as part of an organization will affect others and taking steps to mitigate problems that might emerge for all involved. This is obvious as soon as it is stated, but we have seen multiple useful and beneficial initiatives killed because the political groundwork was not tended. Here are four considerations we've found valuable in instituting effective programs.

Allies

Don't act before you have critical mass. Even if the CEO is a fan, do the work of developing a network of supporters. You will never have enough people on your side, and it is wise to act as though the lack of support from one more person could be enough to end your initiative at any point. For the most part, this involves humbly inquiring about the needs for development that others throughout the leadership see (Schein, 2013) and then returning to them with ideas of how you plan to build on the good work already taking place.

Planting Seeds

The need for change and the value of coaching approaches are not obvious to most people. The kinds of questions you raise in meetings and the articles and research you share with colleagues form the foundation for proposals you may make. Don't hurry or rush. Generally it is better not to start with any program before you have identified the aligned group of believers. This is the educational part of starting a program, and you are planting new seeds with every report on the impact of one component or another and through the excitement generated by small successes.

Continuous Engagement and Growth

You are never done with the political piece. The leadership will change and power will shift from one place to another. Enlist people throughout the leadership, including the board if you have access. Spend time with the loyal opposition even if you have the CEO's support. This may be especially important when you have the sponsorship of one or two key leaders who can provide the financial and people resources necessary to implement a program of coaching. Their support can fool you into complacency with respect to the investments others will have to make and make you forgetful about the need to generate enthusiasm for a new vision.

Decision Points

Once you have agreement for a program, form a cross-functional task group to work on the next phase and the expansion of the system. Be sure to build in evaluation with a clear understanding of the impact on business objectives. That may be the only thing that keeps your initiatives alive as leadership changes.

SAMPLE PATHWAYS

A comprehensive, integrated approach to coaching can begin in a variety of places. It is always useful to think about where you want to end up (begin with a clear and compelling vision), but more often than not, you will begin at a point consistent with the resources available to you. Here are four examples of ways you can start small and leverage the particular kind of success generated by a particular pathway. If you already have some programs that build on coaching approaches, you may find some ideas to answer the "What next?" question.

Start with Individual Coaching

When you begin with executive coaching, you give some leaders the opportunity to sample the most intense and personal form of leadership development. Often those coached become great advocates for the use of coaching. As a human resource leader, you may have a great deal of influence over who gets coaching and which coaches are available to your leaders. Also, because executive coaching is so highly targeted, it is often the case that the changes and growth are noticed by others and witnessed by the leader being coached.

If you have executives who can vouch for the value of the coaching they've received, the next steps are to bring some structure and standards to the processes for coaching. Careful vetting of coaches, evaluation of the results of executive coaching engagements, and close management of the finances lay the foundation for further growth. Once that is in place, it is not difficult to begin to develop internal coaches through professional-level training and certification. While members of the senior leadership may not want to work with internal coaches, it is more cost-effective and much more accessible to have human resource or learning and development professionals who are trained to coach at the same standards.

These steps can be extended through the provision of training programs for mentors to equip them with coaching skills. Internal professional-level coaches are an important resource for mentors and can help ensure that there are fewer failures of mentoring relationships. Also, you will note that in this situation, the extensions of the use of coaching are progressively less funding intensive and represent more impact without a commensurate increase in expenses.

Start with Training HR Leaders to Coach

Human resource leaders across the world are asking for opportunities to be trained at professional coaching levels. You may find that the way to begin your comprehensive approach is by creating an internal coach training program for your staff or with smaller organizations, sending them to respected coach training programs. When HR leaders have the credentials and experience of coaching, they may be seen quite differently by their business partners and their teams. This can form a good basis for other components of an integrated system because the trained coaches are available to work with mentors or train peer coaching advisors. They become resources for whatever other coaching you want to include, such as training managers to use more coaching with their own teams.

Start with Teaching Managers to Coach

We've helped a number of clients start with developing the coaching skills of managers throughout the organization. In several global conglomerates, the sheer number of people they hoped to be touched by this approach was so great that no other initiative was likely to gain sufficient notice. Training is not enough to inspire most managers to coach, so it is necessary to build reward systems around this skill and the outcomes of value. Commitment to guiding visions (such as "every leader a mentor") can begin to shape the culture. Coaching skills training and the use of coaching by managers is best measured by the impact on direct reports and how they contribute to business outcomes. This starting point has been shown to create demand for other forms of coaching because managers need support and guidance to shift from overreliance on telling to incorporating more inquiry and exploration in their conversations.

Sending Senior Leaders to Transformational Programs That Include Coaching

The most common initiating element in our experience has seen the development of sponsors at the more senior level who participate in a transformational leadership development experience including coaching. A major health system embarked on a systematic process of creating a leadership mind-set in all leaders as the result of the chief operating officer's experience in a leadership course. At CCL we have seen top leaders who have participated in such programs go on to become vocal public advocates for leadership development and coaching. When they begin talking in public settings about their growth and the value of coaching, they create a foundation for expanding the availability of these approaches throughout the organization.

HR LEADER ROLES

Responsibility for coaching systems may be lodged with human resources, learning and development, talent management, or even performance improvement. Wherever formally placed, it is useful to think about the roles and responsibilities likely to fall on whoever has taken on the job of making coaching productive for leadership development.

Connection with Performance

Perhaps one of the most important roles is firmly rooting coaching in the strategic plan for leadership development and talent management, which must be driven by the business strategy of the organization. We have often seen orphan programs initially established to address a single problem that no longer has the strategic importance it once had. Many organizations were in a panic to do leadership development during the heady growth days in the previous decade, only to have many of those efforts disappear rapidly in the contracting business environment. However, several elements of leadership development including coaching programs were maintained throughout because they were clearly contributing to the mission of the company. One executive integration program that relied heavily on external coaches continued because it was an integral piece of the talent strategy necessary to meet the needs for this merged global company. The lesson is clear: ensure that the vision for coaching services in your organization clearly spells out the connection with equipping the talent who will drive your business success.

System Integration and Differentiation

Complex systems with multiple components all suffer from lack of transparency from the viewpoint of naive observers and intermittent users. Setting up systems that ensure the most cost-effective solutions for individuals, teams, and the organization requires the HR coaching manager to be able to address confusion about the appropriate solution for the particular situation. As a result, the management of the system and the communications about entry points, procedures for participation, standards for delivery, and the like is a critical function of the coaching manager. This typically requires clarity about the discrete components of the system and the rules governing their use. Who gets access to external professional coaches? Who can access internal professionals? What services are provided for mentoring relationships or matching peers for peer coaching groups? These are questions that must be answered by the architecture of the system and the ways it is tied to existing human resource information systems.

Coaching Evangelist

As is the case for many other services, it is common to find that use is lower than expected unless there are persistent reminders of availability and simple ways to get started. This is true for mentoring programs, executive coaching sessions, peer coaching, and online systems. Because an emotional component is involved in taking initiative, it is necessary for people to find information immediately when potential users are open to a growth experience. Someone could be open because she is inspired and excited about opportunities to grow or it could be the result of a confidence-shattering experience. Either way, readiness for change can be unpredictable. Coaching must be visible in all its modalities when individuals or groups experience the need. Of course, continuous education about what coaching is and does, how it works, and how to access the varieties of coaching services is always needed.

We've seen effective programs that have utilization consistent with anticipated need. In one case, an HR leadership team made coaching utilization and management of the system a high priority in their own planning and acting. In several others, the director of the coaching system created events throughout the year highlighting the value of the coaching services. Annual recognition of mentors and celebration of peer coaching groups seems to be valuable for this. Several companies have used their professional coaches (internal and external) for learning experiences focused on various leadership foci. These include "learn at lunch" or as part of off-site development experiences. Encouraging executives with positive experiences in the coaching system to share what they gained from the process and to demystify the experience can create a climate in which more leaders feel it is worth the effort to participate.

Provide for Management of Coaches

Chapter 5 provides substantial guidance for HR leaders who need to manage internal and external pools of coaches. We have seen coaching pools that were not well managed lead to predatory marketing practices by coaches and the absence of information about the effectiveness of the coaching program. In one case, we discovered that an executive coach had parlayed one coaching engagement into multiple coaching relationships, all unmanaged and costing the company $500,000 per year. While the coaching may have been exemplary, the inability to make the connection between the strategic intentions of the company and the provision of the service was worrisome. The director of coaching services needs to ensure that the right coaches, with the right preparation and the right knowledge of the business and its operations, are matched with the right individuals being coached; that the coaching process is connected to the management structure, and meetings between coach, person being coached, and managers are productive; and that coaching engagements are consistently evaluated for impact.

Educate on Roles and Responsibilities

Each group of players in a comprehensive system has important roles and responsibilities as well as limits. The director of coaching services can make certain the relationships developed through a coaching-involved culture stay healthy and productive by clarifying the roles and responsibilities. Following are some examples of what we mean by roles and responsibilities:

- *Managers.* Managers represent the organization in discussions about the use of executive coaching with one of their direct reports. They use coaching skills in their leadership of their people and with their peers to get the best ideas and the involvement of everyone. They meet with the coach and their direct report to establish goals and expectations for executive coaching when invited.
- *Executives.* Executives serve as sponsors and examples for the organization. Their willingness to talk about how they have used coaching supports the normalization of developmental conversations and relationships. They make themselves available for mentoring.
- *Internal coaches.* Internal coaches are the priests of safety for the coaching services. They must often make clear the limitations of their roles and the balance they strike between their people management obligations and their coaching services.
- *External coaches.* They wisely build strategic alliances with the human resource and learning and development professionals to ensure their services contribute to the overall objectives of the coaching system. They are careful never to solicit additional business except under the guidance of the internal staff and stakeholders. They are wedded to the organization and balance their obligations to those they coach with their priority to support the success of the organization.

WORKING WITH EXTERNAL CONSULTANTS

One of the motivations for this handbook was our experience in many organizations across industries, sectors, and geographies that the success of coaching programs was often tied to the quality of the collaboration between internal professionals and CCL or other firms helping with the architecture of these systems or providing elements of them. When the creation of the approach and the solutions were worked on together and we were clear about our complementary contributions, the impact of these programs could be profound. When the relationships were more transactional and characterized by a purchaser-vendor philosophy, there were as many misses as hits with respect to a positive overall impact on the leadership of the organization. Several lessons have emerged from hundreds of engagements across the world.

Discovery

A joint discovery process leads to well-targeted, appropriately customized solutions when given enough time and access to be done right. Short-circuiting the discovery process is often the basis for the most expensive mistakes. An energy company had spent a lot of money working with a firm to develop a competency model for its executive leadership. Its leaders were loath to invest more and were quite happy with the model. They came to CCL to develop a multirater survey to be used for leader development and wanted to have coaching for executives as part of their development. There was no problem matching survey scales to their competency model, but when we began to explore how the competencies were expected to drive performance, distinct differences emerged among the learning and development staff. They couldn't agree on the behaviors that were needed and were uncertain whether their target audience for the program saw the connections between the competencies and their leadership challenges. Together we embarked on a clarifying discovery process, and both the internal professionals and we were able to make the proposed program more practical and useful as a result of the additional inquiry.

Different Contributions

When involving external consultants in creating these systems, an HR leader has to balance multiple factors. You will have greater experience in your company than most consulting organizations (unless you are inheriting a long-term relationship). They are likely to have a wider experience with different organizations. This can be particularly useful when you need to make the case for your integrated vision because these consultants can be used in communications with senior leaders. It is common for my client contacts to take me along to meetings with their managers and in presentations before the executive leadership group or the board. Our experience and credibility lend greater substance and acceptance because we've seen what works and what doesn't and can be counted on to provide useful guidance.

It is the nature of the HR function to be very careful regarding internal sensitivities, but this stance can be overdone. On more than one occasion, we've had client learning and development managers who wobbled about their direction and decisions. Inquiry showed me that they were uncertain how to respond to questions from senior executives and they overinterpreted questions as opposition. Uncertainty can lead to constant revisions of designs and reporting protocols, but educating senior executives about comprehensive programs and enlisting their support can reduce the likelihood of this happening. The creation of designs for discovery, programs, coaching operations, and the communications about them work best when they are the result of a completely joint effort that comes from the creative learning community formed by the internal coaching management and the consulting professionals.

CONCLUSION

Every organization has unique needs and opportunities to use coaching to develop leadership. Across the board, organizations intent on growth carefully apply the right coaching modalities to save money, experience powerful effects, and benefit the mission of their organizations. Careful thinking about what is to be accomplished and how the whole organization will be engaged can yield sustainable processes far outlasting the formal programs that kick it off. As a human resource professional, you can create lasting change in the culture and practices of your organization.

chapter
FOUR

Evaluating Coaching Interventions

Jennifer Habig and Emily Hoole

Measuring the effectiveness of executive coaching, while difficult, is necessary to the advancement of coaching as a leadership development tool (Kilburg, 2004; Lowman, 2005). Little empirical research supports the effectiveness of executive coaching (Kilburg, 2004), and thus far the field has focused on case studies and survey-based research about the process of coaching to get information (Kilburg, 2004; Lowman, 2001; Grant, 2013). While information about what happened during the coaching and specific case studies can provide great insight and potential hypotheses for more quantitatively based approaches, it cannot provide the foundation necessary for the continued use of coaching as a psychological tool for development. Lowman (2005) writes, "[Psychologists] are of course free to practice coaching from whatever perspective they want, but it [coaching] cannot pretend to be validated or even psychology (at least scientific psychology) if it is not anchored in empirical research" (p. 92).

The good news is that, unlike therapy, the success of executive coaching is more easily defined. Although executives and managers in organizations may face different challenges and opportunities, the goal of coaching is nearly always the same: a substantial change in critical behaviors that will directly or indirectly affect the strategic business goals of the organization in the most efficient and cost effective way. Therefore, measuring the success of executive coaching and, in essence, its value-added requires an evaluation that can track critical behavior change in clients and organizational outcomes as judged by key stakeholders.

The bad news is these behaviors and outcomes are potentially different for each leader receiving coaching depending on her unique skill sets, preferences, and organizational context. Peterson and Kraiger (2004) wrote, "Because coaching is individually customized, the most precise evaluation, as well as the most useful feedback for participants and coaches, will be gained by using customized items related to each person's own development priorities" (p. 274). This is both what makes coaching powerful and what makes it particularly difficult to measure. Unlike other leadership interventions, the uniqueness of coaching requires evaluation focused on the unique, targeted objectives of the leader.

WHY NOW?

The use of coaching continues to rise (see chapter 1 for more details). At the same time, expenses, especially those seen as ancillary, are coming under tighter scrutiny. Internal learning and development experts find themselves having to defend and cut expenses associated with leadership development initiatives.

We hear these common themes from our clients:

> "Development money is tight, and we need to be able to prove the coaching going on in our organization is getting results that matter to those who make decisions about where to allocate resources."
>
> "In order to save money and have coaches who understand our unique business and culture, we plan to use more internal professional coaches. We have to be able to manage the use of multiple types of coaching services within our organization that include both coaching done by external, executive coaches and coaching done by internal professionals and managers."
>
> "Finding and keeping the 'best' coaches (those who get results) is hard, and we need to know which coaches are the most effective in what environments. We need a way to compare impact across coaches."

Any way you look at it, the market is beginning to demand more meaningful data related to the effectiveness of these types of initiatives. What this means for the industry of executive coaching is that we need to find more consistent and valid ways to measure the impact of coaching. We believe these approaches need to keep in mind the following ideas:

- Focus on the creation of a small number of quantifiable and well-accepted measures of coach effectiveness with strong validity evidence. As Greif (2013) noted on the evaluation of coaching in organizations, "It does not make much sense for companies to construct homemade satisfaction scales for the outcome evaluation of HR-programs. *Benchmark-comparison of coaching programs in different organizations or between different types of HR interventions is possible* only if the outcomes are measured by standard scales that have been applied in many different organizations and evaluation studies" (p. 452). This united approach, which will allow for consistency across coaches, organizations, providers, and researchers, is one of the only ways to create a measure of coaching success for future research to address best coaching practices, key coaching skills, and individual difference variables that predict success. One way to determine what makes a great coach is to compare coaching engagements that produce outstanding results to those that were not as successful. By using standard measures and the amount of change, it would be possible to compare highly successful coaching engagements to those that were less successful. These comparisons would help answer many of the questions the field still has:

- Which of our current models of coaching are the most effective?
- What techniques are the most efficient for particular issues, clients, and contexts? In other words, which ones do not just work but work quickly.
- What characteristics do coaches need to be successful (e.g., do they need a warm disposition)?
- What characteristics in the leader tend to be important to success? In other words, who are the best candidates for coaching?

- Use the data to decrease costs associated with coaching.

Once we've answered some of these questions, our findings will aid in the selection and training of coaches, which will decrease the time and cost associated for both internal learning and development experts and external providers. It will also allow us to better predict the types of people, situations, and issues that respond best to coaching, thus decreasing the ineffective or inefficient use of coaching.

WHY CURRENT APPROACHES DON'T WORK AND HOW TO MOVE FORWARD

Current measures of coaching effectiveness used in the field are client-based, self-report scales asking questions about how useful the engagement was for learning and application of new behaviors, how competent the coach was, and how much the coachee enjoyed the process. In general, they focus on both coach-based antecedents and Kirkpatrick's level 1 analysis. Those who take the evaluation one step further usually begin to incorporate the coach's reactions and perception of the process.

The problem with these approaches is twofold. First, the information is arguably coming from one or two of the most biased sources in a coaching engagement: those who participated directly. Asking coaches or leaders to rate how they "feel" the coaching went or if they are "satisfied" with the process is like asking a surgeon or a patient to comment on the success of an operation just after surgery. We can assume the patient didn't enjoy the process and in the short term may actually feel worse. Second, focusing only on what happened in the coaching and not on the changes that occurred because of it at best does nothing to help prove its usefulness and at worst leads to false beliefs about who makes the best coach and what great coaches do that has impact. While it's helpful to hear the surgeon's opinion about whether he or she was able to fix the problem, only time will tell if the outcome is ideal for the patient.

We believe that for the evaluation of executive coaching to be useful to clients and the industry as a whole, we as practitioners need to:

1. Spend time understanding the context for coaching, including the specific needs of the individual, his or her group, and the organization. What makes coaching such a powerful intervention is that it is completely customizable.

2. Use that understanding to focus our evaluation on the achievement of specific goals set during the coaching process. Coaches assist leaders in transforming new insights into actionable goals. A key role of the coach is to help leaders sort through the myriad potential goals the assessment data suggest would be valuable and prioritize them based on the current needs of the organization. The evaluation of any coaching engagement has to include a measure of unique goal achievement as judged by those who can see it.

3. Extrapolate those goals into specific changes in behavior. The evaluation's ability to specifically target and measure behavior change as the result of a coaching engagement is critical. In the past, 360-degree feedback has been used to measure the effectiveness of coaching by both researchers and practitioners (Luthans & Peterson, 2003; Smither, London, Flautt, Vargas, & Kucine, 2003; Thach, 2002). Using competencies with specific behavioral items is a good way to get to specifics. The challenge is twofold: How do you get an accurate measure

of change in these behaviors? And how do you target only those specific areas focused on in each unique engagement?

4. Know the goals and behaviors targeted to get clear about the individual, group, and organizational outcomes expected as a result. In other words, what outcomes will be different if the leader achieves these goals and changes these key behaviors? While coaching is an individual intervention, it can have an impact on direct reports, teams, groups, departments, and, depending on the level of the leader, the organization.

5. Ask about antecedents, context, and reactions in order to test their effect on the outcomes of coaching. People make lots of claims regarding antecedents and process variables that may not matter at all. For example, some people believe having a certification or advanced degree makes someone a better coach. Others believe coaches must have direct experience in the industry or position of the leader to be effective. And still others focus on what happens during the coaching, claiming that all great coaches establish a solid relationship, set a supportive climate, and practice active listening. While any and all of these may in fact matter, all we really know is that not enough data exist to demonstrate the relationship between any one of them and goal attainment, behavioral change, or outcomes that matter to organizations.

6. Ask more than just the leader or the coach about the impact of coaching. Asking for the perceptions of those who work most closely with the leader about the impact of coaching is one of the only ways to get less biased information. Using a system that allows you to ask the client, coach, boss, peers, direct reports, and others about what they have noticed is critical to a better understanding of the real impact of coaching.

7. Check in with key stakeholders along the way. Peterson and Kraiger (2003) state, "If you are interested in ROI and the business impact of coaching, it is essential to gather information from the boss and/or other organizational sponsors at the outset of coaching … regarding their desired outcomes for the coaching and what they perceive the value of those outcomes to be." These stakeholders should include those who suggested the leader receive coaching and, particularly, whoever is defining the outcomes. Are they aligned with the goals set? Have they noticed any early changes? What are they doing to support the process?

8. Take a stance that the effectiveness of any given coach should be determined by the impact and change the leader achieves—not the process he uses. Coaches

are only as effective as the change they are able to evoke. What the leader is able to achieve or strengthen in the organization is the ultimate measure of success for a coach. Clearly there are times that coaching wasn't the right intervention, or the fit was wrong, or the leader wasn't ready, or the organization didn't support the change, but when the amount of change is aggregated over multiple clients across time, it is the most accurate measure of coach effectiveness.

Approaching the evaluation of coaching in organizations with the intent of combining the development of a coaching culture with evaluative thinking can provide a powerful way to foster organizational learning. "Learning organizations [are] organizations where people continually expand their capacity to create the results they truly desire, where new and expansive patterns of thinking are nurtured, where collective aspiration is set free, and where people are continually learning to see the whole together" (Senge, 1990, p. 3). Coaching cultures facilitate ongoing inquiry and continuous development and foster these new and expansive patterns of thinking to create different results; this process is enhanced when evaluative thinking capability is added. This perspective is represented by Torres and Preskill (2001), who define organizational learning as a process of continuous growth and improvement through use of evaluation, embedded in the organization's culture, systems, structure, and leadership, leading to alignment of values, attitudes, and perceptions.

Just as not all organizations are ready to engage in sophisticated coaching interventions, not all organizations are ready to fully engage in evaluative learning. Preskill and Torres (1999) identified the following factors to help organizations assess their level of readiness:

- Senior organizational leadership is willing to commit to evaluation beyond what is required for accountability purposes.
- The organization has a strong and stable senior leadership team.
- The organization engages in periodic organizational assessments such as employee engagement or climate surveys.
- The organization has some form of data management system.
- The team undertaking the evaluation work has administrative support.
- The organization and team have a history of engaging in diverse planning efforts.

When sufficient readiness, commitment, and motivation exist to build a robust evaluation culture, the organization can leverage the dual benefits of a coaching approach and evaluation learning.

When approaching the evaluation of a specific initiative, the place to begin is with the end in mind. Beginning with the end in mind improves the design of the intervention (and evaluation) and can improve the participant experience from the start. This includes close consideration of whether the proposed goals and expectations for the coaching intervention are realistic. Does the intervention support the expected outcomes through realistic time frames, sufficient effort, and funding for what the organization hopes to achieve? An evaluative thinking approach would also examine the underlying theory supporting the outcomes. Does existing psychological, sociological, and organizational development theory support the intervention logic and suggest the intervention will be successful? Is a new, innovative approach or intervention design being implemented, in which case embedding evaluation from the start is even more critical to specify the program theory to be tested? Evaluative thinking during the needs assessment process is also useful in ensuring that a coaching intervention is the right solution to the identified issues. Assessing the pros and cons of various options in relation to the desired outcomes, while exploring the necessary resources and conditions and underlying theoretical basis, is a critical evaluative thinking capability that can save organizations significant time and money by ensuring the right solution is selected and the approach is likely to achieve success. (For more information on evaluating when a coaching solution is the right approach, see chapter 2.) It can also be useful to examine existing evaluation evidence internally or in the literature regarding evidence of impact of a proposed intervention.

EVALUATION APPROACHES AND BEST PRACTICES

When considering building evaluation capability and engaging in meaningful evaluation of coaching, it is important to consider relevant approaches and best practices in the field. CCL's approach to evaluation is participatory and theory-based (Martineau & Hannum, 2008). In our participatory approach, we seek to include key stakeholders, including participants, throughout the evaluation process to reach consensus on the purpose of the evaluation and outcomes to be measured. This approach improves the evaluation design and data collection methods and is important for meaningful interpretation of the results. We also seek to build evaluation capability and evaluative thinking through work with stakeholder groups to advance evaluation practice and organizational learning for future efforts. By "theory-based," we mean designing the evaluation around the intervention theory as articulated with key stakeholders. Development of a logic model or theory of change helps to map out the intervention, resources necessary, conditions required, and short- and long-term outcomes expected from the coaching solution. This does not mean that we do not give appropriate focus to process and contextual factors and keep a sharp eye out for both positive and negative unintended consequences as part of the evaluation process.

Along with advocating for the use of both participatory and theory-based approaches to evaluation, there are a number of best practices for the evaluation of developmental interventions at both the individual and organizational levels. These include multisource evaluation when behavior change or cultural change is an expected outcome, multimethod evaluations to triangulate findings, longitudinal measurement if change over time is expected, strong measurement tools yielding reliable and valid data, and designs that allow for isolation of impact if possible (Hoole & Martineau, 2013).

When behavior change, cultural change, or collective capabilities are the goals of a coaching intervention, multiple perspectives are necessary to evaluate change and impact since these constructs are enacted in shared contexts. A decision point regarding the measurement of these constructs over time is the use of pre- and postmeasurement or the use of retrospective measurement. Within a research paradigm a pre- and posttest approach tends to be the gold standard. There are issues, specifically with response shift bias and rater bias, with a pre/post approach to measuring behavior change, bolstering arguments that a retrospective pretest/posttest is a more appropriate method (Lamb & Tschillard, 2005). Pratt, McGuigan, and Katzev (2000) found that a retrospective pretest methodology produced a more legitimate assessment of program outcomes than did the traditional pretest/posttest methodology when both were tested.

CCL's own experience in the use of pre- and post-360-degree measurement uncovered issues regarding ceiling effects and scale effects. Because leaders who are chosen for a development experience, whether coaching, leadership development, or another type of developmental opportunity, are typically high performing or high potential, they receive ratings at the upper end of the rating scale on most 360-degree items and competencies. This causes a ceiling effect where the range of change is restricted compared to individuals who may have a lower level of competency in certain areas. Scale effects compound the issue with many 360-degree instruments using a five-point scale, so any reported changes on this scale may be very small compared to what raters actually experience (Howland, Martineau, & Craig, 2001). Additional challenges with retaking 360-degree assessments include changes in scope or work situations for leaders, the use of different raters on the second 360-degree leading to a lack of comparability of results, or increased expectations from the same raters resulting in more stringent ratings.

While multisource data can provide the multiple perspectives necessary to explore changes as a result of an intervention, there is also a strong argument for the use of multiple methods to triangulate findings. Data from a single method (survey, interviews, focus groups) may suffer from common measurement bias (Podsakoff, MacKenzie, Lee, & Podsakoff, 2003), leading to lower validity in the interpretation of findings. Designs that include a variety of data sources such as surveys, organizational data (talent data, business performance data), interviews, and focus groups can build a comprehensive and compelling base of evidence. A current shortcoming in the field is the lack of longitudinal designs and evidence to support developmental interventions (Day & Sin, 2011; Hoole & Martineau, 2013). Understanding developmental trajectories will significantly enhance understanding in the field and for practice. Finally, strong designs that allow the isolation of the impact of the intervention will provide the strongest evidence regarding the impact of coaching interventions and the underlying mechanisms necessary for success.

ENGAGING STAKEHOLDERS

Effective stakeholder engagement is a crucial ingredient in the success of organizational evaluation efforts. Stakeholder buy-in and support help to ensure alignment between the goals of the coaching solution and the measurement of expected outcomes, and identification of the types of data that will be valued encourages strong participation in the evaluation process, leads to meaningful interpretation of the results, and ultimately results in effective use of the evaluation data for improvement. Without stakeholder involvement, there is a risk of low participation and results that the organization neither values nor uses, possibly leading to weak support of the intervention.

A coaching intervention or solution can have a variety of stakeholders. These include those who are directly engaged in the initiative as well as those affected by this participation; those funding the intervention, which may include senior management, human resources, or specific business units and departments; and others who are not directly involved but are interested or whose support is critical to the ongoing work itself.

Participants are not considered often enough in most evaluation processes. Their engagement in the evaluation is critical so it can be valuable to have some participants take part in designing the evaluation and as visible and vocal supporters of the evaluation process among their peers. Certainly participant involvement in the sense-making process regarding the results and how to improve the coaching intervention contributes to the overall quality of the evaluation. Managers of those involved in a coaching intervention are also an important stakeholder group. They are often a key source of evaluation data and can be leveraged to encourage the participant to engage in the evaluation process. The role of senior management and other organizational funders is to inform the design and the articulation of what outcomes should be measured to provide evidence of success or progress, along with specifying what types of data are acceptable and compelling. Are self-report data from participants strong enough evidence, or are multisource data needed for this audience? Is it necessary to have data on organizational performance or talent systems, or will stories of individual impact make the case? Along with specifying the types of data acceptable for the outcomes being measured, these stakeholders play a key role in supporting the implementation of any changes as a result of the evaluation. The group responsible for the intervention, typically human resources or a learning and development function, plays the largest role and is the most involved stakeholder group. This group designs and implements the evaluation, leads the process in making sense of the results, and then communicates the results to the key stakeholders and broader organization. Closing the loop by using the results to make changes to enhance the process and impact is the final step.

When looking to begin a stakeholder engagement process, it can be very useful to think about the motivations for each of the groups regarding the program and the evaluation. Understanding why the intervention itself is important to each group and what value they are expecting from the work can be used to build support for the evaluation efforts. Prioritize the stakeholder groups or individuals, and target those most critical to the initiative to be part of the evaluation stakeholder group. Preskill and Jones (2009) outline six primary roles for stakeholders in an evaluation process:

1. *Establish the outcomes or goals of the work.* Ideally this process occurred during the needs assessment phase. Agreement and alignment regarding the outcomes by stakeholders is crucial during the design phase.
2. *Develop and approve the evaluation design.* This includes agreement on the most effective methods to use and the most appropriate sources for evaluation data. Limitations regarding the evaluation process can be identified and discussed at this point to mitigate any disappointment regarding the strength of evaluation evidence produced.
3. *Review the data collection instruments (surveys, interviews).* Review and pilot testing of surveys and interview or focus group protocols can uncover areas of ambiguity or lack of alignment with purposes of the evaluation.
4. *Provide data.* Most stakeholder groups are well positioned to provide some level of evaluation feedback from a process or outcome perspective, or both.
5. *Help to interpret and make meaning of the data.* This is an important step because stakeholders can provide a deeper and more nuanced interpretation of the results or uncover measurement issues that may have an impact on the validity of the findings.
6. *Use the data.* Evaluation can be a meaningless endeavor if no one uses the results. Stakeholders can help to identify the best uses for the findings, from process improvement to building additional support or communicating success.

Preskill and Jones also highlight a variety of challenges in engaging stakeholders in evaluation. The most common barrier is time. The time necessary to engage with a variety of groups and the availability of these stakeholders to dedicate time to the process is challenging in most situations. In some instances, funding is required to involve stakeholders adequately in group processes around design, development, and sense making. Reconciling the different perspectives of stakeholders can be a challenge if there is a lack of agreement regarding approach, results, or the value of the evaluation or the meaning of the outcomes. This is where a prioritization process regarding stakeholder groups can be a useful exercise.

The varying levels of knowledge and sophistication with evaluation among stakeholder groups can increase the time needed to get the best input and output from these groups. In some instances, it is an unfortunate truth that critical stakeholder groups may be indifferent to the evaluation work or do not invest the needed amount of time and effort. Frustration may also arise if key stakeholder groups are unwilling to use the evaluation results. Considering these challenges up front can help guide the development of a successful stakeholder engagement approach.

There are a variety of options for engaging stakeholders in the evaluation process. Interviewing key stakeholders individually or dialogue in a group setting is a good initial first step. Engaging a broad stakeholder group in developing a logic model provides significant value in building a common understanding regarding the intervention, conditions necessary for success, and the intended outcomes. The logic modeling process can then guide the evaluation design and facilitate productive conversations regarding data sources and methods. Stakeholder groups should be engaged again for sense-making sessions after data are collected to explore the results and implications. Stakeholders can also be leveraged for any formal reporting-out sessions to important management groups.

FORMAL EVALUATION OF COACHING INTERVENTIONS

There are three primary reasons to engage in an evaluation process for a specific intervention: evaluation for improvement (formative evaluation), evaluation for impact (summative evaluation), and support of the ongoing development of those involved in the coaching process.

Formative Evaluation

Without a focus on the evaluation of the program, process, or system, an organization will not know which aspects are working and which are not. This can leave an organization with only anecdotal evidence on which to base changes. An important focus for improvement is to understand what is happening at an individual level within coaching engagements, within a program on coaching skills or with broad organizational efforts regarding coaching for development or peer coaching, or from a system perspective regarding the development of a coaching culture. Systemic issues such as utilization or support issues are also uncovered through a focus on evaluation for improvement. Many of these issues may be missed and not corrected if an organization has only an evaluation for impact focus.

The most important role for evaluation for improvement is identification of actions to take to improve the intervention and increase the likelihood of success. This approach uncovers organizational capability and capacity issues to address as well as intervention-specific areas for improvement. Evaluation for improvement can also identify areas of alignment or misalignment with other efforts from the participants' perspective or more broadly. A process and improvement focus will also build organizational capability and capability more broadly in the coaching field regarding optimal conditions for success. Some key questions related to the formative evaluation of executive coaching include:

- What are the critical aspects for executive coaching matching, and what is the most effective matching process?
- What is the optimal length of a coaching engagement?
- How many coaching sessions are needed to achieve a participant's goal or different types of goals?
- What are the important issues related to the modality of coaching?
- What are effective ways to measure and increase readiness for coaching?

These and many other critical questions can be explored and answered through a robust evaluation process.

Summative Evaluation

The second role is evaluation for impact. It is not enough to know how well the process and systems are working if the goals of the intervention are not being achieved. The limited funding in organizations requires demonstrating the value of any investment made in the development of leaders, whether through executive coaching, mentoring, peer coaching, coaching skill building, or coaching culture efforts. Evidence of strong impact also provides a compelling case for sustaining and supporting the expansion of such efforts. Evaluation can be an important component of the development of a coaching culture, fostering inquiry throughout the entire effort, helping to course-correct, and demonstrating evidence along the way.

Evaluation for Development

Finally, at CCL we have found evaluation to be a means of ongoing development for those involved. In an executive coaching engagement, evaluation can be developmental for both the coach and coachee by providing a measure of progress and ongoing feedback. Developmental feedback regarding behavior change at midpoint can help a leader and coach make changes to development plans and actions to increase impact and effectiveness. At a macrolevel, evaluation can point to next steps for development of a group of leaders engaged in a coaching intervention.

We advocate for a comprehensive approach to the evaluation of executive coaching using seven elements (see figure 4.1):

1. Context
   - Organizational context (e.g., developmental climate)
   - Boss support
   - Coachee commitment
   - Recent job or organizational changes
   - Other developmental activities
2. Antecedents
   - Coachee, coach, and rater demographics
   - Reason for engaging in the coaching process
   - Commitment
   - Readiness
3. Process
   - Coaching process
   - Frequency and duration
   - Goal support
   - Satisfaction with the coach
4. Coach behaviors
   - Coachee's perception of the coach's behaviors during the process
5. Goal progress
6. Behavior change
7. Outcomes (individual, direct report, group)

Table 4.1 outlines for these seven elements at what point in the process to collect the data. This approach examines the entirety of an executive coaching engagement and the relevant individual variables and organizational context within which coaching is situated. Best practice in the evaluation field is to

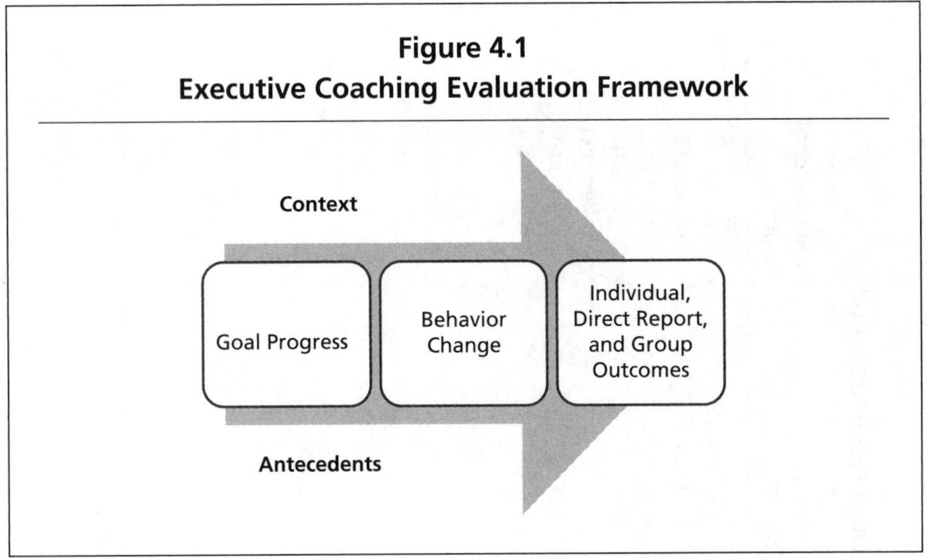

measure change over time. We have found three key times relevant to measure with executive coaching specifically:

- Baseline or at the inception of the coaching process (first coaching session, after each skill-building session)
- A midpoint process and progress check focusing on the coaching engagement, goal progress, and barriers to the process
- On completion of the coaching engagement or some period of time after completion of coaching (e.g., three months) for outcome data

When a pool of coaching hours is being used by a large number of leaders, ongoing usage data for the coaching are also important to track. This approach to timing is also applicable to mentoring or peer coaching interventions. A coaching skill-building intervention may use preprogram data, end-of-training evaluation, and an impact evaluation effort after the application of coaching skills back in the organization.

Research conducted with CCL executive coaching clients (Eckardt, 2013) identified three critical factors to evaluate based on their relationship with goal progress: readiness for coaching, boss support, and self-awareness. This research demonstrates both the importance of readiness for coaching as well as the potential for quality executive coaching to mitigate readiness issues. Higher levels

Table 4.1
Executive Coaching Evaluation Framework Data Collection Points

Context Variables	Individual Variables	Coaching Process	Behavior Change	Organizational Impact
• Boss support for coaching (T2, T3) • Developmental climate of the organization (T3)	• Commitment (T1, T2, T3) • Readiness for coaching (T1) • Increased self-awareness (T1) • Changes in leader situation (T3)	• RACSR coaching behaviors (relationship, assessment, challenge, support, results) (T1, T2, T3) • Frequency of coaching • Duration of coaching • Goal support • Coach quality (T2, T3) • Satisfaction with coaching (T2, T3) • Coaching process (T3)	• Leader goal progress (T2, T3) • Leader behavior change (T2, T3)	• Group and individual impact (T3) • Organizational challenges (T3) • Workplace performance (T3) • Key performance indicators (T3)

Note: Timing: T1, precoaching or after the first session; T2, midpoint; T3, completion or postcoaching.

of readiness can ensure a positive start to a coaching engagement and is predictive of early progress and self-awareness. Readiness measured at the beginning of a coaching engagement was correlated with the level of self-awareness of the leader at midpoint. With a correlation of .39, 15 percent of the variance in self-awareness was explained by readiness. Readiness was more highly correlated ($r = .42$) with goal progress at midpoint, meaning 18 percent of the variance was explained by initial leader readiness to engage in coaching. However, readiness was not correlated with self-awareness or goal progress at the end of a coaching engagement, with the implication that effective executive coaches help coachees overcome any initial issues they might experience.

Of even greater importance for both coaching engagements and the evaluation process is boss support, a critical element in maximizing the impact of developmental interventions. American Express (Leone, 2008) identified five critical elements where boss support positively or negatively affects an individual's developmental progress:

1. Providing support before the leader engages in a developmental experience
2. Providing visible support for the developmental opportunity
3. Meeting with the leader to discuss development needs before the experience
4. Meeting with the leader to discuss development goals
5. Most important, rewarding progress toward developmental goals

Our research substantiates the relationship between boss support and goal progress in the executive coaching context as well. Twenty-nine percent of the variance in the final goal progress was due to how supportive the leader's boss was during the coaching engagement ($r = .54$). Finally, self-awareness, as always, remains a critical focus for leader development no matter the approach. Twenty-eight percent of the variance in goal progress at midpoint was due to the leader's level of self-awareness ($r = .53$). Including these factors in an ongoing evaluation process helps to monitor and adjust for issues relevant to achieving individual goals and ultimately the organizational impact achieved.

Additional coaching evaluation work with clients demonstrated the importance of commitment as a key aspect for goal achievement. Table 4.2 displays the correlations (the statistical strength of the relationship between the variables) between program outcomes and hours of coaching and the leader's commitment to the coaching process. In many cases, there is a positive relationship between

Table 4.2
Relationship of Hours of Coaching and Coaching Commitment to Coaching Outcomes

Correlations with Coaching Outcomes	Hours of Coaching	Commitment to Coaching
Progress toward solving current business challenges	.42	.44
Made progress on development goals	.45	.36
Improved knowledge of strengths and weaknesses	.38	.52
Strengthened leadership capability	*	.45
Improved my business results	*	.44
Improved communication and engagement skills	*	.45
Improved professional relationships with managers and/or key stakeholders	.40	.55

*The correlation between the variables was not statistically significant. $N = 36$.

how committed the leader was to the coaching process and the outcomes, whereas there was no relationship between the number of hours of coaching and the outcome. Both aspects are clearly important to measure in an evaluation process and the results used to drive greater results.

We have also found some strong relationships between the experience of being coached and coaching skill development (see table 4.3). This is an example of an unintended consequence (in this case, positive) and importance of looking for such unintended outcomes. In the case of positive unintended outcomes, how can the organization best leverage such information (e.g., formal incorporation as an intent of the program to strengthen the impact)? When there are unexpected negative outcomes, the goal becomes determining how to mitigate or eliminate them.

COACHING EVALUATION OUTCOMES FRAMEWORK

The value of coaching should be based on the outcomes achieved for the individual and organization, not an evaluation of the process elements or self-reported satisfaction. CCL has developed a rigorous research-based outcomes approach to

Table 4.3
Correlations between Coaching Hours and Commitment and Coaching Skill Development

Correlations with Coaching Skill Development	Hours of Coaching	Coaching Commitment
Increased ability to give appropriate feedback	.49	.55
Increased ability to receive and use feedback	.53	.57
Increased ability to coach others	.59	.58

Note: $N = 36$.

evaluate the impact of executive coaching engagements. To develop our four-level model, we conducted a thorough literature review to understand what was being measured in the field and the research basis for these constructs and approaches. This helped us to understand the current state of practice and level of evaluation evidence in the field. We also sought to understand what business outcomes organizations are seeking to achieve but where evidence is lacking. Our coaching evaluation assessment focuses on outcomes at the individual, direct report, group, and organizational levels, with the specific outcomes selected based on the goals set by the coach and leader for the coaching engagement. Within these four levels there are five types of outcomes (see table 4.4):

1. *Performance outcomes* look at changes in performance for the leader, the leader's direct reports, and the overall performance of the leader's group.
2. *Developmental outcomes* focus on changes for the leader and the leader's direct reports.
3. *Attitudinal outcomes* include dimensions such as engagement, motivation, and job satisfaction.
4. *Interpersonal outcomes* focus on relationships, communication, and collaboration.
5. *Business outcomes* cover a range of measurable business metrics such as growth, revenue, margin, customer satisfaction, and cycle time.

Table 4.4
Executive Coaching Outcomes Framework

	Individual	Direct Reports	Team/Group	Organization
	Focuses on what's different for the individual as a result of his or her behavior change.	Often changes in the coachee directly affect his or her direct reports. Focuses on what's different in the direct reports of the individual being coached as a result of his or her behavior change.	Focuses on what's different for the groups/teams this person leads as a result of his or her behavior change.	Focuses on what's different for the organization (or department) the individual is a part of as a result of his or her behavior change.
Performance	Leadership effectiveness			
	Overall performance	Overall performance	Overall performance	Profitability
	Productivity	Productivity	Productivity	Productivity
	Quality of work	Quality of work	Quality of work	
	Efficiency	Efficiency	Efficiency	Efficiency
Development	Promotability	Promotability	Talent pipeline	
	Retention	Retention	Retention	
	Increase in responsibility	Increase in responsibility		
	Avoiding derailment	Avoiding derailment		

Attitudes	Job satisfaction Engagement Empowerment Morale Organizational commitment Self-confidence Self-efficacy	Job satisfaction Engagement Empowerment Morale Organizational commitment Self-confidence Self-efficacy	Job satisfaction Engagement Empowerment Morale Organizational commitment	
Interpersonal	Relationship quality	Relationship quality	Relationship quality	Relationship quality
	Communication quality	Communication quality	Communication quality	Communication quality
	Decision-making quality	Decision-making quality		
			Collaboration within team	Collaboration with other teams

(*continued*)

Table 4.4 (*Continued*)

	Individual	Direct Reports	Team/Group	Organization
Business			Direction Alignment Commitment	Direction Alignment Commitment Customer service Customer complaints Time to resolution of customer complaints Customer retention and growth Customer growth Sales growth Percentage change in revenue Operating margin

LEVERAGING COACHES IN COACHING EVALUATION

While we caution against the use of coach feedback as the primary measure of the impact of coaching, coaches nevertheless can provide a rich source of data regarding coaching engagements. Typically coaches can share themes about the types of goals being set, organizational barriers that individuals are facing, strengths and challenges of leaders, or reactions to organizational stressors (e.g., merger) and events.

At the beginning of a coaching process, we suggest collecting data regarding the initial coaching session and the coach's perspective on the leader's readiness for coaching. Data regarding the match, fit, or chemistry, when combined with the leader's input on these dimensions, can start to build a research-based understanding of the role these may or may not play in successful coaching. Asking coaches to describe the goals the leaders are pursuing, when combined with a comparative look at how the leaders themselves describe their development goals, provides some useful insight by framing the developmental needs of the group from multiple perspectives.

A midpoint process check-in with coaches to gather data on the coaching process and some initial outcomes can provide critical information for course corrections and improvements. Coach feedback is often most useful in identifying the facilitating factors and barriers the leaders experience to engaging in the coaching process and achieving their development goals. Coaches can also provide deeper and more objective insights into organizational conditions valuable for other leadership development or organizational development work. Obviously you have to be clear in the initial communication to coachees that coaches will be asked for this type of information regarding the leaders and process in a way that protects the leaders' anonymity.

A final area of focus for evaluation with coaches is coach preparation and support. Asking coaches for feedback on the coach onboarding and training process can improve this aspect over time. Questions such as, "What do you wish you had known at the beginning of the coaching engagement?" can identify valuable information to add to coach guides or lists of frequently asked questions. Overall, gathering data from coaches can enhance evaluation efforts and provide unique insights to leverage.

EVALUATION BEYOND EXECUTIVE COACHING

A comprehensive evaluation approach would not just focus on executive coaching engagements within the organizations, but also include other coaching solutions such as coach skill-building efforts and mentoring.

Coach Skill-Building Evaluation

A key focus of these efforts is the development of specific coaching skills and behaviors in the participants and the application of a coaching approach with the participants' direct reports and possibly more broadly in the organization. In this case, a measure of coaching skills and behaviors is important not just for the development process but also to provide baseline information for the evaluation. CCL has developed the Coaching Effectiveness Indicator 360-degree assessment (CCL, 2009) for use in our coach development programs. Ideally measurement would then look at change over time in coaching skills and behaviors, through either a pre- and postmeasurement or use of a retrospective pretest/posttest assessment. Other possible individual-level outcomes to measure for change could be increased self-awareness of impact on others, understanding of personal strengths and needs, and changes in peer networks. At the group and organizational level, some of the changes we have targeted for evaluation as a result of coaching skill development include:

- Appreciation for and leveraging of diverse perspectives
- Ability to handle challenges
- Increased employee engagement
- Increased mentoring within the group or organization
- Development of a coaching culture
- Increased use of feedback to make changes

The facilitators and barriers to applying coaching skills within the organization should also be a key focus for the evaluation effort, along with suggestions to improve the intervention (see table 4.5).

Table 4.5
Examples of Facilitators and Barriers within Organizations for Coach Skill-Building Programs

Facilitators	Barriers
• Relevant program content • Appropriate timing • Supervisor support • Active experimentation • Participant openness to change	• Program targeted at the wrong time in a manager's career • Difficult for managers to change behaviors • Lack of support within the culture for the desired changes • Time demands

Mentoring Program Evaluation

Mentoring programs provide a rich opportunity to explore the impacts on not just the protégé but the mentor as well. In our experience, the mentor gains just as much from the experience, and this should be evaluated. When focusing on the protégé experience, the following are relevant to consider:

- Goal progress and organizational impact
  - Leadership development
  - Professional development
  - Behavior change
- Career advancement
- Intent to remain/retention
- Mentoring process (e.g., mentor availability, organizational support)
- Satisfaction
- Facilitators and barriers experienced

Some slightly different aspects should be taken into account for the mentor portion of the evaluation:

- Training process for mentors
- Mentoring or coaching skill development

- Matching
- Mentoring process (e.g., mentoring interactions and effectiveness)
- Personal development of mentors
- Facilitators and barriers as a mentor

HOW TO MEASURE

We have covered what to measure and when for the evaluation of a variety of coaching interventions. We now turn to a brief overview of how to measure the process, outcomes, and important contextual variables we have introduced.

Surveys

Overall we are advocating the development of common measures to provide consistent, reliable, and valid data to evaluate, research, and advance the field's understanding of coaching. Current practice includes surveys of the leader and the coach with a focus on process and progress. These have a value in the overall coaching evaluation approach but are just a beginning. Surveys can also collect data from managers and HR professionals on the process, support factors, and outcomes of the coaching. Expanding beyond this are surveys including the direct reports and peers of the leader engaged in the coaching intervention to explore behavior change and impact. The most sophisticated approach for gathering multisource data on behavior change and results would be a 360-degree assessment to provide detailed feedback to the leader and coach for development as well as evaluation. Alternatively, a multisource survey could be used with all the rater groups, but individual-level feedback is not provided. This approach misses out on the powerful opportunity to provide ongoing feedback for the leader. The development of standardized surveys or 360-degree assessments may have the greatest potential to influence the practice of coaching but are not the only ways to gather useful evaluation data.

Interviews

Interviews can gather many of the same types of data as surveys, but can also gather more detailed information and stories to provide greater context and deeper understanding of the situation. A common and useful approach is to combine the use of surveys and interviews. Often interviews are used after a survey to explore in more detail issues or opportunities that emerge. Conversely, interviews can be conducted first to identify areas to measure on surveys (e.g., common leadership challenge areas, facilitators, and barriers) to provide more generalizability to the interview data. In our work with clients, we have combined surveys of leaders being coached with interviews with managers and HR business partners.

Organizational Data

HR systems (talent and performance) can often provide data relevant to the coaching efforts, such as retention, promotion, and performance. Tracked over time and in the aggregate, these more objective measures can be linked to the coaching data to generate deeper insights into the process and outcomes of coaching. The use of key performance indicators (e.g., sales, revenue targets, growth targets, margins, employee engagement scores), Lean, or Six Sigma measures (outputs, efficiency) can also build a strong evidence base when combined with additional evaluation data.

Approaches to isolate impact include random assignment, delayed treatment, and longitudinal designs. Many times these are not feasible within organizational contexts, but increased use of such approaches would contribute significantly to the evidence base of coaching.

INFORMAL CHANNELS OF EVALUATIVE INFORMATION

Often when we think about the evaluation of executive coaching, we focus on formal, quantitative, or qualitative ways of getting information. While these are critical to understanding the long-term impact of coaching, effective short-term evaluation of executive coaching programs often uses informal feedback channels.

Using Intake as an Early Gauge of Appropriate Use

Without proper communication about the appropriate use of coaching as a developmental intervention, managers may try to use it as a way to "outsource" the part of their job that has to do with uncomfortable conversations and performance feedback. Having the right data collection channels in place in the beginning can decrease the number of engagements that were likely doomed from the beginning. Typical intake forms include questions for multiple parties (see exhibit 4.1).

Exhibit 4.1
Examples of Intake Form Questions

HR Representative or Manager	Potential Client
How long has this individual been in this role? with the organization?	How would you describe your role?
What is the rationale for executive coaching over other development programs?	What are your three biggest leadership challenges?
Who is initiating the coaching recommendation? Why coaching? Why now? Desired outcomes?	How many direct reports do you have? How are those relationships?
Is the manager (Are you) willing to invest the time necessary and the funding for executive coaching?	Have you ever worked with an executive coach before? If so, how was your experience?
On a scale of 0 to10 (10 being highest), how ready is this individual for executive coaching?	What would you hope is different for you and those around you at the end of this coaching engagement?
How have you determined this readiness?	Describe your ideal coach.
How will success be measured? What will happen if nothing changes?	Are you willing to invest up to X hours a week with an executive coach?

Tracking and Reporting Utilization as a Key Piece of Early Feedback

Whether you are monitoring one or one hundred coaching engagements, being clear about the steps in the process and where people are in it at any given time can be important evaluation data:

- *Early in the process*: How long is it taking for pairs to get started (intake to first session)? Are they completing certain parts of the process (e.g., phone meetings with their coach) but not others (e.g., stakeholder check-in meetings)? Are there specific engagements that are not moving at all?

- *Later in the process*: Are people using their hours within the time frame intended (e.g., three, six, nine months)? Are they using all their hours, or is there a trend in when they begin to fall off?

Open Channels of Communication to Detect Problems

Often practitioners don't use their greatest sources of information early in the process. Coaches and leaders are usually the only people who know early on if the coaching is on the right track. Finding ways to tap into this information quickly leads to corrections that can help the coaching succeed.

Ask the Leader

Sometimes the leader will make an early judgment, accurate or not, that her coach is not the right coach for her. Simple questions asked at the right time can help to correct this:

"Is my coach is a good match for me? Why or why not?"

"Am I comfortable with my coach? Why or why not?"

In addition, it may also be that the leader is not as committed to the process as she needs to be:

"Am I committed to this coaching engagement?"

"Am I committing adequate time to this process?"

Sometimes just asking the question is enough to get the leader past the issue. At other times, it signals that a change may need to occur.

Ask the Coach

Coaches can quickly become sources of information about the organization and the coaching program. Even if you don't have a way to formally track utilization, they can quickly let you know when an engagement is off track (e.g., difficulty scheduling or keeping meetings). They also tend to have great insights into what's working or not from a systems or design perspective (e.g., using nine sessions in six months won't work in this culture; getting interviews with key stakeholders has been difficult). Coaches can be a great source of information about themes and patterns they are noticing across participants and the organization. If this is not a formal part of evaluation, coaches are likely to share issues and struggles with the internal program administrator or to the HR professional leading the initiative through calls or e-mails.

HOW TO USE EVALUATIVE INFORMATION IN PROGRAM DESIGN AND CORRECTION

Once you have set up both formal and informal evaluation channels, it's important to use it to make corrections in the process or design of evaluation programs.

Process Changes

One of the most common early indicators of an issue is low utilization of coaching hours. This could be occurring for many reasons. First, it could be that coaching is not the right answer for the challenges leaders are facing (e.g., performance management, technical skill gaps), and training or mentoring or managing would be a better solution. This lack of alignment can cause the leader to quickly see the coaching as ineffective and a waste of time. This often happens for a certain number of engagements when everyone in a specific group (e.g., leader level, department, team, high potential) gets a coach. Second, low utilization could also be due to lack of adequate communication about the purpose, process, and outcomes of coaching and the importance of this initiative to the execution of current business goals. Third, low utilization could be due to the fact that the coaching hit at a very busy time in the business cycle and can't be made a priority. Be careful about this one. Everyone is always busy, but there are certain times of the year and certain situations that can heavily cut into use.

Another common indicator of a problem is that one or more of the steps is not occurring on a regular basis. Often executive coaching includes the use of assessments, check-ins with the client's boss, or the creation of a development plan. When one of more of these steps either does not occur or causes stress in the system, this is an indication that something may be off.

Design Changes

Engaging in formative evaluation, or evaluation for learning, can lead to design changes for coaching interventions. For executive coaching, the feedback from leaders and coaches may indicate that the number of sessions or the length of time may need to be adjusted for the outcomes desired. Rather than twelve sessions over a six-month time frame, a more reasonable design might be spreading the sessions out over a longer time period. For executive integration for a new senior executive, the coaching intensity may need to be increased to achieve greater success. Feedback from coaches may indicate that they don't have the necessary organizational context information, leading to a redesign of the coaching ramp-up process.

Evaluation of coaching skill building may demonstrate that the target audience is not the appropriate one for the program, leading to changes in program selection or a complete change in the level of leader targeted for the intervention.

One recent client evaluation including both an executive integration process and executive coaching for leaders a level lower in the organization led to the following recommendations:

- Reduce the overall length of engagements.
- Encourage greater human resource business partner involvement in engagements.
- Continue to focus on developing coach knowledge of the business context.
- Increase face-to-face meetings with coaches.
- Use a new survey tool and interview questions for the evaluation.

In the end, not using evaluation data to make changes and improvements is a wasted opportunity and a waste of effort on the part of the organization. Utilization of evaluation and learning from the evaluation process strengthens the organization's overall learning capability and leads to more effective efforts in the future.

MAKING THE BUSINESS CASE WITH EVALUATION DATA

Imagine being able to present the following data to key stakeholders regarding the impact of an executive integration coaching program:

As reported by leaders surveyed

- All reported achieving two or more objectives in their integration plans.
- Ninety-four percent reported achieving early wins and that coaching assisted in these successes.
- Ninety-four percent agreed they made progress toward addressing relevant business challenges.

As reported by managers and human resource business partners interviewed

- Ninety-two percent of managers and 84 percent of human resource business partners agreed that leaders used the authority of their new roles to accomplish business objectives.

- Eighty percent of managers and 72 percent of human resource business partners agreed that leaders established strong, effective networks of relationships to accomplish business objectives: "We were able to bring my team together and have them function well. Through multidisciplinary partnership we delivered over $750 million in cost avoidance to the company."

While word-of-mouth support from those involved in coaching efforts can be effective in communicating value and sharing individual stories highlighting the power of coaching, having strong aggregated data on impact can be crucial for you to garner continued support or expansion of efforts within the organization. Data related to the behavior change and competency development can demonstrate the results of coaching at the individual level, while higher-level data on changes in groups or teams and organizational outcomes demonstrate the ability of coaching to deliver effectively on organizational goals to advance strategy.

CONCLUSION

We hope this chapter has demonstrated the value for the organization in engaging in evaluation of coaching interventions. Doing so builds internal capability and capacity for organizational learning, engages and builds stakeholder support, leads to improved programs with improved results, and builds the business case for coaching efforts throughout the enterprise. Improving the current state of coaching evaluation through more comprehensive approaches and more rigorous methods benefits the field as a whole and all organizations and practitioners engaged in a variety of coaching modalities and related efforts.

chapter
FIVE

Managing Coaches

Johan Naudé and Patrick Stichelmans

If thinking about creating and managing a cadre of executive coaches reminds you too much of herding cats, we promise some help in this chapter. We share our experiences and lessons learned from a decade of managing a globally dispersed community of professional coaches, as well as the experiences of some senior talent and coaching leaders in global organizations. We start with a discussion about using internal or external coaches, and then move on to coach accreditation, selection and training, coaching supervision, orientation to the coaching work, coach matching, quality assurance, and communities of practice. We believe you will find this useful and wish you the best with your coach cadre.

CHOOSING BETWEEN INTERNAL AND EXTERNAL COACHES

When we refer to internal coaches in this chapter, we mean those who have been trained to engage in formal coaching, on a part- or full-time basis, within an organization. Until quite recently, almost all professional coaching in organizations was done by external professionals. As leadership development and coaching become more integrated into organizations, however, internal coaching—by both professionals and line leaders—is also becoming more prevalent. CCL research suggests that leaders attribute as much as 70 percent of their leadership lessons to on-the-job-challenges, 20 percent to experiences in relationships, and only 10 percent to lessons derived from formal classroom activities (McCauley & McCaull, 2013). It may therefore make perfect sense for some companies to accelerate a coaching culture to maximize the developmental potential of both job challenges and coaching relationships. They can do this by not only training line managers in how to informally coach their teams on the job (see Naudé & Plessier, 2014) but also by assigning professional internal coaches.

Benefits of Internal Coaching

Internal coaches, properly selected, trained, and used, can offer a number of benefits to organizations:

- *Cost.* Estimates vary widely, but it is safe to assume that the cost of external coaching is at least twice as high as internal coaching. It is no wonder that HR departments, under pressure to cut costs and yet interested in developing a learning and development culture, are considering a hybrid model with both external and internal coaches.
- *Consistency.* Some organizations have intentionally or unintentionally relied heavily on multiple external independent coaches through personal relationships that HR and other leaders have cultivated with executive coaches over the years. There is nothing wrong with that model as such, but it is not always the best strategy for an organization that needs to be more cost conscious and more strategic about aligning leadership and business strategies. In any case, it makes sense to set common standards for leadership training and coaching frameworks. This can be done by turning to a single provider of external coaches and focusing on developing internal talent and the systems to manage coaching.
- *Scalability.* Enterprise-level interventions increase the likelihood of cascading the benefit of coaching through the organization. If you can train a group of 15 leaders in the organization to become internal coaches and if each of those leaders coaches 10 senior managers, you have reached a potential pool of 150 leaders from which a group of coaching champions can emerge to communicate throughout your organization the benefits of coaching. This approach not only makes coaching more scalable; it also makes it more inclusive.
- *Breaking down silos.* A recurring challenge in many organizations is to get its different parts (whether functions or business units) working seamlessly together. Organizations create complex matrix structures to overcome some of these

barriers. Those are not always effective because they start from the assumption that structures drive behavior, regardless of informal networks or relationships. Internal coaches have the opportunity to strengthen internal networks for the benefit of the organization. As Katharine St. John-Brooks (2014) puts it, "Having internal coaches with a day job in one part of the business working with clients in other parts of the business can play a very positive part in breaking down these structural barriers" (p. 95).

• *Onboarding.* Slow down to speed up. Initially it may be more time-consuming to develop your cadre of well-trained, qualified internal coaches. The advantage comes after the growth pains. Internal coaches have instant, constantly updated knowledge about the company's culture, values, politics, informal networks, and so on. They can be effective if they are able to be objective and curious while avoiding land mines. Internal coaches can also contribute significantly to organizational learning if they capture the themes that arise from coaching and supervision sessions across the enterprise.

Bill Hodgetts, vice president of enterprise coaching and assessment at Fidelity Investments, a US-based global financial services organization, describes his organization's approach to using internal coaches this way:

> For things like onboarding or to help the leader get oriented to the organization, culture, politics etc., internal coaches have an edge over external coaches. The openness to internal coaching here is greater due to the focus on cost and cost cutting. Revenue and profit margins are also clearly driving the decision toward internal coaching. Some organizations tend to use external coaches above a certain level for the perceived status or to make sure they are getting a "neutral" perspective. In different contexts, it can be the inverse. In organizations that are highly secretive or have solid boundaries, internal coaches can be preferred for senior executives as they are considered trustworthy because they are not at risk for sharing the company's secrets. (personal communication, October 14, 2013)

Nedbank, a major banking group in South Africa, offers another example of a successful program of internal coaching (see exhibit 5.1).

Exhibit 5.1
A Case of Successfully Implemented Internal Coaching

Nedbank is one of the four largest banking groups in South Africa as measured by assets. It reaches 6.1 million customers through more than eight hundred outlets across Africa and employs more than twenty-eight thousand people. It also has over sixty internal coaches. Emma van der Merwe, who leads the bank's coaching and mentoring activity, has been in charge of developing the internal coaching system from the outset. She notes, "Internal Nedbank coaches are fully qualified: They are accredited according to the International Coach Federation [ICF] criteria. The majority of our internal coaches spend between 10 and 20 percent of their time coaching, and we have three professionals who spend 100 percent of their time coaching."

Nedbank's primary drivers for using internal coaches are cost, accessibility, and the understanding that internal coaches have of the organization. Van der Merwe adds, "Applicants come mostly from HR, learning and development, and organizational development, yet we also have a few from line management." Coaches are screened in one-on-one and panel interviews and approved for the time commitment by their manager. They then go through a one-year, ICF-accredited coach training program sponsored by Nedbank. All coaches attend supervision sessions as well as a coaching forum, both quarterly, to discuss themes that emerge during the coaching and to continue their professional development.

The use of coaches at Nedbank is on a demand basis as well as integrated into leadership development programs. In addition, internal coaches are being trained to do team coaching. Today, 95 percent of all coaching at Nedbank is done by internal coaches and the remaining coaching, for the executive level and one level below, is provided by external professionals.

Source: Emma van der Merwe, personal communication to the authors, October 22, 2013.

Pitfalls of Internal Coaching

While using leaders in your organization to coach has many benefits, there are also some outcomes and aspects to be monitored.

Credibility This attribute is very much in the eye of the beholder because there are some very competent internal coaches. However, especially for those who coach part time, it is difficult to compete with external coaches when it comes to the number of coaching hours experienced, certified qualifications, and so on. The more that internal coaching is taken seriously within the organization, and as a result produces standards and criteria (who can coach, who can be coached, what credentials are required, what mentoring and supervision are available) and the more value that individual leaders and the organization see in internal coaching, the more credibility is established.

Confidentiality and Power Dynamics The higher an executive rises in the organization, the more difficult it is for him or her to receive unfiltered information about performance (Battley, 2007). An external coach will be more suited to address sensitive performance- or personality-related issues with a greater assurance of confidentiality. From a power dynamics perspective, an external coach may be in a stronger position to "name the elephant in the room" when the elephant is in fact the executive being coached. At Belgian chemicals giant Solvay, this is one of the main reasons that external coaches are preferred. Andrew Foster, senior vice president and chief learning officer, says, "We are asking our leaders to choose a coach they will be comfortable with, but we urge them also to ask themselves the question: 'Is this somebody that will be able to challenge me to see things maybe I don't want to see or raise a topic I might want to avoid?'" (personal communication, October 9, 2013).

Managing Boundaries and Ethical Dilemmas Internal coaches play multiple roles within a corporate system. They may be in charge of human resource development, serve as a business partner to several business units, or have a close personal relationship with one of the respondents in a 360-degree process for someone they coach. An internal coach might have some inside information that might have an impact on the person she is coaching and this was not the case when she started to coach him. A client might share with her that he is thinking of leaving the organization. Maybe she gets a request from a third party interested in information about one of her clients. As with the many other HR roles,

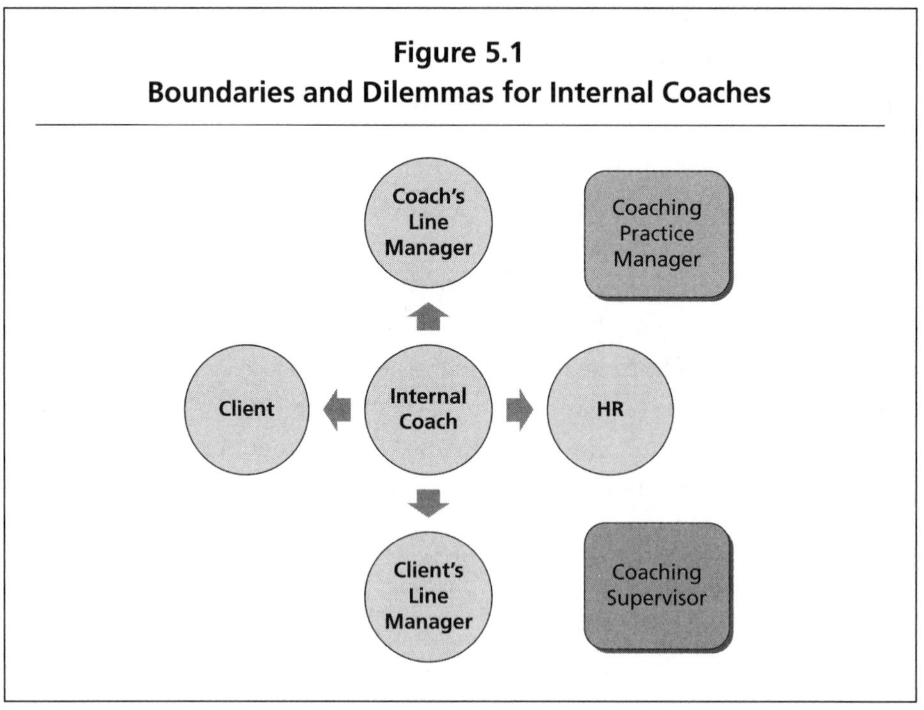

internal coaching can be full of land mines. Given the particular boundary and confidentiality issues of the coaching relationship, however, coach supervision is particularly important. Figure 5.1 illustrates these kinds of entanglements.

Low-Trust Cultures If coaching is seen as a last-ditch effort to rescue or to fix a leader, it will most likely be regarded with suspicion.

Particular Phases in the Organization's Life Cycle When companies are in the midst of difficult times (e.g., mergers and acquisitions, restructuring), coaching in general and internal coaching in particular may be perceived as someone's agenda. At Solvay, alternatives to internal coaches have been used for this reason. Andrew Foster explains: "We have a system of 'confidantes,' usually HR generalists who act as mediators between a boss and one of their direct reports. They would not describe themselves as coaches. The recent history of Solvay has been one of tremendous change in the last 5–6 years in which there has been a lot of anxiety and adapting, which is why we've used 'confidantes' rather than internal coaching at this point. Once we work through all the changes and things settle down, we may pursue the direction of internal coaching" (personal communication, October 9, 2013).

Client Fit Until companies have a sizable, diversified pool of internal coaches, they may not be able to match the ethnic, linguistic, generational, gender, or functional variety of an external pool.

Opportunities and Pitfalls Associated with Managing a Pool of External Executive Coaches

Several models of working with external executive coaches exist today, and many companies use a mix of models.

Multiple Independents In this model, external coaches are deployed on an ad hoc basis, based on local relationships and referrals. It offers the advantage of user friendliness and flexibility, yet fails to provide consistency in terms of the coaching frameworks used, how the matching process works, how coaching is evaluated, and how coaching aligns with the leadership strategy to drive the business strategy.

Boutiques A boutique coaching firm is a collection of coaches operating under one umbrella. Boutique coaching companies often offer the advantage of having a strong local or regional presence or specialty. Coaches operating under the boutique umbrella operate more consistently than a group of independents. However, boutiques lack global presence and scalability. They may claim to have network associations with other boutiques in other regions or parts of the world, but this is often a loose affiliation rather than a systemic collaboration.

Coach Registries A coach registry is a virtual network of coaches who fulfill certain requirements. The largest coach registry is published by the ICF. Anybody with a coaching need can access an ICF-accredited coach practically anywhere in the world. However, there is very little information available about the coaches other than the level of their ICF credential. The coach may be a life, leadership, or career coach. More relevant to the corporate world is CoachSource, the largest virtual network of executive coaches globally. Brian Underhill, CEO and founder of CoachSource, notes,

> Clients were asking for coaches in multiple locations across the globe. They also were not interested in paying for coach travel. This led to the

> creation of Coach Source with 900 coaches worldwide, of which 600 are in North America, 175 in Europe and the Middle East, and 125 in the Asia Pacific region. Prospective coaches fill out an application form online. If they meet the criteria, they are interviewed through Skype and if selected, brought into the pool. Our approach has the advantage of being highly scalable and cost conscious. The disadvantage for some corporations may be that the level of standardization is not nearly as high as with truly integrated networks where coaches share common frameworks and are monitored more closely. (personal communication, 2013)

Integrated Networks Integrated networks work with internal as well as external coaches and have a global presence. They have a consistent onboarding process for their coaches. Stylistically, coaches operating under these networks may be very different, yet they share the same standards and approaches—for example, using assessments, having a behavioral-change-oriented model, being systemic or more psychodynamic. Examples of integrated networks include Korn Ferry, Development Decisions International (DDI), Lee Hecht Harrison (LHH), Right Management, INSEAD, and CCL. Coaching services buyers can work with one provider or with a couple of integrated coaching networks. Global presence, consistent quality, scalability, and seamless orientation of coaches to the client's business are the most important criteria for using this approach. Says Andrew Foster at Solvay:

> Recently I had needs in Shanghai and Sao Paolo and in each instance CCL has been able to provide local coaches able to understand and deal with local issues. The disadvantage of working with independents or with multiple providers like we did in the past is that we were almost starting from scratch every time. There was a lot of unnecessary work being done upfront. One of the advantages of working with a sole provider is that you can define together a framework with clear process steps. The other advantage is that you can build a common database with results. I'm not interested in individual results but in trends and in themes that emerge and that can help me, from a developmental standpoint, to set priorities of how I might decide on what programs are needed. Last but not least, geographic reach is very important for us. (personal communication, October 9, 2013)

Working with integrated networks may not be suitable for every company. It requires a significant initial investment in resources and time to ensure that coaches are oriented to the client's business strategy and culture, as well as to the program specifics. It is also nearly impossible to track assignments and capture themes and patterns without investing in a coaching management technology platform.

SELECTION AND ONBOARDING OF EXECUTIVE COACHES

Imagine you moved to a new country and you're in need of a plumber. You could ask for referrals from neighbors, ask a colleague, or look at ads online. You might meet a few plumbers, ask them to make an offer, and then make a decision. Unless you have a truly unusual plumbing need, you would likely not bother asking any of them to show you their professional license. You probably would not check their credentials with the school they attended. Professional trades like plumbing seem to hold the promise that minimum common standards will be guaranteed.

Not so in coaching. Some observers doubt whether coaching is a real profession. Coaches are not required to have a formal university degree and there is no state-sanctioned licensing as there is for psychologists or lawyers. Coaching does not have enforceable ethical codes of conduct, and numerous accreditation schemes exist, which confuse buyers of coaching services. According to the Sherpa Executive Coaching Survey (2013), 70 percent of executive coaches cite training and certification as their background, twice the number as in the first 2005 survey. Internal coaches, according to the survey, favor university-endorsed programs. Coaches at the midlevel of earnings (in the range of $150 to $300 per hour) favor trade association endorsement, while one in six top-level coaches (earning in excess of $500 per hour) don't believe certification is necessary at all. The most interesting finding is that when asked who is most qualified to certify a training program, most HR and training professionals and most business leaders do not have an opinion.

Coach Accreditation

Coach accreditation is complicated by competition among credentialing organizations for market leadership. Two broad approaches to accreditation have emerged, each of them fragmented with side streets, alleys, and dead ends. The first avenue is academic: postgraduate training in executive coaching is now offered at prestigious business schools, for example. The second avenue has been named "professional" and requires the coach to subscribe to a code of ethics, pursue an accredited coach training program, work a certain number of coaching hours, and pass an exam. The ICF is the best-known global coaching organization and caters to all coaches, whether they are executive, life, or career coaches. Their common approach has the advantage of using a shared coaching language and having a true global presence. However, some experts wonder whether this one-size-fits-all approach might not be similar to applying the same standards to surgeons and general practitioners. What about business leadership coaching standards? Complying with the ICF standards does not guarantee that the coach has strong business acumen or understands psychological and organizational development in any depth.

The Association for Professional Executive Coaching and Supervision, based in the United Kingdom, has a specific executive coaching credential and a high-quality reputation yet lacks global reach, as does the Worldwide Association of Business Coaching. The European Mentoring and Coaching Council (EMCC) offers credentialing as well and, as its name suggests, has its focus on Europe. The Center for Credentialing and Education (CCE), a US-based organization with a long history of credentialing counselors, offers a Board Certified Coach (BCC) credential and a special designation for business leadership coaching. CCE is focused on developing its infrastructure to support coach credentialing globally. The International Society for Coaching Psychology (ISCP) takes a different approach in that it views coaching as a specialized area of psychology. ISCP requires applicants for membership to be trained as psychologists, have at least five years practicing as a coaching psychologist, and provide a letter of reference from another coaching psychologist.

Is accreditation a mere marketing tool, a check-the-box standard for procurement managers in need of criteria to select executive coaches? Or is it an authentic means by which to clarify coach competency? There are many excellent coaches who hesitate to deal with the hassle of an accreditation process. They may have thousands of coaching hours in their experience, have earned credibility and a solid reputation with many clients, and wonder what value the credential will hold for them. Some ask themselves which credentialing process will be truly developmental. And we have seen coaches with multiple credentials fail miserably when working with an approach or in a setting to which they are unaccustomed. In our experience, in less mature markets, a credential is a more effective selection criterion than it is in more mature markets. In less mature markets, a credential helps to distinguish true professionals from more opportunistic entrepreneurs who are attracted to a new profession with few barriers to entry and who may or may not have a talent for coaching.

Interestingly, in research done by Underhill, McAnally, and Koriath (2007), coach credentialing was not viewed by executives as a major factor in choosing a coach. Business experience and ability to establish rapport came in, respectively, first and second place. According to a 2010 survey of forty major buying organizations and nearly three hundred experienced coaches, the majority of them based in the United Kingdom yet operating internationally, qualification and accreditation were losing ground among buyers as indicators of the quality of coaches (Braddick, 2010).

Other Common Selection Criteria

If accreditation offers only very partial information for selecting coaches, what are the other factors buyers may take into account? The Underhill research from 2007 revealed that in interviews, leaders selected coaches on traits such as flexibility, listening skills, and ability to challenge and support. It is generally agreed that those are fundamental coach characteristics to assess in an interview. Yet research from the American Management Association/Institute for Corporate Productivity (2008) found interviews to be less important, in third place as a selection criterion, as compared to business experience and recommendation from a trusted source. Nonetheless, interviews were the strongest predictors of coaching success as reported by the organization. Interestingly, the research found that counseling backgrounds and having a doctorate had no correlation with coaching success. CCL uses the criteria presented in exhibit 5.2 and some of the questions in their initial interviews with candidate coaches.

Exhibit 5.2
CCL's Coach Selection Process

At CCL, new coaches are screened and interviewed on the following criteria:

- Business acumen and understanding of organizational dynamics
- Sensitivity to trust, ethics, and freedom from gender and culture bias

(continued)

Exhibit 5.2 (*Continued*)

- Executive presence
- Strong interpersonal skills—listening, confronting, challenging, candor, trust, warmth, compassion, humor, and rapport
- Assessment skills and instrument knowledge applicable to the client's situation
- Psychological and emotional maturity and stability
- Flexibility; ability to work effectively with a broad range of executives
- Ability to plan, conceptualize, implement, and manage a coaching relationship over time
- Demonstrated knowledge of learning theories and the dynamics of change
- Credibility and authenticity

Possible questions to ask in a coach interview include the following:

- What gives you energy in coaching? With what kind of clients do you do your best work? Your worst?
- How do you develop your practice from a business perspective? What do you focus on and what not?
- Could you describe, confidentially, a recent successful coaching engagement and what you learned from it?
- Could you describe an unsuccessful engagement and what you learned from that?
- Do you have a supervisor, and if so, in what ways do you use supervision?
- How do you deal with a dip in the relationship with your client?
- What tools or models are you drawing from in your practice? What have you learned recently that you have incorporated in your practice?

Just as in any other selection process, coach candidates can slip through the cracks. Perhaps it is because candidates exercise good impression management. Or it may be that an interviewer has a blind spot. Assessment centers are invaluable to the selection process, but they are rarely used in executive coach selection, partly due to the challenges associated with running them and partly due to concerns about the credibility of assessment centers where junior assessors evaluate senior professionals but receive poor or shallow feedback on their work.

CCL'S ASSESSMENT CENTER: NEW COACH ORIENTATION

Coaching at CCL strives to enable leaders to make a more substantial impact on their organizations. CCL's approach makes use of reflection, challenge, and support to help leaders gain new perspectives and insight. Equally important is the potential coach's commitment to action that is aligned with the organization's strategy. CCL adheres to a strict process for selecting new coaches for its network. They must progress through the following steps to meet our minimum qualification requirements:

1. Each candidate has an initial screening interview to ascertain his or her fit for CCL.
2. Approved coach candidates are invited to phase 1 of CCL's New Coach Orientation program, which is approved by ICF for sixty-nine hours of coach-specific training and by CCE toward its BCC credential.
3. As prework, each candidate completes a full assessment suite and significant readings.
4. Candidates attend the one-week, on-site orientation program consisting of in-depth training on CCL's coaching processes.
5. The candidate's coaching sessions are recorded so that CCL can evaluate performance and provide regular developmental feedback using CCL's coaching talent managers and mentor coaches.
6. After successfully passing through phase 1, candidates enter phase 2, where they observe small group facilitation activities in one or two of CCL's open enrollment leadership development programs and conduct feedback coaching sessions under the supervision of CCL mentor coaches. The mentor coaches, along with the CCL coaching talent manager, determine the candidate's readiness for inclusion in the CCL coaching network.
7. Candidates who meet all the specified expectations are invited to join CCL's network of coaches.

Each CCL coach is continually evaluated for quality, consistency of delivery, and professionalism. The coaching talent managers are responsible for quality assurance. The average coachee rating for CCL coaching feedback sessions is 4.70, on a scale of 0 to 5. Coaches who do not maintain a high value rating (at least 4.5) lose opportunities to perform CCL coaching work. The coaching talent managers and community lead coaches also host coach learning sessions, which include best practice discussions as well as opportunities for coaches to hone their coaching skills with each other. CCL coaches have access to each other for peer supervision and support, as well as access to the coaching talent managers and to large pool of coaching supervisors.

COACHING SUPERVISION

Supervision has traditionally been a key part of the professional development of doctors, lawyers, clinical psychologists, and social workers. It has become prominent in coaching only in the past decade, and it may become a coach accreditation requirement in the future judging by the attention it has recently received from international accreditation bodies such as ICF and EMCC. Moreover, as mentoring and supervision are recognized as best practices, pressure will mount to make it a standard of the profession to ensure quality and development of internal coaches. Coaching supervision is well established in the United Kingdom (and growing elsewhere in Europe), with some prominent thought leaders and practitioners such as Peter Hawkins advancing the field.

Supervision remains nascent in the United States. As of March 2014, a Google search for "US coaching supervision" yielded 475 results. In comparison, a search for "UK coaching supervision" resulted in 16,900 matches. As of the writing of this book, there is only one coach supervision credentialing program in the United States, whereas there are several to choose from in western Europe. In the United Kingdom, counselors, psychologists, and coaching professionals with business backgrounds have worked across disciplines to promote and advance the field. By contrast, in the United States, supervision seems isolated within guilds, such as for licensed psychologists. Whatever the contextual differences are, there is a risk associated with underestimating the importance of coaching supervision. How can a coach develop when he has nobody with whom to reflect about a difficult case? What does the coach bring to the session that does not match the need of the client? How can a buyer of coaching services be assured that quality will be delivered and that risks associated with coaching will be managed? Supervision provides an answer to those questions.

Coach Mentoring and Supervision in Practice

Coach mentoring and coaching supervision are overlapping practices with some distinct features. When we refer to coach mentoring in this book, the emphasis is on bringing new coaches up to speed by pairing them with a more experienced coach, not necessarily in terms of years of experience practicing coaching but with regard to certain coaching standards, interventions, or methodologies with which new coaches may be less familiar. At CCL, a mentor coach also supports the new coach as she navigates her way through CCL systems, culture, and the community of peers.

When we refer to coaching supervision, the emphasis is on ensuring that the coach works with the coachee's agenda, not the coach's agenda, that ethical dilemmas are thought through, and generally that the coach's practice is focused on what Hawkins calls "creating a shift in the room"—a shift defined as a key element of transformational coaching in which the coach helps the coachee feel the change that is needed (Hawkins & Smith, 2013). CCL uses the label *coach reviewer* to refer specifically to the standard of listening to and debriefing a recorded coaching session. A debriefing can be from a mentoring or a supervisory perspective.

The Community of Practice of Coach Reviewers

CCL is currently reaping the benefits of having worked for decades with a large, fully integrated network of six hundred coaches who share common standards, common training, and supervision practices. CCL's Europe, Middle East, and Africa regions (EMEA) have served as laboratories for supervision due to the specific nature and challenges of coaching in those environments.

In 2008, CCL EMEA had more than one hundred associate coaches spread over twenty countries and coaching in a dozen languages. While audio reviews of coaches, always with coachee permission, had been an established practice at CCL worldwide for some years, both linguistic and professional development requirements led to the creation of an EMEA community of practice of eight coach reviewers. The reviewer team has a triple mandate: assess, challenge, and support CCL coaches through one-on-one reviews to ensure the highest professional standards are met and that continuous professional development is put into practice; create coach mentoring and supervision capability (each reviewer is led by a certified supervisor); and create a reflective and educational community of practice by discussing standards and best practices that emerge from the reviews and bringing them back to the community of 150 associates through webinars, group supervision sessions, and regional meetings.

From the coach reviews and accompanying interviews we conducted at that time, a number of themes related to coach supervision emerged that we discussed at community-of-practice meetings. That discussion and reflection exercise deepened the coaches' insight into some of their beliefs and assumptions. In the next section we provide examples of those themes.

Examples of Supervision Themes

Virtual Coaching In some coaching programs, coaches and clients meet only or predominantly virtually, a growing trend among many coaching relationships. As a coach, how can you help the client create a shift in a virtual context? What communication patterns should you be aware of that are different from a face-to-face setting?

Challenging Coaching Increasingly clients are required to meet steep challenges in short time frames. When they come to a coaching session, they expect an equally challenging experience to move them forward. While it may be one role of the coach to provide a shelter from the corporate rat race, a safe place to reflect, executives expect to be moved out of their comfort zone. John Blakey and Ian Day (2012) note that traditional coaching approaches have shied away from adopting a more challenging stance because of long-held coaching principles such as being nondirective, building rapport, and holding exclusively to the individual client's agenda (not taking into account the agenda of the client's stakeholders). As reviewers, and in keeping with the CCL's coaching framework RACSR (Relationship, Assessment, Challenge, Support, and Results), which emphasizes the importance of challenge along with support, we discuss and practice what it takes to create enough tension in the room to create a shift. What is the coach's comfort with getting clients out of the comfort zone? What is the client's comfort zone? How can both attitudes be attuned? What are some challenging interventions in dialogue and nondialogue format?

Cross-Cultural Coaching Across CCL, a vast amount of coaching takes place in multicultural settings. As coaches or supervisors, what are the implications of being a member of the predominantly white, Western majority? What does creating trust and intimacy look like when the client's gender, race, religion, or sexual orientation is different from the coach's? As a coach, what assumptions do you make about your clients, their abilities, and their potential? What assumptions stop you from seeing the potential of your clients? How do you deal with your role power as a coach in cultures such as Russia, the Middle East, or sub-Saharan Africa, where power distance is different than it is in Western countries?

Internal or External Supervision?

To date, the majority of supervision happening in corporations has been led by external coaches because they have the expertise and bring a fresh perspective. However, choosing internal or external supervision is not an either-or kind of case. As Katherine Long (2012) rightly points out, there is also a case for building internal supervision capability in organizations that are serious about creating a coaching culture.

COACH CLIENT-SPECIFIC ORIENTATION AND TRAINING

Developing a plan to orient coaches and key stakeholders will depend on how your organization approaches the sourcing of coaches and how it uses coaching. Let's consider how CCL prepares its coaches, who have already been rigorously selected and onboarded into its network, to best support the coaching work CCL carries out with organizations.

We begin by describing what we have found most useful for organizations that are implementing large-scale coaching initiatives, where a globally dispersed cadre of coaches has been selected to support the work. We have identified three major areas to address in orienting and training coaches to support a coaching initiative: orientation to the organization, orientation to the coaching program, and the methodology to use for coach orientation. Several of the components in each of the three areas will apply to a range of coaching program scenarios. This is true for the composition of the coaching cadre (internal, external, sole source provider, multiple boutiques, independent contractors) as well as the size and scope of the coaching initiative (whether the initiative consists of stand-alone engagements versus a large-scale coaching program).

Orientation to the Organization

Orienting coaches to the organization sets them up to be more credible and effective with the leaders they coach: they have an understanding of the business strategy, leadership strategy, organizational culture, change initiatives, and the most salient leadership challenges at the various leader levels in the organization. Tulpa described how important this is and called this setting for coaching the "performance context" (2010, p. 46).

When thinking about what to communicate to coaches about the organization's business strategy, consider the primary drivers for it. The drivers are the intentional choices the organization makes about how to maximize success by leveraging the strengths, weaknesses, threats, and opportunities in the marketplace. The key drivers provide a focus for what leaders need to accomplish. Coaches who understand what those are will be better equipped to support the leaders with whom they work. While it would seem that internal coaches may not need this orientation, we have found that it is not uncommon for managers and leaders to have a poor grasp of the key drivers in their organization's business strategy. Paying attention to this early in the process can highlight gaps in understanding about the business strategy that may be important for the senior leadership team to address.

An organization's leadership strategy takes into account the number and types of leaders who are needed, the skills they need to possess, and the behaviors they need to demonstrate to drive the business strategy (Pasmore, 2009). To the extent your organization is clear about the leadership strategy it needs to support its business, this information is valuable to coaches, especially when it comes to focusing on the behaviors that are essential to supporting the business strategy. For instance, a manufacturing organization moving away from silos and toward more integrated operations, even potentially involving other components of the supply chain, will likely list collaboration and boundary spanning as important behaviors in the leadership strategy. This contextual information will be useful to coaches as the organization navigates this shift. As you consider the orientation requirements for external and internal coaches related to the leadership strategy, you may find that managers and leaders do not understand the leadership strategy as much as they do the business strategy. To this end, we recommend gaining some clarity about leadership strategy prior to orienting your coaching cadre.

Knowledge of the organization's culture increases the chances that the behavioral experiments the coach and leader create will lead to meaningful change and have a positive impact on the leader, her team, and the organization. When thinking about what to communicate to coaches about culture, ask what the explicit rules and values are that shape how people relate to one another in the organization. Also identify the less obvious expectations and norms that are not found in any manual and that shape the way people behave in the organization. Missing the unwritten rules and values can quickly result in someone being marginalized and ineffective. Knowledge of the leadership culture of an organization positions external coaches to be more effective. Internal coaches will need less of an orientation to the basics of the organizational culture.

If the organization is going through any kind of change initiative, be prepared to describe the nature of the change initiative, anticipated time lines, how the initiative is being received, and any challenges the organization faces in helping people make the psychological transition. We know that transition is a psychological process and often lags behind change (Bridges, 1986; Bunker & Wakefield, 2005). Coaches who are well informed can help support their coachees in the transition process.

If available, provide information to the coaches about the leadership challenges at the various leader levels in the organization. To the extent that target populations have been identified for coaching and there are some consistent themes related to the leadership challenges, coaches are better equipped to support their coachees. For instance, people who lead managers tend to be challenged by effectively integrating cross-functional perspectives in decisions or by handling complexity. People leading a business unit or the business may be challenged by balancing trade-offs between the short and the long term or by aligning the organization for strategy implementation. Coaches who are aware of themes like these are in a better position to explore how their coachees are managing these challenges, and they can take a more systemic view when working with multiple leaders in an organization.

Orientation to the Coaching Program

Whether you are using coaching in an ad hoc manner or you have a systemic coaching initiative, there are several important issues to address in orienting coaches and other key stakeholders to the coaching program. Ensuring all stakeholders are clear about the expected outcomes of the coaching program is critical to the success of the initiative. What does the organization hope to gain through the application of coaching? This question needs to be answered clearly, whether for a one-off engagement or a large-scale initiative. Stakeholder responses to this question can be diagnostic of how the organization views coaching and can speak to the organization's developmental stage with regard to readiness for coaching (Frankovelgia & Riddle, 2010).

Whether a one-off coaching engagement or a large-scale, systemic initiative, typically several key stakeholders are involved. Other than the coach and the coachee, the coachee's manager, and perhaps an HR business partner (HRBP) may be involved as part of the accountability and support team. In a large-scale initiative, there are likely to be other key stakeholders who have visibility over the broader program. These stakeholders may be internal and on teams that provide the coaching.

What does the coaching program design entail? Ensuring that stakeholders have a clear understanding of the program design helps with accountability and tracking, which can reduce confusion. For instance, if everyone knows how long the engagements are and the process steps involved, the coachees are more likely to get the support they need to achieve the agreed-on outcomes. What are the steps that have been established that provide a road map for the stakeholders? As coaching has matured as a profession and organizations are increasingly savvy about using coaching, we see increasing consistency in the process steps in coaching engagements. Orienting all stakeholders to these steps enables them to better support the coachee. An example of commonly found process steps follows:

1. A leader is identified for coaching.
2. The coachee is given a couple of coach biographical sketches.
3. There may be a "best fit" call or meeting with each coach.
4. At an introduction and orientation session, the coach and coachee discuss the structure of the engagement.
5. The coach begins an assessment process that may include stakeholder interviews and assessment instruments.
6. The coach meets with the person being coached to report on the assessments, provide insight, and start goal setting.
7. Stakeholder alignment sessions are held around goals and development plan.
8. Coaching is conducted to support the desired outcomes.
9. The coachee (and sometimes the coach) regularly check in with key stakeholders.
10. The coach and coachee create a process to evaluate the impact of the coaching.
11. The coach and coachee engage in the final stakeholder session.

Beyond design and process, consider how issues of boundary management are addressed in an orientation to the coaching program. What does *confidentiality* mean, and what are its limits? What are the expectations about how information is shared and what is shared? Who is the client: the individual coachee, the manager, the organization? Answers to these questions may vary depending on the coaching program design, the stakeholders, and the way that coaching is used in the organization. To the extent there is clarity and a shared understanding about how these issues are addressed, the coaching initiative is likely to run more smoothly, involve more trust, and be more successful in achieving the desired outcomes.

Consider tailoring a coaching program orientation to each stakeholder group involved, as they may have different needs and roles to play in supporting the desired outcomes. What do the coachees have to know about the program? What information should coaches get to best support the program? What do managers benefit from knowing in order to offer the best support to their direct reports through this developmental experience? What information do you need to make available to HR and talent managers so they can take advantage of the program for their people and can provide the requisite support for coachees in the program?

Coachees benefit from knowing why the organization is investing in them and what the organization hopes to gain by their participation in the engagement. Several questions should be addressed to set the stage for coachees to feel good about engaging in the coaching process. Is the coaching reserved for key talent, or are there other considerations in identifying who is invited to participate in the coaching initiative? Beyond an orientation to the design and process steps, what is expected of those being coached? For what are they being held accountable? What resources do they have access to when they have questions or concerns about the coaching engagement? What support can they expect from their manager or from the HRBP? How is confidentiality managed, and what does evaluation of the engagement look like for them?

When focusing on what coaches need, in addition to understanding the coaching design and process steps, there are several considerations. Coaches benefit from knowing how much flexibility they have. Coaching is powerful because it is customized to meet the needs of each individual. While an overarching design and process is valuable, it is important to maintain the flexibility required to optimize the developmental experience for each leader. If a coaching management system is being used, it helps coaches to know the reporting requirements and, if applicable, how to invoice. They also need to know what the expectations are about involvement in any coach community meetings and how to get support when necessary. If coaches are expected to play a significant role in driving the coaching process, this should be clear from the outset. It is not uncommon for coaches to be expected to drive the process by reaching out to key stakeholders to ensure the momentum is sustained and to know how to leverage stakeholders when an engagement seems to be stalling. Something as simple as making sure coaches know that it is vital to develop relationships with their coachee's administrative assistant can help tremendously to facilitate the scheduling of sessions.

The coachee's manager plays a critical role in supporting the direct report's development. Managers need to understand how specifically to provide support in the context of the coaching initiative. It is valuable for them to know the level of access they have to the coach, HR, talent managers, and other resources to ensure they are providing the support and accountability required for a successful developmental experience.

HR and talent partner representatives typically play a key support role. Expectations for their involvement should be clearly articulated in an orientation to the coaching program. What kind of support do they need to provide to the coachee, the manager, and the coach during the process? What resources are available to them when they have concerns about the engagement? For large-scale systemic coaching programs, is there a program manager available to them as a resource? What kinds of information will be available to them through the reporting that is provided? If a coaching management platform is being used, what sort of an orientation makes sense for them to be able to use the system effectively?

Coach Orientation Methodology

If you are a coaching program manager in the organization, you will likely partner closely with internal key stakeholders and key contacts at the coaching services providers you are using to support the initiative. As you think about orienting the various stakeholders to the program, here are some options to consider.

- A guide that is tailored to each stakeholder group can be a useful and user-friendly way to give each stakeholder group access to the basics of the program, including the design, process and logistics.
- Live and recorded webinars for coaches can keep them well informed about the organization and the coaching program.

- To support your HR and talent manager partners, make program-related resources available on an intranet.
- If your organization is using a third-party coaching management system, work with the provider to include an orientation to this system for all key stakeholders who need access.

COACH MATCHING

Once you have identified leaders who will participate in a coaching process, you will want to implement a plan to ensure your leaders are paired with the right coach for them. Based on our experience, we know that providers, clients, coaches, and coachees all tend to place importance on coach matching. If you are working with a coaching provider, they may be well positioned to partner with you in the matching process since they know their coaches well and you have information about your coachees that will be informative in a matching process. First, we consider coach attributes and then take a look at information that is useful to gather about the coachee.

Information about the Coach

Very little research has addressed the topic of coach matching. A 2011 survey identified five coach attributes that are important to address in the coach selection and matching process: an ability to develop critical thinking and action, an ability to develop core management skills and direction, an ability to forge the coaching partnership, the coach's personal profile, and coach experience and qualifications (Gray, Ekinci, & Goregaokar, 2011). The fact that these coach attributes were important in determining coachee commitment to coaching speaks to the importance of taking these attributes into account as part of an overall coach selection and matching process.

The coach's biography can provide some useful information, although it is not a substitute for getting to know the coaches over time and developing a good sense of how they work and with whom they seem to do their best work. A coach's biographical sketch typically contains information about the coach's education and training, professional background and experience, approach to coaching, the range of industries for which he has coached, the leader levels he has coached, and perhaps some personal information. Many coach sketches also contain a photograph of the coach. While most people want to see coach photos, it is good to keep in mind that social desirability biases may come into play, increasing the risk that coaches may be selected based on appearance rather than more relevant factors.

Even with well-planned coach matching, there are times when a coachee will not feel that the chemistry is good between her and her coach. It is a good idea to plan for such a mismatch by having a process in place that all stakeholders are aware of so that there can be a seamless transition to a new coach. This might include another "best-fit" conversation with the coachee and one or two more coaches as well as involvement by other key stakeholders with insight into the type of coach that might be a good fit.

Information about the Coachee

Since matching also relies on having information about the coachee, let's look at what you might want to gather about the coachees so you can share this with your coaches or your provider partner. This is information that will be useful to you, your providers, and the prospective coaches. As you look over the questions in exhibit 5.3, think about which might apply more or less to your situation and whether there are other questions you should consider as part of an intake process. You will notice that some of the questions are quite practical and speak to logistics issues that need to be considered, whereas others are more focused on the coachee's needs and perceptions of readiness to engage in a developmental process.

Exhibit 5.3
Coachee Information for Matching

- What is the name, title, and location of the coachee? For coach matching within a region, location may be less relevant if all coaching is virtual. If much of the work will be done face-to-face, location may be a key variable based on the geographic distribution of the coaching network you are using.
- Can you get a copy of the coachee's résumé or curriculum vitae? Whether you are directly involved in coach matching or providing this information

Exhibit 5.3 (*Continued*)

to a provider partner, the information about the coachee's career path, educational background, and experiences can be useful.

- Is this an existing leader, someone newly hired, an internal promotion, or a lateral move? If an internal promotion, how long has the coachee been with the organization and in the new position? What was the coachee's previous position?
- Will the coachee be receptive to coaching?
- Who are the key stakeholders (e.g., manager and HRBP) who will be involved in supporting the coachee in the developmental process?
- Is the coachee's current position a stretch, or does it come naturally?
- Why coaching, and why now? This speaks to the urgency and potential motivation for coaching. It may also uncover a potential consequence if the coachee does not begin to do something differently.
- What is the purpose of this coaching engagement? If you are using coaching to address a leader at risk for derailment, that is different from supporting a high-potential leader.
- What is the desired outcome?
- What are the coachee's strengths and development needs?
- What type of team does the coachee have? Can you share any special dynamics going on with the coachee's team?
- Do you know anything specific about the coachee's goals and any experience she has already had with coaching? This speaks to the attitude a coachee might have about coaching.
- What might be important to know about a coachee's personality preferences?
- Are there are any personal issues that can be shared (family, education, hobbies, and so on)? This information can provide some useful points of connection for coaches, and it provides a broader picture about the leader's life situation that can be instructive for coaches.

(*continued*)

Exhibit 5.3 (*Continued*)

- Would the coachee prefer a male or a female coach? While some leaders have no clear preference for coach gender, others do express a preference. Sometimes it makes sense to give them what they are asking for, and other times it may warrant a discussion. For instance, some male coachees who are getting feedback that they don't seem to value women may opt for a male coach; in fact, perhaps a female coach might be a better fit to help them develop.
- What kind of coach do you think would be the best fit?
- How soon should this coaching work begin? This is a practical question that may have implications for which coaches are available to support the work. What is intended length of engagement?

QUALITY MANAGEMENT

After making a considerable investment in time and resources to diligently recruit, select, train, and orient your coaches, you want to do the best you can to ensure they are having the desired impact as they coach your leaders. Beyond thinking about how best to evaluate coaching impact, several important considerations relate to how to manage quality. We will focus on three areas related to quality management that precede the end of a coaching engagement or the end of an initiative evaluation. These three areas can be broadly thought of as reporting (data collection and analysis for management of the coaching pool), common challenges and issues, and building and sustaining a community of practice.

Reporting

As coaching has evolved and organizations have become more savvy in their use of coaching services, we have found that organizations are paying more attention to the kinds of data that are useful to have in large-scale coaching initiatives. While there are still many organizations that approach coaching in an ad hoc manner and do not know how much coaching is happening in the organization, how much they are spending on coaching, or what value they are getting from using coaching, we are seeing an increase in the number of organizations that want and expect the kind of reporting that enables them to have a better understanding of the value they are getting from coaching (Frankovelgia & Riddle, 2010). At the crux of the matter is the extent to which they can be confident that coaching is being used as part of a coherent leadership strategy to drive the business strategy. Rather than focusing on internal talent management and performance systems, we will look at the kinds of reporting specific to coaching initiatives. We encourage you to think through how to use your talent and performance systems to leverage the range of reporting data you might benefit from having as part of a coaching initiative.

Spending What kinds of data are important to track? A vice president of talent and coaching practice leader at a global financial services organization recently told us that it is really important to be able to track spending. This concern likely resonates with you. Whether you do this with your internal systems, a coaching vendor's system, or a third-party coaching management system, you want to have good visibility over how much your organization is spending on coaching. It is desirable to be able to track your spending by leader level and by division or business unit.

Utilization Another level of reporting that requires some planning and sufficient human resources or information technology infrastructure is to be able to track coaching utilization or the number of active, inactive, and completed coaching engagements by leader level and division or business unit, as well as by coach. It is also beneficial to track coach selection if you are using a best-fit process where a leader chooses from two or three coaches. As you can imagine, for a large-scale coaching initiative, access to these data on a regular basis enables you to have good visibility over how your coaching initiative is progressing. This level of reporting allows you to see which parts of the organization are using coaching the most and the least, by leader level, enabling you to see how well the coaching utilization aligns with your strategy for coaching. It allows you to make more proactive and strategic decisions. For business units that seem to be nominating a lot of leaders for coaching, are they using the coaching nomination process as intended? For business units that do not seem to be nominating leaders for coaching, what support are they providing their leaders, and is there an opportunity for coaching to be used more strategically? Do the HRBPs have a good understanding of the coaching initiative and how to work with their clients to position coaching?

Tracking Progress Tracking progress within engagements can also be important. There is increasing consistency across executive coaches and coaching providers related to the process steps that occur within an engagement. Look for a tracking system that enables you to see where your leaders are in the coaching process. If too much time elapses between process steps, this may indicate a stalling engagement. Having access to these data at the level of the individual engagement and for the broader initiative provides valuable data to help manage quality.

Goals For large coaching initiatives, we believe it is important to track the goal categories your leaders are working on. It can be value-added to feed this information back into the talent or learning organization to inform other development initiatives by leader level and business unit or division. This information can also be helpful for your coaching cadre as they work with new leaders because it gives them some insight into the challenges that leaders in the organization commonly face. While this can be useful for coaches, they also need to guard against narrowing the focus too quickly by attending more to challenges they expect to find.

Stakeholder Engagement As coaching has evolved, we have learned the importance of thinking about coaching as a team sport. Coaching is more likely to be successful when the manager and HRBP are involved. The increased accountability that results from this approach leads to better traction in engagements and to an increased likelihood of goal attainment (Goldsmith & Morgan, 2004). To monitor stakeholder engagement in the process, we have found it helpful for the coach to be the driver of the process and to reach out regularly to the manager and HRBP. Your coaches can alert you to situations where a manager or HR partner is not as engaged as would be desirable. In situations where HR departments are stretched and cannot be as involved with the engagement as they perhaps might like, coaches can adjust accordingly. In addition to tracking this information from coaches, HR representatives need to be clear about what the escalation process looks like if they have concerns about a coach. When the key stakeholders work together as a team in the best interests of the leader, the results can be impressive.

Technology Over the past few years, as organizations are using coaching more systemically and have an increased need to manage coaching and coaches, we have seen an increased reliance on technology platforms. Many large providers have developed coaching management systems that provide some level of support for the various reporting needs that underpin a robust coaching initiative. Ideally, a coaching management platform would tie into your organization's financial management system to allow more sophisticated tracking of coaching expenditures, and it would have a portal for each stakeholder in the initiative. The coach needs to be able to note when she has had a session, enter some confidential session notes to which she can later refer, and, for external coaches, perhaps invoice for completed work. Coaches and coachees should be able to enter goal and development plans and, ideally, solicit feedback from stakeholders on progress. Some systems with broad capability permit managers to access direct reports' goals and development plans to provide input and support and permit HR offices to view similar information as well as higher-level views of goal trends and other utilization data.

The owners or managers of the coaching program itself need a bird's-eye view that allows them to manage the overall initiative. If you are working with a coaching vendor, it is likely managing the day-to-day work and needs full access to the system. If you are managing the overall coaching initiative, you likely need a dashboard that gives you access to the types of information you want, such as financial data, utilization data, engagement status, goal trends, and perhaps evaluation data.

Common Challenges and Issues

As you think about managing quality in a coaching initiative, be aware of some of the common challenges that arise in these initiatives and what you can do to address and mitigate them. A global financial services organization coaching practice leader has described the importance of thinking about the preengagement phase as a way to increase success:

> How many requests have we received to talk about executive coaching? Not all requests lead to executive coaching. HRBPs are better informed now about when coaching is appropriate. Is there a business need? If this hoped for change is not going to impact the business, we won't pay for it. Is this a real coaching situation—is this an IL [individual leader] issue or a system level issue that is presenting itself as an IL issue? If it is an individual development issue, how open is the individual to getting feedback and coaching? Then we ask are the organizational conditions in place to support this initiative? Is the manager willing to hold the coachee accountable, to support them? (Bill Hodgetts, personal communication, October 14, 2013)

These comments demonstrate the importance of having a clear process in place to determine if coaching is the best fit for a leader. The comments also support the organization's experience that it takes a team to effectively support a coaching engagement. Since coaching takes a team, some of the challenges that arise have to do with the interaction between the key stakeholders in the process. It is important for stakeholders to be clear about their responsibilities in the process, including any agreements about information flow and communication.

While managers are less likely to have difficulty engaging as involved stakeholders, it is not uncommon to find that HRBPs are stretched thin, with a range of responsibilities and too many internal clients to permit them to be as engaged in each initiative as would be ideal. If you anticipate this will be a challenge, consider shifting the "accountability partner" balance on the team toward the manager. Instead of being an equal partner with the manager, keep your HRBP in the loop, and encourage the rest of the team to access them at key transition points in the engagement process.

A common challenge in coaching senior leaders is getting the coaching sessions scheduled because these leaders are so busy. An engagement that is planned for nine months may stretch to fifteen months. We have found that this can be mitigated by coaches getting to know the leader's administrative assistant and ensuring the assistant understands the process and why it is important. When the coach has a good relationship with the administrative assistant, scheduling challenges are less problematic. In the event that scheduling still seems to be a challenge, be prepared with an escalation plan that is clearly communicated to all stakeholders.

BUILDING AND SUSTAINING A PEER LEARNING COMMUNITY OF PRACTICE

Earlier in this chapter, we discussed how important supervision is for coach development. Equally important is the process of coaches learning from each other. This may take the form of group or peer supervision, but it does not have to reach that level to be extremely valuable for both coaches and the organizations deploying the coaches. With a coaching cadre dedicated to supporting your leaders, you want to do all you can to help this cadre as they learn and develop together because this will increase the value delivered to your leaders.

Establishing regular in-person or virtual coach meetings enables you to increase awareness about the range of leadership and business challenges that the leaders being coached are facing. These meetings enable you to leverage the group to address common coaching challenges such as sustaining momentum, scheduling sessions, managing best-fit conversations, and leveraging stakeholders. A format we have found that works well is to meet for forty-five minutes to an hour, taking ten to fifteen minutes to provide an update about any changes in the business that are likely to have an impact on the leaders being coached. The coaches can also contribute as they are likely hearing things from coachees that are pertinent to the cadre.

For each of the sessions, you may want to select one topic for discussion and give the coaches an opportunity to share best practices. Explore whether the coach community meetings can qualify for coaching continuing education through a coach credentialing organization. To the extent you can facilitate this process, it is value-added to those coaches in your cadre who belong to that credentialing organization. For these meetings, we have found that using a virtual meeting platform can help to foster a community of practice. A coaching cadre for a large organization is likely to be geographically dispersed. While it is wonderful to get coaches together in person for community-of-practice meetings, it is not always practical or cost effective. You might also consider leveraging virtual technology for peer supervision case study sessions as described earlier in the chapter.

As you consider other options for nurturing a learning community within your coaching cadre, think about leveraging social media. Many sites allow you to create invitation-only groups and to have multiple conversation threads within a group. Leveraging social media for this purpose allows the whole cadre to benefit from the best practices and lessons of experience supporting your leaders. In addition to supporting a learning community, this approach offers some practical support for your coaching cadre and allows you to stay connected to the issues that are top of mind for your coaches.

CONCLUSION

Coaching in organizations is multifaceted, as evidenced by the range of topics covered in this handbook. As organizations pay more attention to the leadership strategy they need to support their business strategy, we anticipate a shift from a reliance on external coaching to a balanced approach that includes building internal capacity and capability.

We hope this chapter has stimulated your thinking and provided some useful guidelines for how to go about building and managing a coaching pool, including both internal and external professionals, to best support your organization's leadership strategy.

PART TWO

Coaching Guidance for HR Leaders

Many human resource professionals are learning basic coaching skills and doing more coaching than they ever anticipated. Coaching's core conversational approaches and mind-sets can be very helpful equipment for HR leaders who want to add tools for development and problem solving. The basic coaching skills are easy to learn, even if not always easy to do well, but there is a need for targeted reflection on the best ways to approach coaching as an internal professional. The authors of the chapters in part 2 provide coaching guidance from a systems resources point of view, tackling specific populations and situations that human resource leaders will face. The key theme in each of these chapters is that a coaching mind-set can create resource-rich environments in which multiple players work together to enhance the effectiveness of coaching interventions.

Foundational to our thinking about coaching are several elements that are captured in the CCL coaching models. Models ought to provide some common bases for our work within a discipline, and it is wise to avoid turning models into religions, cults, or marketing gimmicks. Here we mention two models that may be referenced in these chapters and provide useful guidance for a coach working in leadership development.

The first model describes the outcomes associated with effective leadership and provides a context for coaching leaders. In an effort to capture the smallest number of critical components associated with effective leadership, William Drath and colleagues at CCL (2008) proposed that effective leadership is evidenced by a clear organizational direction, alignment throughout the organization, and the commitment of the people. Often referred to by its acronym, DAC, this model of leadership impact helps to direct the development of leaders and leadership by describing outcomes that matter to organizations. The DAC model starts from an assumption that leadership in a group or organization is a social function, not the job solely of those who are designated leaders. Leadership, good or bad, emerges within human groups and can be instigated by people in many different roles. Creative leadership ensures that the direction charted is consistent with the mission and values of the organization and that leaders and followers are aligned in their understanding of what actions and effort are required to move in that direction and fulfill the purpose of the organization. Furthermore, creative leadership engages the intellectual, emotional, volitional, and relational sides of the people such that they commit effort, intelligence, and even passion to aiding the organization and their fellows to succeed in that purpose. In a leadership coaching setting, the DAC model provides a framework for assessing gaps and projecting objectives for an individual leader or for a leadership team.

The second model is the coaching framework and is based on a model of effective learning experiences that has guided the design of CCL programs and ensured that participants become more intentional learners. At its core is the idea that we learn best when there is a constructive tension among the elements of an experience. Specifically, CCL asserts that the best learning experiences are marked by healthy assessment, an appropriate level of challenge, and adequate support (ACS). Assessment refers to the ability of the coach to help the person being coached explore her environment, history, and internal dispositions as they affect her perceptions, judgments, and actions. Challenge points to the stretching that is the consequence of new information, new opportunities, and new problems. In coaching, we want to be certain we never protect coachees from the difficulties, including the certainty that they will be periodically confused, uncertain, and in unpleasant emotional states. The coach provides whatever is necessary to ensure that the coachee neither ignores the difficulties nor is overwhelmed by them, but works through them, marshaling whatever internal and external resources are necessary. Support can take many forms. It can be personal affirmation, goal setting, planning for action, and meeting to keep accountability in the conversation. It is support because the coachee experiences it as support, not simply because it was intended as support.

As our coaching practice has developed, we affirmed that the best coaching also creates more effective learners. Also, we have affirmed that coaches can have greater impact by attending to the relationship and the rapport evident in the conversations with those they coach. Coupled with ACS, relationship and rapport flesh out a model we refer to as RACSR (see figure P2.1). However, the unique demands of the coaching situation encouraged us to recognize that coaching will always require attention to the quality of the *relationship* between coach and the one coached and that leadership coaching, because of its place in organizational life, must always keep a focus on results: the outcome of the coaching work. The whole coaching model focuses on results achieved through effective learning in the context of a productive relationship.

We want to move coaching beyond potential overreliance on individual solutions and toward system-based approaches. This means doing individual coaching but also thinking strategically about the range of resources available when change is needed or wanted. The HR leader is uniquely positioned to activate a leader's manager, peers, team leaders, and others in addition to coaching the individual herself. Each of the chapters in part 2 includes lessons drawn from the particular circumstances of interest that can affect the coaching approach. Each chapter also concerns itself with how coaching can activate others in the organization and make use of systems and processes already available. The key is that leadership development takes place in the context of the complex set of relationships and structures of the organization. Wise internal coaches seldom rely solely on their own coaching skills or wisdom, but involve as many elements of the supporting structure as possible.

Coaching by HR or leadership and development leaders seldom takes place under ideal circumstances, so you will find in these chapters strategies and suggestions based on particular cases and the broad experience of CCL coaches worldwide. To say that we want to think systemically does not relieve us of the need for individual action and addressing the particular case.

Within the seven chapters in part 2, the first four are targeted at leadership coaching situations that nearly all human resource leaders face: leaders who are derailing, high-potential leaders, senior leaders, and the business partner for whom an HR leader is responsible. In each chapter, the focus is on the unique

Figure P2.1
CCL's RACSR Model of Coaching

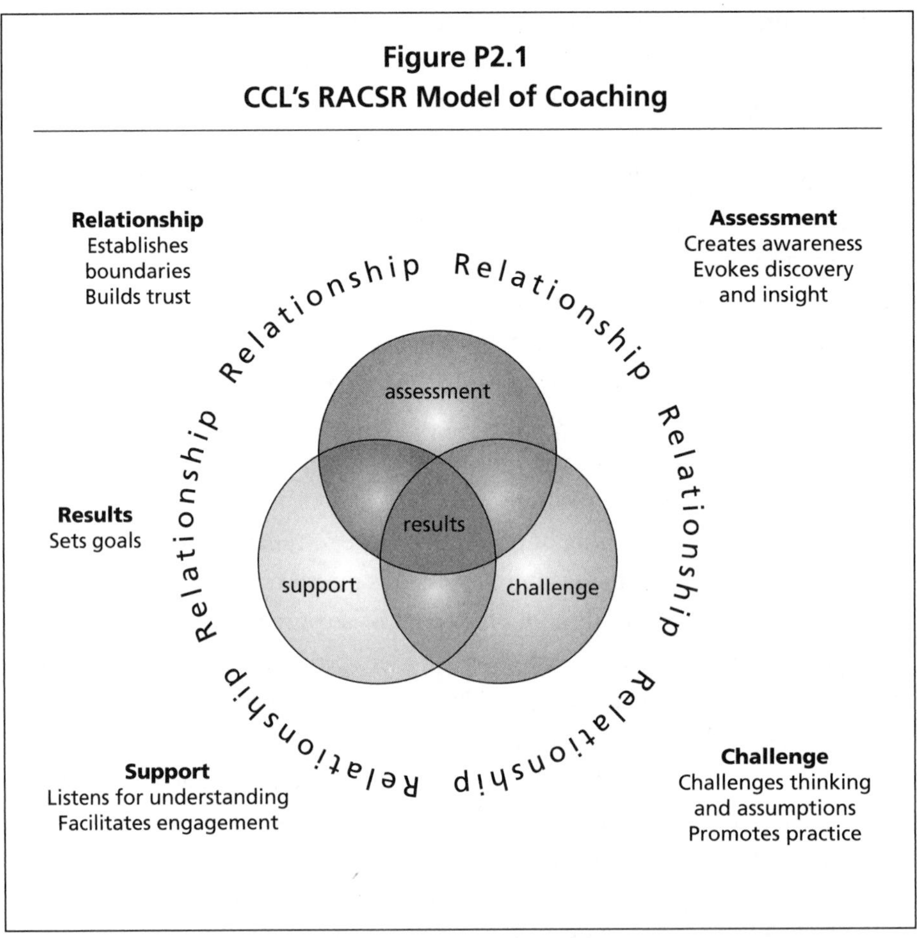

needs and opportunities for leaders in those situations, and you will find guidance for coaching individuals and help thinking through how to engage the other important resources that may be available to you.

The final three chapters address coaching considerations that occur across all leadership coaching situations. We approach complexity from two vantage points: the multicultural context of organizational life in the early twenty-first century and the depth of understanding of an individual's context needed to be an effective coach. Chapter 12, the last one in this part, addresses the ethical questions raised by our need to coach in highly complex and interpersonally risky environments.

chapter
SIX

Coaching the Derailing Leader

Erica Desrosiers and J. Ross Blankenship

Mark is a brilliant and talented design principal at an influential architecture firm in Dallas. His firm has had a hand in designing many of the marquee buildings that shape the Dallas skyline, and his personal touch is often the defining characteristic of these projects. Many clients ask for him by name. His ability to come up with beautiful and functional plans caught the eye of management from his early years at the firm, and over the past ten years he has been heavily groomed for more senior-level roles.

As the head of HR, you have heard that members of Mark's design teams often grumble when they are assigned to his projects and there are rumors of his unwillingness to listen to the input of his teammates. When the announcement was made that Mark would be promoted to serve as the head of design for the firm, there was so much backroom dissent that the CEO caught wind of the rumors and approached you to see what you knew. At the end of your conversation, the CEO tells you directly, "Fix Mark, or find a new head of design."

What do you do?

Situations like this one are all too common in organizations. Many talented individuals seem to be limited by patterns of behavior that threaten their continued success, and human resource leaders are often brought in to fix the problem. This can leave even the most experienced HR leader with limited options

We thank our friends and colleagues who provided valuable feedback on this chapter: Colleen Gentry, Mary Wayne Bush, Tom Vitro, Lee WanVeer, Rob Kaiser, Sarah Evans, Josh Rogers, Baldomero Silva, Harris Ginsberg, Denise Kasper, Jay Porter, Greg Love, Anna Marie Valerio, Tanya Bibby, Ana Teresa Concepcion, Renata Viskanta, and Bill Hodgetts.

to provide help and with tasks that may seem doomed to fail. However, these patterns of behavior, if left unchecked, can lead to an individual's derailment. Research suggests this is often the case, as the rate of ineffective or failed leaders in the workplace is estimated to be as high as 50 percent (Gentry, 2010). Take a minute to think about that statistic: roughly half of the people you know in a leadership position are either leading ineffectively or on the path to derailment.

Derailment is often treated as an individual problem because the outcomes are observed at the individual level. Although much research supports the link between individual behavior and derailment, we believe an individual's derailment cannot be considered in a vacuum. A common intervention for a derailing leader is individual feedback and coaching. We argue that coaching is most effective when it involves as much of the social context of the leader as possible. An individual is part of a broader organizational system that must be taken into account. The individual has an impact on the organization, and the organizational context has an impact on the actions and behaviors of the individual. The organization plays a role in the individual's development (or lack thereof), and individual derailment can have a profound effect on organizational performance. In fact, after surveying senior HR leaders, DeVries and Kaiser (2003) report the organizational cost of a derailed leader at the senior level ranged from $750,000 to $1.5 million. We believe derailment is often preventable, and in fact, organizations can avoid such costs with proper interventions when potential derailment situations arise. In order to accomplish this, HR leaders must be able to identify when an individual may be derailing, how best to intervene, and what to do in the future to prevent similar challenges at the individual and organizational levels.

In this chapter, we draw from the research on derailment and our experiences in organizations to offer suggestions on how to identify and potentially prevent derailment. We begin by describing what derailment is and how it has been defined in the research literature. We then discuss the causes of derailment and provide a framework for assessing derailment potential. Finally, we provide suggestions for how HR leaders can use a coaching mind-set to examine organizational practices and potentially stem derailment in their organizations.

WHAT IS DERAILMENT?

The definitions of *derailment* tend to be broad, ranging from a person with a successful managerial career who nonetheless does not achieve her potential as defined by the organization (McCall, 1998) to losing a position or a voice in organizational decisions, and even being fired (Inyang, 2013). Pioneering research on derailment at the CCL proposed the definition of *derailment* as being "involuntarily plateaued, demoted, or fired below the level of anticipated achievement, or reaching that level only to fail unexpectedly" (Lombardo, Ruderman, & McCauley, 1988, p. 199). Gentry (2010) states it rather plainly as "once-promising talented managers who started strong but ultimately did not go as far as expected" (p. 311).

Prior to derailing, these are the individuals who are viewed as successful in their careers and whose skills and abilities provide a competitive advantage for their organizations (Dries, Vantilborgh, & Pepermans, 2012). They are the those with high potential who rise rapidly through the ranks of their organizations (Derr, Jones, & Toomey, 1988), only to be suddenly knocked off their expected career track. Although there is variation among definitions, they seem to share similar concepts. For the purposes of this chapter, we consider derailment to be the involuntary career plateau or termination of a once highly regarded and successful leader.

WHY DOES DERAILMENT HAPPEN?

Most of the discourse on derailment focuses on what goes wrong with individuals, but this tells only half the story. The systemic forces at the heart of organizational culture play as much a factor in derailment as do individual characteristics and behaviors. Having a basic understanding of the individual and systemic factors contributing to derailment will allow the HR leader to be more adept at identifying derailment and recommending effective interventions.

CCL's research on derailment began in the 1980s with a study by McCall and Lombardo (1983). The authors interviewed managers from Fortune 500 companies to learn how successful executives differed from those who had derailed. They identified four common reasons underlying executive derailment: (1) strengths become weaknesses, (2) weaknesses go undeveloped or ignored, (3) success breeds arrogance, and (4) bad luck. We will take a deeper look into each of these reasons and explore the implications at both the individual and systemic levels.

Strengths Become Weaknesses

When individuals begin their careers, they must develop and demonstrate strong functional skills and technical competence. Excelling in these areas often leads to promotions and steady career progression to roles with increased levels of responsibility. However, as individuals progress to more senior levels of leadership, the importance of functional and technical skills decreases as the importance of leadership skills increases. For example, attention to detail, planning, and execution of tasks is a considerable strength in achieving results early on. However, at higher levels in the organization, overreliance on these strengths may limit a leader's ability to take a more strategic view of the business and focus on the right things. These transitions require leaders to step out of their comfort zone and learn new ways of behaving: less doing, more leading.

Individual Implications The tendency for strengths to become weaknesses can lead to derailment because leaders often play to the technical knowledge, skills, and abilities they have relied on to get to their current level. This is problematic because overusing strengths can create a limited repertoire of leadership capabilities and often goes hand-in-hand with an inadequate pursuit of development opportunities. Furthermore, in times of stress (most days as a leader), people tend to rely on what is comfortable and what comes naturally. As leaders progress to increasingly senior-level positions, they sometimes fail to notice the shift in behavior necessary for their new roles or they notice but are not sure how to adapt. This can cause leaders to apply their strengths improperly or simply overuse them to the point that they become disadvantageous (Kaiser & Overfield, 2011; Goldsmith & Reiter, 2007).

Charan, Drotter, and Noel (2011) discuss the potential derailment resulting from leaders' failure to adapt to increasingly senior roles. They describe the hierarchy of work that exists in most large organizations, which takes the form of six career passages or transitions. Each transition represents a significant change in job demands, requiring new skills, time applications, and work values leaders must master in order to be successful. Because of the natural tendency for people to fall back on the skills, attitudes, and behaviors that have helped them succeed in the past, they sometimes fail to adapt to requirements of a new way of working. As leaders advance from one level to the next, those who attempt to work in the same ways they have in the past will be more likely to derail.

Systemic Implications The challenge of learning and applying new leadership skills and behaviors on the job is compounded by the fact that highly capable individuals are often expected to figure out how to be great leaders on their own. It is also often assumed that an individual who is doing very well in one job will excel in a different job at the next level (Charan et al., 2011). Many organizations thus promote technically proficient employees but fail to adequately prepare them for the transitions, train them for the requirements of new jobs or new levels, or provide ongoing support once leaders take over new roles (Hogan, Hogan, & Kaiser, 2011). Complicating matters is the fact that organizations often place more emphasis and rewards on achieving results as opposed to developing strong leadership skills.

Charan et al. (2011) emphasize the importance of the role of the organization in helping to develop leaders as they move through each passage. They describe most of the leadership development efforts in organizations as ineffective and insufficient because they do not teach leaders what is required at each level. Leaders need to be taught what is different at the next level in terms of skills, time applications, and work values and what will be expected of them. They need to know how to do what is needed and how to adapt to changing environments. If organizations don't recognize the requirements and potential pitfalls associated with each leadership passage, they will not be able to help leaders prepare for new roles and increase the likelihood of their success.

When Joe, a strong operations leader, was promoted to president of his division, Miguel replaced him as the head of operations. Several months after the transition, Joe was getting frustrated with Miguel's performance. He believed Miguel was letting things slip and felt compelled to step in on several occasions to ensure things were running smoothly in operations. Joe sought out the assistance of a coach for Miguel, hoping it would help Miguel adapt. However, after spending time with both Miguel and Joe, the coach realized Joe was the bigger problem. In the discomfort of taking on his new job, Joe had struggled to fully leave the familiarity and mastery of his prior role. He felt he had to step in because of Miguel's failures, but it was Joe's constant meddling that drove Miguel to the point of withdrawal and disengagement. Although the coaching engagement initially concerned Miguel's performance, once the underlying dynamics of the job transition surfaced, the coach was able to work with Joe to focus on the development work he needed to fully take on the role of president.

Weaknesses Go Undeveloped or Ignored

Because leaders are often recognized and rewarded for their strengths in contributing to organizational performance, they tend to rely on what they do well to compensate for what they don't do as well. This presents a similar problem as "strengths becoming weaknesses" because focusing on strengths limits a leader's ability to broaden his capabilities and learn new skills (Kaiser & Overfield, 2011). As a result, strengths are continually developed and applied to new situations while weaknesses are unattended. The leader's manager and the organizational culture may exacerbate the problem by overlooking leadership weaknesses in the face of strong business results. We can all likely think of examples of leaders who have achieved excellent results and were promoted despite clear demonstration of undesirable leadership characteristics.

Individual Implications When an individual's weaknesses go undeveloped or ignored, it is often because they don't receive feedback and lack self-awareness regarding how their behavior is perceived by those around them. They may not seek honest and candid feedback from others, or they may not be around people who will provide them with honest feedback. This is common among senior executives because no one wants to tell the emperor he is not wearing any clothes. Often people feel too threatened or uncomfortable to provide someone with feedback on his weaknesses or challenging behaviors. This only gets worse as leaders advance higher in organizations, because there are fewer people around who are well positioned to provide candid feedback.

It may also be the case that individuals are aware of a weakness or developmental opportunity but do not know what to do with the feedback they're given. They may not know how to operate differently or fear they cannot be equally effective if they do operate differently. They're being asked to flex muscles they haven't been using because they haven't seen the need to use them, and they may have been able to compensate by other means. However, as these individuals continue to advance through their career, the circumstances will demand changes in their behavior and actions. Weaknesses that could be ignored before will be exposed, and they must be addressed before they derail the leader.

Systemic Implications We have pointed out the importance for individuals of seeking and responding to feedback from others. However, managers have a significant responsibility as well to prevent weaknesses from going unchecked by providing their employees with honest feedback and opportunities to receive honest feedback. Not only is it easy to ignore (or miss altogether) developmental opportunities when a leader is otherwise quite successful, managers may also be uncomfortable having the difficult conversations necessary to address performance issues. They may fear the employee's reaction, they may not want to deliver an unpleasant message, or they may simply not know how to have the conversation.

This problem should not be underestimated. Many employees say they don't receive valuable developmental feedback even in their performance evaluation, let alone throughout the rest of the year. It's easy here to point the finger at managers, but often the problem is larger. The organization may speak to the value of feedback, but the underlying culture may not truly promote feedback behaviors and support managers in providing candid feedback. The culture may be "too nice," that is, it's regarded as impolite or disrespectful to say anything that might be perceived as critical of the employee. Or the culture may be so competitive that people are left to fend for themselves. Organizational culture should not be an excuse for managers failing to provide feedback to their employees, but it is certainly a contributing factor that should be considered. It is also important to ensure leaders are taught how to provide feedback effectively. Sharing feedback and having coaching conversations are often skills we assume people should have as they move into people management roles, but this is not always the case. In fact, few are ever taught effective ways of giving feedback. It is the role and responsibility of the organization to ensure the culture supports a feedback-rich environment, where individuals are equipped to provide and receive feedback to improve performance.

Jane was a brilliant finance executive at a moderately sized athletic apparel and sporting goods company. The company was family owned, and most of the leaders (and employees) were men. In fact, it was a significant achievement for Jane to have broken through to the level of leadership she had achieved in the traditionally male environment, which was dominated by men with forceful personalities. However, soon after being promoted, Jane's relationships with her peers began to deteriorate. She was arousing fear and intimidating others, and no one wanted to work with her. After participating in the company's 360-degree feedback process, she received the same feedback she had been receiving for years: she's smart and effective, but her style is abrasive and her approach noncollaborative. She knew this was the perception of her, but she believed this behavior was what had helped her to rise in the organization. After receiving feedback from a coach and discussing her new role, she began to understand that if she didn't make a change, she would not be successful in her new job. She needed to partner with her peers, collaborate, and influence others in a way that hadn't been required before. Her past successes caused the organization to ignore her weaknesses, but with the required shift in her role, her style and behavior now threatened to derail her if left undeveloped.

Success Breeds Arrogance and Overconfidence

After years of continued success and missed opportunities for constructive feedback, an air of invincibility can develop around leaders' abilities and modes of operation (Gentry, 2010). This progressive self-deception can cause them to ignore their mistakes, take a disproportionate amount of the credit for successes, and generally lack the ability to learn from their experiences (Hogan et al., 2011). Though confidence can be a key driver of success, it is critical that leaders' abilities and behaviors are tuned into reality. Increased self-awareness is key. As Sir John Whitmore (1992, p. 34) aptly stated, "I am able to control only that which I am aware of. That which I am unaware of controls me. Awareness empowers me." Honest feedback, reflection, and holding up the mirror to oneself can help leaders learn about developmental areas needing attention and can also shape their understanding of their own strengths in relation to those around them.

Individual Implications As individuals rise through the ranks of an organization, they may gain increasing confidence in their style and ability to achieve results. While demonstrated confidence is an important leadership characteristic, it can cross the line to arrogance where people refuse to listen to others' perspectives and assume they have all the answers. This arrogance can result in a sort of confirmation bias in which leaders may selectively attend to feedback or data supporting their self-perceptions and conclusions, and ignore that which runs counter to their perception of their skills or abilities. This behavior is dangerous for the individual and the organization. Arrogant behaviors can create significant blind spots in leaders and can lead to their taking outsized risks. In addition, developmental feedback may be met with resistance or denial. The longer this problem is allowed to persist, the harder it becomes to mitigate.

Systemic Implications Organizational culture and reward systems may play a key role in feeding the overconfidence of leaders who have been successful. If the culture glorifies high risk taking where taking big risks leads to big rewards, this will reinforce the leader's behavior to continue taking big risks without sufficient input or perspective from others. Furthermore, if systems are designed to reward leaders only for the results they achieve rather than the process by which they achieve them, leaders may develop a sense of arrogance in their ability to achieve certain ends regardless of the means (Peterson, 2008).

Larry graduated with honors from an Ivy League college as an electrical engineer and was immediately accepted into a high-potential leadership development program for a large Fortune 100 aerospace and defense firm. After two years of rotations, he was given a leadership role at one of the businesses and from there achieved a succession of promotions to the level of director. His hard-driving "failure is not an option" style was welcomed, and he developed a reputation as an individual who could "get things done."

During the first years in his role, he was successful, though people complained that he "bulldozed others to get things done" and "never listened to any input." When confronted about these issues, he pointed to his track record saying, "Why does it matter what others think when I have done so well for the company?" When rumors started to circulate that Larry's team members were all looking for other jobs, an HR leader recommended he participate in some development work. Data from a 360-degree assessment and personality test were consistent and not a surprise to Larry, who remarked, "Yes, that's me, but what does it matter since I do the job well?" His manager, HR partner, and coach worked together to help him understand that short-term business results were not the only indicator of success in the leadership roles he aspired to. He came to see that his singular focus on results was actually holding him back from more senior roles in which strategy, collaboration, and ability to get things done through and with others were the keys to success.

Just Plain Bad Luck

McCall and Lombardo (1983) cited the final reason causing leaders to derail as bad luck, factors that are outside their control or the control of the organization. Market changes, mergers, acquisitions, and acts of God are inevitable. However, we suggest that bad luck does not derail; rather, it is an individual's response to bad luck that could threaten to derail her. We know of no leaders who have risen to their current level without facing significant challenges, even failures, early in their career. Those failures may even have been due to factors outside their control, such as the bad luck that McCall and Lombardo suggested. We would argue that "bad luck" may initiate potential derailment, but business failure alone doesn't usually cause derailment.

Individual Implications Derailment occurs when a leader is unable or unwilling to effectively adapt to failure and the changing circumstances that accompany it. Maybe the leader doesn't handle the public relations or communications effectively, or maybe she does not put a working strategy in place quickly enough to deal with the challenge. For example, most people will remember the public relations nightmare that preceded Tony Hayward's resignation as CEO of BP after he commented that he would "like his life back" during the staggering Gulf oil spill crisis. The bottom line is that factors outside of one's control happen all the time. Leaders who derail are those who don't demonstrate the ability to cope with the failure, learn from it, and move on.

Success depends on being able to adapt to changing circumstances, gaining insights, and learning from mistakes along the way. Gilt Group CEO Michelle Peluso refers to it as having grace: "If you're going to take risks and try to step out of your comfort zone, you are going to occasionally fail, make some missteps and disappoint yourself. There are going to be times where you're not going to be the mom you want to be, and sometimes you're not going to be the CEO you want to be. Grace is meeting those moments on the journey, then picking yourself back up, being humble enough to learn and not being too hard on yourself" (Bryant A., 2014, April 20, para. 12). Feedback, coaching, and other types of development work can help leaders become more agile, learn faster, and rely less on old solutions. The more the HR leader can facilitate and encourage these adaptive and forward-looking behaviors in leaders, the better able the leaders will be to avoid derailment in a volatile, uncertain, complex, and ambiguous world.

Systemic Implications Derailment also occurs when organizations fail to make allowances for leaders to learn from their mistakes. Is failure viewed as a learning opportunity or an opportunity for dismissal? How is failure dealt with in your organization? Jack Welch has often discussed the significant failure he experienced early in his career as a young chemical engineer when he blew the roof off a factory and thought he would be fired. Instead, he was asked to think about what he learned from the incident. He described this event as shaping his future approach to leading people and viewing mistakes as opportunities for learning and growth.

When changing circumstances, failures, or bad luck create challenges, agile organizations will maintain some tolerance for the mistakes of their leaders, thereby creating opportunities to learn and develop. Less agile organizations will dismiss leaders who make mistakes and generate fear in those who are still around. Another example is from Linda Wolf, former chairman and CEO of global advertising agency Leo Burnett Worldwide. Midway through her career, she volunteered to lead the group charged with new business development, a bold move at the time, especially for a woman working in an extremely male-dominated field. Her first year in that role, she lost eight of the nine pitches her group made to potential new clients—a terrible result. However, she persevered and invested a significant amount of time and effort to better understand what went wrong, and the agency management remained supportive of her. The following year, she and her team won almost every pitch they made, a phenomenal success. Her story demonstrates not only the value of her resilience as a leader, but also the importance of management support, tolerance of failure, and viewing failure as an opportunity to learn.

HOW CAN YOU HELP?

Because HR professionals have an internal company perspective, they are uniquely positioned to understand derailment issues and potential contributors to derailment in their organization and how best to intervene. HR professionals can and should take an active role in partnering with the business leaders to develop managers and leaders in an effective, timely, and practical way. However, serving in this role requires HR professionals to view themselves as strategic partners in the business, as opposed to the outdated personnel department or the managers of forms and people processes. It also requires business leaders to embrace their roles as developers of talent and not just drivers of financial results. Too often HR is approached by a senior leader who asks to have an executive coach assigned to someone on her team. While the leader may ask the HR professional if it's a good idea, more often than not it seems the manager has already decided on coaching as the solution and is simply approaching HR to take care of the details of finding a coach, handling the paperwork, signing a contract, and scheduling the engagement. While the leader may have the best intentions—trying to help develop the potential coachee—she is outsourcing that development as opposed to taking it on as a part of her responsibility as a leader.

We believe HR professionals can provide far more value to their organizations by collaborating with their business partners to help provide the development and support needed to keep high-potential leaders on track. This includes expertise in the assessment of development needs, identification of gaps, and understanding of the root causes or personality styles underlying certain behaviors and how best to address them. Collaborating in this way requires becoming an informed consultant who is equipped to educate others about derailment, offer a variety of solutions, recommend best practices, and provide guidance on how to turn a developing problem into a developmental opportunity. For the remainder of this chapter, we discuss how HR leaders can help to develop and support those who may be in the process of derailing (and their managers) and how to partner effectively with the business to work toward preventing derailment in their organizations.

At the Individual Level

There are a number of things the HR leader can do individually, and for individuals, to mitigate occurrences of derailment in organizations. Interventions can range from simply increasing their awareness of interpersonal and group behavior in the workplace, to initiating and managing an executive coaching engagement. The key to becoming the most effective HR practitioner you can be is in viewing yourself as an instrument in mitigating derailment. You can influence and support others, and you can guide leaders in seeking the tools and development resources necessary to stay on track. The sections that follow describe a number of the approaches you can take to help prevent individual leaders from derailing.

Cultivate Your Awareness HR professionals can add tremendous value to their organizations if they recognize problematic behaviors in leaders, help them gain self-awareness, and provide developmental opportunities before those behaviors send them off-track. Though it sounds obvious, recognizing problematic behavior starts with knowing your employees personally. Having some familiarity with their strengths, development needs, and performance track record is a critical first step in being able to recognize when things may be going wrong. Sometimes the key to a successful intervention is simply being aware of what's happening with individual leaders, taking note of struggles they may be having or challenges they may be experiencing in working for (or with) certain people. Other times problematic behaviors may surface as questions about a leader's potential or suitability to be promoted. Conversations of this nature are common in organizations and may provide the subtle warning signs an alert HR professional can use to gather more data about potential problems.

Being mindful of what people say about others through informal channels or other networks and tuning in to what's going on in the work environment can provide a great deal of insight. For example, if a leader has an open position on his team and people who seem to be a perfect fit actively avoid the role, there's probably an underlying cause that should be explored. Employees talk about what it's like to work for certain managers, and reputations develop quickly about which ones to work for and which ones to avoid. Gaining a better understanding of why people want to avoid certain leaders is the first step in identifying and ultimately helping those individuals correct a behavior pattern or style that may be putting them at risk for derailment. With this information, exceptional HR professionals can truly demonstrate their value because they are able to sit at the table, hear what's happening in the business, and follow up with leaders and say, "You know, we keep talking about how Jack is struggling. What do you think is going on there? Have you talked to him about it or shared any feedback? What could we be doing to support him more effectively?" Many HR professionals engage only when it's time to talk about performance reviews or other HR processes or they simply react to requests from the business. Proactively engaging in what's happening in the business can help call attention to, and potentially get out in front of, leadership issues before they become problematic.

Follow Up on Red Flags Most HR leaders typically have access to a large amount of data, both formal and informal; they may see year-over-year performance data, 360-degree feedback data, and results from personality assessments or assessment centers, and they may hear the discussions in which performance and potential are reviewed and calibrated. Too often, nothing is done to address potential risk factors until there's a significant behavioral problem and failure to be promoted or termination become the likely outcomes. In order to take action, it's helpful to understand what signs may be indicative of potential derailment. Research at CCL identifies five behavioral themes into which most derailments fall: (1) problems with interpersonal relationships, (2) difficulty leading a team, (3) difficulty changing or adapting, (4) failure to meet business objectives, and (5) too narrow a functional orientation (Gentry & Chappelow, 2009). Table 6.1 provides questions that can be used as a mental checklist in considering whether a leader may be actively derailing or may have the potential to derail.

Act on Your Insights Let's return to Mark, the star architect profiled at the start of the chapter. The HR professional was well aware of grumbling taking place among employees assigned to work on Mark's teams and the rumors of his tendency to be difficult and bull-headed. However, instead of acting on this information and addressing the issue with Mark, his manager, or the CEO, the HR professional allowed the situation to devolve to the point where the CEO

Table 6.1
Questions to Assess Derailment Potential

Factor	Behavior	Considerations
Problems with interpersonal relationships	Insensitive, manipulative, critical, aloof, cold	Does he or she have an authoritarian leadership style? Is he or she volatile or emotionally unpredictable? Does he or she respond to stress by becoming combative?
Difficulty leading a team	Staffing ineffectively, poor leadership skills	Does he or she struggle to motivate team members? Is he or she able to resolve conflict among team members? Does he or she help team members understand how their individual work contributes to the whole?
Difficulty changing or adapting	Responds aggressively to needed feedback, lack of self-awareness	Has he or she adapted to the organizational culture or seem out of place? Does he or she resist learning from his or her mistakes? Is he or she able to use feedback to adjust his or her behavior?
Failure to meet business objectives	No follow-through, overly ambitious	Does he or she prioritize work objectives appropriately? Is he or she overwhelmed by complex tasks? Does he or she struggle to meet the expectations of his or her position?
Too narrow a functional orientation	Overly specialized skill set	Could he or she handle more responsibility? Would he or she be able to manage a different department? Does he or she know how other departments function in the organization?

Source: Adapted from Leslie and Braddy (2013).

approached the HR professional with the ultimatum. Earlier intervention from HR would have likely been more effective, preserved Mark's potential, and left fewer people feeling miserable along the way. Perhaps feedback from Mark's manager could have helped him modify his style, and if working with HR and his manager wasn't helping Mark to make the necessary changes, a coach could have been brought in to assist before the situation reached such a dire point.

Many of us who feel we are progressive consumers of coaching like to say we leverage executive coaching for proactive leadership development and not to fix performance problems. However, a leader who is just starting to derail is often someone who has been highly thought of and has been performing at superior levels. Providing coaching for a derailing leader is not about correcting someone's enduring poor overall performance but rather course-correcting someone who needs an adjustment. If you can catch warning signs early and provide support to a leader before she is off the tracks, it may not require a long-term, costly engagement. When leaders start to fall, you want to catch them before they hit the ground. The HR professional can help them stand back up when they're just starting to trip before they fall and take others down in the process.

Identify Desired Outcomes A mistake that is often made with leaders who have the potential to derail is throwing coaching at them as a cure-all. Once you have identified the behavior that may be problematic to a leader's career, you have to identify what needs to change in order to get the individual back on track. The first step in this process is to consider the ways in which problematic behavior may be affecting others and the individual's ability to achieve results. Consider the viewpoints of the various stakeholders surrounding that leader, and determine how the leader's behavior may be affecting each group (e.g., direct reports, peers, superiors, customers). Sometimes the easiest way to determine the group that is being affected is to look at who brought the problem to your attention. Who have you heard discussing this leader's issues? What effect is her behavior having on others? What type of change is needed to correct these issues? This type of perspective taking will help you determine what kind of intervention will be most effective given the resources available.

Find Out What Feedback Has Been Given (If Any) Although it can be a difficult conversation, asking the leader's manager what has already been done to address the concern will allow you to gather valuable information on the context of the problem. Has the manager given this individual feedback about her behavior? If so, what was the result? If not, why? Taking the time to have this conversation with the manager may alert you to a problem that is bigger than the individual in question. Perhaps the boss is not providing enough support or guidance to allow the individual to succeed. Having a forthright conversation with the manager will allow you to build an image of what this person's work environment looks like and what factors may be playing a role in his derailment that are outside his immediate control.

We recognize the difficult reality of what we're suggesting here. Having conversations with a derailing leader's manager and digging into the situation to see what the manager has or hasn't been doing to help can be very tough and awkward. We don't know a single HR professional who has not had to have this conversation with an internal leader at a level above her own. If you're a director, it can be challenging to tell a senior vice president she is are not doing enough to help her direct report or, worse, that she is getting in their way. However, to achieve the best end result, the message has to be communicated, and it requires the HR professional to be courageous and model the ability to have a difficult conversation when it is necessary.

We don't recommend taking a career-limiting stance and telling someone she is not doing her job. We do recommend building trusting relationships with managers by being willing to have honest conversations about the importance of giving feedback to their employees. This is also a great opportunity for the manager to model the behavior of sharing feedback and guidance in an effective way, an important step in creating a feedback and development culture. The manager is often the best one to share feedback in a way a coach would not be able to do and may need to be reminded of that fact. Just because a leader is senior in the organization doesn't mean she is comfortable having these conversations. The HR professional can help the senior leader by coaching her on the best way to have the feedback conversation.

Determine If Assessments Will Provide Needed Insight In addition to tracking formal and informal feedback discussions and performance measures, assessments can be an important tool in identifying potential risk behaviors. The use of 360-degree feedback and personality measures can be particularly valuable in highlighting tendencies that may already be problematic or may become problematic in the future. While 360-degree feedback is a common method for assessing an individual's behavior by collecting ratings and comments from that individual's boss, peers, and direct reports (Hooijberg & Lane, 2009; Nowack, 2009), personality measures can be used to help identify a leader's natural behavioral style and tendencies and where she might be less comfortable or effective (Hogan & Hogan, 2001). The combination of 360-degree feedback and personality assessments is a beautiful complement of tools. Together, they can capture a leader's natural style or tendency to behave in certain ways, and provide insight into how others are affected by those behaviors. That said, it is critical when administering assessments that a trained feedback facilitator or coach be provided to help those going through the assessment process make sense of their results. Research indicates that the absence of proper support for interpreting results and development planning can not only diminish the potential positive effects of assessment but actually lead to decreased motivation and performance (Nowack & Mashihi, 2012).

Personality Assessments Research indicates the behaviors associated with bad leaders are rather consistent over time, across cultures, and across organizations (J. Hogan et al., 2011; Van Velsor & Leslie, 1995). A key driver of bad leadership, and one that often results in derailment, is an inability to get along with coworkers (i.e., interpersonal relationships). The use of personality assessments, particularly those that highlight "dark side" characteristics (R. Hogan & Hogan, 2001; Kaiser, LeBreton, & Hogan, 2013), can provide rich data on behavioral tendencies that may indicate future derailment potential. If personality assessments are not used routinely in the organization or as part of standard practice, incorporating assessments can add tremendous value for leaders when a trained feedback provider or coach reviews their results with them and facilitates insights from the data. The self-awareness resulting from personality assessments can create "aha" moments for leaders when they see on paper why they tend to act in certain ways and how that might be holding them back.

360-Degree Feedback As potential derailment behaviors become more severe, the interventions typically required to bring about change become more intensive. Sometimes the best way to facilitate development is by presenting the leader with data that provide insight into how others perceive her. Bosses and peers have been shown to be accurate predictors of performance, and direct reports can be a good source of insight into the strengths or deficiencies in leadership style and opportunities for development (Eichinger & Lombardo, 2004). This type of feedback can help leaders gain self-awareness of strengths and weaknesses and how their perception of themselves may differ from how others perceive them (Atwater, Waldman, & Brett, 2002). Using 360-degree feedback successfully requires that the target individual have the opportunity to debrief and discuss the results with someone who is capable of providing certified feedback facilitation. Research has shown that combining 360-degree feedback with a coaching program can be an effective combination for bringing about positive change (Nowack & Mashihi, 2012; Luthans & Peterson, 2003).

John was a successful lawyer who had built up a practice of his own. While his employees appreciated his technical knowledge, they felt understaffed and under pressure. John's inability to delegate and trust others created a rift in the management. Facing the departure of two of the firm's partners (and their books of business), John decided to sell his firm to a larger and more established practice. After the acquisition, senior partners immediately began to get complaints about John's being too high-strung and putting too much pressure on his direct reports (e.g., often sending e-mails throughout the night, asking for replies "ASAP"). The managing partner of the acquiring firm hired a coach to give John one final chance to change his behavior. When the coach conducted a 360-degree feedback assessment, the gap between John's self-ratings and ratings from others was dramatic. Written comments included observations such as, "a belittling approach" and "communication skills need dramatic improvement." John became visibly affected when reviewing the results with the coach and said that he felt "shocked and disappointed" in himself and that "this is the exact opposite of the way in which I want to be regarded." By working with the coach to take action on the feedback, John made dramatic improvements in his behavior and relationships with others and was by all accounts "a changed man" afterward.

Sometimes self-awareness and a little direction are all that are needed to bring about positive change. While this will certainly not always be the case, it is important to remember that leaders do not set out to develop bad habits or a destructive reputation, and when they are given needed feedback, many will be motivated to make changes. If further developmental support is required, the 360-degree feedback process may create an opportunity for the individual to partner with her manager or work with a mentor (see chapter 14) to continue the learning and development process. The assessment may also indicate that only a brief engagement is required for some, while more complex or multifaceted issues may require lengthier and more in-depth interventions.

Sandra, the head of a marketing group, set meetings with her subordinates by sending an invitation in Outlook with no content and the subject line that simply read, "Discussion." Unbeknown to her, these invitations created anxiety and fear in her team members because no one knew what to expect from the meetings even after having been to "discussions" that offered solely positive feedback. After being made aware of this effect by a peer who had overheard some gossip about the habit, Sandra was horrified at having created so much unfounded angst and apologized to her team for the confusion. Admittedly, she was relieved to learn about the issue because she had wondered why her direct reports seemed so timid when coming to meet with her.

Sometimes the solution is as simple as gaining clarity on how others perceive one's words or actions. After all, people do not aspire to be bad leaders. Many leaders who begin derailing are not trying to alienate others; they're simply not paying attention to the way they're doing things. Simply shedding some light on the process by which a leader operates can often have a dramatic effect in its own right.

Peer Coaching The HR professional may recommend peer coaching to individuals who are exhibiting the potential to derail as a low-cost, low-commitment way to start a conversation about how things are going. Peer coaching is "a type of helping relationship in which two people of equal status actively participate in helping each other on specific tasks or problems with a mutual desire to be helpful" (Parker, Hall, & Kram, 2008, p. 499). This practice can be an effective intervention for derailing leaders because a relationship between two people who have similar skills and training can help to remove any evaluative or corrective component of the conversations (Ladyshewsky, 2002). Furthermore, the peer coaching relationship allows the leaders involved to reflect on their own strengths and development needs together (Bennett & Bush, 2014). This can build self-awareness in the individuals and foster organizational awareness of developmental needs that multiple leaders can share. The use of peer coaching in the organization can have a more far-reaching impact in the organization as well: more leaders can be helped and supported, and leadership networks and collaborative relationships can be strengthened. This can be a key first step in developing an organizational culture that thrives on open feedback and mutual support.

Executive Coaching Executive coaching, while more costly than many other interventions and approaches, can be valuable when other attempts have not sufficiently helped or when a leader's issues are particularly deep-seated or complex and would benefit from the robustness of a coaching engagement. Coaching may also be the best solution when a leader's development has some time sensitivity to it and acceleration is required, such as preparing for or dealing with a significant transition or role change. HR professionals can and should consider the situation and context, the leader's issues, and what has been done so far to help the organization take the most appropriate course of action. Often executive coaching can be a highly effective approach for addressing derailment because the coach and client can focus on the issues salient to that leader's situation and help to drive sustainable behavior change.

The HR professional is generally tasked with managing the process, which typically involves finding an appropriate coach, handling the paperwork and contract, and facilitating introductions. However, the HR professional can add even more value in ensuring the effectiveness of the coaching engagement by continuing to stay involved in the engagement and making sure key stakeholders are involved and helping to provide appropriate levels of support for the individual's development. For example, the individual's manager needs to be actively involved in the engagement in many cases but often disengages and trusts the coach to do the work. The HR professional can ensure that the manager stays appropriately engaged and supports the ongoing work, providing input, guidance, and any necessary resources or opportunities along the way. At the time of this writing, CCL is currently engaged in validation studies of a coaching evaluation assessment (CEA), a customizable 360-degree instrument that can track goal progress, changes in critical behaviors, and individual, team, and organizational impact as rated by a leader's stakeholders—the superiors, peers, and direct reports. The CEA provides aggregate data that will allow HR professionals to track coaching engagements and assess the efficacy of the coaching engagement in bringing about meaningful change.

Follow-Up on Development Work

HR professionals are often involved in routine development processes such as 360-degree feedback, and they often have access to the results. However, too often HR professionals see their role as process administrators; they check the box once the assessment process is complete and participants have received their results. This approach fails to take into account that the real work of behavior change occurs after self-awareness has been translated into development goals. Just as it is necessary to provide leaders with guidance as they review and make sense of their assessment results, it is equally necessary that support be built into the development process by involving managers and other stakeholders and scheduling subsequent developmental activities (Nowack, 2009). Furthermore, HR professionals can enhance the effectiveness of this process by checking in with leaders and managers to see if there has been measurable improvement and to make adjustments for ongoing support as needed.

At the Systemic Level Being mindful of the systemic factors in derailment can help determine if the cause of potential derailment behavior is more heavily influenced by situational (e.g., organizational culture) or dispositional (e.g., personality) issues. Researchers have noted the influence of factors such as work-life balance (Gentry, 2010), work overload and stress (Nelson & Hogan, 2009), and whether upper management maintains open lines of communication (Gentry & Shanock, 2008). Systemic solutions can involve pairing appropriate training and development with career advancement and viewing leadership development as a continuous process (Carson et al., 2012; Charan et al., 2011; McCartney & Campbell, 2006), implementing an intensive and honest feedback system within the organizational structure (Inyang, 2013), encouraging upper management to engage with leaders and openly share the organization's mission and values (Gentry & Shanock, 2008), and using good selection techniques to ensure proper job, team, and culture fit with the leader (Charan et al., 2011); McCartney & Campbell, 2006).

We've discussed at length the role of HR in positioning itself better to identify and help prevent the derailment of individuals, but the role of the derailing leader's manager is equally (if not more) critical. Managers often like to hand off people problems to HR, but HR should hold the managers responsible regarding their role in developing their talent, addressing performance, and having difficult conversations. These conversations with managers are not easy, but when conducted with candor, diplomacy, and respect, they can solidify the relationship with the HR professional as a trusted partner.

Selection A key question that can be asked about any struggling leader is, "Is this person in the right seat? The right team? The right organization?" The derailing leader does not necessarily have to be brought back onto the same track but could perhaps be reassigned to a job that is a better match to her knowledge, skills, and abilities. Individuals who are on the track to derailment in one job may be able to excel in a different job (perhaps at a different level) that is better suited to them. Lack of person-job fit can be as damaging to career potential as dysfunctional behavior. On a larger scale, the HR professional may want to consider whether the individual is a fit for the organizational culture. By partnering with managers to employ sound selection methods and by helping to understand what is truly required at different levels, HR can help to decrease incidences of derailment overall.

Managing Transitions Most derailments occur during job transitions, often when leaders are advancing to higher levels in the organization (Gentry & Chappelow, 2009). Managing job transitions is a key area where HR leaders can minimize occurrences of derailment. Well-managed transitions generally consist of two phases where the leader is prepared to make the transition and then integrated into the new position. Many organizations make the mistake of assuming that high-performing individuals will be able to manage such transitions on their own. Providing support for leaders in transition so they are clear about the role they are taking on and assisting them in building relationships with their new boss (and team members) can be a critical way to decrease the likelihood of future derailment. It is equally important to discuss leadership skills essential to success, as they are likely to be different from previous situations the leader has encountered. There are foundational differences in the skills, time applications, and work values required at different levels of leadership, but most organizations fail to recognize those differences and prepare leaders appropriately (Charan et al., 2011).

Monesh was promoted to a role in a different division of his organization to manage a large acquisition that the company had just made, the scope of which was larger than anything he had ever dealt with. It was clear within the first few months that he was struggling. The leadership that he had so clearly demonstrated in his former role was not showing up, and his new leaders were getting frustrated. He too was frustrated, and in a meeting with his HR representative, he openly voiced his concern: "I know what needs to be done. I just don't seem to know what's going on, or how to get things done around here!"

The HR representative suggested sitting down with his manager to discuss the situation and to see what recommendations she would have. In that meeting, it became clear that Monesh's manager had not been able to spend much time with him, despite the importance of his role. The HR professional also realized that

Monesh seemed not to appreciate the importance of getting to know his peers and other functional leaders in this part of the company. The culture of the acquired company he was leading was very different from the parent company's culture, and it seemed that Monesh did not quite see the difference. Once the manager, HR professionals, and Monesh had identified these and other gaps, they created a stakeholder engagement plan and engaged an executive coach for him. In addition, they connected him with a senior leader as a mentor to help him understand and integrate better into the culture.

Partnering with the coach helped Monesh reflect on his own learning and behavior and seek feedback and support for his integration. After several months, Monesh and his manager were pleased that the team was running better and that Monesh was becoming known for his talents as part of the larger leadership team. Monesh himself was more productive and happy and able to fulfill the promise of his being chosen for that role.

CONCLUSION

When it comes to derailment in organizations, HR professionals have powerful tools for reducing and even eliminating its impact. Due to the nature of their roles, they have access to data and information, and they are often called on as a first line of defense to help address leadership issues and challenges. In many instances, the HR professional serves as the coach, whether coaching the derailing leader or the boss. This is an important responsibility for HR professionals, and doing this well makes them infinitely more valuable to the organization. Spotting trouble before others, shining the light on potential leadership challenges, and helping managers deal with those challenges are the behaviors of truly great HR professionals. Holding managers accountable for the right behaviors and speaking truth to power are crucial behaviors for effective HR professionals as well. Underlying all of this is the ability to build trust with the business leaders and partners. Without this foundation of trust, any efforts will be less effective.

HR professionals should rely on their own skills and abilities as a coach, but also know what other systems to activate when the time is right. Furthermore, it is critical to understand that HR is part of the system itself. If HR leaders do not leverage the potential of their role to mitigate the occurrence of derailment, then they are contributing to derailment themselves. Gaining a better understanding of what derailment is and why it occurs will allow HR leaders to play a crucial role in mitigating the effects of derailment and preventing incidences from occurring in the future. By becoming more aware of the effect we can have on the individual and organizational factors contributing to the derailment of leaders, we can work not only to add value to our organizations, but to help salvage people's careers in the process.

chapter
SEVEN

Developing High-Potential Leaders

Kevin O'Gorman

The Introduction to this book argued that most coaching does not take place in formal coaching settings but is a mind-set where leaders, in formal and informal moments, develop thinking, perceiving, and reflecting skills that help them solve problems for themselves and those around them. Sometimes this mind-set is shared broadly enough within an organization to create a culture of coaching. Done well, coaching conversations stimulate people and groups to greater awareness, deeper and broader ways of thinking, and wiser decisions and actions. Nowhere are these outcomes more desirable than in the development of high potentials (HiPo), exceptional leaders who can rapidly broaden, deepen, refine, and advance their understanding, impact, and leadership for an organization's long-term, sustainable success.

HR professionals play a pivotal role in HiPo development. Coaching high-potential talent means asking deeper questions, learning from larger challenges, anticipating higher risk, and offering stronger support. This isn't all that coaches of high-potential leaders need to think about, however. Savvy HR professionals think about the total ecosystem of sustainable development, from the direct coaching of their HiPos to how they might indirectly influence them through the systems and stakeholders who also support their development. This chapter explores these direct and indirect roles, from those focusing on the individual in the near term to those looking at the long-term development of a collective leadership culture that sustains the entire organization.

For all of these goals, HR is ideally situated to provide both direct and indirect resources. HR professionals may coach HiPos, their executive mentors, and other succession stakeholders directly in order to create a skilled and passionate community for leadership development. At the same time, HR's major value may be its indirect support of development resources such as talent systems, succession planning, talent selection, and onboarding practices.

Keeping both direct and indirect approaches in mind, an organization can realize HiPo talent sustainability using coaching, ensuring stakeholder involvement, and managing systems vital to their development. Sustaining high-potential talent requires an organization to attract, develop, and retain leaders with the potential, capacity, and drive to take full accountability for the ongoing success of the enterprise.

NATURE AND SCOPE: COACHING FOR NOW; COACHING FOR THE FUTURE

Too often a HiPo's value is defined in terms of mastering successive positions of responsibility in alignment with the near-term corporate purpose and strategy—that is, how quickly and successfully the HiPo rises in the organization and how well the organization performs as a result. This happens because this is a relatively concrete and measurable value, and in organizational life (and life in general) we prefer tangible results. This focus on results causes us to select, develop, and retain HiPos based on our notions of near- and long-term future needs. We then invest competencies designed to create success within these scenarios.

In a way, this makes perfect sense: HiPos are the organization's way of investing in the future when it doesn't necessarily know what that future might hold. Yet it may miss the mark. As Sydney Finklestein puts it, "The single biggest problem—the fatal flaw in choosing presidents, school board leaders, or football coaches—is that we believe we can predict the future rather than looking for a leader who can quickly adapt to whatever the unpredictable future holds" (2013, para. 4).

What CCL has learned about managing the unknown is that discontinuous, unanticipated change is the kind of existential threat (and opportunity) that emerging leaders have to master together. This capacity for what we call collective generative agility requires more than just the ability to rapidly acquire and assimilate new knowledge. It demands that HiPos question and reconfigure inadequate facts into new meanings, visions, and directions, and they must do this both rapidly and collectively. The question is, How does one coach for this?

COACHING FOR HIGH-POTENTIAL LEADERSHIP

If the focus of coaching high potentials lies with developing a collective response to the unknown, then the enterprise as a whole needs to develop a culture around coaching and systems that broaden and deepen not only HiPos' learning experience but also that of their executive stakeholders and mentors. This establishes the link between mastering collective leadership against the unknown and the development of organizational sustainability.

Unfortunately, no matter how comprehensive the implementation of a succession plan is or how involved the organization is in the commitment to a long-term, strategic plan, the mind-set of many leaders emphasizes short-term goals and what is known. Sustainability in the face of the unknown is set aside for future leaders to figure out. In order to get the most value from high-potential development, HR needs to engage not just HiPos but also executives and other succession stakeholders so they understand the need to balance meeting short-term, known goals with preparing for the unknown.

In the long term, however, it becomes paramount for HiPos to participate in a community of leadership, embodying the change needed in order to anticipate and adapt to the unknown. Leaders in this situation are not responsible for giving followers a sense of purpose, identity, or strategy; rather, they share in the organization's ambiguity and emergent discovery.

One way of looking at these challenges and their differences is through a two-by-two matrix using CCL's assessment, challenge, and support model (ACS), which plays a central role in CCL's RACSR (relationship, assessment, challenge, support, results) coaching model. Figure 7.1 uses the ACS model to characterize the different responses and actions HR can apply to coaching and developing HiPos and their stakeholders.

Where the focus is on individual response in the known present, represented in the lower left of figure 7.1, HR needs to assess, challenge, and support HiPos so they are successful in current circumstances. HR might ask, What remedial and stretch areas will make this person excel? What will make her visible to the right people? What competencies should she focus on in order to support

Figure 7.1
CCL's Assessment, Challenge, and Support Framework for Determining a Course of Developmental Action for HiPos

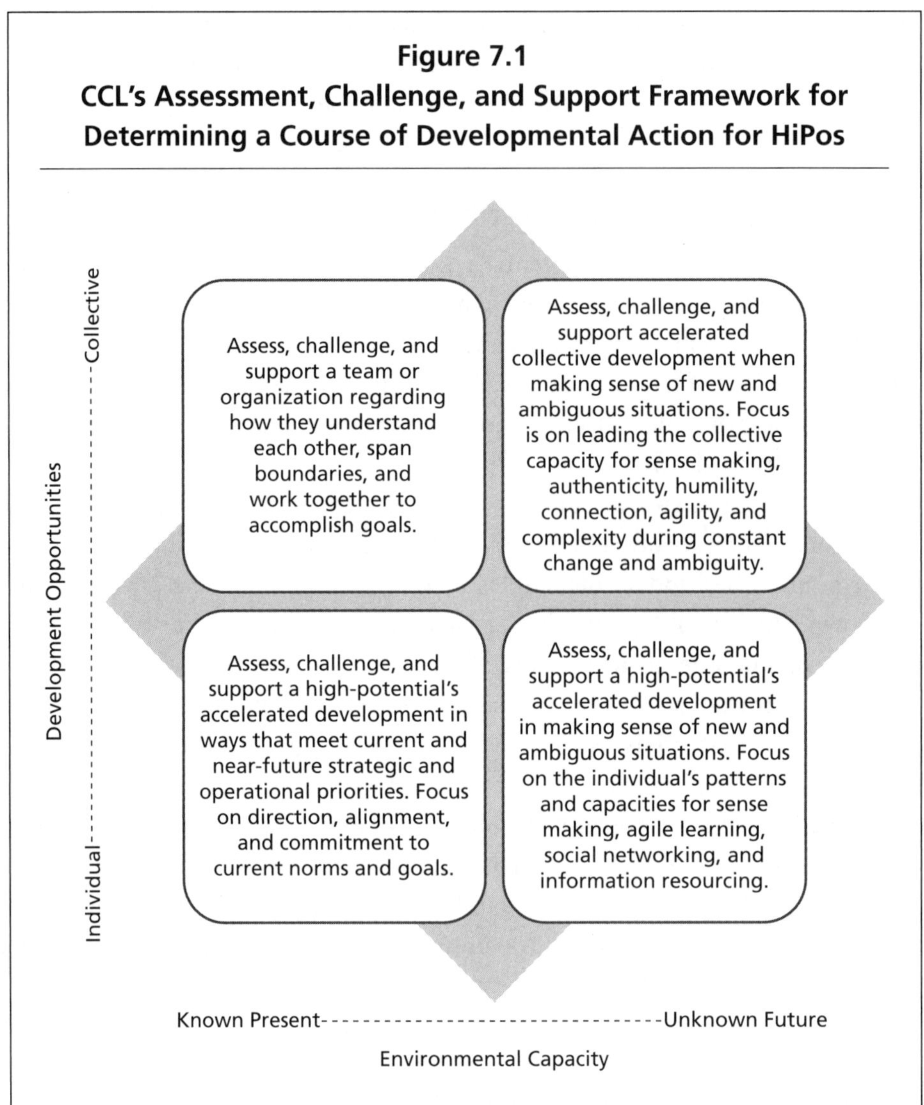

the organization's culture and execute strategy? In these circumstances, HR also has a coaching role with stakeholders. Supporting HiPos means coaching and developing senior leaders into mentors and immediate bosses into developmental allies. Systemically, support could include the creation of performance development plans that include accelerated project and performance milestones or a performance management system with a succession planning track.

Assess, challenge, and support a team or organization regarding how they understand each other, span boundaries, and work together to accomplish goals.
Assess, challenge, and support accelerated collective development when making sense of new and ambiguous situations. Focus is on leading the collective capacity for sense making, authenticity, humility, connection, agility, and complexity during constant change and ambiguity.
Assess, challenge, and support a high-potential's accelerated development in ways that meet current and near-future strategic and operational priorities. Focus on direction, alignment, and commitment to current norms and goals.
Assess, challenge, and support a high-potential's accelerated development in making sense of new and ambiguous situations. Focus on the individual's patterns and capacities for sense making, agile learning, social networking, and information resourcing.
Development Opportunities
Individual------------------------------Collective
Known Present------------------------------Unknown Future
Environmental Capacity

In the circumstances of the collective known present (figure 7.1 upper left), assessment, challenge, and support take into account the immediate environment of the HiPo's team and organization. Individual performance is either enhanced or inhibited by the environment; in some cultures, this is the defining factor. To assess, challenge, and support high-potential leaders as they struggle with and learn to master situations in the moment is the beginning of assessing actual leadership potential. The focus in this situation is on challenging the HiPos to lead while providing support with resources that develop the HiPo's community stakeholders, peers, and report groups. While this must be led and initiated by HiPos, they can benefit from direct coaching and guidance from HR as well as from the development of systems that support (and compensate) team and organizational performance.

In circumstances of the individual and the unknown future (lower right in figure 7.1), personal development takes center stage but with a specific purpose: this is the proving ground for leading in ambiguity. Here, a HiPo leader must be made aware of her relationship with ambiguity, the patterns of sense making and learning she uses in unknown situations, as well as useful patterns she may ignore or discount. For example, does she reach out to others or turn to the web when looking for information? Is her stressor response flight, fight, or freeze? Furthermore, how does the HiPo assess what approach will provide rapid learning in the unknown? Does she demonstrate a practiced response for appreciative inquiry? How open is the HiPo leader to self-discovery as well as the collective discovery that goes with public learning?

The situation of the individual and the unknown future gives HR an opportunity to provide direct coaching and also makes sure those around the HiPo who might have a firmer grasp on new situations are able and willing to assist with transition. In this way, the responsibility and choice of approach when faced with new realities continues to reside with the HiPo, while HR enriches the resources available. Support systems include making sure performance systems (and stakeholders) anticipate a learning curve that might have an impact on short-term performance while the HiPo adjusts to the long-term perspective. In the case of identified HiPos, the curve is steeper and the adjustment time shorter. HR can accelerate the process by providing the assessment, challenge, and support a HiPo needs to survive and perform in the unknown.

In the case of the collective unknown future (top right in figure 7.1), HR moves into the position of both coach and seeker. In this situation, all of the people in the organization are struggling to find their way as both individuals and a collective.

Leadership here is about the ability to maintain direction, alignment, and commitment when direction is unclear and about embracing polarities as people discover and create new rules. This requires that HiPo leaders model and instill what Edgar Schein (2013) calls humble inquiry. Broadly applied, humble inquiry broadens, deepens, refines, and advances our understanding of self, others, systems, and markets. Humble inquiry is not about knowing the answer but about asking different and deeper questions. In the collective unknown future, HR has to coach more broadly than to the individual HiPo and her stakeholders. HR must coach leaders to establish a community of leadership that fosters learning and open dialogue and maintains an open forum for ideas and, perhaps, vociferous debate.

Given the different roles that HR can play in coaching HiPOs, conduct your own assessment. Starting with 100 percent, think about the high-potential needs of your organization within each quadrant and decide where the biggest need is (or should be). Next, assign to each quadrant the quality and quantity of coaching and resources HR currently gives to each quadrant. What gaps and strengths do you notice?

MAPPING 70–20–10 TO THE COACHING OF HIPOS

CCL's lessons of experience research long ago suggested a rough guide to leadership learning. Lombardo and Eichinger (1996) popularized that rough guide as 70–20–10, which is used regularly in the leader development field. The 70–20–10 formula represents the idea that 70 percent of a leader's most significant learning occurs from experience, 20 percent from others, such as bosses and mentors, and 10 percent from formal leadership courses. In 2005, CCL researchers began complementing their US lessons of experience data with findings from China, India, and Singapore. From that work, CCL reported five learning areas broadly shared across those countries (Wilson, Van Velsor, Chandrasekar, & Criswell, 2011):

- Bosses and superiors
- Turnarounds
- Increases in scope
- Horizontal moves
- New initiatives

Each of these kinds of experiences creates coaching opportunities for HiPos (see figure 7.2). In the case of bosses and superiors, leaders benefit from direct

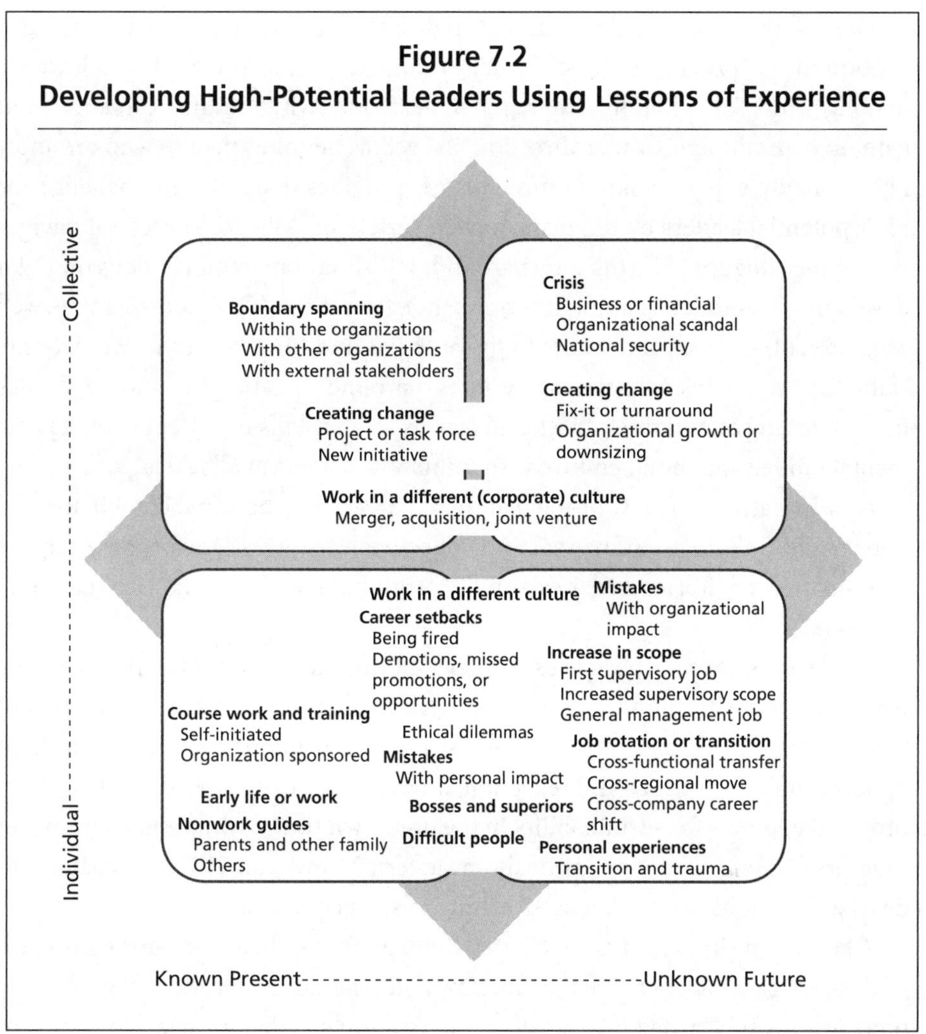

instruction, guidance, feedback, coaching, and mentoring. Since the quality of these high-influence relationships can significantly affect the trajectory of HiPos, HR must take special care to coach not only the HiPo but the enabling environment of his or her bosses and superiors. HR should be aware of how to turn situations into calibrated challenges so that HiPos can learn within the organization's current, known strategy but also as part of a collective in times of crisis and change. What questions can HR ask that will broaden, deepen, refine, and advance executives' understanding that they need to develop HiPos for a sustainable enterprise?

One of the most fertile areas for high-potential development is leading a turnaround, a proving ground for mastering existential threats by collectively making sense of what has to happen next and why. Setting direction and gaining commitment to that direction, as well as aligning people who are most likely already experiencing culture change, provides a significant challenge for high-potential leaders by requiring a wide variety of skills for successful navigation of the situation. During a turnaround, HR should maintain a focus on HiPo development and act as an organizational development (OD) consultant as well as an executive coach if it wants to move HiPos and their bosses forward. Some skills that could become necessary in turnaround situations include a deeper understanding of polarities, trust, and fear, as well as skills to better negotiate new mental models that build culture with influential leaders at all levels.

New initiatives, the last of the five shared areas, may be some combination of known and unknown, individual and collective learning. Many of these require entering new territories under existing strategy, but could become strategic game changers.

While all of these experiences are new and useful to the leader, perhaps only turnarounds create conditions rich enough to use in the moment as examples of how to lead and engage with others in the face of the unknown. With such slight opportunities for practice and reflection, how can HR coach HiPos and their executive stakeholders for sustainability in the unknown future while still counting on them to respond to the needs of the near term? How can HR use coaching to develop individual and collective learning in such conditions?

A key finding in CCL's research is that the experiences that generate the strongest leadership learning are those that are new and different to a leader: "Significantly more lessons are learned from challenging assignments than from any other event cluster, and different assignments sharpen different leadership abilities" (Yip & Wilson, 2010, p. 69). Change can provide significant learning opportunities. With that in mind, HR coaches should pay most attention to the value and depth of the experience they make available to HiPos. The different lessons of experience, as depicted in figure 7.2, may require HR to change the focus of its coaching and development for HiPo, stakeholders, and supporting systems.

To maximize learning, the best coaches use appreciative inquiry to take advantage of the challenge and change the leader is experiencing and provide a reflective frame that addresses what that experience means to the leader. For a HiPo, the long-term question is not *what*, but *if*, and he must navigate ambiguous situations with steady vision. Challenging assignments provide learning opportunities. Coaching can help the HiPo realize the long-term implications of those opportunities.

Developmental relationships often involve one-on-one interactions about issues that occur, with many known variables, under the organization's current strategy. The HiPo may be unaware of variables that are known to the mentor, coach, or manager, and developmental conversations can illuminate them.

In a situation of a collective unknown future, however, leaders need self-awareness, humility, and the mental agility to tackle complex problems. Experiencing adversity is not the same as experiencing challenging assignments. Adverse situations are not sought out intentionally; most people try to avoid the negative emotions that they bring: tension, fear, apprehension, confusion, and disorientation. Intense feelings of loss are common (Moxley & Pulley, 2004). Specific coaching remedies can help. Core development areas for HiPos experiencing adversity are self-awareness, maturity, and self-management of emotions. With the right coaching, HiPos can gain the ability to renew and thrive in circumstances that many others shy away from.

A result of an intentional practice regarding coaching HiPos is a focus on systems supporting the development of collective, high-potential leadership for the unknown. We should turn from asking what specific skills and competencies are required for executing immediate strategy, and ask instead, What will enable the organization to weather a crisis? If direction is lost, is alignment possible? What makes this enterprise worthy of our collective and individual commitment? In the next section, we look at the role of HR in securing a range of HiPo development that leads to ongoing, enterprise-wide, sustainable leadership.

THE ROLES THAT HR AND COACHING PLAY IN HIGH-POTENTIAL DEVELOPMENT

Coaches have to operate within the paradox that all organizations think they are unique and yet they often share the same challenges (Martin, 1983). In a coaching context, CCL's research indicates that "the best executive coaches work well across professions, industries, and organizations," compared with coaches who specialize for one context (Riddle, Zan, & Kuzmyez, 2009). Coaches must work comprehensively and be able to think like a psychologist, a business leader, and an OD management consultant. They must be aware of both individual and collective sustainable development.

Of course, there are various approaches to HiPo development, as they take into account current state and desired future, and HR must shift accordingly. That requires three distinct yet often complementary approaches to HiPo coaching:

- Direct coaching
- Diplomatic influence (creating an invested and enlightened executive stakeholder and HiPo community)
- Strategic design (systems and processes for HiPo development)

These three approaches operate in all four of the quadrants pictured in figure 7.1, and their differences will be addressed below primarily by discussing the contrasts between individual known present and collective unknown future.

Direct Coaching

Direct coaching in the individual known present usually employs clarification of goals, and type and preference from psychological measurements and 360-degree assessment. Direct coaching is a solid foundation for all leaders, but it is even more critical for HiPos, who must also consider things like thought leadership, cross-functional diplomacy, leading rapid transition, making sense of complexity, leading and mentoring leaders, leveraging succession planning, and assessing personal and organizational capacities for mastering disruptive change.

A leader's development is often linked to current business strategy. The goal of coaching is to create self and social awareness when the leader asks, What are my patterns and preferences? What impact do I have on others? Another goal is greater mastery of self in order to intentionally create desired impact as a leader. Some common coaching focuses are influence, communication, political savvy, team leadership, change, and conflict management.

Many of the issues on that list have relevance to the known. In terms of the unknown, they require a discrete set of skills. On the individual level, these skills include agility, pattern identification, deep and detached reflection, thoughtful passion, leveraging polarities, sense making, and increased capabilities and learning capacity. On the organizational level, the skills emphasize deep relationships in open networks across significant boundaries where broadening, deepening, refining, and advancing direction, alignment, and commitment (DAC) as a leadership community are essential for success. For HiPos provisionally entrusted with the future of the organization, personal reflection must be deeper, relationships richer and more far reaching, and their coaches must ask more profound questions.

RACSR: Coaching the Individual and the Organization ACS is the core of CCL's RACSR coaching model: relationship, assessment, challenge, support, results. Applied to both individual and collective coaching, RACSR is a simple and useful way for HR to coach HiPos on today's challenges or on engaging the enterprise for future viability. Using the ACS framework, leaders can connect and make sense of a situation, define the challenge and why it is important, gain support for the learning process, and achieve measurable results.

RACSR can also be useful for HR when it is facilitating a collective leadership gap analysis—a process with multiple assessment options, a number of complementary challenges, and lots of opportunities for HR, executive stakeholders, and peers to provide support for HiPos. If HiPos are viewed as part of a leadership community rather than as isolated individuals, HR can function as both a coach and a diplomat in order to guide a HiPo community with the potential for self-generation and self-management into existence.

HR can use RACSR as a model to help HiPos collectively develop themselves by developing each other as they learn, think, and act together. This should happen early and often.

RACSR can develop the HiPo stakeholder community directly and indirectly at the individual and collective levels. Stakeholders become mentors, guides, advocates, and change agents for a leadership development culture. There is a strong and pivotal role for HR, executive mentors, and coaches to play in the development of this HiPo community learning leadership model. Too many companies focus on performance, but it is development for performance that matters in the long run (B. Pasmore, personal communication, January 4, 2012).

The Dedicated and Detached Coach HR cannot afford to adopt HiPos—that is, to own the HiPos' struggle. The desire to see an individual succeed through personal efforts is understandable; there is much satisfaction to be gained from knowing you had a hand in the development of a future leader. Coaching HiPos holistically, interweaving their professional and personal development, requires addressing the whole person in his or her context, but in some instances it is best to use external coaches who can delve a bit deeper. HiPos who are so mission driven that they live their work may need to reflect on life and leadership as something to both separate and reintegrate, and an external coach can delve more into personal areas of identity and purpose that will help them do that.

Leveraging High-Potential Networks In a CCL survey of managers, 80 percent of respondents believed they had an open and effective network. They did not. Open, diverse, and deep networks provide relationships that generate more (and more diverse) ideas. Leaders who develop networks of unrelated people with diverse perspectives have a steady flow of ideas and potential for cross-boundary convergence across the organization. This is a potential resource for innovating and making sense of situations with new eyes, which are vital for HiPo leadership (Cullen, 2013).

HR has two roles to play here. The first is as a coach, helping to describe the types of networks that provide robust resources and then assisting the HiPo in discovering her natural inclination (or disinclination) to reach out and build open, high-quality relationships across diverse networks. The second role is that of guide, making the case to HiPos and other stakeholders that these types of networks have benefits such as organizational resourcing, sense making, and sustainability.

Developing Difference One way to make room for the long-term unknown is to change the way that HR frames, guides, and develops the thinking of executive stakeholders surrounding diverse HiPo capacities and how they can create sustainability through organizational robustness. Robust diversity of potential leadership comes in many forms. For example, take into account the "odd-angled" leader who may appear to have different values but is simply expressing these values using different notions and perspectives. This person may shine in surprising circumstances. It has been said that Winston Churchill, who was not successful at all of the jobs he held before he became prime minister, was in all of those jobs the prime minister. This did not always endear him to his peers. But at a critical moment, he fit perfectly in a pivotal leadership role that would decide the continued existence of his country (if not its empire). HR can help stakeholders and HiPos alike learn to recognize today's unique leaders as the organization's potential prototypes for agility in the face of the unknown.

Diplomatic Influence

To ensure the future viability of the organization, executives must be responsible for developing those who will lead it. Just as a coach cannot become overly invested in a HiPo's development, senior leadership cannot rely too heavily on HR to develop the organization's next crop of leaders. Overreliance on HR creates a culture where executive leadership abdicates its role as stewards of the company's sustainability.

Who Does What in High-Potential Development? Sometimes it is difficult to redistribute roles and responsibilities. A useful tool for clarifying executive and HR roles in HiPo development is a strengths, weaknesses, opportunities, and threats (SWOT) analysis. As you can see in figure 7.3, executive and HR strengths

Figure 7.3
Using a SWOT Analysis to Distribute Coaching and Development Roles and Responsibilities

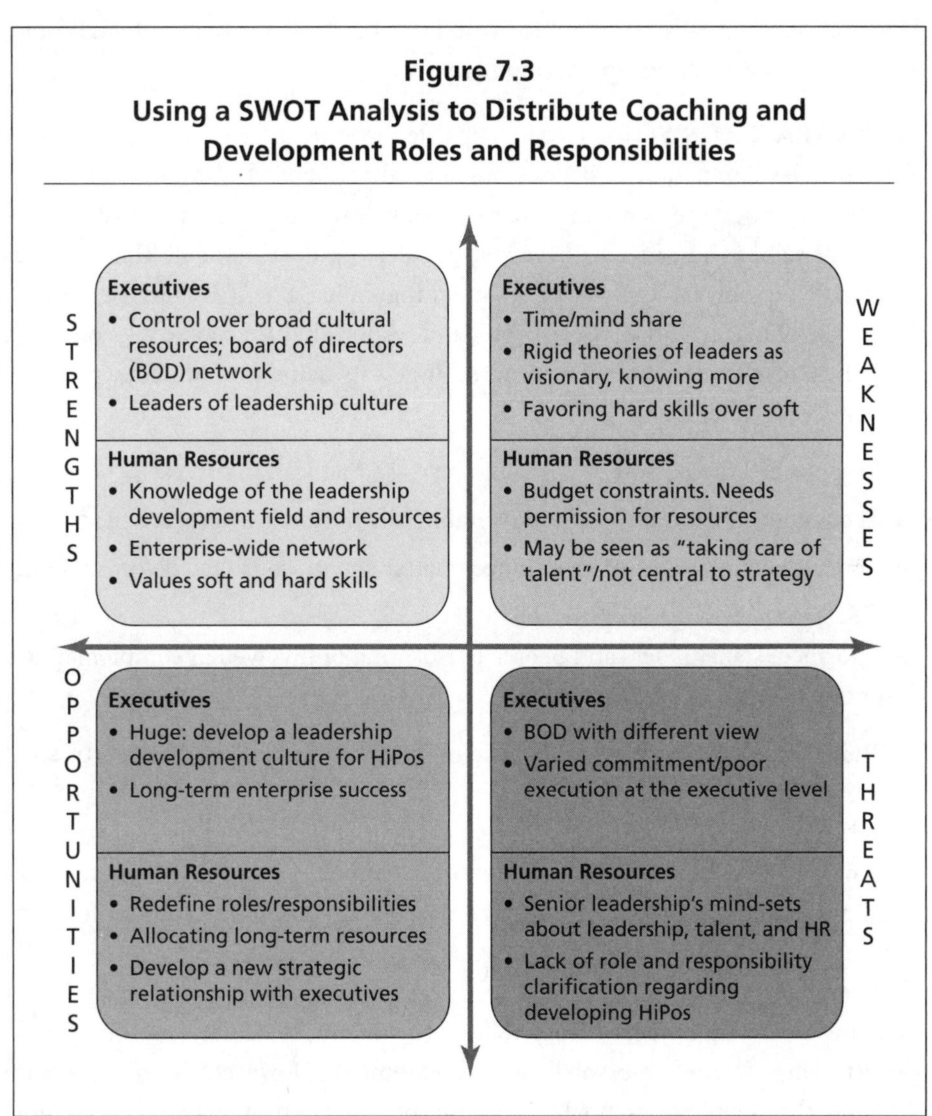

STRENGTHS
Executives
• Control over broad cultural resources; board of directors (BOD) network
• Leaders of leadership culture
Human Resources
• Knowledge of the leadership development field and resources
• Enterprise-wide network
• Values soft and hard skills
WEAKNESSES
Executives
• Time/mind share
• Rigid theories of leaders as visionary, knowing more
• Favoring hard skills over soft
Human Resources
• Budget constraints. Needs permission for resources
• May be seen as "taking care of talent"/not central to strategy
OPPORTUNITIES
Executives
• Huge: develop a leadership development culture for HiPos
• Long-term enterprise success
Human Resources
• Redefine roles/responsibilities
• Allocating long-term resources
• Develop a new strategic relationship with executives
THREATS
Executives
• BOD with different view
• Varied commitment/poor execution at the executive level
Human Resources
• Senior leadership's mind-sets about leadership, talent, and HR
• Lack of role and responsibility clarification regarding developing HiPos

balance the others' weaknesses. Collective and individual opportunities are based on negotiating and clarifying roles and responsibilities. Handling threats may be an educational process and may require mapping the landscape surrounding the development of leaders and what that means to the sustainability of the enterprise and high-potential development.

A series of conversations between HR and stakeholder executives geared toward clarifying roles, developing understanding, and perhaps even coming to a new set of agreements could yield a more strategic way forward. In this case, role clarification is actually a symbol for who is accountable for high potential (and, indeed, all other) leadership development.

Adding RACI A SWOT analysis helps define roles and resources necessary for HiPo development, but it does not formalize them. It also does not create agreement about the ways in which HR and executive leaders must change their interactions in order to have successful HiPo development. That requires influence, diplomacy, and perhaps something called a RACI chart (table 7.1). Use this tool to clarify the types of roles and responsibilities people take on when delivering results on a project or process. It gets its name from the four pieces of information it catalogues:

- **R**esponsible: the person performing the tasks that lead to success
- **A**ccountable: the person held answerable (the buck stops here) for success
- **C**onsulted: the person, often a subject matter expert, consulted before and during the performance of tasks to help ensure success
- **I**nformed: stakeholders and people performing or involved in complementary or interdependent activities

The RACI tool can be especially useful in cross-functional and departmental contexts, which is the case for the example in table 7.1.

When it comes to high-potential development, if you were to place the various roles of HR, executives, HiPos, and their direct managers on a RACI chart, would you be able to decide who is accountable, responsible, consulted, and informed? Take a moment to consider who in your organization takes each role in HiPo development.

Notice the assignments across RACI. Too often HR is seen as the "people department," accountable solely for development. However, HiPo leadership is about the ongoing sustainability of the organization, and therefore it must

Table 7.1
RACI Chart

HiPo Development RACI (Example)	RACI			
Tasks	**Executives**	**HiPo(s)**	**HR**	**Manager**
Resources for HiPo development				
Hi-Po development sponsorship	A	I	C	R
Modeling desired leadership behavior for HiPos	A	I	C	R
Coaching executive stakeholders to become coach-leaders	A		R	
Mentoring HiPos	A	R	C	I
Developing executives as HiPo mentors	A	I	R	I
Direct coaching of HiPos by HR	C	R	A	C
Sourcing external coaches for HiPo development	A	C	R	C
Developing HiPos as mentors	A	R	C	I
HiPo visibility	A	R	I	R
Stretch assignments	A	C	C	R
Action learning	A	I	R	C
Formal programs and conferences	A	R	C	I
Collective: Connections/relationships				
Fostering networks	A	R	C	I
Creating partnerships	A	R	C	I
Using social media for HiPo community support/resources	A	R	C	I
HiPo stakeholder community development	R	A	C	I
Systems and processes				
Performance management system	C	C	A/R	C
Systematic rotation assignments (development path)	A	C	R	C
Succession planning	A/R	I	C	I
Talent selection/identification	A	C	R	C
Communication about HiPo/transparency	A	R	C	I
Integrate HiPo coaching and long-range strategic planning	A	I	R	I
Metrics for HiPo development	A	C	R	I
Metrics for coaching culture development	A	C	R	I
Sponsorship of coaching culture development	A/R			
Sourcing, recruiting, onboarding, and retention of HiPos	A	I	R	C
HiPo competencies, talent identification, and assessment	A	I	R	C
Leadership knowledge management	A	C	R	C
HiPo rewards and recognition	R		A/R	
HiPo talent sharing policies	A	C	R	C
Systematized global practices re HiPo development	C	C	A/R	C
HiPo development integration with business strategy	A	R	C	I

Note: R = responsible; A = accountable; C = consulted; I = informed.

be owned by executive leadership. Executives are then more accountable and responsible for that function than is generally recognized. This is where HR can step into its role as diplomat, influencer, and negotiator. Executives must be established within the culture as more than sponsors. To do this, HR might need to coach and educate the executives themselves or arrange for a third party to fill that role.

Whether or not all of the role designations you map to a RACI chart apply to your long-term goals, where they are applicable, ask yourself what kind of conversations and coaching may need to happen with senior executives to clarify accountability and responsibility for HiPo development. Consider how your current responsibilities were established and if they continue to work as intended as the company and markets change. Then ask yourself what arrangements will most effectively guarantee HiPo development for each capacity listed in figure 7.1—especially for agility in the collective unknown future (top right in figure 7.1).

Holding RACI discussions with stakeholders puts HR firmly in the diplomatic influencer role, blending coaching, influencing, facilitating, and negotiating. In this role, HR is setting up senior leaders with the abilities to make high potentials successful, following the RACSR model.

HiPos go through many transitions and upheavals—points at which a stakeholder's withdrawal of support (particularly at points of failure or learning) could become a roadblock. HR's ability to influence stakeholder thinking before, rather than during, these times requires watching the HiPo ecosystem develop firsthand. This is particularly true for HiPos whose major learning goal is about grappling with the unknown.

In many ways, executives are also learning how to deal with the collective unknown and what will create an agile learning culture capable of navigating it. They are experiencing it in the present and will need to be coached into seeing it as a long-term opportunity and not a short-term irritant. One way HR can do this is by making a business case for development and its impact over the long term. For example, Frank Kalman quotes Amy Edmondson, Novartis Professor of Management and Leadership at Harvard: "The soft skills are the hard skills. People who master the critical leadership skills today are anything but touchy-feely—they're direct, they're clear, they're compassionate, they're no-nonsense. But they're not soft" (2012, para. 7). In the best result, HR coaches become diplomatic influencers for stewardship, and executive management steps up and takes on a more active leadership development role.

Another instance where HR acts as a diplomat and influencer is during succession planning. Succession planning isn't about who will rise to the top of one model or another. It is about developing a leadership community agile enough to operate and engage together when needed. Because executives are accustomed to thinking about HiPo development in terms of the rising star and leader, what is necessary is a mind-set shift in getting executives to spend less time thinking about that and more time thinking about the conditions of the leadership community. It is HR's job to educate executives on what succession planning involves (it is an entire ecosystem, not a path) and how they can negotiate the placement of accountability and responsibility. When coaching both executives and HiPos, it is necessary to assess the ecosystem they have created and then challenge them to evolve it.

When it comes to preparing all leaders, but particularly HiPos, for an uncertain collective future, CCL research highlights the idea that contemporary leaders are called to create space for other people—a space in which people can generate new and different ideas; a space where seemingly disparate departments and people in the organization come together and have a meaningful conversation; a space in which people can be more effective, more agile, and better prepared to respond to complex challenges (Martin, Willburn, Morrow, Downing, & Criswell, 2007).

At the end of the day, HiPos (like everyone else) profit from a culture where development for both the present and the future is standard. The challenge HR faces in its role as a diplomat is to guide this development environment, and the first priority in doing this is guiding the executive leadership.

Strategic Design

At CCL, we have found that leadership development works best when leaders being developed get the best stakeholder and systems support possible. Performance development and management systems designed for the HiPo provide many beneficial results. The components of such systems and accompanying processes support leaders as they move through clearly defined role progressions, accelerate development, and receive continuous feedback to reduce their chances of derailment. But even with a sophisticated, well-planned system, HiPos still leave their organizations.

This loss of talent is not tied to money or perks (Campbell & Smith, 2010). Retention of HiPos relates to an organization's investment, involvement, recognition, and development of their HiPos. Driven, self-directed people want to steer their own course and be recognized for their achievements. They commit more deeply when they are trusted to use their own agency and continue learning with support.

There are inevitable costs of underinvestment in high-potential development, both culturally and systemically. These include discontinuity, churn, instability, and the high costs of losing an asset and having to groom a new one. When designing systems for HiPo development, HR will naturally start with the HiPo and stakeholder communities, but they should also consider the different nature and scope of the areas represented in figure 7.1. What skills must executive stakeholders master to fulfill their roles and responsibilities, for example? Questions about current challenges and needs may lead to answers that satisfy individual, existing, and known issues only; questions about sustainability for the collective future unknown generate very different answers and need different accommodation in a development system design. However, high-potential development is not just about HiPos. It is about the surrounding leadership culture and the support and performance strategies the organization pursues. Is there a coherent leadership strategy in place for your organization that takes both the near and long term into account? Is there a succession plan in place enabling the transfer of leadership knowledge and capability from one set of leaders to the next generation? Who is responsible for HiPos? Who is held accountable?

CONCLUSION

Direct coaching, diplomatic influence, and strategic design are essential roles and responsibilities for HR coaches to act on and to lead when it comes to developing an organization's leaders with the highest potential. Coaching can be used to help HiPos and their stakeholders form developmental partnerships that leverage the organization's culture and systems. It is HR's job to guide, create, and then get out of the way.

HR must also act as an expert and be able to admit to not knowing, declare a development vision, and inquire softly about possibilities. These myriad roles, competencies, relationships, and responsibilities are a daunting mix of direct coaching, diplomatic influence, and systems savvy. Clearly the HR practitioner has some learning ahead, which she can share and use as part of her coaching repertoire with HiPo leaders. That kind of experience, reflected on and shared properly in a coaching, peer, and functional lead context, makes the most compelling case for how to grow as a high-potential leader.

chapter **EIGHT**

Coaching at the Top

Candice C. Frankovelgia

CCL pays very close attention to what it learns from leaders. It has the unique opportunity of having encountered over two thousand C-suite executives in its Leadership at the Peak (LAP) program since 1984. The experience gained from working with these leaders serves as a learning laboratory and a key resource yielding many of the insights contained in this chapter. The intention is to provide an overview of senior leader strengths and challenges, tactics to enhance HR support, and to report further lessons learned since Ted Grubb and Sharon Ting wrote about coaching senior leaders in *The CCL Handbook of Coaching* (2006). Since it is often the result of the strategic support of HR that senior leaders find their way to LAP (an application-only, week-long development experience offered exclusively in Colorado Springs, Switzerland, and Singapore), those lessons of experience are particularly valuable for HR leaders responsible for implementing coaching programs in organizations. We witness significant growth and interpersonal connectedness among leaders in LAP, and this chapter is an opportunity to share our observations.

When leaders who shoulder huge responsibilities have the unique opportunity to be away from the daily demands of the business and in the company of other leaders at similar levels in order to focus exclusively on who they are as a leader, a person, and part of collective, transformational thinking often begins to unfold. Throughout a carefully paced week filled with multiple levels of feedback, experiential exercises, structured reflection, and self-disclosure, senior leaders develop

My thanks to Bill Hodgetts at Fidelity Investments for his thoughtful reflections and contributions to this chapter.

a nuanced picture of how they and others perceive their leadership. What often emerges is recognition of the gaps between who they believe themselves to be (identity) and who they are perceived to be from the outside (reputation). Herein resides a critical enhancement to the ongoing development of the senior leaders in organizations: helping to bridge the gap between a leader's intent and his or her impact.

The heightened responsibility of HR to effectively support senior leaders as they cope with the complexity of current demands is outlined in The Conference Board's CEO Challenge research report (Mitchell, Ray, & van Ark, 2014). The report identified the following key challenges: leading change, managing complexity, entrepreneurial mind-set, integrity, and retaining and developing talent. Despite limitations imposed by confidentiality concerns, role boundaries, accountability, dual roles, and even circumstances of low trust in the culture, there still remains a pivotal role for HR to play in the development of senior leaders within organizations. Although rarely tasked with formal coaching responsibilities for senior executives, the savvy HR leader has the ability to enhance awareness and help leaders learn about the issue beneath the issue in a way that can gradually, and sometimes dramatically, shift the leadership landscape.

Before we get too far, let's define our terms. The word *coaching* has been buried under so many definitions it has virtually lost the merit of a meaningful label. Coaching currently describes a wide range of behavior, including formal coaching engagements, performance enhancement plans, 360-degree debriefing and action planning, informal guidance, onboarding and assimilation, corrective action plans, career planning, and skill building. For the purpose of this chapter, we will rely on the definition our editors provided in the Introduction: "Coaching is a helping relationship with a developmental focus played out in conversations that stimulate the person or group being coached to greater awareness, deeper and broader thought, and wiser decisions and actions." Throughout this chapter, I use *interactions* or *conversations* interchangeably with *coaching*. In helping leaders better understand how they are perceived, whether by the skilled use of catalytic questions, stealth guidance, strategic partnerships with external coaches, or small, consistent, daily interactions that heighten self-awareness and sharpen the thinking of senior leaders regarding people issues, HR leaders are in a unique position to advance the development of senior leaders for individual, team, and organizational benefit.

SENIOR LEADER CHARACTERISTICS

Who are these people bearing such great responsibility? What do they have in common, and what do they look like? Operating in a context of constant, destabilizing change intensified by the 2008 financial crisis, one new leadership characteristic must be added to those that Grubb and Ting identified. Recognizing that every senior leader is unique, the thematic characteristics of senior leaders remain largely consistent over time. After reviewing those common attributes, I identify and discuss this new attribute:

- *Experience.* With most of a beginner's mistakes behind them, top leaders are differentiated by their ability to learn from experience and have a credible list of diverse accomplishments and extensive networks. They know what they are doing and have the track record to prove it. However, this strength also contains the seeds of a weakness. When leaders learn too well what got them to their current roles, they may not recognize that the circumstances have changed and old lessons no longer apply.

- *Ambition and mastery.* This "fire in the belly" quality has been described as confidence, resilience, determination, resourcefulness, and drive, and it is the ticket to entry into the top ranks of leadership. Yet this strength, built on the foundation of individual characteristics, contains one of the most significant potential barriers for leaders in adapting to current demands. The sheer volume of information and complexity of business issues renders it virtually impossible for any single leader to manage alone. Although senior leaders may be skilled and quite comfortable with independent action, the need for collaboration is increasingly important. This doesn't come naturally to many of the leaders we see.

- *Power and control.* Independence and collaboration may be seen as counterforces in the leadership arena but can be usefully conceptualized as a polarity requiring ongoing attention as the leader matures. It is a generalization, but one that is widely experienced, that men tend to rely heavily on exercising power and control in earlier stages of leadership and women tend to be more relational in their influence strategies. As they mature in their leadership role, men tend to gain appreciation and agility in the relational arena, while women gain comfort and agility in the power arena. Increasing awareness of the balance between power or control skills and relational skills is a hallmark of an evolving leader, but complex market forces demand more than a balance. There is an implicit demand to seriously revaluate how to use power in a way that fosters not only individual growth but team and organizational growth as well.

• *Leadership stature.* Frequently referred to as executive presence or polish, this characteristic is often taken for granted until or unless it is found lacking. The leader is the embodiment of the organizational values, and every interaction conveys an impression about the business as well as the person. This elevates executive presence from a nice-to-have attribute to a need-to-have one. The external dimension of leadership stature is a visible representation of the leader's internal sense of self and can be conveyed in myriad ways, including language use, posture, humor, dress, and social poise. These external manifestations of leadership stature can be modified, taught, and managed, but lasting change comes about only when the internal dimension of who they are as a person and a leader is addressed, understood, and evolves. The synergistic potential between the external coach and the internal HR support align roughly according to these distinctions, HR primarily addressing the external presentation and the coach primarily accessing the internal dimensions that give rise to the external manifestations. Later portions of this chapter explore various ways for gaining access to the internal dimensions.

• *Resistance to change.* Marshall Goldsmith's book *What Got You Here Won't Get You There* (Goldsmith & Reiter, 2007) is a popular and accessible study demonstrating how overused or misused strengths often become weaknesses. Successful leaders may be unwilling to let go of the things that created their success despite multiple signals that they no longer work. They often cling tightly to their preference to go it alone or to demonstrate heroic leadership rather than acknowledge that they must now expand their attention in the direction of collective wisdom and collaboration.

• *Rarified air.* Impatience is often worn as a badge of honor among many of the overbooked and overscheduled leaders we encounter. They literally do not have time for nonessentials, but their finger-snapping, watch-tapping message has a dampening effect on collaboration and innovation. Not soliciting or listening to feedback can cost more than time and inefficiency in the long run. It can cost the goodwill and cooperation of the leadership team, and this exacts a significant toll. Before acknowledging that a shift in leadership style or culture is required, many leaders resist stridently and require the leveling effect of outside intervention or

360-degree feedback in order to consider the possibility that a mind-set change may be warranted.

- *Hierarchy effect.* David Campbell, CCL senior research fellow emeritus and author of many effective and widely used leadership assessments, identified and measured this phenomenon wherein the higher a person is in the organizational hierarchy, the more likely she is to have a satisfied view and positive assessment of the organizational climate. Two explanations are possible: "The higher in the organization, the more control over their destiny, the more information and opportunity and the more voice in organizational policies and the better compensated. Why shouldn't they be happier?" Campbell's alternative explanation offers a different causal direction: "The happier you are, the higher you will go" (Campbell & Hyne, 1995, p. 108). Whichever comes first, optimism or satisfaction, we don't often see cranky, pessimistic people in top positions. At least not for long.

- *Legacy.* Turning attention from success to significance is emblematic of maturity that distinguishes good leaders from great ones. Staying in position too long for personal satisfaction limits the ability of a leader to create a lasting legacy and dampens the spirit and potential of rising leaders in the organization. It is unfortunate but not uncommon for leaders to stay in place past the time when they should be focusing on developing and positioning the next-level leader to rise. It often falls to the board to intervene and break this sort of impasse, and boards sometimes turn to HR to craft a solution.

- *Collective learning capacity.* This is the additional attribute alluded to at the start of this list. This capacity refers to the fact that leaders can no longer rely solely on individual competencies, which are necessary but not sufficient. Leaders who recognize that learning takes place not only individually but also collectively differentiate themselves as successful in the current business environment. These leaders are able to tolerate the discomfort of admitting vulnerability and gaps in knowledge in order to step into the challenges necessary to grow. Collective learning capacity is genuine curiosity and willingness to engage in public learning, which means that leaders must acknowledge that they don't have all the answers (McGuire & Rhodes, 2009).

It is also important to consider gender when discussing senior leadership (see exhibit 8.1).

Exhibit 8.1
A Note on Gender

LAP demographics mirror corporate reality at the top of organizations. The average attendance is only 20 percent women. While no quota system for board members has yet been proposed in the United States as it has for European Union and Asian countries, gender diversity is of considerable interest to many shareholders, who cite improved corporate performance for companies with female board representation (Catalyst, 2011). As one of the handful of pioneering women at a previously all-male university in the mid-1970s, I have firsthand experience being one of the few women in a male-dominated institution. This experience introduced the blistering reality that the institutional attributes fostering male excellence are quite different from those fostering female excellence. However, the good news is that the past forty years have seen significant advancement in the acceptance of women, a far cry from the days when my fellow male students asserted their dominance by holding up numeric rating cards like Olympic judges when watching female students walk between classes or in the dining hall.

Still, one truth remains unchanged: the range of perceived positive behavior around assertiveness is much narrower for women than for men. What is considered acceptable assertive behavior for men is often described using less courteous terms when referring to assertive women. Noticing, demonstrating, and responding to assertiveness remain an issue for LAP attendees regardless of gender. This may be particularly acute for this book's readers because the preponderance of HR leadership is female while the preponderance of executive organizational leadership is male.

The bright side of the gender issue is that there may well be a female advantage in that more women may have the collaborative and relational intelligence that many men lack but is demanded of twenty-first-century leaders. Building on the seminal work of *Breaking the Glass Ceiling* (Morrison, White, & Van Velsor, 1992), Ruderman and Rogolsky (2013) have cited authenticity as critical for success in high-achieving women. Experience with LAP participants has shown that the need to live authentically is not gender specific. The intense, compressed, and very personal learning

Exhibit 8.1 (*Continued*)

experience of LAP shows that familiarity opens the door to empathy. It is difficult to marginalize or blame someone once you know her story and see her as a whole person. At the conclusion of the week, we regularly see recognition that personal relationships and collaboration enhance rather than dilute leader effectiveness. This can be a stunning and often emotional realization for leaders accustomed to the isolation of self-reliance.

Ruderman and Rogolsky have identified these hallmarks of living authentically:

- Clarity about one's values, priorities, and preferences
- Acceptance of the need for choices and trade-offs in life
- A strong sense of self-determination
- A willingness to work toward aligning one's values and behaviors
- A high degree of comfort and satisfaction with decisions made earlier in life

For leaders who have built their identity around being experts and highly focused individual achievers, the necessary shift to collective learning and collaborative leadership does not come easily regardless of gender.

COACHING LESSONS FROM LEADERSHIP AT THE PEAK

At the beginning of the LAP experience or any other senior leader development process that CCL addresses, participants typically identify learning goals centered strictly around business themes: leading the organization through transition, creating cultural change, building future leadership capacity, changing strategic direction in response to global fiscal realities, learning to do more with less, consolidating divisions to create efficiencies, strategic agility in response to competitive challenges, and other issues (see exhibit 8.2 for specific success criteria for the HR function). These challenges are real, and leaders can significantly improve in targeted areas using an array of development opportunities. As important as these are, the more compelling issues emerge toward the end of the LAP when trust has been developed and reflection moves to a deeper, personal, and more

Exhibit 8.2
Credibility

A 2014 report identifies twelve critical human capital trends that are the success criteria to measure the effectiveness of the HR function (Deloitte, 2014). Organized into three areas, these trends are:

- *Lead and develop*: The need to broaden, deepen, and accelerate leadership development at all levels; build global workforce capabilities; reenergize corporate learning by putting employees in charge; fix performance management
- *Attract and engage*: The need to develop innovative ways to attract, source, recruit, and access talent; drive passion and engagement in the workforce; use diversity and inclusion as a business strategy; find ways to help overwhelmed employees deal with the flood of information and distractions in the workplace
- *Transform and reinvent*: The need to create a global HR platform that is robust and flexible enough to adapt to local needs; reskill HR teams; take advantage of cloud-based HR technology; implement HR data analytics to achieve business goals

powerful level. These themes have more to do with being seen as the person they want to be, reconciling the gap between who they are from the inside (identity) and who they are from the outside (reputation).

Intent and Impact

We all have multiple stories: who we think we are, who we wish we were, how we think we got to be this way, and how we believe we are being received by others. In the most hopeful scenario, perceptions of our own impact are aligned with how others see us. Yet CCL's long history of measuring executive impact using 360-degree assessments shows that the rate of alignment between self and other perceptions is only about 30 percent on quantitative measures (Campbell, personal communication, 2010). We are not even half right in anticipating how we are viewed! These data can be sliced, diced, and analyzed using myriad variables (age, gender, function, level in organization, type of rater, over versus under rating, scales of most congruence, geographic region, and so forth). All these slices of data have interesting and fruitful implications, yet for the purpose of this chapter, the red warning light concerns the notion that the way we are seen by others is often not the way we see ourselves. Senior leaders have a multitude of stories proportionate to the scope of their responsibilities, the complex array of stakeholders, and the high visibility of their role. There is the story the leader believes to be true from a subjective perspective: the intentions, beliefs, and values that drive behavior. And then there are the multiple stories held by all who are part of that leader's world about that leader based on their experience of impact. It is in the valley between how leaders see themselves and how others see them that leadership misadventures play out.

We've all seen versions of the rift between intent and impact. Leaders attempting to shift the culture from a telling culture to an asking culture believe the endeavor will better prepare the organization to adapt to the changing competitive environment; believe that the reasoning has been made clear and compelling; believe that although it will be a difficult process, it will benefit the organization, employees, and customers; and most of all, believe that their leadership behavior is consistent with this objective. Is this the story that the senior team has about any particular leader's behavior? Is this the story that is being told in the hallways and meeting rooms around the organization? At best, some version of this story will roughly approximate what a leader intends and believes. At worst, the offline conversations suggest a vast chasm between what a leader believes and what the rest of the organization experiences. In the absence of clarifying data and candid conversations, differences between intent and impact are usually viewed negatively. It is not generally habitual to give people the benefit of the doubt and assume positive intent. How can the different perceptions, experiences, and stories be surfaced and addressed in order to keep the organization aligned, committed, and moving in a shared direction?

Show, Don't Tell

Self-awareness is one of the primary tools of the HR leader. Like any other effective leader, HR leaders strive to be aware of the intentions that drive their behavior and to have proficiency in learning about the impact of their behavior. Advancing the art of self-awareness is best done by living it, role modeling, and engaging in timely and courageously truthful conversations while carefully modulating the amount of teaching and telling used while sharing your perceptions. No matter how experienced and well schooled you are in understanding organizational design, business practice, talent management, change leadership, or training and development, your foremost offering to the senior leaders of your organization is your ability to be a role model and walk the talk of self-awareness.

Each senior leader's self-awareness (or lack thereof) shapes the organizational culture in ways that either facilitate or impede the mission of the organization, although this connection may be masked by the sheer wattage of the leader's power, charisma, and intellectual ability. Leaders are often surprised to learn that the emotional tone they establish permeates the organization with astonishing predictability (Algoe & Fredrickson, 2011). Leaders are even more surprised to learn that the emotional tone they intend to convey is often not the tone that people perceive. Although the leader may be the last person to recognize this, the senior HR professional is in a unique position to hold up the mirror and allow the executive to see the often unintended impact and downstream consequences of his behavior.

Your Reactions Constitute Valid Data

The essential tool of leadership is the human being behind the title—the living, breathing person in the role, complete with foibles, unpredictability, and variable reactions to the huge responsibility of the role. Beyond the specific tasks key HR professionals carry out for the organization, perhaps the most vital role they can play is helping to provide an interactive, real-time approximation of an "owner's manual" for the senior leaders they support. Wouldn't it be ideal if senior leaders viewed you as a reliable resource when encountering glitches in the interpersonal arena?

The most successful leaders are the ones whose self-perception is largely aligned with the way others see them—not without flaws but with awareness of strengths and weaknesses plus (importantly) a willingness to continue learning. The essence of your job is to help deal with the inevitable tensions alive in human relationships. This requires you to use sound judgment regarding when to provide input in the moment and when to take notice but to keep your mouth shut. You live in a multidimensional and shifting environment of confidences, boundaries, and balancing truthfulness with risk. Newly minted HR professionals often err on both sides of the safety zone around confidentiality and eventually learn to navigate the optimally effective range within their unique culture. Holding too rigid a line around "protected HR information" can generate the perception that you lack transparency and use policy justifications to avoid true conversations. That perception will break trust as surely but perhaps more subtly than sharing sensitive information unnecessarily, but either way you lose credibility. (Chapter 12 discusses the ethical issues inherent in HR coaching.)

Your job description probably doesn't include the most critical function you provide: inquiring about the intended effect of leadership behaviors and surfacing data when the effect does not match the intent. This puts you in a precarious position of gathering information about impact (from your own emotional, visceral reactions as well as through candid conversations with colleagues) and finding effective ways to share that information back to the leader in a nonjudgmental way that can be heard and acted on. Your goal is to advance senior leaders' learning, thinking, and reflecting abilities while also addressing the solution to the concern at hand. This outcome is crucial for HR leaders and for the senior leaders they support, but for different reasons. For leaders, understanding the impact of their behavior allows course corrections and continuous learning, which expand and enhance effectiveness. For HR leaders, it keeps an endless list of people problems from filling their calendars.

Common Predicaments and Vexations

The most successful leaders are engaged in an ongoing process of becoming more recognizable as the person they want to be. The leaders who learn, adapt, and grow continue to excel in their complex and ever-expanding roles. Leaders who don't learn and adapt are regularly weeded out, but experience shows that new difficulties can surface as responsibility increases and complexity grows. There are some common themes that emerge when a senior leader runs up against a personal limit (charitably referred to as "a learning opportunity") and begins to have an adverse impact on parts or all of the organization. These themes may provide some guidance for your targeted HR support:

- *Going it alone.* Shifting from the individualistic, heroic notion of leader excellence to accepting the reality that interdependence may be required to succeed in the complex business reality is a wall that high achievers, male and female, often hit as they reach a personal limit. Depending on how a leader chooses to identify his strengths, an expert can be expert only at what he is good at. Solo performers are less able to tap into the collective wisdom and the powerful multiplier of collaboration. Truly innovative leaders balance the need for collaboration with knowing when to push forward with decisions others think are crazy. (Steve Jobs comes to mind.)

- *Feedback famine.* Since identity is personality from the inside and reputation is personality from the outside, the only way to close the gap is giving and receiving feedback. Providing feedback (small f, not feedback with a capital F, which invariably creates a bracing for bad news) means weaving observations naturally into the fabric of the workplace through small, daily interactions, letting people know the impact they have on you—both positive and negative. Leaders who believe that yearly performance conversations provide sufficient guidance are often the same ones who avoid ongoing feedback conversations and delegate people issues to HR. This creates a situation where people don't know where they stand and the leader does not know what she doesn't know. This is fertile ground for misperceptions to take hold.

- *Big bark.* In command-and-control cultures, "keeping them on their heels" may once have been a useful leadership tool. As leaders worked their way up the ladder in this sort of environment, they may have learned to exert power and control by fearlessly barking at people as a means of establishing dominance. Not only is this tactic obsolete, it actively works against the collaboration that interdependent cultures require for successful adaptation today.

- *Dirty delegation.* This is a scenario where either the leader does not delegate, thereby creating a cadre of frustrated direct reports while speeding down the fast track to burnout, or the leader overdelegates people issues to HR. This creates a traffic jam at your door and fails to appreciate that all organizational difficulties are essentially people issues.

- *Lack or inappropriate use of humor.* Appropriate humor can be a sophisticated way to protect against stress or anxiety and ease pressure in tense situations. When leaders take themselves so seriously as to eliminate any expression of humor, they risk becoming a dampening cloud over the enterprise. The ability to use humor effectively and even make light of one's own foibles sets a tone of acceptance and heightens the credibility of the leader. Caustic, off-color, or sarcastic humor has an adverse impact on perceptions of leader effectiveness. Humor received the ultimate badge of honor as a measurable leader attribute when it showed up as a scale (Entertaining) on the Campbell Leadership Index (Campbell, 1991). Campbell is fond of saying, "You may have an opinion [about your leadership], but I have data."

- *Defensiveness.* "We're already doing that," or "We've already tried that," or "You don't know all the details about what really happened" are well-worn defensive routines built on the obsolete belief system that the leader must know everything rather than be curious and remain open to the input of others even if it differs from the leader's beliefs. The precondition for a genuine conversation is remaining open to the possibility that the other person could be right. Defensiveness forecloses on the possibility of having a true conversation and seriously impedes leader effectiveness.

- *Impervious to feedback.* In this scenario, behaviorally specific feedback has been delivered by multiple people in multiple venues, yet the leader is unable to incorporate the feedback into behavioral adjustments. People are hired for their capabilities and fired for their personality, and imperviousness to feedback is often the flaw that sends leaders out the door. As you attempt to address this vexation, it may be helpful to remember that fear is usually the root cause. Humane understanding can soften even the most difficult feedback.

- *What's not to get?* In this scenario, the leader believes that he or she has been perfectly clear about direction. Any question from the team is interpreted as a lack of cooperation or a failure of the team without entertaining the possibility that the leader's behavior may be part of the communication breakdown.

Underlying each of these common sources of trouble is a single pervasive limitation: the lack of awareness that the leader's own behavior contributes in some way to the difficult situation she comes to you for help managing. You likely witness endless enactments of the fundamental attribution error (Heider, 1958). This is the tendency to overvalue dispositional or personality-based explanations for behavior while undervaluing situational explanations particularly when the situation may involve the intentional or unintentional behavior of the leader. Exhibit 8.3 shows you how that might look.

Exhibit 8.3
Personality or Behavior?

Imagine the challenge of the most senior HR leader in a large, successful, and nationally visible health care organization who recognizes that the CEO, in the midst of bold organizational restructuring, is entirely unaware of the pervasive informal conversations about her "control freak" tendencies and the chilling effect her behavior has on the productivity and satisfaction of her senior team and the teams they lead. The CEO's national prominence and high-visibility network makes it feel impossible to address any of these behaviors, which the CEO either does not recognize or consistently blames on people or circumstances outside herself. The three times the HR leader attempted to discuss the general issue of workplace morale, the CEO countered with plausible yet dismissive explanations for why people were feeling unhappy at work. The first time it was, "They just didn't get it." The second time it was the "residual effects of the recent restructuring." The third time was the "slow learning curve in response to new electronic operational infrastructure systems." Notably lacking from any of the attributions for malcontent in the workplace is an understanding, however rudimentary, that the low engagement and flat morale had anything to do with her behavior.

Whose Problem Are You Fixing?

A 2013 Survey by the Stanford Business School showed that nearly 66 percent of CEOs do not receive coaching or leadership advice from external coaches while 100 percent of those surveyed stated that they are receptive to making changes based on feedback. This opens up enormous opportunity for internal HR leaders to fill a crucial gap for senior leaders in understanding their impact on the people side of their business. Fully leveraging your role as truth-teller and as a mirror for top leaders is not without risk, but it holds the potential for helping leaders reach the universal aspiration of being seen as the person they want to be.

CEOs don't like spending their time fixing messy people problems, even if they often unwittingly create or perpetuate them. When they come to HR (you) with a plea/request/demand to "fix this problem," you may be tempted to take action.

Acting taps into your strengths and holds the potential for increasing your value by taking some pressure off the boss. But falling into the trap of "fixing" people problems often creates more problems than it solves unless a component of developing the boss's self-awareness is part of the fix (Oncken & Wass, 1999). Otherwise the boss doesn't learn to understand his potential role in creating or maintaining the problem and therefore doesn't develop the skills necessary to resolve interpersonal difficulties that invariably arise out of this blind spot. Lester Tobias (1990) notes that "the greatest mistake we can make is forgetting the need to presume bias" (p. 84).

The pattern will repeat itself with just enough variation to obscure the connection to the source. It creates a steady demand for HR support—but is it the right role for HR to give it?

Simultaneously Addressing Overt and Underlying Issues

Consider these circumstances: your boss asks you to secure conflict resolution, external coaching, or mediation training for two executive vice presidents whose interpersonal tension affects the entire senior team and cascades difficulties to the teams they lead. Tension permeates every meeting; lines are drawn and sides are taken, but the rift is not openly addressed and productivity is spiraling down. As the senior HR officer, you may be pleased to be tapped for your unique skill set, but you know you have only two choices. The first is to simply respond to the overt request of the boss and fix the problem. The second and more difficult is to take on the challenge of addressing the deeper patterns that give rise to the observable problem. How you proceed depends on the credibility you have built and your appetite for taking on a challenge. You have the opportunity to make a lasting difference by not only addressing the issue but also by helping the boss learn more about the role she played in creating or maintaining the problem.

Let's say you have decided on the second course of action. Engaging in a conversation with the boss to fully understand the issue from his perspective can help you surface the subjective perception or mental model about how the problem started. This also releases you from the rushed need to fix things. Fixing the problem itself, without first taking the time to fully understand the other person's frame of reference or mental model, can have the paradoxical effect of entrenching the problem by covertly agreeing with the basic assumptions. Thinking through the situation together, without judgment or predetermined outcome, yields a much greater possibility of creating a lasting solution. The key here is to understand the boss's worldview to create alternative ways to understand the impasse. You may hear things like, "These two people are diametrically opposite types and they push each other's buttons without even realizing it. A comment made by one of them early in their tenure ruptured trust, and it has been impossible to repair. Staff are divided, falling into one or the other camp so the fallout is reaching several layers of the organization." The fundamental attribution error behind all of these statements is that the executive vice presidents are judged to be dispositionally responsible for the difficulty, but the situational variables (including the boss's behavior) are not considered. Before getting into more details about this situation, let's consider the potential underlying mechanism for this disconnect.

Mental Models: Getting at the Underlying Issues

Mental models are deeply ingrained assumptions, generalizations, or even images that influence how we understand the world. They guide what actions we take. Often we are not consciously aware of our mental models or the effects they have on our choices and behavior. Yet they play an important role in filtering information, shaping perception, and defining how we ascribe significance. Fully understanding other people requires discerning the things that are meaningful to them, including the historical or cultural issues that create the unique lens through which they view the world. This understanding helps close the gap between what we think we know and what is actually happening for the other person. Unless you help to surface and understand the mental models that drive behavior on both sides of the issue (in this case, the conflict between the executive vice presidents), your efforts will yield limited or unsustainable results. Worse yet, you run the risk of becoming the person who solves all ensuing people problems without fostering learning or adaptation. Neither option is ideal for you or your organization.

After inquiring and listening carefully, you might now understand the boss's view that the problem is based on inherent traits within each player and that the damage has already been done (also known as "the bad seed hypothesis" or "it's too late now"). Within this mental model, this definition of the problem, the only solution seems to be to fire one or both of the executive vice presidents. Not only is this expensive and disruptive, but it doesn't advance the leader's self-awareness of how she may hold some portion of responsibility. Your task now becomes redefining the problem in a way that allows more options for a solution. Engaging the boss in a genuinely curious and nonjudgmental dialogue to mutually consider how she

Exhibit 8.4
Barriers to HR Effectiveness

Keep a close watch on tendencies that can limit your credibility and impact, such as the following:

- Overidentification with the underdog
- Failing to trust your gut
- Bragging
- Showing off wit or special knowledge
- Name-calling
- Not knowing how to say no
- Fear of hurting others
- Impatience
- Fear of confrontation

may have unwittingly contributed to the onset or perpetuation of the rift begins to open up reflective conversation and potentially broader understanding of the multiple forces at play. This conversational approach brings you into the arena of the boss's sense of identity and requires you to be diligent about withholding judgment. None of us wants our identity tampered with, yet self-improvement beckons us (sometimes drags us kicking and screaming) into portentous territory where we must examine and perhaps modify the established notions we hold about our self.

HR coaches can have their own mental models that interfere with their working with senior leaders. Exhibit 8.4 describes some of the most damaging habits.

Behaviorally Specific Observations

What is your reaction when you see yourself on a video? The perfectly captured image of how you look, move, and sound is accurate—after all, it is recorded. Yet we often recoil in disbelief and fail to recognize that person on the screen. Is that how I really look? Is that how I really sound? Why are my hands moving around so much? or, Why are my movements so mechanical? My body language and my words don't match! Who is that person on the screen? Recorded images are meticulously behaviorally specific and therefore a powerful learning tool. How can your observations as an HR partner serve as a "video recording with benefits"? Simple: the benefit is your ability to share the impact of the behavior on you (the observer)—something the person could not know unless you told her. The more you are able to provide behaviorally specific examples that potentially connect the boss's behavior to the problem formation, the more value you add by holding up the mirror and partnering with the boss to develop greater self-awareness. You begin to close the gap between intent and impact.

Applying this to the executive vice presidents' situation, your specific observations may include that their job descriptions actually contain substantial overlap. More important, when turf issues surface as one-upmanship in executive team meetings, the behavior you see is talking over each other, blocking progress on each other's projects, and going offline to complain about one another. Furthermore, you observe that the boss does not address the behavior but instead tries to offer tactical solutions to disentangle operational problems. Sharing your behavioral observations and noting the impact it had on you (whatever that may have been: frustration, sympathy for the executive vice presidents, dismay that the boss didn't address their behavior, concern about the reaction of more junior members in the meeting) leads to the question of what the boss intended by staying out of the fray. What was the boss's reasoning or belief that prompted that approach?

Don't be lulled into assuming you know what the boss intended: you will probably be wrong. She may have believed she was supporting the executive vice presidents by giving them room to resolve their own issues. Alternatively or additionally, she may have been staying out of it in order to assess their abilities to address conflict. Or there may have been an entirely unexpected intention behind the boss's behavior. You don't know until you ask. Exploring the intentions helps you stay out of the unsupported judgment trap and allows the boss to consciously consider various scenarios. Just having this conversation is helpful in and of itself. Jumping directly into fixing mode to revise job descriptions is a novice's mistake, and it shortchanges deeper exploration. Fixing tactical issues (job description modification) without also addressing the underlying interpersonal drivers (the boss didn't see her part in it) is likely to be wasted energy because unexplored patterns tend to repeat themselves. The problem will resurface in a different version of the same story at a later date.

Identifying and addressing the underlying beliefs, mental models, and meaning-making methods of the senior leader creates a generative partnership that builds the skills of addressing messy people issues that often land at your door. There is an undeniable element of risk in this approach that may cause you to avoid this course of action for good reason. You'll know you're avoiding if you find yourself talking to trusted others about what you "really think is going on," but you are not having this conversation with the key players. Although that response is understandable in the complex power dynamics of an organization, what it actually means is that you have now become part of the problem.

VALUE PROPOSITION

Your value as a trusted advisor depends on your capacity to shine some light into the darker corners of subjective experience where blind spots flourish. Are you willing to provide feedback in such a specific and personal way that it falls into the category of a "video with benefits"? Sharing the impact the behavior had on you, which may or may not be visible to the leader, is your value proposition. The higher a person rises in an organization, the less likely he or she is to receive candid and complete feedback. Ironically, when someone needs it most, useful feedback is nearly impossible to get. By providing succinct, specific, timely, and nonjudgmental observations about the impact of a leader behavior without offering advice or solutions, you advance the leader's self-awareness and create options. Behaviorally specific feedback supports your value proposition. Senior leaders often say as they conclude the LAP experience, "Why hasn't someone told me this before? I wish I had known earlier."

There may be circumstances where you assess that a senior leader you support is not open to feedback, but this assessment may be untested and is less common than many HR leaders believe. When you have irrefutable proof that the boss is not open to feedback, you may be able to demonstrate your effectiveness with others in the CEO's orbit who may not be quite so high on the organization chart and are noticeably more open to feedback. This provides the groundwork for potential future conversations with the boss. Also—and this cannot be overstated—you owe it to yourself and your organization to do a careful self-assessment: Is it your anxiety that keeps you from providing valuable feedback to the boss?

Start with You

Unless you are able to examine your own intentions and seek feedback about your own impact, you are not going to be able to help anyone else do it. Giving and receiving feedback is a skill that requires ongoing practice and refinement. When deciding if and when to provide feedback, ask yourself: "Is it truthful, is it kind, and is it necessary?" If so, give it. There is no need for brutal honesty. You can be both totally kind and totally honest with your feedback.

Clarify Expectations

Whatever your formal role in the organization, be sure to gain an overt agreement about offering observations, providing feedback, and having candid conversations. Seeking permission and clarifying expectations can be as simple as asking, "May I offer an observation?" or, "When you have a little time, I'd like to share some thoughts I have about the situation. Would you be interested?" Assuming someone wants your input without checking first can be a recipe for disaster.

Hold Up the Mirror

Can you articulate the specific behavior that the leader demonstrated and inquire about the intention behind it? Can you use your own reaction or observations about the behavioral reactions of others to help the leader see the difference between the intent and the impact? Can you take the risk of illuminating a blind spot and allow the leader to maintain dignity while he or she ponders alternate possibilities? Can you make the connection that mental models create results that conform to the assumptions?

Anaïs Nin (1962) pointed out that we don't see things as they are but as we are. Treating a person based on your belief that she is a petulant turf protector will elicit petulance and turf protection. Treating a person like a resourceful initiator will elicit an entirely different set of behaviors. If you want to change someone's behavior, direct your first efforts toward changing the way you think about her.

Challenge Assumptions

Once you've developed a track record of providing useful observations and resisted the temptation to tell the leader what should have been done instead (a cardinal mistake), you may want to ask permission to challenge underlying assumptions. For example, a leader who tends to explode and call people out in public may benefit from an offline conversation to inquire about some assumptions. By inquiring about the perceived impact of this behavior, the senior leader is introduced to the possibility that this approach may have outlived its initial purpose (establishing authority, for example). What impact does the leader see as a result? We know that as leaders rise in the organization, they begin to underestimate the value of affirming others' strengths. Comments such as, "I don't want to baby them by complimenting the things they are expected to do," could benefit from further inquiry about the mental models behind such thinking. Are they still relevant? What impact does the lack of positive feedback seem to have?

The crucial and often crippling assumption that becomes clear to LAP participants is that they can no longer delegate, defer, or demand development from others. They must publicly commit to their own inside-out development, recognize capability gaps and vulnerabilities, and engage the team to address the development process. The conscious awareness of the need for collaboration and interdependence is a relatively recent theme in leadership development.

Partner with External Coaches

At the top levels of organizations, if leaders have a coach, it is likely to be an external professional. While coaching within organizations continues to gain prominence, this does not hold true at the highest levels of organizations. Privacy concerns coupled with the legacy reputation of HR as somehow lesser than other leadership roles have created an environment that limits the comfort of top executives in formally seeking advice and guidance from internal coaching partners as compared with external coaches. Despite this reality, your relationship with a leader's external coach holds unique, powerful, and often unexplored potential to assist executives by way of a coordinated inside-outside partnership. You have cultural insights because you see the behavior daily, while the external coach does not. You can provide behavioral observations within the cultural context to fuel the conversations between the coach and the executive. Establishing an overt partnership with the external coach at the beginning of a coaching engagement proves to be an influential way for top leaders to learn about their impact and understand the stories they are creating. Establishing clear guidelines at the outset about what sort of information will be shared and with whom creates comfort for all parties so that they work together in the best interest of advancing top leader development.

Introduce New Information into the Conversation

When used judiciously, forwarding pertinent materials, from journal articles to blogs, can stimulate thoughts and invite conversation. For example, one executive who received an article proposing the ideal praise-to-criticism ratio of five positive comments for every negative comment responded with a quick e-mail reflection: "I think I function at work at roughly 2:1. Maybe closer to 1:1 at home. But probably 10:1 with my dog." This is a productive conversation waiting to happen.

The seed of new information around leadership culture can also find fertile ground, although the growth cycle may be a bit longer. Culture transformation requires leaders to evolve to new mind-sets in order to prepare for future challenges. The new mind-set advances beyond individual to collective leadership and invites long-held leader characteristics to be reconsidered—not a small undertaking.

Leverage Expatriate Assignments and Potential Promotions

Although senior executives do not typically come to HR for development (much less coaching), the unique pressures and widely understood challenges generated by an expatriate assignment can stimulate willingness to grow where previously there had been none. For example, Fidelity Investments, a large, diversified financial services company headquartered in Boston, established an expatriate coaching program for senior leaders offered by internal coaches to ease the transition, anticipate trouble spots, and work with candidates to mitigate concerns. The program achieved immediate acceptance, and executives embraced the opportunity.

Similarly, leaders in the pool of potential successors for next-level positions may be much more willing to seek input and feedback from internal sources. If approached for your thoughts, you have the opportunity to apply your keen behavioral observations and provide considerable fuel for developmental considerations. The key here is allowing the candidate to ask for your input rather than assuming the colleague candidate wants or needs it.

SOME PRODUCTIVE QUESTIONS

Carl Rogers published seminal research in *On Becoming a Person* (1961) to answer the question of how one person can help another person develop. He determined that a certain type of relationship can create within the other person the capacity to grow and develop. This is now commonly referred to as inside-out development. The key aspects that foster a learning environment can be reduced to the following essentials:

- Communicate a desire to understand and appreciate the other perspective.
- Provide structure; then listen.

- Focus on the present.
- Recognize when there is incongruence between experience and awareness (intent and impact).

Questions can provide structure that invites reflection and helps leaders think in terms of behavioral observations, which in turn allows independent choices. Questions can also sensitize leaders to the impact they may have on others by introducing consideration of a third-person perspective. Following are a few questions that we have found fruitful in our coaching work with executives.

Where does leadership reside? Or, What does it take to succeed around here? This question allows the mental model of successful leadership to be surfaced and explored. Is leadership seen as an individual expert, achiever quality, or as a collective, interdependent, and collaborative process? Perhaps it is viewed as existing somewhere along this continuum. Exploring the range of successful leadership blueprints expands the leader's options.

What is your way to manage anxiety, and how will I know? This helps the leader reflect, identify, put into behavioral terms, and make it acceptable to discuss vulnerabilities. This question also helps the leader acknowledge that anxiety is a factor affecting others' behavior as well. Daniel Goleman (2002), whose work in emotional intelligence has had an enduring positive impact on addressing workplace interactions, noted that anxiety often turns even the smartest person into a stupid one.

When you are at your very best, well rested, healthy, and focused, how do you proceed in this sort of situation? This question activates the coach inside the leader and reminds leaders that they often have solutions available to them if they allow themselves time to think things through. As with all other questions, you must remain quiet and allow the leader time to reflect and answer. As you become a partner in development, you get a lot of miles per syllable, so curtail the urge to expound, lecture, and tell.

What would happen if you did nothing about this? Responses provide assessment data about the leader's belief regarding the need to address the issue. If the answer is, "Nothing," you have data that there may not be sufficient motivation or readiness for change. But if a scenario is outlined that points to adverse personal, team, or organizational ramifications, the framework for change is generated by the leader—not by you telling the leader how to change. This creates ownership of the issue that can lead to enduring development. Don't back yourself into the position of pushing or pulling toward change. The leader is the driver.

What do people count on you for? This question elicits a frame of reference regarding the leader's perceptions about what value she brings and surfaces the mental models driving her behavior. If you experience different valuable attributes, your viewpoint expands the leader's perspective. Your behaviorally specific input, including the impact on you, is an irrefutable data point for the leader's consideration. ("You believe that your team counts on you to provide answers, yet when you asked their perspective in the executive team meeting, I saw more energy and ideas flowing from the team than I've seen in months.") You are not telling or advising but reflecting what you felt, saw, and heard. It is up to the leader to decide what to do with the information.

What do you think people call you behind your back? Occasional use of a lighthearted approach can provide a means to sample the accuracy of the leader's awareness about potential vulnerabilities. This may lead to inquiry about your perceptions and open up a meaningful conversation. Don't shy away from answering truthfully and with kindness when asked what you might call her behind her back.

Why does this matter? This is an all-purpose inquiry when a mutually trusting relationship exists and the conversation allows further exposure of mental models behind a leader's approach, action, or reaction. Stick with this one past the initial glib or deflecting response, "It doesn't," or, "Because I said so." Important questions need time, sustained attention, and your silence to allow thoughtful answers to emerge.

WHAT DOESN'T WORK

Carl Rogers's research also identified what does not work in the process of helping another person develop. Paradoxically, these are the very behaviors we repeatedly see in people first learning how to develop others:

- Being directive (telling)
- Giving specific advice (again, telling)

- Getting emotionally involved in finding the solution (telling with animation)
- Assuming a distant, distracted position (vanishing)

Although there are limited times and places where these behaviors may be called for, they are often overused as the default strategy when trying to get someone to change. These well-worn but ineffective strategies are difficult to let go since they are often the very strategies that helped create success in the first place. As any of us who has tried to break a bad habit knows, it is much easier to add a behavior than it is to take one away. So add the behavior of asking in order to let go of the behavior of telling.

CONCLUSION

Beyond anecdotal reports of satisfaction, qualitative research has demonstrated that formal coaching has positive effects on performance and skills, well-being, coping, work attitudes, and goal-directed self-regulation (Theebom, Beersma, & van Vianen, 2014). Yet since the internal HR professional is typically an accessory to the coaching of senior leaders rather than a direct provider of formal coaching, other avenues of providing support should be explored. Helping raise a leader's self-awareness by closing the gap between intent and impact, building trusted relationships, and having candid conversations has not been fully tapped as a leader development tactic by internal HR.

The transformational potential of LAP, as well as other senior-level leadership development experiences, can be extended by trusted HR partners within their organizations. Those partners can support the continuous evolution of the leader by using their internal reactions as data points and engaging in real conversations without resorting to the simplistic and often ineffective tendency to simply tell how someone to develop. A key opportunity for HR to support peak performers in successfully adapting to complex situations is to use behaviorally specific feedback and observations as a means of exploring the gap between intent and impact to support inside-out development. Recognizing that leaders are made, not born, your role as truth teller and human video feedback with benefits opens new territory for supporting leaders and the collaborative leadership culture they intend to create.

chapter
NINE

Coaching Your Business Partner

Florence Plessier and Monica Bortoluzzi

There are plenty of challenges to adding coaching to your repertoire as a human resource business partner (HRBP), but our experience across hundreds of organizations is that your impact can be dramatically increased in this way. We have seen both business performance and people involvement improved when the HRBP is willing to take on the challenges associated with the sometimes conflicting roles. This chapter is designed to help you think about intentionally incorporating coaching in your role as an HRBP. This will not be an introduction to basic coaching. Rather we want to encourage you to think about the places in your work that would benefit from conscious use of a coaching mind-set and behaviors. We assume you are already doing plenty of coaching now and hope to build on that foundation and support your further development through a detailed consideration of the opportunities.

In your HRBP capability, you have a dual loyalty: to the HR function and to the business you are partnering with. You add value by translating the strategy of the business into an HR and people development strategy, enabling the performance of the business today and tomorrow. While line managers may be accountable for the performance of their groups, your guidance and support enable sustained results and improvement over time. By developing managers to become better

We thank the many HR professionals and the HR business partners who have shared their experience with us, in particular, Philippe Brun and Michel Laborie in Europe and Jerry Yap and Praneet Mehrish for their Asian perspective. We also thank David Schlesinger for his contributions to our thinking.

people developers, you contribute to the retention of talent, support the creation of agile and responsive environments, and equip leaders and workers to address multiple challenges. Organizational change and people development are critical missions of your role. Coaching can become the key for enabling long-lasting transformation.

THE HUMAN RESOURCE COACHING LEADER

Coaching stimulates the person or group being coached to greater awareness, deeper and broader thinking, and improved decisions through insights and thoughtful actions. The essential contributions of coaching are:

- Creating awareness of the mental models used to make sense of a specific situation
- Exploring new perspectives that provide the emotional arousal and sense of novelty necessary to initiate change
- Translating intentions into action plans in order to maintain the focus of attention
- Creating the accountability and support mechanisms that allow individuals and groups to repeat a new action until they have developed a new habit

Individual and group change requires these elements, and significant change is unlikely without changes in how people think and act. When you coach in your HRBP role, you create the mental frameworks needed for change and growth. But you may think, *I have so many things for which I am already responsible. Where can I fit coaching into my high-demand world?*

It is not unusual that on any given day, you will be responsible for multiple, competing deliverables. All of the following (and more) could be found in a single day of many HRBPs:

- Preparing a review with your business leader of the people in your department
- Setting up a meeting with the business leader to discuss candidates who were interviewed for a newly created position
- Preparing slides for the talent management strategy meeting to support the business strategy at a critical turnaround moment for the organization
- Fitting a team-building activity into the agenda of a strategic meeting primarily focused on operations

- Reviewing the performance evaluations of key people and exploring developmental opportunities for them
- Being interrupted by a manager coming into your office to discuss a performance issue that she keeps having with one of her direct reports—or by the direct report coming to complain about her boss
- Chasing managers from the department about performance ratings so you can get raises processed
- Being asked for a meeting to talk about an individual's future steps or his resignation

Each of these situations could be approached from a coaching mind-set. Let's review the characteristics of coaching interventions for which you might choose to engage in as an HRBP.

Coaching Interventions Could Be Formal or Casual

Coaching does not have to be contained in a formal setting, scheduled in advance with a predetermined duration. Coaching is a certain kind of conversation for the benefit of the other person's development. As an example, your business leader wants to discuss the low performance of one of her direct reports. You engage in the conversation, listen to the descriptors of low performance, and start wondering whether the direct report has been given specific feedback and recommendations about what he should be doing differently. You confirm your suspicions with a couple of additional questions and realize that this might be a developmental opportunity for the business leader (whom you have noticed can be rather indirect and conflict avoidant). There are various ways to respond:

- Make the problem yours by proposing that you talk to the direct report and explore the issues yourself.
- Give advice, as the people expert, by telling your business leader to give the direct report clearer directions and feedback.
- Advise and problem-solve, almost as a mentor would, by sharing your knowledge on the topic and engaging in an informal conversation around the benefit of feedback.
- Use coaching skills to stimulate the exploration by your business leader about the issue using inquiry, active listening, clarifying questions, and surfacing

expectations and partner around the best solution to create a breakthrough for that direct report.

- Engage the business leader in an informal coaching discussion around what she would like to see her direct report do differently, what has worked in the past, what other behaviors she may want to try, and see her put together a developmental action plan for herself.
- Engage the business leader in a formal coaching process by giving her feedback about her indirect communication style and proposing some meetings to work on modifying her actions.

All of those responses might be useful depending on the situation and the relationship you have with your particular business leader, and each one will create a different outcome in terms of development, time to impact, perception that it creates about you, and results. None is necessarily better or worse, and the choice of approach depends on multiple factors. We define the last three as coaching interventions that are part of the developmental dimension of your role. They are coaching because the intent includes the explicit growth in capability of the manager with whom you are speaking and they keep the onus for thinking and acting on that person.

Coaching Could Take Place with Any Individual or Group

Many individuals and groups could benefit from your coaching role, and we explore them next.

Coaching the Business Leader Serving as a trusted advisor for the leader of the business can have maximum impact on the business itself—its culture and employees. You might be coaching him on one of these topics:

- Managing diversity to ensure a fair evaluation at the people review meeting
- Responding to conflict constructively when he strongly disagrees with peers for the choice of candidate for a new position
- Developing his coaching skills to support the shifts needed to address a challenging turnaround
- Balancing task and people focus in preparing for a strategic meeting
- Providing and soliciting effective feedback to prepare her for annual performance reviews with direct reports

- Influencing upward to support a needed budget request
- Determining a strategic versus tactical emphasis to address the collective feedback that you have had from her team about micromanaging tendencies

Coaching Other Individuals throughout the Organization You are often the person a management team member, a high potential, or any other member of the organization might turn to for developmental discussions. These provide opportunities to you to engage in formal or informal coaching conversations that trigger deeper awareness and new perspectives. Coaching conversations can be about career or performance issues, identification of development opportunities, or addressing cultural or personality differences.

Coaching the Business Management Team Team coaching interventions can generate tremendous impact for the organization. As a member of the management team, the HRBP can enhance the quality of interactions within the management team and leverage organizational performance. This can be done through informal feedback in team meetings, the facilitation of team development off-sites, or modeling a coaching approach using inquiry, exploration of alternatives, and a repeated focus on development.

Coaching Interventions Could Be Responsive or Initiated by You

Coaching may be appropriate as a response to a situation. Many such opportunities arise because problems have surfaced about the leadership of your business partner or as a result of regular 360-degree assessments. Nearly every major structural or business change generates anxiety and spawns problem behavior as people deal with uncertainty about their new roles, new responsibilities, and changing obligations. Leading from the coaching role can provide reassurance about the process needed for adaptation. In fact, these kinds of demands might be seen as a gift to you because they highlight the importance of people strategy in achieving business results. When you engage people through inquiry and invite them to think through solutions on their own, you create an open emotional space and underscore your value as an advisor and coach.

There may be days when the idea of initiating coaching conversations for development may seem like a distant dream, but it is in the strategic choices about these conversations that you are likely to have the greatest long-term impact. Affecting the needed changes in culture to support business transformation and creating the climate for true talent enlargement are the result of identifying leaders with the greatest potential for making a difference. It is in your initiatives that your value as a trusted advisor becomes visible and by which you plant the seeds for a developmental environment. When we reflect on the human resource professionals who have the largest influence within their organizations, nearly all have worked to engage other leaders in expansive conversations to explore their self-awareness, challenge their thinking to find more effective solutions to persistent business and leadership issues, and communicate confidence in the quality and value of those leaders' efforts to grow.

You may want to consider such questions as these when you contemplate the need for your coaching: How developmental is the culture of your company? How have you contributed to shaping your organization's culture? What behaviors do you want to be showing? What are the next steps that you could take?

CHALLENGES TO COACHING AS HUMAN RESOURCE BUSINESS PARTNER

You face at least three types of challenges related to roles, relationships, and skills when you want to play a coaching role more frequently. Do not underestimate these challenges because they can lead to serious problems if you are not well prepared. However, we think it is worth the effort to sort things out to make a coaching contribution. Keep that in mind as we acknowledge and explore the challenges that you might feel as an HRBP coach and turn them into success strategies that will allow you and your organization to fully benefit from the value of coaching as a performance improvement and developmental tool.

Conflicts and Limitations of Role

Prioritizing development in a business context is hard work. There are so many immediate demands on different fronts that we can feel inundated by the urgent and lose the important; fixing rather than developing; providing a solution rather than engaging the partner to explore potential solutions. Development is hard to position as urgent until its lack has created a performance issue. Even then, business drivers might push toward a reaction (getting rid of the person with the performance issue) rather than the developmental option. Time will always be a challenge. What would a short and sharp coaching intervention look like to fit the need for speed while being challenging and provocative? When should you advocate "slowing down to power up"?

Sometimes our best developmental intentions have to be put aside for the benefit of an urgent business concern. Talent choices require judgments about performance, fit, and readiness, and a developmental approach may be an unsupportable luxury at a particular moment. Development implies a strong willingness to fully engage in the learning process and that it is worth it the investment of time and energy. In your role, there is no time and space for development for the sake of development. Development has to be strategically included in the range of choices available to meet the needs of each day. How can you recognize the worthy situations and plan for incorporating developmental investment?

A further limitation related to your role may operate if the company leadership lacks a mature understanding of the value that professional HR has to the organization's success. Are you seen as a strategic partner or only as a support function and an expense? Is there a commitment to funding the continued development of HR business partners, recognizing that people strategy is essential to achieve business objectives? Many organizations still relegate human resources to fixing technical, tactical, or administrative issues. It will be difficult to have the kind of influence the culture and leaders need from you if your organization has a restrictive view of what contribution the HR function can provide, although this may be just the right target for your consultation with senior management.

Managing Multiple Relationships

Coaching manuals and certifying bodies list the quality of the relationship between the coach and the coachee as one of the most important success factors affecting coaching impact (Ting & Riddle, 2006; Habig & Plessier, 2014). What type of relationship does it take to feel comfortable sharing strengths and areas for development but also a sense of self, beliefs, doubts, and fallibility? It takes a relationship grounded on trust. There are some potential challenges for HRBPs related to coaching relationships.

Chemistry For some kinds of coaching or some types of coaching issues, the sense of connection we have with some people and lack with others may influence the opportunities to be their coach. As an HRBP, you don't get to work only with those with whom you have a sense of healthy connection. You have to work with everyone within your scope of responsibility. A substantial body of research supports the idea that outcomes are strongly affected by that fit between coach and coachee (American Management Association, 2008). The consequence is that for some people, you will not be the right coach, and you will have to figure out how to manage the mismatch.

Credibility and Respect If HR's utility is seen as limited to compensation, benefits, and termination procedures, it can feel like a large leap to the trusted role of coach. Also, if you are the first HR leader with coaching skills to work with your business partner, expanding the role definition may require some serious discussions and demonstration of value over time.

Competing Loyalties You will always be playing multiple roles, and they will sometimes be in conflict. What do you do when your devotion to your business partner is tested by her opposition to a significant corporate initiative? Or when he takes actions against staff that skirt the edge of employment standards? Added to these is the persistent problem of managing the information that comes to you. You will regularly have knowledge about a particular person or circumstance that has implications for choices that others are making. As a coach, you will hear opinions and intentions that could require management actions, but which someone may have communicated out of a false belief in your obligation to confidentiality. These are among the most difficult management challenges that you will face, and they will directly affect how you incorporate coaching in your leadership functions. Expressing the limitations of your role and clarifying your obligations to all those with whom you interact can be a burden, but the consequences of not ensuring that clarity can be extremely costly.

Are You Adequately Prepared?

Coaching as an HRBP ranks very high on the scale of complexity. It requires a high level of HR skills, business savvy, a high tolerance for ambiguity, systems thinking, plus a high level of coaching skills, all of them dependent to some degree on your coaching abilities (Ali, Lewis, & McAdams, 2010). It is only over the past decade that formal coaching training has been offered as part of the HR professional curriculum in universities and in continuing education. Before that, HR skills were focused on organization, performance management, and HR processes: compensation and benefits, recruitment, training, personal administration, mobility, and so on. With the emergence of talent management and the challenges around people engagement, developmental skills have become more prominent. Such skills include helping individuals transition, bringing out the best in people, providing feedback for development, helping individuals build confidence, and organizing developmental assignments. In addition, a significant number of HRBPs are not originally HR professionals; they come from sales, finance, R&D, operations, legal, or some other function, and when they were recruited, coaching skills were not necessarily explicit requirements.

We know HR professionals who have natural coaching abilities and have been practicing coaching without putting a name on it. Others have chosen to attend a course with the intention of developing a new set of skills that will enable them to do their work better. However, coaching is an emergent field, and those two populations do not necessarily represent the majority of the senior HR professionals. There is a large discrepancy between the depth and breadth of coaching skills and experience among the HRBP population.

As you reflect on your own experience, we urge you to explore issues of role clarity, relationship, and stakeholder management. The self-assessment depicted in figure 9.1 may be useful as a stimulus to that exploration.

WHY COACHING IS WORTH THE EFFORT

As you engage in coaching conversations, you develop deep relationships that can directly feed your credibility. Being acknowledged as a trustworthy thought partner increases your standing in the eyes of the business and the organization as a whole. By modeling trustworthiness, integrity, and credibility, you are increasing your stature as an HRBP and your potential contribution toward the foundation of a healthy and highly performing organization.

Your position within the system also creates unique opportunities. Given the nature of the HRBP role, you operate at the heart of the system, spanning boundaries between the HR function and the business. Interacting with the business most of the time means partnering with several internal clients belonging to different levels and areas of the organization (one of our clients, for example, was dealing with twelve functions and therefore twelve types of governance within a matrixed organization). Every day you are balancing the operational (e.g., local recruitment) and strategic (workforce planning, talent management, development initiatives) sides of the role. You understand the needs and goals of the different entities you are interacting with. You speak their language and have access to critical information, ongoing sources of feedback, observations, and a number of indicators that provide you with a unique view of the system. This knowledge feeds your view of the organization and can shape the coaching interventions to be attuned to your environment.

Figure 9.1
Self-Reflection: Assessing Yourself

Assessing where you stand will help you be more intentional about how you want to bring coaching into your organization and deciding how you want to grow and stretch yourself as an HRBP coach.

We are proposing that you evaluate your level of feedback and coaching skills, your experience as a coach, your level of confidence, and the level of support and endorsement provided by your organization.

On the continuum below, draw a cross on each line to represent where you see yourself and connect the crosses to obtain an overview.

Skills	No demonstrated skills	←——→	Masterful coaching skills as evaluated by a certifying body[a]
Experience	Never coached before	←——→	Coaching professionally for more than 5 years
Confidence	Uncertain how to start	←——→	Enjoy the challenge and the risk taking of trying
Organizational Endorsement	Top down, feedback, and coaching adverse culture	←——→	Coaching is formally part of your job responsibilities and part of the formal competency framework

Once you have connected the crosses, define your next step on that continuum, reflect on your strengths and development, and explore what it would take to bring you there.

[a]Coaching skills include building rapport, giving feedback, assessing and challenging the person by active listening, rephrasing, questioning, and providing support.

By coaching along polarities such as operational-strategic and local-corporate, you develop a unique understanding of the organization: its current and future challenges, the competing needs of different functions and business units, the key influential players, the hubs of trust (or distrust) within or across departments, the integration (or lack of integration) between populations belonging to different organizations, and so on. Because of that, you play a critical role in breaking silos and creating alignment across the organization. For example, you might find yourself exploring the perspectives of the site management team when interacting with the global head of the business and engaging your business leader toward more empathetic responses to corporate constraints. Or through coaching, you might have gained a deep understanding of the sales manager's challenges and motivation. When the business leader raises suspicions about the good intent of the sales manager, you might be able to use coaching questions to guide him toward a more balanced and positive understanding of his actions.

Specifically, by coaching across multiple organizational layers, you:

- Develop a broad and deep understanding of the organization that will allow you to act as a mirror of the organization itself during your coaching interactions. It will allow your internal client to explore his situation from new angles and viewpoints.
- Get a true sense of the actual climate and bring high-value inputs when the management team explores levels of engagement.
- Can diagnose the level of interdependence and collaboration across the organization and determine the specific interactions or individuals you could coach for maximum impact.
- Can partially map out informal networks and become the connector and the broker that generate alignment across the organization.

As an example of this last layer, you will develop a unique awareness about the informal decision-making processes and have a view on how collective leadership gets expressed or could get expressed in the organization. Because good networks tend to be structurally diverse, connect people across critical boundaries, and consist of quality relationships (Willburn & Cullen, 2013), coaching relationships within the system reinforce organizational health. Each coaching assignment strengthens the relationship between you and the coachee and increases the coachee's ability to improve the quality of his relationship with other members of the organization. As a consequence, increasing the number of your coaching interactions in the organization directly nurtures a higher level of trust, collaboration, and interdependence that will lead to better alignment, commitment, and possibly innovation.

As an HRBP, you have multiple opportunities to coach, and your unique position in the system gives you unique opportunities to add value to the business.

COACHING SUCCESS AS A HUMAN RESOURCE BUSINESS PARTNER

Let us turn to the lessons we've learned talking and working with HRBPs in organizations large and small across multiple sectors, industries, and continents. Common to the lessons we share is an emphasis on knowing your strengths and limitations as a coach, leveraging your position in ethical and professional ways, and persistence in developing your skills and contributions to your organization. These common elements have proven useful as a way of avoiding the land mines that organizational life can present.

Foster a Culture of Development and Feedback

Your position at the heart of the organization gives you the opportunity to become an enabler of a healthy, agile, and high-performing organization. Creating a culture of feedback can be seen as setting the foundation of an organization that learns about itself and therefore naturally adjusts, unfolds, and develops toward its full potential. A culture that values feedback permits the incorporation of coaching conversations across the organization. We believe that effective HR coaches recognize that they are coaching the organization and its teams, as well as the individuals within them.

CCL's research illustrates the correlation between high learning agility and high performance for individuals (Mitchinson & Morris, 2012). Research on learning organizations confirms that this applies similarly at the organizational level (Goh, Elliott, & Quon, 2012). Learning agility is much more than becoming more knowledgeable or skilled; it is about developing a bigger mind, being open and ready to challenge current assumptions, being ready to accept one's own limitations, exploring what else is possible, and testing new ways of making meaning. Becoming a learning-agile organization implies developing a growth mind-set. It implies accepting we are not perfect and that we can grow and explore what we don't know, as well as what we are not yet and believing we can change. Change is an opportunity, not a threat. As a consequence, the HRBP's unique opportunity is to develop the learning agility of the organization and its members. Modeling healthy feedback and encouraging a culture that promotes appropriate feedback can contribute to a more learning-agile organization.

We know how important feedback is for development; it creates novelty (new information) and emotional arousal, two of the essential components for strengthening the synaptic connections that are the cellular basis of learning (Siegel, 2010). Promoting feedback can be the first step of your coaching journey as an HRBP. An organization that successfully develops a feedback culture is one where individuals are able to express disagreement in a respectful and constructive manner. Expressing disagreement implies the ability to engage in a conversation that has the following qualities:

- *Perspective taking.* We feel that we can express our point of view and be open to exploring the point of view of others. We approach the conversation in a facilitative fashion that combines telling our point of view with inquiring about the other's point of view, holding back from coming to conclusions too quickly, and being ready to question our assumptions.
- *Solution focused.* By approaching the conversation as we have described, we may be able to quickly surface misunderstandings, identify points of agreement, or realize that an alternative perspective can be explored. We have transformed dissonance into resonance and are ready to move forward.

Another important purpose of feedback is to surface and reinforce what is successful and positive within the organization and teams and between individuals. A practice of mutual appreciation for what is working well helps us identify the underlying patterns of successful events. Over the long run, it allows the organization to learn from its own strengths and reinforce practices that add value and make a difference from a performance perspective.

You can support the shift toward a feedback culture in the following ways:

- Share with your internal clients your own belief about giving and receiving feedback—how important and useful it is to develop and grow as individuals. Discuss their readiness to:
  - Give feedback in an effective and constructive way

    - Ask for feedback as a powerful way of creating the right organizational climate for openness and learning agility
    - Accept feedback received as a gift with the objective of opening new ways of thinking
- Mentor and equip the team with a proven tool for giving and receiving effective feedback such as the situation-behavior-impact model developed by CCL (Weitzel, 2000).
- Encourage your internal clients to create a developmental network of people that they feel comfortable receiving feedback from.
- Ask for and offer feedback through your own observations as a role model.
- Focus on getting the buy-in of top leadership as feedback role models and develop processes and systems that support a feedback and coaching culture.

Fostering a culture of feedback and development will serve both your HRBP agenda and your HRBP coach agenda

Use and Demonstrate Coaching Skills

As an HRBP coach, you can safely use coaching skills for discovery and exploration in meetings and other interactions in addition to coaching conversations. You may use these skills to identify the best solution in partnership with the business rather than just giving your advice or opinion. Those skills are foundational and create impact, and they are low risk when used.

Genuine and purposeful listening will contribute to finding the best solution to the request and will strengthen your relationship with your counterpart, building trust as the foundation for true partnership. This stance has powerful effects in changing how you are seen and on influencing the climate in your workplace. Your ability to be genuinely curious about the perspectives of others and work to uncover their mental framework, as well as the value of assuming good intentions and competence on the part of others, creates a kind of microclimate that can spread.

Asking open and probing questions will allow you and your internal client to develop a more comprehensive understanding of a situation or a request, the actual goal, and the key drivers behind that goal. Sound questioning will give your internal client the possibility of exploring solutions from a larger number of perspectives. As an example, the head of production requests a team-building activity for his team to boost the level of engagement. You can ask open questions like these:

> "On a scale from 1 to 10, where is the team standing in terms of engagement? What would a 10 look like?"
>
> "What have you tried so far? What worked? What made it work?"

You both may come to the conclusion that the team-building activity is in fact part of a more complex and systemic intervention that may include these activities:

- Clarifying roles and responsibilities within the team
- Actively involving the team in order to prioritize the projects to be accomplished
- Influencing key stakeholders across the organization in order to get approval for additional resources
- Identifying an external coach for an ongoing team coaching process with the objective of rebuilding trust among team members

In those situations, you will apply coaching skills to the exploration of the topic versus the development of the person bringing the topic. Your intent is to assess and gain a better picture of what is requested in a consultative, problem-solving setting. It will help your internal client differentiate the wants from the needs, explore the current and future challenges that have to be overcome in order to achieve the goal, and identify the opportunities that could be unleashed once the goal is achieved.

Match Your Coaching Interventions to Your Level of Experience

Your next steps as an HRBP coach depend on your level of credibility and your experience managing complexity. Developing a feedback culture in your organization or using coaching skills to increase the quality of your interactions is safe and effective whatever your level of skills. Engaging in more formal coaching relationships across the organization is an endeavor for an experienced HRBP coach. Figure 9.2 provides a simple reference to matching the level of coaching to the level of expertise. As an example, a junior HRBP might not see how his relationship with a functional peer has a negative impact on his ability to coach his business leader. Similarly, someone recently appointed to an HRBP role might not recognize the ethical issues involved in conducting an assessment

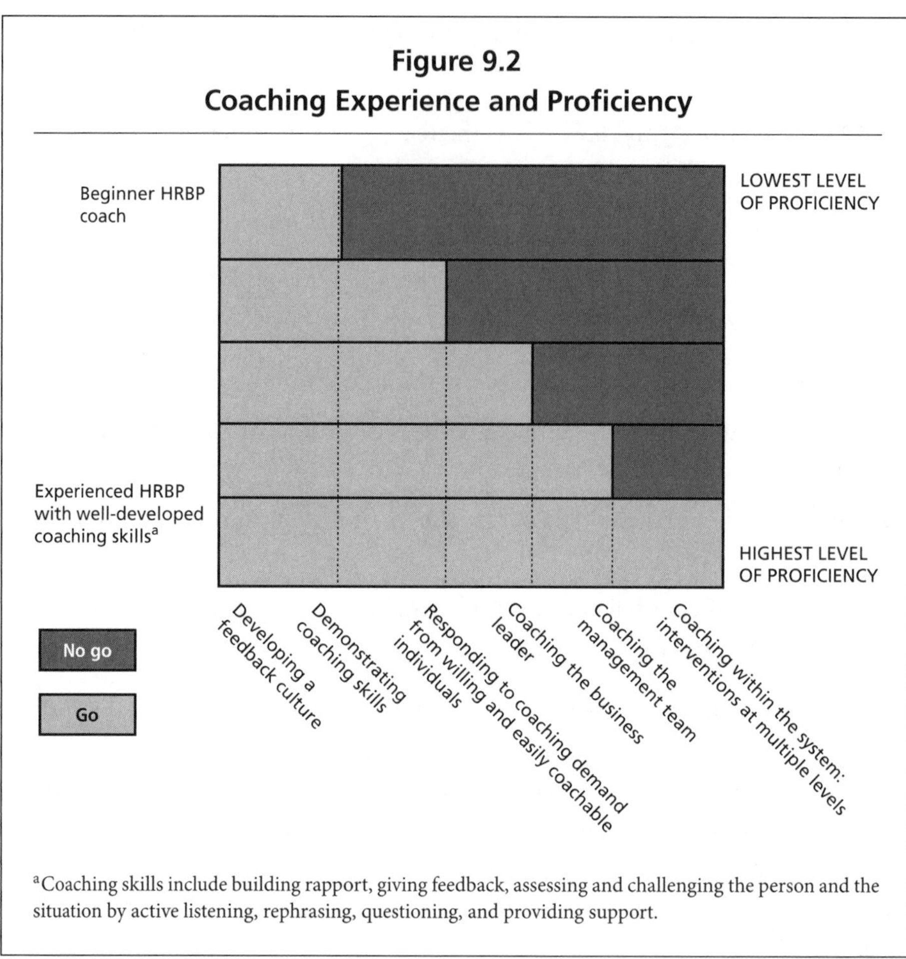

Figure 9.2
Coaching Experience and Proficiency

[a]Coaching skills include building rapport, giving feedback, assessing and challenging the person and the situation by active listening, rephrasing, questioning, and providing support.

debriefing for an individual just before facilitating a talent review meeting where that individual will be evaluated. In contrast, a senior HRBP coach would clearly see the power considerations at play while envisaging two simultaneous formal coaching relationships, one with the leader and one with the leader's direct report. Power, relationships, and ethics are key considerations when coaching as an HRBP, and it takes experience to hold them together while serving an individual demand. The more sophisticated your coaching and HRBP expertise and experience are, the more able you will be.

Accounting for that, we recommend that you systematically develop your coaching capability within the organization: starting with sequential interventions with willing individuals and progressing to multiple assignments with willing individuals with limited power connections before undertaking more complex situations.

Coach Those Who Want It and Are Ready

If you work in a large organization, you will have ample opportunities for coaching others. Ambitious early-career leaders will be looking for feedback and more visible developmental opportunities. Individuals at career transitions of all sorts will have questions about preparing for the changes and will be seeking resources for success in new stages. Workshops and continuing education experiences will often stimulate the kind of mental search that would benefit from a sympathetic and resourceful conversation with a human resource professional.

If you are not overwhelmed with your own unit's demands, the opportunities afforded by making yourself available to coaching those from other units may provide you with a relatively safer set of coaching engagements. There will be fewer direct conflicts of interest since you are not involved in performance evaluation and recommendations for advancement or compensation. However, even coaching those from a colleague's business unit may present hazards if you are not clear about your role and gain agreement in advance that information you develop will not be shared for talent management purposes. Be sure to formalize agreements with other HRBPs if you decide to pursue this avenue, and be certain it includes the proviso that the only person who can report on the coaching content or progress is the person being coached.

As a coach within your own business unit, you have greater leverage because you know more about the people and the dynamics of the group, but you also have greater complexity to manage as a result. The things you know may help or hinder the coaching and the functioning of the unit, and a good deal of the value hinges on your ability to be present to the person you are coaching while keeping the needs of the organization in mind. Be clear with yourself and those with whom you interact about your different roles and the obligations associated with each of them. You are both a coach and a manager. You don't have a choice to be only one or the other, but at any given moment, one may take precedence. When you are a coach, you can be completely present to the person you are coaching. You can be open and receptive to her point of view, even if it has serious limitations or is based on bad information. You can approach the conversation with an exploratory, inquisitive mind and let her discover for herself more complete, thoughtful, and useful understandings.

However, you are always still a human resource professional with legal and professional requirements, and you will always be careful to communicate how those requirements set limits to the coaching conversations and relationship. You will ensure that the person you coach understands the consequences of certain kinds of communication, and you will be certain that his or her manager agrees to respect the space needed for effective coaching conversations.

Avoid the Predictable Pitfalls

All HRBP coaches need to have clear mental checklists of traps that can sidetrack their work and relationships. It is quite hard to recover from broken trust, and being perceived as a lousy coach can have a negative impact on your image as an expert or a business partner. There are some unfortunate situations, actions, and choices that frequently derail the coaching enterprise. Here are the most common.

Losing Track of Your Responsibilities in Each of the Roles You Play It is so engaging and stimulating to coach interesting people and so gratifying to be trusted with sensitive personal and professional information, that HR coaches can forget that their first obligation is to the organization that employs them and those they coach. Alternatively, anxiety about the legal or interpersonal consequences of choices a coachee might make can push an HR coach to flee from the coaching relationship to the relative safety of procedures, rules, and self-protective stances. Keeping track of the multiple roles you play and giving each due respect and consideration is essential if you don't want to undermine all the good that can come from coaching. When should you be concerned? Here are some warning signs:

- You are losing sleep around conflicting loyalties.
- You are having trouble keeping pieces of information in the right boxes.
- You feel personally affected by the topic at hand, or your inner voice is talking to you about your own personal situation and self-interest while you are in the coaching conversation.

Not Every Moment Is a Coachable Moment Not every interaction should be open to greater awareness. There will be situations and people coming to you for expert advice, and you will have to make a choice about the most appropriate way to respond, acknowledging that coaching is just one of the possible responses. Your credibility will rest in the balance of satisfying expectations and stretching them toward growth and development. We recommend starting many responses to questions with a clarification of what's being asked of you and the role you will play. For example, say, "I would like to answer your question as an HR expert. How does that work for you?" Alternatively, you could say something like, "Whom did you come to see? Is it your HR expert for a quick answer or your thinking partner to explore options?"

Overreliance on Challenge or Support Beginning coaches tend to overdo it in one way or another. Either the coach sees the coaching job as upholding high standards and pushing people to live up to them or as warmly supporting whatever they have to say. In the balance of support and challenge, learning can take place. A coach who needs to be liked too much may dilute whatever value he would have by thoughtless affirmation and encouragement. Leaders seldom trust enthusiastic, positive reframing of all they have done. They experience it as patronizing and shallow. Alternatively, a coach who is afraid that her coachee will not show enough early improvement can be punitive or so tough that it undermines the confidence of the coachee, as well as the intimacy of the relationship. We need to constantly monitor the emotional impact of our interactions with those we coach and adjust it so the outcome is learning and change.

Yielding to Organizational Pressure Always having your internal client's best interest at heart is the sine qua non of the transforming experience that coaching promises. As an HRBP coach, that commitment may often be challenged. Your internal client's boss may put pressure on you to impose developmental objectives that your client doesn't want or ask you to report on what you will discuss. You may find you are being asked to take full responsibility for someone else's change or may be asked to coach someone who poses specific difficulties for which you are not prepared. No one will enter a coaching relationship with you if you cannot clarify and maintain the boundaries required. This may require constant revisiting with those whom you coach and their managers (or others involved) about the relationship and its purpose. It also requires that you persistently express the limitations of your role and the potential conflicting wishes with all.

Manipulating This happens when you have an answer in your head and try to drive the conversation through a series of questions to get your business leader to your point of view—through what she thinks to be her own thinking process. If you think the other person would not notice what is happening, think again! There are no good ways to hide that sneaky process from the smart people you are interacting with as an HRBP. Our recommendation is to commit to authenticity. If you have an opinion, share it. Based on your knowledge and experience, your opinion provides an enlightening perspective to your leader. Realize that it is just that, though: an opinion. It can serve as a platform for further awareness and trigger new learning for the leader as you explore the diverging assumptions and beliefs that underlie the opinions both of you hold.

The golden rule is to remember that just as an external coach must be able to recognize a pathological situation and step out of a coaching relationship that she is not equipped to pursue, the HRBP coach must be able to recognize situations where he would become the worst possible coach and bring other coaching resources to address them.

FOCUS YOUR ATTENTION ON YOUR BUSINESS PARTNER

Coaching the business leader and her team is the most important of all the coaching interventions that you can engage in and the most rewarding for its potential multiplying effect. It can elevate your value to the organization and create opportunities for you to increase that value. It can improve your business partner's ability to express his full potential as a leader and communicate effectively who he is, what he intends, and how he will engage his people to achieve their mission. It can start a process of organizational change that is based on the healthy involvement of the human resources within your organization.

We confirmed many of the lessons we've learned through years of work with clients and in a series of interviews with senior human resource professionals. They were unanimous on the preconditions for establishing powerful coaching relationships: chemistry and alignment on values, faith in each other's loyalty, and your partner's genuine belief that your only desire is to see both her and the organization succeed. None of those are likely to be in place when you join a new organization as an HRBP. Each one will require from you a conscious deliberate awareness and effort. As you succeed, it will pay in every dimension of your HRBP role.

It's not surprising how this takes place. It begins when you put your effort into accessing the human being within the leader. Start exploring and sharing each other's strengths and areas for development, work style, values, preferences, and vision for the organization. Some leaders welcome upfront discussions on the topic, while with others, you will gain understanding through informal exploration during work interactions. Your ability to sense and connect to the human being behind the role will play a key role in developing the relationship, as will your ability to talk about yourself and give the business leader access to your authentic self as she opens up to it.

There will be times in your career as an HRBP when the relationship will not work as you want because of chemistry or prejudices. We have all encountered individuals who believe that one must have a management (or a technical) background to be helpful. Female human resource professionals have also been faced with individuals who believe that women are not credible business partners. While such illogical beliefs could be swayed over time by experience, this might not be a fight that you can address and it will most likely eat up your energy. We must always exercise wisdom in choosing our battles, but some are worth choosing. Over time, the opinion of a reluctant business leader might be swayed by recurring positive feedback coming from peers or direct reports about the added value that you brought to them. Your credibility will grow as you serve others.

A successful coaching relationship with one's business partner depends to some extent on a partnership of equals. Chances are that the level of respect that you have for the leader will show in your interactions. Similarly, if you feel intimidated or inferior, it is likely that this is how you would be perceived. If you are ambitious for your business leader's position or if ego matches excite you, you risk a constant arm-wrestling contest where the need to be right may sabotage the healthy exploration of assumptions. You and your partner are complementary: the business leader brings an understanding of the business needs, challenges, and opportunities, and you bring the focus on the pivotal human factor.

Once the chemistry is confirmed as positive and the relationship is seeded, the next challenge is often to facilitate the emergence of the developmental desire of the business leader and establish a recognition of coaching conversations as a developmental tool and to gain appreciation as a coach. HRBPs inherit many types of business leaders: junior or senior, successful or potentially successful, a people person, or a statistical beast. Whoever they are, the organization believes in them, and they have already demonstrated achievement. How able and willing are they to learn? Your role as an HRBP coach will be to continuously nourish their desire to grow and become successful in different ways to cope with change, complexity, and the unpredictability of the business and the economic context. This is where seeking feedback from your business partner and gaining permission to offer it is foundational for further development. Introducing a tool such as CCL's situation-behavior-impact model can give everyone a guide to useful, actionable feedback that diminishes the emotional reactivity resulting when feedback is delivered poorly (Weitzel, 2000).

Recognition for your talent as a coach will happen over time, step by step. It will take many good interactions where the business leader can experience the power of your questions, the pertinence of your feedback, the care for him or her and the mission, and the depth of your listening. This will require active persistence on your part, scheduling time with senior leaders to ensure that leadership questions are added to the operational topics that can swallow up conversations.

Imagine yourself reaching the stage where you coach your business leader and maybe a couple of other high potentials from the organization. You are confident and clear in your dual role, you contract explicitly around confidentiality, you make yourself fully present with each individual, and you have developed a strong relationship with the people you coach. Despite all of these efforts, there are a few negative effects to this that are worth anticipating.

Be mindful that the quality of your relationship with your leader and the intensity of your mutual engagement are visible and envied by your peers or by others in the organization. That can create a distance between you and other organizational members. In the worst-case scenario, it might even result in being perceived as you and your coachee functioning as a couple against others. There are some ways to combat those perceptions:

- Communicate widely about your role and the various hats that you can put on and the boundaries around each of them in team meetings and individually.
- Engage in informal coaching with the team members who might envy the relationship you have with the business leaders.
- Promote the role of internal coaches and support other people to step into that role so it feels less of a privilege.
- Focus your energy on seeding a developmental—coaching and feedback—culture to transform a "taker culture" into a "giver" culture (Grant, 2013).
- Coach and develop your self.

Coaching as an HRBP is more difficult than coaching as an external coach or even as an internal coach from another part of the organization. That is because of the complexity and the challenges associated with being part of the system. Your impact and your ability to enable the transformational work at the level of the organization is directly dependent on your level of coaching skills. A good first step in your coaching developmental journey is using coaching skills and championing a culture of development and feedback to support your role as an HRBP and feed your perceived credibility and strategic value. Understanding how leaders and people develop, promoting feedback, active listening, rephrasing, and questioning seem easily accessible competencies for human resource professionals.

We encourage you to consider deepening your coaching skills for your benefit and your organization's so you can be a role model to the organization. CCL uses the simple RACSR coaching framework to describe the five components that are required to successfully initiate and sustain a developmental journey: relationship, assessment, challenge, support, and results. We have used that model as a map to capture the essential coaching skills where you should invest your developmental effort to become a confident and competent HRBP coach.

We encourage you to assess your current level of comfort (willingness and connection to your natural preferences) and competence (ability and performance) on the dimensions of our RACSR model (Naudé & Plessier, 2014). The importance of meeting regularly with a more senior coach in a supervisor relationship is becoming standard among coaches. Like all other leaders, HR coaches develop through experience, exposure, and courses. As a coach, you have a responsibility to become the better version of yourself and strive to access new level of development.

CONCLUSION

At CCL, we have worked with HR business partners from hundreds of industries and organizations around the globe. The way the HRBP role is conceived and positioned varies significantly among them, as does the use of coaching to perform successfully to support business results. Can HRBPs stimulate an individual or a group to greater awareness, deeper and broader thought, and wiser actions and decision making? We believe it can and that coaching is an essential lever to the individual, team, and organizational transformations that are at the heart of the HRBP's strategic role.

Being a credible HRBP coach requires personal attributes such as impeccable ethics, an egoless desire to be of added value and contribute to the business, a solid sense of self, and a belief in the resourcefulness of individuals and groups. How much the HRBP coach can achieve will depend on her fit with the business leader, her level of development as a coach, and how her efforts are supported or thwarted by the existing organizational culture. Adopting coaching roles in your HR work will have ripple effects on relationships, developmental climates, and engaged performers throughout your organization.

chapter
TEN

Cross-Cultural Coaching

Lize A. E. Booysen

If there were ever a time that leaders could ignore the complex interplay of cultures represented among customers, vendors, workers, and leaders, it no longer exists. No longer a true competitive advantage, the ability to operate in multiple cultural contexts and deal respectfully and sensitively with many cultures is now a basic requirement for all leaders. This is news to no one, but awareness of the challenges far outstrips the capability of many leaders, coaches, and systems to operate successfully across cultures. In 2006, when the first edition of the CCL coaching handbook was published, cross-cultural coaching was an emerging discipline in the United States (Ting & Scisco, 2006; St. Claire-Ostwald, 2007). In Europe, cross-cultural coaching was listed as one of the hottest trends by the United Kingdom–based Association for Coaching in June 2008 (Carter, 2008; Plaister-Ten, 2009), and it remains a growing area. Currently, cross-cultural coaching is still an underresearched area (Abbott, Gilbert, & Rosinski, 2013; Gentry, Allen, Wolf, Manning, & Hernez-Broome, 2011; Plaister-Ten, 2009).

This chapter explores cross-cultural coaching and covers a variety of issues of cultural diversity within the coaching context. I start by distinguishing aspects of coaching from cross-cultural coaching in leadership development, providing some practical guidelines for when cross-cultural coaching is indicated and how it can be integrated into human resource strategy. I then update DeLay and Dalton's (2006) discussion of coaching across cultures to address important issues to consider when coaching and the theoretical frameworks they considered. After this, I review a broad range of theoretical models and research in the field, then consider the implications for practice and the development of competence in effective cross cultural coaching. I conclude this section with an integrated process model for cross-cultural coaching, presenting the practical implications for HR systems and how HR leaders can build professional and systems capabilities in this area. In conclusion, I pose some questions for future consideration in the arena of cross-cultural coaching research and practice.

COACHING AND CROSS-CULTURAL COACHING IN LEADERSHIP DEVELOPMENT

In cross-cultural coaching, the coach helps the coachee through a process of assessment, challenge, reflective and reflexive questioning, and support to make sense of how culture influences his own beliefs and behaviors and that of others he works with. It also addresses how new cultural-rich meaning can be integrated into existing paradigms to enhance learning, understanding, and sense making and develop new ways of seeing. For instance, it can help expatriate managers understand their own culture and work successfully in the host culture and to help global leaders navigate systems of multiple cultures, including their own. Plaister-Ten (2009, p. 77) offered a useful definition for cross-cultural coaching: "Cross-cultural coaching is working with awareness of cultural difference and facilitating culturally determined steps." I argue that cross-cultural coaching optimizes cultural intelligence, agility, and humility through exploring an individual's cultural baggage and cultural, social, and personal identity constellations. The aim is to help leaders understand that what they have learned in their own cultures is not necessarily applicable in others and to challenge and support them as they integrate new learning. Cross-cultural coaching is a distinct specialization in coaching and can make a major contribution in enabling HR practitioners and organizations to prepare and support leaders and organizations to deal with the challenges of the multicultural and global business landscape. As with all other leadership coaching, cross-cultural leadership coaching is a meaning-making process in which the coach helps the coachee to surface and address deeply held beliefs and behaviors arising from cognitive schemas and frameworks. In this case, there is a particular focus on working with schemas shaped by culture and identity construction that underlie beliefs and behaviors that inhibit a coachee's performance in his or her current context.

When Cross-Cultural Coaching Is Indicated

DeLay and Dalton (2006) discussed coaching across cultures in the first edition of the CCL coaching handbook. They singled out two specific instances when cross-cultural coaching is indicated: when the coachee has problems managing effectively and some of the issues may be related to culture, and when the coach is of a different nationality from the coachee and the coachee's coworkers. I propose additional categories of coaching clients or situations that also benefit from cross-cultural coaching, specifically when identity issues around race, gender, ethnicity, age, and sexual orientation are at stake in the relationship: expatriate managers; managers working in international organizations; global managers; managers working in multicultural organizations; and managers working in a merger-and-acquisition environment. Expatriate managers need coaching to better integrate in new host national and organizational cultures and to help them reintegrate into their home countries on their return. Managers working in their own national cultures in internationally owned companies need to navigate multiple cultural boundaries daily. Global managers who work in different national cultures and managers working in multicultural organizations need to integrate multiple cultural and complex realities constantly, and managers in a merger-and-acquisition environment have to deal with different, sometimes opposing, organizational cultures in an adversarial climate in addition to multicultural aspects.

Cross-cultural coaching can be done as part of a specific individual's or group's leader development or as an integrated leadership development endeavor on the organizational level. Abbott et al. (2013, p. 489) proposed the following four areas where cross-culture coaching needs to be practiced:

- Cultural diversity within the practice of coaching and mentoring, particularly on the international level
- Coaching and mentoring in a cross-cultural context (e.g., working with executives on expatriate assignments)
- Coaching and mentoring in diversity and inclusion (working to celebrate and working with diversity as a resource rather than dealing with diversity as a problem)
- Culture as part of a global holistic approach, encompassing cultural intelligence as a resource and dimension of learning for coaching and mentoring situations

Frankolvelgia and Riddle (2010) described five levels of coaching integration in organizations with increasing amounts of complexity and penetration into the processes, systems, and culture of the organization (see chapter 2 for a description of all five levels). At higher levels, coaching is used as leadership development with broad organizational effect, that is, beyond mere education of the individual leader. Similarly, cross-cultural coaching can also function at different levels—for instance, only senior management, or only expatriate managers, or just the global marketing department or the international office. Essentially this is then cross-cultural coaching by exception, organized coaching for specific groups. However, cross-cultural coaching can also be used throughout all levels of an organization and be institutionalized in its culture. It can become a normal component of everyday functioning and even a driver of success in accomplishing the business strategy.

Jenkins (2006) argued that while business leaders do not need to be conversant in cross-cultural research and theory, in order to lead effectively they do need to know how to leverage cultural differences, bridge cultural boundaries, and avoid cultural misunderstanding—and cross-cultural coaching is one way to accomplish this. Rosinski (2003) maintains that clients in cross-cultural coaching relationships are invited to embrace cultural diversity and leverage cultural differences to the advantage of both the leader and the organization. The coaching implication is that while leaders do not need to know or understand cross-cultural research and theory, they do need to be aware of the effect that culture has on their own leadership and that of others. They also should know how to leverage cultural difference, which may require a certain level of knowledge about culture and diversity issues. A basic understanding of cross-cultural dynamics and curiosity about cultures is thus imperative. The implication for cross-cultural coaching is that inclusion of appropriate cross-cultural leadership content needs to be added to the cross-cultural coaching process, and coaches need to be knowledgeable in cross-cultural leadership.

How to Integrate Cross-Cultural Coaching in HR Strategy

HR practitioners can employ the following strategies to enhance a culture of cross-culture coaching in their organization (Anderson, Frankolvelgia, & Hernez-Broome, 2009; Booysen, 2014):

Strategic HR Strategies

- Link cross-cultural coaching to the business strategy by making a business case for cross-cultural coaching.

- Link cross-cultural coaching to individual and group development and performance needs, for instance, through relevant assessments, challenge, and support.
- Recognize and reward cross-cultural coaching behaviors at the individual, group, and unit levels.
- Specifically link managers' key performance areas with cross-cultural coaching competence.

Training and Development Strategies

- Train and develop key HR practitioners to do cross-cultural coaching.
- Coach leadership teams to be sensitive to cultural difference and to be culturally agile.
- Make general cross-cultural education, skills training, and development available to everyone in the organization.
- Make a variety of specific cross-cultural training opportunities available to fulfill individuals' specific training needs.
- Embed cross-cultural coaching in leadership development training and development.
- Develop cross-cultural stretch assignments to further employees' cultural agility.

Support Strategies

- Identify a pool of cross-cultural coaches to use as resources in the organization.
- Seed the organization with leaders and managers who can act as role models and mentors for effective cross-cultural coaching.
- Create cross-cultural boundary-crossing and bridging roles.
- Create safe places for dialogue, apology, and acceptance.

Process and Systems-Level Strategies

- Integrate cross-cultural coaching with other people management processes, such as talent performance appraisals and talent management.
- Audit HR and business strategies, and align with valuing cultural difference best practice.

- Create a safe working environment to deal with cross-cultural conflict, learn, and make mistakes.
- Create an inclusive organizational culture in which cultural differences are valued and celebrated, cross-cultural coaching is the norm, and the organization is seen as culturally intelligent and within a global context.

COACHING ACROSS CULTURES

Social scientists have still not reached consensus on defining the term *culture*. Generally it is used to refer to a set of parameters of collectives that differentiate the collectives from one another in meaningful ways and culminate in a set of values and behavior patterns. Hofstede (1991) and Hofstede, Hofstede, and Minkov (2010, p. 6) define *culture* as "the collective programming of the mind that distinguishes the members of one group or category of people from another." The Global Leadership and Organizational Behavior Effectiveness study, also known as Project Globe (p. 15; Chhokar, Brodbeck, & House, 2007, p. 3; see also House, Hanges, Javidan, Dorfman, & Gupta, 2004) defines culture as "shared motives, values, beliefs, identities, and interpretations or meanings of significant events that resulted from common experiences of members of collectives and are transmitted across age generations."

There is agreement that culture is always a collective phenomenon because it is at least partly shared by people who live or have lived within the same social environment. It derives from one's social environment. Culture is socially constructed. Leadership is also socially constructed and is not a phenomenon that can be isolated from other processes taking place in societies. National culture as a set of values, attitudes, and practices therefore includes those that are relevant to work and organization. These are carried into the workplace as part of the employees' cultural baggage.

Cross-cultural leadership theorists (Chokkar et al., 2007; Dorfman, 1996; Earley & Ang, 2003; Hofstede, 1996; Hofstede et al., 2010; House et al., 2004; Tayeb, 1996; Triandis, 1995; Schwartz, 2006; P. Smith, 2006) agree that there is ample evidence that cultural forces influence many aspects of leadership and that leadership is a universal phenomenon. The basic question under study in cross-cultural leadership is then: "If the phenomenon of leadership is universal and found in all societies, to what extent is leadership culturally contingent?" (Dorfman, 1996, p. 267). This question can be approached in a culture-free or culture-specific way (Dorfman, 1996; House et al., 1997). A culture-free, or universalist, approach proposes that there are universal leadership traits, attributes, behaviors, and theories that remain similar across cultures in the sense that they are comparable, though probably not equally important, across cultures. The culture-specific approach assumes that because cultures are different, leadership processes should reflect these differences and certain leadership constructs and behaviors should be unique to a given culture.

Cross-Cultural Theories and Implicit Cultural Leadership

P. Smith (2006) pointed out that the predominant emphasis in cross-cultural research has been focused on characterizing cultures in terms of values, with recent attention given also to shared beliefs. DeLay and Dalton (2006) explicated Schwartz's (1999) and Hofstede's (1991) foundational value-based cross-cultural frameworks, which explore societal-level interaction and relationships on bipolar dimensions. Schwartz's cultural framework explores individual and group relations, responsible behavior, and interaction with the natural and social world on the following bipolar dimensions: embeddedness versus autonomy (maintenance of the existing social order), hierarchy versus egalitarianism (how responsibility is understood), and mastery versus harmony (the relationship of humans to the natural and social world). Hofstede's (1991, 2006) revised cultural framework addresses similar relations and explores five bipolar dimensions: high-power distance versus low-power distance, individualism versus collectivism, masculinity versus femininity, high uncertainty avoidance versus low uncertainty avoidance, and long-term versus short-term orientation.

Project Globe (House, 1993; House, Hanges, & Ruiz-Quintanilla, 1997) extended Hofstede's dimensions and added humane versus inhumane orientation and high-performance versus low-performance orientation. The Project Globe cultural dimensions are outlined in exhibit 10.1. The Hofstede individualism versus collectivism dimension was augmented by the collectivism scale of Triandis (1995) and formed two distinct dimensions, institutional collectivism and in-group collectivism, and the masculinity versus femininity dimension was extended into two separate dimensions, gender differentiation versus gender egalitarianism and high assertiveness versus low assertiveness. Exhibit 10.2 provides some important caveats and practical implications of measuring and interpreting culture and leadership using fixed dimensions.

Exhibit 10.1
The Project Globe Nine Universal Culture Dimensions

Performance orientation: The degree to which a society encourages high standards of performance and rewards innovation and improvement

Assertiveness: The degree to which individuals are assertive, tough, dominant, and aggressive in social relationships

Future orientation: The extent to which members of a society or an organization believe that their actions will influence their own future

Humane orientation: The degree to which a collective encourages and rewards individuals for being fair, altruistic, generous, kind, and caring to others

Institutional collectivism: The extent to which a society's organizational and institutional norms and practices encourage and reward collective action and collective distribution of resources

In-group collectivism: The degree to which individuals express pride, loyalty, or cohesiveness in their organizations and families

Gender egalitarianism: The degree to which the collective minimizes gender inequality

Power distance: The extent to which a society accepts and endorses authority, power differences, and status privileges

Uncertainty avoidance: The extent to which a society, organization, or group relies on social norms, rules, and procedures to alleviate unpredictability of future events

Source: Adapted from Booysen (2007) based on original discussion from Dorfman (1996), Hofstede (1980, 1991, 1996), House et al. (2004), and Triandis (1995).

Exhibit 10.2
Caveats Using Fixed Culture Dimensions: Practical Coaching

- Cultures are not static; they are dynamic, continually evolving and adapting to changing contexts. The associated beliefs, values, and other elements of culture reflected at a single time may not be the same at later stages.

Exhibit 10.2 (*Continued*)

- Although cultures may appear high or low on a particular dimension in a certain context, this orientation will most likely not be characteristic for all issues or situations.
- There will be individual differences within groups and cultures due to unique personality and social identity differences. There may be highly collectivistic individuals within a highly individualistic society, for example.
- When using dimensions to differentiate between cultures, significant differences within cultures may be overlooked.
- Overlapping cultural entities within an individual's cultural identity structures (social identities), as well as cultures endemic to leadership (masculine leadership culture), must be considered.

While the dimensions are discussed in isolation, in reality they are interrelated and have reciprocal effects on one another, depending on the specific relationship or constellation of the nine dimensions.

These different constellations of interdimensional relationships will manifest in different cultural patterns and manifest differently in leadership depending on the specific constellation.

The nine dimensions can have an impact on and mediate the way other dimensions manifest themselves in a culture. For example, group work in a collectivistic culture should involve active interaction and discussion of issues because everyone should work toward shared outcomes. However, in a collectivistic plus high-power-distance culture (southern Asia, for instance), the group process is more likely to proceed with subdued interaction, a concern for expressed harmony, and a search for public consensus aligned with the apparent wishes of an authority figure.

National culture as a contingency influence on leadership is only one of several other influences.

Source: Schermerhorn and Bond (1997), Dorfman (1996), and Booysen (1999).

Cultural Dimensions and Coaching Strategies

Coachees can use these nine bipolar cultural dimensions to:

- Create a gap analysis of their own culture with some other target cultures by plotting their own and other cultures on the bipolar continuum of each dimension
- Predict how each dimension might influence leadership practices in their own culture or target cultures
- Plot their own "score" on these cultural dimensions and compare with the relevant Project Globe country cluster scores to explore how their own unique personality and social variables might influence their scores
- Identify the five major areas where cultural differences have an impact on their work behaviors and those of others on their teams
- Explore how each dimension can affect and mediate the way other dimensions manifest themselves in a culture

Following are some examples of powerful coaching questions:

General Questions to Create an Awareness of How Culture Influences Behavior

- How does your culture as an American/South African/Canadian influence your worldview? The situation? The context? The problem?
- What aspects of your national culture stand in the way of resolving this issue?
- What aspects of your culture can work for you in this situation?
- What are the differences and similarities between your worldview and theirs?
- How do your own cultural biases worsen the problem?
- What do you need to do to understand their culture better?
- What do you need to do to understand your own culture better?
- What assumptions do you have about your own culture?
- What assumptions do you have about their culture?
- When was the last time you were in a situation where culture differences or similarities played a big part? What happened? What did you learn from that? What did you do? What worked? What might you have done differently?

Questions to Ask When the Coachee Presents a Problem Situation at Work

- Now that you know more about your own culture and that of others, how will you react differently?
- How much influence does cultural difference have in this scenario or context?

Notwithstanding the critique against Project Globe (Hofstede, 2006, 2010; Minkov & Hofstede, 2011; Jepson, 2009; P. Smith, 2006), it is seen as the most comprehensive empirical cross-cultural leadership study to date (Triandis, 2004; Hoppe & Eckert, 2012) and is a useful source for cross-cultural leadership coaching. It is based on the assumption that leader effectiveness is contextual and that it is embedded in the societal and organizational norms, values, and beliefs of the people being led. The key research question was: What is the relationship between culture and leadership attributes?

Project Globe developed and tested the culturally endorsed implicit leadership theory (CLT), an integration of implicit leadership theory (Lord & Maher, 1991), value-belief theory of culture (Hofstede, 1991, 1996), implicit motivation theory (McClelland, 1985), and strategic contingency theory of organizations (Donaldson, 1993; House et al., 2004). In summary, the central theoretical propositions of Project Globe's CLT theory are that the distinctive cultural attributes in a given culture are predictive of the organizational practices of that culture and predictive of leader attributes and behaviors that are most frequently enacted, acceptable, and effective in that culture (House et al., 2004).

Project Globe was the first study to investigate implicit culturally endorsed expectations of leaders on such a broad scale and scope (Hoppe & Eckert, 2012). It investigated sixty-two national cultures and examined both practice (as is) and values (should be). It included 170 international country coinvestigators and sampled 17,300 middle managers. It used a mixed-method research design, including media analyses of unobtrusive leadership measures, in-depth individual interviews, focus groups, and survey research using a questionnaire that measured 9 universal cultural dimensions and 112 leadership attributes in each country. As one of the Globe country coinvestigators, I collected the data for South Africa (white sample), Zimbabwe, and Namibia and coordinated the data collection in Zambia. The most salient findings of the project are briefly summarized in exhibit 10.3.

Exhibit 10.3
Project Globe Findings in a Nutshell

Six Universal Leadership Clusters

- Charismatic/value-based leadership: Reflects the ability to inspire, to motivate, and to expect high performance from others based on strongly held core values
- Team-oriented leadership: Emphasizes team building, collaboration, and common purpose among team members
- Humane-oriented leadership: Emphasizes being supportive, considerate, compassionate, and generous
- Participative leadership: Reflects the degree to which leaders involve others in making and implementing decisions
- Autonomous leadership: Refers to independent and individualistic leadership, which includes being autonomous and unique
- Self-protective leadership: Reflects behaviors that ensure the safety and security of the leader and the group

Ten Country Cluster Leadership Characteristics

- Anglo: Competitive and results oriented
- Confucian Asia: Results driven, encourage group working together over individual goals
- Eastern Europe: Forceful, supportive of coworkers, treat women with equality
- Germanic Europe: Value competition and aggressiveness and more results oriented
- Latin America: Loyal and devoted to families and similar groups
- Latin Europe: Value individual autonomy
- Middle East: Devoted and loyal to their own people; women afforded less status
- Nordic Europe: High priority on long-term success; women treated with greater equality

Exhibit 10.3 (*Continued*)

- Southern Asia: Strong family and deep concern for their communities
- Sub-Sahara Africa: Concerned and sensitive to others, demonstrate strong family loyalty

Twenty-Two Universally Endorsed Leadership Attributes

Trustworthy	Has foresight
Positive	Confidence builder
Intelligent	Win-win problem solver
Administratively skilled	Excellence oriented
Just	Plans ahead
Dynamic	Motivational
Decisive	Communicates
Coordinative	Honest
Encouraging	Motive arouser
Dependable	Effective bargainer
Informed	Team builder

A leader with high levels of integrity, who is value based and charismatic and has good interpersonal skills, will in all probability be universally accepted and seen as effective.

Eight Universally Undesirable Leadership Attributes

Loner	Irritable
Ruthless	Asocial
Nonexplicit	Dictatorial
Noncooperative	Egocentric

A leader who is asocial, malevolent, and self-focused will in all probability be universally perceived as ineffective.

How universally endorsed and undesirable leadership attributes manifest behaviorally is culture contingent, and looks different in different cultures.

Globe found both cultural universals (convergence) and culture specifics (divergence) and grouped the sixty-two nations into ten unique regional country clusters based on their significantly higher or lower scores on the culture dimensions (exhibit 10.3). These clusters provide a convenient way to analyze similarities and differences between cultural groups and to make meaningful generalizations about culture and leadership.

The 112 leadership attributes culminated in six universal leadership dimensions that linked with the country clusters' cultural values and practices. Finally, Project Globe isolated twenty-two universally endorsed and eight universally undesirable leadership attributes (exhibit 10.3). Javidan, House, Dorfman, Hanges, and Sully de Luque (2006, p. 911) pointed out, "Most intriguing from a cross-cultural perspective, however, is the finding that certain aspects of leadership, such as humane and/or participative leadership, are culturally contingent." This is most important in cross-cultural leadership coaching. If universally endorsed leadership includes integrity, being value based and charismatic, and having effective interpersonal skills, what will the cultural manifestations of these attributes look like in different cultures? Also, how can this be enacted within specific organizational cultural constraints? Questions like these stress the importance of viewing cross-cultural coaching not as a one-size-fits-all strategy but as specifically individualized to fit the coachee's agenda, being focused on the relevant cultural contexts or issues, and taking into account the reciprocal nature of the coach's and coachee's respective mental programming.

Project Globe Findings on Coaching Strategies

Coachees can use the six universal leadership clusters and ten country cluster leadership characteristics in a similar way as the nine culture dimensions in these ways:

- Create a gap analysis of their own leadership with some other culture's leadership by allocating scores of low, medium, or high for each leadership cluster.
- Plot their own score on the cluster and compare with the relevant Globe country cluster's dominant leadership characteristics to explore how their own unique personality and social variables might influence their scores.
- Explore how the different combinations of low, medium, and high on each leadership cluster might influence leadership behavior.
- Explore the applicability of these leadership-style clusters in their own organization.

They can also use the list of universally endorsed and undesirable leadership attributes to:

- Shape and develop the twenty-two universally endorsed leadership attributes in their own leadership
- Explore what these twenty-two universally endorsed leadership attributes might look like in different cultural contexts
- Fade the eight universally undesirable leadership attributes in their own leadership
- Explore what the eight universally undesirable leadership attributes might look like in different cultural contexts
- Explore the applicability of these leadership attributes in their own organization

After coachees have explored their own leadership in relationship to the leadership characteristics, coaches could explore the results using the following types of questions:

Examples of Cross-Cultural Coaching Questions

- How do your leadership assessment scores stack up to the universally endorsed leadership attributes?
- What constraints do you experience in your organization? What can you do to change that?
- How do your leadership assessment scores stack up to the universally undesirable leadership attributes?
- Are there some organizational contingencies that force you to display any of the undesirable leadership attributes? What can you do to change that?

National culture as a contingency influence on leadership is only one of several other influences, as Tung and Verbeke (2010) argued: "In some ways, understanding intranational diversity can be more nebulous and challenging when compared with deciphering cross-national distance in cultural dimensions because so many (social identity) variables—such as ethnicity, age, gender, generational differences (for example, first generation Chinese Canadians vis-a-vis second and third generation Chinese Canadians), religion and so on—can come into play in affecting the values, behaviors, and practices of peoples within a given nation state" (p. 1266). It is important not to overemphasize national culture and to ignore the cross-cutting complexity of other social identity variables.

CULTURE, SOCIAL IDENTITIES, AND SOCIAL IDENTITY CONFLICT

I proceed by linking social identity theory (SIT) (Tajfel, 1974; Tajfel & Turner, 1979; Brewer, 2012; Ellemers & Haslam, 2012; Turner & Reynolds, 2012; van Knippenberg, 2011) and social identity conflict management (Hannum, McFeeters, & Booysen, 2010) to cross-cultural leadership coaching. I will show how SIT functions as the interface between the cultural level and the individual personality level of mental programming and meaning making and also explore the implications for leadership coaching.

National Culture, Subcultures, and Individual Behavior

Hofstede (1991) and Hofstede et al. (2010) maintained that human beings have three levels of mental programming: human nature, culture, and individual personality. Societal (or national) culture is layered and contains different levels of socially constructed categories, such as age, gender, race, and ethnicity, which in turn have socially constructed subcultures, such as the different generations, male and female, and different racial and ethnic groups that have significance to a specific society or national culture. Individuals within specific national cultures belong to different categories and subcultures and have unique individual and social identities that influence their behavior. National culture is but one level of influence, alongside a myriad of other levels of cultural influences. Furthermore, culture should be seen as just another contextual factor that needs to be taken into consideration (Booysen, 2007; Hannum, McFeeters, & Booysen, 2010; Lowman, 2007). There is consensus among cross-cultural theorists (Hofstede, 1991, 1996; Hofstede et al., 2010; House et al., 2004; Chhokar et al., 2007) that national cultural (e.g., Dutch, South African, Canadian) dimensions and subcultural (race, gender, sexual orientation) measures have predictive value on a group level but not necessarily on an individual level. On an individual level, personality differences are more salient than cultural differences, and personality is a much more reliable predictor of individual behavior than culture. While culture might be an important force in shaping identity and behavior, it is an unpredictable and unreliable factor in determining any particular individual's values or behavior.

In the same vein, Peterson (2007) pointed out that coaching essentially occurs on an individual level and culture does not predict individual behavior. Yet sensitivity to and understanding of cultural differences can be hugely valuable in coaching. While I agree with Peterson that understanding across cultural differences is valuable in coaching, I believe that it is simply not enough and propose that cross-cultural coaching needs to tap into other theories and models alongside culture theories to bridge this individual-group-level disconnect. SIT is one such theory that can be drawn on in cross-cultural coaching because it explains how individual identity (personal) and group-level (social, collective, cultural) identities integrate and views social identity as part of a person's cultural constellation.

Social Identity Theory: Individual and Collective Social Identities

Some of the most prominent intergroup theories explaining group identity effects on human behavior have been self-categorization (Turner, 1985), social identity theory (Tajfel, 1974), and the extension on social identity theory by Tajfel and Turner in 1979 (Abrams & Hogg, 2004; Ellemers & Haslam, 2012; Ellemers, Spears, & Doosje, 2002; Turner & Reynolds, 2012). Social identity is individuals' sense of who they are based on their group memberships. It is concerned with both the psychological and sociological aspects of group behavior and explains the psychological basis of group behavior, group association and intergroup discrimination, in-group favoritism and out-group derogation, stereotyping, and social identity conflict.

Most important, SIT describes the three psychological processes of social categorization, social identification, and social comparison that explain how people's collective or social identities are different from and integrated with their individual or personal identities:

- *Social categorization*: Individuals often put others (and themselves) into categories. Labeling individuals as black, rich, homosexual, Christian, female, lawyer, or basketball player, for example, is a way of attributing a host of group-specific characteristics to individuals.
- *Social identification*: Individuals associate with certain groups (their in-groups), which serve to bolster their self-esteem and define their behavior and to disassociate with out-groups. This includes a cognitive awareness as well as the emotional significance of belonging.
- *Social comparison*: Individuals compare their groups with other groups, with a favorable bias toward the groups to which they belong (positive discrimination) and competing with groups to which they do not belong.

SIT also focuses on identity management strategies to define own-group belonging and influence, perceived power differentials between in-groups and out-groups, or dominant and subordinate groups (Ellemers & Haslam, 2012; Hofstede et al., 2010).

Three identity management strategies can be used to create and protect positive social identities:

- *Individual mobility*: An individual-level strategy by which individuals may seek to escape, avoid, or deny membership to devalued groups and seek instead to be included in or attempt to pass as a member of the dominant group. For example, female leaders may start to act like men to be accepted in male-dominated leadership positions, or second-generation immigrants may mediate their low status by entering high-status professional groups.
- *Social creativity*: A group-level strategy by which group members redefine or reframe intergroup comparison by representing their own in-group in a positive manner. Examples are using alternative ways of measuring status (such as focusing on friendliness instead of material wealth), or including alternative groups in the comparison (e.g., migrants who do not compare their economic success with that of others in their host countries but rather with that of those in their country of origin), or changing the meaning of low-status group membership ("black is beautiful"). Both individual mobility and social creativity protect only the identity status of the individual in that particular devalued group, not the group-level status.
- *Social competition*: A group-level strategy by which group members engage collectively in conflict to change the status of a particular group. It changes the situation of the group as a whole based on social regulation or political pressure—for instance, gay marriage rights, equal opportunity, or affirmative action.

Social Identity Complexity, Salience, and Simultaneity

Individuals have multiple cross-cutting and intersecting identities (e.g., nationality, ethnicity, gender, language, profession) that they belong to simultaneously (Ferdman, 1995). Identities can be given and fixed (such as ethnicity and gender) or given and transitioning (such as age group). Some identities are chosen (e.g., education and profession), some are fixed (such as parenthood), and some can change (e.g., marital status). Social identities can also become more or less salient in different contexts and in different social identity relativities. Hogg and Terry (2000), Herriot and Scott-Jackson (2002), and Abrams and Hogg (2004) claim that SIT provides an explanation for changes in social identity: as attitudes about the self and perceptions of others about an individual's groups change, his or her social identity evolves and adapts in tandem. The relative importance of social identities varies over time and context. Ellemers and Haslam (2013, p. 391) argue that SIT is a metatheoretical perspective that shows "that in addition to the personal level of self-definition people may also self-define at the group level (and can switch between these different levels)."

Booysen (2007) used SIT alongside Alderfer's (1987) group-embeddedness theory and components of CCL's Leadership Across Differences (LAD) framework to describe the organizational leadership implications of social identity, power shifts, and fault lines in South Africa's subcultural groups in its transition from apartheid to democracy since 1994. Race is found to be the most salient categorization in the South African workplace (Bornman, 1999; Booysen & Nkomo, 2007; Booysen, 2007; Cilliers & Smith, 2006). Booysen (2007, p. 5) writes:

> Alternative social identities, like gender, ethnicity, and professional identity, seem to be embedded within the primary group identification of race as sources of intra-group variation ... For instance, a black female manager, who assigns primacy to her race identity, regards all blacks as part of the in-group. Being a woman and manager describes what kind of black person she is, what makes her more or less similar to others in her in-group category or prototype. This results in the African black woman manager feeling closer to other blacks than to other women or other managers. This dynamic is just more pronounced in contexts where some groups have dominance over others and where some groups are populated more or less prominently by a specific group of people, as explained by the embedded-intergroup theory.

Coaching Implications and Strategies

Coaches, coachees, and all other people at work have unique and overlapping social identity constellations; we all have in-groups and out-groups, or "us" and "them" groups. This dynamic is at play in the workplace and in the coaching context.

The social identity chart in exhibit 10.4 is a useful coaching tool that elucidates our social identity constellation and can be used in a coaching session or

Exhibit 10.4
Social Identity Chart: A Coaching Tool

Instructions

Creating a map of your identity is a way to capture and articulate how you see yourself. You can look clearly at your obvious, surface-level identity and then begin to dig deeper. This can be very useful in exploring how you and others perceive you as a leader.

Using the blank map, follow these instructions to map your own identity.

1. In the outer ring, write words that describe your *given identity*: the attributes or conditions that you had no choice about from birth or later. You may want to include your nationality, age, gender, physical characteristics, certain family roles, possibly religion.
2. In the next ring, list aspects of your *chosen identity*. Consider including your occupation, hobbies, political affiliation, where you live, certain family roles, possibly religion.
3. In the center, write your *core attributes*—traits, behaviors, beliefs, values, and skills that you think make you unique as an individual. Select things that are relatively enduring about you or that are key to who you are today.

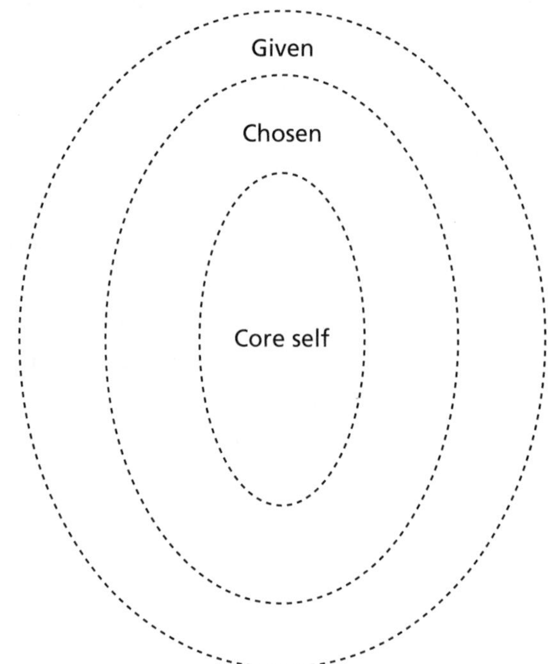

Source: Adapted from Hannum et al. (2010).

as a homework assignment between coaching sessions. Once a coachee completes the social identity chart, the questions in exhibit 10.5 can be used to connect individual and group identity to leadership in the organization.

In summary, SIT functions on both individual and group levels and focuses on cognitive and psychosocial processes of intrapersonal, interpersonal, and

Exhibit 10.5
Social Identity Chart Coaching Questions

- When you look at the identities on your map, what trends do you see?
- Underline the identities that are most important to you.
- How authentically can you live out the underlined identities in your work as a leader?
- What aspects of your identity help you make connections with people at work?
- What aspects of your identity get in the way of making connections with people at work? What gives you the impression that this is the case?
- Are there aspects of your identity that you keep hidden at work?
- What impact might that have on you and those around you?
- Are there perhaps identities that others on your team or your direct reports or peers keep hidden at work?
- What role do you play in their not wanting to show their hidden identities at work?
- How can you create a safer workplace for them to show their full selves at work?
- Which of your social identities have dominant power signatures and bear privilege—for instance, in business organizations, white, male, heteronormative, leader?
- Which of your social identities have subordinate power signatures and bear marginalization—for instance, in business organizations, nonwhite, female, homosexual, nonleader?

Source: Hannum et al. (2010).

group interaction and behavior. It also captures the socially embedded, situated, shared, social, group-located properties (including culture, subcultures, and other categories) of individuals. It should therefore be employed alongside cultural theories and CLT in cross-cultural coaching because it explains the simultaneity of both individual and group (or collective) identities by focusing on the variety of cross-cutting individual and group-located properties, embedded nature, and shifting salience and influence based on context. Individuals' relative positions in society are mediated by their multiple group identities, cultural constellation, and membership group's relative status and power differentials in society. Social identity is thus part and parcel of every individual's cultural constellation and includes national culture, group, and individual social identities. Finally, SIT can be used to explain social identity conflict and boundary-crossing leadership strategies to manage social identity conflict across cultures and in organizations (Nkomo, 2010).

HR practitioners need to be aware of how organizational structures, practices, and systems can marginalize some groups (out-groups) and normalize others (in-groups). They also need to be aware of which groups are privileged and included and which groups are marginalized and excluded and by whom. More important, HR practitioners need to know what can be done about this.

CROSS-CULTURAL COACHING: MANAGING SOCIAL IDENTITY CONFLICT

In a recent study focusing on leadership across differences, CCL researchers investigated how different cultures deal with social identity conflict (Hannum et al., 2010; Ruderman, Glover, Chrobot-Mason, & Ernst, 2010). This twelve-country research project included 2,803 survey respondents, 137 individual interviews, and 24 organizations. The study identified a framework for leading across differences, three role demands placed on leaders when dealing with difference, common exclusionary practices (or triggers) that spark conflict, organizational approaches to dealing with differences, and inclusive leadership strategies to deal with differences. This information can be invaluable to coachees and coaches in cross-cultural coaching. The most important practical applications for cross-cultural leadership coaching from the LAD study are summarized in exhibit 10.6.

Exhibit 10.6
The LAD Findings

- *Differential treatment*: Occurs when individuals or groups perceive they have unequal opportunities or are treated differently from the in-groups. The dominant and nondominant groups may have differing views of what is fair and just—for instance, where all promotions to senior manager positions go to white males or when there are salary differentiations along gender lines.
  - *Possible HR corrective strategies*: Ensure that everyone is treated equally, and take cultural and structural power dynamics into account when dealing with promotions. Do an audit on organizational practices using a cultural lens and implement unbiased practices, for instance, implement "same salary for same work" practices.
- *Assimilation*: Occurs when dominant or in-group members expect others to act just like them and to assimilate or adopt the dominant culture. This is perceived as intolerance of the expression of difference (through religious practices, food or hygiene habits, dress, values, lifestyles, and so on). For instance, a Jewish employee expresses concern about the company policy honoring a Christian holiday, Good Friday, as a paid holiday, saying that if the company recognizes Good Friday as a holiday, it should also recognize other religions' holidays, for example, Yom Kippur. Christian colleagues (the dominant group in this context) resent this perspective and believe that others should adapt to the traditions of "a Christian country."
  - *Possible HR corrective strategies*: The organization could honor both individual and organizational needs by changing Good Friday from a paid holiday to a floating holiday, in which individuals choose whether to take the day off.
- *Insult, exclusion, humiliating acts*: Includes comments and actions that insult or criticize one group relative to another. Offensive remarks, teasing, insults, slurs, and derogatory gestures are related (or seen as related)

(*continued*)

Exhibit 10.6 (*Continued*)

to a person's background or group identity more than to his or her individual characteristics. There are hurt feelings and people take sides. For example, an employee jokes about a colleague's ethnic background, tells sexist jokes, or mocks someone's regional or foreign accent.

- *Possible HR corrective strategy*: Do cultural sensitivity training, create a safe and fair grievance process, and appoint an ombudsman.

- *Different values or beliefs*: Occurs when members of different groups have fundamentally different values and beliefs: one group's "right" is another group's "wrong." Or when one person or group expresses values, it has a negative impact on another person or group in the organization. For instance, employees whose religious beliefs dictate that homosexuality is wrong don't want to collaborate with gay colleagues on a project. Or the majority in an organization does not want to approve medical benefits for same-sex partners.
    - *Possible HR corrective strategies*: Create spaces in which meaningful and respectful dialogue can take place, create safe spaces for civil dissent, and rely on leadership practices that are fair and equitable.
- *Simple contact*: When social tension is unusually high between groups, mere contact can trigger polarization and conflict. People of different groups feel threatened simply by being in the proximity of another group that they perceive as hostile. For example, Israelis and Palestinians required to work together in organizations might find it difficult to do so against the current political background.
    - *Possible HR corrective strategies*: Create superordinate goals for both groups to work toward so no group feels excluded or create a third-party enemy so that groups need to work together to accomplish their goals.

The LAD framework shown in figure 10.1 is based on the metaphor of geological fault lines that create friction when the boundaries rub against each other. Lau and Murnighan (1998, 2005) brought the fault-line analogy into leadership studies and explained it as hypothetical dividing lines that can split organizations into "us" and "them" groups.

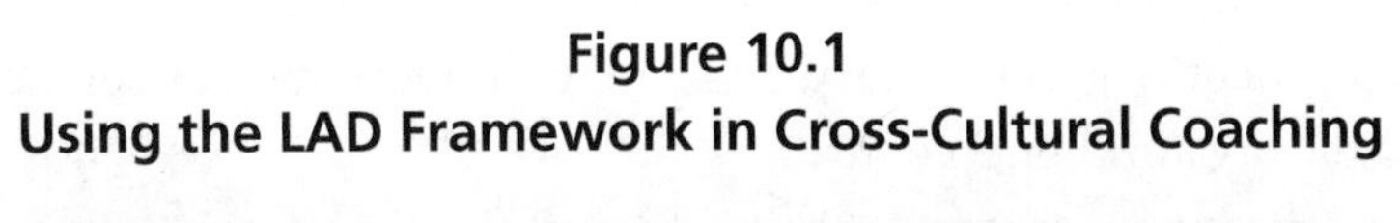

Figure 10.1
Using the LAD Framework in Cross-Cultural Coaching

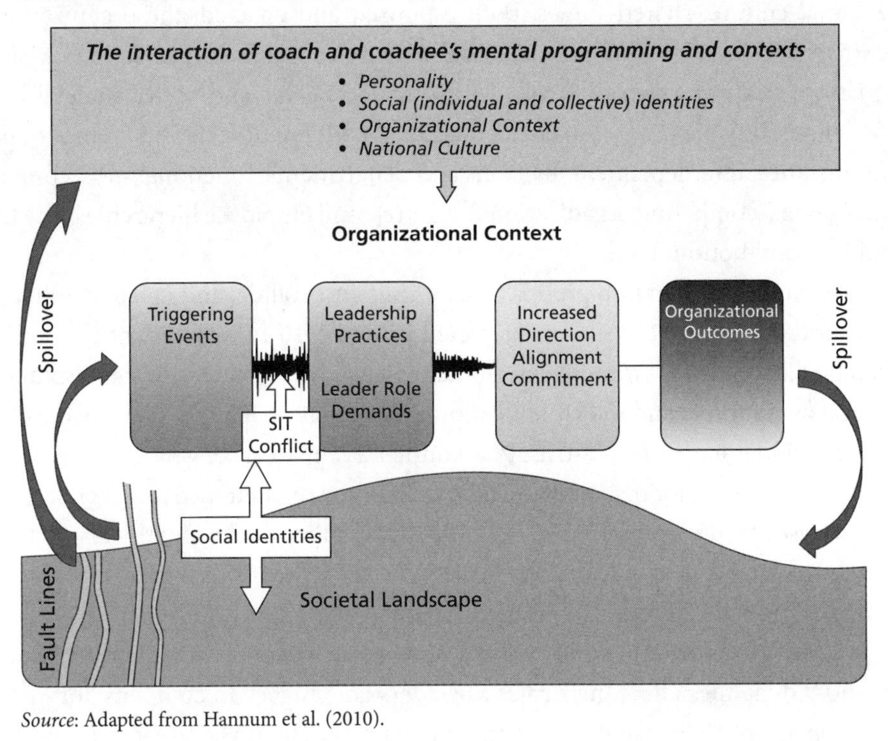

Source: Adapted from Hannum et al. (2010).

In a cross-cultural coaching context, this framework can be a valuable coaching tool to help coachees understand the different dynamics at play of individual and collective social identities and national culture—their own and that of other individuals, groups, or cultures they interact with. The framework also highlights how societal contextual factors and fault lines affect leadership and organizational practices.

The LAD framework suggests that these fault lines (subgroupings such as national culture, race, gender, language, and religion) function on the societal level and spill over into the organizational context. The societal landscape (which includes the demographic, historic, social, legal, and political contexts) influences leaders' and followers' social identity development and awareness, which they carry into their organizational context and specifically leadership practices and expectations. In other words, aspects such as who are the in-groups and out-groups, identity group history, and intergroup anxiety and conflict all spill over into the organizational context.

The organizational context is the next layer of influences. It includes organizational culture; shared values, both espoused and enacted; the organizational climate and practices; human and other resources; and the organization's, vision, mission, strategy, strategic intent, and practices. Over and above societal-level fault lines, organizations also create their own fault lines (or us and them groups), for instance, interdependent divisions and departments, functional silos, competitive teams, competing organizational cultures, and employee hierarchies (the top, middle, and bottom levels).

The fault lines can pull groups apart, grind and collide, and create conflict, or social identity conflict (SIC), as depicted in figure 10.1. Social identity conflicts can be distinguished from interpersonal conflicts by the nature of the disputants' causal attributions and the amplification of the event to a larger collective. When an individual and others attribute a conflict event to race, gender, religion, or sexual preference, for instance, and take sides based on their own race, gender, religion, or sexual preference, it is a social identity conflict. Social identity conflicts are rooted in threats to people's collective need for dignity, safety, recognition, control, and purpose (Haslam, 2001; Simon & Klandermans, 2001; Rothman, 1997).

Leaders and HR practitioners alike need to be aware of how their own social identity dynamics affect their roles as leaders and engage in compensatory practices so as not to be caught up in these dynamics. The LAD research found that leaders and HR practitioners are:

- Often pulled in many directions between conflicting intergroup values, viewpoints, and beliefs. Inclusive leaders need to be unbiased and not influenced by their own, or their group's, values and viewpoints and need to be respectful of everyone's needs and viewpoints.
- Commonly pushed to one side. By definition, a leader is a member of some groups and not others. Groups form perceptions of a leader based solely on social identity grouping. An inclusive leader will focus on practices of fairness and equity to show that he or she is not partial to his or her own group.
- All too frequently caught out of the loop. This is in part due to information filtering, but also in part due to the leader's lack of critical awareness concerning social identity dynamics. Inclusive leaders need to be sensitive to group

dynamics, create an environment of trust and safety, and be accessible in order to be in the loop.

The triggering events in figure 10.1 refer to actions or a series of actions that make social identity inequity or inequality noticeable and can spark social identity conflict. Leaders can engage in effective leadership and HR practices to deal with these social identity conflicts in order to get increased direction, alignment, and commitment from everyone, contributing to positive organizational outcomes. Examples of the five common triggering events and possible HR corrective strategies are discussed in exhibit 10.6.

Best Practice Leadership and HR Strategies for Dealing with Group Difference

The LAD project identified three common approaches organizations used to deal with difference throughout all twelve countries: hands off, direct and control, and cultivate and encourage.

The least effective approach is the hands-off approach, which is based on the assumption that it is not the responsibility of the workplace to deal with issues of difference. In practice, this approach can include doing nothing, letting the situation resolve on its own, denial of the problem, being paralyzed by fear of doing the wrong thing, or not acknowledging conflict. These responses result in blaming the victim or the whistle-blower who identifies potential triggers and venting of emotions without taking action. So more often than not, the conflict and exclusion are just being swept under the rug or left to fester. In South Africa this do-nothing approach is referred to as *ostrich leadership*: managers hide their heads in the sand when there is danger. If they cannot see or hear the danger, they do not have to deal with it because, according to them, it does not exist.

Some direct-and-control approaches, in which authority and organizational rules and regulations are used to manage relationships, are also used to deal with difference. In essence, these practices do not necessarily have to lead to exclusion, provided that the authority, policies, rules, and regulations do not favor one group above another. If cultural inclusion has been institutionalized, these rules and regulations can be valuable tools toward inclusive leadership practice.

Examples of direct-and-control approaches include policies punishing discrimination and harassment and incentivizing equal treatment, performance management systems based on fairness, formalized conflict-management procedures providing fair systems for complaints, and published codes of conduct based on fairness and inclusion.

The underlying assumption of cultivate-and-encourage approaches is that encouraging inclusion, cross-group relationships, and understanding across difference will enhance the viability of the organization — for example:

- Building inclusive organizations through training and development to create awareness and value diversity
- Creating boundary-crossing and bridging roles
- Instilling a climate of respect, equality, and fairness
- Cross-cultural mentoring
- Creating safe spaces for dialogue, apology, and acceptance
- Boundary-spanning leadership practices

Ruderman et al. (2010) identify four key boundary-spanning leadership practices that can be practiced formally by the organization, the leader, or HR or informally by individuals, and can also be used in combination to be even more effective: recategorization or boundary reframing, decategorization or boundary suspending, cross-cutting or boundary weaving, and subcategorization or boundary nesting.

Recategorization or Boundary Reframing These practices emphasize a superordinate identity or set of goals that is inclusive across social groups. For instance, teachers in an environmental school in Israel bring together Israeli and Palestinian teenagers to work together on preserving common natural resources, therefore encouraging the two groups to recategorize each other as stewards of a shared natural resource. Other examples of boundary-reframing tactics include:

- Emphasizing a common destiny or identity such as professional identity (we are all engineers, lawyers, psychologists, or teachers)
- Encouraging all groups to pursue a shared, overarching goal or an all-inclusive organizational mission that brings people together across social identities
- Identifying and facing a competitor common enemy that bonds employees toward the common goal of profitability
- Forging a new identity that transcends differences, for instance, the Rainbow Nation in South Africa or the American Dream.

Decategorization or Boundary Suspending These are practices that emphasize person-based interactions rather than identity group interactions. They are geared toward removing stereotypical categories, maximizing interpersonal relations, and minimizing group differences. For example, a leader in a South African bank uses informal company events to encourage interaction between the black majority and the white minority, who lived in relative isolation and seclusion during apartheid. Other examples of boundary suspending are fostering cross-group friendships through social events, community projects, or "third spaces." Third spaces are neutral zones, where neither of the conflicting parties are in a power position based on space and logistics; examples are meeting places outside the offices of either party or corners and nooks in the organization that are in a neutral space. Third spaces can be physical or virtual or even embedded in shared mental experiences, for instance, shared ideas and ideals—or a combination of these, so that members from different groups can see each other as individuals rather than belonging to a specific group. In addition, dialogue circles can be used to explore individual difference in group belonging.

Cross-Cutting or Boundary Weaving This is a strategy to structure groups so that fault lines that may cause conflict are less obvious. Work teams, for example, are deliberately composed to break down existing fault lines and to have a maximum mix of difference and deliberate mix across boundaries. These practices systematically cross work group roles (job level or occupation) with social identity group membership. For example, the leaders of a US nonprofit sponsors a roundtable forum composed of employees of all levels and social and cultural groups. The forum increases interaction while acting in an advisory capacity on HR and employee practices across boundaries. Other examples are composing a management team that reflects the identities of more than just the dominant group, cutting across the different fault lines; job rotation strategies; virtual teams; and cultural immersion exercises.

Subcategorization or Boundary Nesting These practices structure interactions so that social groups have both distinct and interdependent identities. Groups are valued for their unique contribution and brought together in service of a larger superordinate goal. These practices recognize subgroup membership within a larger organizational context and allow identity groups to be recognized and supported within the context of the larger organization and multiple group belonging. For example, a multinational electronic company creates affinity groups for nondominant or nontraditional groups in which employees have an opportunity to have a voice as a unique group and at the same time contribute to the organizational goals. Other examples of boundary nesting are creating affinity groups for minorities in which social groups have a unique voice as members and input is linked to larger organizational goals (e.g., a professional network of HR practitioners gives expert advice to those in core functions of a manufacturing organization), and promoting events that celebrate the cultures or perspectives of different social identity groups while appreciating similarities and communities of practice.

While organizational contexts usually mirror societal SIC, they also have their fair share of organization-specific SIC. Boundary spanning and inclusive leadership practices can mediate this SIC and exclusive leadership practices can exacerbate it. Leadership actions intending to prevent or resolve SIC can be formal or informal and on individual, group, or organizational levels. Finally, as the right arrow indicates in figure 10.1, there is also a counter spillover or spill back to the societal level from the organizational context.

In conclusion I agree with Reicher, Haslam, and Hopkins (2005) that "leadership is not simply a matter of leaders, or even of leaders and followers ... Rather it has to do with the relationship between leaders and followers within a social group" (p. 566). What needs to be added is that leadership also functions within a specific organizational and societal and national culture context.

Coaching Implications and Questions

I added the top section of figure 10.1 to the original LAD framework to speak specifically to the interaction of the coach and coachee's mental programming and contexts and how that might influence and affect the coaching relationship. Note that the same fault lines that influence the organizational context and inform the triggers that spark SIC also influence the coaching context and have the potential to spark conflict in the coaching relationship. Most important, this will affect the coaching process, focus, and content and certainly the effectiveness of the coaching process. It is therefore imperative in cross-cultural coaching to explore the social identity differences and similarities and possible fault lines that exist in the coaching relationship and also how the social identity constellation of the coachee might affect his or her leadership effectiveness. The use of the self as a coaching instrument in this instance can also be extremely powerful.

Further aspects coaches can explore with their coachees might be these:

- The influence of the leadership role demands on leaders' decisions and practices
- How coachees' individual and collective identities integrate with their culture and organization membership
- How fault lines in their own lives influence their behavior and that of other individuals, groups, and cultures they work with
- Which boundary-spanning practices can be implemented in their organizations to bridge differences
- How to focus more on the similarities in different social identity constellations in order to build alliances, rather than on the differences, which has the potential to cause conflict

Examples of Coaching Questions Targeting Differences

- What can you do to break down some of the fault lines in your team?
- How is your behavior feeding into these fault lines?
- How do existing fault lines in your organization feed into the conflict situation at hand?
- Now that you know more about the leader role demands in leading difference, what will you do differently?

APPLICATION OF CROSS-CULTURAL COACHING MODELS

DeLay and Dalton (2006) gave a comprehensive overview of existing cross-cultural coaching in the first edition of the CCL coaching handbook. Rosinski (2003), Rosinski and Abbott (2006), and Abbott et al. (2013) gave comprehensive overviews of the field of cross-cultural work in coaching and mentoring. Abbott, Stening, Atkins, and Grant (2006) gave a comprehensive discussion of coaching expatriate managers for success.

Rather than presenting another overview in this section, I introduce two new developments in cross-cultural coaching and applications, culture intelligence (CQ) and global mind-sets, and focus on the application of some of the dominant coaching models (Abbott et al. 2006, 2013; Frankovelgia & Riddle, 2010; Plaister-Ten, 2009; Rosinski, 2003). I conclude this section with an integrated framework for developing cultural cross-cultural leadership understanding, or cultural agility, that can be used as a guiding tool in cross-cultural coaching.

Cultural Intelligence

Although most human behavior is embedded in internalized cultural socialization, to a large extent people can step outside their cultural frameworks into other cultural frameworks in order to understand one another better and adapt to different environments and situations. Offerman and Phan (2002), Earley and Peterson (2004), and Van Dyne, Ang, and Livermore (2010) refer to this ability to function successfully in environments where individuals have experienced different programming as cultural intelligence. CQ, they argue, is the capacity to leave behind those intelligent behaviors learned in one cultural context when what is intelligent in another cultural context differs.

Cultural intelligence builds on and extends Goleman's (2002) notion of emotional intelligence and focuses one's capability on effectively understanding and adapting to myriad cultural contexts as an essential skill set needed to lead effectively across cultures. CQ is based on these characteristics:

- *Self-awareness*—understanding the impact of one's own culture and background in terms of the values and biases one brings to the workplace
- *Social awareness*—understanding others and their comparable values, biases, and expectations to manage multiple social realities
- *Behavioral adaptability*—the ability to display appropriate, adaptable, and flexible behaviors and expectations in cross-cultural situations

CQ is in essence the ability to function effectively in a diverse context where the assumptions, values, and traditions of one's upbringing are not uniformly shared with those with whom one works. CQ is a highly useful concept in cross-cultural coaching, (Abbott et al., 2013), and it is malleable and can change based on multicultural experience and cultural exposure (Erez et al., 2013). CQ offers a set of steps and capabilities that allow us to show respect and dignity for others while enhancing our own effectiveness and competitive edge in multicultural and global contexts. Exhibit 10.7 sets out four practical steps toward enhancing CQ through coaching.

Global Mind-Sets

A concept that links closely with CQ is global mind-sets. A global mind-set rests on open-mindedness and a deep awareness of diversity across cultures, combined with the capability of integrating and synthesizing the polarities and cognitive complexities of these diverse viewpoints (Gupta & Govindarajan, 2002; Mosakowski, Calic, & Earley, 2013; Rhinesmith, 1992).

Exhibit 10.7
Building CQ through Coaching

Although the four factors of cultural intelligence do not always develop in one particular order, it can be helpful to think about the four factors of CQ as four steps toward enhanced overall cultural intelligence that can be developed through cross-cultural coaching. Cross-cultural coaches can help coachees to identify, set goals, reframe, and reflect to build CQ.

Step 1: Motivational CQ (drive) gives us the energy and self-confidence to pursue the cultural understanding and planning. The capability to direct attention to cope with ambiguous and unfamiliar cultural situations can be shaped by expatriation, stretch assignments, working in a diverse workforce, and working across boundaries.

Step 2: Cognitive CQ (knowledge) provides us with an understanding of basic cultural cues through, for example, relevant prescribed readings (e.g., this chapter on cross-cultural coaching) or country-specific information for expatriate managers. Testing out of basic cultural assumptions in a safe space can enhance cognitive CQ.

Step 3: Metacognitive CQ (strategy) allows us to draw on our cultural understanding so we can plan and interpret what's going on in diverse contexts. Journaling and reflective and reflexive practice can help coachees to plan, monitor, and revise mental models. Continuous questioning of one's own cultural assumptions is key in this step.

Step 4: *Behavioral CQ* (action) provides us with the ability to engage in effective flexible leadership across cultures. It draws on our interest (drive) and understanding (knowledge and strategy) in order to behave culturally appropriately. Practicing new skills, reporting and reflecting on outcomes of new practices, and situation-behavior-impact analyses can shape new behaviors and action.

Source: Adapted from Van Dyne et al. (2010).

Javidan, Teagarden, and Bowden (2010) interviewed over two hundred global executives and surveyed over six thousand managers and identified a set of individual qualities that are critical for the leaders of tomorrow, which they called a global mind-set. Leaders with a global mind-set are knowledgeable about cultures and doing business in the global arena. They understand the political, economic, social, technological, legal, and environmental (PESTLE) systems in other countries and understand how their global industry works. They are passionate about leveraging diversity and are willing to step out of their own comfort zones and stretch themselves. They can hold the tensions of polarities—they are comfortable with being uncomfortable in uncomfortable environments. They are relational and able to build trusting relationships with people who are different from them by showing dignity, respect, and empathy, and they have good listening skills.

Having a global mind-set, according to Javidan et al. (2010) and Javidan and Walker (2013), requires three qualities:

- *Global intellectual capital*—a manager's knowledge base and how he or she leverages it; global business savvy and competence, cognitive complexity, and cosmopolitan outlook
- *Global psychological capital*—a manager's willingness to engage in a global environment: passion for diversity, adaptability, optimism, quest for adventure, resilience, self-assurance, and confidence
- *Global social capital*—intercultural empathy, cultural sensitivity, interpersonal impact, diplomacy, and the ability to create consensus among divergent views

In their review article of research on global competencies, Bird, Mendenhall, Stevens, and Oddou (2010, p. 811) define *global leadership* as "the process of influencing the thinking, attitudes, and behaviors of a global community to work together synergistically toward a common vision and common goal." They extended the global manager pyramid (Bird & Osland, 2004) and identified fifteen global competency dimensions in six broad categories as depicted in figure 10.2. Cross-cultural coaching should focus on developing these global manager skills.

From figure 10.2 it is clear that leaders with a global mind-set are individuals who have the ability to deal with the complexity, ambiguity, and polarities of cultures without being paralyzed, intimidated, or frustrated by the differences. They do not assume to have the answers but remain curious, open-minded, and humble in their mindful inquiry about others.

Figure 10.2
Global Manager Pyramid

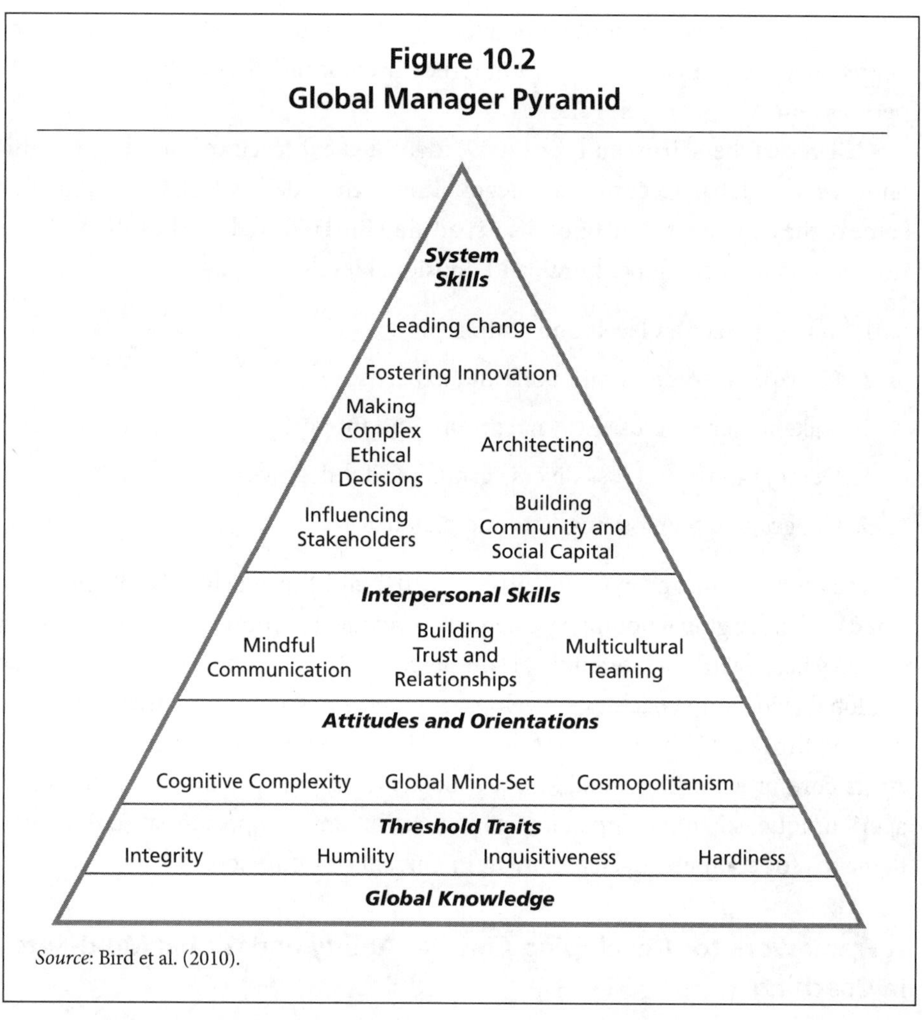

Source: Bird et al. (2010).

Bird, Oikelome, and Amayah (2013) maintained that the term *global* reflects the context in which leadership operates. He argued that global leadership needs to be defined in terms of the manifestation of complexity and boundary spanning since it functions in an extreme context of complexity and involves the creation and navigation of linkages across a myriad boundaries. Complexity involves the interplay of continuous multiplicity (more and different PESTLE influences, stakeholders, cultures), interdependence (mutual interplay and connectedness), ambiguity (confluence of multiplicity and interdependence), and flux (constant motion, whitewater of change, just-in-time actions). Boundary spanning in a global context includes flow (relational aspects using human networks and social capital, to run smooth operations) and presence, which refers to the degree managers must actually "geographically colocate" physically or virtually to perform effectively in their role.

CCL researchers Ernst and Yip (2009) identified five levels of boundaries or differences that global executives are negotiating in their daily work, which illustrate some of the complexity and boundary spanning Bird referred to. These boundaries function on cultural, subcultural, and divisional levels:

1. Vertical—across levels and authority
2. Horizontal—across functions and expertise
3. Stakeholder—across external groups and interests
4. Demographic—across diverse groups and differences
5. Geographic—across markets and distance

The global manager pyramid in figure 10.2 and the coaching strategies (just listed) to bridge global boundary categories provide direction for HR practitioners and coaches regarding intercultural competencies that are important for inclusion in global leadership coaching, development, and assessment initiatives. Mendenhall and Bird (2013) pointed out that global leadership development is hard work. At its core, it is an individual affair; it needs to fit the specific gap of the manager's unique existing competency configuration and the positional (contextual) demands for competency deployment in current or future job.

A Framework for Developing Cultural Agility and Global Mind-Sets in Coaching

DeLay and Dalton (2006) discussed cross-cultural coaching applications, including M. J. Bennett's (1993) useful six-stage developmental model of intercultural sensitivity, with denial of differences at the one extreme and integrating difference on the other extreme of development. Rosinski (2010) adapted Bennett's model as a coaching framework, adding a seventh step in cultural learning, leveraging of differences, which assumes "that individuals can critically think about culture, treasure what they value in their culture, adopt what they believe is valuable from other cultures(s) and synthesize the difference" (p. 136). J. M. Bennett (2014) extended the initial model and showed how it can be used in developing inclusive leadership, where denial of difference manifests in most exclusive and integration in most inclusive practices in this development model.

Figure 10.3 depicts an integration of Rosinski's (2010) and J. M. Bennett's (2014) models. It also extends these models by integrating the research discussed in this chapter on national culture and leadership, culture, social identities and social identity conflict, boundary-spanning practices, cultural intelligence, and global mind-set in a heuristic tool for coaches to use in exploring the landscape of cross-cultural leadership.

Figure 10.3 shows the seven-stage developmental model of intercultural sensitivity, with denial of differences at one extreme and leveraging of differences at the other extreme of development as discussed by M. J. Bennett and Rosinski, as well as J. M. Bennett's addition of inclusive leadership development. Based on the discussion in this chapter, the model can be extended by adding national culture, subcultures, and group and individual social identity as part of the culture; cultural agility, which includes cultural sensitivity, cultural intelligence, and cultural competency; and level of intercultural learning (as part of the ethnorelative stages of development), which includes difference seeking, open and global mind-sets, and boundary-spanning practices. I added the directional arrow lines above the continuum of development stages to indicate how the left side of the continuum indicates negative experiences of difference, whereas the right side indicates positive experience of difference. I also added the directional arrow lines underneath the continuum of development stages, indicating inclusion and exclusion of difference and resultant increase or decrease of intercultural learning. Moreover, I showed how difference avoidance in the left bottom block links up with a closed or parochial mind-set and fault-line-affirming practices, and on the bottom right side how difference seeking links up with an open and global mind-set and boundary-spanning practices.

This framework forms the knowledge base and informs the focus for cross-cultural coaching in the integrated process model for cross-cultural coaching that I discuss next.

AN INTEGRATED PROCESS MODEL FOR CROSS-CULTURAL COACHING

In this section I present a framework for cross-cultural leadership coaching by integrating existing cross-cultural coaching models (Abbott et al., 2013; Anderson et al., 2009; DeLay & Dalton, 2006; Frankovelgia & Riddle, 2010) with CCL's own research on best practices cross-culturally for both executive coaching and

Figure 10.3

Developing Cross-Cultural Understanding: A Coaching Framework

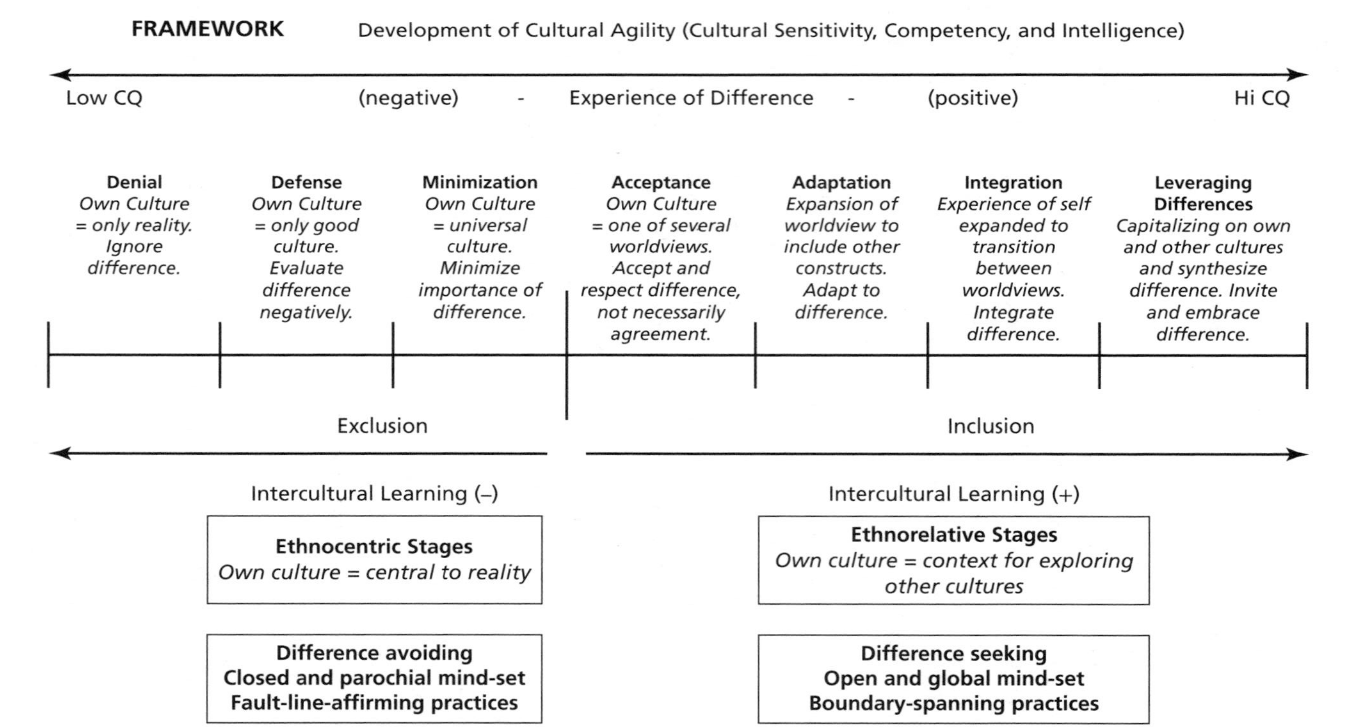

FRAMEWORK Development of Cultural Agility (Cultural Sensitivity, Competency, and Intelligence)

Low CQ (negative) - Experience of Difference - (positive) Hi CQ

Denial	Defense	Minimization	Acceptance	Adaptation	Integration	Leveraging Differences
Own Culture = only reality. Ignore difference.	*Own Culture = only good culture. Evaluate difference negatively.*	*Own Culture = universal culture. Minimize importance of difference.*	*Own Culture = one of several worldviews. Accept and respect difference, not necessarily agreement.*	*Expansion of worldview to include other constructs. Adapt to difference.*	*Experience of self expanded to transition between worldviews. Integrate difference.*	*Capitalizing on own and other cultures and synthesize difference. Invite and embrace difference.*

Exclusion	Inclusion
Intercultural Learning (–)	Intercultural Learning (+)
Ethnocentric Stages *Own culture = central to reality*	**Ethnorelative Stages** *Own culture = context for exploring other cultures*
Difference avoiding **Closed and parochial mind-set** **Fault-line-affirming practices**	**Difference seeking** **Open and global mind-set** **Boundary-spanning practices**

Sources: Adapted from M. J. Bennett (1993), J. M. Bennett (2014), Mendenhall and Bird (2013), Booysen (2014), Hannum et al. (2004), Rosinski (2010), and Van Dyne et al. 2010).

Note: National culture = national culture, subculture, and group and individual social identifies.

feedback coaching (Gentry, Allen, Wolf, Manning, & Hernez-Broome, 2011; Hannum et al., 2010; Ruderman et al., 2010; Ting & Scisco, 2006), following CCL's relationship–assessment challenge support–results (R-ACS-R) process coaching model. This process is embedded in the context of cross-cultural knowledge, practice, and development, as depicted in the X-C (Cross-Cultural) R-ACS-R model in figure 10.4.

DeLay and Dalton (2006) pointed out the US-centric nature of CCL's R-ACS-R model of coaching, where the coach and the coachee collaborate to understand the coachee's development needs, challenge current constraints, explore new possibilities to ensure accountability and support for researching goals, and sustain development. This model is heavily based on the US culture, which is commonly described as individualistic, egalitarian, performance driven, focused on self-mastery, comfortable with change, and action oriented, and might be culturally offensive to individuals in high-power distance cultures, where leaders are not supposed to function in such an enabling way with direct reports. This might also hold true in high-collectivistic societies, where external locus of control tends to be higher than in individualistic societies. In these societies, coachees may feel not in control of their own destinies and might be uncomfortable with being held accountable for their own growth, since they perceive their futures to be in the hands of the leaders or the organization. Another example might be where issues of confidentiality in the coaching relationship are perceived as too individualistic in collectivistic societies and perceived as placing the individual's needs above those of the organization. The whole notion of 360-degree evaluations might be problematic in cultures with high power stratification, collectivism, and humane orientations, where hierarchy, harmony, and face saving are important. Finally, the guiding, rather than expert or controlling, role of the coach might be difficult to accept in cultures with high power stratification and where self-mastery is not so prominent.

While Delay and Dalton (2006) were more critical of the universal appeal of CCL's coaching model, Frankovelgia and Riddle (2010) found that the basic components of CCL's R-ACS-R coaching are applicable in a global environment provided that cross-cultural coaches are acutely aware of their own cultural assumptions and can adapt the coaching practices to the specific cultural contexts. They highlight five components of culture (some overlapping with DeLay

Figure 10.4
Integrated Process Model for Cross-Cultural Coaching

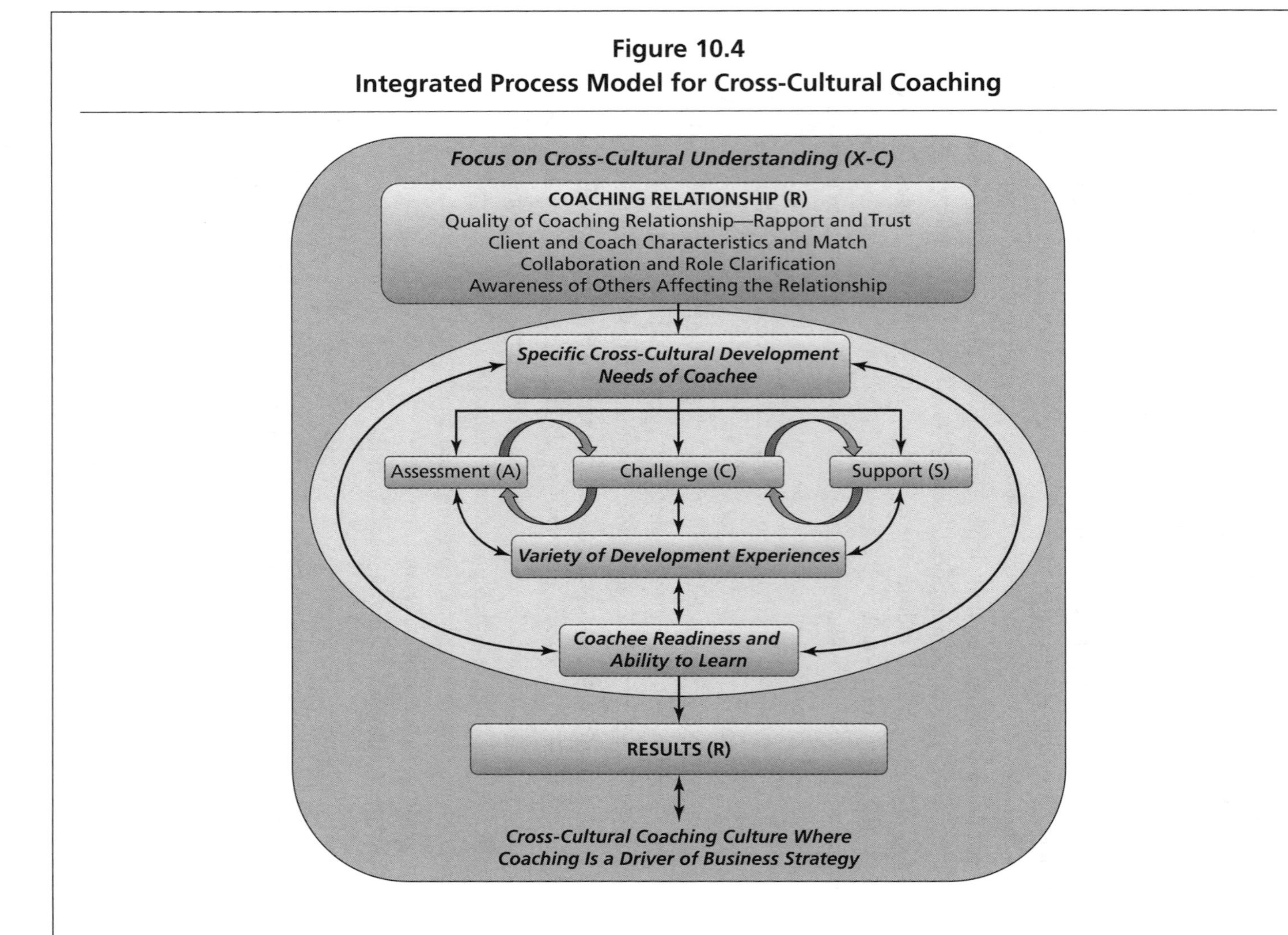

and Dalton's concerns) that can vary across cultures and cross-cultural coaches need to keep in mind:

- Formality, closeness, and spontaneity expected in the coaching relations
- Comfort with assessment methods that involve collecting and quantifying perceptions of leaders' behavior from a variety of people who work with the leader
- Willingness to take on challenges that will stretch an individual beyond existing levels of competence
- How support is expressed and experienced in a coaching relationship
- How results are interpreted, for instance, from a low- or high-performance orientation, or through an individualistic or collectivistic lens

The Cross-Cultural Focus and Context (X-C)

The outside block in figure 10.4 indicates the main focus and context of cross-cultural coaching: focus on cross-cultural understanding. This implies a substantial knowledge component and includes the cross-cultural leadership body of knowledge discussed in this chapter as part of the coaching process and depicted in figure 10.3: influence of national culture on leadership, cross-cultural theories of leadership, implicit cultural leadership, culture, social identities, social conflict, cultural intelligence, and global mind-set. HR can play a strong role in the sourcing, development, and delivery of this knowledge. Ideally cross-cultural coaching would be most effective if it is integrated within the overarching context of leadership development and supported by a cross-cultural coaching culture, where coaching is a driver of the organization's business strategy, as indicated as part of the context of cross-cultural coaching in the outer block in figure 10.4.

Two other areas where HR can play a strong role is in the variety of cross-cultural development experiences and coachee's readiness and ability to learn. Learning is a key component of cross-cultural coaching. The ability to learn is a complex combination of personality and motivational factors and learning experiences. The ability to turn learning into adaptive practice is even more difficult. It is less complex to learn about cross-cultural leadership (to have the knowledge, or "knowing") and more complex to translate knowing into "being" and doing—the practice of cross-cultural leadership, or leading across difference.

Cross-cultural coaching is an individual affair and should be designed to fit individual coachees' and organization needs based on their context, readiness, and capacity. This is indicated in the upper rectangular block in the ellipse in figure 10.4: specific cross-cultural development needs of coachee. Again, HR can play a direct role in surveying and establishing these needs.

Organizational support is thus key to the effectiveness of the coaching process (Booysen, 2014; Gentry et al., 2011), and as indicated in figure 10.4, a number of different HR strategies can be employed to embed organizational support throughout the coaching process and to create a cross-cultural coaching culture.

The Coaching Relationship (R)

The coaching relationship is depicted in the top block of figure 10.4. The quality of cross-cultural coaching relationships is also built on rapport, trust, mutual respect, acceptance, and relational practice, where coaches need to be well prepared and genuinely interested in their coachees' well-being. It should be a collaborative process, with both the coach and coachees playing active roles. There also needs to be awareness of and understanding about other individuals or stakeholders who might affect the coaching relationship.

In addition, for coaches to be optimally effective in a cross-cultural context, they must:

- Be aware of cultural difference and their own cultural biases and assumptions
- Have the ability to adapt their coaching practices to different cultural contexts
- Have a deep understanding and knowledge of cross-cultural leadership dynamics
- Preferably have some personal experience in cultural adaptation and acculturation, and sound appreciation of the cultures of the client and host country in working with expatriate and multinational coachees

If they do not have the last item in the list, they might offend their coachees, thereby losing credibility and neutralizing the power of coaching. The important point is that culture matters even more in the coach-coachee relationship in cross-cultural coaching. The coaching process should revolve around the coachee's agenda and culture, not around the coach's agenda or culture (DeLay & Dalton, 2006; Frankovelgia & Riddle, 2010; Abbott et al., 2006; Gentry et al., 2011).

These qualities make the importance of client and coach characteristic and match a difficult task and a matter of case-by-case examination. Organizations can follow a maximum matched-mix approach: a maximum number of biogeographical variables are matched between the coach and coachee for maximum understanding or, on the other hand, a minimum matched-mix approach for maximum learning.

Assessment in Cross-Cultural Coaching (A)

Assessment creates shared understanding in the coaching relationship and process on the coachee's situation. Through reflective questioning, clarification, and feedback, the coach can guide the coachee toward deeper levels of understanding, self-discovery, and self-awareness. Assessment gives information on the gap between current performance and desired performance and benchmark practices. It clarifies what coachees have to learn, change, or improve and provides a means for critical self-reflection. Assessment also creates opportunities to motivate when coachees receive feedback on progress or effective behavior.

Following are some good-practice cross-cultural leader development assessments based on CCL's coaching process (Booysen, 2014).

Multirater, multisource feedback like 360-degree feedback can be geared to measure specific cross-cultural leadership competencies like inclusive leadership practice, relational practice, dealing with differences, and appreciation for multiple viewpoints. For example, HR practitioners can design or source a 360-degree feedback questionnaire where peers, teams, subordinates, and superiors can give feedback to each other on their level of cross-cultural understanding, cultural intelligence, and global leadership competencies.

Assessments can be focused on cross-cultural leadership practices. Examples are the Global Competencies Inventory (http://kozaigroup.com/inventories/the-global-competencies-inventory-gci), the Intercultural Effectiveness Scale (http://kozaigroup.com/inventories/the-intercultural-effectiveness-scale), the Inclusion Measurement Survey (Davis, 2010), and Global6 (Brodbeck, Ruderman, Glover, Eckert, Hannum, Braddy, & Gentry, 2012).

Other leader development personality and type assessment instruments can also be used to explore areas for further development using a cross-cultural leadership development lens—for example:

- The Workplace Big 5 (Howard & Howard, 2001), to identify the degree to which an individual responds to stress, tolerates sensory stimulation from people and situations, is open to new experiences and new ways of doing things, pushes toward goals, and defers to others

- The FIRO-Business (Schnell & Hammer, 1997), for interpersonal needs such as expressed and wanted, involvement, influence, and connection
- The Myers-Briggs Type Indicator (MBTI; Myers-Briggs & McCauley, 1985), for thinking style preferences
- The Belbin Group Profile (Belbin, 1981), for group action role preferences and styles

The results of such assessments can give HR practitioners and coaches insight into the level of coachees' cultural awareness. Coachees can reflect not only on their own results but also on how their own results might interact with those of their team or work group. HR practitioners can use the results of, for instance, the interpersonal needs (FIRO-Business), cognitive style preferences (MBTI), and group action role preferences (Belbin) assessments in constructing more diverse teams and work groups.

Challenge in Cross-Cultural Coaching (C)

Booysen (2014) maintained that "challenges create disequilibrium, or a sense of a 'disorienting dilemma,' in which known ways of doing are not successful anymore (Mezirow, 2009). These states of disequilibrium cause individuals or collectives to question the appropriateness of their known ways and the adequacy of their existing skills, frameworks, and approaches" (pp. 317–318). Challenges stretch individuals and require them to deal with ambiguity and polarities, force them out of their comfort zones, and help them find new ways of doing through learning and new ways of understanding. McCauley, Van Velsor, and Ruderman (2010) pointed out that the elements (or sources) of a challenge are usually novelty (new experiences, learning new skills), difficult goals (stretch goals), goal setting, conflict or competing values (intrapersonal, interpersonal, group, or social identity conflict), and dealing with adversity (overcoming difficulty or challenging circumstances). In a cross-cultural coaching context, the coachee can be challenged on two levels:

- *Challenge during a coaching session*: In a coaching context, the role of challenge is to primarily establish a clear picture of what is possible for a specific coachee by questioning current constraints and helping him or her explore new possibilities. Coaches also need to challenge existing assumptions, perceptions, and old paradigms through reflective and reflexive questioning in order to encourage new ways of thinking. Coaches need to challenge coachees to set difficult goals, reflect on his or her own practice, and give and receive difficult feedback in an accepting way.

- *Challenge in leadership development*: Challenges in leadership development come in many forms and are dependent on individuals' level of experience and maturity.

Booysen (2014) highlighted some examples of leadership development challenges that HR practitioners can explore as part of the cross-cultural coaching and development process:

- *Developmental and stretch assignments.* For example, expatriate assignments, conflict management resolution between different work teams, or an organizational diagnosis and culture change endeavor can be used to develop cross-cultural leadership capabilities. These assignments help leaders test out and develop new cross-cultural leadership skills and competencies, such as cultural sensitivity and agility, and they heighten awareness of marginalization and privilege and promote questioning of dominant and normative thinking styles and practices.
- *Job rotation and job sharing* across and within functions, horizontal job enlargement, or vertical job enrichment can help leaders develop a deeper understanding of working across different job function levels and silos in the organization. Coachees will gain more insight into how these functions, jobs, and processes all work toward shared goals in the organization and of how silos can be integrated and boundaries spanned.
- *Action learning* (employees learn through working together), individual talent management (the process of attracting and retaining high potential employees), and career paths (charting a course within an organization for an individual's career path and career development) can be included in this level of development.
- *Education, skills training, and development programs* can be categorized as challenges and are useful HR strategies for gaining a variety of development experiences. These are usually done through a combination of on-site and off-site programs and initiatives and have didactic and experiential components.

Inclusive leadership rests on a deep level of consciousness—deep self-awareness as well as an awareness of other perspectives—and an understanding of ethics and social justice issues. Booysen (2014, p. 319) specifically pointed out that leadership development programs "need to meet the learners where they are, which may require differential approaches even within the same group of participants. Aspects such as participants' different learning styles, social identities, leadership levels, and developmental levels all need to be taken into consideration."

Finally, coachees need to be aware of the different leader role demands placed on them when working interculturally and engage in compensatory practices so as not to be caught up in exclusionary and culturally biased practices due to the pressures of these role demands.

Support in Cross-Cultural Coaching (S)

Coaches need to listen for understanding and how coachees can sustain momentum. Emotional support and being there for the coachee through active listening and showing curiosity are supportive behaviors in the coaching process. Other types of support that are more instrumental are to show their commitment and investment in the success of their coachees by helping them think through what they need to do to achieve their coaching goals—for instance, helping them to think through what resources and support they need, that is, who in and outside the organization they might turn to as resources to accomplish their goals. To help them create accountability, coaches can help coachees identify accountability partners inside and outside the work to keep them accountable and sustain the momentum. Additional approaches include establishing rewards for progress made and helping coachees to adjust their goals. It is important for coaches to note that the mere act of intentionally focusing on the other person, being genuinely curious about what he or she is saying, meaning, and needing will go further to address obstacles to effective listening than any other single thing that a coach can do. To stay with the coachee in the here-and-now in the coaching process creates a safe learning process during coaching.

Results in the Cross-Cultural Coaching Process (R)

A series of specific cross-cultural leadership goals linked to the coachee's workplace or home environment, or both, needs to be established during the coaching process. Also, accountability systems need to be fixed in order to build momentum in getting the needed results as the ultimate outcome of the coaching process. It is important for these goals to be challenging and realistic.

For cross-cultural coaching (X-C R-ACS-R) to be effective, coachees and organizations must be committed and have the capacity to support the coaching process. The ACS process plays out in the larger culture of the organization: the more an organization's business strategy and culture are aligned with a cross-culture coaching culture, the more effective cross-cultural coaching will be because the business and HR systems and processes will support and sustain the learning in the coaching process. This will also open up the variety of development experiences and opportunities aligned with cross-cultural coaching and coachee motivation and commitment to cross-cultural development.

CONCLUSION

Culture affects everything we do as individuals and as part of every collective to which we belong. The cultures that have nurtured us are now bounded by those who have provided the rich soil of development for others. As a result, the possibilities for synergy and conflict abound. Coaching as a practice, set of behaviors, mind-set, and profession offers a useful mechanism for creating something positive from the proximity of these worlds of culture, but the best outcomes depend on our readiness. Multicultural competence may have seemed an exotic virtue once, but it is now fundamental to the creation of a positive future in our organizations and in our world.

chapter
ELEVEN

Coaching in Context

The Individual in Relation to Organizational Culture

Elizabeth C. D. Gullette

What comes to mind when you think about coaching a software developer in a high-tech firm? Is it any different from what you imagine when you think about coaching an executive director of a government licensing board? How about a nonprofit youth ballet company's artistic director? For most of us, these descriptions trigger very different images and expectations of the individual based on what we know and what we assume about typical cultures and personalities related to particular industries and occupations. When coaching an individual, there may be good reasons for us to tap into our knowledge and assumptions about her context, but there are also dangers in relying on preconceived notions. This chapter takes a look at how a coach can think about the relationship between a coachee and the coachee's context, particularly the organizational culture, for the benefit of the coaching process. The discussion addresses the issue of coachee-culture fit, the potential benefits provided by a coach's familiarity with the specific industry or occupation of a coachee, and the risks of relying on this familiarity as a lens through which to view the coachee and the value of holding a coaching mind-set as an alternative.

ORGANIZATIONAL CULTURE

There are of course multiple levels of culture for a given individual, since culture is a characteristic of all groups, regardless of size. At a higher or broader level, there are national and ethnic cultures, whereas at the microlevel, there are team and even family cultures, with organizational culture falling somewhere in the middle. Paying attention to the various cultures, or subcultures, within which a leader is embedded is important since they provide different surrounding conditions, influences, and opportunities for the leader. Moreover, certain levels of culture are more relevant than others for certain reasons. For example, the socialization process that a new employee experiences on joining an organization has been shown to be more heavily influenced by the team she joins than by the broader organization, an insight that has implications for onboarding efforts. Since the influence of national and ethnic cultures is so fundamental and the implications of this level of culture to coaching so important, this topic is addressed separately and extensively in chapter 10. The focus of this chapter is organizational culture, and subcultures as they are relevant.

Organizational culture has been described by Edgar Schein (1992) as the implicit shared values, beliefs, and assumptions that influence how individuals in an organization think, behave, and react to their environment. This work context is a critical factor for a coach, whether external or internal, to remain fully aware of in a coaching engagement. Schein (1996) has pointed out the common failure of scholars, to which we can add practitioners, to fully and equally take into account both the individual and the organizational, or systemic, perspective when addressing issues within the bounds of organizations. For coaches, the one-on-one, confidential (albeit limited) nature of the relationship with a coachee makes this potential to focus on the individual at the expense of the system even greater. This happens in spite of well-meaning attempts to broaden our definition of the client to the organization, to view the coaching process as a team effort involving the coachee's manager and HR business partner, and so on.

How Organizational Culture Is Relevant to Coaching

For coaches to keep in mind the dual focus of individual and organizational culture is worthwhile for several reasons. In the case of leadership or executive coaching, coaches must recognize that leader and culture are intertwined and mutually influential. This is at its most obvious in the case of founders, whose own values, beliefs, habits, and personality contribute substantially to the organization's culture, though successive leaders influence the culture as well (Schein, 1992). In more established organizations, we often see this direction of influence manifest as leaders attempting intentional culture change in response to some threat or opportunity. Unfortunately, change is not easy to accomplish because culture is a powerful force once in place. As Schein reflected, "We did not grasp that norms held tacitly across large social units were much more likely *to change leaders than to be changed by them*" (1996, p. 231, my emphasis). For those of us engaged in coaching leaders with the goal of change, this statement is a bit unsettling. The prospect that a leader's potential for change and agency is significantly constrained by her surrounding culture might be discouraging. However, we know very well that leaders do change their behavior, grow, develop skills, expand their perspectives, and achieve other goals in coaching. So we are left with a recognition of the push-and-pull, back-and-forth relationship between leaders and culture. This is a relationship in which culture exerts a strong influence and may even impose the parameters within which leaders can change—but also a culture that leaders can influence, possibly even modifying the parameters themselves.

The Individual in Relation to Culture

Theological ethicist Richard Niebuhr (1951) proposed an interesting framework for thinking about the relationship of the individual to the prevailing culture. Niebuhr talked about being "against culture," "of culture," "above culture," "in paradoxical relation to culture," and "transforming culture." He was specifically talking about Christ and Christians in relation to culture during a time of significant debate within the Protestant movement of the early twentieth century. Despite what may seem a very specific application, aspects of this framework can be useful as we consider the various relationships that a leader could have with his or her culture and the implications of each for coaching. We'll take a look at a few in particular.

Against Culture A leader who is against the culture of her organization sees it as undesirable in some way, wrong for where the organization needs to go, and she therefore rejects it. Such a leader may point out or criticize what is wrong, act in ways that conflict with the prevailing culture, or attempt culture change. Many stories of "slash-and-burn" CEOs illustrate this type of relationship with culture. Ron Johnson, for example, who fell precipitously from favor as CEO of JCPenney, first managed to alienate customers and employees alike, not only by getting rid of sales events and slashing jobs but by his evident disdain for the organization's members and its culture. As Joseph Guinto (2013) notes in an aptly titled article, "Who Wrecked J.C. Penney?" "Johnson's team declared the headquarters to be 'overstaffed and underproductive.' As proof, they claimed that employees in

Plano had watched 5 million YouTube videos in a single month and that a third of the time headquarters employees spent on the internet was for purposes unrelated to work ... Most of the current J.C. Penney employees ... were enraged by the implication that headquarters staff was unproductive."

A more nuanced example is that of Peter Löscher, appointed in 2007 as the first CEO of Siemens AG in its 160-year history to come from outside the company. As Löscher (2012) noted, "I arrived at Siemens at a very difficult moment. The company faced allegations of bribery in several countries, and eventually it paid $1.6 billion in fines ... Siemens had to change ... Within months of my taking over, we replaced about 80 percent of the top level of executives, 70 percent of the next level down, and 40 percent of the level below that. I fundamentally changed how our managing board made decisions." In addition, he introduced new lines of business and new initiatives, from green energy to diversity. While Löscher ultimately failed to deliver the financial results expected by investors and was ousted in 2013, he came into his role as a stark contrast to the prevailing leadership culture then embroiled in controversy. His efforts to change the prevailing approach to decision making were at least in part in response to conversations with employees who were frustrated with slowness and bureaucracy, demonstrating a very different attitude than Ron Johnson displayed. Löscher undoubtedly affected the culture of Siemens, although his legacy is mixed.

Depending on the leader's competence in areas such as emotional intelligence, influence, and instilling a vision, not to mention delivering results, she may be more or less effective as a leader in an opposing relation to the culture. Coaching this leader would need to take into account this relationship, the leader's goals for the organization and herself, and her skill and competencies in moving toward those goals.

Of the Culture Being of the culture implies that the leader is fully integrated, or assimilated, into the organization's culture. It may be that there is a close leader-culture fit, which I discuss in more detail shortly, or it may be that the leader accommodates the culture. Consider one global consumer products company we worked with, headquartered in Japan and founded over a hundred years ago. Although the organization had grown through acquisitions in other regions of the world, all of the senior leaders were based in Japan and remained closely identified with the company's established culture, seeking to infuse it into a global culture. Everyone we met in the organization deeply respected the values and behaviors these leaders lived by and promoted. Unfortunately, some aspects of the home base culture were difficult to export or to scale to a global organization, and the leaders could not see this. For example, a prevailing cultural expectation of lifetime employment was at odds with the need to streamline the workforce when acquiring more than one similar business if those acquisitions were expected to add value and not just cost. Similarly, the headquarters culture was male dominated, with no female senior leaders, which was at odds with the existing diversity in Western business units and seemed to present an ultimate glass ceiling in the organization. The highest-level executives' inability to step back from the prevailing culture to clearly assess which aspects supported their business strategy and which did not created substantial frustration among the company's leaders throughout the world.

While this example illustrates problems that can result from leaders being of the culture, there is nothing inherently problematic about this identification. It depends on the needs and goals of the leader and organization. Questions for a leader, and his coach, in such cases include:

- How aware are you of your own personality, values, assumptions, and behaviors, and how aware are you of the values, assumptions, and behaviors held within and promoted by the surrounding culture?
- Is that alignment desirable?
- What are the implications of overidentifying with the prevailing culture for your individual and organizational goals?

There may be both costs and benefits to a leader's identifying so closely with the organization's culture, depending on her goals. There may be strengths to leverage from this alignment as well as challenges to overcome. A coach's attunement to these issues can prove valuable to a leader's own reflection and actions.

Above Culture A leader who is above the culture may have some of the same differences as one against the culture, but she may not reject the organizational culture or push against it as much as simply separate from it, continuing to work in her own way while letting others work in their way. This acceptance of the differences without accommodation or conflict, as with other relationships to culture, may or may not be what is best in leading the organization. Understanding it and asking that question is something a coach can challenge a leader to do, promoting self-awareness and an intentional process going forward.

Understanding an Individual's Culture: Balancing Specific and General Information

Clearly organizational culture represents a powerful backdrop for understanding an individual's situation and is a profound influence to consider. The coach's discernment of the organizational culture takes place on two levels:

1. The specific, granular assessment of the leader's actual context through observation, interviews, conversation, and data within the organization, which is relevant in that an individual's fit with his or her culture has implications for coaching.
2. The more general, broader understanding, or assumptions, of the culture based on knowledge of similar organizations (i.e., of an industry). This is relevant because there are industry-specific variables that may serve a coach well to be knowledgeable about (e.g., jargon, competitive pressures, common dimensions of culture) in terms of credibility and quicker understanding of the coachee's situation and perspective, for example—but also may bias the coach's view of the coachee to the extent the assumptions do not apply to the individual.

Ideally, being mindful of the first—the importance of assessing the actual, specific organizational culture of a coachee—can help mitigate the risks associated with the second, namely, assuming one understands a coachee—his situation, his style, his preferences, his strengths, or his challenges. This must be combined, of course, with solid, objective assessment of the individual.

Coachee-Culture Fit

There is ample evidence that individuals are attracted to and remain in environments that fit their personality and values (Schneider, 1987). As might be expected, then, an individual's performance, tenure, and well-being are enhanced when there is alignment between the person and his work context. This is referred to as person-environment or person-organization fit (Caplan, 1987). Using Niebuhr's framework, we might think of this phenomenon as being of the culture and that this kind of relationship is the most comfortable for employees. Schneider's (1987) attraction-selection-attrition (ASA) framework draws on this mutually reinforcing relationship, proposing that "people make the place." Specifically, the ASA cycle is one in which individuals are attracted to organizations similar to them; they are then selected by organizations because of those similarities, and they remain in organizations that fit well or leave if the fit is not as good as they had hoped. This cycle begins with the founder embedding her own values, beliefs, and personality into the organization's culture. Looking at these person-based factors helps shed light on organizational attributes such as structure, processes, technology, and culture, in addition to external determinants, which may at times be overemphasized.

In fact, evidence suggests that both person-based factors and factors in the external environment (e.g., social, economic, technological) are important contributors to an organization's behavior, similar to the nature and nurture influences on individual personality. These external influences will be addressed next, and they certainly fit theory and the ASA cycle to reinforce the importance of assessing a coachee's work context, including culture, as part of gaining an understanding of the coachee and how fit with the organization may relate to performance and well-being and, by extension, potential development goals in coaching. If a person is not performing well, for example, one would presumably look carefully at what might be contributing to this. Is there a lack of skill? A resource problem? A knowledge gap? Assessing the fit between the person and the culture can provide additional information of value: for example, is this a traditional command-and-control manager in a culture that is less hierarchical and more empowering of employees?

When Fit Is Desirable Since coaching is essentially an intervention to boost an individual's performance and well-being in the context of her organization, one might conclude that coaching should aim to move a coachee toward closer alignment with her culture if such alignment (person-environment fit) is associated with positive outcomes. Helping the authoritarian manager to become more like other managers in the organization, more aligned with the culture, by teaching and promoting a management style that empowers others, for example, could indeed lead to improved performance on her team—and ultimately less stress for her. This would be akin to helping the person become more of the culture.

Indeed, often what prompts a coaching intervention is the fact that an individual is not representative of the surrounding culture and the ways this lack of alignment or fit manifests. This mismatch may be problematic for both the individual, who may feel out of place, uncomfortable, or even incompetent, as well as for those around him. Whether adapting to the culture is desirable depends on the individual's goals and the goals of the organization. Gaining clarity on this is critical because it can be incredibly challenging for a person to adapt to an unfamiliar environment or one that is not a natural fit. If deemed desirable, the value of coaching for an individual who wants to make this effort, typically involving both behavior and attitude change, could be tremendous. Among other things, coaching can help a coachee tap his or her internal motivation by surfacing broader goals and values the change would connect to. Coaching can help a coachee identify resources, such as role models or mentors, that would support the change goal, and it can promote and reinforce the practice of new behaviors and new perspectives until they take root.

When Fit Is Not Necessarily Desirable Assessing the fit between individual and organizational culture can clarify areas of alignment that can be left as is, or possibly leveraged, as well as areas of misalignment affecting a coachee's performance or well-being, and merit attention in coaching. However, when it comes to leaders in particular, a sole focus on promoting alignment between individual and culture could pose problems because the very role of a leader is at times to serve as an agent of change. This factor can apply to an individual in a subgroup or to a team member. The leader promoting change need not be in a formal leadership role.

Supporting the importance of this objective role of a leader, Schein (1992) argued for the value of a leader standing outside or on the margin of the organizational culture to be able to understand and question it. We can think of that position as above the culture. Such objectivity is aided by awareness of one's own degree of alignment with the culture and the consideration of whether convergence or divergence in particular areas is desirable for a leader. In other words, it is not simply a matter of assessing fit, but also of determining whether alignment is desirable based on the broader goals of the leader, perhaps to shift the culture to be more innovative or collaborative. Once a leader moves from a more removed relationship to culture, observing from outside, to a more active engagement with the culture, she shifts from being above the culture to being against the culture. A coach's explicit framing of these shifts can provide a helpful road map for a leader setting out to make changes in the organization's embedded ways of thinking and acting.

This issue is the focus of the leader-culture fit, which draws attention to the degree of match between leader and culture on any given attribute and the importance of taking this into account in leadership coaching (Nieminen, Biermeier-Hanson, & Denison, 2013). Viewed simply, a leader can be low or high in an attribute and a culture can be low or high in an attribute, producing matched highs, matched lows, unmatched highs (high in leader, low in culture), and unmatched lows (low in leader, high in culture). An example of a matched high might be the case of a leader who engages in a high degree of collaboration within a culture that is highly collaborative. Alternatively, a leader who is highly collaborative in a very competitive culture represents an unmatched high.

Importantly, it is not assumed that a match, or alignment, is the preferred configuration. In the example of an unmatched high related to collaboration, the leader may need to be a change agent in moving the organizational culture away from competition and toward collaboration. Already being good at collaboration is a strength for this leader to leverage: she can serve as a role model, share stories of the benefits of collaboration in her personal experience, and teach collaborative behaviors based on knowing what has worked for her. Promoting reflection and insight in such a leader can be a valuable role for a coach to play, as the leader needs to be consciously aware of how she does what she does if she hopes to teach others to do it.

Maintaining an awareness of a coachee's organizational culture, then, is an important element of a coach's focus for several reasons. First, on the most basic level, it can serve as a reminder that there may be limits on what are reasonable goals and actions for the coachee. Second, a lens related to coachee-culture fit provides diagnostic information relevant to a coachee's performance and well-being. Third, keeping in mind a coachee's fit with the organizational culture is important because it permits the identification of areas of leader-culture convergence and divergence. The coach and coachee can make intentional use of either condition in support of the leader's ultimate goals, understanding that these may need to involve some degree of culture change.

The Evolution of a Leader's Fit with Culture

For the sake of clarity, we've been focusing on an either-or proposition—that fit may or may not be desirable, depending on the goals of the individual and the needs of the organization. In many instances, it may be useful to think more in terms of timing or the developmental point of a leader in an organization. A leader first entering an organization is at a different stage in relation to the culture than a tenured leader who long ago established credibility, a record of performance, and strong interpersonal ties.

The leader new in role, even if brought in to shake things up, brings in new ideas, or otherwise change (to go against the culture), will likely fail if he pushes this agenda too early. Consider the example of an executive in a pharmaceutical company who was brought in from the outside to develop a new business model for the organization, which was facing increased competition from the biotechnology sector and a dwindling pipeline of new drugs. Her personality was characterized by a high degree of originality and openness to change. In addition, she was low on dimensions of perfectionism and being systematic. This personality configuration contrasted sharply with the prevailing culture of precision, risk aversion, and a tendency toward perfectionism. Clearly this individual's personality and her experience in innovative roles made her a great fit for the new thinking and change required in the task she had been given. However, her coach realized that this executive would have to consider very carefully the fact that she was surrounded by, and reliant on, people who were, whether naturally or as a result of their own successful integration into the culture, risk averse, data driven, methodical, and uncomfortable with change. She had to manage her own urge to move quickly in new directions and her ability to see the future more clearly than others with a need to build trust and create a bridging vision that could move people along without overwhelming them. This took some time, some relationship building, asking questions, listening, and soliciting thinking partners in the development of possible future scenarios.

As chapter 15 points out, the transition period for a new leader is a critical inflection point during which intentional focus should be placed on learning about, joining, and integrating with the existing culture. A new leader has to prove himself by delivering early results, getting to know the key stakeholders and constituents, and generally demonstrating he respects and wants to add value to the group. Over time and with visible evidence of these efforts to adopt and integrate into the culture, the leader is more likely to be viewed as credible and having the right to question that culture and even attempt to change it. A coach with this developmental perspective in mind can help a leader navigate this process to improve the probability he is successful in ultimately achieving his agenda.

INDUSTRY-SPECIFIC KNOWLEDGE: RELEVANCE TO COACHING

Should a coach have knowledge of or experience in the industry of his coachee? At CCL, we hear this request fairly frequently from clients. To understand how widespread this interest is, we surveyed internal HR professionals involved in coaching and leadership development to find out just where they, often charged with contracting executive coaches, stand on this and related questions. We also surveyed external professional coaches to gain their perspective for this chapter. Among the 142 respondents, about two-thirds of the internal HR professionals believe that it is somewhat or very important for the external coaches they hire to have specific industry experience, as compared to only about half of external coaches who hold this view (see figure 11.1).

Why might it be important or valuable for a coach to have specific industry knowledge? How important is this to a coaching engagement? In part, the answer

Figure 11.1
Development Professionals' View of the Importance of Industry-Specific Experience for Coaches

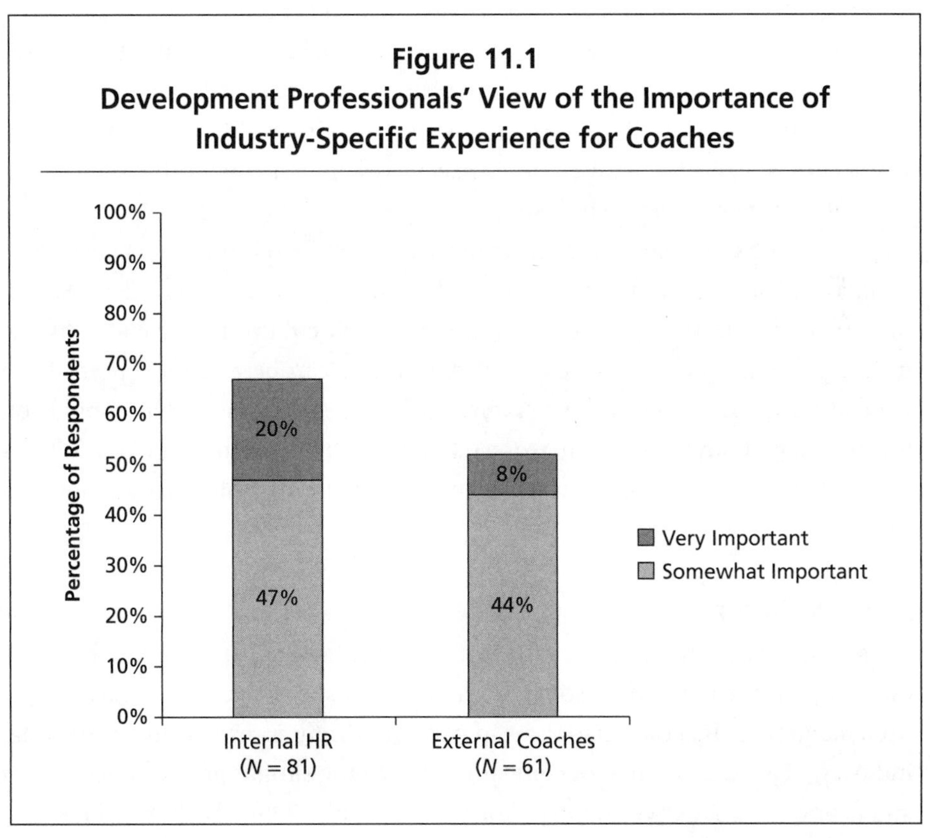

to these questions depends on one's definition of coaching, whether it is more inclined toward consulting and advising or, as CCL defines it, more toward facilitating development through eliciting and promoting self-awareness, insight, new perspectives, and new behaviors. Viewed in this light, coaching progress and success are less dependent on content knowledge and more dependent on process knowledge and skill. So in-depth knowledge of an industry for a developmentally oriented coach who is insightful and highly skilled may not necessarily influence the ultimate outcome of coaching, which is the achievement of the coachee's goals and her learning and growth. This may be one reason that only 8 percent of the external coaches surveyed said that industry-specific experience is very important compared to 20 percent of internals.

However, industry familiarity can be helpful to the rapport building involved in coaching, and it may be helpful in assessment, especially early in the coaching assignment. Most people would agree that understanding the jargon, acronyms, business issues, and general context in which the coachee is embedded can lend credibility to the coach and create a sense of shared experience. My background doing research and clinical work in an academic medical center and then working in a health care consulting firm, for example, has made it easier to enter into the coaching and consulting relationships I've had with health-related nonprofits, physician leadership initiatives, nurse executives, and clients in the biopharmaceutical and medical device industries.

In terms of assessment, one of the more compelling reasons for a coach to be familiar with a coachee's industry is related to the importance of considering organizational culture in coaching. If an organization's culture is influenced by the industry it is in, then knowing about an industry can be a vantage point from which to understand a coachee's culture and some of the issues that impinge on her. But do we know whether there is a relationship between industry and culture? Certainly the vast majority of respondents to our survey believe so, as shown in figure 11.2.

Industry Cultures

Organizational culture is influenced by numerous factors. The role of a founder's own individual traits and, to some extent, those of successive leaders has already been mentioned. In addition to those idiosyncratic influences, research shows that industry, defined as a group of companies producing similar products or services and facing a similar environment (Konrad & Susanj, 1996), also has an influence

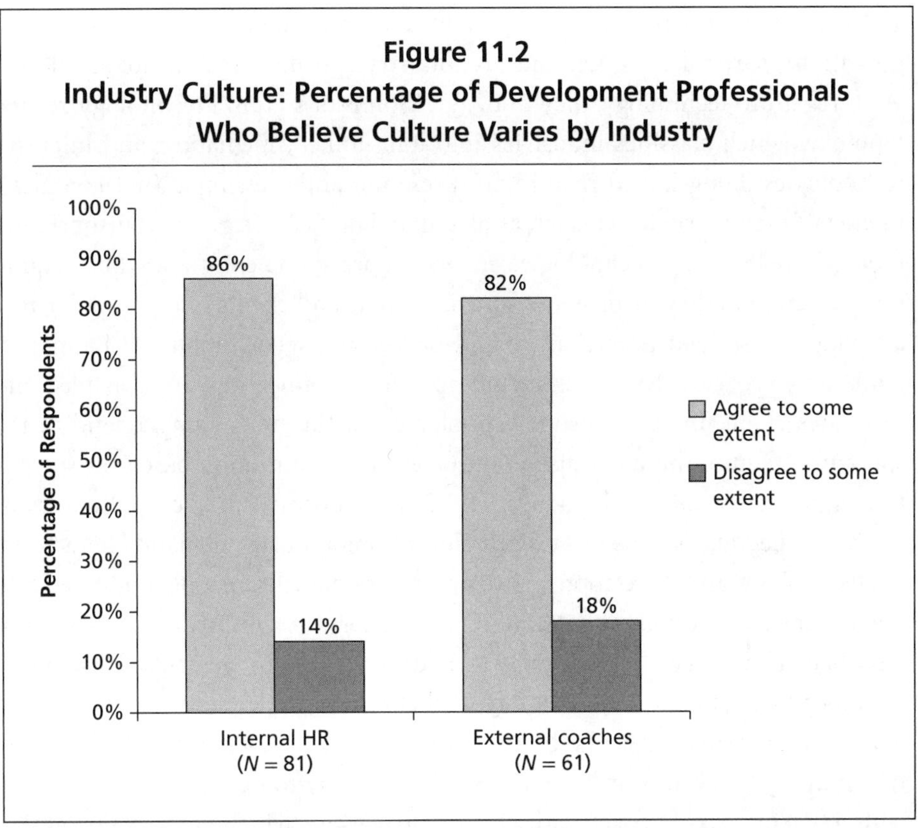

on culture. Indeed, certain dimensions of culture have been found to vary more between distinct industries than within a given industry, meaning organizations within a specific industry tend to have in common certain cultural characteristics (Chatman & Jehn, 1994; Konrad & Susanj, 1996). This is presumably because external factors in the environment impose certain constraints on industries and require certain similar responses and adaptations, which result in converging structures, processes, and cultural characteristics within a given industry.

Factors in the environment that have been shown to influence the development of an industry's culture include economic, social, and technological variables. The economic environment involves the nature and degree of competition and the amount of room for additional growth in the competitive environment. The social environment involves the rules and expectations of the society and social structures in which organizations operate. The technological environment relates to what technology is used to get the work done (Konrad & Susanj, 1996).

Chatman and Jehn (1994) highlight the importance of technology and growth in particular as relevant to industry-specific organizational culture. With regard to technology, they draw on Thompson's (1967) technology-related typology, which classifies industries into long-linked, mediating, and intensive technologies. Long-linked require no discretion and are simple (not complex), predictable, and structured, such as assembly line tasks (e.g., the transportation industry). Mediating technologies involve more complexity and thus require more discretion; they involve first sorting "inputs and clients into groups" before applying "prescribed procedures based on those categorizations" (Chatman & Jehn, 1994, p. 526). Examples include product engineering firms, banks, and insurance claim units. Intensive technologies, at the most complex end of the spectrum, require the most discretion or even customization based on specific task or project needs and characterize R&D units, hospitals, and consulting firms.

Even reflecting on this brief discussion of one industry demand characteristic, technology, and its relationship to organizational culture, one might begin to make some assumptions about culture and leadership within an organization in a particular industry—for example, related to the encouragement of discretion, tolerance for ambiguity, and comfort with complexity. Not surprisingly, a coach with experience in a particular industry would likely have a schema of that industry and predict, even if unconsciously, what is likely to exist in an organization within that industry. A coach with a history of working with high-tech Silicon Valley firms, for example, may develop an expectation of leaders as highly intelligent, entrepreneurial, forward thinking, and comfortable with complexity, while their surrounding cultures are characterized by a fast pace and near-zealous appreciation for personal discretion and ingenuity.

Growth was also highlighted by Chatman and Jehn (1994) as important in relation to industry culture. The idea here is that low growth places constraints requiring certain common approaches and behaviors, for example, related to efficiency and risk aversion, while inhibiting others. In a high-growth industry, by contrast, firms will presumably experience increasing revenues and opportunities promoting a culture of innovation and risk taking.

Other aspects of culture shown to be more strongly related to industry than organization include innovation, stability, people orientation, easygoingness, detail orientation, and team orientation (Chapman & Jehn, 1994).

We can see, then that an organization's culture can be influenced by its industry. Industry knowledge can be an advantage to coaches; however, it is critical to acknowledge that such a perspective is by definition at a high level and so can be somewhat general and involve assumptions. If that's the case, then what coaches do with their general knowledge in a specific coaching encounter matters a great deal. The point is not that knowing about typical themes and patterns is inherently bad; coaches gain useful contextual information from knowing that certain dimensions of culture are more prominent in the financial industry than in engineering firms, for example. Rather, the point is that there are both benefits and drawbacks to generalizing in the context of coaching individuals, and it is incumbent on coaches, whether external or internal to an organization, to be cognizant of how we use generalized information. Does it form a framework that prompts us to ask confirming or disconfirming questions? This use can be valuable. Or does it form a lens through which we view an individual and make assumptions about him or her? For example, a coach might think, "I'm working with a surgical team and assume key issues for the female nurse vis-à-vis the male doctor involving power and gender." Unexamined assumptions can get us into trouble, whereas examined assumptions provide an informed basis for challenging them and give us a foundation for asking the right kinds of questions.

So knowledge of or experience in an industry may contribute to our assumptions about a given organizational culture and, by extension, a given leader. Another salient factor underpinning assumptions about a leader and, especially his immediate subculture, is his occupation or the profession represented by his team or functional department, for example, information technology, human resources, or accounting. Finally, and not independent of either the broader industry relationship to organizational culture or the subculture of the occupational or functional group based on the attraction-selection-attrition (ASA) framework, is the concept of modal personality, or shared personality characteristics in an organization. This refers to the most common or average personality traits in a given type of organization or subgroup.

Industry Personalities

As noted previously, a founder's personality has been found to influence the emerging and the subsequent organization's culture, and the ASA framework suggests the organization attracts people with similar personal characteristics as the founder (Schneider, 1987). Indeed, this has been found to be true. Top organizational leaders' unique profile of personality and values aligns to those of the organization, and these leaders play a unique role in shaping the organization's culture to become somewhat homogeneous in terms of both personality and values (Giberson, Resick, & Dickson, 2005). That process has been described as one in which "leaders embed their personality into the organizations they lead by surrounding themselves with individuals who are similar to themselves" (p. 1007).

One of the ways that individuals self-select into groups before even joining the workforce is by declaring a college major or selecting a vocation. This could be seen as one step in the process of finding the right organizational fit. In studying this relationship, Judge and Cable (1997) found business majors favored innovative and aggressive cultures, whereas engineering majors favored supportive cultures and disliked what were termed "outcome-oriented" cultures. Personality traits have also been found to cluster within industries (Schneider, Smith, Taylor, & Fleenor, 1998).

Many people have an intuitive sense that there is a relationship between personality and one's choice of organization, occupation, or function. Organizations tend to have common personalities, so the research support for this connection is not surprising. What may be more surprising is how many people do not expect this to be true. In our survey of development professionals, 46 percent of internal HR respondents and 48 percent of external coaches disagreed to some extent with the statement that personality varies by industry. One convincing example of this relationship comes from our own work with a global strategy consulting firm, in which we found over 80 percent of leaders showed NTJ patterns (Intuitive, Thinking, Judging) on the Myers-Briggs Type Indicator.

For practicing coaches, understanding this tendency for personalities to be somewhat similar within an industry and, even more so due to founder and leader factors already mentioned, within a given organization, may provide some useful contextual information and prepare us for certain challenges or to adapt in some way. For example, the majority of our surveyed external coaches reported they adjust the way they coach, at least sometimes, in response to both the culture of the organization (93 percent of respondents) and the personality of the individual (97 percent), as shown in more detail in figure 11.3.

An assumption one might hear about a leader in an organization largely of chemical engineers, for example, is that she will likely have a personality style oriented toward concrete, fact-based information; an analytical, objective approach to making decisions; and a structured, systematic way of managing her work and time. While having some general expectations for the culture based on typical

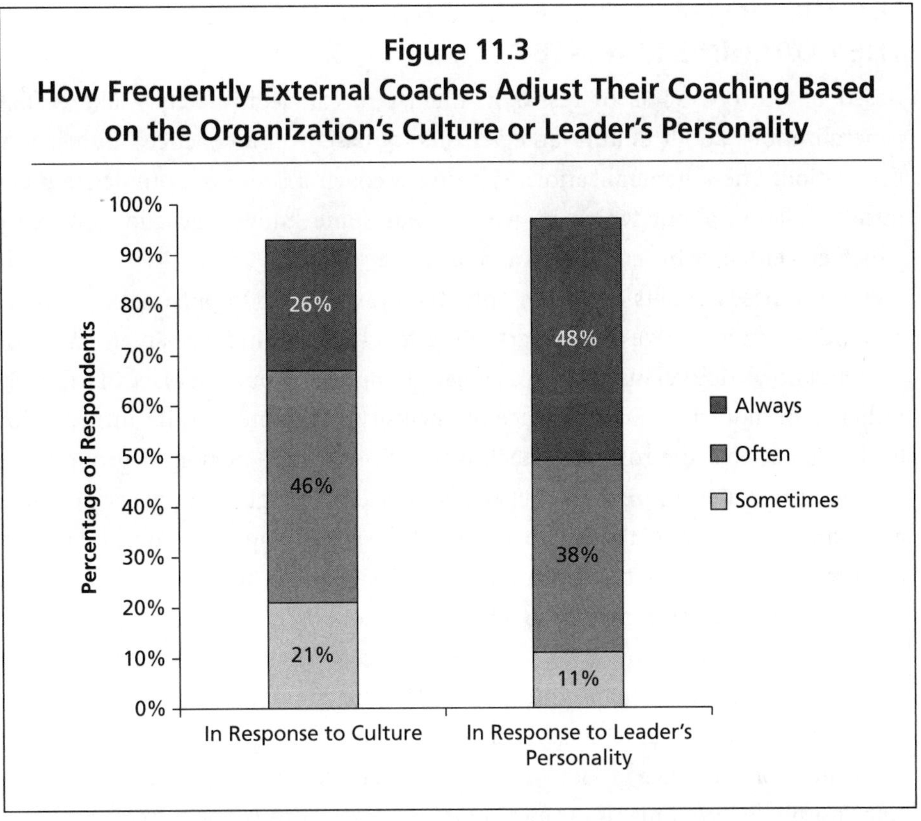

Figure 11.3
How Frequently External Coaches Adjust Their Coaching Based on the Organization's Culture or Leader's Personality

personalities may be useful, having specific expectations for the leader you are coaching is not.

COACH PREPARATION FOR AN ENGAGEMENT

Regardless of whether a coach has specific experience in or knowledge of an industry, it is important for any coach to do homework to understand the company and industry in which he will be coaching a leader. When engaging in large-scale executive coaching work, CCL always treats the cadre of coaches as a community of practice and ensures an onboarding process including familiarizing coaches with the organization, its business, strategy, challenges, environment, and so on. We typically hold periodic teleconferences with this community to share business updates, trends, and themes to continue to deepen coaches' understanding of the client organization. (Chapter 5 provides detail about the process and issues related to coach preparation.)

LETTING GO OF KNOWLEDGE AND ASSUMPTIONS: THE COACHING MIND-SET

Based on various areas of research, then, one can legitimately make certain generalizations about culture and personality based on a coachee's industry or occupation. These generalizations can give a coach a sense of confidence going into a situation about which he feels he has some knowledge and familiarity, which can enhance his credibility and promote rapport.

But do these benefits outweigh potential drawbacks? Do personal experience and industry knowledge on the part of the coach lead to more of an emphasis on content knowledge versus process use (i.e., giving advice out of a place of expertise rather than inquiring out of a place of curiosity)? As noted in the Introduction to this handbook, the role of a coach is to "stimulate the person or group being coached to greater awareness, deeper and broader thought, and wiser decisions and actions." Its aim is "the improvement of the perceiving, thinking, and reflecting process" that leads to "the solution to the concern at hand." Leading to a solution is very different from providing a solution.

Perhaps even more important, does experience in an industry, especially if only in one organization, actually interfere with a coach's ability to see the unique, idiosyncratic individual who is his or her coachee? Does general knowledge lead to assumptions that are in fact stereotypes? If so, this is antithetical to coaching since no single individual is ever an actual representative of the stereotype.

These are obviously not yes or no questions or intended to inform coach selection. Rather, they are questions for reflection. For organizations selecting coaches to work with their leaders, this discussion should suggest that industry experience on the part of the coach need not be a prime consideration, and there are other criteria more important, such as the coach's experience coaching leaders, references from other coaches, educational as well as work background, and the fit between coach and coachee, typically gauged by the coachee herself prior to contracting. Part of this fit admittedly involves the coach's credibility. But credibility can come from a variety of sources.

These questions about industry knowledge, culture, and fit should provoke reflection and exploration on the part of the coach, and they can even be leveraged in coaching conversations to help a leader explore his own assumptions and stereotypes of those around him. A colleague of mine who is a superb coach has been politically active as a citizen and volunteer throughout his adulthood. Through various political campaigns and their aftermath, his firsthand exposure to the political appointment process at the state level jaded him over time. When he took on a coaching engagement with a state employee who served as the executive director of a profession's regulatory board, a political appointment, he realized he had to confront some biases and negative assumptions that had crept into his mind-set. Specifically he recognized, in a peer supervision conversation, that he expected the leader to be "slick" and not particularly qualified for his position. While it was difficult for him to let go of these expectations entirely, being aware of them allowed him to hold them as hypotheses rather than conclusions. In fact, the evidence he found did not support the hypotheses: the executive director was committed, energetic, well meaning, mostly qualified, and had a strong sense of integrity even if he did lack certain management skills. This coach had to continue to be mindful of his biases creeping in—for example, guarding against expectations about resource constraints and limited promotion potential to dampen the individual's motivation to learn and develop as a leader. This was not at all true, and in fact the coaching work moved over time from an initial focus on behavior change and skill acquisition to a deeper process of challenging thinking and possibilities contributing to more strategic thinking and more tolerance for others' differing viewpoints.

How might a coachee be influenced by assumptions about individuals in his culture? One sales executive whom I coached provides an example. He found it easy to lead his own commercial organization, but he had difficulty working effectively with his peers from other parts of the company (e.g., R&D, legal and compliance, finance). A key issue we revisited regularly as he worked to develop these relationships and expand his influence was his judgments of them as "wonks." The culture of the organization outside sales was heavily influenced by the scientist founders and leaders. The culture tended to be somewhat introverted, deliberative, and political (people kept their cards close to the chest), whereas this leader was extraverted, experimental, and very direct. His inability to break in to the circle of his peer group reinforced his own conclusion that everyone around him embodied the introverted, deliberative, political culture.

Part of our work for this coachee was to consider the key individuals in his network as individuals, surfacing the assumptions and judgments he harbored about them, and then to leverage his strength in exploration and experimentation to set out to disprove his assumptions with each individual. As you might imagine, many of his peers turned out to be fairly representative of the culture; however, there were a few exceptions. This realization was not only enough to help him question his own assumptions more directly (a desirable coaching outcome in itself), but these individuals were able to serve as points of entry for him to integrate more effectively in the group and exert more influence. Most important, he became more successful in interacting with the remaining group members—those whose style was more aligned with the prevailing culture—over time as he became less frustrated and was more visibly effective working with the few who were less similar to the prevailing culture.

Clarifying explicitly the potential benefits as well as drawbacks of preconceived knowledge in a given situation enables a coach to draw value while remaining clear-eyed and taking an individualized stance. More broadly, this type of reflection on the part of a coach is a fundamental force in her continued development. This is the rationale behind the rise of coaching supervision, an activity that has always been integral to other helping professions such as counseling and therapy. Coaching supervision has become more popular as its value has become clearer, making itself important to the practices that contribute to effective coaching. These include maintaining a coaching mind-set, with its stance of learning and curiosity, primary reliance on inquiry and elicitation, and use of a framework for approaching the work (such as CCL's RACSR: relationship, assessment, challenge, support, results).

We might take a moment here to explain what is meant by a coaching mind-set. It is a perspective informed by knowledge bases and any number of experiences but in which that very knowledge and experience take a background position to curiosity, inquiry, and full presence. One way for a coach to think about this is to think of herself as a student, because even if the coach is very familiar with a particular industry or organization, the coachee will always know much more about his world than his coach and can therefore play the role of teacher even as he himself learns.

CONCLUSION

To help understand both the common contextual factors to hold as a backdrop and the critical importance of maintaining an individual-oriented stance, this chapter suggests that coaches hold a dual lens. It discusses cultural characteristics, common personality traits, and leadership demands specific to certain industries, while also making the case for approaching each individual within that generalized context as an unknown.

We hope this discussion provides helpful guidance for your thinking and practice as a coach, particularly in the assessment of leaders, the clarification of their development needs, and the ongoing reflection and practice we encourage them to engage in as they grow and develop in their own organizational context. A second goal has been to stimulate deeper reflection on the mind-set that we as coaches bring to each unique relationship with a leader and promote greater awareness of our assumptions and biases as well as our opportunity to learn from them in order to best help them.

chapter TWELVE

Ethical Considerations for the Human Resource Coach

Maggie Sass and Barbara Fly-Dierks

Ethics is an important consideration in any coaching relationship, but it is especially critical in human resource coaching because of the unique challenges internal HR and organizational development (OD) professionals have in simultaneously navigating multiple roles and maintaining appropriate boundaries. For any given employee, an HR professional may participate in hiring and selection, development reviews, work audits, disciplinary matters, and coaching. Coaching in this environment requires not only discretion and boundary management but also an ethical framework for how information should be used in each type of role activity, whether for selection or development. The role may also complicate personal relationships at work. For example, internal HR coaches may be required to make recommendations about employees they are coaching and with whom they are close colleagues, may be asked to keep pertinent organizational information confidential that could adversely affect leaders (i.e., their coachees), or may be required to coach an employee as a last resort before termination.

Internal coaching is different from external executive coaching in a number of ways, including contracting, personal boundaries, and confidentiality. HR professionals may have less control over contracting than external coaches, so they may find themselves in a situation in which they are managing complicated relationships such as coaching an employee and her direct report or coaching an employee who wants to discuss a problem involving someone the HR professional knows well. The HR professional will find herself having to manage the interests of the organization and the individual—being privy to information an external coach would not have access to—and struggling to support and challenge a coachee without compromising her obligations and responsibilities to the organization. Walker-Fraser (2011) argues that "the challenge for HR professionals is to have a systematic approach to goal setting, expectation and evaluation, while allowing for flexibility in addressing contextual-cultural issues, in alignment with business objectives" (p. 73). Leadership coaching in an organization has always complicated the question, "Who is the client?" but an HR professional practicing coaching may be even more conflicted about loyalties and confidentiality than the average external coach. The HR coach may feel torn between protecting employees from exploitation by the organization and providing information to the organization that can help inform decisions about talent, placement, and promotions. Such issues happen less with upfront contracting around confidentiality, so it is good to have clear guidelines within the organization about what will and will not be shared outside the coaching relationship.

HR coaches come from a variety of backgrounds. Professionals in HR and OD roles may have academic backgrounds and experience in education, business, human services, organizational development, and technology, to name just a few. They may belong to established professions such as psychology that have enforceable ethics codes (e.g., American Psychological Association), although coaching ethics and standards remain largely voluntary because coaching has yet to be differentiated as its own profession. However, regardless of training or professional experience, people in HR and OD need to understand the ethics of coaching and how to incorporate ethics into their work (Lowman, 2013). The Center for Creative Leadership (CCL) has produced a statement of coaching ethics and professional standards to summarize common international standards of professional conduct for leadership coaching and demonstrate CCL's commitment to them. Ethical codes from professional bodies including the APA, the Center for Credentialing and Education, and the International Coach Federation were selected as statements to provide guidance to coaches since they were all created by organizations with a significant history of human service in coaching, counseling, or consulting; have direct relevance to leadership coaching; and are internationally recognized. CCL believes that the most useful approach to providing ethical direction in coaching is to acknowledge various coaching-relevant ethical codes and provide guidance for their use. CCL's coaching supervisors including licensed psychologists serve as an important safeguard for the application of appropriate standards in CCL's own external coaching services as well.

HUMAN RESOURCE COACHING DEFINED

Coaching, for purposes of this chapter, is defined in the Introduction to this handbook as a "helping relationship with a developmental focus played out in conversations that stimulate the person or group being coached to greater awareness, deeper and broader thought, and wiser decisions and actions." Such coaching conversations may occur in an HR role as formally contracted coaching engagements with employees or as informal on-the-fly opportunities.

Formal contracted coaching engagements are usually distinguished by an established contract between two or three parties. For example, a human resource business partner (HRBP) may contract for a coaching engagement with both an employee and her boss to prepare the employee for a new role in the organization. In this type of coaching relationship, the HR professional needs to have transparent conversations with both the boss and the direct report seeking coaching about managing the multiple relationships, confidentiality, and limits to confidentiality (see exhibit 12.1). Other issues to consider include the time line for the coaching engagement, including number of sessions and frequency; expectations of both the boss and the direct report (the coachee); and any type of formal evaluation or measurement related to the engagement (Fielder & Starr, 2008).

Exhibit 12.1
Confidentiality Discussion Topics

- Always discuss the limits of confidentiality. Information that will be shared includes:
  - Illegal activities
  - Child or elder abuse
  - Threats to safety of self or others
- Always discuss what will be held confidential. Information that will not be shared includes:
  - Venting about one's boss
  - Venting about coworkers
  - Future job plans (e.g., plans to leave the company)

(*continued*)

Exhibit 12.1 (*Continued*)

- Future family plans (e.g., an impending move, increase in family size, spouse work relocation)
- Assessment results

- Always discuss what the coachee consents to have shared, which might include:
  - High-level themes (without identifying information), such as dissatisfaction with benefits or working environment. We recommend this be discussed during each coaching session if the coach has any question about whether information is to be held in confidence. In those circumstances, the coach might say something like "I think your boss would really enjoy hearing this. Do you want this held confidential, or may I share it with him?"
- Always discuss what the coach will be able to share, which can include:
  - Company vision, policy
  - Public knowledge regarding the company's strategic direction, acquisitions, general policy
  - Job opportunities that have been posted internally
- Always discuss what the coach will not be able to share, which can include:
  - Any insider information (e.g., pending acquisitions or sales)
  - Information shared in conversations with the coachee's boss, unless expressly stated
  - Content of coaching conversations with coworkers

Having conversations both at the beginning and during the coaching engagement will help ensure that there are no misunderstandings. We also recommend that if information is to be shared, such as that described in exhibit 12.1, the coach help the coachee consider sharing the information herself. If the coach believes the information is important or helpful for the boss to know (e.g., the results of a personality assessment), the coach should secure consent from the coachee in writing. Better yet, the coach can leave it in the hands of the coachee and let her decide when and where to share such information.

Informal coaching can be conceptualized as one-off or ad hoc developmental conversations. Similar to formally contracted coaching engagements, these conversations are opportunities for an HR professional to listen, probe to help clarify the issues and possibilities for action, and challenge thinking and assumptions to open up new possibilities. Although a valuable skill, informal coaching is different from a defined coaching relationship or engagement in which boundaries and confidentiality are more clearly outlined, and so it is important for an HR professional to understand the ethical implications of coaching someone about information the coachee wants kept private. Consider the following scenario. An employee shares with an HRBP in an informal coaching conversation that he is frustrated with his boss because the boss is using company resources to help get his side business up and running. Although the conversation may be informal, the HR professional can never truly be in a coaching relationship without being clear about the limits to confidentiality. The following questions may arise: Is this information confidential? Should the HRBP report this information? What are the limits to confidentiality in an informal conversation? It is important for HR professionals to be clear within their organization and with the employees with whom they work about confidentiality and its limits within informal relationships, just as it is in formal coaching relationships.

ETHICAL FRAMEWORK FOR HR COACHING

There are two broad areas to consider in the context of ethics and coaching. The first relates to the appropriate use of coaching by HR and OD specialists and includes issues such as role conflict, confidentiality, and managing personal and professional boundaries in coaching. The second relates to the space outside the appropriate use of coaching, which is distinguished by the issues of concern and depth of intervention needed. For example, if an employee were to approach an HR coach with a serious life crisis (e.g., divorce, death of a loved one, struggles with depression or anxiety at a clinical level), a coaching conversation might help the person clarify what she needs to do to get help and support through this time. For example, the coach can speak to the coachee's manager about workload help, provide guidance for the coachee to seek an employee assistance program consultation, or seek outside help from a health care professional. However, a coaching conversation would not generally address the crisis-related issues directly in terms of providing guidance, consultation, or advice. There will be times when an employee reveals information, asks for help, or discusses a topic that can make the HR professional feel out of her depth, but if she stays in the role of coach, these difficult cases can be less intimidating. The challenge is not to give in to the urge to fix the coachee's problem or situation but rather to help the leader identify the problem, facilitate the discussion, and collaborate with her coach to come up with possible solutions and a preferred plan of action.

To understand how ethics fits into the HR professional's coaching role, we look to Wooten's (2001) evaluation of ethical dilemmas, which provides a taxonomy of ethical dilemma categories. These include misrepresentation and collusion, misuse of data, manipulation and coercion, value and goal conflict, and technical ineptness. These categories can serve as a framework to understand issues specific to coaching in the HR role.

In table 12.1, we compare Wooten's framework with the more practical application work of St. John-Brooks (2010) in which she surveyed internal HR coaches regarding the types of ethical dilemmas they encounter. Interestingly, the ten most commonly reported ethical dilemmas in HR coaching that she found mostly overlap Wooten's categories of misuse of data, manipulation and coercion, and value and goal conflict.

NAVIGATING DILEMMAS

The HR coach faces some unique challenges given the nature of the role. He faces potential conflicts of interest ("misuse of data" in table 12.1) or role conflicts among parties, including stakeholders; in addition, among those parties, there may not be shared agreement on what is considered the real target of coaching ("value and goal conflict" in table 12.1); and he may be privy to confidential information and feel a burden to act on the information ("misuse of data" in table 12.1). One of the keys to alleviating potential ethical dilemmas or challenges is to keep in mind the definition of coaching expressed previously in this chapter and in this book's Introduction. The coach facilitates learning, acts as a sounding board, and asks tough questions, all in the service of the coachee's development. It follows, then, that the coach will not, and should not, be focused on what to do with information the coachee is revealing. In addition, recall the importance of establishing from the outset a clear coaching contract and of having a frank discussion with a clear understanding of the limits of confidentiality (see exhibit 12.1 for examples).

Table 12.1
Top Ethical Categories and Dilemmas Facing Internal Coaches

Wooten's (2001) Ethical Category	Definition	St. John-Brooks's (2010) Internal Coaches' Top Ten Ethical Dilemmas
Misrepresentation and collusion	Human resource management professional misrepresents his or her skill base, education, expertise, certification, or specialized training	
Misuse of data	Voluntary consent or confidentiality of organization members is violated or abridged or data are distorted, deleted, or not reported	• Third parties in the organization wanting information or feedback about the client • Being told by a client about inappropriate comments or behavior by a third party and not being able to act on the information • Client's personal issues having an impact on performance (but the client not wanting anyone else to know) • Knowing something about the client or the client's future that he or she doesn't know (and you can't reveal this information) • Being unable to use information that could benefit the coachee's team or the entire organization

(continued)

Table 12.1 (*Continued*)

Wooten's (2001) Ethical Category	Definition	St. John-Brooks's (2010) Internal Coaches' Top Ten Ethical Dilemmas
Manipulation and coercion	Implementation of HR roles, practices, or programs requires organizational members to abridge their personal values or needs against their will	• Client attempting to use sessions to further her own agenda (by influencing the coach) (Wooten speaks to coach manipulation but not coachee manipulation of the coach.)
Value and goal conflict	Conflict or ambiguity concerning whose needs will be fulfilled by meeting specific goals.	• Role conflict. Where the coach is coaching a client on whom, or on whose work area, the coach's job (separate from the coaching role) impinges • Client wanting to discuss an issue involving someone the coach knows well or works with • Where relationships between clients can set up difficulties • Client wanting to discuss leaving the organization
Technical ineptness	Lack of knowledge or skill in the use of techniques or procedures to diagnose human resource management issues	

The following cases provide examples of typical internal ethical scenarios and allow a broader discussion around ways to contract about and think through some HR coach challenges. We provide helpful questions the HR coach can ask himself about ethical situations and also types of questions the coach can use in typical coaching sessions that demonstrate commitment to ethical practice.

Legal Issues

It is important to clarify the distinction between legal issues in human resource management (HRM) and ethical dilemmas. Laws are rules that have been approved and are enforced by a government body. In HR, for example, there are laws that protect against unlawful discrimination in hiring based on race, age, or gender. Ethics principles, as opposed to laws, are rules of conduct based on right and wrong ways to approach situations (de Jong, 2006). There can be differences of opinions on how to approach ethical issues because people differ in their interpretations of what is right and wrong.

Misrepresentation and Collusion

As Wooten (2001) suggests, misrepresentation and collusion is a category of ethical dilemmas that directly applies to the roles and responsibilities of HR professionals. It is most relevant in the context of HR coaching as it applies to professional competence. HR professionals receive a variety of educational training and can earn a range of unique HR certifications (e.g., HR Certification Institute's PHR or HRMP certification), assessment certifications (e.g., a 360-degree feedback instrument certification), or specialized HR training (e.g., CCL's Coaching for HR Professional course). It is important for HR professionals to be clear about the competencies in which they have expertise and those outside their training or experience. If an HR or OD professional is asked to coach an employee and does not feel prepared for the role or competent to take on that assignment, it is important to be transparent. Doing so might open up opportunities to approach a supervisor with requests for coach training, learn coaching techniques and best practices from resources such as coaching handbooks and relevant journal articles, and receive direction and supervision from someone in the company more experienced in coaching. Consider how the case that follows illustrates this topic.

The Not-So-Legal Eagle

Matthew has been coaching a regional manager, Pam, on performance issues. He discovers some legal violations of pay practices are being condoned at the next level of management. During a coaching session, Pam appears nervous and fidgety, playing with her watch and twisting her wedding ring as she reveals this information to him. She mentions that a similar issue came up several years ago when she was with another organization, but she never told anyone. Pam indicates she wants to do "the right thing" this time, but is afraid of being fired. Matthew has no legal training but decides to advise Pam on handling legal violations.

DISCUSSION

Matthew is clearly practicing outside his competency of skills and education. This situation actually has two problems: Matthew's lack of training in legal issues regarding violations of pay practices and the violation of pay practices being condoned at the upper levels of management. The first problem is created because of something the coach is doing or attempting to do (give advice); the second problem originated elsewhere but is something that has come to the coach's attention (illegal pay practices).

This scenario may be a bit different from other scenarios because it involves legal issues. The crux of the matter is that it is unethical for Matthew to provide any legal advice to Pam. It is ethical, however, for him to help Pam explore the dilemma created in her current situation. Legal issues, by their very nature, complicate the coaching situation. The dilemma becomes how to ensure that potentially illegal activity is addressed. To help Pam develop her thinking and behavioral response to the situation remains an important coaching opportunity. Matthew has the opportunity to model self-awareness and self-management by being open with her about his lack of legal training and by recommending that she meet with an internal legal expert.

If there are practices occurring in the organization that are clearly illegal, the HR professional's responsibility is to the larger organization. This supersedes the coaching relationship and is the reason whistle-blower policies have been put into place. It is important to know your organization's practices and policies around whistle-blower issues. These kinds of issues must be spelled out in the initial contracting phase, as noted in exhibit 12.1.

QUESTIONS

Matthew should ask himself several questions about this dilemma to clarify the circumstances:

- Do I need to be clear that I have no formal legal training? Am I competent to help solve this coachee's issue?
- What category of ethical issue (or issues) does this fall into, and why?
- What organizational policies are in place to help me deal with this situation?
- Do I need to remind Pam about the limits of confidentiality?
- What is Pam's agenda around this issue?
- Do I have personal biases that could be affecting my ability to coach?
- What is my legal responsibility? What is my ethical responsibility?

COACHING QUESTIONS

Matthew might ask in his coaching sessions with Pam questions such as these:

- What does "doing the right thing" mean to you?
- What assumptions are you making about what happens if you reveal what you have discovered?
- Are you sharing this issue so that I can do something about it, or do you want to address this on your own?
- What is the potential impact of doing nothing?
- What are some possible courses of action you can take?
- What kinds of things have you thought about since the previous incident that may be influencing how you are thinking about this situation?

(*continued*)

- What do you wish you had done or could go back and do differently?
- What kind of support do you need, and from whom, in order to take the next steps?
- What do the next steps look like?

Misuse of Data

Misuse of data can pose a number of ethical issues in coaching, such as breach of confidentiality and inappropriate use of employee data. In an organizational context, it is critical for the HR coach to be clear with both the leader being coached and the sponsor of the coaching, such as the employee's boss or a division head, so that each party understands the context of the coaching as well as the role of each person and that each party independently agrees to the coaching engagement. Lowman (2013) suggests that it is the responsibility of the coach to explore whether an employee has been pressured into a coaching relationship and then to determine together the course of action—a continuation of the engagement or something different. Lowman also suggests that voluntary consent in coaching is often compromised in organizational contexts. Consider, for example, an HR professional who is required to coach a derailing employee who does not want to be coached or is told that coaching is being used as a last resort before terminating an employee. In this case, it would be prudent for an HR coach to determine how transparent she can be with the employee about the circumstances that have brought her to the coaching engagement and work through any issues the employee may have about participating in the engagement.

Confidentiality in coaching is an integral part of building the relationship between a coach and coachee. It helps to establish trust and the sense of safety necessary for an effective coaching relationship. Even more than external coaches, HR coaches find themselves in a unique position in terms of confidentiality because they are bound by loyalties to both the organization and individual employees. An internal coach will need to be clear with coachees about the areas he will not be able to keep confidential so that the coachee has a choice about what to reveal and what to keep private (Sugarman, 1992). An HR coach will also need to explain to the organization the types of information he can share and those he will not disclose (See exhibit 12.1 for a discussion of these issues.) It is typically valuable for the coachee to be the one to provide updates (e.g., to her boss) so as to promote alignment and encourage a developmental component to that relationship.

Many of the common issues in confidentiality reported by St. John-Brooks (2010) relate to the organization's wanting information about a coaching client, a coaching client disclosing personal issues that he does not want shared with the organization, or the HR coach being unable to use information obtained from a coaching conversation that would be helpful for the organization. In all of these cases, it is the responsibility of the HR coach to simultaneously hold information from both the organization and the individual but to draw clear lines around what is shared and with whom. It can be helpful for HR coaches to put equal emphasis on thinking through confidentiality issues ahead of time as well as incorporating limits in the coaching contracting discussion. Discussing issues around confidentiality can often be uncomfortable, but the more dialogue there is on the subject, the more clarity the HR coach, the coachee, and the organization will have regarding expectations.

It is also paramount for HR professionals to protect confidential information, such as health information and behavioral or 360-degree assessment data, as well as to ensure that such materials and information are used only for their intended purposes. HR coaches can avoid a number of potential ethical problems if they are upfront with their organizations about the purpose and use of various coaching tools, if they maintain that such materials and information are to be used in developmental ways only, and if they specify that all data related to the coachee belong to the coachee. Consider the following case.

The Diagnosis Dilemma

Jim has been coaching Susan, who is being considered for a promotion to a critical position in the organization. Susan has confided in Jim that she is undergoing treatment for breast cancer but has not disclosed this to anyone else because she feels it will hurt her chances of gaining the promotion. Jim has been asked to provide a professional recommendation for Susan not as her coach but as her HR business representative.

(*continued*)

DISCUSSION

This situation may seem complicated but it is quite common. Many times HR coaches are asked to provide advice to hiring managers about talent (hiring and firing), which may be complicated by existing coaching relationships with the same employees. In this case, Jim should have discussed confidentiality issues with Susan before the start of the coaching engagement to make her aware that her personal health issues and development needs would be kept confidential. Should Jim decide that he could provide a professional recommendation without compromising his coaching relationship, there will be no ethical issue. However, if Jim feels as though the information he is privy to will affect his judgment, he needs to be clear with the organization that he cannot represent Susan as her HRBP because he is also her coach.

QUESTIONS

Jim might ask himself questions about this dilemma that include these:

- What category of ethical issue (or issues) does this fall into, and why?
- Where does my primary responsibility lie?
- What is the impact if I reveal the information?
- What is the impact if I don't reveal the information?
- Can I maintain dual relationships with the same coachee and still do no harm?
- How can I best support Susan as her coach as she faces her dilemma?
- Am I making assumptions that a medical condition will necessarily negatively affect her performance?
- What support can I or the organization offer Susan when and if she reveals her medical condition?
- Am I challenging myself to remain in a coaching role?
- Do I feel confident in Susan's ability and therefore feel comfortable providing a professional recommendation? Would I have had a different answer to this question had she not revealed the information to me?

COACHING QUESTIONS

In his coaching sessions with Susan, Jim might ask questions such as these:

- You've shared with me your health situation. What do you see as the potential impact of your health issues on taking a critical position?
- What concerns do you have in discussing your health with me and the potential impact on being considered for the promotion?
- What assumptions about this situation may be at play here?
- How might you challenge the assumptions?
- What, if anything, does the organization need to know about your health issues to make the best decision about the promotion? Why?
- How might your health issues affect your ability to perform in the new role?
- How might you work around these potential complications?
- Tell me about your support network inside and outside work.
- How can you leverage these networks?
- How can you set yourself up to succeed?
- What are you most afraid of?

Manipulation and Coercion

Manipulation and coercion as conceptualized by Wooten (2001) occur "when particular HR roles or practices required organizational members to abridge their personal values or needs against their will" (p. 166). This type of ethical dilemma could arise when either the coach or coachee uses the coaching relationship to exert power over the other party. Our understanding of coaching suggests that both the coach and coachee are equal members of a collaborative relationship. HR coaches need to be clear that the coaching relationship and topics discussed during coaching sessions, within the limits of confidentiality, should not be used to take advantage of or provide an advantage to a coachee. For example, if a coach shared information with a coachee about a job opening in the company that had not been advertised yet, that information could provide an advantage. Alternatively, if a coach coerced a coaching client to put in a good word to her boss by threatening to reveal privileged information shared by the coachee, that would disadvantage the coachee. Nor should the coaching relationship be used as a way for coachees to manipulate coaches. St. John-Brooks (2010) found that one of the top ten ethical issues in internal coaching was coercion on the part of the coachee to use coaching to further her own agenda. If a coach suspects that the coachee intends to manipulate the relationship, it would be prudent to speak to the coachee about this and potentially transfer him to a different HR coach. The following case illustrates this category of ethical dilemmas.

The Vine Climber

Ashley has been coaching Samantha, a higher-level manager not in Ashley's direct reporting structure. Samantha has learned that her boss is being terminated and suggests to Ashley that she wants her to do something to enable Samantha to move into her boss's role. Because Samantha outranks her, even though she is not a direct superior, Ashley feels pressured to take action or be in danger of losing her job.

DISCUSSION

Ashley finds herself coaching a superior. Although Samantha is not in her direct reporting structure, this creates, not surprisingly, discomfort for Ashley. Samantha evidently feels comfortable and safe enough in the relationship that she has asked her coach to help her get promoted, but it will be necessary for Ashley to challenge Samantha's assumption that because she is in HR, she can or will exert influence. It might be appropriate to point out to Samantha the coercion she feels, the inappropriateness of being put in this dual-role position, and the problems the power differential is creating.

Regardless of the power differentials in this case, Samantha's request of Ashley is inappropriate and unethical. It will be important for Ashley and Samantha to revisit boundaries and role expectations (contracting) and make clear their roles and the limits of the purview of coaching. It is necessary to make it clear that the request is outside the bounds of their coaching relationship.

QUESTIONS

Ashley might ask herself questions about this dilemma that include these:

- What type of ethical situation is this? What motives, fears, or desires might be behind Samantha's request?
- Does Samantha truly want to engage in the coaching relationship, with the goal of growth and development?
- How can I use this coaching opportunity to facilitate Samantha's growth and self-development?
- Have I set clear boundaries, clarified my role, and focused on the goals of coaching?
- How can I ensure I keep the focus on Samantha and her development?
- Am I afraid to be completely honest because Samantha outranks me? With what impact?
- Am I afraid that if I don't honor her request, it will have a negative impact on me?

COACHING QUESTIONS

Ashley might ask in her coaching sessions with Samantha questions such as these:

- Let's talk about how this puts me in a difficult situation: I'm your coach, but you do outrank me. What might be the implications of this? When you ask me to use my influence to help you move into your boss's role, are you asking me as the HR manager or as your coach?
- How can we talk about this openly while both committing to honoring our roles as coach and coachee rather than my role as your HR manager?
- What are your expectations about my ability to influence? Are they reasonable, or do we need to talk about how to reset them?

Value and Goal Conflict

The value and goal conflict category of HR coaching ethics includes conflicts of interest, the issue of balancing employee and organizational interests, and boundary management. Of St. John-Brooks's (2010) top ten most common ethical dilemmas, four fall into this category, suggesting it is a common area for

HR coaches struggling with ethical concerns. HR coaches will need to think through issues related to role conflict and the types of boundaries they set within their coaching practice about people or issues they will discuss. To think the matter through, the coach can ask herself the following types of questions:

- Can I be nonbiased in discussing someone I know?
- Will I be able to leave information I know about this person at the door and discuss only information provided by the coachee?
- Will I be able to listen to information about my friend and not get defensive?
- Does my friendship with this employee affect my ability to be a good coach?

With all of these questions, we encourage transparency whenever possible. For example, the coach may say to the coachee, "I know Chris very well and will need to consider if I can listen to your criticism of him without becoming defensive." This self-reflection and critical thinking provide a good model for self-development and growth. HR and OD professionals are often the only coaches in an organization, so it can be tricky to step away from a coaching engagement from a resource perspective. It is important to set clear guidelines within the HR function in order to protect internal coaches in the event they feel strongly about stepping away from a coaching engagement due to conflicts of interest or other ethical concerns. The following case highlights some important questions to consider when value or goal conflict ethical issues arise.

Which Hat Should I Wear?

Julie, the HR manager, has been coaching Brian for a year. As a result of the impact of his coaching and his growth as an employee, he has received a promotion he's been working toward for two years. After six months in his new role, Brian has decided it is time to leave the organization and has applied to a competitor organization. If he wins the job, he will receive a significant increase in salary and responsibility. He has asked Julie to write a recommendation for him as his personal coach, not as the HR manager.

DISCUSSION

As an HR professional, Julie has a vested interest in retaining quality employees. In her role as coach, it is inevitable that she will learn confidential information about a coachee's satisfaction with his job or plans to leave or stay with the organization. In cases such as this, the dual roles become evident. It is not the goal of the HR coach to avoid any possible dual-role relationship; rather, it is to recognize they will occur and develop strategies for handling the situation.

Julie will do well to recall that the essence of coaching is a helping relationship with a developmental focus played out in a conversation. Julie has clearly been placed in a dual-role position: she is Brian's coach and has developed a collaborative, facilitative relationship built on trust and mutuality, but she is also the HR manager. As the HR manager, she might feel pressure to influence Brian, a valued employee, to remain with the company. She may, for example, be able to offer him a better compensation package, but as Brian's coach, she may know that Brian has not been happy in the organization and might be a better fit with the new organization. As his coach, she may have coached him to explore options outside the organization because of a values conflict with the organization. As his coach, she will not encourage him to stay; rather, she will encourage him to look at the data and explore the options. However, writing a letter of recommendation is incompatible with the neutrality needed by the coaching role, and many organizations have strict policies governing communications about current or former employees.

QUESTIONS

Julie might ask herself questions about this dilemma that include these:

- What type of ethical issue does this fall into?
- Are there policies in place to help me deal with this situation?
- How can I manage my two conflicting roles: that of HR professional and that of Brian's coach?
- How and with what can I be transparent? For example, can I say something such as, "Your request for a recommendation puts me in a difficult position because as your HR manager, I very much want you to remain in the organization, but as your coach, I know you've been fundamentally unhappy here"?
- Is it appropriate to make a recommendation as a coach? As a former coach?

(*continued*)

- How can I "keep my coaching hat on" and support Brian in his own growth and development and not fall into the trap of providing answers?

COACHING QUESTIONS

In her coaching sessions with Brian, Julie might ask questions such as these:

- Tell me about your thought processes in asking me to write a recommendation for you as your coach.
- Let's talk about how this creates a bit of a dilemma for me: I'm your coach and encourage your growth and self-development, but I am also your HR manager and have a vested interest in keeping quality talent in the organization.
- Let's talk through the potential positive and negative consequences of my writing a recommendation for you.
- How can we be most transparent so there is no misunderstanding? For example, if I write a recommendation as your coach, it will not be a secret that I am also the HR manager with this company.
- In what ways might that have a potential adverse impact?
- In what ways might that have potential positive impacts?

Technical Ineptness

Similar to the misrepresentation and collusion category, technical ineptness is a category of ethical issues connected with a lack of knowledge or skill to effectively address issues. This category is relevant to HR coaching in the event a coach finds herself unable to appropriately address topics in coaching or to navigate situations that would require a referral of a coachee to a professional more skilled in related issues (e.g., doctor, psychologist, therapist). HR coaches need to be clear with coachees when they find themselves outside their areas of expertise. However, it is also important to remember that coaches should not be playing a subject matter expert role, but should be working more as a thought partner, in which process expertise includes asking challenging questions and using supporting statements to promote reflection and clarity. Consider the following case.

The Bridge over Troubled Waters

The company has begun a reduction in force (RIF) as a result of an enterprise-wide downsizing initiative. Lucy, who has been in HR for six months and is new to the organization, decides the survivors of the layoff need special attention. However, she has no training around the impact of downsizing on organizations or its employees. In addition, she has no training in handling complex psychological issues or assessing counseling needs. She dives in anyway.

DISCUSSION

Dealing with a downsizing is a specialized skill within HR. While Lucy is enthusiastic and well meaning, she lacks competence in this area. She has never been through an RIF or downsizing initiative, and she is a relatively inexperienced HR professional who makes up for lack of experience with abundant enthusiasm and a desire to help. If Lucy can focus her approach as a coach rather than as a self-proclaimed expert, she will be able to help her coworkers address their issues rather than succumbing to the temptation to fix their problems resulting from the RIF.

QUESTIONS

Lucy might ask herself questions about this dilemma that include these:

- What type of ethical situation is this? Why?
- In what ways can I be transparent about what is happening with this RIF?
- What are the limits of my expertise around downsizing initiatives or RIFs?
- What do I need to do to coach within the limits of my expertise?
- How can I effectively balance my roles as coach and HR representative?
- How can I be transparent about which role I am playing?
- Given my lack of knowledge and training, how can I best coach and serve my clients?

(*continued*)

COACHING QUESTIONS

Lucy might pose questions such as these to the people she is coaching through the RIF:

- What kind of support can I give you during this difficult time?
- What resources would be helpful to you during this difficult time?
- What do you need from me as your coach?
- What do you need from me as your HR representative?
- Let's discuss which role I will be playing and agree [contract] on the rules of confidentiality and on my role as your coach [or your HR representative].
- Which role, HR representative or coach, do you see as of more use to you?
- What do you see as your options going forward, given the downsizing and that you will be leaving (or staying)?
- What are potential obstacles you will face if you remain in the organization?
- What are some options for addressing those obstacles?
- What are the potential obstacles you will face if you are transitioned out of the organization?
- What are some options for addressing those obstacles?
- What are your biggest fears, expectations, and beliefs as you remain in [or leave] the organization?

ORGANIZATIONAL SUPPORT FOR HR COACHING

Internal HR practitioners do not necessarily have the education and expertise needed to manage the ethical situations that will arise in coaching on their own. In our experience, it behooves the organization to provide the following kinds of support.

Ethical Guidelines or Contract

It is valuable for organizations to have clearly stated ethical guidelines and to provide guidance to HR coaches for addressing situations as they arise in coaching.

One benefit of having guidelines is that the coach not only has the support of the organization but also a way to make decisions based on clear guidelines. Too many times, coaches are left to their own devices to make things up as they go along when guidelines and practices are not clear.

In addition, beyond a specific ethical code, a decision tree or model will help provide a more detailed level of support and help identify organizational resources for certain dilemmas (e.g., in the case of suspected legal or company policy violations, the decision tree might indicate that an employee consult his supervisor/HR representative).

Coach Supervision and Mentoring

Coach supervision provides an opportunity for the coach, whether internal or external, rookie or seasoned, to have a place in which to explore his own efficacy, learn and practice techniques, and get feedback on how he is developing as a coach. It also provides an opportunity for checks and balances. For example, a coach supervisor or mentor might say to a coach, "I wonder if you are focusing on the wrong thing, solving the coachee's problem rather than creating an environment where the coachee can grapple with her own issues and solve them. How can you shift the focus?" (For some additional thoughts on coach supervision, see chapter 5.)

Ethics Training

Workshops that provide training on real-life ethical dilemmas an HR coach may face are very beneficial (Craft, 2010). For example, a workshop might use case studies to highlight common ethical issues and address them in small and large group discussions based on established organizational guidelines. A workbook of case studies and best-practice decision-making strategies would be a natural outgrowth of this collection of cases.

For another training resource, consider collecting ethical dilemmas submitted anonymously by HR coaches to provide a living document with sample dilemmas that include best practices for dealing with similar issues. An ongoing and evolving resource like this shows that the organization has a commitment to managing ethical issues as they arise and that it invites dialogue regarding ethical dilemmas. Coaches can begin to look at situations through the ethical assessment lens. This in turn supports ethical practice and critical thinking as part of the organizational culture rather than an ad hoc approach. In reality, ethical issues can arise on a daily basis, and the more that HR coaches are equipped with the necessary tools of the trade, the greater the positive impact on the individual and the organization will be.

Coaching Resource Libraries

Consider making space available where an HR coach can ask questions and find answers and resources such as sample cases, ethical codes of conduct, decision-making models, and internal experts in HR policy, practice, and procedures (e.g., legal versus ethical issues, HR law, employment relations and practices). CCL has such a resource, collected digitally, which it calls "Coaches' Corner."

CONCLUSION

Ethical issues are an inevitable component of the HR professional's experience, particularly in coaching relationships. It is not our contention that an organization will be able to eliminate ethical issues and dilemmas, but there are a number of ways to manage situations as they arise and provide resources to HR professionals to help navigate potentially ethical gray areas.

By its very nature, HR coaching is the work of managing competing interests and information from both the organization and individual employees and therefore requires the HR coach to embrace the tension that inevitably arises as part of the role. In the case of Jim and Susan, in which Jim knows confidential information about Susan that might have a negative impact on her being considered for a promotion if it is used as part of an internal decision-making process, Jim did not solicit the information; Susan volunteered it. Even so, the ethical dilemma arises from the revealed information. It may feel difficult for the HR professional to ignore this information when providing a recommendation. It is much like a jury being told to disregard information that was revealed in court but has been disallowed. It has to be a conscious and intentional process. The HR coach has to hold on to this information, not run from it, and hold herself to the highest standard of ethical behavior. This alone may contribute in important ways to the coaching relationship and the development of the coachee.

This chapter has provided a framework, sample cases, and practical questions to help guide HR coaches as they navigate the ethical issues that inevitably arise in coaching situations. We hope this chapter serves as an aid in honing their ability to navigate ethical dilemmas and come out on the other side more informed, more competent, and more confident. And, above all, the chapter's purpose is to ensure that the development of the coachee remains the primary goal of coaching.

PART THREE

Special Applications of Coaching

The use of coaching as a developmental conversation and an ongoing developmental process creates opportunities for utilizing a variety of applications benefiting individuals, groups, and organizations. In part 3, we highlight some specific circumstances and opportunities where coaching can play a unique role or has been underused to date, and where broader application could lead to increased impact in organizations. The applications explored in the following chapters range from the individual level, to teams at various levels within organizations, including the formation of senior leadership teams, and all the way up to the organizational level and large-scale changes and transformation efforts.

Throughout this handbook, we have highlighted opportunities and areas where coaching breaks from the confines of executive coaching and moves into much broader applications. Mentoring programs, for example, can be a valuable talent management tool, especially when used as a component of a broader talent strategy to promote development, retention, and engagement by connecting leaders at higher levels in the organization to newer or younger leadership talent. Chapter 14 provides an overview of mentoring, including what it is, what the individual and organizational benefits can include, and the strategic and operational considerations of designing and implementing formal mentoring programs. Chapter 13 highlights a process CCL collaboratively developed with others to introduce coaching approaches in a wide variety of situations, from grassroots communities in developing countries to transformational efforts with prison populations. In addition, chapter 19 describes CCL's efforts to take coaching to young people and others outside the corporate coaching paradigm. We hope these chapters highlight for you the deep power of coaching for individuals, groups, and communities.

Teams play a critical role in organizational life and organizational success. They are critical units in most organizations, given the increasing complexity of work and the resulting need for collaboration. When functioning well, teams can serve as key levers in organizational performance, leadership, and change. When not functioning well, they can inhibit those outcomes. Drawing on CCL's research and practical experience working with teams, chapter 16 reviews various approaches to team coaching, including the process of team coaching, its emergent nature, common targets of intervention, required capabilities and competencies of team coaching practitioners, and foundational frameworks and theories that inform such work.

Teams are of special significance to HR leaders who serve on senior executive teams and play a key role in supporting the teams' optimal functioning. From an HR perspective, how can coaching help to ensure successful transitions of senior executives into the organization and on to the top leadership team and support the creation of highly effective senior executive teams? Leaders who are new to their roles face unique challenges that put them at risk of failure, whether they are hired externally or promoted from within. Executive integration coaching, which focuses on the successful transition of a new leader into his or her role, has proven a powerful tool to mitigate the risk of failure. Drawing on CCL's work in this area, chapter 15 provides a practical overview of the executive integration coaching process, laying out the success factors targeted in such coaching and the key steps involved. Moving from the integration of new executives into the organization to executive team functioning, chapter 17 explores how a senior HR leader can work with the CEO and the rest of leadership to define the membership, roles, group dynamics, governance processes and standards, and stakeholder management of the senior executive team.

At an even broader scale, what is the role of coaching in supporting large-scale transformation efforts within an organization? Change management is almost a constant within organizations today, and coaching can play a key role in supporting the senior executive team, and managers at other levels, to be change leaders as well as change managers. In our experience, change efforts quite often fail because the leadership aspects of such work are not attended to throughout the process. Chapter 18 explores principles for organizational transformation and the need to balance the role of leader coach for members of the senior team to develop the capabilities they need to lead change and the role of serving as an organizational leadership guide to build the organizational capabilities necessary for successful transformation efforts.

By broadening the conversation regarding opportunities to apply coaching within organizations, we hope part 3 provides some fresh thinking for you as an HR leader to expand your set of coaching tools.

chapter
THIRTEEN

Coaching for All

Creative Leadership Conversations with Peers

Philomena Rego, TZiPi Radonsky, Lyndon Rego, and Patrick Williams

How does a company reconcile the demands of fiscal realities (paying the bills, continuing its work) with its larger vision to benefit the world? This challenge affects organizations of all kinds throughout the world, and the Center for Creative Leadership is not immune from the contradictions between its practical needs and its world-changing vision ("To advance the understanding, practice, and development of leadership for the benefit of society worldwide"). CCL decided early in its existence to regularly and persistently push development into new populations such as youth leadership and more recently into new areas around the world. The question that drives us is, "How can we make leadership development a democratic endeavor, not limited by ability to pay nor by cultural assumptions?"

The initiatives characterizing our answers to this question have been incubated in an inclusive global team operating under the banner of Leadership Beyond Boundaries (LBB) (CCL, 2013). One initiative focuses on the application of coaching skills as a core element of development and incorporates it into group programs, leader training, and peer coaching. This chapter shares a little of the design of Creative Leadership Conversations, the program that includes all of these elements, and describes some of the settings in which the approach has proven valuable.

CREATIVE LEADERSHIP CONVERSATIONS

The idea for Creative Leadership Conversations (CLC) developed from the appreciation of the power of deep and open dialogue to change how we see ourselves, our relationships, and our communities. We took a cue from Pat Williams, who had created a nonprofit organization, Coaching the Global Village, to address the question, "Can we create a means where two people can sit under a baobab tree and be engaged in a creative and collaborative conversation that builds and strengthens relationships while inspiring new thinking and broader horizons?" When he heard about LBB, he connected with the other authors to create the CLC approach and resources. In this chapter we refer to these resources as the CLC tool kit.

CLC is a means for individuals and organizations to develop their coaching skills, extend the power of coaching into a range of developmental conversations, and create a coaching culture. CLC has been used around the world in a variety of applications, from teaching coaching to consultants in Latin America to helping prisoners in North America shift perspective; from equipping nongovernmental organization workers in Africa to better engage stakeholders to enabling nuns in India to renew their commitments to their calling and to each other. In many of these applications, CLC is used as a mechanism for peer-to-peer interaction that moves people beyond reliance on roles defined by power, social standing, authority, or tradition to a readiness to assist others in their own learning.

The CLC tool kit brings together a wide range of resources for leadership development and coaching skills and provides a common language that is easy to grasp and has proven readily understandable in different places and with different populations. Attentive readers will recognize echoes of the CCL coaching framework (RACSR: relationship, assessment, challenge, support, results) in the CLC model, but it has been adapted to LBB work. Figure 13.1 provides an overview of the tool kit's elements. At the center is the idea of relationship ("You + I"), which is surrounded by three concentric circles that represent different domains of interest. Each domain involves relationships of one sort or another as a focus and a mechanism for growth.

The first domain, *Be*, builds on the recognition that we come to understand ourselves through our relationships with others. In dialogue with another person, we find our own beliefs, values, habits, desires, motivation, and identity thrown into high relief. The domain of being is the first focus, and it relates clearly to the broad description of assessment in the CCL coaching framework. In the coaching framework, assessment covers self-awareness, attention to feedback and our impact on

Figure 13.1
Elements of the Creative Leadership Conversations Tool Kit

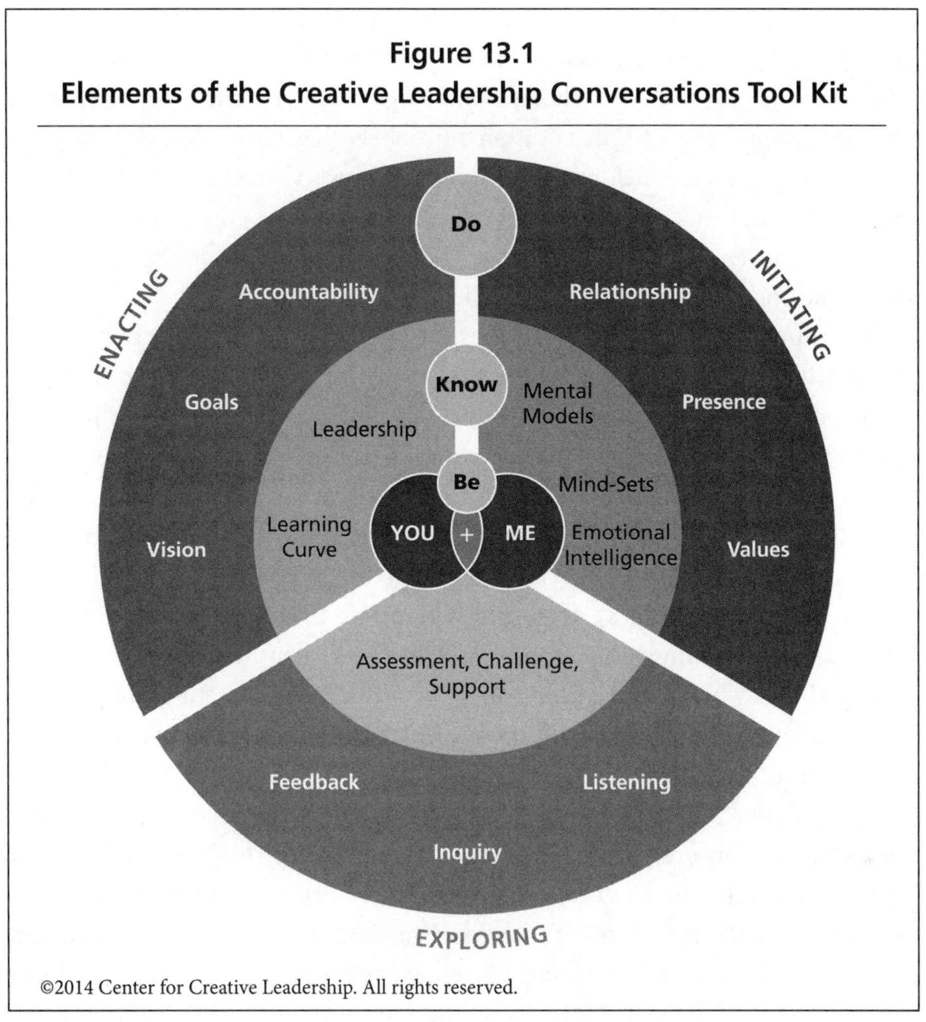

others, and engagement with one's inner life (attitudes, mind-set, values). *Be* points to our identity, but positions it as a relational dimension, which is appropriate for a leadership development domain. This domain also includes an assumption of collaboration, which allows the LBB team to present the CLC model so that it is understood in both individualistic and collectivist cultural settings. (The Be-Know-Do model has its origin in the *US Army Leadership Manual*, later popularized by Hesselbein & Shinseki, 2004.) In the framework of creative conversations, be, know, and do are treated as domains of belief, knowledge, and skill that are made available during and as a result of coaching sessions.

The second domain, *Know*, captures the range of theories and cognitive tools that enable a common language with which to conduct creative conversations. This part of the model includes other CCL models, such as assessment-challenge-support (ACS), in addition to models that have wide circulation in human development, such as emotional intelligence (Goleman, 2002). While it is not necessary to know all of these models in order to engage in the kind of coaching conversations offered by the CLC, the range included speaks to self, other, and community development of leadership.

The third domain, *Do*, encompasses a variety of actions and activities associated with structuring creative conversations. They are grouped according to the hypothesized progress of steps in the CLC process, beginning with *initiating* actions followed by *exploring* and *enacting*. Initiating actions represent the kind of offering of oneself we make in starting a conversation when we are truly interested in the other person. CLC brings some helpful structure to the encounter (a design to the relationship), exposes who we are (identity), and says what we value (values). Exploring actions are the responsive elements of a conversation, including hearing what the other person has said, exploring further through inquiry, and sharing how it affects us as feedback. Enacting completes the narrative by urging collaboration on creating something together that expresses the new reality associated with our conversations.

The CLC tool kit has been used to extend coaching into environments beyond the traditional corporate setting. It adopts as its aim sharing tools and practices and demonstrating that all of us can create a healthier, more interesting, and more vital world through the right kind of conversations. LBB has shown that the CLC tool kit can be readily adopted in widely divergent settings and adapted to particular communities with benefits that are not dependent on a single cultural lens.

CLC IN THE WORLD

CLC and peer coaching skills programs have been offered in Cameroon, Chile, El Salvador, Singapore, Ethiopia, India, Haiti, Jamaica, and the United States to a wide range of audiences, including directors of HR and senior training officers, college heads and school principals, teachers and professors, counselors and extension workers, medical doctors and nurses, police and prisoners, managers and supervisors, government leaders and religious workers.

Preparing Government Leaders to Develop Other Leaders

The Management Institute for National Development (MIND) in Jamaica has hosted both customized and open enrollment CLC programs for the public, as well as the social services sector. A driver has been the national Vision 2030, which aims for Jamaica to achieve developed country status by the year 2030 (Planning Institute of Jamaica, 2007). Vision 2030 is based on seven guiding principles that put people at the center of Jamaica's development. Transformational leadership is first among these principles.

The participants in the MIND CLC programs include mostly senior and middle managers. Managers in Jamaica typically focus on performance development, where telling, problem solving, and giving advice are the norm. The CLC approach of eliciting the involvement and best thinking of the whole team is significantly different—eye opening and challenging for the participants in fact. Many participants found it difficult to let go of familiar and comfortable control-based leadership approaches and to embrace a different way of leading. The CLC approach creates a safe environment that helps participants experiment with engaging others in a partnership of equals. The deep sharing at the outset of the process creates trust and connection around shared values, backgrounds, and challenges. With greater awareness of commonalities, participants are asked to turn the mirror inward and question their own assumptions and the impact of their assumptions on themselves and others. As one of the participants put it, "This is a call for paradigm shift. We cannot continue the way we have been doing things and leading ourselves and others and expecting different results" (personal communication, November 29, 2013). The previous way of leading, he explained, had created a culture of dependency, failing to think, and victimization.

As the CLC process unfolded, MIND participants worked to co-create new approaches to leading that was more responsive to Vision 2030. They used the tools of inquiry to encourage answers from their coach peers. One participant noted how important it was to learn that the person being coached has all the answers needed; there is not any need to "fix" him. That frees coaching from performance reviews (the past) and sends it toward aspirations and goals (the future). A number of participants agreed that this realization shifted their interactions. In the words of one school counselor attending the session, "When a student comes to me, the focus of my thoughts is to find out what is important and what do they want to achieve."

Reinvigorating a Community of Nuns

One of the first CLC programs served a group of nuns who were running an AIDS treatment and community outreach program. The sister in charge of the facility commissioned the program because she wanted to develop her skills and those of her staff so that they could help the clients with more empathy and compassion. She said that she discovered in the CLC process that the quality of her listening was poor. "I was hearing them," she said, "but not really listening."

At the conclusion of the program, the nuns committed to engage with others without judgment and to be curious about alternative perspectives. A week or so later, the sister reported that she had noticed a difference. The nuns had been using the new practices and had changed how they were interacting with each other, the staff, patients, and children. Some of the sisters who were least expected to change had actually changed the most. She noted that she had become intentional in building relationships and listening, and that she didn't have to try so hard to come up with powerful questions because she was already connected with others. She observed that using the skills and engaging her staff in a productive way resulted in improved relationships and a positive impact on those they serve.

In another example, the LBB team delivered a two-day coaching program to twenty-six nuns and four staff members in the United States with the goal of helping veteran community members to coach new members of the community and develop a coaching culture within the community. The program aimed to improve communication, ward off conflict, and create both formal and informal opportunities for coaching throughout the community. The core knowledge shift these participants experienced was that leadership is an activity that everyone can practice; it is not a position. The training was followed by six hours of coaching by volunteer coaches for each participant and six monthly calls to develop their learning. In practicing coaching and sharing their real-life issues and dreams, the participants deepened their relationships with each other. One of the sisters said that she had no idea how intimate and connected she would feel with the other participants. Another commented that now when she leads a meeting, she thinks, "What would be a question to open this conversation right now?"

Transforming Prisoners

A dramatic application of the CLC model occurred in prisons through the Reconstruct Program led by a prisoner, Talib Shakir, who at the age of seventeen received a life sentence, with probation at twenty years. (His parole was denied in 2014, and he transferred to a different prison, where he continues to appeal his sentence.) During his incarceration, he has embraced the opportunity to reevaluate his life and turn it around. He reflected on what it takes to break the cycle of violence, crime, and recidivism. While in prison, Shakir originally worked with outreach groups and at-risk teens and youth through efforts commonly known as "scared straight." What he realized was that once a person's actions reach the stage where a scared straight intervention might be prescribed, it's no longer possible to scare them straight. Another approach was needed, and he drew on his own experiences for lessons to inspire change in at-risk youth. He also sought new tools that could change the minds and hearts of those on whom he was focused.

When he encountered coaching and a book by Patrick Williams and Diane Menendez (2007), he began to actively practice the skills. He writes:

> I believe that I am a living proof that with the right people in your life, taking the right steps in life and having the right opportunities, that coaching can play a critical and important role in successful re-entry of many prisoners. I cannot tell you of the difference in the lives of the guys that I am in contact with through coaching that are better men today as a result of having been coached. I had one guy tell me today that he had chills and goose bumps after the session due to the impact of having [been] asked a powerful and thought provoking question. That feeling led him to do the things that he knows that he needs to do but just needed a little help getting there. I have come to believe that most people don't care what you know until they know that you care. That is what makes coaching a powerful tool of change! (Coaching the Global Village, 2013)

Reconstruct provided a pilot coach training program for a group of inmates to give them new communication strategies for talking with their families on visitations, interacting with other men, and transforming potential conflict situations into a two-way discussion with new levels of listening and learning. The anecdotal evidence from participants was striking in its strong praise for the impact on the individual prisoners, and a second program is nearing completion as this book goes to press.

CONCLUSION

We share these examples and the CLC model to encourage you, as an HR professional, to think of applications for coaching skills development in more settings and with more populations than you may have anticipated. These changes in mind-set, attitude, and behavior may be quite small, but they can have a dramatic impact on the climate and culture of an organization or a community. When practiced persistently through repeated creative leadership conversations, coaching practices can turn climates of distrust and internal competition toward practices of appreciation, collaboration, and even compassion. The key to getting those results is creating opportunities for people to engage in candid, courageous, and creative conversations with each other. CLC is based on the understanding that these coaching skills—listening, inquiry, and feedback—can be learned, and when they are consistently practiced, they can transform lives, teams, organizations, and communities.

chapter
FOURTEEN

Mentoring for Leadership Development

William A. Gentry

The Center for Creative Leadership (CCL), through its Europe, Middle East, and Africa (EMEA) office, recently partnered with a global health and hygiene product manufacturer on the design, implementation, and training of a mentoring initiative. The program targets a specific group of managers in the organization whose scope and responsibilities are becoming broader and more global in nature. The initiative includes several of the best practices for formal mentoring programs that we discuss in this chapter:

- *Organizational support.* The CEO and other high-ranking organizational leaders have publicly supported and sponsored the initiative. There are also "mentoring champions" across the entire organization who support the matching of mentors to mentees and act as a conduit between the mentor-mentee pair and the organization to discuss what is working and what is not.
- *Intentional mentor-mentee matching.* Program designers created a template outlining criteria for the matching process and factors to guide the choice of mentors and mentees.
- *Confidentiality and trust.* Although the mentoring initiative started in HR, the ownership has moved to the business units. Confidentiality among mentor and

Thanks to Rob Elsey, André Keil, Nigel Murphy, and Rich Walsh for their work in mentoring and for providing examples and stories of how CCL has worked with individuals and organizations in its own mentoring activities.

mentee and the supervisors of both has been managed, as confidentiality is an important aspect of mentoring relationships.

- *Training and orientation of mentor and mentee.* All parties involved develop a common schema or model of mentoring through consistent informational materials and group training sessions. These provide mentors with information about the purpose of the initiative, skills, style, and how to manage the life cycle of the relationship and connections to other mentors in what becomes a supportive peer network. The sessions provide similarly relevant training to mentees.
- *Guidance on meeting frequency and format.* The formal relationships last between six and nine months, though some have lasted longer. Most meetings are virtual because the organization is global; however, an initial face-to-face meeting, when possible, is beneficial to mentors and mentees. Meetings generally take place every three to four weeks for the first few months, with more flexibility thereafter.
- *Evaluation of the mentoring program.* The mentoring program is still an active initiative in the organization. However, there are some positive initial findings:
  - Mentees are transitioning into new roles more quickly and with better success.
  - Mentees are getting better guidance on how to effectively manage large multifunctional teams.
  - Mentees are building networks more quickly and with the right people.

MENTORING: HOW IT ALL GOT STARTED

The concept of mentoring dates back to Homer's *Odyssey*. Before leaving to fight in the Trojan War, the main character, Odysseus, entrusted his older friend Mentor (in fact the goddess Athena) to teach and educate his son, Telemachus. The term *mentor* has since become proverbial for a faithful, trusted, or wise advisor. In fact, mentoring has been part of the fabric of our everyday lives throughout history. (See exhibit 14.1 for popular examples.)

Exhibit 14.1
Famous Mentoring Relationships

We each have our own ideas, vision, or image of what a mentor is, what a mentoring relationship looks like, and circumstances in which a mentor is used. And these ideas can be very different from each other. The focus of this chapter is on mentoring in a workplace setting. But mentoring can take place anywhere, such as in community service and outreach (think Big Brothers/Big Sisters mentoring program) or in educational settings (teacher advising a student).

So no matter where you look, more than likely you will find something that resembles a mentoring relationship. Do these sound familiar?

- In well-known professional relationships:
    - Psychologist Sigmund Freud mentored his protégé, Carl Jung
    - Anne Sullivan teaching Helen Keller
    - Novelist Gertrude Stein and Ernest Hemingway
    - Haydn and Beethoven
    - Oscar Hammerstein and Stephen Sondheim
- In the business world:
    - Andrew Carnegie and Charles Schwab
    - Larry Summers and Sheryl Sandberg
- In books or movies:
    - Obi Wan Kenobi and Yoda instructing Luke Skywalker in the *Star Wars* movies
    - Mr. Miyagi and Daniel LaRusso from *The Karate Kid*
    - Professor Dumbledore and Harry Potter
- In sports:
    - Trainer Angelo Dundee with boxer Muhammad Ali
    - Basketball coach John Wooden and Bill Walton

(*continued*)

Exhibit 14.1 (*Continued*)

- Golf instructor Harvey Penick and Ben Crenshaw
- Golf peers Seve Ballesteros and José María Olazábal
- In entertainment and pop culture:
  - Singer/songwriter Woody Guthrie and Bob Dylan
  - Musicians Dr. Dre and Eminem
  - Television producer Lorne Michaels and actress Tina Fey
  - Coaches who mentor inexperienced singers or dancers in reality television talent shows

Social scientists have taken particular interest in the concept of mentoring in traditional workplace contexts, beginning in the 1970s and 1980s with the landmark and seminal works *Seasons of a Man's Life* (Levinson, Darrow, Klein, Levinson, & McKee, 1978) and *Mentoring at Work* (Kram, 1985). Practitioners and human resource (HR) professionals have also examined and employed mentoring as a powerful form of training and development for decades, in a variety of formal and informal settings. A 2011 survey stated that at least 70 percent of Fortune 500 companies had a mentoring initiative (Carver, 2011).

Many of you are HR professionals or leaders in your organization who play the role of coach or play active roles in the implementation of coaching initiatives in organizations. You may also be involved in mentoring experiences and processes. The terms *coaching* and *mentoring* are frequently used interchangeably, and you may be confused as to what the similarities and differences are between coaching and mentoring. So let's be clear from the start on what we mean by *coaching* and what we mean by *mentoring*. Based on the summary of Murphy and Kram (2014) and our work at CCL (e.g., Hart, 2009), there are definite differences, although both are clearly relationship focused and developmental in nature. The focus of coaching is more for building capacity, especially as it relates to current effectiveness or preparation for a relatively near-term change or increase in responsibility. The focus of mentoring is more on a person's career path, with mentors leveraging their positions in organizations and their personal expertise to sponsor mentees and transfer needed knowledge to their mentees. This handbook notes that coaching can be developmental and stimulates a person's awareness to make wiser decisions and act accordingly. Coaching tends to involve conversations that are task, behavior, or goal oriented in nature, focusing on short- to intermediate-term results and goals. Results are highly important in coaching, as CCL's coaching framework (RACSR: relationship, assessment, challenge, support, results) suggests. The strong focus on actionable learning, short-term to intermediate results, and development for enhanced performance is characteristic of coaching in the workplace.

Mentoring is much broader and more expansive. It is more multifunctional and multifaceted than coaching, and the underlying goal of mentoring may be more long term in nature. The focus for mentoring is less on short-term or intermediate goals and usually more on the broad career development and success of an individual, focusing on experience, expertise, and personal growth. Personal and professional development is the main purpose of mentoring (Murphy & Kram, 2014). Mentors may also give more direct advice, whereas coaches may ask questions more. Mentoring uses a variety of activities that include coaching conversations, as well as other functions of support, such as sponsorship, protection, and role modeling.

Because this handbook is focused on creating coaching cultures within organizations through an array of activities with multiple entry points, mentoring initiatives should be thought of as one of many services and strategies that contribute to a culture of learning or of development. Mentoring programs can be vital for a leader to develop or as part of a leadership development initiative (McCauley, 2006; McCauley & Guthrie, 2007). Mentoring initiatives can be used in conjunction with other services that this handbook explores, such as peer coaching or team coaching.

The first part of this chapter provides an overview of what mentoring is (and is not) in a workplace context and the roles mentors play in a mentoring relationship. Then I explain how both parties of the mentoring relationship, the mentor who provides mentoring and the mentee or protégé who receives mentoring, benefit from actively engaging in the relationship, as well as how the organization as a whole may benefit from high-quality mentoring relationships. In the next section of the chapter, I discuss best practices for formal mentoring programs in organizations as a practical discussion of how HR professionals and leaders can maximize the positive outcomes that formalized mentoring can bring. The third section looks at where mentoring research and practice may be taking the field in the future.

BACKGROUND AND DEFINING WHAT MENTORING IS AND ISN'T

Characteristics of Mentoring

Several characteristics describe mentoring (Eby, Rhodes, & Allen, 2007). First, though it may be obvious, is that mentoring involves two people, and it is a unique relationship between them. No two mentoring relationships are alike; some mentoring relationships may change the life of the person mentored for the better, and others may be superficial and trivial (Levinson et al., 1978). Second, mentoring involves learning and knowledge acquisition, particularly of the person being mentored (the mentee), but the mentor learns during the mentoring process as well (Ramaswami & Dreher, 2007). Third, mentoring is a process in which the mentor provides different types of support functions to the mentee, mainly emotional/psychosocial and career related (Kram, 1985). Fourth, mentoring is a reciprocal, mutually beneficial relationship that benefits both the mentee and the mentor. Finally, mentoring relationships are dynamic: the relationship can change over time, and the impact of mentoring on both parties can be greater as time goes by (Kram, 1985). You may initially think that other types of relationships are similar, but as exhibit 14.2 explains, mentoring is quite distinctive.

Exhibit 14.2
Distinctive Mentoring Characteristics

Mentoring is a dynamic, unique relationship between two people in which one person intentionally provides various types of support for the other but both parties acquire knowledge and benefit from the experience. Other types of relationships could be seen in similar ways: role model–observer, teacher-student, supervisor-subordinate, and professional coach-client relationships (Eby et al., 2007; see also Baek-Kyoo, Sushko, & McLean, 2012). Though these are similar and may have some overlap, mentoring differs from these other relationships too. Keep in mind these characteristics specific to mentoring relationships:

- Requires interaction
- Can vary from very distant to extremely close

Exhibit 14.2 (*Continued*)

- Can have a much broader scope of influence
- Has more variation in mutual learning of both parties
- Has varying power differences
- Can be formal or informal
- Can be spontaneous or planned
- Can happen in any context, such as in academia, the larger community, and, the focus of this chapter, the workplace
- Can be open to anyone, for anyone to be a mentor or mentee, inside or outside the organization

Functions of Mentoring

Mentoring research (Kram, 1985) has found that a mentor assists a mentee by providing two types of mentoring functions:

- Career-related support
- Emotional and psychosocial support

These two major functions, and the categories that are part of each, fit well with what CCL (Hart, 2009) believes successful mentors should do:

- Develop and manage relationships
- Survey the environment for threats and opportunities
- Sponsor the mentee's developmental activities
- Guide and counsel
- Teach
- Model effective behavior
- Motivate and inspire

These align well with what CCL believes is needed for any developmental experience to succeed: assessment, challenge, and support (ACS; Van Velsor, McCauley, & Ruderman, 2010), the core of the RACSR coaching framework.

Career-Related Support Career-related support is possible because of a mentor's senior position, experience, and influence. This helps the mentee understand organizational life, gain exposure, and obtain promotions. It may also help the mentor to develop a reputation within the organization for developing talent and support. Mentoring theory identifies five observable career-related functions and behaviors (Kram, 1985):

1. *Sponsorship.* Mentors help build the reputation of a mentee within the organization. Mentors also help the mentee obtain lateral or upward job opportunities.
2. *Exposure and visibility.* A mentor assigns key tasks and responsibilities to a mentee so that the mentee can come into contact with high-ranking or more senior-level managers. By doing so, mentors also help mentees gain knowledge about organizational life and different parts of the organization that may become of interest in the mentee's future.
3. *Coaching.* Within the context of mentoring, the function of coaching increases the mentee's knowledge and understanding of the world of work. By providing coaching, the mentor passes on advice, shares ideas, provides feedback, and demonstrates different perspectives to the mentee. This handbook's general use of the term *coaching* may be broader, particularly related to a coaching culture in an organization, or an elicitive or inquiry-based process or method to assess, challenge, support, and move a coachee toward targeted results.
4. *Protection.* Many times mentees may not know or are uninformed about what projects to get involved in or the pros and cons of working with certain people. Mentors provide protection by shielding a mentee from harm and reducing pursuit of unnecessary risks.
5. *Challenging assignments.* A mentor may assign challenging work assignments to a mentee to help the mentee develop necessary competencies such as managerial or work-related competencies. Doing so will help the mentee become prepared to move upward in the organization.

Emotional and Psychosocial Support Mentees often find great support from their mentors that can enhance their competence, identity, self-worth, and effectiveness. Emotional and psychosocial support is a second category of mentoring functions and depends more on the quality of the mentoring relationship than does career-related support and may affect relationships not only internal to the organization but also outside the organization. According to mentoring theory (Kram, 1985), there are four observable emotional/psychosocial functions and behaviors that mentors do:

1. *Role modeling.* The most frequently reported emotional and psychosocial behavior is role modeling. As a mentor sets an example for how to act and work, a mentee will identify with the mentor, attempting to model the mentor's attitudes, values, and behavior.
2. *Acceptance and confirmation.* A mentor gives support, trust, and encouragement to the mentee to help him or her take risks and develop a professional identity.
3. *Counseling.* A mentor acts as an active listener or a sounding board to help a mentee with anxiety- or fear-provoking problems.
4. *Friendship.* A mentor gives respect and support to a mentee. The result is mutual liking, understanding, and information sharing about work and life.

Mentors have the ability to serve all of these functions at one time or another, but may not serve all of them at one given time. Mentors may provide a variety of these functions over the course of the entire mentoring relationship. Furthermore, they may perform some of these functions more for some mentees and other functions for other mentees.

Benefits of Mentoring

Most of the commonly known benefits of mentoring are focused on the mentee, which makes sense because the mentee is usually the main focus of any mentoring relationship. But research shows that mentoring can benefit the mentor and implies organizational benefits as well.

Benefits for the Mentee Research has shown just how crucial mentoring is to a mentee's career and personal life (Noe, Greenberger, & Wang, 2002). As shown in table 14.1, mentees definitely receive objective career benefits through mentoring, but there are also subjective career outcomes—affective benefits that the mentee experiences (Allen, Eby, Poteet, Lentz, & Lima, 2004). Though not measured objectively, subjective career outcomes are still important to assess because they are issues many organizations want to know about their employees. In addition, they are indirectly related to bottom-line organizational performance.

Table 14.1
Mentoring Career Benefits

	Mentees	Mentors
Objective career outcomes	Higher salaries and compensation Higher promotion rates and number of promotions (Allen et al., 2004; Chao, Walz, & Gardner, 1992; Dreher & Ash, 1990; Fagenson, 1989; Scandura, 1992; Whitely, Dougherty, & Dreher, 1991)	Higher salaries and compensation Higher promotion rates and number of promotions (Allen, Eby, & Lentz, 2006a; Bozionelos, Bozionelos, Kostopoulos, & Polychroniou, 2011; Eby, Durley, Evans, & Ragins, 2006; Ghosh & Reio, 2013)
Subjective career outcomes	Better organizational socialization Higher job satisfaction Higher general satisfaction More career mobility/ opportunity and recognition Higher career satisfaction and career commitment Lower turnover intentions (Allen et al., 2004; Chao et al., 1992; Fagenson, 1989; Koberg, Boss, & Goodman, 1998; Noe, 1988)	More organizational commitment Enhanced leadership Greater affective well-being Higher job satisfaction Lower turnover intentions (Chun, Sosik, & Yun, 2012; Ghosh & Reio, 2013; Lentz & Allen, 2009)
How mentoring benefits each party	Human capital Movement capital Social/political capital and signaling Path-goal clarity Values clarity (Ramaswami & Dreher, 2007)	Human capital Movement capital Optimal resource usage Social/political capital and signaling Identity validation Relational gains (Ramaswami & Dreher, 2007)

The positive outcomes for mentees are primarily the result of receiving career-related and emotional and psychosocial support, leading to five possible types of impacts (Ramaswami & Dreher, 2007) as displayed in table 14.1 and detailed below:

1. *Human capital.* When being mentored, the mentee acquires all sorts of knowledge, skills, and abilities through challenging assignments, coaching, and role modeling received from a mentor. This is meant to boost or enrich the mentee's performance. The mentee learns new or different ways of doing things and receives ongoing positive, as well as constructive and developmental, feedback on his or her performance.
2. *Movement capital.* When a mentee receives mentoring, he or she is provided with exposure and visibility. Specifically, mentees get opportunities to meet key stakeholders, meet people with formal and informal power in the organizational hierarchy, and socialize with these important people—for example, by being invited to a leadership meeting or to work on a task force that will make recommendations to senior management. Many of these people may be leading high-profile projects or have power and influence over salary and promotion. As a result, mentees may be more likely to move around the organization, as such moves are sponsored by the mentor and organization. This will enhance the networking and socializing that he or she needs to perform well on the job.
3. *Social/political capital and signaling.* In mentoring relationships, mentees gain legitimacy and exposure by being introduced to key stakeholders, decision makers, and senior leaders who may be able to influence the career progression of the mentee in the future. When meeting these people, the mentee can learn more about the politics inside the organization. By getting advice and coaching from his or her mentor, the mentee will signal to others that he or she will be able to network with these powerful and influential people and navigate the politics in every organization. The mentor can provide direction and advice on how to be politically savvy, a skill associated with better performance and higher promotability (Ferris, Davidson, & Perrewé, 2005; Ferris, Treadway, Brouer, & Munyon, 2012; Gentry, Gilmore, Shuffler, & Leslie, 2012; Gentry & Leslie, 2012).
4. *Path-goal clarity.* Mentees receive coaching, counseling, and advice on how to achieve career goals from mentors. Mentors help mentees gain insight into

their own developmental needs, help mentees understand their strengths and weaknesses, and provide feedback that nonmentored individuals do not receive. Mentors help mentees build up their own self-confidence, self-efficacy, and motivation to achieve goals, which are inevitably tied to objective and subjective career success.

5. *Values clarity*. Mentors provide mentees a sense of clarity beyond just path-goal clarity in the course of a mentoring relationship. Mentees are able to gain clarity around current work-life situations and how the current state of affairs at work helps or hinders their career progression. They gain perspective on how their values, work and professional identity, and work and life centrality all play a part in furthering their own objective and subjective career success. This sort of self-enlightenment and opportunity for self-reflection aided by a mentor is something that nonmentored individuals usually do not get.

Benefits for the Mentor With so much of the mentoring research focused on the mentee, many would think that mentoring benefits only the one receiving it. However, researchers have begun to explore the mentoring relationship from the perspective of the mentor (Allen, 2007; Allen, Lentz, & Day, 2006). As you may have experienced in your own life, mentoring is not a one-way, unidirectional relationship, but rather a reciprocal and collaborative relationship that benefits both parties. Mentors gain personal satisfaction, are able to build a network of supporters through their cadre of mentees, can obtain job-related and organizational news or other pieces of relevant information from their mentees, and become better at their jobs through the mentoring process (Allen & Eby, 2003; Allen, Poteet, & Burroughs, 1997; Bozionelos, 2004; Ragins & Scandura, 1999). Table 14.1 shows objective and subjective career outcomes for mentors and the reasons that mentoring is likely beneficial for mentors—for example:

1. *Human capital*. Mentors can learn many things from their mentees. They can get awareness of the latest trends in the field or new developments in the field. As an example, if mentors are in a mentoring relationship with a mentee from a different demographic background, the mentor can gain better knowledge of how to deal with diversity. All of this knowledge acquisition can enhance the mentor's performance, which can be tied to the mentor's objective and subjective career success.

2. *Movement capital.* Mentoring can benefit a mentor as the mentee moves across and up the organization. In response to the mentor's devoting time and effort to the mentee, the mentee may feel as if he or she needs to "reciprocate" and provide the mentor with similar opportunities of movement possibilities, or knowledge about other opportunities that may not have been possible without the mentoring relationship. For instance, a mentee may let a mentor know of an opening in her division that would represent a reasonable promotion opportunity for the mentor.
3. *Optimal resource use.* By giving a mentee work, the mentor may potentially be decreasing the amount of time, energy, and work he or she has to do. This lessens responsibilities in some areas so the mentor can focus on more important and possibly high-profile work and responsibility. Proper delegation to mentees can help the mentor divert, enhance, or increase his or her capacity of work and responsibility that can inevitably improve the mentor's job performance and objective and subjective career outcomes. Delegating effectively can have its rewards.
4. *Social/political capital and signaling.* By mentoring others, a mentor can expand his or her power base or reputation. The more mentees a mentor has, the more likely those mentees will want to reciprocate the time, effort, and energy given to them in the relationship by providing feedback, news, and information, thus building up social/political capital. Also, if mentors are successful at mentoring others, the mentor's reputation will build. This increase of reputation can act as a signal to others that the mentor is someone who has an eye for talent and has the knowledge and capability to cultivate talent. This reputation can be crucial for attaining rewards, promotions, and salary increases, as well as for increasing subjective career success outcomes such as job satisfaction or organizational commitment.
5. *Identity validation.* By participating in a mentoring relationship, mentors can enhance their own self-awareness, self-discovery, and growth as a leader, which are all part of identity validation. Mentoring others can lead to a heightened sense of self-worth and personal and professional satisfaction and could revitalize one's job or career (Schulz, 1995). For many people, leaving a legacy is a top priority. Mentors can leave a legacy by mentoring others and feel a sense of purpose, fulfillment, and confirmation at work

(Kram, 1985). When mentors feel they are helping others, they in fact are also helping themselves, increasing their subjective career success.

6. *Relational gains.* As the mentoring relationship grows and matures, the mentor may feel a strong emotional bond with the mentee that can be beneficial for the physical and mental health of a mentor. This may increase the mentor's job and life satisfaction and commitment to the organization.

The story of Conrad and Akilah illustrates the ways in which a mentoring relationship can benefit both the mentor (Conrad) and mentee (Akilah).

Conrad and Akilah

Conrad was a middle-aged German working for the research arm of a global chemical company in Europe. In the mentoring program in his organization, he was paired with Akilah, a young Middle Eastern female chemist with high potential in the organization. Both benefited from their mentoring relationship that formally lasted eighteen months.

Conrad gave Akilah a challenging assignment of fixing a struggling product line and continually provided ongoing feedback on how well she was doing based on his observations (human capital). During this time, Conrad introduced Akilah to high-ranking members in the organization before she gave a presentation about her work in an important quarterly meeting. Coincidentally to Akilah (but not Conrad), they were also influential parties in the year-end talent discussions (movement capital; social/political capital and signaling). Conrad also talked to Akilah about her career aspirations. Akilah hoped to get an assignment in China and eventually become vice president of the product development group. Conrad discussed with her the best way to go about that (path-goal clarity) and how those career aspirations would align with her own values, needs, and identity inside and outside the organization (values clarity).

Conrad also benefited from this mentoring relationship. Leveraging her background, Akilah helped Conrad develop a much more global perspective on their customers as well as understanding the value of some newer research methods (human capital). During and after the mentoring relationship, Akilah felt indebted to his mentoring, and she regularly let Conrad know of job opportunities inside and outside the organization through her own networks (movement capital). When Conrad gave Akilah that challenging job assignment, it freed up his time so he could spend more time on a safety issue that could have brought a lot of trouble to the organization if not given attention (optimal resource use). With Akilah's reputation growing in the organization and her success in dealing with the challenging assignment, Conrad became known as a talent scout and a cultivator of talent, which increased his own reputation (social/political capital and signaling). The mentoring relationship also helped infuse a renewed sense of vigor for his work (identify validation). Coincidentally, Conrad's children were about to go to college, and he was feeling rather alone in life. Being a mentor to Akilah brought an emotional attachment and friendship that helped counteract those feelings of loneliness and sadness outside the workplace (relational gains).

In the end, the mentoring relationship helped both Akilah and Conrad. Akilah was able to get an assignment in China that she believed would not have been possible without Conrad's mentoring. She is well on her way to become a vice president. Conrad had a renewed sense of self-worth and motivation. After five very productive years in the organization, a job offer from another organization that Akilah mentioned to Conrad long after their formal relationship ended was too good to pass up. The job would allow Conrad to be closer to his children and grandchildren. Despite changes in roles and location, this valuable partnership benefited both Conrad the mentor and Akilah the mentee.

Benefits for the Organization

As an HR professional focused on leveraging the talent in your organization, you are likely thinking about many potential benefits of mentoring for your organization based on the preceding discussion. Or you are nodding your head because you have firsthand knowledge of it. The research is a little behind in this area, however, and is shown usually through case studies and organizational reports (B. Garvey & Garrett-Harris, 2005). However, we can assume theoretically that mentoring benefits the organization in the long run, even if indirectly (Baugh & Fagenson-Eland, 2007; Tong & Kram, 2013). As an example, when people receive mentoring, they usually feel less stress (Baugh, Lankau, & Scandura, 1996; Kram & Hall, 1991; Nielson, Carlson, & Lankau, 2001). Logically, the less stress they have, the healthier they usually are, which in general is associated with lower rates of absenteeism, tardiness, and turnover. From a research perspective, more work needs to be done in uncovering the exact impact of mentoring programs on bottom-line organizational outcomes.

Mentoring Is Not Always Beneficial

Most mentoring relationships are positive. Yet some may be marginally beneficial, and some relationships may in fact be dysfunctional and destructive to the mentee or mentor (Eby, 2007; Scandura, 1998), which can inevitably hurt the organization. Research suggests what may lead to bad mentoring relationships (Eby, 2007; Eby & McManus, 2004):

- Mentor-mentee mismatch in values, personalities, or work style
- Neglect and lack of interest
- Unwillingness to learn from both parties
- Manipulation, deception, or self-interest
- Inability to take part in a quality relationship in general

Exhibit 14.3 offers lessons CCL has learned in helping troubled mentoring relationships. Such difficulties can result, for example, from a mentor feeling that he or she would be better off spending time on other work or fulfilling other responsibilities (Ragins & Cotton, 1993; Ragins & Scandura, 1999) or due to a poorly performing mentee reflecting badly on the mentor (Ragins & Cotton, 1993; Ragins & Scandura, 1999).

Similarly, the mentee does not always benefit from a mentoring relationship, which can be costly, for example, if the mentee relies too much on the mentor. If taken to the extreme, harassment, jealousy, exploitation, abuse, neglect, and sabotage could be outcomes of a dysfunctional mentoring relationship (Dougherty, Turban, & Haggard, 2007; Eby, 2007; Eby & Lockwood, 2005; Eby & McManus, 2004; Kram, 1985). Mentees in a dysfunctional relationship may even have increased stress and depressed mood, and experience withdrawal behaviors such as absenteeism or turnover intentions and lessened job satisfaction (Eby & Allen, 2002; Ragins, Cotton, & Miller, 2000; Scandura & Hamilton, 2002), which can directly affect organizations.

Exhibit 14.3
Lessons from Troubled Mentoring Relationships

At times, CCL is brought into an organization to strengthen (or fix) mentoring initiatives that are not going well. One public services organization had mixed results with its mentoring program, and CCL was brought in. Through interviews, CCL found that both mentors and mentees saw the program as a waste of time. Several times mentors and mentees said something to the effect of, "I didn't know my partner, and I wasn't clear on how they might help me or I might help them." In reflecting on how the program could be more valuable, mentors and mentees both usually said:

"Provide insight into why mentoring is important to our organization."

"Provide clarity on what is expected of mentors and mentees."

"Provide support in doing a good job in mentoring."

In short, there are pros and cons of mentoring relationships that must be assessed. All involved should understand what mentors and mentees bring to the table. For instance, mentors should understand the time, energy, and resources it takes to mentor others. Mentees should understand that a mentor is just one of many people who can help him or her in performance and development issues.

CONSIDERATIONS FOR SETTING UP A MENTORING PROGRAM

Informal Mentoring Programs

According to Eby et al. (2007), mentoring "relationships that develop naturally or spontaneously without outside assistance are considered informal mentoring" (p. 12). Informal mentoring relationships are initiated, maintained, and terminated by the mentor and mentee without official organizational involvement, and there is no prescribed frequency or length of time to be involved in the relationship (Baugh & Fagenson-Eland, 2007; Finkelstein & Poteet, 2007; Ramaswami & Dreher, 2007). Many of us have likely experienced or witnessed these informal mentoring relationships. They occur mainly due to mutual attraction and interest of mentor and mentee. And they may be more beneficial than formal mentoring (Baugh & Fagenson-Eland, 2007). Compared to those in formal mentoring programs, mentees in informal mentoring relationship have been shown to receive more career and emotional and psychosocial functions from their mentors and have higher-quality mentoring relationships (Allen, Day, & Lentz, 2005; Chao et al., 1992; Fagenson-Eland, Marks, & Amendola, 1997). Furthermore, informal mentoring can have a larger and more significant effect on career outcomes of mentees than formal mentoring (Underhill, 2006). So informal mentoring is one powerful relationship that you should encourage and support in your workplace.

Mentoring as Part of the Responsibilities of Leaders and Supervisors

Though separate from formal programs, an important role and responsibility of successful supervisors and leaders is mentoring their direct reports. Mentoring is an essential behavior to consider in the development and performance of managers and leaders (Allio, 2005; D. Day, 2000; Muldoon & Miller, 2005; Palus, Horth, Selvin, & Pulley, 2003; Stead, 2005). Think about your organization right now. With limited dollars in development budgets and with modern organizations becoming flatter, managers have to spend more time and effort in coaching and mentoring their direct reports to be successful (Agarwal, Angst, & Magni, 2009; Ellinger, Ellinger, & Keller, 2003; Murrell, Crosby, & Ely, 1999; Richard, Ismail, Bhuian, & Taylor, 2008; Sosik & Jung, 2010).

Mentoring as a specific responsibility of supervisors and managers can have a positive impact on direct reports, including higher levels of career mentoring, job performance, and affective commitment compared to those without managerial mentors (Brashear, Bellenger, Boles, & Barksdale, 2006; Payne & Huffman, 2005; Scandura & Williams, 2004). My own research at CCL indicates that managers who mentor others are seen as more effective at their job by their boss and more promotable by their boss and peers (Gentry & Sosik, 2010; Gentry, Weber, & Sadri, 2008). As with more formal mentor-mentee relationship, managers who mentor their direct reports:

- Are seen as more effective and efficient in their job
- Gain information and support from their direct reports
- Expand their power base and reputation
- Are seen by upper management as having good judgment, reputation, and credibility

- Gain increased recognition, influence, clout, visibility, legitimacy, respect, and admiration

Organizations and HR professionals should support and reinforce the role that mentoring has for leaders in their organization because mentoring and leadership are inextricably tied together (Godshalk & Sosik, 2007).

Formal Mentoring Programs

Finkelstein and Poteet (2007) provide a good working definition of a formal mentoring program:

> A formal mentoring program occurs when an organization officially supports and sanctions mentoring relationships. In these programs, organizations play a role in facilitating mentoring relationships by providing some level of structure, guidelines, policies, and assistance for starting, maintaining, and ending mentor-protégé relationships. (p. 346)

Despite the popularity of formal mentoring programs in Fortune 500 companies, research shows they have produced mixed results (table 14.2).

Table 14.2
Advantages and Disadvantages of Formal Mentoring Programs

Advantages of Formal Mentoring Programs	Disadvantages of Formal Mentoring Programs
• Seen as a perk by employees • Used as a recruitment and retention strategy for employees • Used as a succession-planning tool for organizations • Used as a way to groom high-potential employees or those in underrepresented groups	When compared to mentees in informal relationships, mentees in formal mentoring programs may: • Receive less mentoring • Receive lower-quality mentoring • Receive fewer psychosocial/emotional and career-related mentoring functions from their mentors • Have lower compensation

Sources: Finkelstein and Poteet (2007); Underhill (2006); Allen et al. (2005); Chao et al. (1992); Ragins and Cotton (1999); Wanberg, Welsh, and Hezlett (2003).

The benefits of formal mentoring programs can be maximized when the mentees are highly satisfied with their mentors (Ramaswami & Dreher, 2007; Wanberg et al., 2003). Surveying mentees at points in the engagement can be useful to assess satisfaction, as can simply checking in and asking for feedback from the mentee.

In summary, there are three key recommendations regarding organizational promotion of mentoring. First, encourage employees to be proactive in participating in informal mentoring relationships. Second, make sure that managers understand that a role they also need to play while managing others is that of a mentor to their direct reports. Finally, make sure that the mentee's satisfaction is a top priority in formal mentoring programs.

Best Practices for Formal Mentoring Programs

If you ensure certain best practices are followed in setting up and managing formal mentoring programs, the benefits will grow. Research on success criteria for formal mentoring programs, along with CCL's experience in partnering with organizations to build their mentoring programs (see exhibit 14.4 for suggested resources), suggests the following best practices for organizations across sectors.

Exhibit 14.4
Suggested Resources on Formal Mentoring Programs

For more information on best practices in formal mentoring programs, I recommend this reading list:

- Book chapters by Baugh and Fagenson-Eland (2007), Finkelstein and Poteet (2007), and Stokes and Merrick (2013) give a detailed list of best practices and in-depth analysis of academic and outside literature in support of many of these best practices.
- A book chapter by Sontag, Vappie, and Wanberg (2007) provides a good overview and case study of a mentoring program and what occurred from a practical perspective from beginning to end.
- Allen, Finkelstein, and Poteet's (2009) book *Designing Workplace Mentoring Programs: An Evidence-Based Approach* is a great resource for the design, development, and operation of formal mentoring programs. It includes a host of useful tools, resources, and case studies.

Organizational Support

One of the most crucial factors in successful implementation of any development initiative is organizational support. CCL has firsthand experience with this reality, for example, in implementing 360-degree processes in organizations (Fleenor, Taylor, & Chappelow, 2008). The same is true for mentoring. Many of us have witnessed the relationship between the level of support employees have for an initiative and the support given by the organization and its leaders. The culture and systems of the organization may also play a big part in the overall success of any mentoring program. If the organization's reward system, culture, and norms encourage learning and development and supportive relationships, mentoring programs should be more effective (Allen, 2004; Aryee, Chay, & Chew, 1996; Kram, 1985; Parise & Forret, 2008).

CCL and others (Burke & McKeen, 1989; Catalyst, 1993; Cunningham, 1993; Keele, Bucker, & Bushnell, 1987) note several ways organizations can readily show their support:

- Have open communication about the program
- Have formal and high-ranking leaders talk about the importance of the program
- Have formal and high-ranking leaders actively participate in the program
- Link mentoring programs to the organization's mission statements
- Link mentoring programs to reward systems
- Change the work designs and systems to be more in line with mentoring programs

Above all, participants of the mentoring program must feel that their organization and management support the program. Involving senior stakeholders, getting their buy-in, commitment, and validation of the program, and serving as champions of the program, are all crucial (Allen et al., 2006a; Klasen & Clutterbuck, 2002; Parise & Forret, 2008).

Program Objectives

CCL also recognizes that for a development initiative to be successful, clear goals need to be established (Fleenor et al., 2008). If an organization wants to implement a formal mentoring program, the organization must understand the purpose behind the program and the goals. Clarity of purpose and goals will influence the structure of the program, who will participate in the program, and under what conditions participants will engage in the program (Eby & Lockwood, 2005; Megginson, Clutterbuck, Garvey, Stokes, & Garrett-Harris, 2006). A needs assessment for mentoring and a culture assessment of the support for mentoring in the organization would obviously need to be conducted (Catalyst, 1993). Mentoring programs may fulfill the following needs (Catalyst, 1993; Eddy, Tannenbaum, Alliger, D'Abate, & Givens, 2001):

- Succession planning or grooming people for senior management
- Skill improvement
- Retention
- Diversity awareness and increase
- Relationship and network building

Organizations must ensure the mentoring program fits the needs of the organization, is linked to the organization's strategy, and has clear objectives that are regularly communicated (Baugh & Fagenson-Eland, 2007; Finkelstein & Poteet, 2007). Furthermore, organizations need to understand that a mentoring program inevitably involves an interpersonal relationship between two people, and any decision regarding design and structure should be made with the intent to improve relational processes between mentor and mentee (Allen et al., 2009).

Selection and Participation of the Participants

As part of the needs assessment and clarification of the program's purpose, there is the inevitable discussion around who should be mentees and who should be the mentors of those mentees. Exhibit 14.5 discusses the four key phases CCL believes are critical for mentoring partnerships.

However the participants of the mentoring program are chosen, it is recommended that the mentoring program is voluntary with no detrimental consequences for not wanting to participate or deciding to withdraw from the program. Mandatory participation may cause resentment, decreasing the satisfaction with and time dedicated to the program (Finkelstein & Poteet, 2007).

Exhibit 14.5
Four Key Phases of Mentoring Partnerships

In our work with the Leaders Counsel, CCL isolated four key phases to highly effective mentoring partnerships, as described by faculty member Rich Walsh:

- *Formation*: Partners meet, establish goals, and understand mutual expectations and concerns.
- *Alignment*: Apply available resources, closely monitor, coach, and adjust accordingly.
- *Experimentation*: Collaboratively introduce new ideas, challenge assumptions, build momentum toward goals, and provide ongoing feedback.
- *Completion and transfer*: Measure impact, debrief key lessons learned, finish the mentoring relationship, and transfer recommendations to others.

Working with a global steel manufacturer, CCL helped establish a model in selecting nominees and later supporting mentors and mentees through each of the four phases. This was a collaborative approach with the organization, mentors, and mentees to ensure success.

Mentors Organizations should carefully consider the ability and willingness of a person to be a mentor when creating a formal program. Catalyst (1993) and Finkelstein and Poteet (2007) bring up good questions to think about:

- Should mentors be experienced professionals and leaders in organizations?
- Should they be from groups such as organizational functions or based on demographics?
- Should a mentee have only one mentor or more than one?
- Should participation as a mentor be voluntary, or should there be a nomination process?

While there are no clear-cut answers, you should make every effort for mentors to:

- Have the motivation to be a mentor and want to dedicate the time and effort a mentoring relationship needs (Burke & McKeen, 1989; Eddy et al., 2001). Research shows that a mentor's voluntary participation is positively related to perceiving rewarding experiences and negatively related to seeing mentoring as more trouble than it was worth (Parise & Forret, 2008).
- Have their readiness assessed (see Hart, 2009, for a list of readiness questions mentors should ask themselves). Previous experience as a mentee or mentor, locus of control, and wanting to be promoted are all beneficial characteristics of mentors, particularly around willingness to mentor others (Allen, Poteet, Russell, & Dobbins, 1997; Allen, Russell, & Maetzke, 1997; Ragins & Scandura, 1999).
- Be empathetic and want to help others; be a good role model of what the organization wants mentees to be or behave as; and be a good communicator, be confident, patient, and trusting and have appropriate business or technical knowledge and skills to pass on to the mentee (Allen, 2003; Allen, Poteet, & Burroughs, 1997; Catalyst, 1993; Cunningham, 1993; Eddy et al., 2001; Messmer, 2001; Tyler, 1998).

Mentees In some mentoring programs, being a mentee is voluntary; in others there is a nomination process. Who is to be a mentee is usually a by-product of the purpose behind the mentoring program. The top groups usually targeted for mentoring programs are (Eddy et al., 2001):

- Newly hired employees
- Anyone in the organization (voluntary)
- High-potential employees
- Those in professional or managerial positions

Mentees should not be selected primarily or only because of demographic characteristics such as education, socioeconomic status, age, or rank (Dougherty et al., 2007; Wanberg et al., 2003). Instead, consider the following findings, which are consistent with the training and development literature showing that those who are more successful after training have a high motivation to learn and an internal locus of control (Colquitt, LePine, & Noe, 2000):

- Those who are mentored tend to have a higher need for power and achievement than those who are not mentees (Fagenson, 1989, 1992).
- It is preferable for mentees to have a strong achievement orientation, be assertive, be willing to take the initiative, and have a learning goal orientation (Cunningham, 1993; Finkelstein & Poteet, 2007).
- Mentees with more extraversion and openness to experience tend to receive more mentoring (Bozionelos, 2004).
- Career variables such as career motivation and career self-efficacy are related to mentees' benefiting from mentors (R. Day & Allen, 2004).
- Mentees with an internal locus of control, higher emotional stability, self-monitoring, and mentoring experience, part of what Turban and Dougherty (1994) call a "proactive personality," are more likely to initiate and receive mentoring.

Matching Once an available pool of mentors and mentees is identified, how should a mentee be matched with a suitable mentor? Should the organization drive the matching process, or should the mentor and mentee be proactive in the matching? Should matching be left to some statistical algorithm that matches personality and interests like an online dating site? Should it be completely random? Exhibit 14.6 offers an example of how CCL helped one organization with the process of matching mentors and mentees.

The matching process should not be random or exclude input from the parties involved. It is best if the mentor and mentee have some voice in the matching process (Burke & McKeen, 1989; Murray, 1991; Wilson & Elman, 1990), which allows them to feel more buy-in and commitment to the mentoring program and more satisfied with the program itself (Allen et al., 2006a; Allen, Eby, & Lentz, 2006b). Organizations should stay away from randomly matching mentees with mentors and should use a variety of factors when matching, including the needs and objectives of the mentoring program and the culture of the organization (Finkelstein & Poteet, 2007). This can become particularly relevant when there are direct or indirect reporting relationships between a potential mentor and mentee. Three possible ways to match people are:

- Administrator assignment
- Choice based
- Assessment based

Exhibit 14.6
Matching Mentors and Mentees

Matching mentors and mentees can be difficult, but is important to the overall success of any mentoring effort. In working with a global services company interested in peer mentoring, CCL helped create a process for forming mentoring pairs.

1. Mentors and mentees were nominated by their vice president and then encouraged to participate in the mentoring program by their direct manager. During that initial discussion, program objectives were shared, and then potential goals of the nominee were developed.
2. Each nominee was asked to select from several high-level organizational goals and then to add goals.
3. Nominees were matched for any reciprocal knowledge of different parts of the organization. For example, a sales leader who wanted to learn marketing was paired with a marketing leader who wanted to learn sales.
4. Matching took into account when there was a mutual desire to gain cross-cultural, cross-gender, or cross-generational awareness. Whenever possible, leaders were paired with individuals with different backgrounds and experiences.

The matching was then agreed to by the mentor and mentee. The pairs participated together in a mentoring training and orientation session to kick the program off.

Above all else, the needs assessment of the mentoring program should be a driving force for how mentors and mentees are to be matched. Having a mentor who is at a higher organizational level with no direct reporting relationship and from a different department tends to be most beneficial to the mentee because it helps broaden the networks of each party and brings in new perspectives (Ragins et al., 2000). Proximity can also be important, although a challenge for many national or global organizations (Eby & Lockwood, 2005). Perceived similarity between mentor and mentee can be an important factor for matching (Allen & Eby, 2003;

Ensher & Murphy, 1997; Turban, Dougherty, & Lee, 2002). And, finally, matching is enhanced when there is a good fit between mentor and mentee on factors including the following (Hart, 2009):

- Values
- Aspirations
- Subject matter overlap
- Attitude style
- Compatibility of work styles
- Amount of time devoted to the mentoring relationship

Whatever matching process is used, program administrators should be aware of the difficulty any relationships can have at the beginning, including how demanding relationships can be or the anxiety of meeting someone new. Activities to build camaraderie can help (Blake-Beard, O'Neill, & McGowan, 2007). Hart (2009) in his work at CCL gives several examples of how to build the relationship:

- Ask questions concerning comfort level or how likable or respectful the other person is.
- Inquire what a person can offer in this relationship.
- Get to know the person by collecting formal or informal data through interviews, 360-degree assessments, or observation, obviously with the individual's permission.

Research suggests that there are certain characteristics that mentors and mentees want from each other (Allen, 2004; Allen et al., 1997; Allen, Poteet, & Russell, 2000; Finkelstein, Allen, Ritchie, Lynch, & Montei, 2012; Olian, Carroll, Giannantonio, & Feren, 1988). Mentors tend to want mentees who have:

- Motivation
- Competence
- Honesty
- Confidence
- Dependability
- A strong learning orientation and a willingness to learn

Mentees usually want mentors who are:

- High in interpersonal competence
- Good communicators
- Well liked and highly respected

Program Elements

There are a variety of program elements to consider after you have matched mentors and mentees in order to ensure a successful relationship.

Training and Orientation Once the participants are known and matched, a training session should cover the following critical elements (for more details, see Baugh & Fagenson-Eland, 2007; R. Garvey & Westlander, 2013; Finkelstein & Poteet, 2007):

- A clear definition of mentoring, roles, and responsibilities
- Suggestions for how to be successful and avoid failure as a mentor and mentee
- Benefits of the mentoring program
- Overview of learning styles
- Interpersonal skills training, including how to handle challenges and conflicts
- Clarification of goals and expectations

Keep in mind that the needs assessment and purpose of the program should guide the expectations of the relationship. Moreover, mentors and mentees should set goals, expectations, and responsibilities, preferably together.

Meeting Frequency and Format Proximity plays an important part in the mentoring process. The more frequently a mentor and mentee can meet face-to-face, particularly at the beginning of the relationship, the better (Mendelson, Barnes, & Horn, 1989). It is recommended that the mentor and mentee meet face-to-face at least once, preferably early on (Finkelstein & Poteet, 2007). The frequency, duration, format, and methodology behind the meeting should be clear, and expectations should be agreed on by both parties and followed throughout the relationship (Baugh & Fagenson-Eland, 2007; Finkelstein & Poteet, 2007).

Usually a mentoring program lasts six to twenty-four months, with the goals of the program determining the length of the mentoring relationship (Finkelstein & Poteet, 2007; Forret, Turban, & Dougherty, 1996).

Evaluation The evaluation of any program should not be forgotten. CCL has a strong tradition of evaluation in leadership development (Hannum, Martineau, & Reinelt, 2007; Martineau & Hannum, 2008). Evaluation should be part of the whole process, from the needs assessment at the beginning, to monitoring in the middle, through to the end (Stokes & Merrick, 2013). Part of the evaluation process should be monitoring how well (or poorly) mentoring relationships are going, progress being made, and if suggested or needed changes should be made midstream. These types of inputs should be gathered from program participants on a regular basis (e.g., quarterly). There should also be a way to formally end mentoring relationships that are not working or are not up to standard during the program (Eddy et al., 2001). (See chapter 2 for more detail on needs assessment and chapter 4 for evaluation.)

Evaluation is crucial in determining if the program reached the intended goals and to understand its overall success. There are many ways to gather data when evaluating mentoring programs, including end-of-program surveys, reports, interviews, and even 360-degree evaluations (Catalyst, 1993; Eddy et al., 2001). Examples of the types of data evaluations should gather include (see Finkelstein & Poteet, 2007, for more detail):

- Career progress
- Frequency of meetings between mentors and mentees
- Quality of the relationship from both the mentor and mentee perspective
- The knowledge and skills developed or enhanced for mentor and mentee
- Mentor and mentee satisfaction with the program
- Ideas on how to improve any future mentoring programs

While organizations desire retention rate and succession planning information from evaluations, mentors are more concerned with information around helping others and positive feedback, and mentees value information on encouragement and support, skill improvement, gaining access to and increasing and enhancing their networks, and becoming more successful after the mentoring program (Eddy et al., 2001).

Through our work with the Leaders Counsel, CCL has found some common evaluation measures and outcomes of mentoring programs:

- Retention
- Promotability or increases in responsibilities

- Global awareness and readiness for new and evolving roles
- Innovation and speed for new ideas to get to market
- The willingness of those being mentored to later mentor others

Having a solid evaluation means having solid research methods to enhance the robustness and findings of any evaluation. (Chapter 4 of Craig & Hannum, 2007, offers detailed information about program evaluations.)

THE FUTURE OF MENTORING

Some questions are emerging in the mentoring literature that will move the field forward:

- How does mentoring work in a global context?
- What are the advantages and disadvantages of e-mentoring?
- Is the classic older mentor–younger mentee approach to a mentoring relationship still viable?
- Should we even be talking about mentoring, or should we change our way of thinking?

Mentoring in a Global Context

The world is no doubt global. While some evidence indicates that mentoring may be viewed similarly and can be beneficial across various cultures (Hu, Pellegrini, & Scandura, 2011; Yang et al., 2011; China: Liu, Liu, Kwan, & Mao, 2009; India: Haynes & Ghosh, 2012), most of the mentoring research and well-known practices come from the United States. More research and understanding is needed to understand the meaning and value of mentoring around the world. For instance, Clutterbuck (2007) discusses the evolution of mentoring in Europe, which has gone from mentor as a source of knowledge transfer to mentor as a resource; a one-way learning relationship to a mutual learning relationship; doing and guiding to more reflecting, questioning, and dialogue; one long relationship to multiple relationships.

The most recent cross-cultural research from the GLOBE (Global Leadership and Organizational Behavior Effectiveness) project, which includes data from 825 organizations in 62 cultures, shows nine dimensions on which national cultures vary (House, Hanges, Javidan, Dorfman, & Gupta, 2004). According to Clutterbuck (2007), two may be relevant to the study and practice of mentoring: power distance and individualism-collectivism. Power distance is "the degree to which members of an organization or society expect and agree that power should be stratified and concentrated at higher levels of an organization or government" (House & Javidan, 2004, p. 12). Some cultures that are high in power distance may find the mentoring relationship more difficult to participate in, given power structures that make it difficult to challenge and admit mistakes or weaknesses (saving face). Second, mentors in more individualistic cultures (compared to collectivistic cultures) may have a tougher time if the focus of the mentoring relationship is too much on the mentee's personal career progression.

Performance orientation is another potentially important cultural factor to consider with regard to mentoring. My own research at CCL (Gentry et al., 2008) using managers from thirty-three countries showed that the positive relationship between supervisory mentoring and managerial performance is even stronger in countries that are higher in performance orientation, "the degree to which an organization or society encourages and rewards group members for performance improvement and excellence" (House & Javidan, 2004, p. 13). Societies high in performance orientation value setting ambitious goals, have high expectations for people, intellectually challenge others, value training and development, reward individual performance and achievement, and view feedback as essential for improvement (Javidan, 2004). These descriptors of cultures high in performance orientation align well with what mentors are expected to do. The benefits of mentoring may be even more important in high-performance orientation cultures.

If culture is explicitly taken into account in a mentoring relationship, mentors and mentees may gain further knowledge about the role of cultural diversity and orientation, furthering the knowledge of both mentor and mentee and their cultural intelligence (CQ) and intercultural competence (Abbott, Gilbert, & Rosinski, 2013). This is an area where mentoring could be useful.

Mentoring in a cross-cultural context may also be useful when it comes to expatriate assignments. An expat may benefit from mentoring by someone in the host country, and the mentor may benefit as well (Shen & Kram, 2011; Zhuang, Wu, & Wen, 2013). One powerful example comes from work CCL did with a vice president in an organization who was hired in Europe and placed on the East Coast of the United States. The vice president found himself struggling with the cultural adjustment and the fact that his wife and children remained in Europe for the first year of employment. Life in the United States was significantly different from what he had expected from conversations during the hiring process. He was paired with two mentors, one in the United States for the local role and the other a colleague in Europe who had returned from the same assignment, to address cultural changes, separations, and managing personal relationships. Ultimately the vice president asked the company to place him in the London office to be closer to his family, as his wife was not interested in moving to the United States after hearing about her husband's challenges. In the end, the vice president was reassigned and, importantly, retained by the company. It was a win-win for the company and the vice president, as well as both mentors who were advocates for retaining and repatriating him.

Interestingly, coaching research may give insight into cultural differences that could be found in the way mentoring is used, practiced, or understood across cultures. My research at CCL shows many similarities and subtle differences in the best practices of coaches in Europe and Asia (Gentry, Manning, Wolf, Hernez-Broome, & Allen, 2013) and the characteristics of coaches and clients needed for effective coaching engagements (Gentry, Wolf, Manning, Hernez-Broome, & Allen, 2011). These ideas could be easily transferred to a mentoring relationship, and research is needed to test these assumptions. For instance, the way a mentor is seen and understood as an authority figure across cultures may differ. In some cultures, authority figures are more approachable than in others. So the ways in which cultures view authority figures could affect the mentoring relationship, as well as how cultures view personal space and use of time (Abbott et al., 2013; Gilbert & Rosinski, 2008). Furthermore, the gender or nationality of the mentor compared to the mentee may be an issue in some contexts (Abbott et al., 2013). Clutterbuck (2007) suggested that mentoring across cultures can be beneficial under the following conditions:

- The focus is on mutual learning.
- The supporters of the mentoring program are culturally diverse themselves and can serve as resources.
- The training of mentors and mentees addresses cultural differences and how to build a dialogue around diversity.
- The mentoring program takes into account the cultural differences of the local talent versus the culture of the home organization.

CCL has had great success in working with organizations on mentoring in a global context. One such initiative was with a global office furniture designer and manufacturer. The mentoring program was part of a more comprehensive leadership initiative that included twenty-four senior leaders from the Americas, EMEA, and Asia Pacific. The nine-month program started with a five-day face-to-face development experience. In the early stages of the initiative, the group was divided into three smaller groups of eight leaders who were supported by a highly experienced leadership coach. Each of the three smaller groups was also sponsored (or mentored) by a member of the executive team. The aim of the experience was to strengthen these leaders' ability to work across the organization, build strong global networks, give the leaders exposure to executives, and gain exposure to key talent. Each team met weekly over the nine-month period and monthly with the executive sponsor (or mentor). This was a development experience for both leaders as mentees as well as the executives who sponsored the teams.

E-Mentoring and Virtual Mentoring

Given the discussion of working in a global context, mentoring often must be done virtually. Thus, e-mentoring and virtual mentoring (using electronic means such as e-mail, chat rooms, and social media as the main channel of communication) are worth mentioning (Ensher & Murphy, 2007; Hamilton & Scandura, 2003). While both formal mentoring and e-mentoring are meant to provide support (Ensher, Huen, & Blanchard, 2003), e-mentoring may be especially beneficial to those who may not have the opportunity to get mentoring due to cost, geographic constraints, or other limitations (Single & Single, 2005). There are several advantages to e-mentoring (Ensher & Murphy, 2007; Hamilton & Scandura, 2003; Single & Single, 2005):

- Low cost
- Greater access to mentors over many time zones
- Equalization of status
- Less emphasis on demographic differences
- Increased participation, particularly by those who are shy or who have poor social skills
- Increased organizational connectedness
- Amount of interaction between mentor and mentee is known

Some research has explored the benefits of e-mentoring for the mentor and mentee (see Ensher & Murphy, 2007, and Ghods & Boyce, 2013, for detailed information and summary of the studies that have examined this). If e-mentoring is used, the same best practices for formal mentoring programs should also apply, from a preliminary needs assessment to evaluation and everything in between, with the added awareness of technology feasibility and functionality that must be addressed (Ghods & Boyce, 2013). While there are some upsides, there are also disadvantages of e-mentoring compared to face-to-face mentoring (Ensher & Murphy, 2007; B. Garvey, Stokes, & Megginson, 2009):

- Lack of access due to geographic or technological boundaries
- Inability to understand how people are feeling through observation of nonverbal behaviors
- Chances of misinterpretation of written communication or lack of writing skill
- Fears of lack of confidentiality and privacy
- Lack of technology or skill in technology

Peer Mentoring

The world has changed, and with changing organizational career dynamics, so too has the thinking of what mentoring really means and who can be mentors and mentees. Downsizing, layoffs, changing organizational structures, flatter organizations, and decreasing numbers of senior leaders available to be mentors have contributed to the increase in peer mentoring (Tong & Kram, 2013). Such mentoring involves a peer-to-peer relationship between employees working at a similar level, which runs counter to the conventional, hierarchical relationship between older seasoned mentor and younger inexperienced mentee (Tong & Kram, 2013). Peer mentoring can provide complementarity, mutuality, and reciprocity that other mentoring relationships may not (Kram & Isabella, 1985; McManus & Russell, 2007). Many of the benefits that come from a traditional mentor-mentee relationship also benefit the two parties in a peer mentoring relationship, with the added benefit of playing a role in the socialization process of new employees and information sharing (Bryant, 2005; Eby, 1997; Kram, 1985). Having a peer as a mentor may have some benefits as compared to having a higher-ranking person as a mentor. With hierarchical constraints lifted, peer mentors may be better able to share things readily, communicate freely, and support and collaborate more easily (Kram & Isabella, 1985). Peer mentoring relationships may be beneficial for mutual learning and support among peers (Delong, Gabarro, & Lees, 2008; McManus & Russell, 2007; Parker, Hall, & Kram, 2008).

Increasingly, leaders at high levels of organizations must broaden their experiences and global perspectives (Walsh & Trovas, 2014). One way they do this is by expanding their responsibility to multiple functional areas. In one high-tech company, a vice president of marketing was asked to oversee marketing and information technology; CCL arranged for this leader to be paired with another vice president of information technology at a different company, which enhanced the mentee's effectiveness in the expanded role.

Developmental Networks

Kram and Higgins (2008) suggest that the traditional mentor-mentee relationship no longer works because individual senior mentors cannot keep up with changes in the workplace. People should invest time, energy, and resources in developmental networks instead. Developmental networks consist of a select group of people who provide advice, support, and certain "holding behaviors" such as confirmation, contradiction, and continuity that are necessary for personal growth and effectiveness (Dobrow, Chandler, Murphy, & Kram, 2012; Ghosh, Haynes, & Kram, 2013). These authors suggest that mentoring should no longer be looked at in the traditional way as a single, one-on-one relationship. Rather, it should be a constellation of relationships (Higgins & Kram, 2001) that includes multiple mentors, across multiple levels, using intra- and extraorganizational relationships. For instance, these relationships should include:

- Bosses
- Peers
- Direct reports
- Those in professional organizations
- Leaders in the firm
- Personal support systems from:
  - Community
  - Family
  - Educational and school experiences

All of these parties can act as learning partners for an individual. Though the research on developmental networks is limited, it is starting to grow, and its benefits are starting to surface. Developmental networks provide instrumental functions such as career advancement and success (Bozionelos, 2006; Chandler, Kram, & Yip, 2011). Research my colleagues and I have conducted with managers from Europe indicates that successful leaders leveraged developmental networks including people from both within their organizations (bosses, peers, and colleagues) and outside the organizations, such as friends and family members, former professors, and previous bosses and mentors from former organizations (Eckert, Ruderman, Gentry, & Stawiski, 2012; Gentry, Stawiski, Eckert, & Ruderman, 2013). Organizations should consider encouraging this among their employees. Organizations also should encourage their employees to be masters of their own mentoring because people need to be more proactive and more purposeful when it comes to mentoring in today's workplace, asking others to be part of their developmental network but being purposeful in terms of who they ask, why they are asking these people, and the reasons they want them in their developmental network.

CONCLUSION

Mentoring benefits mentees, mentors, and their organization when done right. For formal mentoring programs, several best practices and the involvement of key stakeholders can ensure the success of the program for all parties. HR professionals, executives, leaders in organizations, and those in mentoring relationships should be mindful of the context of organizations today. Several things may need to change when it comes to the classic and formal older mentor–younger mentee dynamic. You may want to emphasize the importance of leaders mentoring their direct reports. You should understand and support the fact that each employee should be more proactive and purposeful when it comes to finding a mentor, and in mentoring others, through formal and informal means, in developmental networks with people in the formal hierarchy or peers inside organizations, across time zones, and with knowledgeable others outside the organization. A proactive person purposeful in his or her own mentoring and developmental relationships is the key characteristic of twenty-first-century workplace mentoring going forward, much different from what has traditionally been thought of in the past four decades.

chapter FIFTEEN

Executive Coaching for Onboarding

Robert Elsey and Douglas D. Riddle

Today's business environment is fast paced, confusing, demanding, and stressful—on a good day. On tougher days, which seem to be more frequent for many of us, the work experience can become volatile, uncertain, complex, ambiguous, and filled with overwhelming personal and organizational pressures. With such demanding environments also comes the ever-increasing expectation on performance—not just performance at some future date but high levels of performance today and every other day. These forces pressure companies to find the right leadership talent, capable of navigating the demands and uncertainties of business while building a resilient and sustainable organization for the future. As a result, talent recruitment and retention processes take center stage for most organizations.

THE IMPORTANCE OF HIRING AND RETAINING TOP TALENT

The process of securing, integrating, and developing key leadership talent to fulfill exceptional performance demands can be a resource-intensive, time-consuming, and costly endeavor and makes hiring the best executive talent a critical element to ensure the organization is able to adapt and thrive. Organizations that develop effective methods and practices to support newly acquired or newly promoted leaders maximize success and minimize potential talent loss or failures and provide a potential recruiting differentiator.

Executives want to work for organizations where they can envision a healthy career and can access support systems that help them grow and thrive. Strong talent development programs can be effective enticements for top talent. Leaders and potential future leaders desire to work for companies that demonstrate as much commitment to employee development as the company does to the bottom-line business results. And with historically consistent executive failure and loss rates hovering around 30 to 50 percent within the first two years of employment, any activities that promote sustainable talent success serve an organization's goals of retaining top performers. No organization wants or can afford highly visible talent failures or repeated failures of their executives or high potentials. A track record like this can mar a company's reputation and ability to attract and retain top talent.

Drawing on CCL's experience in this specific area of executive coaching, this chapter offers a practical framework and advice about design considerations and implementation for executive integration coaching.

EXECUTIVE INTEGRATION COACHING AND ONBOARDING: WHAT'S THE DIFFERENCE?

With such risky return rates on talent hiring, one popular practice to fortify the newly hired executive is to provide an immediate, robust, orientation program to help effectively integrate the executive during the early phases of transition. By frontloading the transition process with a variety of support tools and methods, an organization can promote positive long-term productivity and employment satisfaction and reduce turnover. One effective method that has gained traction in the past decade we are calling *executive integration coaching*.

A more familiar term among organizations for orienting a new employee is *onboarding*. Typically onboarding refers to an administrative orientation process associated with starting a new job in a new company, including completing the necessary HR paperwork and orienting the employee to rules, regulations, company mission, history, and so on. Executive integration coaching extends the purposes and methods of onboarding. Rather than viewing the orientation of a new executive as an administrative process, we encourage HR to see orientation more broadly as a whole integration process. Executive integration refers to a time-sensitive process of intentional early support—scaffolding that supports the newly hired leader through her transition period. The process helps to clarify and align stakeholder expectations about the new executive's role (beyond the job description) and helps to build consensus about this person's short- and long-term goals, how she can effectively leverage available resources, and how she can interact with networks and stakeholders to ensure that she and the company achieve a successful transition.

An organization may use executive integration coaching for a variety of reasons, but mostly related to transition periods, which often include a new role, developing a high-potential leader for an upcoming promotion or expanded role, or supporting leaders through a merger and acquisition, organizational restructuring, workforce realignment, cultural transformation, or the redefinition of the organization's strategy and work processes. All of these circumstances and others require quick acquisition of new skills or competencies.

The Promise of Executive Integration Coaching

"Failure to launch" is not a phrase you want to use when referring to a newly hired leader. Making an early investment in talent is essential to a successful transition. Not only does early support reveal the value an organization places on talent, it reduces costly talent failures and increases productivity. Stepping into a new role is challenging for most people, and that is especially true for an executive, where there may be additional pressures of visibility, scrutiny, and ultimate accountability thrust on him quickly. The executive who agrees to take a different leadership position shares a risk with the organization, and both are betting on the contributions and leadership the change in role will bring. Both the executive and the organization share the significant burdens of producing a return on investment (ROI) and the ultimate goal of producing positive results. How an organization demonstrates early investment in its people sends a message about what level of commitment it makes to support and develop talent. The value of installing effective executive integration coaching programs to prepare new leaders for the typical challenges they will encounter during the first three to six months of a new role and surfacing organization-specific challenges cannot be overstated. Early support processes facilitate and accelerate connections within smaller groups and across broader networks and can reduce the lag from the hiring date to productivity and contribution. ROI from such a coaching program may be assessed through both short- and long-term achievements, such as productivity, talent retention during economic growth cycles, lower turnover rates, and higher sustained employee satisfaction, all of which lead to organizational loyalty.

Implementing an Integration Program

There are many ways to build an integration program. Often the first choice made concerns how much of the program the organization will manage versus what parts might be contracted for through a vendor. Program management may be divided, or it may be managed by one party or the other. Organizations with larger talent development departments and broader, dedicated resources can be more self-reliant when building and implementing large-scale executive integration coaching programs. Organizations that are resource constrained may require external partnerships to build and support the program (and that is more frequently the case).

Organizations that approach the onboarding process as a companywide initiative rather than as an ad hoc approach or an administrative process should honestly assess the resources and ability of their internal talent teams to support executive integration. As with any other companywide initiative, unforeseen obstacles can quickly escalate into critical problems and require significant attention and resources. For this reason, organizations often enlist external experts rather than attempting to manage the process themselves. Partnering with an experienced coaching organization offers many benefits, including deep expertise, a broad and scalable resource network, dependability, and sustainability.

Two critical components a coaching vendor brings to the integration process are a sophisticated executive coach network and the administrative and operational infrastructures required to implement and manage large-scale efforts. This helps organizations reduce overextension of their internal talent departments. Cost is a factor, of course. It may cost more to hire experts in the short run, but ultimately it may save more than enough resources to make up the difference. For example, hidden costs might include the number of people required to support the effort and the amount of time it takes to build, launch, implement, manage, and evaluate these types of programs. Although not exactly grounded in economic practice, the adage "you get what you pay for" is generally applicable when it comes to executive integration coaching. Organizations should consider carefully and fully the criteria they will use to enter the best and most appropriate vendor partnership. That critical decision can sometimes mean the difference between success and failure.

The Importance of Partnership

The relationship of the organization and its coaching vendor is critical to the success of this use of coaching. Healthy team dynamics can often produce high-performance results, and unhealthy dynamics can stall or prevent productive efforts. Therefore, an organization should spend a little extra time getting to know its potential partner before making any decision. One interview is not sufficient. The larger the coaching initiative is, the more time you will likely be working with your partner. Choose smartly and make the investment in time because it will pay dividends over the course of the program.

Start by asking your own team what it perceives is needed from a partner, and then use that information to assess whether a potential partner's core capabilities and experience are a good fit to those needs. In addition, consider the interpersonal chemistry of the vendors you interview. Collaborations of this kind usually require extended work interactions over time to ensure mutual success. Depending on the scope of the work, you and your partner will spend a considerable amount of time together before the initiative formally launches. A vendor with practical executive coaching experience can help you avoid typical pitfalls and can forecast critical issues early. Although downward pricing pressures can weigh heavily on vendor selection, often there is a strong, positive relationship between experience, quality, outcomes, and price. Opt for the experience, quality, and outcomes that you need rather than the price you want. There's nothing worse than a high-visibility talent initiative going poorly in an organization. It takes a long time to reset institutional memories of a mediocre or failed program.

After Selecting a Partner, What Then?

Once a partner organization has been selected and the work contracted, many other decisions need to be made, even if the selection process included a comprehensive proposal. Moving from proposal to implementation requires strong communication and partnership between the two organizations. Dedicating the first few meetings to reviewing the design, clarifying operational and administrative functions, clarifying how the team will communicate and work together, assigning roles and responsibilities, determining oversight and management, and overall good project management are critical. Don't shortchange these early conversations, as many assumptions can go uncovered and lead to miscommunication. As is often the case, once a project is in full swing, unexpected situations arise and must be addressed swiftly. Creating a classic project management task chart like a role, accountable, consulted, informed (RACI) matrix (see exhibit 7.1 in chapter 7), or a similar decision-based framework can be a good starting point. It is likely that many team member assumptions will surface as this document is completed. Exhibit 15.1 covers many of the issues you and your partner should address at the start of an executive integration program.

In addition to the issues listed in exhibit 15.1, it is also critical to settle on a clear and shared definition of *confidentiality*. It is best to discuss at length how confidentiality is defined in the context of the integration work to ensure that all members of the team agree before any rollout takes place. Leaders participating in

Exhibit 15.1
Critical Topics to Discuss with a Partner

- Purpose of the work
- Expected outcomes and goals of the program (individual, teams, organization)
- Identification of all stakeholders affected by the work
- Standardization versus customized engagements
- Formal launch and stakeholder communication strategy
- Need and types of program collateral materials
- Operational and administrative platforms and capabilities or limitations
- Use of different types of individual or team assessments
- Decisions on which development goal forms to use and their interface with existing forms, platforms, or processes
- How goal progress and engagement impact will be tracked, measured, and reported back to various stakeholder groups
- Types and frequency of reports (e.g., utilization reports, dashboard reports, goal progress reports)
- Escalation processes for when an engagement stalls, a system or process isn't working, or there's a problem with a participant or a coach
- Methods of data collection, types of measures to evaluate quality, impact, and benefits from the onboarding program: aggregated individual, team, and organizational-level data
- How ROI will be determined if necessary

such a coaching process often want to know what the boundaries of confidentiality are between themselves, the coach, and any other stakeholders in the process (such as their boss or human resource business partner). Consider what confidentiality means for the organization-vendor team. Are all team members privy to the same levels of information about such areas as the coachee, her goals, overall goal data and themes, evaluation data, and decision making?

As with any other well-executed initiative, engage the team early and work through the details. The larger the scale of the work is, the more critical these early conversations become. Regular team check-in meetings can build trust in the relationship and promote a strong partnership and quality output.

THE COACHING WORK

Before covering the elements of a program design, we should address the nature of the coaching work because this can influence the program's design. In executive coaching generally, the coach and executive commit to a formal, ongoing relationship to accomplish specific goals. Executive coaching broadly defined is a highly flexible process with customized goals, usually developmental in nature, with self-, other-, or situational awareness at the core of work goals. Much of the coaching work is spent identifying historical personal and career themes and patterns, which mental models and behavioral choices have advanced or retarded the leader's career progress, and how these patterns fit with the new expectations and goals for both the role and the leader given their current state of functioning. Executive integration coaching can also be a formal, ongoing process, but it is usually much more abbreviated in time and includes more structured processes, methods, and targeted transition activities than traditional executive coaching. Executive integration coaching's key purpose is to help accelerate a leader's integration into his new role, with his new team, with the new company and culture and to advance the leader's understanding and readiness to accomplish the work.

As a component of executive integration, coaching powerfully engages self-awareness by encouraging a leader to think about thinking—metathinking, if you will (Riddle, 2009). As leaders explore their mental models and paradigms, they gain awareness and can conceivably develop a more intentional approach to managing their thoughts and behaviors. This process of self-awareness and learning accelerates the journey to effective leader. As self-, other-, and situational awareness grows, the tendency to blame others or circumstances recedes and ownership increases. The leader becomes a more effective learner as the process of learning itself comes under his intentional control.

Perhaps more so than in traditional developmental executive coaching, the executive integration coach plays the role of guide and advisor as the executive moves through the key tasks associated with successful integration. The coach works to ensure that the demands for performance do not eclipse the need for rapid learning and assimilation of lessons. A leader who feels the pressure to prove herself too early may actually lag in achieving high contribution. The leader must develop proper tools to ensure early and continued effectiveness; otherwise, she risks getting stuck in reactive patterns of doing the job but does not make any significant contribution. High-impact integration coaching can help prevent such plateaus.

Getting started on the integration process quickly after hiring is best. Within the first thirty to forty-five days of hiring, the new executive should be paired with a coach to conduct the executive integration work, which may span three to six months. This early partnership often launches a set of steps and activities for the leader to complete. Many of these activities involve success factors that we described previously as targets of specific actions or performance needs. The period from six to eighteen months may move away from the integration and early performance focus and toward a broader, developmentally focused process to address how to sustain patterns of thinking and acting over time and achieve sustainable performance and success in the role.

EXECUTIVE INTEGRATION FRAMEWORK

Michael Watkins speaks of three pillars that are the three imperatives companies must address in onboarding new leadership: politics, culture, and expectations (2003; see also Betof & Betof, 2010). Our model incorporates Watkins's three pillars, and it also includes the practical focus on the scope of authority and responsibility that comes with the leader's new position and the unique contribution that a leader makes when authentically engaged. This last element is the unique stamp successful executives always place on their leadership: the combination of personality and talent that can come from no one else.

Five factors demand a significant portion of the attention and energy of a leader in a new position. If they are ignored or only half-heartedly addressed, the leader may struggle with taking on a new role. Executive integration coaching works best when it addresses these five factors.

Factor 1: Job Scope and Organizational Roles

The mental adjustment to a new job begins with an understanding of the position's scope of responsibility and authority. This is part of mapping the landscape of the circumstances in which a leader must function. Such mapping goes beyond the job description to include the identification of what is needed to achieve business results and instigate organizational change. It includes information about the roles the leader is expected or permitted to play in the organization, along with the comprehensive knowledge of the company and its business (e.g., products and services, core values, executive organization, business priorities, standards of conduct, financials). Learning these elements provides the first set of data that allow diagnosis of the business unit needs and the creation of the preliminary targets for business advancement.

Factor 2: Relationship Network (People and Politics)

Establishing the right kind of relationships with the right people sets an executive on track for success. Good relationships build the social capital of the leader, which is the basis for everything he or she accomplishes. Building a strong and effective network is the most important first step in avoiding the land mines associated with bad politics. Relationships are the primary lever through which executives accomplish their work.

Assessing the political situation begins with getting good guidance about who can affect the executive's success. The new leader's manager and the human resource leader can provide that guidance. A newly hired executive should always ask, "Who else do I need to know to be effective here?" Administrative staff members are often the keenest observers of company politics, with knowledge of who is listened to, respected, or ignored in the organization. Interviews should be arranged with all potential stakeholders, including managers, peers, and team members. Questions to be raised in those conversations include what the leader and the person interviewed owe each other, what resources they can contribute to each other, and how they will communicate. An executive transition coach can be extraordinarily helpful in preparing for the interviews and guiding the leader into an exploration of the lessons learned, as well as helping to plan how to develop, strengthen, and sustain effective relationships.

Factor 3: House Rules (Culture)

In order to make changes in organizational culture or to influence it to be more productive, an executive must first demonstrate an understanding of the prevailing culture and a willingness to "play well" in it. Leaders first gain credibility as people who can read and respond appropriately to the unwritten rules and invisible values that shape how people in an organization deal with each other. In the same way that summer visitors to a community have no voice on the practices of the year-round residents, an executive has to demonstrate respect for and understanding of the organizational culture. Here is an example from our experience. When a new operations director came into a global consulting company, her impatience with the collaborative style of the organization and her terse e-mails were interpreted as arrogance. As she learned to match her messages to the unwritten e-mail protocols of the company, her disciplined approach to business operations began to be appreciated and her influence increased.

Culture affects such items as how meetings are conducted (highly structured or casual, for example), how formal communications are expected to be (e-mail stating just the facts or e-mails with a formal greeting and ending ("Dear ___" and "Warm regards," for example), behavior in meetings (competitive participation or mutual affirmation), and what kind of contributions are most valued (individual or collaborative). Because culture is sometimes seen as a group's personality, that group can be complementary or in conflict with the personality of the individual leader. There are implications to either scenario, which an integration coach can help a leader understand and leverage.

Assessing culture requires the use of several learning methods, including guided observation and reflection and the involvement of "culture guides" (long-time employees who can draw attention to footholds and handholds and point out treacherous ground). The new leader's objective is to learn how to operate in the culture, not to simply accommodate it. Neither ignoring the culture nor mindlessly fitting in will work to shape a more effective culture (see chapter 11). The executive must treat his or her involvement in the organizational or group culture as a learning experience, not as a rite of initiation. As acceptance grows, the executive is able to advocate changes in culture that can improve the functioning of the unit and equip it for more effective performance.

Factor 4: What Matters (Expectations)

It is common knowledge that job descriptions and organization charts are incomplete guides to what a leader will be responsible for or have the authority to change. Healthy organizations and executives persistently work to surface the unexpressed (and sometimes unaware) expectations that people have about executives. The importance of expectations is amplified when it comes to achieving early wins in a new position or with a new set of responsibilities. Clear expectations and mutual understanding encourage production of the right results that will be well received.

The executive should be led to discover and manage the expectations that come with the position. Does she expect that her manager will know what she does not yet understand without being told? Does she expect that she will be given some significant period of time before showing meaningful business results? Also, the executive will need to inquire about the expectations of her team, manager, and other stakeholders. Which team members expect that the executive will be directive enough that they can confidently throw themselves into particular tasks? Which team members anticipate being told expected outcomes but count on being left to figure out the best way to deliver those? Can the executive read the behavior of her manager and navigate the differences between what is said and what is actually rewarded? The leadership transition coach provides a safe, constructive environment to make sense of what is heard and observed and can guide the leader to more effective negotiations of appropriate expectations.

Factor 5: Authentic Contribution

True effectiveness in a new position involves more than meeting the expectations of others; it requires making a contribution based on unique character and talents. In the same way that a skilled writer gains influence only when she finds her own voice, so a leader who inspires commitment in others brings character, personality, gifts, and passion to the business. This is why the cornerstone of leadership effectiveness is self-awareness. The creation of feedback mechanisms with trusted associates, the use of 360-degree multirater instruments and personality assessments, and observation of one's impact on others can contribute to self-knowledge that helps a leader create significant value by his or her leadership.

The final factor focuses attention on leveraging one's unique gifts and viewpoint and applying them to the leadership task. The most powerful leader is the most authentic leader. The leadership transition coach works toward completion of the integration program by helping the leader plan continuous development through learning experiences and identify the ways his or her characteristics can help shape the job, the team, and the organization's success.

DESIGNING AN EXECUTIVE INTEGRATION COACHING PROGRAM

There are many considerations when designing an onboarding program. Creating an efficient but effective program requires a breadth of information about the organization establishing the program, its culture, and the purpose of the program and the participants. It's also good practice to assess the overall organizational readiness for a program of this nature (see chapter 2). Often such initiatives require strong internal champions for resource support, especially to sustain the effort. Depending on the size of the organization and the number of anticipated leaders to participate, it may be a multiyear, multisite-based effort that requires a few consistent, visible champions to gain traction. Also, understanding typical challenges faced by newly appointed leaders, current organizational challenges, and cultural nuances can inform some of the design decisions. This information helps focus the scope of the program and its purpose.

Executive integration programs may have both primary and secondary goals. Primary goals include integrating the executive into her role, and secondary goals may focus on shifting the organizational culture or supporting a broader talent development strategy. Surfacing the key drivers of the effort will inform the best design choices. Make good design decisions early. Ultimately your organization will want to know if the program is worth the investment, what the program's impact was, what an evaluation of the program reveals, and in general what the ROI was. Keep these questions in mind to inform the program design and then produce the right type of outcomes and data.

Because the express purpose of integration coaching is to help the new leader quickly assimilate to his role, the program's central design adheres to those individual goals. However, additional aspects should be considered. The notion of customizing each engagement may sound appealing from the standpoint of a highly personalized coaching experience; however, the broader the program's scope and rollout, the more a standardized design may be preferred, if for no other reason than pure operational resourcing efficiency and cost management. This one decision about the level of standardization may potentially alter many design decisions.

Phases of an Executive Integration Coaching Engagement

Integration program designs may include many of the following phases, but not all are necessary. Depending on the length of each engagement and the resources and time allotted, a design may omit or consolidate some of these steps:

1. Program launch
2. Leader-coach matching process
3. Introductory conversation with the selected coach and a review of the program
4. Assessments: Formal instruments and interviews
5. Insight session and formal integration plan developed
6. Alignment session to gain the boss's support and agreement on goals
7. Integration coaching work
8. Team integration workshop with the leader's team (optional)
9. Reassessment to gather feedback and determine goal progress
10. Transition and final alignment, recommendations for next year in role

The Launch Strategy

Once the coaching program has been designed and is ready to install, attention should be given to a formal launch strategy for the new program. Articulating clear value propositions about the benefits of the program for the various internal stakeholder groups and developing compelling collateral materials can be an effective way to encourage quick adoption and participation. A combination of materials like program pamphlets, electronic and social media welcome videos or webinars, along with information on HR or talent intranet sites, can dramatically increase visibility, accelerate socialization of the program offering, and stimulate interest and uptake. There are many campaign elements to address prior to an organizational launch. Each of these can be scaled to fit your organization.

Assessment and Evaluation

Assessments used in the program can include informal and formal measures. Informal measures may include a biographical career history, résumé, and performance evaluations. Formal measures may be a 360-degree feedback instrument, stakeholder interviews, at least one personality type or leadership-style profile, and any assessment data previously gathered by the organization. How confidentiality has been defined for the initiative and how the core question of who owns the data has been answered will inform how assessment data are selected and assessment reports distributed. CCL strongly advocates that only the coach and coachee are privy to all the assessment data. This is not to say that the leader doesn't share the broader themes, patterns, and implications extracted from the compiled data, but that the data reports themselves are not shared but instead used to help inform the development of the newly installed leader during the coaching sessions. The effect of this position is to place ownership of the coaching work squarely on the shoulders of the coachee. After a thorough debriefing of all the data with the coach, the coachee is able to process, own, and socialize the implications of the data. This is the first step of a leader owning the integration work ahead. It requires the leader to put voice to their data and make a declaration of intention to work the plan.

Decisions about the kind and the methods of evaluation to be used to measure the program's impact are also an important component of integration coaching. At the outset of any design, consider the various types of measurements that will be used or produced to evaluate the process. Performing a good evaluation takes time and attention, so do not leave it until the end to plan. Instead, early on, determine what type of evaluation data will be meaningful, what data are relevant, how the data will be collected, how data will be reported and to whom, and how success will be defined. Ask also if it's important to gather evaluation data at the leader, team, and organizational levels or only the leader level. Will you evaluate the coaches? If so, how will that evaluation be handled? Answering these questions early can have implications for how you structure the program design or how coaches might be asked to approach the work.

For example, CCL's Coaching Evaluation Assessment is designed to measure a participant's progress on each of her goals as well as to measure coach efficacy. The assessment provides many of the evaluation data points and reports that organizations frequently ask for when designing executive integrations programs, including aggregate reports to demonstrate the program's overall impact.

CONCLUSION

This chapter provides a brief overview of executive integration coaching for HR leaders and others responsible for organizational planning and talent management. It advocates the active involvement of professional transition coaches, but that is a decision each organization must make. The basic factors that lead to successful executive effectiveness are the same in any type or size of organization. Executives must know what is required, what authority comes with the role, and who has influence or resources. They must understand the cultural practices that define acceptance or rejection from the group, surface and address unspoken assumptions and expectations, and find an authentic expression of their contributions. Organizational support for accomplishing these tasks reduces the time it takes for executives to become full contributors and equips those executives to perform at a high level in typical situations so as to be effective at handling disruptive change.

chapter SIXTEEN

Team Coaching

Elizabeth C. D. Gullette

Teams are critical units within most organizations today, given the increasing complexity of work and the resulting need for coordination and collaboration across interdependent tasks. Ironically, while the emergence of teams has been a response to complexity, it is also true that teams themselves add complexity to organizations in that they are dynamic collections of individuals within a multilevel system. When functioning well, teams can be valuable levers of organizational performance, combining diverse skill sets and experience and permitting quick, flexible responses. When they are ineffective, they fail to deliver on their promise and can create headaches for those on and around them. Given the stakes, as well as the complexity, what can coaching-oriented human resource partners do to enhance the functioning and performance of teams in their organizations? This chapter addresses that question.

BUILDING A TEAM'S CAPACITY TO PERFORM

Team coaching can be thought of as an intentional intervention to develop the shared leadership capacity of a team by teaching and promoting the use of task and team-oriented process skills that drive performance. This view emerges from the recognition that the levers of performance within a team are found in processes the members engage in and the shared mental models and team learning that result from these.

A Point of View on Team Coaching

Our approach to team coaching is both developmental and performance oriented, taking into account the organizational context. This is analogous to CCL's perspective on individual leadership coaching expanded to a larger system. As defined in the Introduction to this handbook, coaching is based on relationships, where developmental conversations help those being coached to gain awareness, expand their thinking, and make wiser decisions. Coaching also develops one's ability to analyze, think, reflect, and solve problems, which helps turn experiences into knowledge. As this definition makes clear, coaching is not primarily a didactic approach, involving teaching of content or advising, although this may be appropriate at times. Instead, coaching tends to be a more emergent process of inquiry, dialogue, and reflection that addresses the unique issues, needs, and goals as co-discovered by the coach and the party being coached (whether individual or team). The fundamental methodology of coaching, whether in an individual or team context, involves facilitating development with attention to process, or what might be termed *developmental process facilitation.*

Team coaching is differentiated from individual coaching in that the target system of the intervention is a group, which brings group identity, group dynamics, and group process to the foreground. Moreover, the group is specifically a team, which implies some degree of interdependence in working toward a shared goal or goals.

In addition, whereas tasks, projects, work relationships, and organizational context form the backdrop for the key issues in individual coaching, this dyadic coaching process is nonetheless generally removed from the individual in the act of working (the coach and individual sit together in an office or on the phone and have a conversation about work). By contrast, the business at hand and work context for the team are the actual setting for team coaching, since a coach enters the team's field as they work together in regular meetings and any off-sites the team may have. The same dynamics and processes that the team uses to engage in any aspect of work together are visible or can be discerned over time as a coach builds trust with the team.

Why Team Coaching?

Although on rare occasions a team leader seeks help for an already good team in order to raise its performance to an even higher level or create a high-performance team, external professionals or internal HR partners are typically called in to help a team when its members face challenges or problems that get in the way of effective performance. You may have experienced team problems yourself as a member of a team at some point and have probably witnessed struggling teams so you can easily list some of the most common problems that occur on teams—for example:

- Problems with communication
- Lack of coordination
- Conflict
- Issues with trust
- Disruptive or domineering behavior by one or a few team members
- Ineffective decision making
- Unequal effort or contribution among members

These issues can stem from problems with either the initial formation of the team or poor processes applied by established teams. Formation problems might start with selecting the wrong members in the first place, whether for expediency, political reasons, or lack of forethought. Pulling together a group of individuals who do not bring the combined skills, knowledge, and experience to best meet the demands of the team purpose ensures a weak foundation that is difficult, if not impossible, to overcome. How the team is structured relates to this as well: being overly inclusive, for example, can be a knee-jerk alternative to being strategic, such as by creating a core team of strong members who can tap a broader network of others for information or targeted help. Another formation-stage problem, lack of clarity around the purpose or goals of the team, can underlie symptoms involving, for example, conflict, communication, and coordination. Similarly, inattention to chartering and the creation of explicit norms can open the way for disruptive behavior by individuals that does not get addressed, lack of effective decision-making and conflict-resolution processes, and so on. Failure to orient members to each other so as to understand and respect the skills, talents, and experience that each can contribute to their shared effort also gets a team off on the wrong foot since this mutual understanding promotes trust as well as more efficient and effective use of resources.

More established teams can experience problems when they do not use effective task and team-related processes. For example, they may fail to develop and apply task-appropriate performance strategies to get work done together efficiently and effectively. They may not engage in deep enough dialogue to thoroughly understand issues and the multiple perspectives held by team members.

And, of course, they may continue to engage in problematic interpersonal behavior if norms were never developed or enforced.

Any of these issues can be magnified by the fact that many teams are virtual or dispersed and many, if not most, are made up of individuals who are members of multiple teams and therefore cannot devote all of their time, attention, and energy to any one team (Maynard, Mathieu, Rapp, & Gilson, 2012). These realities intensify the need for the clarifying and aligning functions accomplished in effective formation as well as intentional, strategic, effective task and team processes at all points.

This brief overview of common challenges and potential intervention points covers some of the most important factors to consider in assessing a team. We now go into more detail to understand teams, their functioning, their pain points, and potential steps for a coach to take in order to help a team.

ASSESSMENT: TEAM DISCOVERY AND DIAGNOSIS

To engage effectively in team coaching, you will want to understand as much about teams as possible to guide your thinking and action. One of the basic considerations in your assessment is what type of team you are working with. What are some of the characteristics of the team, what is its purpose, and what features of this team are similar to or different from other teams and how do these bear on the team's functioning?

Team Types

As you think about the range of teams in your own organization and others you've been a part of, you can probably identify many of the features that characterize particular teams (summarized in table 16.1). For example, teams can vary according to their function, their purpose, or the degree of power they hold, among other things. They can be classified by the following functions: production, service, management, project focused, or committee (Sundstrom, McIntyre, Halfhill, & Richards, 2000). It can also be useful to think of teams in terms of features or contextual factors that are particularly salient, such as being a virtual team, a strategy team, or an operations committee.

It may be especially helpful when dealing with a team to think about the factors that underlie these various categorizations and labels, since the underlying dimensions offer information about where potential problems may arise and which

Table 16.1
Summary of Key Factors to Consider in Understanding a Specific Team

Factor	Examples
Purpose	Enterprise leadership, strategy formulation, operations, product development, talent development
Function	Production, service, management, project focused, committee
Environment and context	Market conditions, location, orientation (internal and external), stakeholders/clients
Interdependence	Goals, tasks, work flows, knowledge sharing
Team composition	Size, structure, capabilities, diversity, geographic distribution/virtuality, membership stability
Temporal characteristics	Developmental stage, work phase

interventions may be most valuable. Researchers studying the effectiveness of teams have helped to clarify several of these dimensions (Kozlowski & Bell, 2012).

Environment and Context What is the external environment or organizational context within which the team is working? Is the team an internally oriented work team focused on improving operational processes, with its clients being other internal production teams? Or are they working on an external customer engagement strategy and so cross boundaries outside the business? Are they an executive team responsible for strategy and reporting to a board of directors? Is the team's broader market environment dynamic and fast changing or relatively stable? What's the competition like? How connected to the system outside the team does it need to be?

These factors are important for a team coach to take into account because a team's performance has been shown to be related to the degree to which the team is aware of and deals well with its environment and constituencies, for example, by communicating to key stakeholders, scanning the environment for information relevant to important decisions, and leveraging technologies and resources to get work done.

Interdependence How interdependent is the team in terms of its goals as well as team member roles and their processes? Some teams are closer to collections of fairly independent individuals, each with his or her own tasks that require minimal coordination, whereas other teams are responsible for highly interdependent joint work and outcomes. The more interdependent the team is on each other throughout the work flow, the more important are alignment, communication, mutual understanding, and shared knowledge. Do team members have a clear strategy for how they will approach their work together? Do they know how to approach creating such a strategy? Do they ask each other for help and keep each other informed so work flow is efficient and leverages the right people at the right time in the right sequence? These are questions a team coach can assess and help to improve if needed.

Team Composition Is the team composed of the right members to address its purpose and goals? Is it diverse enough to include multiple perspectives, experiences, and skill sets that will enhance the team's thinking and working and yet not so diverse that effective communication and mutual understanding would require more time or resources than the team has available? Is the team colocated or geographically dispersed? What are the implications of this on their ability to establish a strong foundation with clear norms, an understanding of what each other brings to the team, and how they will communicate and coordinate their work? More face-to-face time together during the initial phase of a team's life cycle and during task preparation is generally helpful for ultimate performance (Maynard et al., 2012). Discussing team composition with the team leader or sponsor when a team is already formed and working can be a difficult conversation since there may not be interest or willingness in moving people off or on the team. Nevertheless, having the explicit conversation is still important in that it raises awareness of the issue, it could lead to some restructuring if needed, and it may lead to more intentional, strategic talent allocation to teams in the future.

A final team membership variable to consider is the stability of the team itself. How new are the members to the team? How stable is the membership? It is difficult for a team to develop the necessary shared knowledge, alignment, and trust to be effective without some degree of stability. So too it is important to engage in some level of "re-formation" work when a new member joins for the same reasons initial formation work is important: to get to know each other's strengths, style, and experience and to begin the process of developing shared knowledge.

This step is often overlooked by a team leader and can be an important point for an HR partner to raise and perhaps help with.

Developmental Stage and Work Phase Where is the team in time? That is, at what point is the team in its life cycle (e.g., formation phase, permanent and mature, wrapping up as a temporary project team), and where is the team in its workload cycle (e.g., in a lull, just beginning a project, in the grip of high workload demands)? A team that is just forming is at a key developmental point that a coach can help with tremendously. A long-established team may be challenged by a sense of inertia, an overly insular focus, and groupthink that could reduce their ability to innovate or solve problems creatively. Understanding where a team is in the cycle of work is also critical, as it is typically more effective to work with a team on issues that require stepping back and engaging in dialogue, practicing new skills, or working through long-standing conflicts when they are not in the throes of a difficult project with looming deadlines.

Case Examples

Two examples illustrate how teams can vary on the dimensions we've been discussing. As you read them, consider implications for how you would coach each team, including further questions you would have as part of your assessment and potential areas that you would address to improve their functioning.

Team 1 is a relatively homogeneous team in terms of demographics, skill, and experience (low diversity) that has been together for several years (mature in life cycle) in a single-factory manufacturing firm (relatively simple context, no geographic or spatial distribution). The members have to coordinate their work within the team and with the packaging and shipping teams in their plant (low to medium need for boundary spanning or connecting outside the team); their current challenge is responding to high seasonal demand (high task or workload demand) for their main product in their country (relatively low environmental complexity).

Team 2 is a newly formed (formation phase in life cycle), multicultural production team with members of varying backgrounds (high diversity) within a global organization that is integrating recently acquired businesses across regions into a matrix structure (high organizational and environmental context complexity); team members are located in different countries in North America, Europe, and Asia, and they interact virtually (geographically distributed). Their current challenge is responding to high seasonal demand (high task or workload demand) for their main product across several regions (relatively high environmental complexity).

If we simply categorized these teams by function, we could say that both are production teams. While that is a start, we would clearly miss a great deal of important information that differentiates the teams, despite their common challenge of dealing with a spike in demand. The characteristics of each team, based on where they fall along the various dimensions, provide potential targets to evaluate and intervene as necessary to improve the functioning of the team. If a team coach is called in to help one of these teams because conflict is emerging, for example, knowing that both teams are production teams facing increased demand for their product is of minimal help; it does little to illuminate potential problem areas or intervention points. By contrast, knowing that a team is just forming and doing so across multiple boundaries (e.g., demographic, cultural) and time zones in a dynamic context of organizational transformation, with its accompanying ambiguity and uncertainty, can be very helpful in clarifying areas where the team may need to do some work to enhance its functioning. For example, we know that team member orientation to each other and to their goals is important during the formation phase. We also know that shared mental models are important for teams to have so that they can respond quickly and in sync when demands are high and there is little time for coordination and communication. Coaching to help a team such as this get oriented to each other and develop more shared mental models is likely to be of more benefit than the same coaching would be to the homogeneous, single-factory team that has been together for some time and likely has significant overlap in their mental models already.

Different types of teams have different needs, and, equally important, different characteristics of teams beyond their broad type that can guide what to look for and how best to help a team. Characteristics or factors to think about in assessing a team include:

- The complexity of the context the team is in, the degree to which team members need to connect with others outside the team and span boundaries,
- The degree of interdependence within the team and its work,
- The diversity of the team (e.g., culture, background, demographics, personality),
- The distribution of the team (e.g., virtual),

- The stability of the team and its members, and
- Where the team is in its life cycle, as well as in its project time line or workload.

One last consideration in thinking about what type of team you are dealing with relates to what its purpose is and, by extension, its expected output. Is it a strategic plan? Decisions? A project? Implementation of the marketing plan? While this is related to its function, it is more specific than that. However, the purpose or expected output of a team relates directly to how one defines the effectiveness of that team. Does it produce the expected product? Does it make the required decisions? Does it produce a strong strategic plan? Does it implement a new information technology system smoothly, on time, and within budget? This leads us into a consideration of team effectiveness. How is it defined for any given team—and what characterizes high performance in teams?

WHAT MAKES A TEAM EFFECTIVE?

For HR professionals concerned with the performance of teams within an organization, understanding what factors contribute to effectiveness is a prerequisite to determining how to intervene if things are not going well. Hackman and colleagues (Hackman & Morris, 1975; Hackman & Wageman, 2005) have clarified three components of team effectiveness:

1. Group performance (output) meets or exceeds the expectations and standards of the team's clients.
2. Team members experience learning and satisfaction.
3. The team's potential for interdependent work in the future is enhanced.

Think about teams in your organization with these three criteria in mind. There may be a team, for example, that delivers at a high level of quality but is moving so fast or is so burdened with work that the members are getting burned out. In this case, there may be little time for learning and little satisfaction. Nor is it likely that the team will be able to sustain itself for the long term or remain viable because there is little opportunity for it to engage in what Hackman and Wageman (2005) call "the social processes the team uses in carrying out the work [which] enhance members' capability of working together interdependently in the future" (p. 272). Alternatively, you may know of a team in which members are learning and get along very well but they are not performing to expectations. In neither of these cases would the team be considered effective.

Team Process

What a group does to achieve the desired level of performance, satisfaction, and longer-term viability is the group's process. Figure 16.1 illustrates how specific behavioral processes can support effective outcomes, in part by contributing to the development of what we might call productive states—less visible but important conditions or interim outcomes.

There are several ways of categorizing team processes, and each provides a lens that can be helpful to a team coach in assessing a team and where the opportunities for improvement may lie. One traditional categorization of team-related processes breaks them into task work and teamwork.

Figure 16.1
Assessing a Team's Effectiveness: What You See and What's Behind It

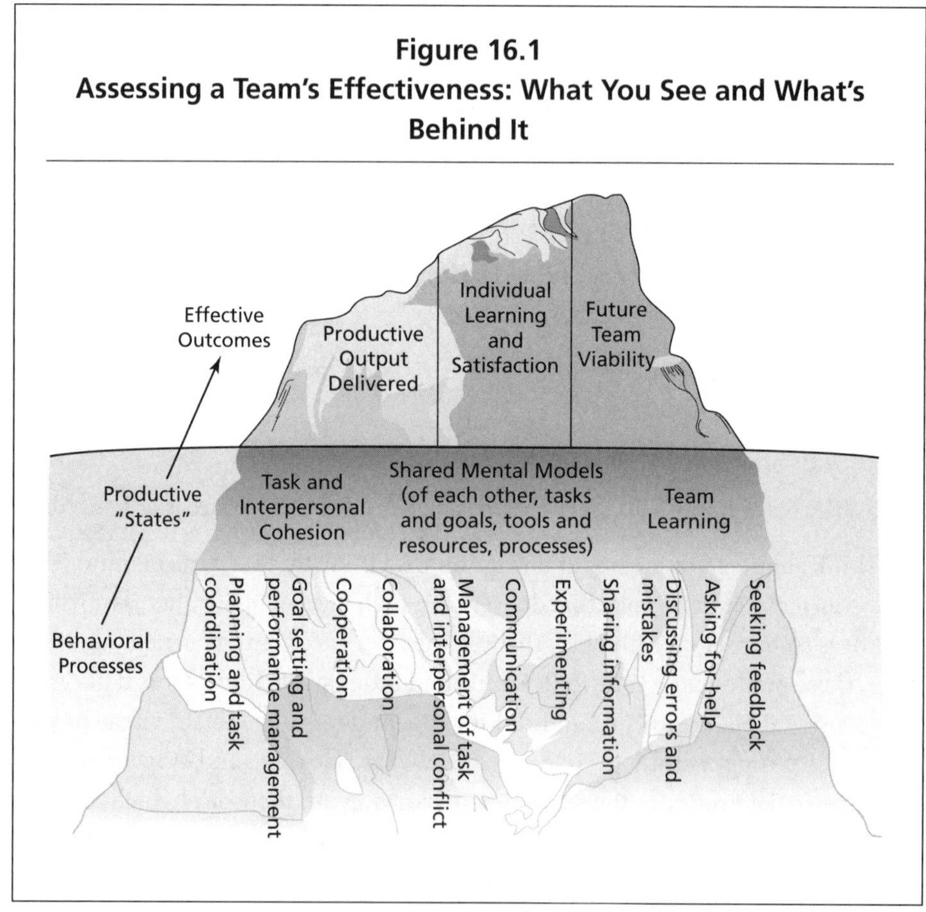

Task Work and Teamwork *Task work* refers to behaviors that address the work or output the team is responsible for and may involve technical expertise, exchanging of information, making plans, allocating resources, solving problems, and so on. *Teamwork* in this specific use refers to the interaction of the team members, or the prosocial behaviors that maintain effective relationships.

Keeping this frame in mind—the existence of both task work and teamwork processes—can help guide the assessment of a team and lessen the risk of focusing solely on team dynamics and interpersonal relations. These are an important piece of the puzzle, but for work teams, equal attention must also be paid to the processes in getting the work done.

Team Member Knowledge, Skills, and Abilities One way to look at team processes more granularly is to specify the domains of individual team member knowledge, skills, and abilities (KSAs) underlying them. Stevens and Campion (1994), for example, identified fourteen KSAs essential to effective team processes. These domains provide helpful targets for a team coach, as well as team leaders and members, to pay attention to. The fourteen KSAs are divided into two main categories and further subdivided as follows:

1. Interpersonal KSAs
   - Conflict resolution (e.g., "to recognize and encourage desirable, but discourage undesirable team conflict," "to recognize the source and type of conflict confronting the team and to implement an appropriate conflict resolution strategy"; p. 505)
   - Collaborative problem solving
   - Communication
2. Self-management
   - Goal setting and performance management
   - Planning and task coordination

Cognitive, Affective, and Behavioral Processes.

Kozlowski and Bell (2012) also provided a helpful frame for assessing a team's effectiveness and identifying target areas for coaching by categorizing team processes in terms of cognitive, affective or motivational, and behavioral mechanisms.

Looking at each of these carefully, one can see the connections with task work and teamwork processes as well as the underlying KSAs. We will focus on those that have been found to be most central to team performance.

Cognitive Processes Two key cognitive constructs relate to team performance: shared mental models and team learning.

A team's shared mental models can be about each other, their tasks and goals, the tools and resources they have available, and the appropriate processes to use to accomplish their work (Cannon-Bowers, Salas, & Converse, 1993). Having shared understanding about these domains is thought to improve team performance by promoting more accurate expectations and greater alignment in approaching tasks (Salas & Cannon-Bowers, 2001). Clearly, one important area for a team coach to assess in some way, even informally, is the degree of shared understanding on the team, specifically in these domains. At CCL, we believe that interviewing each team member during the assessment phase of team coaching is important for a variety of reasons. One of the more important is to gauge the degree of shared understanding, or alignment, regarding issues such as the team's purpose and goals, performance, and processes.

A second cognitive construct considered important for team effectiveness is team learning. Team learning involves gaining new knowledge and perspectives together in the course of shared experience. Teams engage in learning behaviors when they seek feedback, ask for help, discuss errors and mistakes, share information, and experiment. These behaviors in turn are associated with enhanced team performance. It is important to note that engaging in such behaviors involves interpersonal risk, so promoting a climate of psychological safety on the team is an important foundation for encouraging learning behaviors.

Psychological safety is more than just interpersonal trust. It also involves respect for each other's competence and care for each other as human beings. While this does not mean that team members need to be friends, it does suggest that not liking each other imposes a limit on the level of safety and therefore the degree to which members will take the risks necessary to discuss mistakes, admit weakness and failure, and engage in other vulnerable behaviors required for learning. Assessing the degree of psychological safety and the general climate for learning may surface one or more points of entry for team coaching. It may be useful, for example, to work with the team to promote awareness of and appreciation for each team member's competence, getting to know them beyond their work roles to have a deeper appreciation of their full humanity, what's important to them, and so on.

Team members will be much more likely to engage, speak up, provide feedback, ask questions, say, "I don't know" or "I don't understand," admit mistakes, and even dig into the root cause of errors if they are confident that they will not be embarrassed or punished in some way (Edmondson, 1999). A team that engages in such learning behaviors is more likely to perform well because, among other things, they will not repeat the same mistakes and will be able to adapt and flex, not sticking with the current direction so as to avoid admitting error (i.e., save face).

Affective Processes The discussion of psychological safety moves us into the area of affective, or motivational, team process variables. Two in particular are associated with team effectiveness: cohesion and conflict. Cohesion, broadly defined as a force that brings team members together, can be interpersonal or task related, as can conflict, an opposite force that tends to push people apart. Both cohesion and conflict may have benefits as well as downsides.

Task cohesion, as the name implies, is about shared commitment to the group and its goals, which should enhance team member motivation to work harder than they otherwise might. Interpersonal cohesion, also as the name implies, involves positive feelings about each other or, quite simply, liking each other. For the most part, interpersonal cohesion promotes open, effective communication and other mutually beneficial, collaborative behaviors.

Teams can experience both task-related conflict and interpersonal conflict. Task-related conflict, also referred to as cognitive conflict, may actually be important for teams to engage in, at least to a moderate degree. However, interpersonal conflict is generally detrimental to teams. Engaging in moderate cognitive conflict and working through different and initially unreconciled views, ideas, or knowledge about an issue can be a key process driving the development of shared mental models (e.g., aligned expectations), which we've already highlighted as important to team effectiveness. Thinking about, sharing, discussing, and developing multiple ideas leads to more thorough consideration of alternatives and better decision making, in addition to promoting shared mental models (Ensley & Pearce, 2001).

There is a need for balance in these two affective variables, cohesion and cognitive conflict. While team cohesion is typically related to higher performance, too much interpersonal cohesion in the absence of cognitive conflict can be associated with group-think ("the tendency for groups to pressure consensus and conformity"; Kozlowski & Ilgen, 2006, citing Janis, 1972), without adequate consideration of multiple viewpoints and options. Thus, one of the most important areas where a team coach can add value to a team is in ensuring team members have the necessary skills to engage in productive cognitive conflict. Equally important is ensuring the necessary climate of psychological safety and the norms to promote this type of thinking, sharing, discussing, and developing of multiple, and sometimes conflicting, ideas. A team coach must also be able to discriminate between types of conflict and recognize sources of conflict, as well as teach teams related skills, to be able to encourage the good and discourage the bad.

What specific skills and abilities does a team coach promote toward this end? Stevens and Campion (1994) advocate for employing a win-win negotiation strategy as one example. In our CCL work with teams, we also emphasize dialogue skills that involve balancing advocacy and inquiry to surface assumptions, clarify perspectives, make reasoning explicit, and generally keep the discussion focused on the task and a productive resolution of any conflicts.

Behavioral Processes Behavioral constructs found to be important for team effectiveness include coordination, cooperation, and communication. Coordination refers to team member activities, or task work processes, that ensure efficient progress on interdependent work: planning a task strategy, sharing information, or being ready to and contributing at the right time and in the right way. Cooperation on the part of team members involves willingness and effort to do one's part toward the joint work. Communication, of course, is not independent of collaboration and cooperation but really is in service of them and can relate to both task work and teamwork. "Task work communication involves exchanging task-related information and developing team solutions to problems. Teamwork communication focuses on establishing patterns of interaction and enhancing their quality" (Kozlowski & Bell, 2012, p. 442).

The importance of communication to team effectiveness is both profound and commonsensical. One doesn't have to be a research scientist to rightly identify communication as one of the most important processes in any interpersonal relationship, including teaming. However, elements of communication that are related to effectiveness are important to clarify so as to guide intervention if necessary. The specific KSAs that Stevens and Campion (1994) related to the communication subcategory are instructive here:

- An understanding of communication networks and the ability to use them.
- Communicating "openly and supportively" (p. 505).
- A focus on behaviors or events rather than personal factors, which is also a key tenet of CCL's straightforward, nonevaluative, behaviorally anchored feedback model—situation, behavior, impact (SBI)—which aims to avoid judgments and interpretations by focusing on observable behavior.
- Validating others' views and statements.
- Building on what others have said. We've all been in conversations in which others are obviously just waiting to make their point without regard for what others say. This disjointed communication misses opportunities for learning from each other's perspectives and for integrating multiple views.
- Owning one's communication, which is also integral to CCL's SBI model in two ways: first, speaking in the first person ("I" statements) rather than in the second person ("you"), which is a fairly common recommendation; and, second, the speaker states the impact of the behavior on him or her (or on a process or outcome as long as it is observable rather than interpreted).
- Active, nonevaluative listening.
- "Ritual greetings and small talk, and a recognition of their importance" (p. 505), which relate to psychological safety and interpersonal cohesion.

One interesting way to think about communication on teams is in terms of ratios. John Gottman has convincingly demonstrated that a ratio of five positive interactions to one negative interaction predicts long-lasting, satisfying relationships, whereas a ratio closer to one-to-one, meaning just as much negative as positive interaction, is predictive of divorce or break-up later on (Gottman, 1994; Ryan, Gottman, Murray, Carrère, & Swanson, 2000). For example, you might wonder how your friends, Anne and Olivier, stay together since they seem to argue so much. However, as long as they have about five times the amount of positive communication to make up for their arguing, they should be okay (at least, statistically).

Others have extrapolated from these findings to different contexts. For example, at CCL we teach the SBI feedback model to encourage greater sharing of positive and constructive feedback for developmental purposes. We emphasize the importance of providing a greater proportion of positive feedback because practical experience convinces us that people are less defensive in receiving feedback if they believe you have good intentions. Providing frequent positive feedback is a way of demonstrating good intentions and is a form of open, supportive, validating communication. In addition, positive feedback is more likely to enhance self-esteem, whereas constructive feedback, many would agree, can sting a bit. I have heard colleagues use the analogy of a bank account: it's important to make enough deposits (positive feedback) so that there is a positive balance before one can make withdrawals (constructive feedback) and you always want to have a positive balance (higher ratio of positive to constructive).

The balance between inquiry and advocacy in team communication is another example of this concept. The importance of inquiry is prominent in the work of several organizational learning theorists (Argyris & Schön, 1978; Senge, 1990; Ross & Roberts, 1994) who view inquiry—asking questions, clarifying, exploring—as opening up possibilities, increasing understanding, and therefore leading to more effective action. They recommend balancing advocacy—arguing for one's position and narrowing toward closure—with inquiry. Consider a team faced with shrinking revenue that prompts its members to rethink their strategy and find solutions. Unless the problem is crystal clear, simple, and obviously addressable with a straightforward fix, there will have to be some discussion to clarify the nature of the problem, its potential roots, and possible solutions. A team member who simply and adamantly advocates for the position that "we just need to cut marketing expenses immediately" may prevent adequate exploration of the causative factors and the best short- and long-term action to take. Obviously there is a time and a place for advocacy as well, but balancing such advocacy with inquiry to clarify and understand the issues and their interconnections—for example, by asking, "How does that relate to our broader goals?"—may prove smarter in the end, even if it takes a bit longer. Coaching teams to balance inquiry and advocacy and promoting the practice of asking, exploring, and deepening dialogue is a clear way to promote team learning and the development of shared mental models when they are at a point in their work cycle that permits this type of stepping back.

One final consideration when thinking about team communication relates to the direction of that communication, whether focused inwardly on the team or outward to stakeholders beyond the team and even beyond the organization. Many have pointed to the importance of teams paying attention to and interacting with their external context. The definition of team effectiveness mentioned earlier, for example, includes both internal and external aspects. Group performance is defined as the team's product or output meeting or exceeding clients' expectations.

Whoever those clients are, they are external to the team. Indeed teams with a strong external orientation have been shown to perform more highly than those with less of an external perspective (Ancona, 1990). That may involve attending to the environment outside the team and the organization by environmental scanning or performing a SWOT (strengths, weaknesses, opportunities, and threats) analysis, for example. Another key aspect of an external orientation is communication with those outside the group, such as with other functional areas, customers, or suppliers.

Such cross-boundary interaction provides opportunities to learn and gain new ideas and perspectives, which has been shown to beget more new ideas within a team. In other words, there is a connection between external communication and that highly sought golden egg, innovation (Hülsheger, Anderson, & Salgado, 2009). Dyer, Gregersen, and Christensen (2009), in an article entitled "The Innovator's DNA," described five skills of innovative leaders, based on empirical research, that included networking with (i.e., communicating with) diverse others for the sake of gaining new ideas and perspectives. They distinguish the networking that many leaders do for a variety of other reasons from this special type of networking, which intentionally seeks out people with ideas and perspectives different from their own to expand their thinking. Given the tendency for groups to become insular and complacent as they become more and more comfortable with each other (further along on their developmental trajectory), developing a habit of communicating externally to keep ideas fresh is worth coaching teams to do.

Coaching to Improve Team Effectiveness: Summary

Given the vast body of knowledge on team effectiveness and team performance, what are the most important things to keep in mind? For me as a team coach, the first is to know what defines effectiveness for the specific team I am working with. What is its purpose, and what is expected of it? While that will vary, certainly that the output needs to meet or exceed the standards of the team's clients is not in question. This could be considered the first rule of team performance.

I would also want to ensure that the experience of being on the team is fulfilling to the members and that they are learning and growing as individuals and, importantly, as a team. This implies a climate of psychological safety and that the task and the teamwork processes they engage in are effective and productive. These practices include engaging in deep enough dialogue to develop shared mental models, even if this involves some cognitive or task-oriented conflict, coordinating to move interdependent work forward, and communicating in ways that promote divergent thinking first—alternatives, exploration, new perspectives, new discovery—and then alignment. This requires more positive, supportive, encouraging communications than negative, but not solely positive, which may indicate or lead to cohesion without cognitive conflict and its benefits. This also requires balancing advocacy with inquiry to promote exploration, full understanding, systemic perspectives, consideration of minority views, and ultimately alignment.

Establishing a firm foundation for these effective team learning practices is critical and involves establishing norms that promote seeking feedback, discussing errors and mistakes, sharing information, and experimenting. Imagining a team engaging in these behaviors brings to mind activity, dialogue, energy, engagement. Often what we see is the opposite: holding back, restraint, constraint, discomfort, uncertainty. The former are promoted in a climate of psychological safety. The latter result in the absence of psychological safety and the absence of skills to engage in inquiry, dialogue, feedback, and exploration. If team coaching targets nothing beyond creating psychological safety and teaching and promoting the practice of skills for inquiry, dialogue, and feedback, it will move most teams to a much higher level.

An interesting note that bears surfacing is that the processes and behaviors we promote in team coaching and encourage team members to develop and practice largely overlap with what has been referred to as shared team leadership, as opposed to more traditional hierarchical team leadership. Not surprisingly, shared team leadership has been shown to be related to team performance (Hoch & Kozlowski, 2012). This is why I consider team coaching to be an intentional intervention to develop the shared leadership capacity of a team by teaching and promoting the use of task and team-oriented process skills that drive performance.

WHEN TO DO WHAT: THE TEMPORAL DYNAMICS OF TEAMS

Considering the array of variables important to team effectiveness, it is easy to succumb to the danger of viewing teams as static rather than dynamic—thinking in terms of a snapshot of how they coordinate, cooperate, and communicate, for example, rather than a movie of how they engage in these processes over time. This is problematic since some processes are more important at certain times than at others, some issues are more likely to surface at certain times than at others, and, importantly, a team coaching intervention may be more effective at certain times than at others.

Two time-related dimensions are important to consider in relation to teams. The first is the team's development, or where the group is in its life cycle. The second is where the team is in its workload cycle: in the course of a project, on a particular task, or in terms of how burdened they are with task demands at any given point.

Team Life Cycle: A Developmental Perspective

A team's development refers to its growth and change over time as members interact and as it adapts to changing conditions (Kozlowski & Ilgen, 2006). Many stage models of group development have been proposed and essentially capture the basic stages that many readers are no doubt familiar with as described by Tuckman (1965), based on his review of encounter and therapy groups. Organizational scholars point out that the groups that such models were based on are different in important ways from work teams, for example, in the fact that work teams have tasks, goals, and structures that encounter groups do not. Such differences mean that while nonwork team group development models are helpful as a starting point, clarifying some of the more specific temporal factors unique to work teams is important.

One area of general agreement is the significance of the initial formation phase in a team's development. Establishing psychological safety, orienting team members to each other, and other socialization functions are critical regardless of group type. For work teams, this orientation and socialization process involves agreeing on their purpose in addition to team members gaining a mutual understanding of what each other brings to the group in terms of knowledge, beliefs, experience, strengths, talents, personality, and preferences. In other words, this is a process of developing shared mental models of each other. Not only is this mutual understanding important to be able to establish roles and figure out how best to work together, but the self-revelation in the process builds cohesion.

The formation work of a team is critical to team performance. Unfortunately, shared understanding does not spontaneously occur within a group. Instead, team members have to "engage in purposeful interpersonal interactions directed toward understanding their teammates' roles and capabilities" (Pearsall, Ellis, & Bell, 2010, p. 192). Team coaches can contribute substantially to the promotion of this purposeful activity. Given the significance of intentional team formation work, and the particular importance of senior teams in organizations, the topic of senior team formation forms the focus of a separate chapter (chapter 17).

Team Workload Cycle

When a team has moved beyond formation, it is essentially in work mode. While the team may continue to mature and will likely experience some disruptions with membership changes requiring a degree of "re-forming," there is really no evidence of generalizable postformation stages of development (see Hackman & Wageman, 2005). Instead, we can think of postformation as the point at which task work functions become more prominent, and so the effectiveness of teams in engaging in task-related processes is of interest to the coach. Postformation, a team cycles through phases of lower and higher work demands. These variations in a team's workload and demands create different needs from a team leader or, by extension, a team coach. During lower task load, a leader can provide the most value by offering what Kozlowski et al. (1996) refer to as "instruction," whereas in high task load conditions, the role is to provide "intervention." This same thinking can be applied to the role of a coach—although with any team coaching, it is expected that one of the outcomes the coach focuses on is the transfer of coaching skills to the leader (if there is a formal team leader).

Instruction refers to promoting team alignment around goals and roles, such as through goal setting and feedback, and encouraging team learning and coherence so there is a strong foundation for working together under more intense conditions. At the beginning of a task or project, for example, task work processes such as goal setting and planning are priorities. At a time like this, the work demands are typically not yet at their peak, so there is opportunity to direct attention to processes that prepare the team to work seamlessly and efficiently together when work demands go up and the team is in nose-to-the-grindstone mode.

In these more demanding conditions, the intervention function is most helpful. Initially this involves prioritizing and planning for contingencies, but as the demands increase and, with them, the pace and ambiguity, the role of leadership (or coaching) involves assessing and monitoring the internal and external situation and revising or refocusing on goals as appropriate. For example, in the midst of a fast-paced project with many interdependent tasks, changes coming at the team from the outside at every turn, there is a need to focus more narrowly on each next step so as to not get bogged down with what could be an overwhelming "big picture." Figure 16.2 provides an illustration of how team coaching might be used at various points in a team's life and work cycle.

Figure 16.2

Team Coaching in the Context of a Team's Life and Work Cycle

Work Cycle
Higher workload demands (e.g., project/work/year midpoint)
Lower workload demands (e.g., project start, fiscal year start)
Lower workload demands (e.g., project close, fiscal year close)
Higher workload demands (e.g., project/work/year midpoint)
Lower workload demands (e.g., project close, fiscal year close)
Life Cycle
Formation
Ongoing Teamwork with Membership Changes (reformation)
Team End (e.g., project team)
Team Coaching
Member orientation, chartering/ purpose, norms, aligning around goals and roles
Promoting team alignment goalsetting and feedback, encouraging team learning and cohesion
Work start: goalsetting, planning
Increasing demands: prioritizing, contingency planning
With increased pace and ambiguity: assess, monitor, refine goals, refocus
As work comes to a close or at planned "time-out": review and reflection for learning and alignment
Ongoing time-relevent team coaching by team leader and shared by team

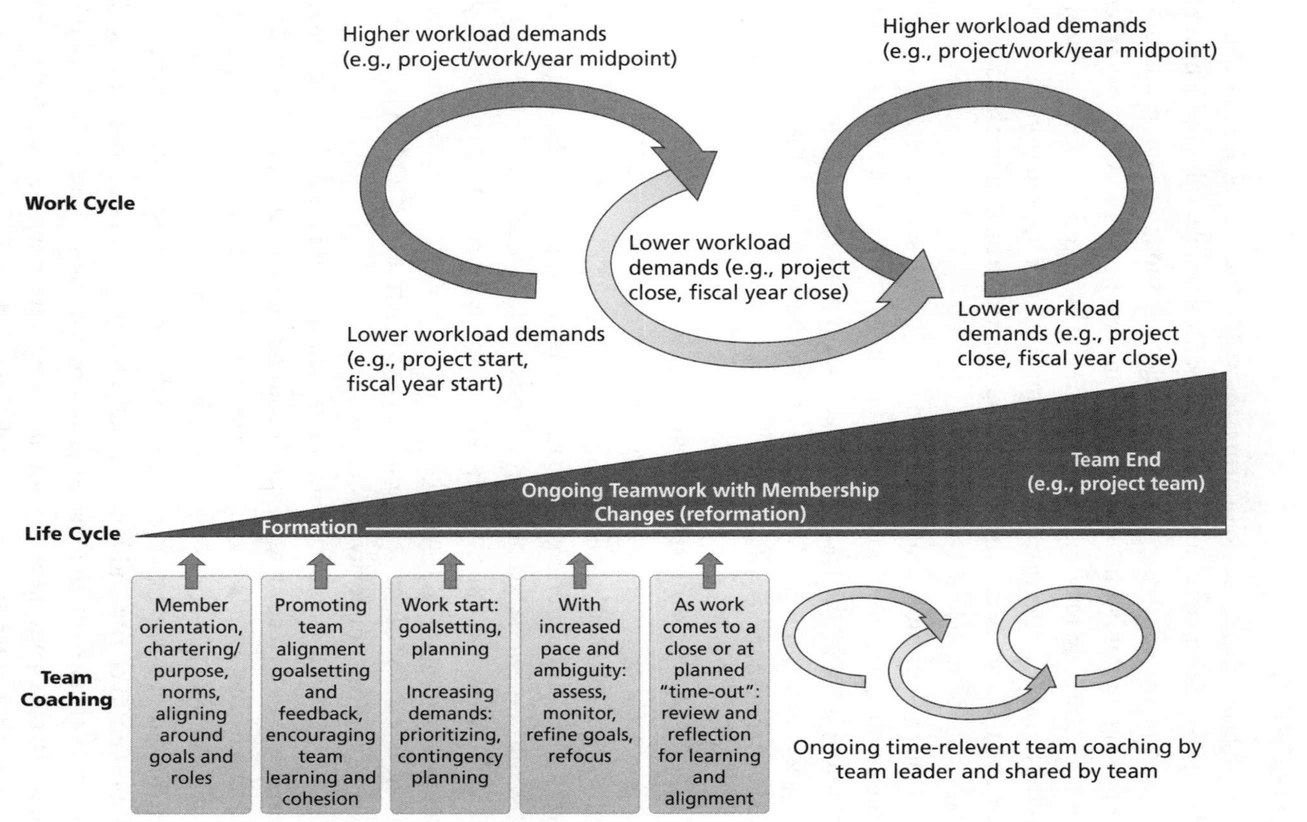

PULLING IT ALL TOGETHER: THE PROCESS OF TEAM COACHING

Viewing coaching as we do informs the process that we engage in when we coach. Being an elicitive, developmental activity, for example, rules out a heavy emphasis on training or advising in team coaching, although where teams lack certain knowledge or skill, addressing this gap can certainly be part of the overall coaching process. Similarly, focusing on the business at hand and the organizational context as the learning platform means that team building removed from the purpose and tasks of the team is not stressed, although early formation work may err more in this direction than later coaching.

One way to think about team coaching is as a sort of dance among process consultation, the provision of tools and frameworks, and facilitating the application of them by the team to task and team processes to improve their specific targeted areas while working on the team's business, with the aim of enhancing team effectiveness.

CCL's RACSR Coaching Framework

CCL's coaching framework, as shown in figure P2.1 at the start of part 2, is built on our core assessment, challenge, and support (ACS) framework for development, with the critical addition of attention to relationship and results (RACSR). The RACSR framework has become a fundamental process guide for our executive coaching as well as our coaching skills training. The comprehensive and dynamic yet simple framework is equally relevant for team coaching. We have found that using an explicit framework fosters a coaching mind-set and an increased appreciation for the complexity of coaching.

The RACSR framework promotes collaboration in eliciting insight and awareness as well as identification of strengths, gaps, and goals to guide ongoing coaching. The framework emphasizes the importance of a trusting relationship with a coach, a relationship in which issues of boundaries and confidentiality are unique and more complex than in dyadic coaching relationships, but no less important to clarify and honor. Finally, the framework encourages the dynamic use of both support and challenge to promote new thinking, new perspectives, new behaviors, and new ways of functioning together. As we frequently say, this framework is intended to advance disciplined thinking about the various aspects of a coaching mind-set and behavior and not to be approached formulaically. The elements of the RACSR as applied to teams follow:

1. *Relationship*: Establishing rapport, boundaries, and trust, which includes an initial contracting discussion with the team.
2. *Assessment*: Assessing the team to develop shared insight regarding key team variables (e.g., purpose, goals, task, and team processes) and to integrate this information into an understanding of strengths and development opportunities that serve as potential foci of the ongoing coaching work. This is analogous to assessing personality, competencies, and performance in an individual.
3. *Challenge*: Challenging group thinking, perspectives, assumptions, and practices to promote the ability of the team to observe itself and become aware of other possibilities.
4. *Support*: Listening for understanding, facilitating the engagement of all team members as they are challenged by the coaching, and helping the team remove obstacles to their effective functioning and the achievement of their goals.
5. *Results*: Setting goals in team coaching is no less important than in individual coaching, although this is sometimes less explicit than it should be. Goal setting, or the identification of problems to improve on, is heavily informed by assessment and should involve all team members to promote buy-in.

Establishing the Relationship, Engaging in Assessment, and Targeting Results

So what might the process of team coaching look like in practice? First, the need for team coaching is surfaced. For an external coach or an organization like CCL, this typically comes as a client request. For an internal HR professional, this could come in many forms—as a direct request to you because a new team is forming or a team intervention is desired, as complaints to you about the team from within or outside of it, or through your own observation of dysfunction or ineffectiveness. It could also come about as part of a broader initiative or changes within the organization that the team has to rise to the occasion to deal with, for example, an executive team involved in organization transformation, as discussed in detail in chapter 18.

Regardless of the way in which the need for team coaching surfaces, the initial activities in relationship-building and assessment should follow. These processes involve fairly straightforward activities that are no doubt familiar to many: discovery, diagnosis, contracting, and, throughout, establishment and deepening of rapport. The coach's relationship with a team is by nature more complicated than with an individual. Attention must be paid to maintaining a focus on team-level work and a systems perspective and not aligning with one or more individuals or viewing behavior in isolation from the system's influences. Contracting with a team establishes the purpose, structure, and parameters (including confidentiality and its limits) of the engagement, makes them explicit, and allows all parties to commit to the process as informed participants.

What we refer to as assessment at CCL includes both formal and informal assessment. Importantly, while assessment is more prominent early on, it is an ongoing process. As noted above, the point of assessment is to develop shared insight and understanding. All of the team-related frameworks and variables discussed thus far present potential targets for a team coach's assessment activity.

These areas include what type of team it is and where it falls on the various dimensions that may characterize a team. What is its purpose, and what are its goals? Who is on the team—composition, diversity, geographic distribution? Are roles established and clear? How clear and aligned are team members on all of these factors? Are individuals known to each other and mutually respected? What is the current functioning of the team: its dynamics (e.g., level of trust, quality of interactions, climate) and task and teamwork processes (e.g., problem solving, decision making, conflict management)? What is the level of cohesion and coordination? How is the communication? How effective is the team? This includes clarifying what constitutes performance in terms of the productive output expected (e.g., product, service, decisions, and plans). It also includes the degree of team member learning and satisfaction and the sustainability of the team.

We typically interview each member of a team and select stakeholders to interview as well in order to assess these factors. Synthesizing the interview data allows the additional appraisal of the degree to which there is alignment. This addresses the question, To what extent are team members' mental models shared? Interview data also provide insight into how well the team is performing and how effective its processes are. We may use assessment instruments if we believe they would provide important information regarding data not discoverable in the interviews. We may use individual-level assessments as well. Although these do not provide information on team functioning, they can be useful for certain reasons, such as to understand the diversity of personalities on the team or to provide the basis for a team-building element, such as during formation or as needed later to promote mutual understanding and cohesion.

One of the ways to begin to gain alignment and begin the reflective process of encouraging the team to be aware of its dynamics and processes is to share back such interview and other data for the team to sort through and engage in meaning making around. The coach should also pay attention to what the data reveal about how much skill building or skill training will be required and how much safety and trust there is to inform the coaching approach. For example, a climate lower in trust may require that the work be done in a progressive way, starting in small, safe steps, versus in the full system from the beginning.

A similar judgment must be made, based on level of trust or safety, about the degree to which verbatim interview data are revealed to the team versus summarized themes and outliers. Either way, the process of reviewing and making sense of the interview data can be a valuable activity for the team to engage in together and this is often the first session after the assessment interviews. The coach, however, is not making sense of these data for the first time with the team but should review the information ahead of time in order to identify any frameworks or tools that will be useful for the team to have right away. This allows the coach to provide just-in-time training or skill development to be immediately applied to the team's own content and process—not only in the initial session but also in ongoing sessions.

For example, framing the importance of an external perspective and external communication can provide a benchmark for the team members as they review their own data and realize that they may need to make a shift in focus to take external stakeholders and constituents more into account. Similarly, having baseline information about the potential benefits of task conflict and disadvantages of interpersonal conflict may be a helpful frame as they review their own responses to questions about dynamics and conflict. And knowing dialogue that balances advocacy with inquiry is associated with higher-performance teams can serve as an incentive to learn some basic dialogue skills to use in discussing the assessment data and in future interactions.

As should be clear from these examples, the team's work to understand, make sense of, and draw conclusions from their data can lead to the identification of targets for the team coaching work. Other assessment data contributing to the identification of targets include information gleaned through good questions and team discussion of what they see as their strengths, weaknesses, challenges, and opportunities for improvement. This identification of target areas in team coaching is analogous to goal setting and development planning in individual coaching and in both cases corresponds to the results element of the RACSR model.

Challenging and Supporting the Team in Achieving Results

Obviously relationship building and maintenance continue throughout the coaching process. As noted, assessment continues throughout team coaching as well, albeit less formally, generally in the form of observation, feedback, and inquiry on the part of the coach and the team members themselves. As team coaching proceeds, the coach facilitates the development of the team to improve in whatever areas it has identified need enhancement, such as conflict management or decision-making processes. Moving the team toward the results it has identified as important is achieved through the complementary processes of challenge and support.

At CCL, we frequently hear from participants in our coaching skills programs that the connotations they have for the term *challenge* are somewhat different from the way we advocate its use in coaching, which requires clarification. While some use this word to mean "confront a person" or "conflict with a person," at CCL we apply it not to individuals but to thinking, perspectives, and assumptions. Challenging in coaching, then, is about prompting an individual or group to reflect on their implicit beliefs and practices, to surface and question their assumptions, and entertain other perspectives. Challenge as such prompts questioning, awareness, and an expanded view of what is possible and what alternatives exist. This allows the team to make intentional choices about its behavior and to practice new skills, promoting practice and stretch being key aspects of challenge. For example, taking a time-out when a team discussion has devolved and individuals are simply advocating loudly and angrily for their positions to ask the team what is going on and whether they are moving toward their goals is a way to challenge. Specifically, these questions challenge their automatic behaviors, prompt them to practice reflection and self-management, and stretch to try alternative behaviors such as taking a deep breath, explicitly stating their assumptions, and inquiring about another's reasons for reaching a particular conclusion.

As you can see, although team coaching is not primarily a didactic approach, challenging a team to see things differently and develop new approaches can involve providing frameworks and models as well as teaching tools or new skills.

This is why we can view team coaching as a sort of dance between process consultation, the provision of tools and frameworks, and facilitating the application of them by the team to task and team processes to improve their specific targeted areas while working on the team's business, with the aim of enhancing team effectiveness.

Questions a team coach asks might include, "What's going on here?" "What don't you know about this issue?" or "What will be the most useful process for you to use to make this decision?" A coach also can challenge a team by holding back and allowing its members to work through their own issue and encourage a retrospective review afterward to prompt them to identify missed opportunities or ineffective strategies. Challenge can also involve having a team engage in practice with a tool or skill, for example, by asking them to "practice listening and using inquiry rather than advocacy as you talk about a key problem the team faces" and then debriefing the experience for learning.

The Evolution of the Team Coaching Process

Once any formation, training, or skill development functions of coaching are accomplished in the team's development work, the role of the coach involves more process consultation, observing the functioning of the team in dealing with its business at hand, and intervening less frequently, primarily when processes are ineffective and could be improved. A key goal is to use a coaching approach that prompts the team to reflect on their process and come up with more effective behaviors, approaches, or solutions.

Another shift the coach makes, in addition to moving from a training and skill-building function into a process-consultation function, is when the team moves from low task load to high task load. When the demands on the team are manageable or even relatively low and attention can and should be paid to the team's development in terms of skill building and shared mental model convergence, the coaching should shift when the team is under high demand to focus on helping it deal with the high task demands, which take priority. This may involve prompting the group to break larger goals down into smaller goals, or what might be called manageable chunks. The coach can also help the team to focus on one step at a time to maintain alignment, engagement, and momentum and a sense of control rather than chaos.

The length of any given team coaching engagement, whether by an external professional or an internal HR partner, will depend on the needs of the team and how effectively they are able to take on shared leadership and self-coaching. At CCL, we often work with a team over a year or so, joining the members for regular team meetings and off-sites every month or two, though the schedule varies greatly. Depending on the individual leadership development needs of team members, we may also provide executive coaching to one or more members, including the team leader. Similarly, if there are broader organizational changes under way, we may work with the executive team, and other teams as relevant, to promote positive, effective changes on this larger scale (described in chapter 18).

Case Examples

Consider the team described earlier in this chapter that was just forming and included a diverse membership across multiple time zones in a dynamic context of organizational transformation. A team coach called in to help this team with a high level of conflict might be particularly aware of the challenges for this team to get to know each other and develop shared understanding of each team member's strengths, talents, and role contributions, as well as shared understanding of the team's purpose and goals. Without these shared mental models, there is unlikely to be the trust, unspoken understanding, and quick coordination required during a high-demand period. A coach might first gather input from each team member related to the team's purpose, goals, and functioning and then share this back in a virtual meeting that is intentionally designed to promote increased self-disclosure, vulnerability, and shared understanding as a foundation for discussing norms for communicating and working effectively together. The establishment or refinement of clear norms and goals is important for ultimate task work but it also contributes to the team's development of interpersonal cohesion. In this case, norms might include respect for and accommodation of team members in all time zones, as basic as that might sound. Setting a mutually workable time to meet by videoconference or perhaps a rotating schedule so team meetings are not always late at night for one person or subset could promote cross-boundary awareness as well as a sense of inclusion and respect, not to mention boost the probability of attendance. A next step for this coaching might be to teach some basic dialogue and problem-solving tools and have the team use them (practice) to surface assumptions, gain alignment, and identify possible solutions to a key problem.

In a second case, a colleague and I were recently asked to work with a management team that many would not even define as a team because of its size: twenty-two people, at varying levels of leadership. Nonetheless, these individuals had shared goals and interdependent tasks, and they needed to work effectively together. We were told that they had formed six months previously and were meeting twice a week. However, top executives were still making most of the decisions for which the team was ostensibly responsible, there was grumbling behind the scenes, and meetings were dominated by a few individuals. The client request was to help them become more effective together so they could ensure that the organization implemented its strategy successfully.

Assessment of the team included interviews and observation of a half-day team meeting. After the data from these were reviewed, we added an individual personality instrument to the assessment process because interviews and observation suggested that there had never been a real formation phase and there was little cohesion, with an absence of substantive discussion (in fact, discussion was extremely limited, superficial, and engaged in by just a few people, suggesting low trust and, likely, lack of dialogue proficiency). Moreover, while there was an official charter that we, the coaches, received from the chief operating officer, interviews revealed large gaps in knowledge about the purpose of the team, lack of alignment around team goals, and very little attention to the external environment. There were no explicit team norms either.

An initial session with this team involved an interweaving of activities to promote interpersonal familiarity and understanding, effective dialogue, processing of the charter, and creation of shared norms, as well as the identification on the part of the team of other target areas they believed were important to address over time. Because the team was large and trust was fairly low, we used a progressive approach similar to CCL's boundary-spanning practices. These begin with buffering, which refers to defining and initially maintaining boundaries to create psychological safety. Following that, we used the practice of reflecting, that is, looking past what separates parties while keeping the boundary intact. It uncovers the differences and the commonalities among groups (Ernst & Chrobot-Mason, 2011).

In the context of the team coaching, the individual personality assessment created the focus for the buffering: individuals reflected on their results as well as their broader strengths, talents, and potential contributions to the group. They then reflected this with partners, increasing each other's shared understanding and creating a foundation for role clarity. With some degree of trust, safety, and sense of acceptance established, this discussion and self-revelation then moved to the whole group setting for further reflection.

In order to promote robust dialogue that would allow the team to tackle their own work, rather than leave decisions to the CEO and COO, we provided brief training on the use of inquiry, emphasizing in particular assessment and challenge questions to deepen the conversation and uncover issues and assumptions that are not typically surfaced in normal discussions. Team members applied these in groups of three to real issues that the team and organization faced. The slightly larger group, as compared to the first discussion held in pairs, was a small stretch in terms of safety and permitted one person to observe at a time and subsequently provide feedback, another skill we taught and that we encouraged in practice.

The iterative approach was also used to promote the skill of balancing inquiry and advocacy. The application in this case was done in groups of six, a further stretch that extended the psychological safety from the previous groups of three; the focus was on the charter document. In order to encourage constructive dialogue and knowing that there was not uniform agreement with aspects of the charter, we created a structured process that gave permission and, in fact, set an expectation, for everyone to raise concerns and disagreements. Another way of saying this is that we normalized, or created a norm for, raising concerns and disagreeing. To do this, we asked groups to engage in dialogue and identify their top three concerns. This was followed by a large group dialogue about the concerns and areas of agreement, which was extremely free flowing. I intentionally use the term *dialogue* rather than simply *discussion*, because we explicitly encouraged the application of skills that were previously learned and practiced, including inquiry, challenge, and surfacing assumptions.

Additional work with this team involved observing and coaching to reinforce the team's new norms, skills, and processes in the service of alignment and better effectiveness. This was generally in the context of their team meetings, in which they engaged in their ongoing work together. As they gradually became more adept at engaging in group dialogue that really dug into issues, uncovered assumptions, and led to better decisions, team members became more confident in their own process interventions—calling "time-out" or prompting the group to reflect with a question, for example. They did not shy away from tough issues as much as they had in the past, which led them to grapple with strategic and organizational culture issues that they had avoided previously. After several months, the team was holding each other accountable to their agreed-on norms and was clear on their purpose and goals, able to engage in robust dialogue and handle some conflict, make better decisions, and learn together. Although they still had some gaps, they felt capable of continuing their developmental work together, and everyone was engaged and committed to the work.

A Note about Team Size

While there is no hard-and-fast rule about the optimal team size, most people agree that a team can be too large, and many tend to think of this cutoff as ten to twelve. The right number of people, though, depends on a variety of factors, including how much work needs to be accomplished, how much coordination is required, how many different skill sets will be most valuable, and so on. One approach to working with a team that is particularly large is to consult with the team leader about structure and design, to challenge the thinking of the leader to consider whether the size makes sense for the intended purpose and what the composition should look like. If the conclusion is that the proposed structure makes sense, or if for whatever reason (e.g., political) the team size will remain as is, then the team coach adapts.

The second case example reflects some of this adaptation. The progressive approach we took to promote the development of psychological safety, trust, and open dialogue may not be necessary to the same degree with smaller teams. A team coach may need to make other adaptations as well. For example, as the team gets bigger, obviously the effort to create shared mental models becomes more complicated and may take more work and more time. Similarly and related, team dialogue is more complicated in that more perspectives are potentially being shared. In order to have dialogue that leads to shared understanding, the various perspectives need to be remembered and interwoven into the discussion. To do this, certain communication tools become particularly important, including summarizing understanding after individuals talk and building on what each other says so that each perspective is incorporated into succeeding comments and statements and, in essence, become embedded and part of the memory. A team coach needs to be alert to the opportunity to facilitate the use of such tools and skills. While this is most easily done when teams are meeting in person, it can also be done virtually on conference calls and in e-mail or similar online discussions. Another technique that can be helpful in this regard is to periodically summarize the discussion to this point, which a coach can prompt team members to do as a matter of course. And, finally, a common but valuable approach to capturing or creating a team memory is to document key points that come up in the conversation on a flip chart or board.

Intervening with Individuals in Team Coaching

Much of this discussion has been about working with the team at the team level. This focus is critical but does not mean that the team coach loses sight of the individuals as individuals, since team functioning is affected by factors at the individual level. These could include individuals who are disruptive, dominate, or are not at the same level of awareness, skill, or competence as other members regarding teamwork or task work. In this last case, the individual (and team, by extension) may benefit from some specific training or development experience outside the team, such as a leadership development program, a skill program, a course, management training, or individual coaching. Someone who is disruptive requires feedback and expectation setting first and foremost, along the lines of performance management. Beyond that, such a person may also require individual coaching to support behavior change based on the explicit feedback about behavioral expectations, assuming he or she acknowledges the behavior and expresses a willingness to change. The same would apply to a dominating individual who may or may not be aware of his or her impact: feedback and possibly individual coaching as required.

Finally, individual attention should be paid to the team leader with a goal of transferring the team coaching, team facilitation, and process consultation skills to the team leader as well as a general expectation that the team itself will become better able to attend to teamwork as well as task processes. An explicit focus on the team leader to increasingly use the skills of team coaching and process consultation and facilitation, as appropriate, and to understand issues of timing in order to be most effective is warranted.

SPECIFIC APPLICATIONS OF TEAM COACHING

While teams can take many forms and the range of tasks and outputs they are responsible for is vast, certain challenges emerge for teams fairly commonly. The challenges facing teams derive from the types of issues we've been discussing:

- Not establishing firm foundations, such as clarifying and locking hands on the purpose, or identity, of the team and its goals as well as getting to know each other well enough to understand strengths, talents, personalities, and values
- Teaming in the incredibly complex, dynamic environments by which most teams are surrounded
- The need to develop learning agility
- Ineffective or dysfunctional teamwork and task work processes

These challenges and the symptoms that show up as team problems are not necessarily independent of each other, and in many cases, they overlap significantly. We will also address some of the unique needs of specific types of teams that tend to be the most common targets of team coaching in today's organizations.

Failure to Establish a Firm Foundation

The significance of the team formation phase is indisputable, as it establishes a firm foundation from which to work. The foundations for a team include its purpose or identity, its goals, and the mutual understanding and bonds among members. Clarifying and "locking hands" on the purpose, or identity, of the team and its goals is an example of establishing a firm foundation. So too is the team's activity of getting to know each other as people, including strengths and weaknesses, talents, values, and motivators, so that roles can be established, mutual understanding begins, and interpersonal practices that make the establishment of shared mental models possible begin to take root. Inadequately addressing the critical tasks of formation prevents the development of shared mental models and psychological safety that allow seamless, flexible, quick task accomplishment and ongoing learning later.

It is important to bear in mind that keeping the foundations of a team strong, like maintaining a healthy root system in a plant, is an ongoing process. And even if it generally fades to more of a background issue beyond the initial formation of the team, there are times in the life cycle of the team when attention to foundations reemerges as important, such as when team membership changes. If a new member joins the team, it is important for that person to be oriented to the team, and vice versa. This is not purely a socializing function or one-directional. Instead, this is a mutual process that allows for shared mental models to emerge about each other (who they are, what they bring, and what role they will play); about the team's purpose, goals, and tasks; about the tools and resources they have available; and about the team and task processes they will use (Cannon-Bowers et al., 1993).

Failure to establish this foundation in the beginning or to revisit it when there are changes prevents this emergence of shared understanding that is so critical to effective task accomplishment, especially in high-demand situations, as well as to the ability of the team to learn and grow together. These failures directly relate to the factors that define high performance for a team: group performance that meets or exceeds stakeholder expectations, team member learning and satisfaction, and group health and viability.

And while many teams and team leaders would prefer to "skip the warm, fuzzy stuff" and "get down to business," not "slowing down to power up" can cause problems later. Skipping this foundation building at the beginning of the team's life cycle and thereafter prevents the opportunity to deepen familiarity, create shared understanding, and build trust. This will manifest itself on a team as dysfunction: lack of direction and alignment, conflict, distrust, clique and political alliance formation, disengaged meetings and discussions, hallway conversations, mixed messages coming from the group, and so on.

The Need to Slow Down to Power Up

The US military in the 1990s coined the acronym VUCA to describe the increasingly volatile, uncertain, complex, and ambiguous environment it was facing. The term has since been widely applied to the world of business and organizations (Smith & Rao, 1994). However, the fact that phrases such as "increasingly fast pace of change" and "ever-more dynamic environment" have become well worn in describing organizations does not make them any less true. The interdependence inherent within organizations, among organizations, and within the broader systems of which they are a part — societal, governmental, and economic, combined with the geographic spread of organizations and their constituents — creates massive complexity in our work world. Amid this complexity are found almost constant change and challenges that are new, have not yet been encountered, and require new thinking and new solutions. Heifetz and Laurie (1997) talked about these as "adaptive change" and "adaptive challenges" and noted that "solutions to adaptive challenges reside ... in the collective intelligence of employees at all levels, who need to use one another as resources, often across boundaries, and learn their way to those solutions" (p. 124).

All of this means that teams should work interdependently, no matter how fluid the context, by learning together as they go. However, without explicit acknowledgment of these surrounding challenges and the specific adaptations they require, teams may not rise to the challenge. Instead, they may deal with the rapid pace by succumbing to it, as if carried downstream by a strong, fast-moving current. They might skim over discussions without delving into deeper dialogue about underlying issues. They rely on advocacy at the expense of inquiry, do not span boundaries, and maintain relatively superficial relationships that don't allow the development of trust, mutual respect, and shared mental models. In other words, they never "slow down to power up," as we say at CCL, a key tenet of our organizational transformation work (see chapter 18).

Developing Learning Agility

While there may be value in a team engaging in activities unrelated to work (e.g., social simulations, experiential activities), particularly to contribute to the socialization involved in formation, at some point team coaching must get to a point where it uses the team's own organizational environment and real work as the learning context and content. This is because observing and directly working with the real issues allows the most immediate transfer of learning. In other words, reflection on real work allows for abstraction and application of learning to new, other, and emerging work challenges, enhancing the team's effectiveness in doing their work. This reflection, abstraction, and application process is at the very heart of coaching. It is also the very description of learning agility, which has been defined as "the willingness and ability to learn from experience, and subsequently apply that learning to perform successfully under new or first-time conditions" (DeMeuse, Dai, & Hallenbeck, 2010, citing Lombardo & Eichinger, 2000). Coaching in general, and team coaching in particular, can serve as a critical support for leaders to learn from business challenges and the daily challenges of leading as a team.

Improving Dysfunction

While working effectively together begins with a positive, constructive formation phase and the establishment of a firm foundation, what it looks like in actual practice on an ongoing basis can be captured quite well by calling on teamwork and task work processes and constructs. In particular, common team process failures or dysfunction tend to relate to cohesion, conflict management, problem solving, decision making, communication (e.g., a lack of breadth or depth, advocacy over inquiry), accountability (performance management), collaboration, and team learning behaviors (e.g., feedback, discussing mistakes). These issues are not mutually exclusive and may even contribute to or reinforce each other. For example, good communication and cohesion breed shared understanding and better decision making; good decisions inspire trust within the team, which enhances confidence and a sense of safety, promoting more open discussion of mistakes for increased learning.

Common Issues for Unique Types of Teams

As should be obvious by now, one size does not fit all in team coaching due to the multitude of variables that may be important to consider with any team. However, it should also be obvious that there are some fairly straightforward places to look for the root of problems and some key interventions that may prove quite valuable for many teams. Understanding the type of team and characteristics of it that may impede its functioning is a starting point. Assessing the degree of clarity and alignment around core issues, such as the team's purpose and goals, is next, followed by clarifying how the team is doing with regard to important task and teamwork processes. Beyond this, there are some specific issues related to unique types of teams commonly found in organizations today that CCL's research and practical experience allows us to highlight for consideration.

Coaching a Leadership Team A leadership team is a decision-making team that is often made up of representatives of specific functions and thus responsible for both high-level (e.g., enterprise) goals and their own organization's or function's goals. The tension between independence and interdependence is salient for such teams. They also need to be strategic, so attending to both their degree of connection with their external environment and their effectiveness at engaging in processes that relate to large-scope information gathering, effective meaning making, and good decision making is key. In terms of their formation, the creation of team identity, effective group functioning, and leadership practices in the service of its primary functions of setting direction (vision, strategy, communication), creating alignment throughout the organization (communication; attention to structure, design, rewards/incentives, and process; developing teams), and building the commitment needed to accomplish organizational objectives (communication, inspirational leadership) are fundamental.

Coaching a Cross-Functional Project Team The use of project teams convened to accomplish specific projects is common today. They are, by definition, cross-functional, task focused, and often time limited. This means that effective project management (involving a variety of task work processes) is critical, as are boundary-spanning practices that permit the development of shared mental models, including dialogue. Decision making and collaboration can be particularly important process areas around which to work with such a team.

Action Learning Teams Action learning teams are specific types of cross-functional project teams convened with both a project or task focus and a leadership development goal. Action learning projects are becoming increasingly important in organizations' talent development initiatives, and CCL has been working with many of these organizations to design, frame up, and coach teams through this process. We have found that champions or project sponsors from higher-level leadership are important to the success of these initiatives. This is both to ensure that the projects are important to the organization and that there is visible support for the projects and teams. An action learning coach plays an important role in the learning of the team, focusing members' attention on their developmental outcome throughout the process by using inquiry and prompting reflection, even as they push ahead on their project work. Action learning coaching is unique in this regard: it is specifically intended to foster leadership learning and development at both the individual and team levels within the context of a specific project.

Group Coaching Group coaching can mean a variety of things, but at its most basic refers to coaching of a group that is not an interdependent team. This can mean coaching provided by a coach, whether an external professional or an internal HR partner, to a collection of individuals as either a cost-saving strategy as compared to one-on-one coaching, or as a way to intentionally leverage common themes and challenges and the potential for peer learning, as with a group from the same functional area. At CCL, we have also used a group coaching approach that involves teaching a group of individuals engaged in a development process some basic coaching skills so they can serve as peer coaches to each other in implementing their development plans over time. In group coaching, there is generally not a group-level outcome targeted as there is in team coaching (since there is not a shared task or goal that the group is responsible for achieving), so most of the team-level processes discussed in this chapter do not directly apply. Instead, the goal is typically related more to individual development, whether of general leadership competence or of one or more specific competencies or skills.

TOOLS USED IN TEAM COACHING

Team coaching is an emergent process that involves attention to group dynamics and process and requires agility on the part of the coach. The most fundamental tools for the coach to use are keen observation, thorough assessment (formal and informal, including diagnostic interviews), elicitive inquiry (asking good questions), and feedback. These form the basic building blocks of effective developmental process facilitation. Often the most critical activities for teams to engage in, and therefore for coaches to promote, are robust dialogue, reflection, constructive feedback, conflict management, effective decision making, and group learning. Tools should be introduced to the team only in the service of such outcomes and only based on the unique, emergent needs of the team in question. Tools that we use at CCL include these:

- Explorer Tools (Visual Explorer, Leadership Metaphor Explorer, Collaborative Trust Explorer) to engage the "whole brain" and promote more expansive thinking as well as provide shared language to talk about team phenomena
- Building blocks of team dialogue
  - Inquiry for team dialogue (assessment and challenge questions)
  - Balancing advocacy and inquiry
  - Situation behavior impact feedback model
- Process debriefing tools, such as understanding the level of agreement using Fist of Five, uncovering issues by listing Benefits/Concerns, or capturing process issues by focusing on What Is Working/Not Working
- SWOT analysis
- Storytelling
- Experiential activities that pull out certain behaviors or processes that need to be addressed, for example, Colourblind or Challenging Assumptions (RSVP Design Ltd., www.rsvpdesign.co.uk)
- Boundary-spanning tools (see Ernst & Chrobot-Mason, 2011)

CONCLUSION

Team coaching enhances the effectiveness of teams by developing the shared leadership capacity of the interdependent group. The targets of team coaching are the task and team-oriented process skills that drive performance, ongoing learning, and long-term group health. The process involves the key activities of relationship building, assessment, challenge, support, and driving results. By having a framework in mind to guide discovery of what is behind problems a team may be having and to guide how you approach the process of coaching the team to rise above its challenges, you will be better equipped to promote the effectiveness of the teams in your organization and the learning, development, and satisfaction of the individuals forming and performing on those teams.

chapter SEVENTEEN

Senior Team Coaching

Douglas D. Riddle

Every human resource professional has opinions about the executive leadership group of his or her organization. Some have the opportunity to work with the group's members. This chapter provides guidance about the opportunities and risks associated with coaching the senior executive group as it seeks greater leadership effectiveness.

There are three main approaches to coaching the senior leadership team that can involve HR leaders. You may be the primary contact and guide for an external professional who is engaged to coach the team through its development at various stages. You may be the coach to the team leader who wants to be a better coach for her team, or you may be engaged to provide some team and individual coaching for the senior team yourself. This chapter focuses most of its attention on the work you might do as a coach, but the issues and opportunities it addresses also have importance if you are providing guidance to an external professional or the team leader.

Across the many organizations my colleagues and I at the Center for Creative Leadership have worked with through the years, few maximize the benefit available to the executive leadership group through judicious involvement of HR leadership. In many organizations, the HR function is seen as managing processes and procedures and having little of substance to contribute to the effective exercise of executive leadership. There are many reasons for this. Certainly many senior HR leaders came of age when HR was devoted to compensation, employee relations, and people crises (Lawler, 2008; Ryan, 2005). Such leaders may feel ill equipped to have a positive impact on the functioning of the business unit leadership. However, more contemporary HR leaders with backgrounds in group process, strategic deployment of people resources, and organizational development may have insights and tools that can remove many of the self-imposed limitations on senior team performance.

There are significant benefits to involving a well-equipped HR leader in advancing the performance and development activities of the senior team. The right person, one who has developed deep and trusting relationships with members of the senior team, holds substantial knowledge of internal culture and practices and maintains sufficient distance from the political turbulence associated with negotiating resources and power. That position, if combined with appropriate training, makes the HR leader an especially valuable coach for the team, particularly if the team is committed to improving its performance over time.

WHY SENIOR LEADERSHIP GROUPS NEED COACHING

The senior executive function of an organization may or may not need a team to work well (Wageman, Nunes, Burruss, & Hackman, 2008). Our experience with large, complex organizations suggests that when an organization has multiple sites and operates in multiple markets or has a complex mix of services or products, the coordination of those components becomes more important. There's nothing magical about working as a team, but several conditions require collaboration or a common mind-set. The senior leadership needs to be able to sample information from the customer base and the competitive environment. The first challenge is to be able to attend to the large quantities of data available to most organizations. The second is to be able to draw inferences based on the interaction of these forces and form a comprehensive view of the factors of importance. These specific tasks may require a group of leaders to acquire, understand, interpret, and draw conclusions that can benefit the whole enterprise. In particular, the health and well-being of the whole organization always requires some restraints and constraints for one function over another.

A president or chief executive may be able to perform all those functions in an organization with unique focus or a single market but will require a cabinet of committed partners otherwise. In most organizations, the executive benefits from a group who can work well together while bringing a heterogeneous set of experiences and mental frameworks to the tasks. This means they will have to be able to acknowledge and value differences yet apply them in the service of a joint task. All the issues referenced in chapter 16 affect such a group: competition, hyperindividualism, unclear goals and norms of behavior, conflicts of judgment, and diverse viewpoints.

Senior teams in Western organizations can benefit from coaching because collaborative, joint leadership practices demand a mind-set that is largely bred out of leaders. Historically a leader's ability to really hear and receive the thinking of others while persistently seeking joint solutions has not been rewarded in Western organizations. Instead, unbridled competition with a superficially friendly face is the norm. The consequence is that most important conversations take place everywhere except in group meetings. They happen before or after these meetings, in the hallway or the pub or on the golf course, but not in the scheduled meeting. Meetings are reserved for posturing and competitive positioning, primarily through the presentation of reports. Creating a highly functioning group of senior leaders requires significantly different ways of thinking and acting from what feels natural in Western culture. Coaching allows a group of strong leaders to add the capacity for listening, receptive thinking, and collaborative problem solving to their repertoire.

HOW HR LEADERS BECOME SENIOR TEAM COACHES

In a few senior teams, the head of HR is called on to play a coaching or developmental role with the whole team. Unfortunately, this is still the exception rather than the rule. Across the globe, many senior groups do not yet include a head of people resources as a member of the executive team. It is still not uncommon to have the head of HR report to the chief financial officer. Even when the HR head is a member of the senior leadership team, she may not be called on to help the group focus on its own operations and leadership effectiveness. Especially when the senior group uses its meetings mostly for reports by each function (and expert specialization is seen as a sacred element of the team's respect for each other), the opportunities for the head of HR to affect the senior group's functioning are limited. For that to change, the HR leader and his CEO and president must agree on the value of making the working of the group a focus. The CEO must be willing to enlist the HR leader in using her expertise in group dynamics and performance for the benefit of the leadership.

There are three primary alternative paths that lead to HR leaders' taking on coaching roles with senior executives: access via partner coattails, access via talent processes, and access via crisis. As is widely suspected, few HR leaders are seen as having the gravitas, business savvy, or intellectual horsepower to gain the trust of senior business leaders (Ryan, 2005; Lawler, 2008). Human resource professionals collaborate in the caricature by agreeing to play it safe when unhelpful attitudes and group practices should be challenged. Perhaps allowing human resources to be left as a cost center rather than a source of market advantage contributes to the reticence. Smart human resource professionals, however, will be unrelenting in their commitment to ensuring that the human dimensions of organizational success are always in view and the costs of disengaged or ineffective leadership are never ignored. This can be risky and requires both courage and intelligent judgment to successfully execute.

Access via Partner Coattails

In our experience, some vice presidents of human resources became indispensable when they were lower-level managers or directors working with business leaders who led a group or division. In one case, the head of sales for the European office took his HR business partner with him when he was promoted to global head of sales. These relationships are characterized by high degrees of interaction and consultation. Several HR leaders told us that they commonly speak with their business partners several times each day.

In most cases, these relationships work through individual consultation rather than through real connection with the whole team. In addition, the HR leader may be seen as belonging to the team leader and not the whole group. Also, members of the senior team may be likely to have their own HR partners from whom they seek advice and with whom they consult on people management issues. However, we know of several savvy HR leaders who have collaborated with their president to introduce learning practices into the ongoing work of the group or have played other coaching roles with the whole team. We introduce some of the key themes for those conversations later in the chapter.

Access via Talent Processes

Several HR leaders we know who work with the executive team started with a limited role, such as the responsibility of driving the talent review for senior leaders, but then they saw their scope of influence expand. Often they were asked to create dossiers for the top leaders and provide those for the chief executive and the rest of the group. The most strategic HR leaders found in this task an opportunity to raise important questions about the culture and leadership climate required for the future success of the organization. In one case, this led to a fruitful conversation about the kinds of relationships and the ways of operating modeled by the executive leadership group itself. The senior vice president of HR was then able to challenge the group to incorporate a focus on group reflection and learning processes, which allowed them to set goals to improve their effectiveness in decision making, communications, and strategic direction. Occasionally this tactic is referred to as "coaching up." It is essentially founded on the unquestionable competence of the HR professional and her long-standing credibility with leadership.

Access via Crisis

Sadly, in several nonprofit organizations and a few commercial companies with which we've worked, the opportunity for coaching the executive leadership group emerged as a reaction to the helpless panic engendered by a significant crisis within the organization. Often that crisis was manifest within the senior leadership itself. In one company, the fragile cooperation everyone wanted after acquiring a regional competitor was shattered early in the life of the merged organization. The former president of the smaller firm walked out in frustration at what he experienced as inadequate attention to the values and knowledge his company had brought to the combined company. The regional leaders who had come with him were rumored to be readying a mass exodus. The vice president of HR, not normally a member of the executive team, was suddenly thrust into the mix to see what could be done to repair relations with this regional division. As a result of spending time with the disaffected leaders, he was able to provide some important direct feedback that led to deep and critical reflection by the executive team. Team members had previously avoided considering how their behavior and climate might be affecting the merging of cultures.

Establishing Value

How does the human resource professional establish her value to the senior leadership team? Two critical areas deserve focus. One is the approach of the human resource professional and the other is the level of professional skill exhibited.

Approach We have noticed that some HR professionals appear to gain instant recognition and are sought out by business leaders for consultation and guidance. They show up with a readiness to listen—what Edgar Schein (2013) calls "humble inquiry" — and an appreciation for what's working well. This can be a challenge for younger HR professionals who may feel it is important to demonstrate their intelligence and insight, but many (perhaps most) executives are sufficiently competitive that displays of brilliance (not to be confused with true discernment) may tend to provoke a compulsive need to demonstrate their own competence or assert their authority. Similarly, the habit of "trying to be helpful" starts from an assumption that solving problems makes one valuable. However, this form of helpfulness tends to remind leaders they are aware of more problems than you are. This approach also does not take seriously enough the senior leader's conundrum: "I know more than you do, but I'm not smart enough to solve all I'm faced with."

This element can be tricky because our leadership language and the descriptions in this chapter rely on ideas such as gravitas, credibility, and presence. The challenge for younger professionals is that these words are often associated with age and experience. The paradox is that younger professionals who adopt the mannerisms or patterns of older leaders may simply amplify the impression of inexperience or appear to be faking it. In our experience, many younger HR professionals get the hearing they deserve because of the quality of their thinking and the clear-eyed analysis of the systemic issues affecting senior management. Our experience suggests that authenticity and a commitment to the truth are what lead others to see us as serious contributors.

The second element of approach relates to one's attitude toward and behavior in the context of the highly political environment of senior leadership. Conflicting expectations and demands from multiple constituencies are in the nature of senior leadership. Can you rise above the fray and make a genuine contribution to enterprise leadership? The most effective HR leaders make clear their commitment to the enterprise and its customers and never overpromise or allow themselves to be overallied with one leader or group over others. Are you seen as the president's person or the corporation's leader?

The third element of approach requires striking the balance between a commitment to the truth and sensitivity to the risks associated with it, for you and others. Can the leaders with whom you work count on you to tell them the truth about themselves and their impact on others, but also feel confident that you will not savage them with the information? Truth conveyed with kindness and thoughtfulness that communicates some sensitivity to the emotional impact is always valuable, though not always welcomed initially. We have learned through painful experience the dangers of straying too far to one side or the other. Too much concern for saving leaders from bad news or challenging feedback leaves them persuaded you may have nothing of importance to offer. Yet too much casual confidence in the receptivity and readiness for tough messages possessed by senior team members can lead to emotional shutdown or rejection of the process. The balance between these poles has to be constantly adapted in light of the quality of the relationship and our perception of the emotional state of those with whom we are working.

Professional Skill Professional skill level has everything to do with the way the HR leader manages the roles available to play in the work of the senior team. What is it that senior team leaders want from their advisors? Each wants something different, of course, but all want someone who is an equal with respect to his or her knowledge of and commitment to the business. We've heard descriptions like "sparring partner" and "sounding board" from CEOs when they talk about the HR leaders they value or wish they had. It takes an extraordinary level of confidence in one's usefulness and indifference to the power differential to be useful to a CEO or head of a major leadership team. But confidence without expertise may result in an invitation to leave the organization.

One HR leader with whom we've worked saw his star rise because of brief hallway conversations with the president of the company in which he would ask about the anticipated consequences of leadership or market decisions the leadership team was making. His acuity was noted—particularly his ability to predict the ready acceptance or rejection of contemplated actions. Many CEOs have plenty of data about the potential financial consequences of product choices or various future scenarios, but they don't begin to have enough information about the human reactions that make one scenario more likely than another.

The point of having an expert in human resources is so that the human costs and human responses can be estimated with greater accuracy. Another HR leader coach for the senior team of a major electronics firm was tapped for this role because of the way she carried on the annual review of senior talent within the organization. The CEO was generally dismissive of HR and organizational development work, which he saw primarily in terms of pacifying the troops. When he found her willing to take on other senior leaders during the talent review of the top three hundred and make the connection between their leadership behavior and the performance of their units, he began to find it useful to consult about his own immediate team. In time, this led to more formal roles for this HR leader in advising that group.

As long as organizations are full of humans, the expert who knows how people function in groups and how teams are developed and learn is going to have the most opportunities to work at enhancing the performance of senior teams.

CHARACTERISTICS OF SENIOR TEAMS

Senior leadership teams or executive groups or top teams are made of the folks who are supposed to be responsible for setting the direction for the whole organization. We will start with the realization that the term *team* is used quite loosely with respect to the senior leadership group in most organizations (Wageman et al., 2008). It can refer to a wide variety of groupings of leaders with either shared responsibilities or regular interaction. However, a useful, and aspirational, description of teams comes from Jon Katzenbach and Douglas Smith (1993): "A team is a small number of people with complementary skills who are committed to a common purpose, set of performance goals, and approach for which they hold themselves mutually accountable" (p. 112). Many senior leadership groups hold themselves out to be teams, but in some cases, the evidence is difficult to reconcile with the aspiration. In fact, a significant challenge for team coaches is to recognize the differences between the aspirational intentions of senior leadership and the actual practices and resulting performance of senior leadership groups.

Let's review some of the realities of senior leadership groups and see how they may shape the opportunities for coaching solutions. In addition to Katzenbach and Smith's description, Wageman et al. (2008) note something we have encountered repeatedly: it is often hard to know who is and who should be on the senior leadership team. The formation of senior teams tends to be ad hoc, based on multiple factors including the functional structure of the organization, the informal power and influence dynamics, and the varying information needs. We have grown accustomed to a confused and uncertain look from clients when we ask, "Who are the members of the executive team?" A frequent response is, "Do you mean who attends executive leadership meetings or who is officially a member?" In some cases, central staff members who prepare the reports for the senior group are more consistently present than some of the official members.

We have yet to encounter an executive leadership group that was formed in a strategic fashion because of complementary skills. This is different from many project or management teams in organizations where the membership is explicitly identified for representative or functional purposes. As a result, much of the research and folklore about project teams cannot be applied to senior teams. Senior teams often have more fluid boundaries. Membership is most strongly determined by the wishes of the CEO or president of the organization. However, the more teamlike the senior leadership group is, the more likely that the membership and structure represent an approach based on shared commitments and a process of engagement. As a CEO or the board expresses a determination for more of a leadership team, the processes of involvement for a larger group in establishing strategy and gaining alignment across the organization are strengthened.

Katzenbach and Smith (1993) suggest that a team is also committed to a common purpose, a common set of performance goals, and a common approach. In fact, these are the primary challenges for a leadership group and should be an explicit set of objectives. For this discussion, the common purpose is the joint leadership of the enterprise. Senior leadership teams (we will continue to use the term loosely) may or may not be prepared to lead the whole enterprise (Wheelan, 2003; Katzenbach & Beckett, 1996). Few have explicitly addressed questions about balancing the performance of the various functions with the overall enterprise performance for which they are responsible. It is easy to see why the pressure to maximize the success of the function or division for which they are responsible can readily trump the choices needed for maximizing enterprise success. These inherent role conflicts are manifest in the reward and recognition systems and in the perceptions of the majority of employees of the enterprise. The chief financial officer is rewarded for the management of the finances and is seen as the money person by nearly everyone in the company. Her important role as a member of the senior team may not be visible either within the team where she is expected to sound the alarm over financial concerns or across the organization to the same extent. In addition, performance bonuses in most companies are tied to functional performance and only slightly to impact or contribution to enterprise performance. Senior team members may be rewarded for overall organizational performance, but what is missing is recognition of contributions that cross boundaries or for specifically collaborative behavior.

So we may say that what sets senior leadership groups apart from other teams is not the people in them (they all started out in other teams anyway) but the peculiar circumstances or ecology of the senior team. It begins with the fact this typically very small group stands at the intersection of powerful constituencies. There is the board, which is concerned with long-term success and the continuing viability of the organization. In many cases, there are stockholders, who may be primarily concerned with and vocal about the quarterly statements and the value of their ownership. In family businesses, there may be the whole range of generations, each of which sees the success of the business in different terms with levels of distrust or low respect for the wisdom of the other generations. Each of the senior team members is responsible for a function or functions whose success may be measured quite differently from how their fellows on the team are measured. In addition, each member has some amount of loyalty to the leaders and workers in his function. I haven't even mentioned the customers, suppliers, or unions in this pressure cooker yet. No other group in any organization stands in quite the same position relative to the competing demands of different stakeholders. And lest we forget, these are usually people who are used to high achievement and used to shaping their own destinies. They have careers and professional standing among peers across industries or professions, such as the chief legal officer who is also a board member of the Association of Corporate Counsel. So we must add her own internal pressures, including professional identity, to this mix.

Finally, it turns out that senior teams are unique with respect to the personalities of their members. Through its work with senior leaders, CCL has noted that conceptual thinkers are overrepresented among senior leadership. CCL's database of senior leaders is loaded with people with high dominance, a high need to exercise control, and impatience with human frailty. Is it any surprise that senior team meetings demonstrate a lack of listening to each other, a competition among ideas, and struggles to contain the energy associated with self-promotion? With the right leadership and under the skies of strong human values, these characteristics can lead to innovative thinking, dynamic communication, high engagement, and an exciting place to work. In the absence of that socializing commitment, senior leadership groups can be chaotic, frustrating, and destructive environments that can spread dissatisfaction throughout an organization. Human resource professionals are in a unique position to catalyze a powerfully productive and virtuous leadership community through coaching this group.

What to Focus On

So you have moved into a position in which you can advise the CEO or president of your organization on human resource and team development issues. Note that team coaching does not always mean being physically or virtually in the presence of the group. It can mean working with one person or part of the team, but with a clear recognition of the team dynamics and the impact of any actions or initiatives on the team. What should you be looking for, and where can you add the most value? A few areas emerge consistently in the life of senior executive groups. I briefly review four important opportunities for valuable effects in the functioning of senior teams:

- The need for operating agreements within the group
- Smart procedures for onboarding new members of the team
- The role that the head of the group plays
- Defining shared obligations

Group Operating Agreements The chief information officer for a major company described all the surprises she experienced when joining the new organization. The senior group operated without an agenda or minutes, and accountability for follow-up seemed to be haphazard or operate under rules that she couldn't discern. She had become convinced that decisions were driven by the passion of whoever would not give up a position or whoever was "loudest the longest." She was not reassured when we noted that these characteristics were not that unusual among senior teams. She was experiencing the confusion associated with the absence of operating agreements.

Operating agreements must come from the operational needs of the team. As a seasoned professional, you will observe a variety of ways that the senior team is not functioning optimally. It is easy to make the case and design a discussion to remedy what you have observed. However, what seems obvious is exactly the thing that requires verification. Follow-up interviews can explore what meaning the patterns you observe have for the group members and those they lead. What appears to be wasteful conflict may be treasured heterogeneity of thinking to the team members. It will not be a good target for team coaching. Conversations with team members are needed to ensure that what is salient to the HR professional is significant to the team participants (see exhibit 17.1 for example discussion questions). Nothing is gained by generating new dissatisfaction about things unimportant to the team.

Making agreements about how the team will operate seems like wasted effort until things break down as a result of misunderstandings, poorly communicated expectations, and violations of values. Consultants and academics may make the threshold seem higher and harder than it needs to be because experience with multiple teams leads to expanding lists of the many ways things can go wrong. This in

Exhibit 17.1
No Script, But a Trail to Follow

Although there can never be a script for coaching conversations, some questions regularly contribute to useful conversations:

- Do we believe our meetings have the right balance of reporting, gaining agreement or alignment, and deciding?
- Do we believe our meetings have the right balance of problem solving and strategic thinking?
- Are we comfortable that we always know what to tell our own teams about what was discussed, the disagreements involved, and our process?
- Do we have confidence that all of us are operating with the same assumptions?
- Do we have confidence that we are all using similar standards for communicating decisions about policy and strategy and that we are holding our own teams responsible at the same levels?

turn leads to a large number of prescriptions for agreements (Marshall & Dobbins, 2009). However, it is unlikely that all of those failures will occur with your leadership team, so it may be wise to focus only on those that emerge within the life of the group you want to develop. The most prominent needs for explicit agreement tend to be about how decisions are made, how meetings are run and for what purposes, and how information is communicated within and beyond the group.

Invited to consult to the CEO on the effectiveness of his "cabinet," the senior vice president of human resources noted that a good deal of time in meetings was taken up with debating various viewpoints without any decisions being reached. Further exploration with the CEO surfaced his lack of clarity about whether he was seeking advice, consultation, or a decision from the group in any given situation. The team was given the opportunity to wrestle with improving their performance in decision making and reached an agreement that anyone presenting an issue (including the CEO) had the obligation to identify the type of response he or she wanted: affirmation, a decision, or guidance. The consequence was that many more items were addressed in the same time and with much less pontification.

While there are innumerable ways misunderstandings arise and the resulting erroneous conclusions lead us astray, it is important to implement preventive approaches that are reasonable and make sense to the members of the team. Be cautious about planning processes and team-building exercises that distort the importance of these agreements. The purpose of the senior leadership team is to lead the enterprise, not to create ideal norms and internal processes. The mental and emotional investment of team members is critical to coaching success and must be earned. Overdoing team development is no better than ignoring it. Both lead to resistance or inaction and further conflict within the team. We are aiming for "good enough" dialogue and "good enough" group processes to accomplish what is needed.

Onboarding New Team Members Every time a new member joins the team, there is the possibility of either increased fragmentation and subgroup formation or improved group ownership of its culture and processes. Remarkably, most senior teams appear to think a friendly "welcome aboard" is sufficient investment in a new team member.

Whether a new team member comes from outside the organization or is promoted from within, the transition period is a significant time of risk and possible reward. The HR team coach can make an important contribution by asking what needs to be done to ensure that several key tasks are tackled early in the tenure (Riddle, 2009; see also chapter 15). Perhaps the two most important tasks are the development of the right relationship network and the clarification of expectations by stakeholders. These are both activities that need the involvement of the whole group of executive leaders to be sufficiently useful. The coach has an opportunity to insert questions about the essential connections for the new members and encourage the team to think this through in the context of the organizational matrix. Who does she need to know? Who are the key information expediters (gossip) and influence nodes (e.g., administrative assistants who have longer tenure than most of the senior leaders)? What are the lessons we've each learned about what the emotional land mines are in this organization? What have our own missteps taught us? These questions get to the fundamentals of any organization and the visible, tangible elements of the corporate culture. They are always more important in the early days of a new senior team leader than any consultant's model of the culture. The way that the coach raises questions about the culture and ensures appropriate nonjudgmental feedback about cultural intelligence can shape whether new members of the executive group contribute to a collaborative environment or end up leading schism or leaving.

When I refer to smart procedures for onboarding, I am specifically targeting the emotional, relational, and cultural factors that affect the perception that a new person is going to belong to the "tribe"—or not. Even when a new leader has been installed with the mandate to shake things up or to change the culture, he is not likely to have any lasting impact if he does not first join the existing culture and show proper respect to those he is called to lead and with whom he will have to work. Smart leadership groups take seriously the value of advising newcomers (new to the organization or to the position) on the social dynamics, the politics, and the people who exert influence on the hearts and minds of their colleagues.

Leader of the Pack No one disputes the importance of the personal leadership style of the team leader, but oddly, the role and mutual expectations of the leadership team and its head are seldom the focus of attention. This may be because it is risky to raise questions about the CEO, and certainly one would not venture to initiate these conversations in the group meeting itself. However, much of the conflict and fuzzy performance of senior leadership is a consequence of difficulty reading the intentions and desires of the CEO or president. Ambiguous messages from the top about intent and expectations lead to competing theories among the team and to conflict that can be highly disruptive to the effective executive function.

An example is useful here. We were called to work with the enterprise leadership in a financial services firm in the United States. The founder was distressed by significant conflict between two of the most senior executives on the senior leadership teams. The CEO and president were lifelong friends who had started the firm together decades earlier, but warfare within the senior leadership was shredding the company's performance and talent was leaking out every door and window. Our discovery process uncovered that the long-term success of the firm had allowed the CEO to gradually withdraw from active engagement, and in the reduced availability of his calming presence, the president's emotional volatility had led to open conflict with another senior leader who had joined the firm within the previous three years. The CEO's wishes were that everybody could be like a big family, but a series of personal changes and attention to some major hobbies meant that he was weakly urging better behavior from a distance. A climate of distrust and tension had come to dominate the leadership group. The head of human resources had been neutralized over time and had little power; he did not sit on the inner council but still had as much access to all the players as he wanted. In coaching the HR leader, we were able to find a metaphor that he could use with the CEO to reactivate his supervisory role: the paterfamilias (the father figure in a family). Armed with this metaphor, the HR head was able to connect the deep desire of the CEO for healthier relations within his team with how he played his role. The CEO recognized he would have to be a stronger father figure if his desire for more of a family dynamic was to be realized. This in turn led the group to recognize that they needed to work harder at developing teamwork if they were to regain lost ground.

Frequently neither the team nor the leader knows how to talk about their relationship. We arrive at organizational life with deeply ingrained expectations that are seldom the focus of reflection and about which we do not typically have appropriate language. In the past, leadership studies focused more attention on leadership and followership, but that language is not as common now. However, the mutuality of the relationship between the team and the leader requires that the obligations be negotiated in each direction. The team coach can raise questions about what team members need from the CEO and what he expects of them. The power imputed to the CEO's role is effective because it is shared, but defining the ways a particular senior team will share authority is rarely incorporated in senior team discussions. Examples include what responsibility the team or the CEO has when there is conflict within the team, what degree of freedom will be most helpful in meeting mission targets, and how mutual accountability will be accomplished.

Where Collaboration Is Needed As noted earlier, not all organizations need the top leadership to think and behave as a team. However, all senior leadership groups need to collaborate intensely on some things for the benefit of the whole enterprise (Wageman et al., 2008). What are those things? Facilitating that conversation may be the most useful function of internal coaching: to get the senior group to decide what things require them to be a team, to collaborate. This is not an easy question to answer because the group may not be truly collaborating on any work at all. It is possible in many organizations to go through the strategic planning process, the annual budgeting, the capital expenses decisions, and many more enterprise-affecting exercises treating them as horse-trading events. In a horse-trading event, the assumption is that through competitive negotiations, the best overall solution will emerge. However, this game is rigged to maintain the status quo, with continued resource benefits accruing to those who already receive the most and the persistent inattention to emergent trends that have fuzzy business and financial models. Unfortunately, those may shape the future of the markets in which you compete. It is only when a group makes a conscious decision to operate as the thought leaders for the whole enterprise and when team processes and practices facilitate this mind-set that they become enterprise leaders.

This reality drives a concern with some forms of team development for senior leaders. A certain amount of team coaching requires a continuing focus on getting along with each other, building trust, and improving communications within the team. While these characteristics are useful, they are also irrelevant if the senior leaders are not keeping their eyes on their obligations as leaders of the organization and its business. The social dynamics of the prevailing culture will often trump the best intentions and efforts of team development exercises if they are not tied directly and explicitly to the performance of the organization in fulfillment of its mission. Group conversations or activities that have only very loose or indirect connection to the mission and the business models will be seen as a distraction by the most responsible members of the senior leadership. By contrast, better communications skills or a higher level of trust among the group targeted because they are learning better ways to solve business problems as a leadership team will be understood to be of critical importance. You maintain your credibility as a valuable contributor to the leadership team when you keep the connection between the questions you ask and the performance of the group on its key metrics explicit.

This also means developing the right metrics for team development. If, for instance, the company you serve has determined it must be more agile in a changing marketplace, it is right to ask what the senior team can do to improve that. When they ask their direct reports, they may find that an agile organization requires as much distributed leadership as possible and quick turnaround of decisions to enable units and groups to take action or change direction. Your work coaching the senior team will certainly include asking team members what feedback they have received on these critical issues and ensuring that they are having those conversations with those who report to them. They will need to work together to determine what they can do to access better data, acquire timely analysis, and address significant concerns more rapidly to get to the right decisions faster. There are so many elements involved in pushing authority out from the center and speeding up decision making that the senior team will need to focus on this repeatedly. In addition, because it is hard to change whole systems, their enthusiasm may lag, so keeping this kind of question on the table on an ongoing basis will require a coach who can keep it visible. This kind of question and the need to collaborate better to solve it are examples of the connections between group process and business performance that establish the credibility of the coach and the process of coaching. When they work, they lay the foundation for more collaboration in areas where it is needed.

Doing the Coaching

Current practice in coaching senior teams requires an ecological perspective. This means that coaching the team takes place when the team is together, when you are encountering one or a few members, and when you are engaged in conversations with those in their social neighborhoods (such as with a board member or one of their direct reports). Coaching cannot be limited to a particular setting or place but must be seen as activities from a particular mind-set. While there are specific times and places when you may be considered to be coaching, it should be seen as an interlocking set of activities that leverages your relationships for the benefit of the team. It is this unique relationship that makes it coaching, not the activities themselves or the focus of your conversations.

In other words, you will be understood to be coaching the team if you establish the value of doing some process consultation of team meetings or when you create team development experiences or off-sites that combine attention to the team process and relationships with a focus on strategic planning or problem solving. However, your regular conversations with team members and engagement about their roles and intentions, their engagement and impact, are also part of coaching the team. In particular, your conversations with the team leader about process and practice encourage her to keep a focus on the how the team can learn from its experiences and improve its performance through a learning attitude. In all of these situations, the effective team coach uses conversations to keep the ownership of the group process in the hands of the group members. You are equipping them to bring intention to the climate they create rather than seeing it as something with which they have to cope or complain about.

Problem Opportunities: "What Do I Do about . . . ?" The opportunity to coach a senior executive group also brings opportunities to tackle larger problems. What will you do about the skeptical member or the oppositional leader? What will you do about schisms within the group based on demographic, historical, or values differences? As a coach, you have no authority beyond your credibility as an honorable broker and the quality of the relationships you build with senior leaders. It is important in our model to recognize that your job is not to fix the problems of the senior leadership group but to give them the opportunity to take hold of their own processes, practices, and performance. Your role is to work with the team leader to create a safe and fair environment for that to take place.

What Contributes to a Safe and Fair Environment? There are a number of actions you may take to help ensure a minimum of explosive or destructive incidents in the working of the senior team. First, you should never walk into a team meeting without knowing the viewpoints or positions of key influencers on the team. Much of the work of team coaching takes place in the ongoing conversations of discovery that allow you to coach the team through the individual members. Continuous inquiry and genuine interest in the viewpoints and concerns of the team members is one of the active ingredients for team coaching.

Never allow yourself to think you are manipulating the team process or that you can fix differences between members. It is tempting to allow team members to use your good office to convey messages or frame issues in ways they want to see them. It is also tempting to allow yourself to be seduced by the impression of specialness that is the product of having secret knowledge entrusted to you. One HR leader we worked with found herself in an uncomfortable place when the head of marketing confided that he and the chief operating officer were working to push the unpopular chief financial officer out of the company. Of course, she could not reveal this information to anyone. Neither could she make any headway on senior team performance in the face of this state of affairs. She was effectively neutralized as a team coach.

This happens in particular when ideas of confidentiality become rigid rules and the mission and purpose of the senior team are undermined by the need to follow those rules. This is not a simple matter. Clarity about one's values and the effect on behavior is essential to avoid being stuck in such a conundrum.

Your value as a team coach rests on your ability to stay an honest broker for the right kind of climate. To do that, you want to know each person's viewpoint on critical points of division so they can be raised in calm and straightforward ways that show that diversity of opinion can be constructive. In addition, these individual conversations allow you to coach team members on appropriate ways to express differences without ad hominem attacks or deliberately provocative ways of stating them.

See Intensity, Passion, and Conflict as Necessary Your demeanor and that of the team leader communicate whether what is happening in the group is catastrophic or expected and welcomed. Normalizing the group's process and describing it as valuable, even when conversation becomes heated, builds confidence in the capacity of the group to handle conflict and work things through. This also means meetings are never ended just because of increased volatility but continued even if all that can be done at the moment is a summary of the positions and a description of the next focus for attention on the topic.

Honesty and Respect Are the Law The clear expectations of the team leader that people will communicate with honesty and respect for each other must be made explicit. People must understand they can express a range of emotion, but they must aim it properly. Blaming, indirect criticism, and sarcasm cannot be tolerated. These are the circumstances that cry out for team operating agreements that include behavioral norms for meetings and other contexts and that are renewed regularly.

Don't Coach When Managing Is Needed Coaching is not a cure-all for everything that can go wrong among senior leadership. I've already discussed the incredible pressure evoked by the competing forces working on the group. Some problems in team leadership are solvable only by direct management when there are willful, repeated violations of group norms. A professional coach, whether from human resources or brought in from outside, will recognize when circumstances grow beyond the scope of her role or expertise. When that happens, the coach has the opportunity to identify the nature of the problems and ensure they are visible to those who should take responsibility for solving them.

Bring a Team to Coach the Team: Using External Vendors It is likely that you will be working with external team coaches or consultants at various times whether or not you are also coaching the senior executive team. From our point of view, it is best that you think of these experts as members of your team rather than hired help who will take care of the work. We have often found that internal human resource professionals are not prepared to take advantage of the collaborative opportunities afforded by a coaching initiative and stand by without full engagement in the process.

Wise external professionals recognize that you will be present in the organization's life long after the present initiative has faded into happy memory and will use your involvement in the process as a mechanism to ensure the changes started in the engagement continue to bear fruit. On many occasions, we have had internal HR leaders deeply involved in selecting our team to work with their organization and free and open with valuable information about their observations, only to step away when the planning and execution of the interventions begin. Our practice is to seek the involvement of internal professional staff as much as possible without compromising their role as clients. To whatever extent you feel comfortable, we encourage participation in less politically sensitive portions of the discovery work and again in analysis of the data generated (without having access to the raw data from interviews or surveys, which might compromise the anonymity of the respondents). Internal professionals have knowledge of political sensitivities and group dynamics that an external provider can never uncover in early encounters. Your participation through regular meetings for discussion of findings and planning for solutions can amplify the impact of these leadership development activities in the short term and over time.

CONCLUSION

It is not a given that internal human resource leaders will have the obligation or opportunity to coach the senior executive group of their organization, but they have a unique vantage point and a valuable contribution to make. We have suggested ways to use that vantage point as a jumping-off place for improving the work of the senior leadership, but it will require establishing your credibility, creating the environment for growth, and taking appropriate risks for the sake of that influence. There is no single right way to accomplish these things, but the effects can be wide ranging because of the central role that the leadership team plays in the creation of climate and culture in an organization. It is up to human resource professionals and leaders to make learning and development for individuals and teams a core focus for the organization if it is to compete successfully in our volatile and complex environment.

chapter EIGHTEEN

Transforming Organizations

Coaching and Guiding Senior Teams

John B. McGuire and Candice C. Frankovelgia

A declaration of interdependence is under way across organizations. Everything in our world is, or will be, connected. But interdependent, collaborative work is not a natural act in most organizations. Everyone says they want changes in leadership behavior, to be more collaborative in work processes and shared systems, but mostly that hasn't happened. How did we get here? How can we get beyond here to there? The Center for Creative Leadership (CCL) has been asking these questions and finding answers through action research and development practices (see table 18.1 for some of the work that has shaped our thinking about action research). A shift in mind-set is usually required for genuinely collaborative work. We believe that new ways of learning and working are needed to foster leadership for an interdependent world (McGuire & Palus, in press).

The goal of culture transformation work and to moving toward interdependence is to purposefully and actively build capability for new ways of working. It allows for the new thinking, beliefs, tools, and decision processes that will result in the organization's successfully adapting to business challenge changes.

What we've said here might seem a bit heady or academic, but we intend this chapter to be a very down-to-earth and practical guide for the what and the how-to of developing senior teams and organizational transformation through the leadership culture. We balance theory and application—stories about what and how we did this work, lessons learned, and guidelines, principles, and tips. We believe you will find this chapter a resource to use and return to.

Table 18.1
Methods and Tools Supporting Action Development and Interdependent Mind-Sets

Method or Tool	Description	Source or Reference
Difficult conversations (two-column exercise)	Examining the assumptions, frames, and feelings left unspoken in a conflictual conversation	Argyris, Putnam, & Smith, 1985; Senge, Kleiner, Roberts, Ross, & Smith, 1994
Learning pathways grid	Systematic analysis of a difficult conversation in terms of actual versus desired frames, actions, and outcomes	Taylor, Rudolph, & Foldy, 2008
Action logics instrument with coaching groups	Assessment of individual action logics (mind-sets), supported by trained coaches and peer dialogues	Rooke & Torbert, 2005
Mapping organizational action-logic history	Understanding company history by tracing its history of development in action logics	Torbert & Associates, 2004
Culture mapping tool	Group exercise in which an organization's culture is mapped and reflected on, with an appraisal of the organization's actual and desired culture, according to two dimensions and four types	Cameron & Quinn, 1999; Slobodnik & Slobodnik, 1998
Business process analysis and mapping	Analysis of value-creating activities for specific products and services and aligning them into a "value stream" while eliminating activities that don't add value	Womack & Jones, 2003
Organizational leadership quick tools	A series of real-time, action development learning tools focused on strategy, culture and direction, alignment, commitment	McGuire & Palus, in press

Table 18.1 (*Continued*)

Method or Tool	Description	Source or Reference
Action inquiry: Four parts of speech	Encourages framing, illustrating, advocating, and inquiring for effective communication in support of collaborative inquiry	Torbert & Associates, 2004
Group dialogue	Conversation models that support the construction of shared meaning through exploring diversity in assumptions and perspectives	Isaacs, 1999; Palus & Drath, 2001; McGuire & Palus, 2003
Putting something in the middle	Mediated dialogue using Visual Explorer and other media	Palus & Drath, 2001
Visual explorer	A tool that uses visual imagery and the resultant metaphors to mediate group dialogue	Palus & Horth, 2004
First- and second-person journaling	Research staff keep personal as well as group journals of observations and experiences related to projects	LeCompte & Schensul, 1999
Body sculpting of roles and relationships	Group workshop exercise in which people from diverse roles collectively, physically modeled their actual and desired interdependencies with each other, using physical postures in relation to one another as the metaphoric device to support group reflection	Moreno, 1977
Culture walk-about tool	Ethnographic tool to capture subjective and objective observations in first-, second-, and third-person modes	LeCompte & Schensul, 1999

(*continued*)

Table 18.1 (*Continued*)

Method or Tool	Description	Source or Reference
Open space technology	A tool for establishing effective affinity groups amid diverse interests; used in a variety of ways, including forming discussion groups at workshops and seeding idea communities	Owen, 1997
Idea communities	Interest- and passion-driven greenhouses of future R&D efforts, leading in some cases to fully established communities of practice	Lave & Wenger, 1991

Source: McGuire, Palus, and Torbert (2007).

TRANSFORMATION OBLIGATION

When Winston Churchill said, "It's difficult to look further than you can see," he could have been speaking for leaders of organizations today. Before 2008, when we spoke to executive groups, ideas like interdependent systems and collaborative work were given courteous nods or responded to with good, if skeptical, questions. Since the global recession, executive groups have displayed new awareness and absolute consensus that they are inside and part of a new and evolving interdependent world and that they have an absolute requirement to develop leadership capable of dealing with the complexity, ambiguity, and uncertainty that it brings every day. Leaders across the globe are beginning to understand that we live in an interdependent world and that leadership must rise up to face that challenge. This awareness is catapulting us beyond our twentieth-century mind-sets.

Here is a story to make the point practical. A few years ago, we spent time with dozens of senior leaders from the construction industry. As we engaged them about their most significant challenges in a shifting world, this example of a change in belief and practice emerged:

> Before the global financial crisis, we spent huge amounts of time in competing over pricing in the proposal process—we all believed that

we would get better margins if we could out-maneuver the other guy. But since the crisis, everything is too tight to waste time in this competitive and time-consuming process. Now, because we need to rely on both efficiency and effectiveness, all of our time spent in pricing and proposals is focused in collaborating (instead of negotiating) with our suppliers and our customers. It is faster, easier, and more productive for all of us. (Personal communication, 2011)

Change is inevitable—but why transformation? By *transformation* we mean an enterprise-wide change in leadership mind-set (culture) combined with changes in strategy, systems, structure, processes, and talent. In our work, we've identified important skills that organizations need in the future—leading people, strategic development, inspiring commitment, and managing change—and that these are among the weakest skills for leaders today. At the same time, we have found that approaches focusing on flexibility, collaboration, crossing boundaries, and collective leadership are increasingly important and necessary to the basics of the bottom line.

Change within a function or business unit around one capability (such as strategic intent or innovation) is important and useful, and it may be the entry point for organizational transformation. However, when we talk about transformation, we mean advancement in the leadership culture that expands executive-to-enterprise-wide capability to deal with perpetual "wicked complex" challenges that are not going to go away.

CHANGE LEADERSHIP IS THE WAY: OUR TRANSFORMATION FRAMEWORK

Change management + change leadership = Transformation. We introduce this simple yet profound idea early in this chapter in order to get your attention. The twentieth century mind-set was all about treating everything as objects to manage—not only systems, structures, and processes but also people. Change management is about managing business systems—things that fit into a spreadsheet and a Gantt chart. Change management is necessary and half of the picture, but not the most interesting half. Change leadership is often the missing half and is about leading in the human system. Figure 18.1 illustrates the balance between the

Figure 18.1
A Question of Balance

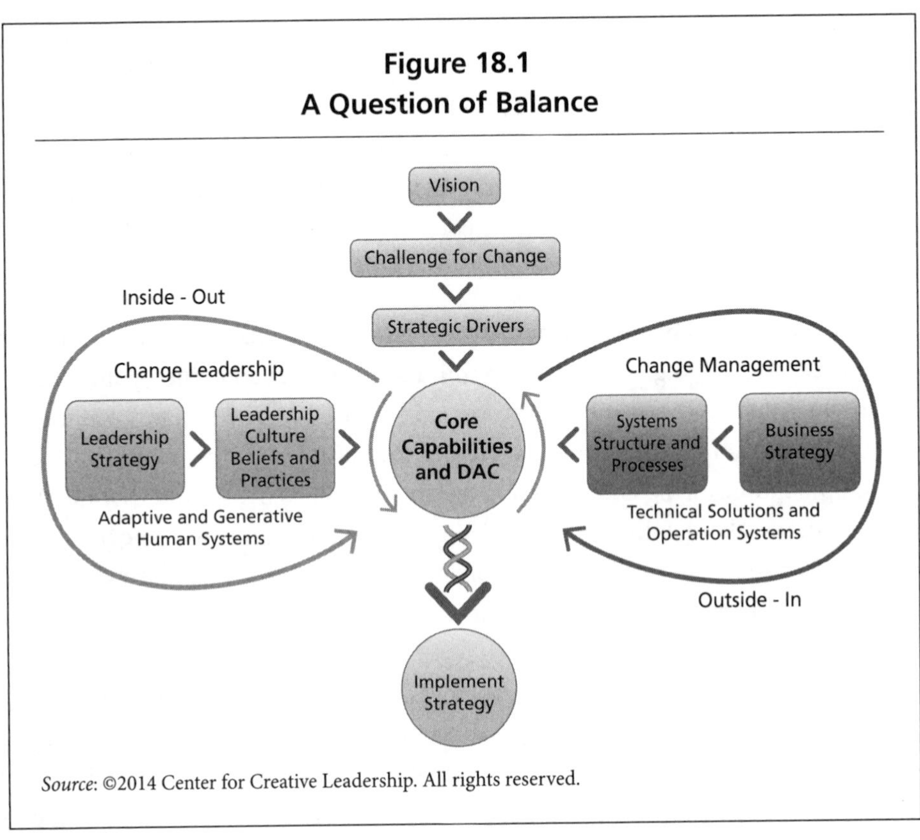

two kinds of systems. Change leadership is about devising the leadership strategy necessary for the execution of the business strategy (McGuire & Rhodes, 2009).

For decades, the field of change management has performed dismally, yielding a one-in-four chance of success (Cameron & Quinn, 1999). This well-established track record is not good enough. At the beginning of the twenty-first century, we began to practice change leadership with clients in concert with their change management efforts. This was the start of introducing the work of leadership strategy in unison with organizational strategy. Our core purpose in pioneering this work for over a decade has been to improve the probability of success for our clients' change and transformation efforts (Dinwoodie, Quinn, & McGuire, 2014). We discovered five principles for improving the probability of success in transformation:

Principle 1: Culture change is a guided, public learning process where personal risk taking and shared insights lead to superior solutions. You cannot manage people into change. With proper guidance, we can discover that change also holds innovation, creativity, and joy.

Principle 2: Executives do the change work first. They must lead by engagement and example in the transformation process.

Principle 3: Developing vertical capability through both-and thinking is a shared goal. Dealing with increased, emerging complexity requires more mature mind-sets and elevated thought and action.

Principle 4: Leadership culture changes through advancing beliefs and practices (behaviors) simultaneously. Best beliefs drive best practices drive best beliefs; develop mutually reinforcing beliefs and practices in parallel.

Principle 5: Sustainable culture change is a learn-as-you-go process embedded in the work of the organization. In this leadership culture, leaders apply new beliefs and practices through prototypes in action development, learning new ways of working together across the organization.

Feel the Heat or See the Light

Leaders who seek experienced input from successful agents when facing massive change are the ones who are smart enough to know what they don't know—that change is accelerating and daunting in an ever-shifting landscape. One of our most successful clients told us they could not imagine doing the hard work of transformation from a burning platform; at least they had a healthy company as a base to work from. In this new century and the global new world order, everything has shifted. Here's what CEO Samuel Palmisano had to say about a study done by IBM:

> What we've heard (from 1500 CEO's) is that events, threats and opportunities aren't just coming at us faster and with less predictability; they are converging and influencing each other to create entirely unique situations. These first-of-their-kind developments require unprecedented degrees of creativity—which has become a more important leadership quality than attributes like management discipline, rigor or operational acumen. There is a fundamental shift in the way the world works... with challenges and opportunities... [we are experiencing] a Smarter Planet. (IBM, 2010)

Since the global financial crisis and into this decade, we have heard from our clients a change in requirement for leadership development, and with it comes a shift in language reflecting the way they are thinking about leadership and change. Some call it a requirement for leadership's creativity and innovation, some call it collaborative culture or coaching/learning culture, and others name it a mind-set of strategic intent—but no matter what new term they choose to express their requirements, we see their need as an organization-wide capability of interdependent leadership. Leadership for an interdependent world is collaborative leadership that is fast and agile, capable of both-and strategic thinking and learning, and composed of leaders who are accountable for their own piece (e.g., business unit/function) of the emerging puzzle and enterprise, taking responsibility on behalf of the whole.

Too many leaders today are being pushed into this new world without frames for understanding what is happening to them. However, some are embracing the "smarter planet" concept and wading into the future with open arms. Let's explore the differences and share some lessons learned about how to shift a leadership team into more leaders who can see the light.

A few clients do see the light; they are intent on industry leadership, creating new markets or market niche mastery, and are driven by a vision of a different future. These clients present with a conscious intent of transformation. This sounds like an ideal situation, but we've seen it have negative unintended consequences if the leaders move too quickly or fail to get enough leadership capability ramped up before charging ahead with change into the whole organization. More commonly, we see organizations that feel the heat; they are struggling with complicated choices and inadequate capability while recognizing that something different needs to happen. The consistent theme, whether seeing the light or feeling the heat, is that the senior leaders must be able to recognize their own need to change themselves or they will not be able to lead the transformation their organization requires to remain viable.

Note that we have discovered over time the importance of a shared language during transformation work. Furthermore, we have come to understand that our language, which expresses the concepts we have developed in close concert with any number of clients over the years, is not necessarily common to all organizations. To better communicate our ideas in this chapter, we provide in exhibit 18.1 the terms and definitions we use in our action research and transformation development work.

Exhibit 18.1
Toward Shared Terms

Leader	The role of a person who participates in the process of leadership
Leadership	The social processes producing the outcomes of direction, alignment, and commitment among people with shared work
Leadership culture	The self-reinforcing web of individual and collective beliefs and practices in a collective for producing the outcomes of shared direction, alignment, and commitment
Leadership development	The expansion of a collective's capacity for producing shared direction (D), alignment (A), and commitment (C)
DAC	The outcomes of the social process of leadership are shared direction, alignment, and commitment
Interdependent	A form of leadership culture or mind-set based in the collaboration of otherwise independent leaders and groups
Independent	A form of leadership culture or mind-set based in heroic individual achievement
Dependent	A form of leadership culture or mind-set based in conformance or tradition
Vertical development	Transformation of leadership cultures or mind-sets from dependent, to independent, to interdependent, such that each more capable successive stage transcends yet includes earlier ones
SOGI	The social processes of leadership operate, and can be developed and analyzed, at four nested levels: individual (I), group (G), organizational (O), and societal (S)

(*continued*)

Exhibit 18.1 (*Continued*)

Culture tools	Tools and methods to help people see and experience, reflect on, and then begin to intentionally and strategically shape their culture. "Quick" tools are portable and adaptable with ease-of-use for groups.
Discovery	Beginning, and then tracking, the process of culture change by deeply understanding the future vision and strategic purpose to be pursued
Public learning	Learning as a group activity, such that potentially difficult topics require social risk taking and personal vulnerability as they are explored with the goal of shared insights and better solutions
Four arts: dialogue, headroom, inside out, boundary spanning	Practices that extend internal experiences that expand public learning across human and system boundaries, and channel better design choices into organizational action
Dialogue	A public learning conversation that temporarily suspends judgment and explores underlying assumptions across differing perspectives with the goal of shared learning and deeper mutual insight
Headroom	The time and space to model risk taking in public that explores breaking old patterns and experimenting with new behaviors and that lifts up, or vertically advances, the leadership culture toward interdependence
Inside out	The subjective, internal individual development experience of focus on imagination, intuition, curiosity, emotions, identity, beliefs, and values
Boundary spanning	Seeing, bridging, and leveraging five types of group boundaries: horizontal, vertical, demographic, geographic, and stakeholder

Exhibit 18.1 (*Continued*)

Both-and	Engaging beyond the binary defaults to either-or thinking; adoption of double-loop learning and the practices of dialectical and intersystemic being and doing
Beliefs in action story telling	A type of dialogue using personal and shared stories about experiences in the organization that illustrate how changing beliefs result in different kinds of actions and a changing set of outcomes
Prototypes	The experimental efforts or pilot projects sponsored by senior teams to test and learn about organizational applications of the emerging leadership culture in the process of strategy execution

LESSON 1: STRATEGY EXECUTION DRIVES TRANSFORMATION

Just because you have talented leadership, a proven track record, and experienced professionals with good intentions heading toward the same objective, do not jump to conclusions and assume you can do the job the way it needs to be done in the current environment. Many stellar-looking strategy ships run aground on the shoals of change. Most organizations' complex business strategies require a kind of learning-ready, collaborative (interdependent) leadership capability that the organization does not have.

The logic goes like this: "In our organizations, we are forced to create strategies that respond to our increasingly complex, competitive, global environment. Implementation of those strategies requires elevated leadership mind-sets equal to the strategic task, but we do not yet have mind-sets that are collaborative, cross-boundary, and oriented to agile learning and see whole systems that are capable of being enterprise competent, not just business unit or function competent." Today in most organizations, we have mind-sets (think *cultures*) that see leadership either (1) as people in authority or (2) as knowledge and expertise held by only certain individuals. In either case, the organization cannot implement the complex strategy because it does not yet have the culture where leadership is (3) a collective activity, with the shared interdependent mind-set required to do so. It's a simple equation: the current leadership capability does not equal what is required to succeed.

Leadership Development as Public Learning

If we accept the proposition of leadership development as a learning process, we might also adopt the simple formula of action + reflection = learning. The key to transformation is a learn-as-you-go process that is done in public with others, actively owning outcomes and reflecting together to discover better and better options and decisions. Applying this concept is foundational to individuals' self-knowledge in forming a team, as well as the leadership collective that is leading the transformation further into the culture. This kind of learning process requires assisting senior leaders in breaking through and out of their individual and organizational defensive routines (Argyris, 1995).

Frustrated executives work harder and longer these days. People at every level are overwhelmed, guarded, and cynical, making them appear uncooperative, when the problem often resides in the lack of shared leadership capability. The shift in focus must include and then go beyond the development of the individual leader in order to transcend into the unfolding, emergent realization of leadership as a social phenomenon—a collective activity.

To get there requires two shifts in thinking about talent and leadership:

1. Beyond *individual competencies*, we must embrace *organizational leadership capabilities.* Even Dave Ulrich (2010), Rensis Likert Professor at the Ross School of Business, University of Michigan, is now talking about a post-competency era. No single, heroic leader is capable of dealing with the level of complexity in our VUCA (volatile, uncertain, complex, and ambiguous) world.
2. Beyond the *individual as leader* (a heroic idea) and into the view of *leadership as a shared collective activity.* We define leadership as a social process that achieves direction, alignment, and commitment (DAC), and the leadership culture with its beliefs and practices is the vehicle for the social process (Drath et al., 2008).

Here is another story to illustrate what we mean. A high-tech organization we know hit the market-shifted-and-we-didn't-see-it-coming wall, with performance numbers dropping like a rock. In reaction, its leaders spent three long days in a strategy-making session. These were smart, successful people working in a fast-changing environment. Their situation-responsive strategy-building work was solid, and they had devised a good plan. Toward the end of the session, the leader asked only one question about the talent to execute the strategy: "Do we have the head count to pull this off?" The intervention that was necessary with this team was to use a collaborative, action inquiry approach to challenge the assumption (belief) that head count or capacity was sufficient to address the task of collective, shared capability (Torbert & Associates, 2004).

While we are empathetic to the difficulties of matching talent to strategic requirements, this example is not unique. Head count and collective capability are not the same thing, and the gap can be a show stopper. Understanding the leap from developing the competencies of individual leaders to what it takes to develop shared, collective leadership capability is a stretch for many senior leaders, yet it is an idea whose time has come. This is why CCL has introduced this concept and its related leadership strategy service in order to assist clients with the integration and coordination of their talent needs in alignment with the culture, strategy, and organization design required to succeed (Pasmore, 2009).

Two Client Illustrations

A traditional health care provider came to CCL seeking assistance in becoming an integrated health care system in a highly politicized and visible regional environment. The CEO was a transformational thinker, clearly envisioned the end goal, and was fully prepared to devote whatever time and resources were required in order to achieve the transformation. We assembled a leadership development team based on our understanding of their complex needs and brought together CCL specialists for individuals, teams, and coaching, as well as organizational transformation and health care. The health system had skilled individual leaders with impressive track records who struggled to work together to deal effectively with difficult challenges and to view their obstacles from a variety of fresh perspectives.

It soon became clear that serious issues in readiness for transformation were present. The health care provider operated in silos and defaulted to traditional hierarchical boundaries, and as a result, turf battles predictably and regularly erupted.

The more resistance shown by various factions of the senior team, the more transformational and far reaching the CEO's efforts became. CCL's organizational leader guide activities had to take a back seat to individual leader coach activities in order to help the CEO and each team member become aware of the impact of different tolerance levels for the speed of change. Specifically, coaching was used to help members learn to identify and disclose the intention behind their behavior and seek to understand the impact their behavior had on others. This was an entirely new skill for them to develop. Core to this is the usual shocking reality that others almost never see senior leaders as these leaders see themselves.

Our second story is about an urban transport company that came to us with an imperative to transform in order to be ready for the market shift they saw coming. With some baseline individual development completed, we rapidly moved into the work of executive team development. Instead of a team, what we found was a group of individuals, strong performers all, competing with each other from their silos and triangulating each other through going to the boss to complain about the other guy. They would also make public comments (digs, really), often with humor, to take competitive shots at their colleagues (they called these "drive-bys").

Our first business with them was to move this independent, competitive belief and practice toward an interdependent belief and practice based on collaboration and learning. In this intervention, we used the arts of transformation (see lesson 4) to generate a learning environment and enabled people to practice public learning with each other directly through dialogue. This meant that individual team members were no longer allowed to get at other teammates by going through the team leader or using blame-focused drive-bys. The new behavior was to go directly to teammates with feedback. If a team member did go indirectly to the team leader or any other colleague with business about someone else, they were to be redirected to the person for whom the feedback was intended. This new practice quickly enhanced both feedback and learning among team members by enabling direct communication and building trust.

Key Lessons from Our Work

We will return to these two cases because they reveal valuable experience. But first we share some of the lessons we've drawn from this work:

- The transformation work of the organization may be parallel with individual and team work, but organizational transformation can never be ahead of the individual readiness of the players.

- At the beginning of transformation work, the readiness of the team leader and team members to transform is determined more by willingness than ability.
- Individual leaders never see themselves as others see them; only a learning process of feedback and coaching closes this gap.
- Public learning, first in closed sessions with teammates and later in more public arenas, is the learning platform of transformation.
- When teams slow down to power up, key beliefs (mind-sets and culture) begin to shift as they make action development (strategy implementation) decisions that drive new behaviors (practices).

With learning being an action + reflection activity, our development task is to assist teams in appropriate and effective ways to do reflection with each other using a variety of tools that result in stronger feedback loops. These interactions lead to the establishment of a learning environment within the team. Team norms (or beliefs and practices) emerge to become cornerstones of the new leadership culture they have worked to create.

The lessons we have learned suggest that organizations should continue to seek more of a balance between developing (coaching) individual leaders and developing the collective capabilities of the organization. The common thread of experience in our transformation practice is a powerful one: choosing the right leadership culture is the difference between success and failure. And the route to developing a reliable leadership culture capable of facing today and tomorrow's challenges flows from individual leaders, through groups and teams, and then into and across the leadership culture.

LESSON 2: COMBINING SKILL SETS OF COACH AND GUIDE YIELDS ALCHEMY OF TRANSFORMATION

We have already suggested that transformation through senior leaders occurs in two overlapping realms or dimensions. First, individual leaders must learn to give and receive feedback and to see themselves as others see them. From there they can form a trust-based team that can act, reflect, and learn together. This is foundational to forming an interpersonally healthy, trusting team. This work of the team is about who we are.

Second, as the team builds trust and its capacity to learn, the members of the team must begin to develop the complex mind-sets (both individual and collective) required to run the business. Complex strategic challenges require senior leadership to carry out the organization's work in a different way. The senior team must first practice and then demonstrate the beliefs and practices of an advanced leadership culture before they ask others to do so. As they invite others to join in the transformation process across the enterprise, they become leaders developing leaders. This work of the senior team is about what we will do.

To summarize, the early, deeper focus of who we are is identity work that develops from individual to team. It progresses from the individual leader to the leadership team. This work must be grounded in and applied to the organization's work. The what-we-will-do work is collective work of the team to the organization. It progresses from the team's new way of working, now applied to the organization.

Early in the transformation process, the work that bridges the identity and collective realms is a focus on team roles, agenda management that separates operations from strategy work, (re)visiting strategic intent, and the identification of strategic drivers and key organizational capabilities. Dialogues about the kind of leadership culture and mind-sets necessary for implementing shifting strategies in response to volatile markets require agile work that do not and cannot proceed in linear fashion.

Key Development Roles

In our transformation practice, we always work with a team in groups of two, three, or more. The complexity of transformation demands many hands. In order to work with senior teams that are developing a learning environment and process to change the fundamental operations of the organization, it is essential that coaching partners function mutually in the learning process. This is a complex task requiring intention and role clarity between facilitators. As we have developed our craft, we have come to see that we play two essential roles in the transformation process. The first is leader coach. Expertise in individual leader development and group dynamics belongs primarily to the field of behavioral science, and executive coaches have applied this expertise in the business arena with great success. In the role of leader coach, the focus is on activities relating to self-awareness, identity, power dynamics, role clarity, and interpersonal styles. Particular attention is focused on the team leader because her behavior has the most powerful shaping effect on the team dynamic. When we work with senior teams on transformation, one member of the CCL team is dedicated as a coach to the leader (with protocols on confidentiality made explicit). The leader's development process gains transparency as it evolves as public learning, a key attribute of successful change. Other team members have access to individual coaching as needed. The territory of the coach role in development is individual to team.

The second role is organizational leadership guide. Expertise in business and organizational dynamics belongs primarily to the field of organizational development. It focuses on and features activities for developing capabilities across the enterprise that are applied directly to the organization's work. In this role, the focus is on activities having to do with collective learning methodologies, strategy execution, design thinking, and prototype production (pilots) across the enterprise. Those activities entail team dynamics and learning, enabling the implementation of business and leadership strategies requiring complex systems thinking and cross-boundary work. This advisory consultative practitioner role acts as an organizational guide. In this role, the guide assists teams in substantially improving collaborative leadership and organizational capabilities. The territory of the guide role in development is team to organization.

When the leader coach role and the organizational leadership guide role are combined into a leadership development design, the result is more than one plus one; it is exponential. At the center of the two roles is the readiness of individual leaders to wholly engage within the team in order to connect in the work of running the business. The sole purpose of coaching in the individual-to-team work is to enable the work of the guide to move toward the higher-level outcomes of the team-to-organization work. The two roles are aligned to assist senior leaders and their teams to get ready to face and pursue complex challenges and the transformation required for ongoing strategic work.

Transformation Methodology

We briefly introduce our transformation methodology here because it is useful to discern how the roles of coach and guide shift in importance and active focus over time. Initially the work is concentrated on coaching leaders; however, it quickly advances into organizational guide work that operates in parallel to coaching. As senior team transformation work takes hold, senior leaders will seek to extend and experiment with the transformation in early prototypes (pilot projects) within other teams or work groups where key, strategic organizational change needs to happen. These sponsoring senior leaders will need to ensure that the prototype teams are also getting the kind of leader coaching and organizational leadership guidance they require. Whether senior leaders have developed the ability to provide these roles themselves or need additional help, the dance of the two roles is recreated as each subsequent prototype team moves first toward a healthy team and then into healthy organizational work, all within the transformation process.

As distinct from change management, our change leadership methodology is distinguished by slowing down to power up in the first few phases of work. We intend for senior leadership to have the development time necessary to achieve its own team readiness in order to lead others and the organization into the complex work of transformation.

Our transformation methodology uses four broad, overlapping, reinforcing phases and has two essential ideas. In the initial phases, we insist on improving the probability of success by ensuring organizational readiness to do the required work. This work is not for everyone. We measure readiness early by senior leaders' willingness and ability to engage in the learning and change process. As the work advances, we build culture change—first within work groups and then across those groups—that moves toward a critical mass for enterprise-wide change. Our goal is to involve everyone in the organization in a learning process that creates trust, ownership, and increasing forms of interdependence. These nonlinear, overlapping, and parallel phases often look something like the representation in figure 18.2:

Phase 1. Discovery: Determining willingness—establishing the feasibility of entering the change process

Phase 2. Readiness: Developing understanding—developing a deeper appreciation of the long-term implications of integrating a new culture into the organization's work; pilot-testing initial prototypes for early learning

Phase 3. Prototype: Framing the change process—practicing interdependent leadership through mapping business and leadership strategies, the learning process, and organizational work targets

Phase 4. Capability: Building capability—implementing, simultaneously and in parallel, what is already established in parts into the whole organization

We have provided examples of the phases in table 18.2.

Table 18.2
Transformation Methodology Descriptions and Examples

Phase	Description	Examples
1. Discovery: Determining willingness	Develop connections within senior leadership: engagement for development.	• Engage senior leadership through interviews, team processes, collaborative inquiry. • Explore alignment of strategy, culture, talent, and organizational design. • Leaders themselves uncover and identify the culture changes required to achieve strategic success.
2. Readiness: Developing understanding	Apply the culture transformation method in senior teams; senior leadership grasps and appreciates the implication of the real change required and the implication for impact on the organization.	• Slow down to power up; practice the arts of transformation behind closed doors; experiment with dialogue, public learning, feedback, and both-and thinking. • Senior leaders generate and practice new beliefs and behaviors within the work of the team and work of the organization. • Launch and learn outside the team from experimental change prototypes within senior leaders' territories.
3. Prototype: Framing the change process	Prototype and practice the emerging leadership culture; scenario plans for enterprise transformation of the culture in and across the organization's work.	• Map business and leadership strategies' target work processes. • Scope the work across divisions, partners, governance, and communities; engage senior leadership sponsors and stage the work. • Leaders develop leaders' readiness; prepare senior leaders to do the development work of the leadership culture.

(*continued*)

Table 18.2 (*Continued*)

Phase	Description	Examples
4. Capability: Building capability	Implement the culture enterprise-wide; build sustaining capability and capacity for future challenges.	• Action development workshops; charter cross-functional work groups for strategy implementation. • Boundary-spanning skill building for teams connecting with teams. • Feedback and learning loops; beliefs in action stories.

Figure 18.2
Phases of Transformation Methodology

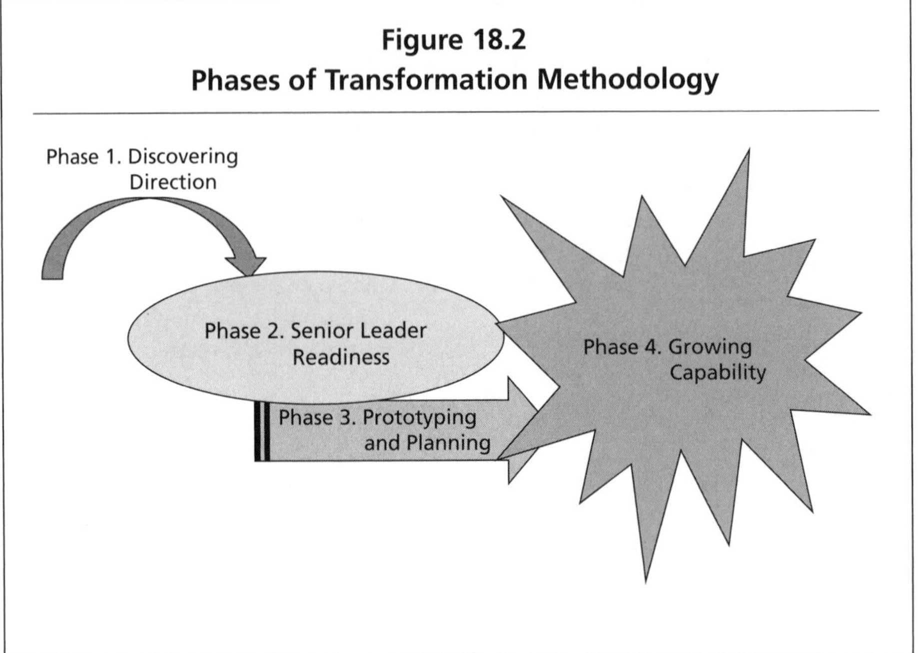

LESSON 3: THE VERTICAL SHIFT IN LEADERSHIP CULTURE IS TRANSFORMATION

All organizations must adapt and change, and executives know it because complexity is accelerating everywhere. Conventional change efforts continue to fail. Behind closed doors, senior leaders are speaking a different, unconventional truth. Increasingly they are questioning the incessant reorganizing, reengineering, and restructuring in the name of efficiency. Strategies that should work fall apart instead, and operational decisions that once were clear-cut are now complicated and ambiguous. What these conventional approaches fail to account for is that adaptation to new systems, structures, and processes required by complex strategies must be advanced through new mind-sets, assumptions, and beliefs that live in the culture.

However useful for individuals, most traditional leader development is competency based—advancing skills on a horizontal scale. We continue to introduce vertical development—an elevation of mind-sets toward more and more sophisticated capabilities in leadership thought and action (Petrie, 2014; Rooke & Torbert, 2005; Wilber, 2000). Let us explain a little more about what we mean by vertical development (for individuals and the culture). A hierarchy of culture exists, and each successive culture is increasingly capable of dealing with more complexity, more ambiguity, and more uncertainty. This means that earlier forms of culture (mind-set) are likely conservative, holding power at the top, whereas more developed mature cultures enable learning and collaborative leadership as a collective process (what we refer to as postconventional). Therefore, the work of transformation is to elevate (vertical development) the culture from an earlier mind-set to a later, more mature and sophisticated, complex mind-set (McGuire & Rhodes, 2009).

Beliefs drive leaders' decisions, and repeated patterns of decisions in collective leadership become organizational practices. If you want best practices, invest in best beliefs. This is the realm of leadership culture. We often ask senior leaders, "How many decisions do you make every day?" Answers vary from dozens to hundreds, but laughter is the most prominent response. They understand that they are unconsciously competent about most decisions—we make them conscious about the assumptions and beliefs their decisions are based on. Through this learning process, leaders become aware of the beliefs as drivers of their behavior.

Back to Our Stories

As the health system we told you about earlier began to make progress in its transformation, the CEO mandated that he and his team take regularly scheduled days at CCL to learn to have productive conversations about key issues that guided their beliefs and behavior. Unhappy team members grumbled about taking time away from the tactical, operational issues that were in fact life-or-death in a hospital setting. The CEO did not waiver and took considerable heat for doing so. He created the opportunity for his team to give him feedback about how his vision for integration affected them. He shared his motivations and aspirations; he did not back away from having the difficult conversations and admitted mistakes publicly. He made explicit why it was important for the chief medical officer to understand the impact of clinical decisions on the chief information officer and vice versa, why strategy could not be placed at the end of the line of tactical topics at executive team meetings. Complaints that had previously been relegated to water-cooler conversations were given center stage and discussed openly in order to find solutions and avoid wasting time and squandering goodwill. Throughout this process, it became quite clear who on the team was aligned with the direction. Those who were committed stayed, while others selected out. These changes were accepted as natural consequences of the new style of leadership. The grinding work of transformation continued despite several changes on the leadership team.

Let's return to the story of the urban transport company. The senior team continued down their pathway and persisted for a time in behaving as though competition between silos was beneficial. Through dialogue, however, they were able to see that a belief in internal competition came from an independent mind-set, limited by either-or thinking, and that compromise and limited cooperation were the best they could ever achieve given their assumptions and beliefs (mind-set). Over time they came to experience the advantages of an interdependent culture. Both-and thinking led to cross-boundary work. For example, on the eve of losing a large university client, a weekend crisis with the client's equipment and systems opened up a short window requiring a higher level of service. The company's newly developing agile responsiveness to clients included actions that worked not only across the company's regional management boundaries for resourcing and equipment, but also involved experts from headquarters, resulting in comprehensive and high-quality services. Customer-driven quality response to the crisis was only the beginning. As customer satisfaction grew, the demand for increasingly more product and services grew in kind over the next several quarters.

These client-driven behaviors would not have occurred before the transformation work. The impact was far beyond client retention as the service revenue grew by several factors with the transport company shift to a new leadership mind-set through the customer-driven belief and practice. With such early encounters and prototype efforts in the day-to-day work, senior leaders began to have experience in the transformation process. The action development experiences of consciously shifting to new beliefs and mind-sets resulted in very different practices and outcomes.

As we continued the organizational leadership guide role within the team, we created the conditions for a shared experience of the comprehensive change in beliefs among team members. In fact, we conducted a three day off-site focused solely on new leadership beliefs as the drivers of transformation. In this way, we ramped up our role as guide and created the opportunity first for transformation work within the team and then the team leading transformation across the enterprise. One of their four beliefs became "customer-driven," and Living the Beliefs became a credo.

The Nature of Leadership Culture

Culture is fundamentally about the interpretive process through which people make meaning of the world and is the source of the tools they create to deal with the world. Leadership culture drives the social process leaders use to create shared direction, alignment, and commitment throughout the organization.

The goal of culture transformation work is to purposefully and actively build capability for new ways of working. It allows the new thinking, beliefs, tools, and processes that will result in the organization successfully adapting to business challenge changes. However, business strategy will likely require different culture and capability in various parts of the organization. Therefore, discerning the levels of challenge and complexity across and in different parts of the organization is key to understanding the types of culture required from place to place. Culture change is hard, so be sure exactly where you have to have it for organizational success.

Leadership culture can be understood in terms of three essential leadership mind-sets (what we also refer to as "leadership logics") that drive leadership behaviors (McGuire et al., 2007), as illustrated in figure 18.3.

Dependent Leadership Culture Dependent leadership cultures hold only people in positions of authority responsible for leadership. Authority and control are held at the top. Success depends on obedience to authority and loyalty. Mastery and recognition of work operate primarily at the level of technical expertise. Open conflict is not embraced. Other characteristics associated with dependent cultures are a conservative approach to change, an emphasis on keeping things running smoothly, and the tendency to publicly smooth over

Figure 18.3
Leadership Culture and Mind-Sets

Leadership Culture		Leadership Mind-Set
Interdependent	Leadership is a **collective** activity.	Collaborator
Independent	Leadership emerges out of **individual knowledge and expertise.**	Achiever
Dependent	**People in authority** are responsible for leadership.	Conformer

mistakes. Leadership development experiences may be made available to others, but generally senior leaders do not participate. Transformation readiness is often restricted and selective. Development activities for this type of culture are often at the individual and team level and contained within a specific part of the organization.

Independent Leadership Culture Independent leadership cultures assume that leadership emerges as needed from a variety of individuals based on knowledge and expertise. Authority and control are distributed through the ranks. Independent cultures value decentralized decision making, individual responsibility and expertise, and competition among experts. Independent cultures focus on success by adapting faster and better than the competition. Success means mastery of systems that produce results in an individual's own domain, and it eventually contributes to the success of the organization, though indirectly. Mistakes may be treated as opportunities to learn. Other characteristics associated with independent cultures are individual performance as an important source of success and status and an emphasis on taking calculated risks, having open disagreement, and taking independent actions within functions or work groups.

In independent cultures, leadership development activities may be undertaken by senior leaders, but they mostly occur behind closed doors, in separate and contained pockets. Transformation readiness is often good in independent cultures. Development activities can often be practiced within the team and then within the organization in parallel.

Interdependent Leadership Culture Interdependent leadership cultures view leadership as a collective activity that requires mutual inquiry, learning, and a collaborative capacity to work with complex challenges. Authority and control are shared based on mutually shared strategic competence for the whole organization. The mind-set tends toward collaborating in a changing world so that new organizational orders and structures can emerge through collective work. Mistakes are embraced as opportunities for individual, team, and organizational learning, and both positive and negative feedback are valued as essential tools for collective success. Other characteristics associated with interdependent cultures include the ability to work effectively across organizational boundaries, openness and candor, and synergies being sought across the whole enterprise. Leadership development activities are required of the senior leaders and conducted in visible and public forums for the advantage and participation of all.

Although we find that almost all of our clients require more interdependent cultures at the top and in certain strategic portions of their organizations, the principle of transforming culture remains the same: transform the leadership culture to the level of mind-set required for the strategic future of the organization. Culture transformation is hard work and should be pursued only when necessary.

Matching the Culture to the Need

While there is nothing inherently better about one culture compared with another, organizations must match the leadership culture to the operational need. Asking a command-and-control (dependent) culture, for example, to implement an innovative, agile strategy is a recipe for disaster. In contrast, an interdependent organization is better poised to handle a high caliber of complexity and challenge. As a more fluid organization, it will be able to draw on individual talent, connect effectively across boundaries, and adapt as needed. A more sophisticated use of culture types is the matching of subcultures within and across an organization—perhaps conformers in finance, achievers in sales, and collaborators at the top and across the supply chain.

Here we want to say two things that may seem contradictory. On the one hand, organizations may have dependent or independent subcultures perfectly suited for the work they do and the strategy they pursue. On the other hand, we say that all organizations are being pushed or pulled into greater interdependence. We see that almost everywhere at the senior leadership level in organizations, but not necessarily in every part of every organization. However, don't confuse the need for applying the clear trend of interdependence in senior leadership with the need for other types of culture in, for example, the sales, purchasing, or accounting functions in your organization.

Developing leadership culture is about growing leadership talent to the needed level of capability. To break through the current capability ceiling, organizational leaders must take the time to connect two critical factors. First, they have to know where their target cultures for change are located in the hierarchy of cultures, and then they need to measure the required growth and investment needed to hit that target. Investing first in knowing what your current culture is and what it is not capable of will save an organization dollars and time. Second, you have to understand the feasibility of successful transformation for the strategic drivers and core capabilities needed for your business and leadership strategy to succeed. It is the job of leadership to ensure that smart strategies can be wisely implemented.

By choosing the right level of leadership culture that your organization absolutely requires for its future, your leadership talent as a collective can advance to new levels of organizational capability that secures success. When the level of leadership culture aligns with your business strategy, your performance can be stellar.

LESSON 4: TRANSFORMATION IS THE ART OF CULTIVATING LEADERSHIP MIND-SETS

The four arts of vertical development—dialogue, headroom, boundary spanning, and inside out—are the core approaches we use in the learning process that enables the elevation of mind-sets (see exhibit 18.2). CCL has a robust set of tools for practicing these approaches and to engage teams directly in the collaborative learning process (Palus, McGuire, & Ernst, 2011).

Exhibit 18.2
The Four Arts of Vertical Development

Dialogue

Through collaborative inquiry and creative conversations (see chapter 13), people reflect on unquestioned assumptions and difficult topics, find common ground, and cocreate multiple solutions that allow the best ideas to win. Using mediated dialogue, we help groups deal with complex or potentially divisive issues by putting something in the middle that objectifies and represents the issue at hand.

Headroom

Organizations need to have the time, space, risk taking, learning, and modeling to lift the entire leadership culture to a new interdependent order of thought and action. This requires collective public learning. By raising the ceiling beyond conventional thought and action, headroom creates room to explore, experiment, and practice—to break out of old patterns and try new behaviors.

Boundary Spanning

To advance a leadership culture, leaders at all levels must practice the art of seeing, bridging, and leveraging five types of group boundaries: horizontal, vertical, demographic, geographic, and stakeholder, first within one's own team and then across teams.

Inside Out

This art focuses on the values, beliefs, identity, emotions, intuition, curiosity, imagination, and leadership mind-sets of individuals, which can then be applied to the external (outside-in) challenges and dilemmas of the organization.

Back to Our Stories

The coaching leader's work in the health system with which we were involved included the initial interviews, diagnosis, and data synthesis that led us to design and deliver an initial two-day development session for the senior leadership team (SLT), with regularly scheduled sessions after. Ongoing coaching with the CEO and senior team members generated various experiences to meet emerging needs for individual development. When some team members complained about another member of the team, the CEO addressed the issue directly, provided clear and candid feedback, and set expectations, which included having the team member who was the target of complaint address the rest of the team to get direct feedback. Granted, this created enormous discomfort in and around the team because it radically departed from the way the team had previously operated. In pursuing the move to a new culture, the CEO asked us to facilitate difficult one-on-one conversations between members of the SLT and other key stakeholders, regardless of where they sat in the organization. When the CEO identified a hot spot—obstacles to progress or failure to advance a project (often due to past events or lack of trust)—steps were taken to address it openly and directly. The CEO consistently blocked and redirected unhealthy communication habits. While this was moving the transformation in a positive direction, it also created tension across the enterprise.

Several months into the intensive work, as a result of the greater capability for transformation demonstrated by the SLT, we facilitated a leadership strategy session with a wider group of the health system's stakeholders (including physicians, training and development staff, and communications staff), plus the SLT. This was the first of several projects that the team launched in order to practice, on a limited basis, the interdependent beliefs and practices emerging in the SLT. This boundary-spanning session created an environment with sufficient headroom to produce a collaborative vision behind which stakeholders could align. It became clear that physicians' leadership development was an emerging need; consequently, physician leadership team (PLT) sessions were cocreated and launched. Collaborative teaming sessions (a prototype effort aimed at contributing to forming the new culture) were held to clarify team operating agreements, including decision making, confidentiality, and handling of conflict. The result of this relentless approach to addressing any emerging issue was that it surfaced beliefs and perceptions that before were hidden and undiscussed. Lack of trust emerged as a frequent refrain. The often repeated statement, "We don't trust leadership," seemed to be a shorthand way of saying, "We don't trust leadership to do things the way we are used to."

Stepping up to the challenge, the SLT launched an enterprise-wide "trust immersion" session where the leadership team addressed several previously undiscussable issues and followed up with regular meetings of "trust teams" (yet another way to drive the culture change down into and across the system) that were cofacilitated by a health care system member deeper in the organization, a health system SLT member, and a CCL coach. A group of self-identified change agents, including members of the PLT and the SLT, became the change leadership team known as the "guiding coalition." Interspersed over the course of our two-year transformation partnership were development opportunities including a day-long session to introduce new ways to address issues, solve problems, and develop new opportunities. The health system SLT and CCL teams each had its level of leadership mind-sets (logics) assessed and debriefed by a third party. As a result of these efforts, an entirely new leadership mind-set based on building trust took hold at the top in the formal leadership at the health system and cascaded though the system. Not everyone was comfortable with the new reality, to be sure. But from this story, we hope you can see how effective the four arts can be in practice.

At the urban transport company, the organizational leadership guide work was preceded by leader coaching in the first phase of individual work and teamwork with the executive team. Through their own measures of culture, capabilities, strategy, and gaps, executive team members tested their willingness and ability to engage in transformation work. Initially they discovered their inability to have truly collaborative conversations, observed a divide in understanding of the company's strategy, and acknowledged their shaky trust in one another. They faced up to their avoidance of conflict and found a willingness to participate in leader coaching work to create a trust basis for organizational work.

Throughout that first year of work, the executive team faced emerging business challenges, launched strategic groups, established foundational beliefs for the new culture, and pursued the goal of attaining industry leadership. We used pilot programs to help the company prototype and test the new culture. A strong joint commitment allowed CCL to attend executive team meetings and participate directly in their organizational work interventions. This provided a practice field for developing new behaviors and beliefs with the team and in the pilots and prototypes. For example, the executive team created four strategy teams that spanned boundaries, including non–executive team members from across the enterprise, to focus on prototypes in areas like strategic finance, operations, and environmental excellence. They also established a leadership strategy team hosted by the CEO. Our early work with the executive team and through the prototypes was already transforming the culture across select work groups. The organization's response to one business challenge stands out as an exemplary prototype in the pursuit of industry leadership.

The company took a risk in abandoning a base revenue stream by attacking an industry-standard solution with a more expensive but operationally superior eco-friendly product. It made great strides in working collaboratively in field teams that piloted safe, quality installation, and it pursued efficiency goals and better margins. One executive team meeting was a turning point in these efforts. By using the four arts, in particular, the inside-out and headroom-creating processes, a hidden belief (assumption) was unearthed. While the executives had aspired to an interdependent culture for the company's top one hundred leaders, they had assumed that the frontline, customer-facing, union member technicians would continue to be managed as a traditional command-and-control dependent culture. During a mind-set-expanding dialogue, they discovered and confronted this belief. They were stunned by the implications of their belief and assumptions. They had increasingly discussed how a customer-driven future and the crucial growth of the company's service business depended on the technician-customer relationship. How (they asked themselves) could technicians, the most important link to customers, *not* be engaged in the culture of interdependent collaboration? This learning was foundational for planning the next phase of taking transformation across the whole enterprise and resulted in branch-level interventions that engaged everyone in the organization.

Subsequently, the executive team formed and defined four new beliefs as transformational drivers around which it could unite:

1. Be customer driven in every thought and action—why we work together.
2. Conduct business with interdependent collaborative mind-sets—how we align our work.
3. Take 100 percent responsibility for the enterprise—what we all own.
4. Expect integrity as the value base for everything we do—who we are.

Most important, it developed these beliefs as levers in action development work (the pilot project prototypes that tested business strategy implementation) to achieve its industry leadership targets. The four beliefs formed by the executive team also launched the company's effort to build an environment of leaders developing leaders, a crucial step into the next phase of the transformation process.

LESSON 5: THE ART OF CHANGE LEADERSHIP IS GETTING STRATEGY AND CULTURE ALIGNED

An organization's business strategy shows up in its choices, whether those choices are made consciously or not. This is also true of leadership culture and its beliefs and practices. The strategy shows up in the kind of people systems the senior team chooses to manage and develop. This all has tremendous implications for leadership development systems and programs, but it is much more than that.

Executive and leadership teams bear a responsibility to make the organization's strategies conscious and explicit. They need to be as aware and diligent about the leadership strategy as they are about the business strategy. Moving the choices that are an expression of strategy into the team's zone of intentional change can vastly increase the feasibility of change.

The future lies in leadership practices that align vision, strategic drivers, and core capabilities. An organization must first get the business strategy right and then work on the leadership strategy in parallel. When the organization can get both strategies to operate as one, the probability of successful transformation increases tremendously. We provide some advice on just that in exhibit 18.3.

Exhibit 18.3
Nine Strategies for Change: Essential Strategic Advice

1. *Don't hand transformation work off to HR.* Shifting the work to a function makes transformation appear to be a program, and the feasibility of success will drop several points. Organizational transformation belongs to the whole enterprise, and all senior leaders must own it. The HR function can provide expertise and project management. Only senior leaders together (including the organization's human resource leader) can create change through repeated, consistent, daily behavior visible to all.
2. *Begin privately within the senior leadership team.* Jump-start the change work behind closed doors. Try it out, practice, and learn together before you go public. Timing and speed of adopting new behavior are important.

(*continued*)

Exhibit 18.3 (*Continued*)

3. *Be willing to give the time.* Taking time to learn is necessary. When the team shifts its perception of time from a constraint to a resource for learning, transformation is happening.
4. *Practice strategic leadership.* Think of strategy building as a learning process (Hughes, Beatty, & Dinwoodie, 2014). The feasibility and probability of success increase when continuous learning occurs across key dimensions of executing strategy.
5. *Find the team's center.* Determine the senior leadership culture and mind-set. Find the mind-set center of gravity. Try to understand the variety of mind-sets in power and the key roles they play in the team and organization. It takes only a few interdependent collaborator mind-sets to lead others forward (it helps if one of them is the CEO).
6. *Separate strategy from operations.* Use the senior team's agenda to manage simple ways to conduct operational meetings while also making open times to practice the four arts of transformation in strategic dialogues. Provide at least two open sessions a year for a few days to think strategically together about where you are and where you are going. Slow down to power up.
7. *Identify sails and anchors.* Which members will push for and support change, and which ones will likely resist? Make two lists. Go to the anchors (resisters) and see if you can get them to be at least neutral and to practice do-no-harm. Elevate the sails by placing them on visible projects. Encourage them to connect with others and generate excitement for the advancement of the new culture through beliefs-in-action stories.
8. *Have the difficult conversations.* Undiscussable topics, sacred cows, and conflict avoidance have to stop in order to make way for a transformative environment. Practice the four arts to create that environment.
9. *Balance "what" and "how" questions with "why" and "what if" questions.* Practice curiosity and imagination. Ask provocative questions. Inquire more; advocate less.

Choosing the Change Leadership Team

Change is less likely to come if the CEO, COO, or other major power brokers are authoritarian, control-minded conflict avoiders or pleasers. The same is true if, outside the team's immediate sphere of influence, there sits another key player in a powerful and influential position who opposes leadership culture change. On the senior team itself, it takes only one powerful detractor to seriously damage or even sink the ship of change. If people in a key line of business, an important geographical area, or an essential function see their executive vice president, for example, defying the change in word or deed, they won't support the change and may actively work against it.

To mitigate these problems, you can create what we call a change leadership team (CLT) made up of key executive team members plus other prominent, influential leaders. Choose members whose behavior, mind-set, and enthusiasm move the culture in the desired direction. They are influential leaders across functions and business units that may be down a few layers into the organization — company folk heroes, a maven or two, informal leaders who have influence across the system, members of the governing board, and representatives from the supply chain and from client and constituent groups. The CLT is an extension of the senior team, not a replacement for it. By creating a CLT, you can build a powerful set of stakeholders with a collective, cross-boundary voice for change. Using a CLT has several advantages over relying solely on an existing senior leader team:

- Strengthen a weak core leadership mind-set on the executive team.
- Advocate on behalf of the organization and so extend leadership development.
- Extend progress on key operations initiatives through prototypes and change work.
- Anticipate change and create consistency when senior team membership changes.
- Serve an interim, progressive change strategy function when key executive players are not yet on board with the change work.

LESSON 6: PRACTITIONERS BRING LEARNING TOOLS AND AGILE MIND-SETS TO THE EXPERIENCE OF TRANSFORMATION

The history of change management teaches us that a simple approach does not work in a complex challenge. Change is very difficult. Our experience with clients has helped us identify themes and patterns, tools, and frameworks that help transform leaders, teams, and organizations.

Change Leadership Core Lessons

The lessons of change leadership are hard won. Some of the central lessons are as follows:

- Bigger minds are needed to keep pace with rapidly changing reality. Reality is leaping ahead of our collective development. We need new thinking and new ways of working together in order to keep up. Most organizations are behind in development to move up the hierarchy of culture, and it takes an even greater move to thrive in the face of change.
- Change requires new mind-sets, not just new skills. Our organizations have become savvy developers of individual leader competencies. In doing so, we have overrelied on the function to manage change through individual skill development. Executives have not yet sufficiently considered the need to advance their individual and collective leadership mind-sets.
- Hidden assumptions and beliefs must be unearthed. Unexamined beliefs control an organization and prevent any meaningful change. Years of valuing hierarchy, status, authority, and control—even if unstated—lead to assumptions and behaviors that are out of date, unnecessary, unhelpful, and at odds with transformative goals and strategic direction.
- Organizational change requires leaders to change. Change the culture—change yourself: that's the new reality. Senior executives who move the needle toward organizational transformation also experience significant personal transformation. That commitment to personal change is a fundamental part of readiness to take on the leadership and management challenges of change to build a sustainable future.

- It takes a new kind of hard work. Stop calling them "soft skills." Developing new beliefs and mind-sets is hard—maybe the hardest work leaders will ever do. The leadership practices that new beliefs and mind-sets generate will permanently alter the way leadership is experienced and accomplished. Developing a new mind-set is much harder than managing spreadsheets or the next restructuring. If it was easy, everyone would be doing it.

Readiness Factors for the Senior Team

Following are key factors to consider when undertaking transformational change:

- The executive team is engaged as both enabler and participant in the change process. It is important that leaders do not move too fast for the organization to see and absorb the change in the organization's work—not just what is being said about the work. Culture change is successful only when executives understand they must do the change work first.
- Leadership development is part of the organization's cultural history. The organization has experience with and appreciation for leadership development as a means of building leadership capacity. The leadership culture has seen positive effects from its previous leader development efforts.
- Senior leaders know that the missing piece in change is the leadership culture. Not only is the senior team clear about the need to improve operations, but it sees that the lever for lasting improvement lies in leadership. Team members often do not know how the connection between the two works, but they often share a belief that alignment of leadership lies somewhere in the culture.
- The senior team is willing to engage in emergent work. Organizational cultural change is not a management program with guaranteed deliverables but a trail that leaders blaze along the way. This requires a willingness to develop their ability to tolerate uncertainty and ambiguity.
- The senior team recognizes the need for cross-boundary work. This is often expressed as breaking down silos or described as a horizontal process work where peerlike relationships are required to cooperate and collaborate. This can include crossing the boundaries of functions, alliances, agencies, suppliers, and other entities.

The more that these factors are present, the more likely it is the transformation effort will have a good start and proceed toward success.

A PRACTITIONER'S LOOK IN THE REARVIEW MIRROR

You might assume that CCL's highly trained professionals in individual, team, and organizational leadership would know better than to assume that they are immune to the same forces CCL's clients wrestle with every day. We take some solace in the fact that we can learn from our mistakes, and this chapter is an application of those lessons learned.

During one of our recent transformation client team experiences, we shared many observations, learned powerful lessons, and gained deeper insights. We believe that similar experiences and lessons occur simultaneously within our clients' senior teams. We are sharing these observations, lessons, and insights as a summary to this chapter in order to illustrate the parallels that we encounter in partnership with our clients. It is to some degree an explanation of the degree of deep regard and connection that we take together into an intentional future:

- Beware of working from assumptions not made fully explicit. This challenge is sneaky, because many of us have worked together successfully over time and appear to hold similar views. We became confused with one another because we were facing different challenges and working from different assumptions. We learned that we had to take time to dig several layers down to reveal individual beliefs and identify where our own thinking diverged from that of others.
- We fell into the trap of having conversations that advanced our thinking with a subset of the team and failed to sufficiently bring absent members up to speed. Complex travel schedules are the routine in complex organizations. When travelers returned, we assumed they would be able to get onboard with our advancements with minimal explication. We took the time to get them up to speed—but not enough time or with enough detail. This left some team members dismayed and disoriented.
- We had to go back repeatedly to reset our overarching understanding of what our (shifting) objectives were becoming. Rapid developments with clients brought us repeatedly into new territory, and we had to go back and rethink our objectives at regular intervals in order to keep our direction and behaviors aligned. We needed to consistently test our hypotheses and learn.
- We continuously discovered the need to practice the four arts ourselves.
- Whenever we thought we had clear insight into system dynamics (ours and our clients), we had to recognize our own blind spots to our personal contributions to those dynamics.

- Taking ourselves too seriously sapped our energy. We solved more problems more effectively when we thought we were off the clock and unwinding together. A little laughter and lightness allowed us to see the issues from an entirely new perspective. The notion of serious play took on fresh meaning and we were able to apply ourselves with renewed vigor (Schrage, 2000).
- Seeking new and unexpected development opportunities became necessary, both individually and especially as a team, because what we used to feel capable of doing was no longer sufficient to meet the needs of the task at hand.

CONCLUSION

In hindsight, the ability of the CCL transformation teams to learn in partnership with CCL's client organizations has proved to be transformational system change in action. Combining the coaching role with the organizational guide role in oscillating fashion to meet emerging client needs creates a virtuous learning cycle to assist senior teams lead organization transformation. As Chris Argyris has taught us, success in the marketplace increasingly depends on learning, yet most people do not know how to learn. In many ways our transformation practice is dedicated to the principle of learning how to learn continuously, alongside our clients, and in the face of our collective future's unfolding and daunting challenges. We believe it is a principle worth following and a value worth pursuing.

chapter
NINETEEN

Coaching beyond the Organization

Joel F. Wright

How can we hone the leadership capabilities and coaching capabilities of more professionals in organizations and those soon to enter the work world? One way is in implementing a multilayered leadership solution—a model that can be used to develop large numbers of leadership coaches in organizations alongside community youth initiatives.

Leadership and coaching capabilities are interdependent capabilities that can enhance the purpose of one's life and one's effectiveness. Many individuals in organizations recognize the need for their culture and employees to embody leadership coaching practices, but a number of factors, including resources, can make widespread skill development challenging. For several years at CCL, we have been exploring ways to expand access and address two needs regularly brought to our attention:

1. Increase the coaching capabilities in organizations and communities.
2. Develop young people with life and leadership skills for employment and citizenship.

I thank Beth Gullette, Cindy McCauley, Ellen Van Velsor, Laura Weber, Preston Yarborough, Marin Burton, Lyndon Rego, Sarah Stawiski, and Sarah Miller for insights into writing and editing this chapter. Also, thanks to our community partners and their staff and volunteers who worked with the Center for Creative Leadership and are part of the Leadership Beyond Boundaries movement: the Golden LEAF Foundation, the YMCA of Greensboro, the Office of Leadership and Service Learning at the University of North Carolina at Greensboro, Ravenscroft School, Southern Methodist University's Hart Center for Engineering Leadership, and the Milton Hershey School. Finally, thanks to the entire Leadership Beyond Boundaries team and CCL, who have invested many long hours to advance this work in service of our mission and have bettered young people, communities, organizations, and the world. It's an honor serving with all of you.

CCL's Leadership Beyond Boundaries (LBB) group developed a multilayered leadership program model as one possible solution to these challenges. This model was informed by global immersions and CCL's accumulated knowledge from decades of training global leaders. We had concluded that many people do not receive leadership education or training until they are already in management or formal leadership positions, and many managers, whether new or experienced, lack the mentoring, coaching, facilitation, or leadership abilities to support and develop their teams. Multilayered leadership solutions emerged as a result of building on CCL's rich legacy of research and experience and combining it with LBB's innovative approaches.

This chapter reviews CCL's genesis of a multilayered leadership solution, with attention to how such an approach can develop coaching capabilities and better prepare young people for work and life. This chapter:

- Describes multilayered leadership solutions
- Explains LBB and how it developed multilayered leadership solutions
- Shares the importance of focusing on young people and leadership coaching for adults
- Introduces the building blocks of a multilayered leadership solution
- Presents two multilayered leadership solutions
- Invokes a call to action

WHAT IS A MULTILAYERED LEADERSHIP SOLUTION?

This chapter offers examples of multilayered leadership solutions—those with multiple levels of learning and impact as part of their design. Our multilayered leadership programs target young people in high school or college who are paired with a developmental coach in a group leadership coaching model. Youth, mentors and coaches, and groups and facilitators all develop their leadership capacity. In developing these leadership solutions, we have taken a design thinking approach, listening to what the world needs and connecting stakeholder resources to create positive outcomes for everyone. The multilayered solutions in this chapter address three challenges we believe are interrelated:

1. Developing young people with personal and professional leadership skills for work and life

2. Enhancing the coaching and leadership capabilities of employees in the work world and community
3. Cascading the impact into applicable domains of one's life: work, family, friends, school, and community, for example, through service-learning or in the workplace

The multilayered leadership solutions discussed in this chapter run about eight months each year. In groups of five to eight, participants and developmental coaches work in leadership workshops with experiential activities, discussion, and reflection that keep participants active, engaged, and practicing leadership concepts together. Figure 19.1 provides a visual representation of the multilayered leadership process.

Evaluation data from the multilayered leadership programs shared in this chapter demonstrate a positive impact on both leadership coaches and youth. Across both programs, leadership coaches agreed or strongly agreed that their effectiveness at work had been enhanced (Center for Creative Leadership and ETR Services, 2013; Stawiski, 2013). Young people who participated in these programs demonstrated a shift in thinking about their identity and their role in creating positive change (Miller, Van Velsor, Wright, & Champion, in press; Stawiski, 2013).

Figure 19.1
Multilayered Leadership Solution

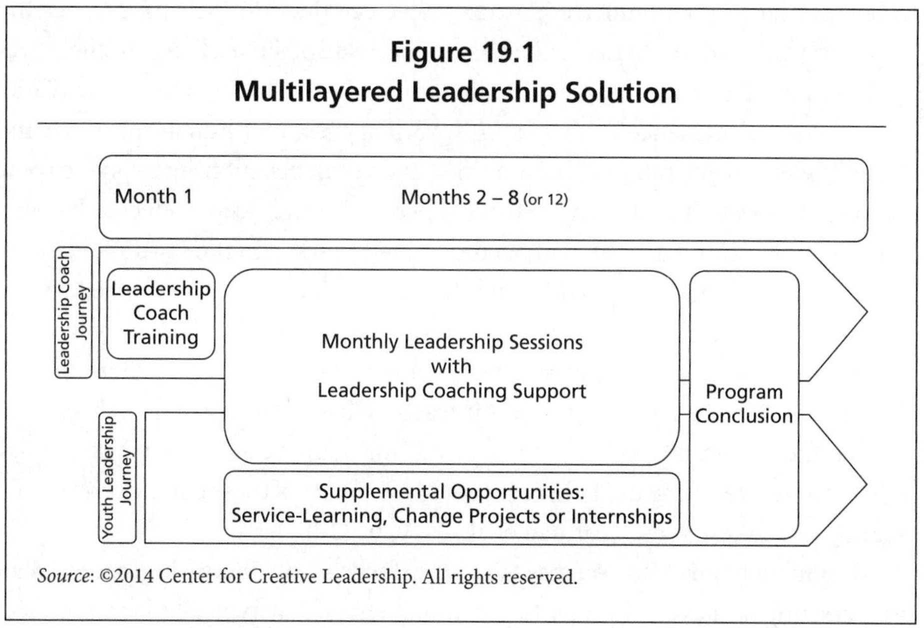

Source:

The data demonstrate that participation in multilayered leadership programs results in young people and the leadership coaches acquiring tangible skills that prepare them for working, leading with others, and living a life of purpose. Through these programs, organizations have the opportunity to develop their staff and young people in the community, a solution for more productive work environments and a stronger leadership pipeline.

The emergence of multilayered leadership solutions came from insights in the field coupled with research and leadership program evaluations. We next look at the origins of LBB, the CCL division that works with younger populations, and how we came to use a multilayered leadership approach. We believe this background can be instructive as you contemplate how to develop a leadership and coaching solution for your context.

LEADERSHIP BEYOND BOUNDARIES

In 2006, CCL launched an initiative we now call Leadership Beyond Boundaries (LBB), which focuses on democratizing leadership development. Our work is to explore and expand new leadership solutions that increase access to high-quality, developmentally appropriate leadership content, thereby enabling all people to learn and grow as leaders and citizens (Altman, Rego, & Harrison, 2010). The model we use to communicate how all people can develop their own leadership capacity, work and live better with others, and create positive change in their lives and communities is: Leading Self, Leading with Others, and Changing Your World.

Lessons and evidence from our LBB work suggest that human resource and talent leaders, organizations, communities, and youth benefit from applying some of the practices and tools that we discuss here. We were deeply affected by what one young African man who had been recruited to serve in the Lord's Resistance Army, a paramilitary group, said about the need for increased access to leadership development. Following an experience with CCL, he shared: "Where you come from, this leadership teaching may result in better management, better business practices. But here, here in Uganda this teaching has the ability to save lives. This region, these governments have been at war for many years. If they heard today what you were teaching us I believe we could end many of these conflicts. We could see an end to these wars" (Altman et al., 2010, p. 222).

Throughout our LBB journey, we have focused on increasing accessibility and creating scalable solutions to reach audiences that typically lack access to leadership development. We were guided in our thinking by such questions as: What would organizations, communities, and the world look like if more people had access to leadership development? How can organizations expand their leadership offerings to more employees? How do we help individuals and collectives develop these skills earlier in life for greater impact? How could organizations and communities come together to create positive impact from which all stakeholders would benefit? Our experience suggests more people could realize their talents and potential and live, lead, and work more effectively with others to develop a more just and peaceful world.

Through our LBB work, we have leveraged the research, knowledge, and experience generated throughout CCL, the broader field of leadership development, and our LBB community partners. All of these have informed the design and prototyping approach we've employed in developing our multilayered leadership solutions.

WHY FOCUS ON YOUNG PEOPLE?

Increasingly a wide range of evidence from research, experience, and evaluations is signaling the need to develop leaders earlier in life. For years, CCL faculty have passed on participant comments from our executive leadership development trainings exclaiming, "I wish I got this when I was younger." During our research work in India in 2006, our LBB team met with forty-three organizations and nearly two hundred individuals (young professionals and organizational and educational leaders) and learned about their rapidly growing business environment and the talent challenges such growth places on organizations. Developing talent was a key issue identified by those within corporations. We consistently heard how young professionals in India lacked the skills needed as they entered the workforce. The prevailing perspective that both young professionals and their employers voiced was that these skills needed to be acquired prior to entering the workforce. One corporate leader even went so far as to say, "Only 20 percent of the graduates [of universities] are employable" (Wright, Rego, & Rego, 2007, p. 2).

Further confirming what we were hearing in India, a report by the US-based National Association of Colleges and Employers (2012) reported that 80 percent of respondents in their research selected the demonstration of leadership skills as the top attribute employers hire for after filtering for grade point average. In the research study, Expanding the Leadership Equation—Developing Next-Generation Leaders, my colleague and I shared data collected from 462 survey respondents from all sectors of the economy, organizational levels, and age ranges that found over 95 percent of respondents believe leadership development should start by age twenty-one. In addition, the majority of respondents (84 percent) believe leadership development opportunities should be offered to all youth, and 90 percent feel it should be part of every student's educational experience (Van Velsor & Wright, 2012).

Secondary and postsecondary schools are also recognizing their roles in developing leadership skills for younger people. At Southern Methodist University's School of Engineering, the Hart Center for Engineering Leadership was created to help develop both the technical and soft skills of all undergraduate engineers and computer scientists to enable them to lead teams, solve tough problems, and make a difference in the world. In South Africa, the African Leadership Academy (ALA) was founded in 2004 to develop the next generation of African Leaders. ALA recruits young people fifteen to nineteen years old from across Africa who demonstrate initiative and have passion for their continent. At ALA students complete a rigorous, hands-on leadership education that couples rich practice opportunities, mentoring and coaching, and more. Ravenscroft School, a pre-K to 12th grade independent school in Raleigh, North Carolina, has launched the Lead from Here initiative to help all students develop as citizen leaders. This initiative is accelerating the school's ability to deliver on its mission: to nurture individual potential and prepare students to thrive in a complex and interdependent world.

While the need to develop leaders earlier is not a new concept, the need to formalize leadership development, begin it even earlier, and make it accessible to all young people is the new challenge and opportunity.

Need for Leadership Coaching

Leader development and coaching are interdependent. If young people need leadership coaching and employees in the work world need to hone their leadership capabilities, how do we connect these two developmental needs? This connection is what helped us develop our multilayered leadership solutions.

From young professionals entering the workforce, we often hear the hunger to be mentored, coached, and guided by those above and around them. While ideally the immediate managers of these young professionals could play the role of a coach, they often lack the skills themselves to do this task adequately. In India, we heard how many of these supervisors are young professionals themselves and still learning basic managerial skills. One young manager admitted that he was "not experienced to facilitate difficult situations in the office" and that "initially it was difficult to disassociate personal ambition and views from the situation at hand." Another young professional shared that young managers are often "prepared to manage the process but not people" and need to "learn how to communicate, how to get people to do their work, how to develop support, and convince/negotiate with people." The impact of this dearth of coaching capabilities within young managers was expressed by a comment from one senior executive who shared his biggest fear: that a young manager might effectively "kill" unidentified emerging talent and drive them out of the organization (Wright et al., 2006). These examples highlight two challenges: the need for those in supervisory roles to have better leadership and coaching capabilities and the importance of supporting young professionals when they transition into an organization.

Even younger audiences need coaching and mentoring too. While Big Brothers/Big Sisters and other mentoring programs that pair youth with more experienced adults have been around for quite some time, not all youth development and youth leadership development programs incorporate formal mentoring or coaching. This is a missed opportunity for extending a young person's learning; we were reminded of this during the creation of one of our early youth leadership development programs.

Early in LBB's journey, we connected with a local YMCA director of teen programs who recognized the value of leadership development for the summer camp counselors on his staff. These camp counselors ranged in age from their midteens to early twenties. Most had never experienced formal leadership training. Recognizing an opportunity to prototype in our backyard, we designed a half-day leadership development experience for these YMCA camp counselors.

The immediate feedback of our prototype proved positive and provided insight for refining the prototype and increasing our knowledge about how to develop a multilayered leadership solution. Collectively, the YMCA camp counselors shared that they learned leadership from the inside out. They gained awareness of their strengths and preferences and how these affected their ability to work, live, and lead with others. The development experience helped them learn how to work more effectively with others and begin to see themselves as leaders. The director of camp counselors was ecstatic about the powerful transformation he witnessed in his staff.

The camp counselors who participated blossomed in ways they had never before imagined. They had never grasped the concept of themselves as leaders prior to the program. Now they did, and the realization caused a foundational identity shift.

The director began seeing his team step up and take on more senior roles, welcome greater responsibility, and improve their problem-solving and decision-making skills. Anecdotes emerged about how their leadership experience and journey was helping them in school, both in secondary and postsecondary education. Many on the team believed that the program helped them provide concrete examples of their leadership during their college application and interview process.

One-time, stand-alone programs can create positive impact. Deeper impact, however, can be achieved when ongoing coaching and mentoring supplement the initial programming. In this example, the YMCA director provided the supplemental support once the initial program finished. Some of the impact we witnessed was the result of this director's skilled developmental coaching.

The impact the director had as a coach helped us see the benefit of developmental coaching for younger audiences. Coaching is consistently ranked as one of the most powerful parts of our executive programs and is critical in supporting the learning journey of participants. Coaching would now become a core component of our youth leadership programs as well.

CORE BUILDING BLOCKS OF A MULTILAYERED LEADERSHIP PROGRAM

Implementing a multilayered leadership program is a complex task requiring intentional development and engagement in creating a leadership learning culture. In such a culture, a community of support is foundational to assisting everyone on their leader development journey. Headroom, the time for reflection, questioning, and exploration, must be provided. This opportunity for meaning making, critical thinking, and practice weaves together to deepen participants' understanding of the concepts taught and to accelerate learning. With a multilayered leadership approach, leadership coaches and youth learn tools and models and explore leadership concepts together.

A leadership learning culture evolves when:

1. Developmental frameworks, philosophies, and pedagogies are consistently communicated and modeled.
2. Staff and leadership coaches are intentionally trained.
3. Curriculum centers on experiential learning.

Central to our work at CCL is grounding our programs in research-based models, pedagogy, and expertise of those versed in these practices. Our multilayered leadership solutions are no different. Our biggest challenge comes in preparing leadership coaches and partner community organizations' staff.

Leadership coaches and staff need to set the tone. Both play strategic roles. Staff generally facilitate program experiences and act as overall guides to leadership coaches and coachees. Leadership coaches become small group facilitators and are at the forefront of relationship management and engagement within multilayered leadership programs. Leadership coaches are an extension of the core staff team and should be seen as partners in creating a leadership learning culture. Both community staff and leadership coaches are required to attend a training that introduces everyone to foundational models, philosophies, and pedagogies. This consistent exposure establishes a base from which a leadership learning culture can flourish.

Developmental Frameworks, Philosophies, and Pedagogies

Creating a leadership learning culture requires everyone, staff and volunteers, to operate together. Max Klau points to the importance of having consistent leadership philosophies and models in "Exploring Youth Leadership in Theory and Practice" (2006). He explored two research questions while evaluating three youth leadership education programs: "What conceptions of leadership inform the work of youth leadership educators in the field today?" and "What pedagogical techniques are employed by programs to teach the mode of leadership they espouse?" Although the programs he observed are not representative of the entire field, one of the major findings is the confusion and mixed messages participants receive when staff, volunteers, and program designers are not aligned around governing models. Imagine one person promoting the belief that leaders are born or that leaders are extraverts while another professes that anyone can develop his or her leadership potential. Confusing messages like these can be corrected through intentional, explicit, and consistent use of core models, philosophies, and pedagogies.

In implementing our multilayered leadership programs, we have discovered what models serve us best in creating effective leadership coaches and a consistent leadership learning culture. The following questions are at the core of our models:

1. What is your leadership development philosophy?
2. What is your definition of leadership?
3. What is your learning and development model?

The answers to these questions are embedded in the following models:

- Leading self, leading with others, changing your world
- Direction, alignment, commitment
- Assessment, challenge, and support

These models are some of the building blocks of our multilayered leadership programs. Learning about these models and what makes a solid leadership learning culture can support developmental coaches in creating a more intentional culture at work, resulting in increased support for fellow staff, more effective teams, and achievement of results.

Youth Leadership Development Framework Knowing your own leadership philosophy as a coach, architect of a program, or leader of others can heavily influence the culture you desire to create. In our multilayered leadership programs, coaches learn about CCL's leadership philosophy, which serves them in their occupation or other areas of their life. For decades, CCL's research has supported the concept that everyone can learn and grow in their leadership potential.

The model our LBB team uses to communicate the philosophy that everyone can expand their leadership capacity is: Leading Self, Leading with Others, and Changing Your World (see figure 19.2).

This model is LBB's evolution of CCL's earlier version: Understand Self to Lead Self; Understand Others to Lead Others; and Understand Change to Lead Change (typically within an organization). While both models work well, we have discovered that the earlier version is too complex and the emphasis on leading others and leading change is too hierarchal and positional for young people. Leading Self, Leading with Others, and Changing Your World is simpler and more empowering for audiences today.

This model starts with Leading Self because CCL approaches leader development as an inside-out process in which one must first learn about self. Leading with Others focuses on the multiple challenges and opportunities that arise when working, living, and leading with other people. Changing Your World, with the emphasis on *your* instead of *the*, makes it more concrete. Sometimes when people hear the call to action of "change the world," they find the message overwhelming. Change *your* world enables people to define their desired scope.

Leading Self, Leading with Others, and Changing Your World is an interdependent model that is flexible and provides multiple entry points and opportunities for

Figure 19.2
Youth Leadership Development Framework

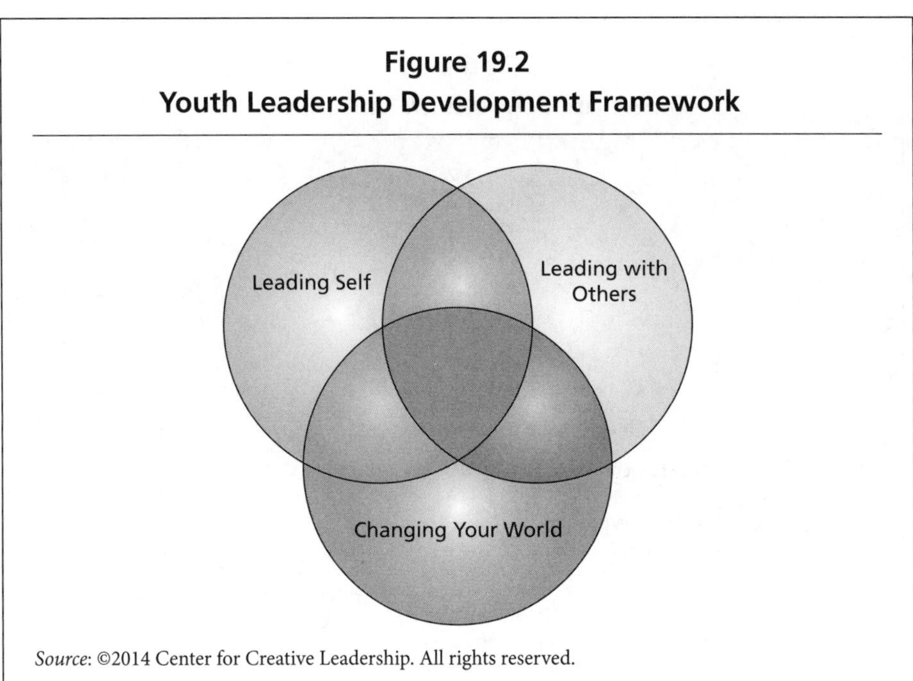

Source: ©2014 Center for Creative Leadership. All rights reserved.

learning within each intersection. For example, many people do not see themselves as leaders and thus might enter this model through the Changing Your World door because of having a service orientation. What often happens is that the service experience connects them to a cause and the need to learn how to work with and lead others to be more effective and have greater impact. The service experience of Changing Your World can also be an inside-out process connecting with Leading Self, as it provides the opportunity to assess what motivates one, what one values, and what skills one needs to improve in order to work better.

Building a collective mind-set around this model helps coaches learn how to communicate and support young people as they discover interests, passions, and skills they will need for the rest of their life. Evidence from our multilayered leadership solutions will show how learning how to facilitate this leadership philosophy with young people can support the application of this model within the work world.

Direction, Alignment, and Commitment At CCL, we believe the three outcomes of effective leadership are direction, alignment, and commitment (DAC; see figure 19.3). Setting direction is about clarifying and agreeing on the vision or

Figure 19.3
Direction, Alignment, Commitment

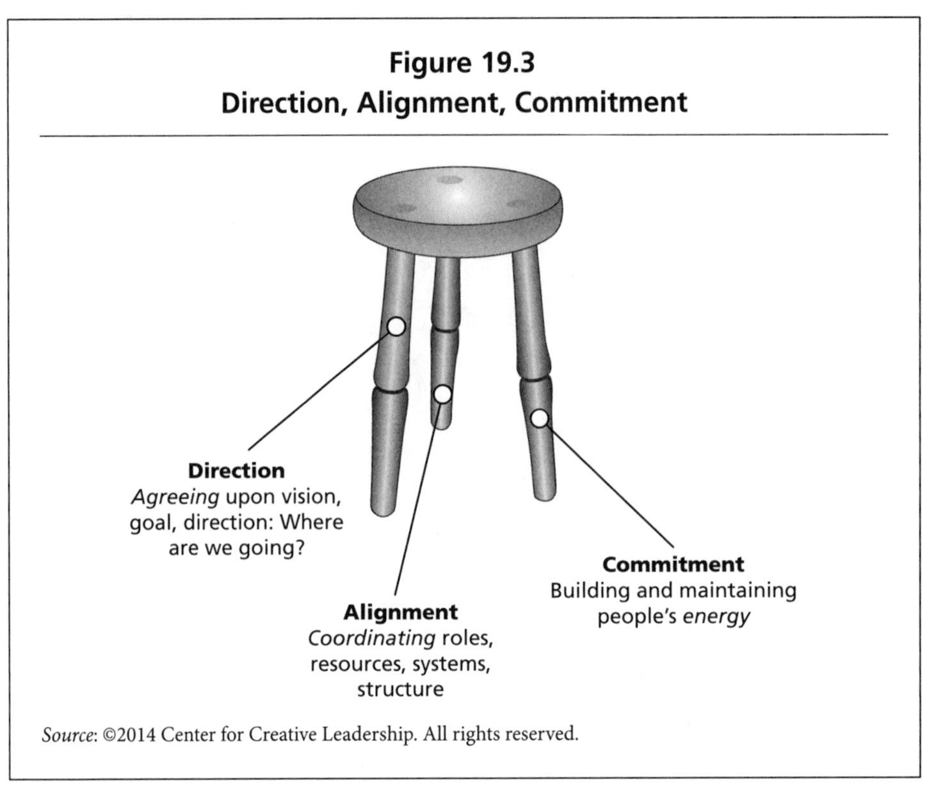
Direction
Agreeing upon vision, goal, direction: Where are we going?
Alignment
Coordinating roles, resources, systems, structure
Commitment
Building and maintaining people's *energy*

goal. Creating alignment is about coordinating all of the roles, resources, systems, and structures necessary to accomplish the direction. Building commitment is about engaging, motivating, and sustaining the energy, individually and collectively, to achieve the direction. This model has been well received globally and can apply to individuals or collectives in virtually any context. Coaches and youth alike find multiple opportunities in and out of the program to apply and practice this model.

For individuals, direction can involve setting a goal or creating a vision for the future. Achieving the goal requires aligning and coordinating all the disparate pieces that support the direction. These might include various resources: funding, transportation, and technology, for example. One aspect of aligning resources might be to create a plan or strategy to achieve the direction. Commitment, sustaining the energy, is the final ongoing work. What will keep one's energy up to stay on target, especially when obstacles emerge? This may change as one's emotions, interests, and work preferences shift when working and leading with others.

With groups, DAC operates fairly similarly to the individual case except that group members are required to step up and step back throughout the process. Direction, that is, clarifying a goal or direction, typically takes more time to establish together. Selecting a vision that doesn't resonate with a portion of the population can affect the group's commitment. Alignment takes on an entirely new level of complexity because it requires systems, resources, and role clarity to achieve. Commitment is more challenging as well because more people with varied values and motivations are involved.

The DAC model also interacts with the leadership philosophy: Leading Self, Leading with Others, and Changing Your World. Both DAC and this leadership philosophy promote the understanding that leadership is not solely positional: anyone can lead.

DAC is a powerful learning tool, and applying it can transform how people understand and enact leadership. Leaders we've worked with often share the model with others or use it as a diagnostic tool. Students at Ravenscroft School are now saying, "We're not DAC-ing!" This recognition is profound in helping their team to pause and reassess their leadership by asking:

- Are we clear on where we're going? (direction)
- Are we all clear on our plan and our role? What other resources might we need to achieve our direction? (alignment)
- How committed are we to our direction? (commitment)

DAC and the leadership philosophy are core models that create a common language. Creating a common language assists the development of a leadership learning culture.

RACSR: Relationship, Assessment, Challenge, Support, Results One of CCL's core developmental models refers to the components of an effective learning experience: assessment, challenge, and support (ACS). As noted elsewhere in this handbook and described in depth in the first volume of *The CCL Handbook of Coaching* (Ting & Scisco, 2006), CCL's coaching framework extends this model to include relationship as the container in which development occurs, with a focus on results (figure 19.4) as the intended outcome.

Relationships are foundational to the learning and development that occurs in coaching. Since the work of developing individuals as leaders is deeply personal, a high degree of trust is needed in a coaching relationship. Assessment is

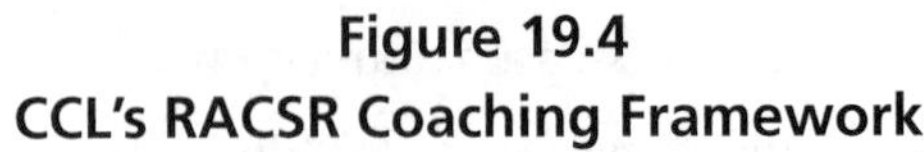

Figure 19.4
CCL's RACSR Coaching Framework

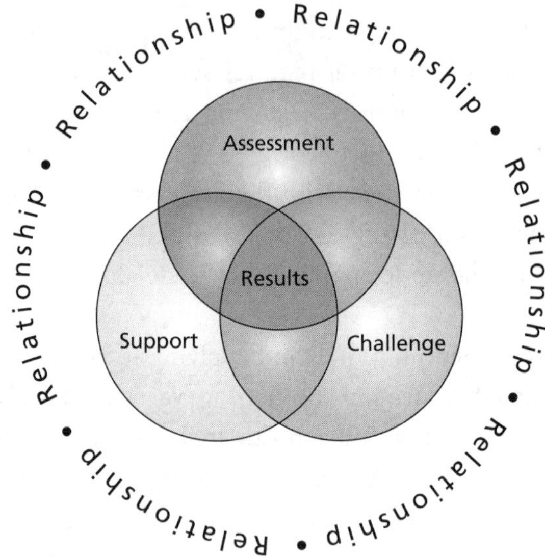

Source: ©2014 Center for Creative Leadership. All rights reserved.

the process of understanding who you are and where you are right now. CCL uses a variety of assessments, both formal instruments and informal meaning-making tools, including inquiry, observation and feedback, as well as other creative means to help individuals take a deeper look at themselves and what is needed to advance their personal leadership journey. Challenge involves being prompted to think and behave in new ways and being stretched through developmental assignments, development in place, or other opportunities to practice, learn, and grow.

Support is critical for the individual to achieve results. Support means locating and establishing the necessary assets, approaches, and internal reserves that will help someone successfully navigate and learn during this challenge. Coaches and mentors are often the most formal of support relationships, but colleagues, supervisors, friends, and family members can also have an impact on an individual's learning journey. A learning culture can also have an impact on one's engagement, trust, and results. Support is often an afterthought or a poorly planned dimension of development. When finding support, it is important to: reflect on the preferred ways for the coach and coachee to define and enact support, figure out ways to support oneself by creating enough time and space to reflect and prepare and developing mechanisms that help one cope with stress or unexpected situations, and find a variety of sources of support. Results, CCL believes, happen when assessment, challenge, and support are found in the right ratio and surrounded by a relationship of trust.

This model forms the basis for development to take place. Leadership coaches often cite this model as a resource that has served them in better supporting learning and development of others.

Experiential Learning

The ratio 70–20–10 speaks to the importance of learning by doing and is central to how our multilayered leadership solutions function. Using this as a guide, we plan for participants to spend about 70 percent of their time in experiential work: coaches in their role as leadership coaches and youth participating in internships, service experiences, or experiential activities. Another 20 percent of learning is intended to come from leadership coaching: youth from leadership coaches and leadership coaches from CCL staff. And the final 10 percent of time is spent in more formal training with lecture and sharing of models. This multilayered process provides a launch pad stemming from a common language, grounded in consistent models and built on relationships.

Because people often learn best by doing, we use experiential education pedagogy to guide our program design and process. The Association for Experiential Education (2014) offers the following definition of experiential learning: "Experiential education is a philosophy that informs many methodologies, in which educators purposefully engage with learners in direct experience and focused reflection in order to increase knowledge, develop skills, clarify values, and develop people's capacity to contribute to their communities" (para. 2).

In designing multilayered leadership programs, we strive for our program modules to be research based, with "teach" components being short and concrete while the bulk of time is spent on experiential activities that provide deeper learning and practice. As in sports, "practice, practice, practice" is the mantra. Multilayered leadership solutions strike a good balance between theory and practice.

Learning Curve

"What got you here will not get you there." This statement is commonly uttered around CCL to acknowledge the learning journey, including learning dips, one must traverse to achieve ongoing effectiveness and positive impact. The model we use to help people understand and embrace the learning curve is perhaps the one that connects all of the other elements because it is symbolic of the life and leadership journey we are all on (figure 19.5).

CCL's emphasis on learning as a vital capability of a leader comes from more than three decades of research and experience consistently demonstrating that everyone can learn and grow as a leader. This means everyone has leadership potential and through consistent exposure, practice, feedback, and reflection, individuals can learn to be more effective.

Carol Dweck's work has helped us connect and communicate how one's mind-set influences one's engagement in the learning journey. Dweck's work

Figure 19.5
Learning Curve

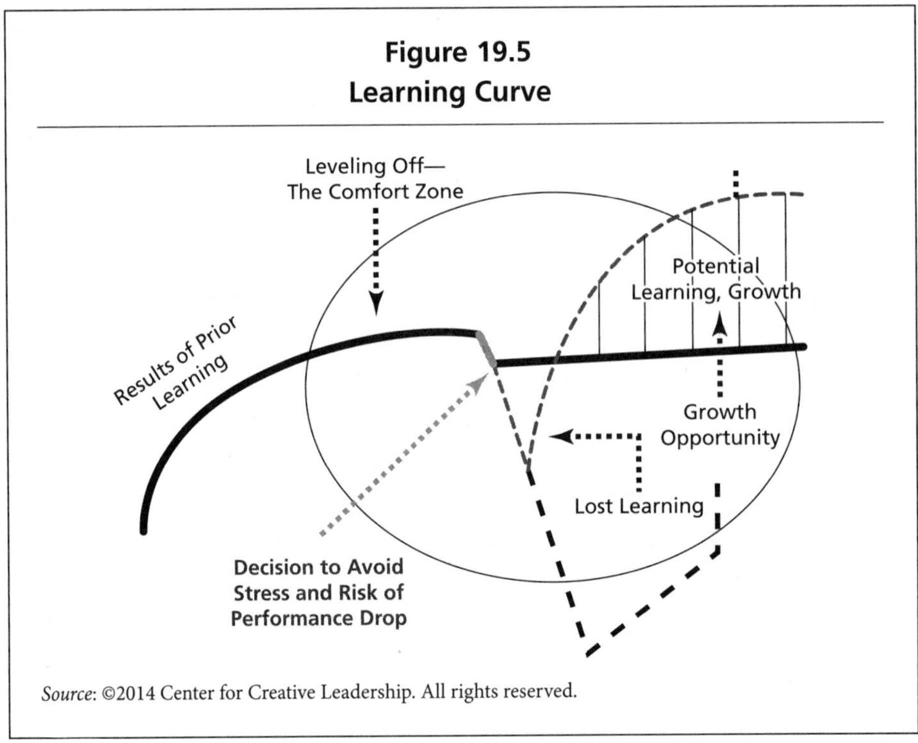

focuses on how mind-set—as growth or fixed—contributes to how one engages with challenge, effort, obstacles, criticism, feedback, and the success of others. In her work with students, she explains how using the language of "hard work" as opposed to being "smart" encouraged participants in her study to step up and take on a more difficult challenge as opposed to quitting or taking an easier challenge (Dweck, 2006). CCL's research connects with Dweck's in its emphasis on learning and feedback as important ongoing components to leader development.

Intentional Training of Leadership Coaches

One of the critical challenges we faced in developing multilayered leadership solutions is ramping up leadership coaches to the appropriate level. The leadership coaching role is perhaps the most important one in the program. Therefore, leadership coaches are required to attend a leadership coach training. From this initial training through to the conclusion of the overall initiative, our focus is on increasing the awareness, understanding, and application of foundational models, philosophies, and pedagogies so leadership coaches can effectively support the development of their coachees. Coaches learn the program models, including Leading Self, Leading with Others, Changing Your World; RACSR; and DAC as well as their underlying philosophy. CCL staff provide ongoing support through one-on-one feedback sessions, monthly facilitated leadership coaching calls, group meetings, guidebooks, and additional exposure and practice during regularly delivered programs. By the end of the year-long program, more than 77 percent of leadership coaches report that the program enhanced their effectiveness at work and in their community.

Impact of Culture on Learning and Development

Culture has an impact on learning and development. Whether in a corporation, nonprofit, school, community, family, or program, the culture—the way people interact, engage, and support each other—influences how individuals learn and develop. Creating the right culture begins with staff modeling the philosophy and pedagogy the program seeks to impart. We often hear, "You were modeling what you were teaching." This embodiment of the leadership philosophy, application of the models, and belief in what we do is what we seek to inspire in those who join the culture.

MULTILAYERED LEADERSHIP DEVELOPMENT PROGRAMS: EXAMPLES

Through the work of LBB, we have developed, piloted, and evaluated several multilayered leadership programs for young people. In this section, we provide an overview of two of the most robust of these: the Golden LEAF Scholars Leadership Program and the YMCA Leadership and Mentoring Program. Each focuses on different age groups, but both develop young people and enhance the coaching capabilities of those supporting them.

Golden LEAF Scholars Leadership Program

The Golden LEAF Scholars Leadership Program (GLSLP) runs annually and serves college students in a four-year freshman-to-senior-year design. This program serves students from rural, tobacco-dependent, economically distressed communities. Its goals are to:

1. Assist scholars in developing the skills they need for the work world
2. Help young people see rural North Carolina as a viable place to live, work, and raise their families
3. Increase the leadership capacity of rural North Carolina

Scholars This program is open to college students who have a four-year scholarship from the Golden LEAF Foundation (GLF) to attend a four-year postsecondary academic institution in North Carolina.[1] The three components of the program are leadership development training offered by the Center for Creative Leadership, a paid summer internship in a rural state community, and a leadership coaching component using coaches from rural North Carolina. In addition to the internships, all scholars conduct a summer leadership project that deepens their connection and network within a rural community.

The GLSLP runs from January through September, starting and ending with formal face-to-face leadership development programs. Participants, referred to as scholars since they must first have been awarded the scholarship from the GLF, enter in their freshman year of college. Each scholar is assigned a coach. Both scholars and coaches attend the January conference where they form a coaching group in which there are five scholars per coach. Each coach supports the scholars in a group coaching format during conferences and individually by phone from February to August. Coaching support is designed to help scholars set and keep their personal and professional goals, find and succeed in an internship, and forge connections with individuals who live in rural North Carolina.

Stipends provided to the scholars help them obtain and participate in internships by allowing them to explore their career interests without being limited by financial constraints. The stipend is also a financial asset to rural businesses, which can employ scholars as interns at no expense. Funds for the stipends and other program components are provided by the Golden LEAF Foundation, and CCL administers them.

Leadership Coaches A crucial aspect of the program is the role of the coach. Without the coach, the program could become a very segmented checklist of experiences: January retreat, internship, summer project, September retreat. However, in this program, the coach connects all programmatic components and developmental models. Their engagement with the program begins with a day-long training. They then begin their work with the scholars at the leadership conference in January. After this intensive beginning, the coach is responsible for providing monthly phone coaching to each scholar. The initial conference provides a foundation by creating a leadership learning culture among the coaches and the scholars. From this initial conference, coaches support scholars' ongoing learning and development over the eight-month leadership journey. They also improve their own leadership skills, alongside the students.

Evaluation A standard practice when CCL launches a new program and one of this magnitude is to include an evaluation plan that provides both formative data, allowing us to course-correct, and summative data to identify short-, medium-, and long-term impacts. Evaluation from the past four years demonstrates our effectiveness to date in achieving our goals with the GLSLP and provides evidence to key stakeholders that contributes to the sustainability of the program.

Data from the 2013 program year point to the significant impact the program is having on coaches' leadership effectiveness, work performance, and career goals. As shown in figure 19.6, 100 percent of coaches enhanced their own leadership through the program, 77 percent increased their effectiveness at work, and over 60 percent found the program helped them clarify and achieve career goals. These findings are consistent with the two previous program years (Stawiski, 2013).

Figure 19.6
Coaches' Perceptions of Program's Impact on Them

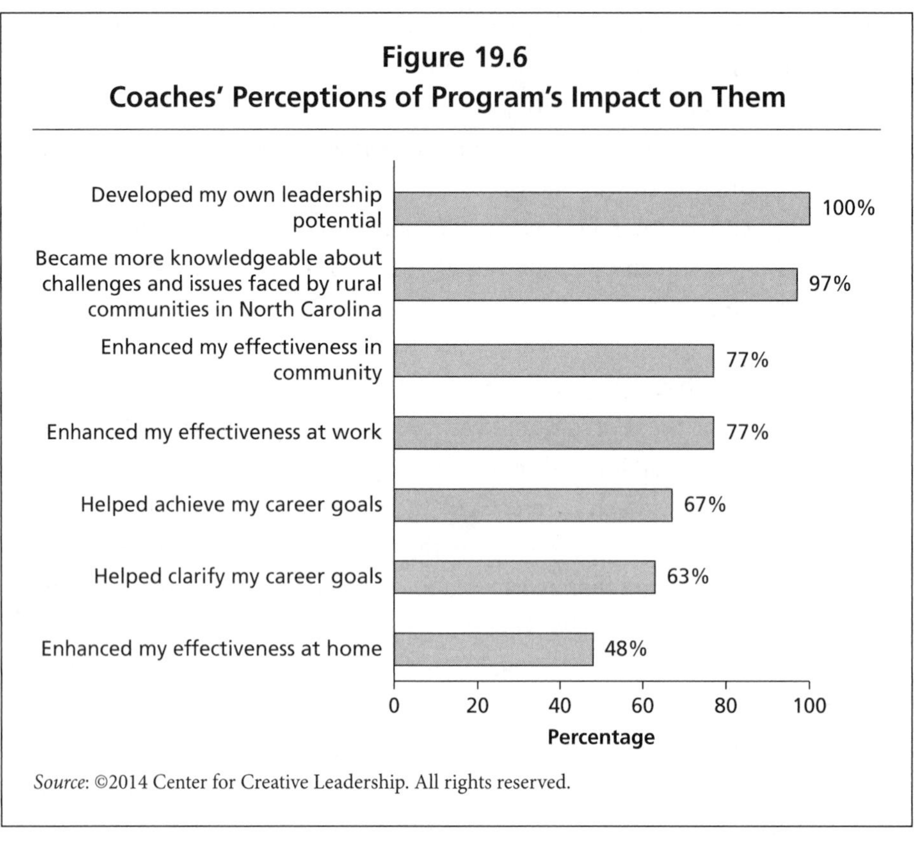

Open-ended comments also demonstrated the program's impact on coaches. As the following comments of Golden LEAF Scholars and leadership coaches (Stawiski, 2013) illustrate, many coaches gained valuable skills that were applicable to their work, home, and communities:

> "Professionally, the program has given me an opportunity to practice my leadership skills and develop my coaching philosophy."
>
> "Personally, I have enhanced my coaching/mentoring skills. Professionally, I have further developed my network of professionals and my contribution to my community."
>
> "I have been able to grow as a person at home with my son, work, and community. I use the facilitation techniques."
>
> "The program sustained my commitment to my community and fueled my 'spark,' reenergized I should say!"

> This program "definitely motivated me to increase my work efforts in rural NC. It helped open my eyes to the opportunities in entrepreneurship in these rural communities."

Focus group data revealed the importance of making intergenerational connections (between the coach and coachee), a challenge often identified by individuals in organizations. Across our multilayered leadership programs, we commonly hear a shift in perspective from concern to appreciation and hope among older generations in relation to younger ones. For instance, in the GLSLP, one leadership coach said he gained greater appreciation for college students and all they have to juggle. Another coach noted that an article she had recently read stated that if you do not have anyone under thirty years old on your contact list, you are in trouble. This coach was delighted and exclaimed, "Now I have five!"

This GLSLP program is creating powerful impact and is a model for how youth, coaches, organizations, and communities can benefit from multilayered leadership solutions. Now in its fourth year, the GLSLP serves more than three hundred college students and forty-five coaches annually. Our 2013 year-end evaluation found that scholars in all cohorts rated their leadership skills considerably higher than they were the previous year. Moreover, internship sites rated GLSLP scholars higher than their contemporaries on leadership attributes and professionalism (Stawiski, 2013). In the 2013 program year, 217 scholars worked approximately 49,000 hours, contributing almost $950,000 to 150 businesses and organizations across rural North Carolina.

Already there is much evidence for the benefits that such programs can have on all of the stakeholders: students, adult coaches, employers, and society at large. We're cautiously optimistic that this leadership and coaching program will increase the leadership capacity in rural North Carolina, which can address some of the social and economic challenges that exist.

YMCA Leadership and Mentoring Program

> The story I have about the leadership program is that in school I was making bad grades . . . The leadership program helped me see what I needed to do and helped me mature in multiple areas—values, and who I am, what I need to listen to and what I don't need to listen to . . . Mentors here at the leadership program . . . gave me a visual for what I want to be when I grow up—you know, I want to help people . . . After attending these sessions, my image of a leader has

completely changed because it has informed me that a leader can come from anywhere, at any time, and can look any way. So that's changed a lot since I have started. (Center for Creative Leadership, 2011)

The YMCA Leadership and Mentoring Program (LAMP)[2] is nested within the YMCA Black and Latino Achievers program at the Hayes-Taylor YMCA in Greensboro, North Carolina. The program is a national program model adopted and adapted by local YMCAs that focuses on college readiness for young people aged thirteen to eighteen. At the Hayes-Taylor YMCA, existing programming involved SAT preparation, college tours, community service, and skill-based programming occurring once a month. Our goal was to enhance this core programming with a second monthly gathering for LAMP.

LAMP is a high-quality, research-based leadership development curriculum for youth (figure 19.7). Youth develop the life and leadership skills that will aid

Figure 19.7
LAMP

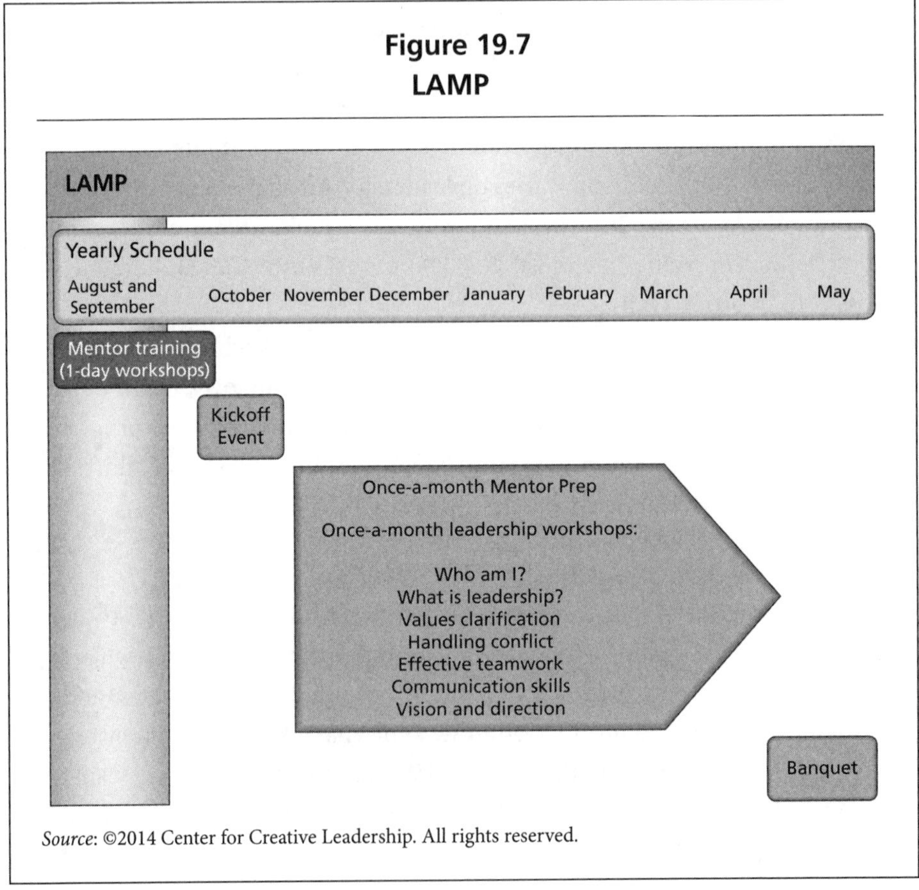

Source:

them in school, life, and future careers. It is not a cohort-based model: students and mentors can join the program at the start of each academic year. Each fall starts with a half-day experiential learning retreat to promote relationships and teach leadership coaches the RACSR model. Once a month for seven months, there is a workshop lasting two and a half hours for students and leadership coaches focusing on leadership-related activities done in small groups called "family groups." There is no requirement of prior involvement in the program; participants can choose to remain in the program for the full four-year, twenty-eight-workshop design.

Although leadership coaches have their own training prior to the start of every year, they experience the LAMP curriculum simultaneously with the youth. Coaches also prepare each month through a mentor preparation session. This double dose for leadership coaches, as active participants and small group facilitators, reinforces the leadership lessons and provides multiple opportunities for leaders to practice and model what they are learning.

The Curriculum The LAMP curriculum is organized around seven themes and is designed as a four-year program, supporting youth as they learn and grow through their high school years. The seven themes are summarized in table 19.1.

Developmental Coaching in LAMP Mentoring plays a key role in this program and is done in the family groups, typically four to six students with one adult mentor and one college student mentor. We also use family groups to provide an extra measure of safety to participants and mentors alike. Many youth-serving organizations have rules against youth being mentored one-on-one or meeting off-site, so this group mentoring model helps ensure that risk management controls are in place. If mentors want more interaction with Achievers outside the program, they can find opportunities to volunteer for additional activities at the YMCA.

We have found the combination of younger and older mentors to be especially helpful to youth because they are exposed to different mentoring styles and different life stages. Having college students as role models provides high school–aged youth with information and motivation for a postsecondary education.

While mentors give a significant amount of time and knowledge to the Achievers, they also reap the benefits of this investment both personally and professionally. Ninety-two percent of mentors report increasing their ability

Table 19.1
LAMP Curriculum

Theme	Green Series	Orange Series	Blue Series	Purple Series
Who Am I	Who Am I and How Do I Be My Best Self	Stress and Self Talk	What Is Personality	Who Am I
What Is Leadership	What Is Leadership	Leadership Styles	Time Management	What Is Authentic Leadership
Values Clarification	Values in Action	Values Proposition	Recognizing Others' Values	Values & Actions: True to You
Handling Conflict	Caution in Conflict	Conflict	Conflict Conversations	Handling Hot Button Conflicts
Communication Skills	Nonverbal Communication	Communication Improve	Public Speaking	Communications
Effective Teamwork	How Can I Be an Effective Team Member	We're All in This Together	Team Formation	How Does Leadership Exist in Teams
Vision and Direction	Changing the Story in My Community	Using SMART Goals to Achieve Your Vision	Connecting Inspiration and Vision	How Do I Get to Where I Want to Go

Source: ©2014 Center for Creative Leadership. All rights reserved.

to promote a climate of collaboration when working with others, 83 percent report improved ability to facilitate learning, and a similar proportion report a greater ability to improve group engagement (78 percent) and group effectiveness (79 percent) (Miller et al., in press). These skills are in high demand in the work world.

A CALL TO ACTION

What would the world look like if more corporations or organizations partnered with communities to implement multilayered leadership solutions? I believe employees would be more effective at work, at home, in their community, and with friends. I believe young people would embody the skills employers are seeking and would be empowered to create a more intentional life and enact more positive impact in the world. I believe communities would become stronger as the overall leadership capacity of its young people, employees, citizens, and organizations expands.

We have learned a great deal through prototyping these programs with our gracious community partners. Two of the most compelling lessons are:

1. Leadership coaching develops both the coachee and the coach.
2. Leadership coaching shifts the perspective of cross-generational interactions.

Across the world, in India at the Welingkar Institute of Management Development and Research (WE School) and the Institute for Future Education, Entrepreneurship and Leadership (iFEEL), CCL has trained more than five hundred business students, developed more than fifty faculty trainers/mentors, and completed some one hundred team projects. Eighty percent of faculty from the WE School and iFEEL report increasing mentoring skills and all of the faculty report an increase in their facilitation skills.

Youth in these programs regularly reflect on improving their ability to lead with others as the result of increased awareness of personal preferences and values; they also learn about what motivates others. These changes facilitate a leader-identity shift that increases a young person's confidence to lead his or her life and enact positive change.

From our programs, we have heard about cross-generational empathy increasing between parents and children, community members, teachers, and students. As one leadership coach said, empathy between groups smoothes the road:

> Many people my age think it's impossible to relate to the younger generation, but if you sit down and talk with them, you realize that we share many of the same problems. The leadership skills taught by CCL are applicable to anyone. Being able to interact with a group of young people and discover that we face similar issues, such as conflict resolution and committing to goals, showed them that being a leader is a continuous process that doesn't end once you become a successful adult. (Center for Creative Leadership and Rotary District 7680, 2011)

At the Milton Hershey School, a private boarding school in Hershey, Pennsylvania, that serves children in financial and social need, a version of a multilayered leadership program is being implemented within the Dearden Leadership Academy. After only two years, evidence is pointing to a reduction in discipline issues within student "homes," groups of eight to twelve students living together with "house parents," married couples who serve as mentors and guides for the children. A home life director from the administration worked with a high school girl to prepare for a discussion with her house parents using a CCL feedback model. Following this leadership coaching moment, the girl found time to deliver her feedback. The result was a transformed relationship with her house parents.

Innovative multilayered leadership solutions offer advantages over traditional coaching and mentoring programs. Struggles typically identified in these mentoring/coaching programs include recruiting and retaining volunteers, bridging the relationship divide, and having enough volunteers to match with coachees. Many of these issues can be addressed by borrowing elements of a multilayered leadership solution: leadership content serving as the experiential and relational bridge between coach and coachee; leadership coaching skill development supporting the personal and professional growth of the leadership coach, which brings added value to the volunteer role and can be leveraged to recruit and retain volunteers; and group mentoring that can reach more young people. All of these benefits can help unleash untapped leadership potential.

At CCL, we believe there are exciting applications for scaling this work and are fascinated with the implications of corporations and community organizations partnering to implement multilayered leadership programs. In this model, all coaches would be from the same organization and would learn the same leadership language throughout the leadership development process and coaching process. Working with young people would foster cross-generational understanding, and working with the community could benefit the image of an organization. We anticipate that the gains in leadership culture from multilayered leadership solutions could be monumental.

A corporate-community partnership can start with what we call listening tours, a period of time in which information and ideas are gathered. Robert Greenleaf, in his book *Servant Leadership* (2002), described the listening approach taken by a leader assuming the lead position in a large, challenging public institution. The new leader spent three months listening to the challenges and realities in his organization. From something as seemingly simple as listening, "this able man learned and received the insights needed to set the right course" (p. 30).

The listening tour CCL began in 2006 provided the early insights into what would inform our multilayered leadership solutions approach and what now could point to the importance of corporate-community partnerships. I recall one of my early inspirations. It came when I was sitting outside on a restaurant patio in Bangalore, India. I felt as if I were in an intellectual bubble, stimulated by a blend of spicy food, the buzz of a hustling and bustling entrepreneurial city, and a captivating conversation. The young manager I dined with related that he had taken it upon himself to provide his team with the opportunity to leave the oasis of his organization and do something inspiring in the community. This idea resulted in increased employee engagement, a more connected team, and increased productivity. And it didn't stop there. Like a seed of hope spreading, other teams learned of the experience and joined. More energy spread across the organization, boosting company morale and impact further. This simple idea that cost relatively little brought significant personal and professional rewards.

For me, this conversation crystallized years of contemplation about how organizations and communities could be better interdependent partners in addressing multiple challenges while producing beneficial results for all stakeholders. If one individual in one corporation could create such positive impact, how could something similar be built, replicated, and scaled for even greater impact?

CONCLUSION

What might be possible in your community? How could corporations and community organizations come together to develop the right leadership solution for it? What might your organization and community look like after implementing something together? What might be possible if more people in the world had access to leadership and coaching solutions? Go and lead now. Listen and then develop a solution that will serve individuals and collectives in your community, empowering all people to create a more just and peaceful world.

NOTES

1. The Golden LEAF foundation was established as a nonprofit organization in 1999 under the 1999 Master Tobacco Settlement to provide assistance to

economically affected or tobacco-dependent regions of North Carolina. The Golden LEAF Foundation funds the GLSLP.

2. Funding for the first two years of this program came from the YMCA of Greensboro and was later supplemented by a four-year federal grant that CCL was awarded: FY 09 Recovery Act Local Youth Mentoring Initiative of the Office of Juvenile Justice and Delinquency Prevention, Department of Justice (award 2009-SC-B9–0015). We are grateful for the support of both of these organizations and for the work and dedication of the staff at the Greensboro Y.

REFERENCES

Abbott, G., Gilbert, K., & Rosinski, P. (2013). Cross-cultural working in coaching and mentoring. In J. Passmore, D. B. Peterson, & T. Freire (Eds.), *The Wiley-Blackwell handbook of the psychology of coaching and mentoring* (pp. 483–500). Chichester, UK: Wiley.

Abbott, G. N., Stening, B. W., Atkins, P.W.B., & Grant, A. M. (2006). Coaching expatriate managers for success: Adding value beyond training and mentoring. *Asia Pacific Journal of Human Resources, 44*(3), 295–317. http://www.researchgate.net/publication/234377643_Coaching_Expatriate_Managers_for_Success_Adding_Value_Beyond_Training_and_Mentoring

Abel, A. L. (2011). *It's about trust and training: Examining your organization's internal coaching practice.* New York, NY: The Conference Board.

Abel, A. L., & Nair, S. (2012). *Executive coaching survey: 2012 edition.* New York, NY: The Conference Board.

Abel, A. L., Ray, R. L., & Roi, R. (2013). *Strategic leadership development: Global trends and approaches.* New York, NY: The Conference Board.

Abrams, D., & Hogg, M. A. (2004). Metatheory: Lessons from social identity research. *Personality and Social Psychology Review, 8*(2), 98–106.

Agarwal, R., Angst, C. M., & Magni, M. (2009). The performance effects of coaching: A multilevel analysis using hierarchical linear modeling. *International Journal of Human Resource Management, 20,* 2110–2134.

Alderfer, C. (1987). An intergroup perspective on group dynamics. In J. W. Lorsch (Ed.), *Handbook of organizational behavior* (pp. 190–222). Englewood Cliffs, NJ: Prentice Hall.

Algoe, S. B., & Fredrickson, B. L. (2011). Emotional fitness and the movement of affective science from lab to field. *American Psychologist*, *66*(1), 35–42.

Ali, Y., Lewis, N., & McAdams, C. K. (2010). Case study: Building an internal coaching capacity: The American Cancer Society coach cadre model. *Industrial and Commercial Training*, *42*(5), 240–246.

Allen, T. D. (2003). Mentoring others: A dispositional and motivational approach. *Journal of Vocational Behavior*, *62*, 134–154.

Allen, T. D. (2004). Protégé selection by mentors: Contributing individual and organizational factors. *Journal of Vocational Behavior*, *65*, 469–483.

Allen, T. D. (2007). Mentoring relationships from the perspective of the mentor. In B. R. Ragins & K. E. Kram (Eds.), *The handbook of mentoring at work: Theory, research and practice* (pp. 123–147). Thousand Oaks, CA: Sage.

Allen, T. D., Day, R., & Lentz, E. (2005). The role of interpersonal comfort in mentoring relationships. *Journal of Career Development*, *31*(3), 155–169.

Allen, T. D., & Eby, L. T. (2003). Relationship effectiveness for mentors: Factors associated with learning and quality. *Journal of Management*, *29*, 469–486.

Allen, T. D., Eby, L. T., & Lentz, E. (2006a). Mentorship behaviors and mentorship quality associated with formal mentoring programs: Closing the gap between research and practice. *Journal of Applied Psychology*, *91*, 567–578.

Allen, T. D., Eby, L. T., & Lentz, E. (2006b). The relationship between formal mentoring program characteristics and perceived program effectiveness. *Personnel Psychology*, *59*, 125–153.

Allen, T. D., Eby, L. T., Poteet, M. L., Lentz, E., & Lima, L. (2004). Career benefits associated with mentoring for protégés: A meta-analysis. *Journal of Applied Psychology*, *89*, 127–136.

Allen, T. D., Finkelstein, L. M., & Poteet, M. L. (2009). *Designing workplace mentoring programs: An evidence-based approach*. Malden, MA: Wiley.

Allen, T. D., Lentz, E., & Day, R. (2006). Career success outcomes associated with mentoring others: A comparison of mentors and nonmentors. *Journal of Career Development*, *32*, 272–285.

Allen, T. D., Poteet, M. L., & Burroughs, S. M. (1997). The mentor's perspective: A qualitative inquiry and future research agenda. *Journal of Vocational Behavior*, *51*, 70–89.

Allen, T. D., Poteet, M. L., & Russell, J. (2000). Protégé selection by mentors: What makes the difference? *Journal of Organizational Behavior*, *21*, 271–282.

Allen, T. D., Poteet, M. L., Russell, J., & Dobbins, G. H. (1997). A field study of factors related to supervisors' willingness to mentor others. *Journal of Vocational Behavior, 50,* 1–22.

Allen, T. D., Russell, J.E.A., & Maetzke, S. B. (1997). Formal peer mentoring: Factors related to protégés' satisfaction and willingness to mentor others. *Group and Organization Management, 22,* 488–507.

Allio, R. J. (2005). Informed viewpoint article: Leadership development: Teaching versus learning. *Management Decision, 43* (7–8), 1071–1077.

Altman, D., Rego, L., & Harrison III, S. (2010). Democratizing leader development. In C. McCauley, E. Van Velsor, & M. Ruderman (Eds.), *The Center for Creative Leadership handbook of leadership development* (3rd ed., pp. 220–250). San Francisco, CA: Jossey-Bass.

American Management Association/Institute for Corporate Productivity. (2008). *Coaching: A global study of successful practices: Current trends and future possibilities, 2008–2018.* Retrieved from http://www.opm.gov/WIKI/uploads/docs/Wiki/OPM/training/i4cp-coaching.pdf

Ancona, D. G. (1990). Outward bound: Strategies for team survival in the organization. *Academy of Management Journal, 33*(2), 334–365.

Anderson, M. C., Frankovelgia, C., & Hernez-Broome, G. (2009). Business leaders reflect on coaching cultures. *Leadership in Action, 28*(6), 20–22.

Argyris, C. (1995). *On organizational learning*. Cambridge, MA: Blackwell.

Argyris, C., Putnam, R., & Smith, D. (1985). *Action science: Concepts, methods, and skills for research and intervention.* San Francisco, CA: Jossey-Bass.

Argyris, C., & Schön, D. (1978). *Organizational learning.* London: Addison-Wesley.

Aryee, S., Chay, Y. W., & Chew, J. (1996). The motivation to mentor among managerial employees. *Group and Organization Management, 21,* 261–277.

Association for Experiential Education. (2014). *What is experiential education?* Retrieved from http://www.aee.org/whatIsEE

Atwater, L. E., Waldman, D. A., & Brett, J. F. (2002). Understanding and optimising multisource feedback. *Human Resource Management, 41*(2), 193–208.

Baek-Kyoo, B. J., Sushko, J. S., & McLean, G. N. (2012). Multiple faces of coaching: Manager-as-coach, executive coaching, and formal mentoring. *Organization Development Journal, 30*(1), 19–38.

Battley, S. (2007). Executive coaching myths. *Leader to Leader, 44,* 20–25.

Baugh, S. G., & Fagenson-Eland, E. A. (2007). Formal mentoring programs: A "poor cousin" to informal relationships? In B. R. Ragins & K. E. Kram (Eds.),

The handbook of mentoring at work: Theory, research and practice (pp. 249–271). Thousand Oaks, CA: Sage.

Baugh, S. G., Lankau, M. J., & Scandura, T. A. (1996). An investigation of the effects of protégé gender on responses to mentoring. *Journal of Vocational Behavior, 49*, 309–323.

Belbin, R. M. (1981). *Management teams: Why they succeed or fail.* Oxford, UK: Butterworth-Heinemann.

Bennett, J. L., & Bush, M. W. (2014). *Coaching for change.* New York, NY: Routledge.

Bennett, J. M. (2014). Intercultural competence: Vital perspectives for diversity and inclusion. In B. Ferdman & B. Deane (Eds.), *Diversity at work: The practice of inclusion* (pp. 155–176). San Francisco, CA: Jossey-Bass.

Bennett, M. J. (1993). Cultural marginality: Identity issues in intercultural training. In R. M. Paige (Ed.), *Education for the intercultural experience* (pp. 109–136). Yarmouth, ME: Intercultural Press.

Berke, D., Kossler, M. E., & Wakefield, M. (2008). *Developing leadership talent.* San Francisco, CA: Pfeiffer and Center for Creative Leadership.

Betof, E., & Betof, N. (2010). *Just promoted! A 12 month road map for success in your new leadership role.* New York, NY: McGraw-Hill.

Bhasin, M. K., Dusek, J. A., Chang, B.-H., Joseph, M. G., Denninger, J. W., Fricchione, G. L., & Libermann, T. A. (2013). Relaxation response induces temporal transcriptome changes in energy metabolism, insulin secretion and inflammatory pathways, *PLoS ONE 8*(5): e62817. http://www.plosone.org/article/info%3Adoi%2F10.1371%2Fjournal.pone.0062817

Bird, A., Mendenhall, M., Stevens, M. J., & Oddou, G. (2010). Defining the content domain of intercultural competence for global leaders. *Journal of Managerial Psychology, 25*(8), 810–828. http://www.emeraldinsight.com/doi/abs/10.1108/02683941011089107

Bird, A., Oikelome, F., & Amayah, A. T. (2013). *Global leadership: Clarity around concepts and complications in practice symposium.* International Leadership Association, Montreal, Canada.

Bird, A., & Osland, J. (2004). Global competencies: An introduction. In H. Lane, M. Maznevski, M. Mendenhall, & J. McNett (Eds.), *Handbook of global management* (pp. 57–80). Oxford: Blackwell.

Blake-Beard, S. D., O'Neill, R. M., & McGowan, E. M. (2007). Blind dates? The importance of matching in successful formal mentoring relationships. In

B. R. Ragins & K. E. Kram (Eds.), *The handbook of mentoring at work: Theory, research and practice* (pp. 617–632). Thousand Oaks, CA: Sage.

Blakey, J., & Day, I. (2012). *Challenging coaching: Going beyond traditional coaching to face the facts.* New York, NY: Nicholas Brealey.

Booysen, L.A.E. (1999). Male and female managers: Gender influences on South African managers in retail banking. *South African Journal of Labour Relations, 23*(2/3), 25–35.

Booysen, L.A.E. (2007). Societal power shifts and changing social identities in South Africa: Workplace implications. *Southern African Journal of Economic and Management Sciences, 10*(1), 1–20.

Booysen, L.A.E. (2014). The development of inclusive leadership practice and processes. In B. Ferdman & B. Deane (Eds.), *Diversity at work: The practice of inclusion* (pp. 296–329). San Francisco, CA: Jossey-Bass.

Booysen, L.A.E., & Nkomo, S. M. (2007). The tea incident: Racial division at Insurance Incorporated—a teaching case. *International Journal on Diversity in Organisations, Communities and Nations, 7*(5), 97–106.

Bornman, E. (1999). Predictors of ethnic identification in a transitionary South Africa. *South African Journal of Psychology, 29*(2), 62–72.

Bozionelos, N. (2004). Mentoring provided: Relation to mentor's career success, personality, and mentoring received. *Journal of Vocational Behavior, 64*, 24–46.

Bozionelos, N. (2006). Mentoring and expressive network resources: Their relationship with career success and emotional exhaustion among Hellenes employees involved in emotion work. *International Journal of Human Resource Management, 17*, 362–378.

Bozionelos, N., Bozionelos, G., Kostopoulos, K., & Polychroniou, P. (2011). How providing mentoring relates to career success and organizational commitment: A study in the general managerial population. *Career Development International, 16*, 446–468.

Braddick, C. (2010). *More process, less insight? Survey report: Trends in executive coach selection.* London: Graham Braddick Partnership. Retrieved from http://www.carolbraddick.com/pdf/MoreProcess_LessInsight_Oct2010.pdf

Brashear, T. G., Bellenger, D. N., Boles, J. S., & Barksdale, H. C., Jr. (2006). An exploratory study of the relative effectiveness of different types of sales force mentors. *Journal of Personal Selling and Sales Management, 26*(1), 7–18.

Brewer, M. B. (2012). Optimal distinctiveness theory: Its history and development. In P.A.M. Van Lange, A. W. Kruglanski, & E. T. Higgins (Eds.), *Handbook of theories of social psychologies* (pp. 81–98). Thousand Oaks, CA: Sage.

Bridges, W. (1986). Managing organizational transitions. *Organizational Dynamics, 15*(1), 24–33.

Brodbeck, F. C., Ruderman, M. N., Glover, S., Eckert, R., Hannum, K. M., Braddy, P. W., & Gentry, W. A. (2012). *Global6 report*. Greensboro, NC: Center for Creative Leadership.

Bryant, A. (2014, April 20). Michelle Peluso of Gilt Groupe: I don't need an ivory tower (or an office). *New York Times*. Retrieved from http://www.nytimes.com/2014/04/20/business/michelle-peluso-of-gilt-groupe-i-dont-need-an-ivory-tower-or-an-office.html?_r=0

Bryant, S. E. (2005). The impact of peer mentoring on organizational knowledge creation and sharing: An empirical study in a software firm. *Group and Organization Management, 30*, 319–338.

Bunker, K., & Wakefield, M. (2005). *Leading with authenticity in times of transition*. Greensboro, NC: Center for Creative Leadership.

Burke, R. J., & McKeen, C. A. (1989). Developing formal mentoring programs in organizations. *Business Quarterly, 53*(3), 76–79.

Byrne, J. C., & Rees, R. T. (2006). *The successful leadership development program: How to build it and how to keep it going*. San Francisco, CA: Jossey-Bass.

Cameron, K., & Quinn, R. (1999). *Diagnosing and changing organizational culture*. Boston, MA: Addison-Wesley.

Campbell, D. P. (1991). *Manual for the Campbell Leadership Index [CLI]*. Minneapolis, MN: National Computer Systems.

Campbell, D. P., & Hyne, S. A. (1995). *Manual for the Campbell Organizational Survey* (2nd ed.). Minneapolis, MN: National Computer Systems.

Campbell, M., & Smith. R. (2010). *High potential talent: A view from inside the leadership pipeline (White Paper)*. Greensboro, NC: Center for Creative Leadership.

Cannon-Bowers, J. A., Salas, E., & Converse, S. A. (1993). Shared mental models in expert team decision making. In N. J. Castellan (Ed.), *Individual and group decision making* (pp. 221–246). Hillsdale, NJ: Erlbaum.

Caplan, R. D. (1987). Person-environment fit theory and organizations: Commensurate dimensions, time perspectives, and mechanisms. *Journal of Vocational Behavior, 31*(3), 248–267.

Carson, M. A., Shanock, L. R., Heggestad, E. D., Andrew, A. M., Pugh, S. D., & Walter, M. (2012). The relationship between dysfunctional interpersonal tendencies, derailment potential behavior, and turnover. *Journal of Business and*

Psychology, 27(3), 291–304. http://link.springer.com/article/10.1007%2Fs10869-011-9239-0#page-1

Carter, D. (2008, May). Diversity in European coaching. *Training Journal,* 6–7.

Carver, B. N. (2011). The hows and whys of groups mentoring. *Industrial and Commercial Training, 43*(1), 49–52.

Catalyst. (1993). *Mentoring: A guide to corporate programs and practices.* New York, NY: Catalyst.

Catalyst. (2011). *The bottom line: Corporate performance and women's representation on boards (2004–2008).* New York, NY: Catalyst.

Center for Creative Leadership. (2008). *Driving performance: Why leadership development matters in difficult times* (White paper). Retrieved from http://www.ccl.org/leadership/pdf/landing/DrivingPerformance.pdf

Center for Creative Leadership. (2009). *Coaching Effectiveness Indicator.* Greensboro, NC: Author.

Center for Creative Leadership. (2011). *The YMCA black and Latino achievers leadership and mentoring program* (Flyer). Greensboro, NC: Author.

Center for Creative Leadership. (2013). *Leadership Beyond Boundaries (LBB).* Retrieved from http://www.ccl.org/Leadership/research/gvol.aspx

Center for Creative Leadership and ETR Services. (2013). *Golden Leaf Foundation: Scholars leadership program: 2013 Final evaluation report.* Greensboro, NC: CCL Evaluation Center and ETR Services.

Center for Creative Leadership and Rotary District 7680. (2011). *Rotary seminar for tomorrow's leaders* [Flyer]. Greensboro, NC: Author.

Chandler, D. E., Kram, K. E., & Yip, J. (2011). Mentoring at work: New questions, methodologies, and theoretical perspectives. *Academy of Management Annals, 5*(1), 519–570.

Chao, G. T., Walz, P. M., & Gardner, P. D. (1992). Formal and informal mentorships: A comparison on mentoring functions and contrast with nonmentored counterparts. *Personnel Psychology, 45,* 619–636.

Charan, R., Drotter, S., & Noel, J. (2011). *The leadership pipeline: How to build the leadership powered company.* San Francisco, CA: Jossey-Bass.

Chatman, J., & Jehn, K. (1994). Assessing the relationship between industry characteristics and organizational culture: How different can you be? *Academy of Management Journal, 37*(3), 522–553.

Chhokar, J. S., Brodbeck, F. C., & House, R. J. (2007). *Culture and leadership across the world: The GLOBE book of in-depth studies of 25 societies*. Mahwah, NJ: Erlbaum.

Chun, J. U., Sosik, J. J., & Yun, N. Y. (2012). A longitudinal study of mentor and protégé outcomes in formal mentoring relationships. *Journal of Organizational Behavior, 33*, 1071–1094.

Cilliers, F., & Smith, B. (2006). A systems psychodynamic interpretation to South African diversity dynamics: A comparative study. *South African Journal of Labour Relations, 30*(2), 5–18.

Clutterbuck, D. (2007). An international perspective on mentoring. In B. R. Ragins & K. E. Kram (Eds.), *The handbook of mentoring at work: Theory, research and practice* (pp. 633–655). Thousand Oaks, CA: Sage.

Coaching the Global Village. (2013). *The reconstruct program*. Retrieved from http://coachingtheglobalvillage.org/the-reconstruct-program/

Coffman, C. W. (2000, October 9). Is your company bleeding talent? *Gallup Business Journal*. Retrieved from http://businessjournal.gallup.com/content/292/your-company-bleeding-talent.aspx

Colquitt, J. A., LePine, J. A., & Noe, R. A. (2000). Toward an integrative theory of training motivation: A meta-analytic path analysis of 20 years of research. *Journal of Applied Psychology, 85*, 678–707.

Cooperrider, D. L., & Srivastva, S. (1987). Appreciative inquiry in organizational life. In R. W. Woodman & W. A. Pasmore (Eds.), *Research in organizational change and development* (Vol. 1, pp. 129–169). Stamford, CT: JAI Press.

Coutu, D., Kauffman, C., Charan, R., Peterson, D. B., Maccoby, M., Scoular, P., & Grant, A. M. (2009). What can coaches do for you? *Harvard Business Review, 87*(1), 91–97.

Craft, J. L. (2010). Making the case for ongoing and interactive organizational ethics training. *Human Resource Development International, 13*, 599–606.

Craig, S. B., & Hannum, K. M. (2007). Experimental and quasi-experimental evaluations. In K. M. Hannum, J. W. Martineau, & C. Reinelt (Eds.), *The handbook of leadership development evaluation* (pp. 19–47). San Francisco, CA: Jossey-Bass.

Cullen, K. L. (2013, November). *Leveraging networks for leadership and organizational direction: Proven and cutting-edge approaches*. Keynote presentation at the Leading Insights Summit, Boston, MA. Retrieved from http://www.slideshare.net/ActivateNetworks/cisummit-2013-kristin-cullen-leveraging-networks-in-leadership-and-organizaional-d

Cunningham, J. B. (1993). Facilitating a mentorship programme. *Leadership and Organization Development Journal, 14*(4), 15–20.

Davis, E. (2010, July 14). Inclusion measurement: Tracking the intangible. *Trend-Watcher*, 504. Retrieved from http://www.i4cp.com/trendwatchers/2010/07/14/inclusion-measurement-tracking-the-intangible

Day, D., & Sin, H.-P. (2011). Longitudinal tests of an integrative model of leader development: Charting and understanding developmental trajectories. *Leadership Quarterly, 22*, 545–560.

Day, D. V. (2000). Leadership development: A review in context. *Leadership Quarterly, 11*, 581–613.

Day, R., & Allen, T. D. (2004). The relationship between career motivation and self-efficacy with protégé career success. *Journal of Vocational Behavior, 64*, 72–91.

de Jong, A. (2006). Coaching ethics. In J. Passmore (Ed.), *Excellence in coaching: The industry guide*. London: Kogan Page.

DeLay, L., & Dalton, M. (2006). Coaching across cultures. In S. Ting & P. Scisco (Eds.), *CCL handbook of coaching: A guide for the leader coach* (pp. 122–148). San Francisco: Jossey-Bass.

Deloitte. (2014). *Human capital trends* (Report). Retrieved from www.deloitte.com

Deloitte Development. (2014). *Global human capital trends 2014: Engaging the 21st century workforce*. London: Author.

Delong, T. J., Gabarro, J. J., & Lees, R. J. (2008). Why mentoring matters in a hyper-competitive world. *Harvard Business Review, 86*(1), 115–121.

DeMeuse, K. P., Dai, G., & Hallenbeck, G. S. (2010). Learning agility: A construct whose time has come. *Consulting Psychology Journal: Practice and Research, 62*(2), 119–130.

Derr, C. B., Jones, C., & Toomey, E. L. (1988). Managing high-potential employees: Current practices in thirty-three U.S. corporations. *Human Resource Management, 27*(3), 273–290.

DeVries, D. L., & Kaiser, R. B. (2003, November). *Going sour in the suite: What you can do about executive derailment*. Presented at the Maximizing Executive Effectiveness: Developing Your Senior Leadership workshop Human Resources Planning Society, Miami, FL. Retrieved from http://kaplandevries.com/thought-leadership/more/94

Dinwoodie, D. L., Quinn, L., & McGuire, J. B. (2014). *Bridging the strategy/performance gap* (White Paper). Greensboro, NC: Center for Creative Leadership.

Dobrow, S. R., Chandler, D. E., Murphy, W. M., & Kram, K. E. (2012). A review of developmental networks: Incorporating a mutuality perspective. *Journal of Management, 38*, 210–242.

Donaldson, L. (1993). *Anti-management theories of organization: A critique of paradigm proliferation.* Cambridge: Cambridge University Press.

Dorfman, P. W. (1996). Part II: Topical issues in international management research. In J. Punnitt & O. Shanker (Eds.), *International and cross-cultural leadership* (pp. 267–276). Cambridge, MA: Blackwell.

Dougherty, T. W., Turban, D. B., & Haggard, D. L. (2007). Naturally occurring mentoring relationships involving workplace employees. In T. D. Allen & L. T. Eby (Eds.), *Blackwell handbook of mentoring: A multiple perspectives approach* (pp. 139–158). London: Blackwell.

Drath, W. H., McCauley, C. D., Palus, C. J., Van Velsor, E., O'Connor, P. M., & McGuire, J. B. (2008). Direction, alignment, commitment: Toward a more integrative ontology of leadership. *Leadership Quarterly, 19*(6), 635–653.

Dreher, G. F., & Ash, R. A. (1990). A comparative study of mentoring among men and women in managerial, professional, and technical positions. *Journal of Applied Psychology, 75*, 539–546.

Dries, N., Vantilborgh, T., & Pepermans, R. (2012). The role of learning agility and career variety in the identification and development of high potential employees. *Personnel Review, 41*(3), 340–358. http://www.emeraldinsight.com/doi/abs/10.1108/00483481211212977

Dweck, C. (2006). *Mindset.* New York, NY: Ballantine Books.

Dyer, J. H., Gregersen, H. B., & Christensen, C. M. (2009, December). The innovator's DNA. *Harvard Business Review, 87*(12), 61–67.

Earley, P. C., & Ang, S. (2003). *Cultural intelligence: Individual interactions across cultures.* Palo Alto, CA: Stanford University Press.

Early, P. C., & Peterson, R. S. (2004). The elusive cultural chameleon: Cultural intelligence as a new approach to intercultural training for the global manager. *Academy of Management Learning and Education, 3*(1), 100–115.

Eby, L. T. (1997). Alternative forms of mentoring in changing organizational environments: A conceptual extension of the mentoring literature. *Journal of Vocational Behavior, 51*, 125–144.

Eby, L. T. (2007). Understanding relational problems in mentoring. In B. R. Ragins & K. E. Kram (Eds.), *The handbook of mentoring at work: Theory, research and practice* (pp. 323–344). Thousand Oaks, CA: Sage.

Eby, L. T., & Allen, T. D. (2002). Further investigation of protégés' negative mentoring experiences: Patterns and outcomes. *Group and Organization Management, 27*, 456–479.

Eby, L. T., Durley, J., Evans, S. C., & Ragins, B. R. (2006). The relationship between short-term mentoring benefits and long-term mentor outcomes. *Journal of Vocational Behavior, 69*, 424–444.

Eby, L. T., & Lockwood, A. (2005). Protégés' and mentors' reactions to participating in formal mentoring programs: A qualitative investigation. *Journal of Vocational Behavior, 67*, 441–458.

Eby, L. T., & McManus, S. E. (2004). The protégé's role in negative mentoring experiences. *Journal of Vocational Behavior, 65*, 255–275.

Eby, L. T., Rhodes, J. E., & Allen, T. D. (2007). Definition and evolution of mentoring. In T. D. Allen & L. T. Eby (Eds.), *Blackwell handbook of mentoring: A multiple perspectives approach* (pp. 7–20). London: Blackwell.

Eckardt, A. M. (2013). *Executive coaching: What's personality got to do with it? Exploring the role of personality in the achievement of coaching outcomes moderated by boss support.* Unpublished bachelor's thesis, University of Surrey, Guilford, UK.

Eckert, R., Ruderman, M., Gentry, W. A., & Stawiski, S. (2012). *Through the looking glass: How relationships shape managerial careers* (White Paper). Greensboro, NC: Center for Creative Leadership. Retrieved from http://www.ccl.org/leadership/pdf/research/ThroughTheLookingGlass.pdf

Eddy, E., Tannenbaum, S., Alliger, G., D'Abate, C., & Givens, S. (2001). *Mentoring in industry: The top 10 issues when building and supporting a mentoring program* (Technical report). Naval Air Warfare Center Training Systems Division.

Edmondson, A. (1999). Psychological safety and learning behavior in work teams. *Administrative Science Quarterly, 44*(2), 350–383.

Eichinger, R. W., & Lombardo, M. M. (2004). Patterns of rater accuracy in 360-degree feedback. *Human Resource Planning, 10*, 23–26.

Ellemers, N., & Haslam, S. A. (2012). Social identity theory. In P.A.M. Van Lange, A. W. Kruglanski, & E. T. Higgins (Eds.), *Handbook of theories of social psychologies* (pp. 379–398). Thousand Oaks, CA: Sage.

Ellemers, N., Spears, R., & Doosje, B. (2002). Self and social identity. *Annual Review of Psychology. 53*, 161–186.

Ellinger, A. D., Ellinger, A. E., & Keller, S. B. (2003). Supervisory coaching behavior, employee satisfaction, and warehouse employee performance: A dyadic perspective in the distribution industry. *Human Resource Development Quarterly, 14*, 435–458.

Elliott, J. P. (2010). *How to accelerate leadership readiness and development in uncertain times.* New York, NY: Sibson Consulting.

Ensher, E. A., Huen, C., & Blanchard, A. (2003). Online mentoring and computer-mediated communication: New directions in research. *Journal of Vocational Behavior, 63*, 264–288.

Ensher, E. A., & Murphy, S. E. (1997). Effects of race, gender, perceived similarity, and contact on mentor relationships. *Journal of Vocational Behavior, 50*, 460–481.

Ensher, E. A., & Murphy, S. E. (2007). E-mentoring: Next-generation research strategies and suggestions. In B. R. Ragins & K. E. Kram (Eds.), *The handbook of mentoring at work: Theory, research and practice* (pp. 299–322). Thousand Oaks, CA: Sage.

Ensley, M. D., & Pearce, C. L. (2001). Shared cognition in top management teams: Implications for new venture performance. *Journal of Organizational Behavior, 22*(2), 145–160.

Erez, M., Lisak, A., Harush, R., Glikson, E., Nouri, R., & Shokef, E. (2013). Going global: Developing management students' global characteristics through multicultural team project. *Academy of Management Learning and Education, 12*(3), 330–355.

Ernst, C., & Chrobot-Mason, D. (2011). *Boundary spanning leadership: Six practices for solving problems, driving innovation, and transforming organizations.* New York, NY: McGraw-Hill.

Ernst, C., & Yip, J. (2009). Boundary spanning leadership: Tactics to bridge social identity groups in organizations. In T. L. Pittinsky (Ed.), *Crossing the divide: Intergroup leadership in a world of difference.* Boston, MA: Harvard Business School Press.

Executive Coaching Forum. (2008). *The executive coaching handbook: Principles and guidelines for a successful coaching partnership* (4th ed.). Retrieved from www.instituteofcoaching.org/images/pdfs/ExecutiveCoachingHandbook.pdf

Fagenson, E. A. (1989). The mentor advantage: Perceived career/job experiences of protégés versus non-protégés. *Journal of Organizational Behavior*, *10*, 309–320.

Fagenson, E. A. (1992). Mentoring—who needs it? A comparison of protégés' and non-protégés; needs for power, achievement, affiliation, and autonomy. *Journal of Vocational Behavior*, *41*, 48–60.

Fagenson-Eland, E. A., Marks, M. A., & Amendola, K. L. (1997). Perceptions of mentoring relationships. *Journal of Vocational Behavior*, *51*, 29–42.

Ferdman, B. M. (1995). Cultural identity and diversity in organisations: Bridging the gap between group differences and individual uniqueness. In M. M. Chemers, S. Oskamp, & M. A. Costanzo (Eds.), *Diversity in organisations: New perspectives for a changing workplace* (pp. 37–49). London: Sage.

Ferris, G. R., Davidson, S. L., & Perrewé, P. L. (2005). *Political skill at work: Impact on work effectiveness*. Mountain View, CA: Davies-Black.

Ferris, G. R., Treadway, D. C., Brouer, R. L., & Munyon, T. P. (2012). Political skill in the organizational sciences. In G. R. Ferris & D. C. Treadway (Eds.), *Politics in organizations: Theory and research considerations* (pp. 487–529). New York, NY: Routledge/Taylor and Francis.

Fielder, J. H., & Starr, L. J. (2008). What's the big deal about coaching contracts? *International Journal of Coaching in Organizations*, *6*, 15–27.

Finkelstein, L. M., Allen, T. D., Ritchie, T. D., Lynch, J. E., & Montei, M. S. (2012). A dyadic examination of the role of relationship characteristics and age on relationship satisfaction in a formal mentoring programme. *European Journal of Work and Organizational Psychology*, *21*, 803–827.

Finkelstein, L. M., & Poteet, M. L. (2007). Best practices in workplace formal mentoring programs. In T. D. Allen & L. T. Eby (Eds.), *Blackwell handbook of mentoring: A multiple perspectives approach* (pp. 345–367). London: Blackwell.

Finklestein, S. (2013, September). *A fatal flaw when choosing the right leader, BBC Capital: Syd weighs in*. Retrieved from http://www.bbc.com/capital/story/20130919-a-fatal-flaw-in-choosing-leaders

Fleenor, J. W., Taylor, S., & Chappelow, C. (2008). *Leveraging the impact of 360-degree feedback*. San Francisco, CA: Jossey-Bass/Pfeiffer.

Forret, M. L., Turban, D. B., & Dougherty, T. W. (1996). Issues facing organizations when implementing formal mentoring programmes. *Leadership and Organization Development Journal*, *17*, 27–30.

Foster, S. (2014). *Coaching 2.0: The next generation of coaching in organizations* (Kenexa Corporate Report). Somers, NY: IBM Corporation.

Frankovelgia, C. C., & Riddle, D. D. (2010). Leadership coaching. In C. D. McCauley, M. N. Ruderman, & E. Van Velsor (Eds.), *The Center for Creative Leadership handbook of leadership development* (3rd ed., pp. 125–146). San Francisco, CA: Jossey-Bass.

Frisch, M. (2001). The emerging role of the internal coach. *Consulting Psychology Journal: Practice and Research, 53*(4), 240–250.

Garvey, B., & Garrett-Harris, R. (2005). *The benefits of mentoring: A literature review, a report for East Mentors Forum Sheffield*. Sheffield: Coaching and Mentoring Research Unit, Sheffield Hallam University.

Garvey, B., Stokes, P., & Megginson, D. (2009). *Coaching and mentoring theory and practice*. London: Sage.

Garvey, R., & Westlander, G. (2013). Training mentors: Behaviors which bring positive outcomes in mentoring. In J. Passmore, D. B. Peterson, & T. Freire (Eds.), *The Wiley-Blackwell handbook of the psychology of coaching and mentoring* (pp. 243–265). Chichester, UK: Wiley.

Gentry, W. A. (2010). Derailment: How successful leaders avoid it. In E. Biech (Ed.), *The ASTD leadership handbook* (pp. 311–324). Alexandria, VA: ASTD Press.

Gentry, W. A., Allen, L. W., Wolf, A. K., Manning, L., & Hernez-Broome, G. (2011). Coach and client characteristics that Asian and European coaches believe are needed for effective coaching engagements. *International Journal of Mentoring and Coaching, 4*(2), 56–123.

Gentry, W. A., & Chappelow, C. (2009). Managerial derailment: Weaknesses that can be fixed. In R. B. Kaiser (Ed.), *The perils of accentuating the positive* (pp. 97–114). Tulsa, OK: Hogan Press.

Gentry, W. A., Gilmore, D. C., Shuffler, M. L., & Leslie, J. B. (2012). Political skill as an indicator of promotability among multiple rater sources. *Journal of Organizational Behavior, 33*, 89–104.

Gentry, W. A., & Leslie, J. B. (2012). *Developing political savvy*. Greensboro, NC: Center for Creative Leadership.

Gentry, W. A., Manning, L., Wolf, A. K., Hernez-Broome, G., & Allen, L. W. (2013). What coaches believe are best practices for coaching: A qualitative study of interviews from coaches residing in Asia and Europe. *Journal of Leadership Studies, 7*(2), 18–31.

Gentry, W. A., & Shanock, L. R. (2008). Views of managerial derailment from above and below: The importance of a good relationship with upper management and putting people at ease. *Journal of Applied Social Psychology, 38*(10), 2469–2494.

Gentry, W. A., & Sosik, J. J. (2010). Developmental relationships and managerial promotability in organizations: A multisource study. *Journal of Vocational Behavior, 77*, 266–278.

Gentry, W. A., Stawiski, S. A., Eckert, R. H., & Ruderman, M. N. (2013). *Crafting your career: Cultural variations in career relevant relationships* (White Paper). Greensboro, NC: Center for Creative Leadership. Retrieved from http://www.ccl.org/leadership/pdf/research/craftingYourCareer.pdf

Gentry, W. A., Weber, T. J., & Sadri, G. (2008). Examining career-related mentoring and managerial performance across cultures: A multilevel analysis. *Journal of Vocational Behavior, 72*, 241–253.

Gentry, W. A., Wolf, A. K., Manning, L., Hernez-Broome, G., & Allen, L. W. (2011). Coach and client characteristics that Asian and European coaches believe are needed for effective coaching engagements. *International Journal of Mentoring and Coaching, 9*(2), 56–79.

Ghods, N., & Boyce, C. (2013). Virtual coaching and mentoring. In J. Passmore, D. B. Peterson, & T. Freire (Eds.), *The Wiley-Blackwell handbook of the psychology of coaching and mentoring* (pp. 501–523). Chichester, UK: Wiley.

Ghosh, R., Haynes, R. K., & Kram, K. E. (2013). Developmental networks at work: Holding environments for leader development. *Career Development International, 18*, 232–256.

Ghosh, R., & Reio, T. G., Jr. (2013). Career benefits associated with mentoring for mentors: A meta-analysis. *Journal of Vocational Behavior, 83*, 106–116.

Giberson, T. R., Resick, C. J., & Dickson, M. W. (2005). Embedding leader characteristics: An examination of homogeneity of personality and values in organizations. *Journal of Applied Psychology, 90*(5), 1002–1010.

Gilbert, K., & Rosinski, P. (2008). Accessing cultural orientations: The online culture orientation framework assessment as a tool for coaching. *Coaching: An International Journal of Theory and Practice, 1*(1), 81–92.

Godshalk, V. M., & Sosik, J. J. (2007). Mentoring and leadership: Standing at the crossroads of theory, research, and practice. In B. R. Ragins & K. E. Kram (Eds.), *The handbook of mentoring at work: Theory, research and practice* (pp. 149–178). Thousand Oaks, CA: Sage.

Goh, S. C., Elliott, C., & Quon, T. K. (2012). The relationship between learning capability and organizational performance: A meta-analytic examination. *Learning Organization, 19*(2), 92–108.

Goldsmith, M., & Morgan, H. (2004). Leadership is a contact sport: The "follow-up factor" in management development. *Strategy + Business, 36*, 70–79.

Goldsmith, M., & Reiter, M. (2007). *What got you here won't get you there: How successful people become even more successful*. New York, NY: Hyperion.

Goleman, D. (2002). *Working with emotional intelligence*. New York, NY: Bantam Books.

Gottman, J. M. (1994). *What predicts divorce?* Hillsdale, NJ: Erlbaum.

Grant, A. M. (2013). *Give and take: Why helping others drives our success*. New York, NY: Penguin.

Gray, D. E., Ekinci, Y., & Goregaokar, H. (2011). A five-dimensional model of attributes: Some precursors of executive coach selection. *International Journal of Selection and Assessment, 9*(4), 415–428.

Greenleaf, R. K. (2002). *Servant leadership: A journey into the nature of legitimate power and greatness* (25th anniversary ed.). Mahwah, NJ: Paulist Press.

Greif, S. (2013). Conducting organizational-based evaluations of coaching and mentoring programs. In J. Passmore, D. B. Peterson, & T. Freire (Eds.), *The Wiley-Blackwell handbook of the psychology of coaching and mentoring* (pp. 443–470). Malden, MA: Wiley-Blackwell.

Grubb, T., & Ting, S. (2006). Coaching senior leaders. In S. Ting & P. Scisco (Eds.), *The CCL handbook of coaching* (pp. 149–175). San Francisco, CA: Jossey-Bass.

Guinto, J. (2013, November). *Who wrecked J.C. Penney? D Magazine*. Retrieved from http://www.dmagazine.com/publications/d-ceo/2013/november/who-wrecked-jc-penney

Gupta, A. K., & Govindarajan, V. (2002). Cultivating a global mindset. *Academy of Management Perspectives, 16*(1), 116–126.

Habig, J., & Plessier, F. (2014, March). Measuring the impact. *Training Journal*, 64–69.

Hackman, J. R., & Morris, G. (1975). Group tasks, group interaction process and group performance effectiveness: A review and proposed integration. In L. Berkowitz (Ed.), *Advances in experimental social psychology* (Vol. 8, pp. 45–99). New York, NY: Academic Press.

Hackman, R., & Wageman, R. (2005). A theory of team coaching. *Academy of Management Review, 30*(2), 269–287.

Hamilton, B. A., & Scandura, T. A. (2003). E-mentoring: Implications for organizational learning and development in a wired world. *Organizational Dynamics, 31*, 388–402.

Hannum, K. M., Martineau, J. W., & Reinelt, C. (Eds.). (2007). *The handbook of leadership development evaluation*. San Francisco, CA: Jossey-Bass.

Hannum, K. M., McFeeters, B. B., & Booysen, L.A.E. (2010). *Leading across differences: Cases and perspectives*. San Francisco, CA: Jossey-Bass/Pfeiffer.

Hanson, B. Z. (2007). *Why coaching programs fail* (Canadian Management Center White Paper). Retrieved from http://cmcoutperform.com/why-coaching-programs-fail

Hart, E. W. (2009). *Seven keys to successful mentoring*. Greensboro, NC: Center for Creative Leadership.

Hart, E. W. (2011). *Feedback in performance reviews*. Greensboro, NC: Center for Creative Leadership.

Haslam, S. A. (2001). *Psychology in organisations: The social identity approach*. London: Sage.

Hawkins, P., & Smith, N. (2013). *Coaching, mentoring and organizational consultancy: Supervision, skills and development*. Berkshire, UK: Open University Press.

Haynes, R. K., & Ghosh, R. (2012). Towards mentoring the Indian organizational woman: Propositions, considerations, and first steps. *Journal of World Business, 47*(2), 186–193.

Heider, F. (1958). *The psychology of interpersonal relations*. New York, NY: Wiley.

Heifetz, R. A., & Laurie, D. L. (1997). The work of leadership. *Harvard Business Review, 75*(1), 124–134.

Herriot, P., & Scott-Jackson, W. (2002). Globalization, social identities and employment. *British Journal of Management, 13*, 249–257.

Hesselbein, F., & Shinseki, E. K. (2004). *Be, know, do: Leadership the army way*. San Francisco, CA: Jossey-Bass.

Higgins, M. C., & Kram, K. E. (2001). Reconceptualizing mentoring at work: A developmental network perspective. *Academy of Management Review, 26*(2), 264–288.

Hoch, J. E., & Kozlowski, S.W.J. (2012). Leading virtual teams: Hierarchical leadership, structural supports, and shared team leadership. *Journal of Applied Psychology, 99*(3), 390–403.

Hofstede, G. (1980). *Culture's consequences: International differences in work-related values*. Beverly Hills, CA: Sage.

Hofstede, G. (1991). *Cultures and organisations: Software of the mind*. London: McGraw-Hill.

Hofstede, G. (1996). Cultural constraints in management theories. In R. M. Steers, L. W. Porter, & G. A. Bigley (Eds.), *Motivation and leadership at work* (6th ed., pp. 425–439). New York, NY: McGraw-Hill.

Hofstede, G. (2006). What did GLOBE really measure? Researchers' minds versus respondents' minds. *Journal of International Business Studies, 37*(6), 882–896. https://ideas.repec.org/p/ner/tilbur/urnnbnnlui12-194534.html

Hofstede, G. (2010). The GLOBE debate: Back to relevance. *Journal of International Business Studies, 41*(8), 1339–1346. http://www.palgrave-journals.com/jibs/journal/v41/n8/abs/jibs201031a.html

Hofstede, G., Hofstede, G. J., & Minkov, M. (2010). *Cultures and organisations: Software of the mind* (3rd ed.). New York, NY: McGraw-Hill International.

Hogan, J., Hogan, R., & Kaiser, R. B. (2011). Management derailment: Personality assessment and mitigation. In S. Zedeck (Ed.), *APA handbook of industrial and organizational psychology* (pp. 1–28). Washington, DC: American Psychological Association.

Hogan, R., & Hogan, J. (2001, June). Assessing leadership: A view from the dark side. *International Journal of Selection and Assessment, 9*, 40–51.

Hogg, M. A., & Terry, D. J. (2000). Social identity and self-categorization processes in organizational contexts. *Academy of Management Review, 25*(1), 121–140.

Hooijberg, R., & Lane, N. (2009). Using multisource feedback coaching effectively in executive education. *Academy of Management Learning and Education, 8*(4), 483–493.

Hoole, E., & Martineau, J. (2013). Evaluation methods. In D. Day (Ed.), *The Oxford handbook of leadership and organizations*. New York, NY: Oxford University Press.

Hoppe, M., & Eckert, R. (2012). *Leader effectiveness and culture: The GLOBE study* (Research Review). Retrieved from http://www.ccl.org/leadership/pdf/assessments/GlobeStudy.pdf

House, R. J. (1993). *Prospectus: The GLOBE study* (Unpublished Manuscript).

House, R. J., Hanges, P. J., Javidan, M., Dorfman, P. W., & Gupta, V. (2004). *Culture, leadership, and organizations: The GLOBE study of 62 societies*. Thousand Oaks, CA: Sage.

House, R. J., Hanges, P. J., & Ruiz-Quintanilla, S. A. (1997). GLOBE: The global leadership and organisational behaviour effectiveness: Research program, *Polish Psychological Bulletin, 28*(3), 215–230.

House, R. J., & Javidan, M. (2004). Overview of GLOBE. In R. J. House, P. J. Hanges, M. Javidan, P. W. Dorfman, & V. Gupta (Eds.), *Culture, leadership, and organizations: The GLOBE study of 62 societies* (pp. 9–28). Thousand Oaks, CA: Sage.

Howard, P. J., & Howard, J. M. (2001). *The owner's manual for personality at work: How the big five personality traits affect performance, communication, teamwork, leadership, and sales.* Charlotte, NC: Bard Press.

Howland, B., Martineau, J., & Craig, S. B. (2001). *Leadership development success: A client report.* Greensboro, NC: Center for Creative Leadership.

Hu, C., Pellegrini, E. K., & Scandura, T. A. (2011). Measurement invariance in mentoring research: A cross-cultural examination across Taiwan and the U.S. *Journal of Vocational Behavior, 78*, 274–282.

Hughes, R., Beatty, K. C., & Dinwoodie, D. (2014). *Becoming a strategic leader: Your role in your organization's enduring success.* San Francisco, CA: Jossey-Bass.

Hülsheger, U. R., Anderson, N., & Salgado, J. F. (2009). Team-level predictors of innovation at work: A comprehensive meta-analysis spanning three decades of research. *Journal of Applied Psychology, 94*(5), 1128–1145.

Human Capital Institute. (2012). *Scaling executive coaching across the enterprise: The key to developing tomorrow's talent.* Retrieved from http://www.lhh.com/en-US/thought-leadership/Documents/2013-LHH-Scaling-Executive-Coaching-Across-the-Enterprise.pdf

Hunt, J. M., & Weintraub, J. R. (2007). *The coaching organization: A strategy for developing leaders.* Thousand Oaks, CA: Sage.

IBM Corporation (2010, May). *Capitalizing on complexity: Insights from the Global Chief Executive Officer Study.* Retrieved from http://www.inspireimagineinnovate.com/PDF/Capitalizing-on-Complexity-IBM-Study.pdf

Inyang, B. J. (2013). Exploring the concept of leadership derailment: Defining new research agenda. *International Journal of Business and Management, 8*(16), 78–86. http://www.ccsenet.org/journal/index.php/ijbm/article/view/27572

Isaacs, W. (1999). *Dialogue and the art of thinking together.* New York, NY: Random House.

Janis, I. L. (1972). *Victims of groupthink.* Boston, MA: Houghton Mifflin.

Javidan, M. (2004). Performance orientation. In R. J. House, P. J. Hanges, M. Javidan, P. W. Dorfman, & V. Gupta (Eds.), *Culture, leadership, and organizations: The GLOBE study of 62 societies* (pp. 239–281). Thousand Oaks, CA: Sage.

Javidan, M., House, R. J., Dorfman, P. W., Hanges, P. J., & Sully de Luque, M. (2006). Conceptualizing and measuring cultures and their consequences: A comparative review of GLOBE's and Hofstede's approaches. *Journal of International Business Studies, 37*(6), 897–914. 10.1057/palgrave.jibs.8400234

Javidan, M., Teagarden, M. B., & Bowden, D. E. (2010, April). Making it overseas: Developing the skills you need to succeed as an international leader. *Harvard Business Review,* 109–113.

Javidan, M., & Walker, J. (2013). *Developing your global mindset: The handbook for successful global leaders.* Edina, MN: Beaver's Pond Press.

Jenkins, J. (2006). Coaching meets the cross-cultural challenge. *Leadership in Action, 26*(5), 23–24.

Jepson, D. (2009). Studying leadership at cross-country level: A critical analysis. *Leadership, 5*(1), 61–81.

Joo, B.-K., Sushko, J. S., McLean, G. N. (2012). Multiple faces of coaching: Manager-as-coach, executive coaching, and formal mentoring. *Organization Development Journal, 30*(1), 19–38.

Judge, T. A., & Cable, D. M. (1997). Applicant personality, organizational culture, and organization attraction. *Personnel Psychology, 50*(2), 359–394.

Kaiser, R. B., LeBreton, J. M., & Hogan, J. (2013). The dark side of personality and extreme leader behavior. *Applied Psychology: An International Review.* http://onlinelibrary.wiley.com/doi/10.1111/apps.12024/abstract

Kaiser, R. B., & Overfield, D. V. (2011). Strengths, strengths overused, and lopsided leadership. *Consulting Psychology Journal: Practice and Research, 63*(2), 89–109. http://insightu.net/content/pdf/strengths.pdf

Kalman, F. (2012, December 17). Has executive education gone soft? *Chief Learning Officer.* Retrieved from http://clomedia.com/articles/view/has-executive-education-gone-soft

Katzenbach, J. R., & Beckett, F. (1996). *Real change leaders: How you can create growth and high performance at your company.* New York, NY: Time Business.

Katzenbach, J. R., & Smith, D. K. (1993). The discipline of teams. *Harvard Business Review, 71*(2), 111–120.

Keele, R. L., Bucker, K., & Bushnell, S. J. (1987). Formal mentoring programs are no panacea. *Management Review, 76*(2), 67–68.

Kilburg, R. R. (2004). Trudging toward Dodoville: Conceptual approaches and case studies in executive coaching. *Consulting Psychology Journal: Practice and Research, 56*, 203–213.

Klasen, N., & Clutterbuck, D. (2002). *Implementing mentoring schemes: A practical guide to successful programs*. London: Butterworth-Heinemann.

Klau, M. (2006). Exploring youth leadership in theory and practice. *New Directions for Youth Development, 109*, 57–87. http://onlinelibrary.wiley.com/doi/10.1002/yd.155/pdf

Knights, A., & Poppleton, A. (2008). *Coaching in organizations*. Hertfordshire, UK: Ashridge Business School.

Koberg, C. S., Boss, R. W., & Goodman, E. (1998). Factors and outcomes associated with mentoring among health-care professionals. *Journal of Vocational Behavior, 53*, 58–72.

Konrad, E., & Susanj, Z. (1996). Influences of industry on organizational culture and climate. *Review of Psychology, 3*(1–2), 3–10.

Kozlowski, S.W.J., & Bell, B. S. (2012). Work groups and teams in organizations. In N. W. Schmitt & S. Highhouse (Eds.), *Handbook of psychology, vol. 12: Industrial and organizational psychology* (2nd ed., pp. 412–469). London, UK: Wiley.

Kozlowski, S. W., Gully, S. M., McHugh, P. P., Salas, E., & Cannon-Bowers, J. A. (1996). A dynamic theory of leadership and team effectiveness: Developmental and task contingent leader roles. *Research in Personnel and Human Resources Management, 14*, 253–306.

Kozlowski, S. W., & Ilgen, D. R. (2006). Enhancing the effectiveness of work groups and teams. *Psychological Science in the Public Interest, 7*(3), 77–124.

Kram, K. E. (1985). *Mentoring at work*. Glenview, IL: Scott, Foresman.

Kram, K. E., & Hall, D. (1991). Mentoring as an antidote to stress during corporate trauma. *Human Resource Management, 28*, 493–510.

Kram, K. E., & Higgins, M. C. (2008, September 22). A new approach to mentoring. *Wall Street Journal*. Retrieved from http://online.wsj.com/news/articles/SB122160063875344843

Kram, K. E., & Higgins, M. C. (2009). *A new mindset on mentoring: Creating developmental networks at work*. Cambridge, MA: MIT Press.

Kram, K. E., & Isabella, L. A. (1985). Mentoring alternatives: The role of peer relationships in career development. *Academy of Management Journal, 28*, 110–132.

Ladyshewsky, R. K. (2002). A quasi-experimental study of the differences in performance and clinical reasoning using individual learning versus reciprocal peer coaching. *Physiotherapy Theory and Practice, 18,* 17–31.

Lamb, T. A., & Tschillard, R. (2005). *Evaluating learning in professional development workshops: Using the retrospective pretest.* Retrieved from www.nsdc.org

Lamoureux, K. (2007). *High-impact leadership development: Trends, best practices, industry solutions and vendor profiles.* Oakland, CA: Bersin & Associates.

Lau, D. C., & Murnighan, J. K. (1998). Demographic diversity and faultlines: The compositional dynamics of organizational groups. *Academy of Management Review, 23,* 325–340.

Lau, D. C., & Murnighan, J. K. (2005). Interactions within groups and subgroups: The effects of demographic faultlines. *Academy of Management Journal, 48,* 645–659.

Lave, J., & Wenger, E. (1991). *Situated learning: Legitimate peripheral participation.* Cambridge: Cambridge University Press.

Lawler, E. E. (2008). The HR department: Give it more respect. *Wall Street Journal.* Retrieved from http://online.wsj.com/news/articles/SB120468005346212087

LeCompte, M. D., & Schensul, J. J. (1999). *Analyzing and interpreting ethnographic data.* Walnut Creek, CA: AltaMira Press.

Lentz, E., & Allen, T. D. (2009). The role of mentoring others in the career plateauing phenomenon. *Group and Organization Management, 34,* 358–384.

Leone, P. (2008, March). Take your ROI to level 6. *Training Industry Quarterly,* pp. 15–19.

Leslie, J. B. & Braddy, P. W. (2013). *Benchmarks.* Greensboro, NC: Center for Creative Leadership.

Levinson, D. J., Darrow, C. N., Klein, E. B., Levinson, M. H., & McKee, B. (1978). *Seasons of a man's life.* New York, NY: Knopf.

Littlefield, A., & Mage, G. (2010). *Coaching 2.0: The next generation of coaching in organizations* (Corporate Report). Wayne, PA: Kenexa.

Liu, D., Liu, J., Kwan, H. K., & Mao, Y. (2009). What can I gain as a mentor? The effect of mentoring on the job performance and social status of mentors in China. *Journal of Occupational and Organizational Psychology, 82,* 871–895.

Lombardo, M. M., & Eichinger, R. W. (1996). *The career architect development planner.* Minneapolis, MN: Lominger.

Lombardo, M. M., & Eichinger, R. W. (2000). High potentials as high learners. *Human Resource Management, 39*(4), 321–329.

Lombardo, M. M., Ruderman, M. N., & McCauley, C. D. (1988). Explanations of success and derailment in upper-level management positions. *Journal of Business and Psychology, 2*(3), 199–216. http://link.springer.com/article/10.1007%2FBF01014038#

Long, K. (2012). Building internal supervision capability in organizations. *The OCM Coach and Mentor Journal.* Retrieved from http://www.theocm.co.uk/downloads/Coach_as_Supervisor_Case_Study.pdf

Lord, R. G., & Maher, K. J. (1991). *Leadership and information processing: Linking perceptions and performance.* Boston, MA: Unwin-Hyman.

Löscher, P. (2012, November). The CEO of Siemens on using a scandal to drive change. *Harvard Business Review.* Retrieved from http://hbr.org/product/the-ceo-of-siemens-on-using-a-scandal-to-drive-change/an/R1211A-PDF-ENG

Lowman, R. L. (2001). Constructing a literature from case studies: Promise and limitations of the method. *Consulting Psychology Journal: Practice and Research, 53*(2), 119–123.

Lowman, R. L. (2005). Executive coaching: The road to Dodoville needs paving with more than good assumptions. *Consulting Psychology Journal: Practice and Research, 57*, 90–96.

Lowman, R. L. (2007). Coaching and consulting in multicultural contexts, integrating themes and issues. *Consulting Psychology Journal: Practice and Research, 59*(4), 296–303. http://psycnet.apa.org/psycinfo/2008-00338-007

Lowman, R. L. (2013). Coaching ethics. In J. Passmore, D. Peterson, & T. Freire (Eds.), *The Wiley-Blackwell handbook of the psychology of coaching and mentoring* (pp. 68–88). Oxford, UK: Wiley.

Luthans, F., & Peterson, S. (2003). 360-degree feedback with systematic coaching: Empirical analysis suggests a winning combination. *Human Resource Management, 42*(3), 243–256.

Marshall, E. M., & Dobbins, T. (2009). *The potential and challenges of consensus decision-making* (White Paper). Greensboro, NC: Center for Creative Leadership.

Martin, A., Willburn, P., Morrow, P., Downing, K., Criswell, C. (2007). *The changing nature of leadership* (White Paper). Greensboro, NC: Center for Creative Leadership.

Martin, J. (1983). The uniqueness paradox in organizational stories. *Administrative Science Quarterly, 28*, 438–453.

Martineau, J. W., & Hannum, K. M. (2008). *Evaluating the impact of leadership development: A professional guide.* Greensboro, NC: Center for Creative Leadership.

Maynard, M. T., Mathieu, J. E., Rapp, T. L., & Gilson, L. L. (2012). Something(s) old and something(s) new: Modeling drivers of global virtual team effectiveness. *Journal of Organizational Behavior, 33*, 342–365.

McCall, M. (1998). *High flyers.* Boston: Harvard Business School Press.

McCall, M. W., Jr., & Lombardo, M. M. (1983). *Off the track: Why and how successful executives get derailed.* Greensboro, NC: Center for Creative Leadership.

McCartney, W. W., & Campbell, C. R. (2006). Leadership, management, and derailment: A model of individual success and failure. *Leadership and Organization Development Journal, 27*(3), 190–202. http://www.emeraldinsight.com/doi/abs/10.1108/01437730610657712

McCauley, C. D. (2006). *Developmental assignments: Creating learning experiences without changing jobs.* Greensboro, NC: Center for Creative Leadership.

McCauley, C. (2013). *My love-hate relationships with 70–20–10* [Web log post]. Retrieved from http://www.experiencedrivendevelopment.com/my-love-hate-relationship-70-20-10/

McCauley, C. D., DeRue, D. S., Yost, P. R., & Taylor, S. (2013). *Experience-driven leader development: Models, tools, best practices, and advice for on-the-job development.* San Francisco, CA: Wiley.

McCauley, C. D., & Guthrie, V. A. (2007). Designing relationships for learning into leader development programs. In B. R. Ragins & K. E. Kram (Eds.), *The handbook of mentoring at work: Theory, research, and practice* (pp. 573–591). Thousand Oaks, CA: Sage.

McCauley, C. D., & McCaull, M. W. (2013). *Using experience to develop leadership talent: How organizations leverage on-the-job development.* San Francisco, CA: Jossey-Bass/Pfeiffer.

McCauley, C., Van Velsor, E., & Ruderman, M. (2010). Introduction: Our view of leadership development. In E. Van Velsor, C. D. McCauley, & M. N. Ruderman (Eds.), *The Center for Creative Leadership handbook of leadership development* (3rd ed., pp. 1–27). San Francisco, CA: Jossey-Bass.

McClelland, D. C. (1985). *Human motivation.* Glenview, IL: Scott-Foresman.

McGuire, J. B., & Palus, C. J. (2003). Using dialogue as a tool for better leadership. *Leadership in Action, 23*(1), 8–11.

McGuire, J. B., & Palus, C. J. (In press). Toward interdependent leadership culture: A transformation case study of KONE Americas. In D. D. Warrick & J. Muller (Eds.), *Learning from real world cases: Lessons in changing culture*. Oxford, UK: Rossi Smith.

McGuire, J. B., Palus, C. J., and Torbert, W. (2007). Toward interdependent organizing and researching. In A. B. Rami Shani, S. A. Mohrman, W. H. Pasmore, B. Stymne, & N. Adler (Eds.), *The handbook of collaborative management research*. London: Sage.

McGuire, J. B., & Rhodes, G. (2009). *Transforming your leadership culture*. Greensboro, NC: Center for Creative Leadership.

McManus, S. E., & Russell, J. E. (2007). Peer mentoring relationships. In B. R. Ragins & K. E. Kram (Eds.), *The handbook of mentoring at work: Theory, research, and practice* (pp. 273–298). Thousand Oaks, CA: Sage.

Megginson, D., Clutterbuck, D., Garvey, B., Stokes, P., & Garrett-Harris, R. (Eds.). (2006). *Mentoring in action*. London: Kogan Page.

Meister, J., & Willyerd, K. (2010). *The 2020 workplace: How innovative companies attract, develop, and keep tomorrow's employees*. New York, NY: HarperCollins.

Mendelson, J. L., Barnes, A. K., & Horn, G. (1989). The guiding light to corporate culture. *Personnel Administrator*, *34*(7), 70–72.

Mendenhall, M. E., & Bird, A. (2013). In search of global leadership. *Organizational Dynamics*, *42*, 167–174.

Messmer, M. (2001). *Human resource kit for dummies*. New York, NY: Wiley.

Mezirow, J. (2009). *Transformative learning in practice*. San Francisco, CA: Jossey-Bass.

Michaelson, M., & Anderson, J. (2008). *The L3 leadership "state of being": A holistic approach to leadership*. Glendora, CA: Glowan Consulting Group.

Miller, S., Van Velsor, E., Wright, J., & Champion, H. (In press). *LAMP facilitators training manual*. Greensboro, NC: Center for Creative Leadership.

Minkov, M., & Hofstede, G. (2011). The evolution of Hofstede's doctrine. *Cross Cultural Management: An International Journal*, *18*(1), 10–20. http://www.researchgate.net/publication/230557684_The_evolution_of_Hofstede's_doctrine

Mitchell, C., Ray, R., & van Ark, B. (2013). *CEO challenge 2013*. New York, NY: Conference Board.

Mitchell, C., Ray, R. L., & van Ark, B. (2014). *The Conference Board CEO Challenge 2014: People and performance*. New York, NY: Conference Board.

Mitchinson, A., & Morris, R. (2012). *Learning about learning agility*. Greensboro, NC: Center for Creative Leadership.

Moreno, J. L. (1977). *Psychodrama* (4th ed.). New York, NY: Beacon House.

Morrison, A. M., White, R. P., & Van Velsor, E. (1992). *Breaking the glass ceiling*. Greensboro, NC: Center for Creative Leadership.

Mosakowski, E., Calic, G., & Earley, P. C. (2013). Cultures as learning laboratories: What makes some more effective than others. *Academy of Management Learning and Education, 12*(3), 512–526. http://amle.aom.org/content/early/2013/07/08/amle.2013.0149?related-urls=yes&legid=amle;amle.2013.0149v1

Moxley, R. S., & Pulley, M. L. (2004). Hardships. In C. D. McCauley & E. Van Velsor (Eds.), *Handbook of leadership development* (2nd ed., pp. 183–203). San Francisco, CA: Jossey-Bass.

Muldoon, S. D., & Miller, S. (2005). Leadership: Interpreting life patterns and their managerial significance. *Journal of Management Development, 24*, 132–144.

Murphy, W. M., & Kram, K. E. (2014). *Strategic relationships at work: Creating your circle of mentors, sponsors, and peers for success in business and life*. New York, NY: McGraw-Hill.

Murray, M. (1991). *Beyond the myths and magic of mentoring*. San Francisco, CA: Jossey-Bass.

Murrell, A. J., Crosby, F. J., & Ely, R. J. (1999). *Mentoring dilemmas: Developmental relationships within multicultural organizations*. Mahwah, NJ: Erlbaum.

Myers-Briggs, I., & McCauley, M. H. (1985). *Manual: A guide to the development and use of the Myers-Briggs Type Indicator* (2nd ed.). Palo Alto, CA: Consulting Psychologists Press.

National Association of Colleges and Employers. (2012). *Job outlook 2013*. Bethlehem, PA: Author.

Naudé, J., & Plessier, F. (2014). *Becoming a leader coach: A step by step guide to developing your people*. Greensboro, NC: Center for Creative Leadership.

Nelson, E., & Hogan, R. (2009). Coaching on the dark side. *International Coaching Psychology Review, 4*(1), 7–19.

Niebuhr, H. R. (1951). *Christ and culture*. San Francisco, CA: HarperCollins.

Nielson, T. R., Carlson, D. S., & Lankau, M. J. (2001). The supportive mentor as a means of reducing work-family conflict. *Journal of Vocational Behavior, 59*, 364–381.

Nieminen, L., Biermeier-Hanson, B., & Denison, D. (2013). Aligning leadership and organizational culture: The leader–culture fit framework for coaching organizational leaders. *Consulting Psychology Journal: Practice and Research, 65*(3), 177–198.

Nin, A. (1962). *Seduction of the Minotaur*. Denver, CO: Alan Swallow.

Nkomo, S. M. (2010). Social identity: Understanding the in-group/out-group phenomenon. In K. Hannum, B. B. McFeeters, & L.A.E Booysen (Eds.), *Leading across differences: Cases and perspectives* (pp. 73–80). San Francisco, CA: Jossey-Bass/Pfeiffer.

Noe, R. A. (1988). An investigation of the determinants of successful assigned mentoring relationships. *Personnel Psychology, 41*, 457–479.

Noe, R. A., Greenberger, D. B., & Wang, S. (2002). Mentoring: What we know and where we might go. In G. R. Ferris & J. J. Martocchio (Eds.), *Research in personnel and human resources management* (Vol. 21, pp. 129–173). Oxford, UK: Elsevier.

Nowack, K. M. (2009). Leveraging multirater feedback to facilitate successful behavioral change. *Consulting Psychology Journal: Practice and Research, 61*(4), 280–297. https://www.envisialearning.com/system/resources/69/Leveraging_360_Feedback_to_Facilitate_Successful_Behavior_Change_Consulting_Psychology_Practice_and_Research_Nowack_2009.pdf?1275611561

Nowack, K. M., & Mashihi, S. (2012). Evidence-based answers to 15 questions about leveraging 360-degree feedback. *Consulting Psychology Journal: Practice and Research, 64*(3), 157–182. http://www.apa.org/pubs/journals/features/cpb-64-3-157.pdf

Offerman, L. R., & Phan, L. U. (2002). Culturally intelligent leadership for a diverse world. In R. E. Riggio, S. E. Murphy, & F. J. Pirozzolo (Eds.), *Multiple intelligences and leadership* (pp. 187–214). London: Erlbaum.

Olian, J. D., Carroll, S., Giannantonio, C. M., & Feren, D. (1988). What do protégés look for in a mentor? Results of three experimental studies. *Journal of Vocational Behavior, 33*, 15–37.

Oncken, W., & Wass, D. L. (1999). Management time: Who's got the monkey? *Harvard Business Review, 77*(6), 178–197.

Orenstein, R. L. (2006). Measuring executive coaching efficacy? The answer was right here all the time. *Consulting Psychology Journal: Practice and Research, 58*, 106–116.

Osland, J. S., & Bird, A. (2005). Global leaders as experts. In W. H. Mobley & E. Weldon (Eds.), *Advances in global leadership* (Vol. 4, pp. 123–142). Bingley, UK: Emerald Group.

Owen, H. (1997). *Open space technology* (2nd ed.). San Francisco, CA: Berrett-Koehler.

Palus, C. J., & Drath, W. H. (2001). Putting something in the middle: An approach to dialogue. *Reflections, 3*(2), 28–39.

Palus, C. J., & Horth, D. M. (2004). *Visual explorer: Picturing approaches to complex challenges.* Greensboro, NC: Center for Creative Leadership.

Palus, C. J., Horth, D. M., Selvin, A. M., & Pulley, M. L. (2003). Exploration for development: Developing leadership by making shared sense of complex challenges. *Consulting Psychology Journal: Practice and Research, 55,* 26–40.

Palus, C. J., McGuire, J. B., & Ernst, C. (2011). *Developing interdependent leadership.* In S. Snook, N. Nohria, & R. Khurana (Eds.), *The handbook for teaching leadership: Knowing, doing, and being*. Thousand Oaks, CA: Sage.

Parise, M. R., & Forret, M. L. (2008). Formal mentoring programs: The relationship of program design and support to mentors' perceptions of benefits and costs. *Journal of Vocational Behavior, 72,* 225–240.

Parker, P., Hall, D. T., & Kram, K. E. (2008). Peer coaching: A relational process for accelerating career learning. *Academy of Management and Learning, 7*(4), 487–503.

Pasmore, B. (2009). *Developing a leadership strategy* (White Paper). Greensboro, NC: Center for Creative Leadership.

Passmore, J., Peterson, D. B., & Freire, T. (2012). *The Wiley-Blackwell handbook of the psychology of coaching and mentoring*. San Francisco, CA: Jossey-Bass.

Payne, S. C., & Huffman, A. H. (2005). A longitudinal examination of the influence of mentoring on organizational commitment and turnover. *Academy of Management Journal, 48,* 158–168.

Pearsall, M. J., Ellis, A.P.J., & Bell, B. S. (2010). Building the infrastructure: The effects of role identification behaviors on team cognition development and performance. *Journal of Applied Psychology, 95*(1), 192–200.

Peterson, D. B. (2007). Executive coaching in a cross-cultural context. *Consulting Psychology Journal: Practice and Research, 59*(4), 261–271. http://connection.ebscohost.com/c/articles/28836994/executive-coaching-cross-cultural-context

Peterson, D. (2008). High potential, high risk. *HR Magazine, 53*(3), 85–87.

Peterson, D. (2009). Does your coach give you value for your money? *Harvard Business Review, 87*(1), 95.

Peterson, D. B. (2010). Good to great coaching: Accelerating the journey. In G. Hernez-Broome & L. A. Boyce (Eds.), *Advancing executive coaching: Setting the course for leadership coaching*. San Francisco: Jossey-Bass.

Peterson, D. (2011, March 30). *Creating a coaching culture in your organization.* Presentation to The Conference Board, New York, NY.

Peterson, D. B., & Kraiger, K. (2004). A practical guide to evaluating coaching: Translating state-of-the-art techniques to the real world. In J. E. Edwards, J. C. Scott, & N. S. Raju (Eds.), *The human resources program evaluation handbook* (pp. 262–282). Thousand Oaks, CA: Sage.

Petrie, N. (2014). *Vertical leadership development part 1: Developing leaders for a complex world* (White Paper). Greensboro, NC: Center for Creative Leadership.

Plaister-Ten, J. (2009). Towards greater cultural understanding in coaching. *International Journal of Evidence Based Coaching and Mentoring, Special Issue, 3,* 64–81.

Planning Institute of Jamaica. (2007). *Vision 2030 Jamaica: National development plan.* Retrieved from http://www.vision2030.gov.jm/Overview/Guiding Principles.aspx

Podsakoff, P. M., MacKenzie, S. B., Lee, J., & Podsakoff, N. P. (2003). Common method biases in behavioral research: A critical review of the literature and recommended remedies. *Journal of Applied Psychology, 88,* 879–903.

Pomerleau, M., Silvert, H., WanVeer, L., Desrosiers, E., & Henderson, M. (2011). *The 2010 executive coaching survey* (Report 1464). New York, NY: The Conference Board.

Pratt, C., McGuigan, W., & Katzev, A. (2000). Measuring program outcomes using retrospective pre-test methodology. *American Journal of Evaluation, 21,* 341–350.

Preskill, H., & Jones, N. (2009). *A practical guide for engaging stakeholders in developing evaluation questions.* Retrieved from http://www.rwjf.org/content/dam/web-assets/2009/01/a-practical-guide-for-engaging-stakeholders-in-developing-evalua

Preskill, H., & Torres, R. T. (1999). *Evaluative inquiry for learning in organizations.* Thousand Oaks, CA: Sage.

Ragins, B. R., & Cotton, J. L. (1993). Gender and willingness to mentor in organizations. *Journal of Management, 19,* 97–111.

Ragins, B. R., & Cotton, J. L. (1999). Mentor functions and outcomes: A comparison of men and women in formal and informal mentoring relationships. *Journal of Applied Psychology, 84*, 529–550.

Ragins, B. R., Cotton, J. L., & Miller, J. S. (2000). Marginal mentoring: The effects of type of mentor, quality of relationship, and program design on work and career attitudes. *Academy of Management Journal, 43*, 1177–1194.

Ragins, B. R., & Scandura, T. A. (1999). Burden of blessing? Expected costs and benefits of being a mentor. *Journal of Organizational Behavior, 20*, 493–509.

Ramaswami, A., & Dreher, G. F. (2007). The benefits associated with workplace mentoring relationships. In T. D. Allen & L. T. Eby (Eds.), *Blackwell handbook of mentoring: A multiple perspectives approach* (pp. 211–231). London, UK: Blackwell.

Reicher, S. D., Haslam, S. A., & Hopkins, N. (2005). Social identity and the dynamics of leadership: Leaders and followers as collaborative agents in the transformation of social reality. *Leadership Quarterly, 16*, 547–568.

Rhinesmith, S. H. (1992). Global mindsets for global managers. *Training and Development, 46*(10), 63–69.

Richard, O. C., Ismail, K. M., Bhuian, S. N., & Taylor, E. C. (2008). Mentoring in supervisor-subordinate dyads: Antecedents, consequences, and test of a mediation model of mentorship. *Journal of Business Research, 62*(11), 1110–1118.

Riddle, D. (2009). *Executive integration: Equipping transitioning leaders for success* (White Paper). Greensboro, NC: Center for Creative Leadership.

Riddle, D., & Pothier, N. (2010). What clients want: Coaching in organizational context. In G. Hernez-Broome & L. Boyce (Eds.), *Advancing executive coaching: Setting the course for successful leadership coaching*. Hoboken, NJ: Wiley.

Riddle, D., Zan, L., & Kuzmyez, D. (2009). Five myths about executive coaching. *Leadership in Action, 29*(5), 19–21.

Rogers, C. (1961). *On becoming a person*. Boston, MA: Houghton Mifflin.

Rooke, D., & Torbert, W. (2005, April). Seven transformations of leadership. *Harvard Business Review*, 66–77.

Rosinski, P. (2003). *Coaching across cultures: New tools for leveraging national, corporate and professional differences*. London, UK: Nicholas Brealey.

Rosinski, P. (2010). *Global coaching: An integrated approach for long-lasting results*. London, UK: Nicholas Brealey.

Rosinski, P., & Abbott, G. N. (2006). Coaching from a cultural perspective. In D. R. Stober & A. M. Grant (Eds.), *Evidence based coaching handbook: Putting best practices to work for your clients* (pp. 255–275). Hoboken, NJ: Wiley.

Ross, R., & Roberts, C. (1994). Balancing inquiry and advocacy. In P. M. Senge, A. Kleiner, C. Roberts, R. B. Ross, & B. J. Smith (Eds.), *The fifth discipline fieldbook* (pp. 253–259). New York, NY: Doubleday

Rothman, J. (1997). *Resolving identity-based conflict in nations, organisations, and communities.* San Francisco, CA: Jossey-Bass.

Ruderman, M. N., Glover, S., Chrobot-Mason, D., & Ernst, C. (2010). Leadership practices across social identity groups. In K. Hannum, B. B. McFeeters, & L.A.E Booysen (Eds.), *Leading across differences: Cases and perspectives* (pp. 95–114). San Francisco, CA: Jossey-Bass/Pfeiffer.

Ruderman, M. N., & Rogolsky, S. (2013). *Getting real: How high-achieving women can lead authentically* (White Paper). Greensboro, NC: Center for Creative Leadership.

Ryan, K. D., Gottman, J. M., Murray, J. D., Carrère, S., & Swanson, C. (2000). Theoretical and mathematical modeling of marriage. In M. D. Lewis, & I. Granic (Eds.), *Emotion, development and self-organization: Dynamic systems approaches to emotional development* (pp. 349–373). Cambridge: Cambridge University Press.

Ryan, L. (2005, May 31). Why HR gets no respect. *Bloomberg Businessweek.* Retrieved from http://www.businessweek.com/stories/2005-05-31/why-hr-gets-no-respect

Sahin, F. (2012). The mediating effect of leader-member exchange on the relationship between theory X and Y management styles and affective commitment: A multilevel analysis. *Journal of Management and Organization, 18*(2), 159–174.

Salas, E., & Cannon-Bowers, J. A. (2001). Special issue preface. *Journal of Organizational Behavior, 88*(22), 87–88.

Scandura, T. A. (1992). Mentorship and career mobility: An empirical investigation. *Journal of Organizational Behavior, 13*, 169–174.

Scandura, T. A. (1998). Dysfunctional mentoring relationships and outcomes. *Journal of Management, 24*, 449–467.

Scandura, T. A., & Hamilton, B. A. (2002). Enhancing performance through mentoring. In S. Sonnentag (Ed.), *The psychological management of individual performance: A handbook in the psychology of management in organizations* (pp. 293–308). Chichester, UK: Wiley.

Scandura, T. A., & Williams, E. A. (2004). Mentoring and transformational leadership: The role of supervisory career mentoring. *Journal of Vocational Behavior, 65*, 448–468.

Schein, E. (1992). *Organizational culture and leadership* (2nd ed.). San Francisco, CA: Jossey-Bass.

Schein, E. H. (1996). Culture: The missing concept in organization studies. *Administrative Science Quarterly, 41*(2), 229–240.

Schein, E. H. (2013). *Humble inquiry: The gentle art of asking instead of telling*. San Francisco, CA: Berrett-Koehler.

Schermerhorn, J. R., Jr., & Bond, M. H. (1997). Cross-cultural leadership dynamics in collectivism and high power distance settings. *Leadership and Organisational Development Journal, 18*(4), 187–193.

Schneider, B. (1987). The people make the place. *Personnel Psychology, 40*(3), 437–453.

Schneider, B., Smith, D. B., Taylor, S., & Fleenor, J. (1998). Personality and organizations: A test of the homogeneity of personality hypothesis. *Journal of Applied Psychology, 83*(3), 462–470.

Schnell, E., & Hammer, A. (1997). *Integrating the FIRO-B with the MBTI: Relationships, case examples, and interpretation strategies*. Palo Alto, CA: Davies-Black.

Schrage, M. (2000). *Serious play: How the world's best companies simulate and innovate*. Boston, MA: Harvard Business Press.

Schulz, S. F. (1995). The benefits of mentoring. In M. W. Galbraith & N. H. Cohen (Eds.), *Mentoring: New strategies and challenges* (Vol. 66, pp. 57–68). San Francisco, CA: Jossey-Bass.

Schwartz, S. H. (1999). Cultural value differences: Some implications for work. *Applied Psychology: An International Review, 48*, 23–47.

Schwartz, S. H. (2006). A theory of cultural value orientations: Explication and applications. *Comparative Sociology, 5*, 137–182.

Senge, P. (1990). *The fifth discipline: The art and practice of the learning organization*. New York, NY: Doubleday.

Senge, P. (2000). *The leadership of profound change*. Knoxville, TN: SPC Press.

Senge, P. M., Kleiner, A., Roberts, C., Ross, R. B., & Smith, B. J. (1994). *The fifth discipline fieldbook*. New York, NY: Crown Business.

Shen, Y., & Kram, K. E. (2011). Expatriates' developmental networks: Network diversity, base, and support functions. *Career Development International, 16*, 528–552.

Sherpa Coaching. (2013). *Eighth annual executive coaching survey 2013: At the summit*. Cincinnati, OH: Author.

Siegel, D. (2010). *Mindsight: The new science of personal transformation*. New York, NY: Bantam.

Simon, B., & Klandermans, B. (2001). Politicized collective identity: A social psychological analysis. *American Psychologist, 56*, 319–331.

Single, P. B., & Single, R. (2005). E-mentoring for social equity: Review of research to inform program development. *Mentoring and Tutoring: Partnership in Learning, 13*, 301–320.

Slobodnik, A., & Slobodnik, D. (1998, April 30). *Change management in a human systems model: Four systems types*. Presented at the M&A Process Conference, Toronto.

Smith, L., & Rao, R. (1994, September 19). *New ideas from the army (really). Fortune Magazine*. Retrieved from http://money.cnn.com/magazines/fortune/fortune_archive/1994/09/19/79743/index.htm

Smith, P. B. (2006). When elephants fight, the grass gets trampled: The GLOBE and Hofstede projects. *Journal of International Business Studies, 37*(6), 915–921. 10.1057/palgrave.jibs.8400235

Smither, J. W., London, M., Flautt, R., Vargas, Y., & Kucine, I. (2003). Can working with an executive coach improve multi-source feedback ratings over time? A quasi-experimental field study. *Personnel Psychology, 56*, 23–44.

Snook, S., Nohria, N., & Khurana, R. (Eds.). (2012). *The handbook for teaching leadership*. Thousand Oaks, CA: Sage.

Sontag, L., Vappie, K., & Wanberg, C. R. (2007). The practice of mentoring. In B. R. Ragins & K. E. Kram (Eds.), *The handbook of mentoring at work: Theory, research and practice* (pp. 593–616). Thousand Oaks, CA: Sage.

Sosik, J. J., & Jung, D. I. (2010). *Full range leadership development: Pathways for people, profit and planet*. New York, NY: Routledge.

St. Claire-Ostwald, B. (2007). Carrying cultural baggage: The contribution of socio-cultural anthropology to cross-cultural coaching. *International Journal of Evidence Based Coaching and Mentoring, 5*(2), 45–52.

St. John-Brooks, K. (2010). Moral support. *Coaching at Work, 5*(1), 48–51.

St. John-Brooks, K. (2014). *Internal coaching: The inside story*. London, UK: Karnac Books.

Stagl, K. C., Salas, E. B., & Burke, C. S. (2007). Best practices in team leadership: What team leaders do to facilitate team effectiveness. In J. A. Conger & R. Riggio (Eds.), *The practice of leadership: Developing the next generation of leaders* (pp. 172–197). San Francisco, CA: Jossey-Bass.

Stawiski, S. (2013). *Golden LEAF Scholars Leadership Program, 2012–2013* (Interim Report). Greensboro, NC: Center for Creative Leadership.

Stead, V. (2005). Mentoring: A model for leadership development? *International Journal of Training and Development*, *9*, 170–184.

Stevens, M. J., & Campion, M. A. (1994). The knowledge, skill, and ability requirements for teamwork: Implications for human resource management. *Journal of Management*, *20*(2), 503–530.

Stokes, P., & Merrick, L. (2013). Designing mentoring schemes for organizations. In J. Passmore, D. B. Peterson, & T. Freire (Eds.), *The Wiley-Blackwell handbook of the psychology of coaching and mentoring* (pp. 197–216). Chichester, UK: Wiley.

Sugarman, L. (1992). Ethical issues in counselling at work. *British Journal of Guidance and Counselling*, *20*, 64–74.

Sundstrom, E., McIntyre, M., Halfhill, T., & Richards, H. (2000). Work groups from the Hawthorne studies to work teams of the 1990s and beyond. *Group Dynamics: Theory, Research, and Practice*, *4*, 44–67.

Tajfel, H. (1974). Social identity and intergroup behaviour. *Social Science Information*, *13*, 65–93.

Tajfel, H., & Turner, J. C. (1979). An integrative theory of intergroup conflict. In W. G. Austin & S. Worchel (Eds.), *The social psychology of intergroup relations* (pp. 33–47). Monterey, CA: Brooks & Cole.

Tayeb, M. H. (1996). *The management of a multicultural workforce*. New York, NY: Wiley.

Taylor, S. S., Rudolph, J. W., & Foldy, E. G. (2008). Teaching reflective practice: Key concepts, stages, and practices. In P. Reason & H. Bradbury (Eds.), *The SAGE handbook of action research* (2nd ed., pp. 656–668). London: Sage.

Thach, E. C. (2002). The impact of executive coaching and 360-degree feedback on leadership effectiveness. *Leadership and Organizational Development Journal*, *23*, 205–214.

Theebom, T., Beersma, B., & van Vianen, A. (2014). Does coaching work? A meta-analysis on the effects of coaching on individual level outcomes in an organizational context. *Journal of Positive Psychology*, *9*(1), 1–18.

Thompson, J. (1967). *Organizations in action*. New York, NY: McGraw-Hill.

Ting, S., & Riddle, D. (2006). A framework for leadership development coaching. In S. Ting and P. Scisco (Eds.), *The Center for Creative Leadership handbook of coaching* (pp. 34–62). San Francisco, CA: Wiley.

Ting, S., & Scisco, P. (Eds.). (2006). *The CCL handbook of coaching: A guide for leader coach*. San Francisco, CA: Jossey-Bass.

Tobias, L. L. (1990). *Psychological consulting to management: A clinician's perspective*. New York, NY: Brunner/Mazel.

Tong, C., & Kram, K. E. (2013). The efficacy of mentoring—the benefits for mentees, mentors, and organizations. In J. Passmore, D. B. Peterson, & T. Freire (Eds.), *The Wiley-Blackwell handbook of the psychology of coaching and mentoring* (pp. 217–242). Chichester, UK: Wiley.

Torbert, B., & Associates. (2004). *Action Inquiry: The secret of timely and transforming leadership*. San Francisco, CA: Berrett-Koehler.

Torres, R. T., & Preskill, H. (2001). Evaluation and organizational learning: Past, present, and future. *American Journal of Evaluation*, *22*(3), 387–395.

Triandis, H. C. (1995). A theoretical framework for the study of diversity. In M. M. Chemers, S. Oskamp, & M. A. Costanzo (Eds.), *Diversity in organisations: New perspectives for a changing workplace* (p. 11). London: Sage.

Triandis, H. C. (2004). Cultural intelligence in organizations. *Group and Organization Management*, *31*, 20–26.

Tuckman, B. W. (1965). Developmental sequence in small groups. *Psychological Bulletin*, *63*(6), 384–399.

Tuckman, B. W., & Jensen, M.A.C. (1977). Stages in small group development revisited. *Group and Organizational Studies*, *2*, 419–427.

Tulpa, K. (2010). Leveraging the coaching investment. In J. Passmore (Ed.), *Excellence in coaching: The industry guide* (2nd ed., pp. 44–62). London, UK. Kogan Page.

Tung, R. L., & Verbeke, A. (2010). Beyond Hofstede and GLOBE: Improving the quality of cross-cultural research. *Journal of International Business Studies*, *41*, 1259–1274. http://econpapers.repec.org/article/paljintbs/v_3a41_3ay_3a2010_3ai_3a8_3ap_3a1259-1274.htm

Turban, D. B., & Dougherty, T. W. (1994). Role of protégé personality in receipt of mentoring and career success. *Academy of Management Journal*, *37*, 688–702.

Turban, D. B., Dougherty, T. W., & Lee, F. K. (2002). Gender, race, and perceived similarity effects in developmental relationships: The moderating role of relationship duration. *Journal of Vocational Behavior, 61*, 240–262.

Turner, J. C. (1985). Social categorization and the self-concept: A social cognitive theory of group behaviour. In E. J. Lawler (Ed.), *Advances in group processes* (pp. 2, 77–122). Greenwich, CT: JAI Press.

Turner, J. C., & Reynolds, K. J. (2012). Self-categorization theory. In P.A.M. Van Lange, A. W. Kruglanski, & E. T. Higgins (Eds.), *Handbook of theories of social psychologies* (pp. 399–417). Thousand Oaks, CA: Sage.

Tyler, K. (1998, April). Mentoring programs link employees and experienced executives. *HRMagazine, 43*(5), 98–103.

Ulrich, D. (Ed.). (2010). *Leadership in Asia: Challenges, opportunities, and strategies from top global leaders*. New York, NY: McGraw-Hill.

Underhill, B. O., McAnally, K., & Koriath, J. J. (2007). *Executive coaching for results: The definitive guide to developing organizational leaders*. San Francisco, CA: Berrett-Koehler.

Underhill, C. M. (2006). The effectiveness of mentoring programs in corporate settings: A meta-analytical review of the literature. *Journal of Vocational Behavior, 68*(2), 292–307.

Van Dyne, L., Ang, S., & Livermore, D. (2010). In K. Hannum, B. B. McFeeters, & L.A.E Booysen (Eds.), *Leading across differences: Cases and perspectives* (pp. 131–138). San Francisco, CA: Jossey-Bass/Pfeiffer.

van Knippenberg, D. (2011). Embodying who we are: Leader group prototypicality and leadership effectiveness. *Leadership Quarterly, 22*(6), 1078.

Van Velsor, E., & Leslie, J. B. (1995). Why executives derail: Perspectives across time and cultures. *Academy of Management Executive, 9*(4), 62–73.

Van Velsor, E., McCauley, C. D., & Ruderman, M. N. (Eds.). (2010). *The Center for Creative Leadership handbook of leadership development* (3rd ed.). San Francisco, CA: Wiley.

Van Velsor, E., & Wright, J. (2012). *Expanding the leadership equation—developing next-generation leaders*. Greensboro, NC: Center for Creative Leadership.

Wageman, R., Nunes, D. A., Burruss, J. A., & Hackman, J. R. (2008). *Senior leadership teams: What it takes to make them great*. Boston, MA: Harvard Business School Press.

Walker-Fraser, A. (2011). An HR perspective on executive coaching for organizational learning. *International Journal of Evidence Based Coaching and Mentoring, 9*, 67–79.

Walsh, R. J., & Trovas, S. A. (2014). *Leading with impact: How functional leaders face challenges, focus development, and boost performance* (White Paper). Greensboro, NC: Center for Creative Leadership.

Wanberg, C. R., Welsh, E. T., & Hezlett, S. A. (2003). Mentoring research: A review and dynamic process model. In J. J. Martocchio & G. R. Ferris (Eds.), *Research in personnel and human resources management* (Vol. 22, pp. 39–124). Oxford: Elsevier.

Watkins, M. (2003). *The first 90 days: Critical success strategies for new leaders at all levels*. Cambridge, MA: Harvard Business School Press.

Watkins, M. D. (2012, June). How managers become leaders. *Harvard Business Review*.

Weitzel, S. R. (2000). *Feedback that works: How to build and deliver your message*. Greensboro, NC: Center for Creative Leadership.

Wheelan, S. A. (2003). An initial exploration of the internal dynamics of leadership teams. *Consulting Psychology Journal: Practice and Research, 55*, 179–188.

Whitely, W., Dougherty, T. W., & Dreher, G. F. (1991). Relationship of career mentoring and socioeconomic origin to managers' and professionals' early career progress. *Academy of Management Journal, 34*, 331–351.

Whitmore, J. (1992). *Coaching for performance*. London: Nicholas Brealey Publishing.

Wilber, K. (2000). *Integral psychology*. Boston, MA: Shambhala.

Willburn, P., & Cullen, K. L. (2013). *A leader's network: How to help your talent invest in the right relationships at the right time*. Greensboro, NC: Center for Creative Leadership.

Williams, P., & Menendez, D. (2007). *Becoming a professional life coach: Lessons from the Institute of Life Coach Training*. New York, NY: Norton.

Wilson, J. A., & Elman, N. S. (1990). Organizational benefits of mentoring. *Academy of Management Executive, 4*(4), 88–94.

Wilson, M. S., Van Velsor, E., Chandrasekar, A., & Criswell, C. (2011). *Grooming top leaders: Cultural perspectives from China, India, Singapore and the United States* (White Paper). Greensboro, NC: Center for Creative Leadership.

Womack, J. P., & Jones, D. T. (2003). *Lean thinking: Banish waste and create wealth in your corporation*. New York, NY: Simon & Schuster.

Wooten, K. C. (2001). Ethical dilemmas in human resource management: An application of a multidimensional framework, a unifying taxonomy, and applicable codes. *Human Resource Management Review, 11*, 159–175.

Wright, J., Rego, P., & Rego, L. (2007). *India young professionals report*. Greensboro, NC: Center for Creative Leadership.

Yang, L.-Q., Xu, X., Allen, T. D., Shi, K., Zhang, X., & Lou, Z. (2011). Mentoring in China: Enhanced understanding and association with occupational stress. *Journal of Business and Psychology, 26*, 485–499.

Yip, J., & Wilson, M. (2010). Learning from experience. In E. Van Velsor, C. D. McCauley, & M. N. Ruderman (Eds.), *The Center for Creative Leadership handbook of leadership development* (3rd ed.). San Francisco: Jossey-Bass.

Zhuang, W.-L., Wu, M., & Wen, S.-L. (2013). Relationship of mentoring functions to expatriate adjustments: Comparing home country mentorship and host country mentorship. *International Journal of Human Resource Management, 24*(1), 35–49.

NAME INDEX

Page numbers in italics refer to tables, figures, and exhibits.

M

S

T

SUBJECT INDEX

Page numbers in italics refer to tables, figures, and exhibits.

B

C

D

E

G

H

J

K

L

M

N

O

P

Q

R

S

U

V

W

Y

ABOUT THE CENTER FOR CREATIVE LEADERSHIP

The Center for Creative Leadership (CCL) is a top-ranked global provider of leadership development. By leveraging the power of leadership to drive results that matter most to clients, CCL transforms individual leaders, teams, organizations, and society. Our array of cutting-edge solutions is steeped in extensive research and experience gained from working with hundreds of thousands of leaders at all levels. Ranked among the world's Top 5 providers of executive education by *Financial Times* and in the Top 10 by *Bloomberg BusinessWeek*, CCL has offices in Greensboro, North Carolina; Colorado Springs, Colorado; San Diego, California; Brussels, Belgium; Moscow, Russia; Addis Ababa, Ethiopia; Johannesburg, South Africa; Singapore; Gurgaon, India; and Shanghai, China.